Introduction to Expert Systems

INTERNATIONAL COMPUTER SCIENCE SERIES

Consulting Editor **A D McGettrick** University of Strathclyde

SELECTED TITLES IN THE SERIES

THIRD EDITION

Introduction to Expert Systems

Peter Jackson

West Group, Rochester, NY

ADDISON-WESLEY

Harlow, England • Reading, Massachusetts • Menlo Park, California
New York • Don Mills, Ontario • Amsterdam • Bonn • Sydney • Singapore
Tokyo • Madrid • San Juan • Milan • Mexico City • Seoul • Taipei

Addison Wesley Longman Limited
Edinburgh Gate
Harlow
Essex CM20 2JE
England

and Associated Companies throughout the World.

Line illustrations by Margaret Macknelly, Tadley, UK.
Typeset in Sabon Roman by 42
Printed and bound in The United States of America

This edition first printed 1998
Second edition first published 1990, and reprinted 7 times
First edition first published 1986, reprinted 3 times

ISBN 0-201-87686-8

British Library Cataloguing-in-Publication Data
A catalogue record for this book is available from the British Library

Publishers' Acknowledgments
The publishers are grateful to the following for permission to reproduce the material cited: Figures 10.4 and 10.5 from Prerau D.S. (1990), reprinted by permission of Addison Wesley Longman US; Figures 11.4 and 11.5, from Clancey W.J. (1987a), copyright The MIT Press.

Preface

The third edition of this book was written with four kinds of reader in mind:

- *general readers* who want a treatment of the field that has both breadth and technical depth;
- *teachers and students* who want an authoritative text that covers all areas of expert systems that might figure in a first graduate or undergraduate course;
- *software engineers* who are interested in gaining expertise in this area and want a practical guide with some theoretical basis;
- *researchers or research students* who are interested in introductory treatments of advanced topics.

This preface is meant as a guide for these different kinds of reader.

For the general reader

I have tried to write chapters so that they open with a fairly conversational style and then progressively get more technical. The idea is that later sections of a chapter can be passed over without losing the big picture. Certain chapters and sections are specifically marked with a [†], and these can be skipped – permanently, if you so desire.

The key chapters to read are the following.

1. What Are Expert Systems?
2. An Overview of Artificial Intelligence
3. Knowledge Representation
5. Rule-Based Systems
6. Associative Nets and Frame Systems
9. Representing Uncertainty
10. Knowledge Acquisition
11. Heuristic Classification (I)
14. Constructive Problem Solving (I)
16. Designing for Explanation
17. Tools for Building Expert Systems
20. Machine Learning
22. Case-Based Reasoning
24. Summary and Conclusion

Other chapters should be regarded as optional, depending on the reader's taste and interest.

For students and teachers

A good first course in expert systems for undergraduates could be based on the following chapters.

1. What Are Expert Systems?
2. An Overview of Artificial Intelligence
3. Knowledge Representation
5. Rule-Based Systems
6. Associative Nets and Frame Systems
9. Representing Uncertainty
10. Knowledge Acquisition
11. Heuristic Classification (I)
14. Constructive Problem Solving (I)
16. Designing for Explanation
17. Tools for Building Expert Systems
24. Summary and Conclusion
Appendix. CLIPS Programming

CLIPS makes a good vehicle for relatively simple exercises that do not require a great deal of coding.

For a more advanced, graduate-level course, following on from an introductory class in artificial intelligence, I would recommend the following.

1. What Are Expert Systems?
5. Rule-Based Systems
6. Associative Nets and Frame Systems
7. Object-Oriented Programming
9. Representing Uncertainty
10. Knowledge Acquisition
11. Heuristic Classification (I)
12. Heuristic Classification (II)
14. Constructive Problem Solving (I)
15. Constructive Problem Solving (II)
16. Designing for Explanation
17. Tools for Building Expert Systems
24. Summary and Conclusion
Appendix. CLIPS Programming

For software engineers

Software engineers whose interest in expert systems is primarily practical should concentrate on the following chapters.

4. Symbolic Computation
5. Rule-Based Systems
7. Object-Oriented Programming
8. Logic Programming

11.   Heuristic Classification (I)
12.   Heuristic Classification (II)
14.   Constructive Problem Solving (I)
15.   Constructive Problem Solving (II)
16.   Designing for Explanation
17.   Tools for Building Expert Systems
18.   Blackboard Architectures
19.   Truth Maintenance Systems
Appendix. CLIPS Programming

Other chapters can be read on an 'as needed' basis.

For the researcher

The later chapters of the book provide overviews of recent research in areas adjacent to the expert system mainstream, and these can be read in conjunction with some earlier chapters which serve as an introduction.

3.   Knowledge Representation
5.   Rule-Based Systems
6.   Associative Nets and Frame Systems
8.   Logic Programming
9.   Representing Uncertainty
10.   Knowledge Acquisition
13.   Hierarchical Hypothesize and Test
16.   Designing for Explanation
18.   Blackboard Architectures
19.   Truth Maintenance Systems
20.   Machine Learning
21.   Belief Networks
22.   Case-Based Reasoning
23.   Hybrid Systems

In general, the third edition is less linear than either the first or the second. Material is organized more according to issues and topics, and less according to the systems being discussed. I have also provided more programming examples, exercises, and boxes which contain little asides.

Supplementary materials

I will also maintain a page at the following World Wide Web address to provide additional materials associated with the book.

http://members.aol.com/JacksonPE/music1/introduc.htm

The reader will find links on this page to downloadable CLIPS code and some presentation materials.

Such materials can also be accessed via the publisher by searching for the book under

http://www.awl-he.com/computing

I hope that you enjoy reading this book as much as I enjoyed researching and writing it.

Peter Jackson
Rochester, NY

Contents

What Are Expert Systems?

You are having a bad day with your personal computer. You have just upgraded your favorite word processor, and now when you click the icon you get an error message, such as

```
"Call to Undefined Link."
```

Like most error messages, this is about as helpful as a fortune cookie from Mars. You blow the whole directory away and reinstall, to no avail. You tinker with various initialization files, but nothing works.

Finally, you break down and call customer support. Your luck changes and you get someone who knows what they are talking about. He tells you to blow away half a dozen old dynamic link libraries in a system directory and reinstall. You do it, it works, and your blood pressure returns to normal.

Whatever expertise may be in this domain, it is clear that the technical support person has it and you don't. You may have a Ph.D. in Computer Science, you may be a wiz programmer, but you couldn't do their job unless you underwent the right training and somehow acquired their troubleshooting experience. So expertise isn't just possessing knowledge or having qualifications; it is a highly specialized set of skills that have been honed in a particular situation for a specific purpose. As such, being an expert is quite distinct from having an education.

1.1   The nature of expertise

That being said, under what conditions would you feel happy in calling a computer program an expert?

- It seems reasonable to insist that the program *possess knowledge*. Merely possessing an algorithm, for example some kind of checklist of things to test, is not really sufficient. This would be like giving someone off the street a list of questions and answers and expecting them to perform the technical support task. Sooner or later, they will be 'found out.'
- This knowledge must be focused upon a *specific domain*. A random collection of names, dates, places, and old proverbs is not the kind of knowledge that provides the basis of expertise. Knowledge implies organization and integration, in that different pieces of knowledge relate to each other and bring each other to mind.
- Finally, this knowledge must be capable of *solving problems* directly. Merely demonstrating knowledge relevant to technical support, for example, is not the same as being able to perform the task on demand. Similarly, having access to online documentation is not the same as having a person or program attempt to solve your problem.

Let us put these considerations together to produce the following definition of an expert system.

An *expert system* is a computer program that represents and reasons with knowledge of some specialist subject with a view to solving problems or giving advice.

An expert system may completely fulfill a function that normally requires human expertise, or it may play the role of an assistant to a human decision maker. In other words, the client may interact with the program directly, or interact with a human expert who interacts with the program. The decision maker may be an expert in his own right, in which case the program may justify its existence by improving his productivity. Alternatively, the human collaborator may be someone who is capable of attaining expert levels of performance given some technical assistance from the program. Getting the right allocation of function between person and machine is often the key to successful expert systems deployment.

Expert systems technology derives from the research discipline of *Artificial Intelligence* (AI): a branch of Computer Science concerned with the design and implementation of programs which are capable of emulating human cognitive skills such as problem solving, visual perception and language understanding. This technology has been successfully applied to a diverse range of domains, including organic chemistry, mineral exploration, and internal medicine. Typical tasks for expert systems involve:

- the interpretation of data (such as sonar signals),
- diagnosis of malfunctions (such as equipment faults or human diseases),
- structural analysis of complex objects (such as chemical compounds),
- configuration of complex objects (such as computer systems), and
- planning sequences of actions (such as might be performed by robots).

Although more conventional programs have been known to perform similar tasks in similar domains, we shall argue in the next section that expert systems are sufficiently different from such programs to form a distinct and identifiable class. There is no precise definition of an expert system that is guaranteed to satisfy everyone; hence the blandness of the definition given above. However, there are a number of features which are sufficiently important that an expert system should really exhibit all of them to some degree.

1.2 The characteristics of an expert system

An expert system can be distinguished from a more conventional applications program in that:

- It *simulates human reasoning* about a problem domain, rather than simulating the domain itself. This distinguishes expert systems from more familiar programs that involve mathematical modeling or computer animation. This is not to say that the program is a faithful psychological model of the expert, merely that the focus is upon emulating an expert's problem solving abilities, that is, performing some portion of the relevant tasks as well as, or better than, the expert.
- It performs reasoning over *representations of human knowledge*, in addition to doing numerical calculations or data retrieval. The knowledge in the program is normally expressed in some special-purpose language and kept separate from the code that performs the reasoning. These distinct program modules are referred to as the *knowledge base* and the *inference engine*, respectively.
- It solves problems by *heuristic* or *approximate methods* which, unlike algorithmic solutions, are not guaranteed to succeed. A heuristic is essentially a rule of thumb which encodes a piece of knowledge about how to solve problems in some domain. Such methods are approximate in the sense that (i) they do not require perfect data and (ii) the solutions derived by the system may be proposed with varying degrees of certainty.

An expert system differs from other kinds of artificial intelligence program in that:

- It deals with subject matter of *realistic complexity* that normally requires a considerable amount of human expertise. Many AI programs are really research vehicles, and may therefore focus upon abstract mathematical problems or simplified versions of real problems (sometimes called 'toy' problems) in order to gain insights or refine techniques. Expert systems, on the other hand, solve problems of genuine scientific or commercial interest.
- It must exhibit *high performance* in terms of speed and reliability in order to be a useful tool. AI research vehicles may not run very fast, and may well contain bugs: they are programs, not supported software. But an expert system must propose solutions in a reasonable time and be right most of the time, that is, at least as often as a human expert.
- It must be capable of *explaining and justifying solutions* or recommendations in order to convince the user that its reasoning is in fact correct. Research programs are typically only run by their creators, or by other personnel in similar laboratories. An expert system will be run by a wider range of users, and should therefore be designed in such a way that its workings are rather more transparent.

The term *knowledge-based system* is sometimes used as a synonym for 'expert system' although, strictly speaking, the former is more general. A knowledge-based system is any system which performs a task by applying rules of thumb to a symbolic representation of knowledge, instead of employing mostly algorithmic or statistical methods. Thus a program capable of conversing about the weather would be a knowledge-based system, even if that program did not embody any expertise in meteorology, but an expert system in the domain of meteorology ought to be able to provide us with weather forecasts.

In summary, expert systems encode the domain-dependent knowledge of everyday practitioners in some field, and use this knowledge to solve problems, instead of using comparatively domain-independent methods derived from computer science or mathematics. The process of constructing an expert system is often called *knowledge engineering*, and is considered to be 'applied artificial intelligence' (Feigenbaum, 1977). We shall further develop the distinction between the knowledge engineering approach and more conventional computer science approaches to problem solving in Chapters 2 and 3.

The rest of this chapter has the following plan. Four fundamental topics are identified which are intimately related to the theory and practice of expert systems development, and these are briefly discussed with a view to introducing some terminology and giving the reader an overview. The final section poses the question 'What is the state of the art?' and provides a chapter plan for the rest of the book.

1.3 Fundamental topics in expert systems

Given that expert systems research has grown out of more general concerns in artificial intelligence, it is not surprising that it maintains strong intellectual links with related topics in its parent discipline. Some of these links are outlined in the following sections, with references to the general literature. There are also forward references to chapters of this book which have a bearing on the various topics.

1.3.1 Acquiring knowledge

Buchanan *et al.* (1983) define knowledge acquisition as follows.

> [Knowledge acquisition is] 'the transfer and transformation of potential problem-solving expertise from some knowledge source to a program'.

This transfer is usually accomplished by a series of lengthy and intensive interviews between a knowledge engineer, who is normally a computer specialist, and a domain expert who is able to articulate his expertise to some degree. It is estimated that this form of labor produces between two and five units of knowledge (for example, rules of thumb) per day. This rather low output has led researchers to look upon knowledge acquisition as 'the bottleneck problem' of expert systems applications (Feigenbaum, 1977).

There are a number of reasons why productivity is typically so poor; here are some of them.

- Specialist fields have their own jargon, and it is often difficult for experts to communicate their knowledge in everyday language (see Box 1.1). Analyzing the concepts behind the jargon is rarely straightforward, since these concepts need not admit of precise mathematical or logical definition. For example, a military strategist may speak of the 'aggressive posture' of a foreign power without being able to specify exactly what distinguishes such a posture from a non-threatening one.

- The facts and principles underlying many domains of interest cannot be characterized precisely in terms of a mathematical theory or a deterministic model whose properties are well understood. Thus a financial expert may know that certain events cause the stock market to go up or down, but the exact mechanisms that mediate these effects, and the magnitude of the effects themselves, cannot be identified or predicted with certainty. Statistical models may enable us to make rather general, long-term predictions, but they do not normally sanction specific courses of action in the short term.

- Experts need to know more than the mere facts or principles of a domain in order to solve problems. For example, they usually know which kinds of information are relevant to which kinds of judgment, how reliable different information sources are, and how to make hard problems easier by splitting them into subproblems which can be solved more or less independently. Eliciting this kind of knowledge, which is normally based on personal experience rather than formal training, is much more difficult than eliciting either particular facts or general principles.

- Human expertise, even in a relatively narrow domain, is often set in a broader context that involves a good deal of commonsense knowledge about the everyday world. Consider legal experts involved in litigation. It is difficult to delineate the amount and nature of general knowledge needed to deal with an arbitrary case.

BOX 1.1

Forgotten Passwords

If you have a memory like mine, you probably forget your passwords on various machines quite frequently. How does your system administrator, let's call him Sam, reset your password? Our budding knowledge engineer, Ken, tries to find out.

> *Sam*: Well, if it's a YP password, I first log on as root on the YP master.
> Ken: Er, what's the YP master?
> *Sam*: It's the diskfull machine that contains a database of network information.
> Ken: 'Diskfull' meaning – ?
> *Sam*: – it has the OS installed on local disk.
> Ken: Ah. (*Scribbles furiously.*) So you log on ...
> *Sam*: As root. Then I edit the password datafile, remove the encrypted entry, and make the new password map.
> Ken: ... password map. (*Attempting humor.*) What happens if you forget *your* password?
> *Sam*: On a diskfull system, I could reboot to single user mode, or I could load MINIROOT so I can edit */etc/password*. Or I could reload the whole system, which I'd rather not do. Root passwords aren't usually included in YP. On a diskless client I could use the *passwd* command.
> Ken: Oh. (*Sorry he asked.*)

Poor Ken is struggling. He might have had an easier time if he had glanced at the System Administrator's Guide prior to the interview to get some basic terminology.

Dissatisfaction with the interview method has led some researchers to try to automate the process of knowledge acquisition. One area of research concerns *automated knowledge elicitation*, in which an expert's knowledge is transferred to a computer program as a side effect of a person–machine dialogue (see Chapter 10 *et seq.*). Other researchers have looked to the subfield of AI known as *machine learning* for a solution to the bottleneck problem. The idea is that a computing system could perhaps learn to solve problems in much the same way that humans do, that is to say, by example (see Chapter 20).

1.3.2 Representing knowledge

Knowledge representation is a substantial subfield in its own right, which shares many concerns with both formal philosophy and cognitive psychology. It is concerned with the ways in which information might be stored and associated in the human brain, usually from a logical, rather than a biological, perspective. In other words, it is not typically concerned with the physical details of how knowledge is encoded, but rather with what the overall conceptual scheme might look like.

BOX 1.2

Syntax and Semantics in the Family

A basic part of knowledge representation, which is so obvious that it is often not stressed, is that a representation should somehow "standardize" the syntactic variety of English. Thus the sentences

'Sam is the father of Bill'.
'Sam is Bill's father.'
'Bill's father is Sam.'
'Bill has Sam for a father.'

all have the same fundamental meaning (semantic content), and should therefore be rendered in the same way. In a representation, we try to relate form and meaning more simply than in English, in that expressions with the same or similar meaning should look the same or similar. Thus the above sentences might be mapped to the expression

```
father(sam, bill).
```

The semantics of this expression must specify (amongst other things) that the first name stands for the parent and the second name stands for the child, and not vice versa.

We can also see that the sentences

'Sam is the father of Jill'
'Bill has Sam for a father.'

share meaning in a manner that is more evident when we render them as

```
father(sam, bill).
father(sam, jill).
```

We shall say more about syntax and semantics in Chapters 3 and 8.

In the 1970s, knowledge representation research attempted to address such questions as how human memory works, proposing theories of reminding, recognition, and recall. Some of the resultant theories led to computer programs which tried to simulate different ways in which concepts might be associated, so that a computer application would somehow always be able to find the right piece of knowledge at the right time when solving some problem. Over time, the psychological veracity of these theories became less important than their utility as vehicles for experimenting with new data and control structures, at least from an AI point of view.

Knowledge representation in the large has always been, and is likely to remain, a controversial topic. Philosophers and psychologists have sometimes been shocked by the hubris of AI researchers who talk rather glibly about human knowledge in a jargon that freely mixes terminology from logic, linguistics, philosophy, psychology, and computer science. On the other hand, the computer metaphor has provided a novel means of asking, and occasionally answering, difficult questions which have languished for centuries in the realm of metaphysics.

In the world of expert systems, knowledge representation is mostly concerned with finding ways in which large bodies of useful information can be formally described for the purposes of symbolic computation. *Formally described* means rendered in some unambiguous language or notation which has a well-defined *syntax* governing the form of expressions in the language, and a well-defined *semantics* which reveals the meaning of such expressions by virtue of their form. We can put off a discussion of syntax and semantics until Chapter 3.

Symbolic computation means non-numeric computations in which the symbols and symbol structures can be construed as standing for (*representing*) various concepts and relationships between them. We shall likewise put off a discussion of symbolic computation until Chapter 4. But see Box 1.2 for an example of symbolic representation.

AI researchers have expended a good deal of effort in constructing *representation languages*, that is, computer languages that are oriented towards organizing descriptions of objects and ideas, rather than stating sequences of instructions or storing simple data elements. The main criteria for assessing a representation of knowledge are logical adequacy, heuristic power, and notational convenience; these terms deserve some explanation.

- *Logical adequacy* means that the representation should be capable of making all the distinctions that you want to make. For example, it is not possible to represent the idea that every drug has some undesirable side effect unless you are able to distinguish between the designation of a particular drug and a particular side effect (for example, aspirin aggravates ulcers) and the more general statement to the effect that: 'for any drug, there is an undesirable side effect associated with it.'
- *Heuristic power* means that as well as having an expressive representation language, there must be some way of using representations so constructed and interpreted to solve problems. It is often the case that the more expressive the language, in terms of the number of semantic distinctions that it can make, the more difficult it is to control the drawing of inferences during problem solving. Many of the formalisms that have found favor with practitioners may seem quite restricted in terms of their powers of expression when compared with English or even

standard logic. Yet they frequently gain in heuristic power as a consequence; that is, it is relatively easy to bring the right knowledge to bear at the right time. Knowing which areas of knowledge are most relevant to which problems is one of the things that distinguishes the expert from the amateur or the merely well-read.

- *Notational convenience* is a virtue because most expert systems applications require the encoding of substantial amounts of knowledge, and this task will not be an enviable one if the conventions of the representation language are too complicated. The resulting expressions should be relatively easy to write and to read, and it should be possible to understand their meaning without knowing how the computer will actually interpret them. The term *declarative* is often used to describe code which is essentially descriptive and can therefore be understood without knowing what states a real or virtual machine will go through at execution time.

Several conventions for coding knowledge have been suggested, including *production rules* (Davis and King, 1977), *structured objects* (Findler, 1979) and *logic programs* (Kowalski, 1979). Most expert systems use one or more of these formalisms, and their pros and cons are still a source of controversy among theoreticians. A number of such formalisms are critically reviewed in Chapters 5–8, while software tools for constructing such representations are described in Chapters 17, 18 and 19.

Most of the code examples in this book use the CLIPS language, which combines production rules with structured objects. The appendix provides a reasonably thorough introduction to the main concepts and constructs of CLIPS, with many code examples. There the reader will find a non-trivial program which exercises most of the interesting features of CLIPS and demonstrates many of the AI techniques discussed in Chapters 1–3.

1.3.3   Controlling reasoning

Expert systems design involves paying close attention to the details of how knowledge is accessed and applied during the search for a solution (Davis, 1980a). Knowing what one knows, and knowing when and how to use it, is an important part of expertise; this is usually termed *metaknowledge*, that is, knowledge about knowledge. Solving non-trivial problems implies a certain level of *planning* and *control* when choosing what questions to ask, what tests to perform, and so on.

Different strategies for bringing domain-specific knowledge to bear will generally have marked effects upon the performance characteristics of programs. They determine the manner in which a program *searches* for a solution in some space of alternatives (see Chapters 2 and 3). It will not normally be the case that the data given to a knowledge-based program will be sufficient for the program to deduce exactly where it should look in this space.

Most knowledge representation formalisms can be employed under a variety of *control regimes* (see Box 1.3), and expert systems researchers are continuing to experiment in this area. The systems reviewed in the later chapters have been specially chosen to illustrate the many different ways in which the problem of control can be tackled. Each has something to offer the student of expert systems research and development.

BOX 1.3

Automotive Aggravation

Imagine that your car is difficult to start, and when running exhibits loss of power. These symptoms are not, in themselves, sufficient for you to decide whether you should look for a fault in the electrical system or the fuel system of your car. Yet your knowledge of cars might tell you that it is worth running some additional checks before calling a mechanic. Perhaps the mixture is wrong, so look at the exhaust smoke and the coating on the spark plugs. Maybe the distributor is faulty, so see if the cap is damaged in some way. These rather specific heuristics are not guaranteed to locate the fault, but with luck they may take you to the heart of the problem more quickly than running an exhaustive set of routine checks over the car's components.

Even if you are mystified by the symptoms of your sick vehicle, you probably know enough to perform global checks before very specific checks, for example, to see if there is a strong spark at the plugs (which would tend to rule out an electrical fault) before testing the battery for flatness. Even in the absence of specific heuristics, the more methodical your procedures, the greater the chance that you will find the fault quickly. The general heuristic that says

'test whole modules before testing their components'

could form part of a *control regime*: a strategy for applying knowledge in some systematic way. Another heuristic might be

'replace cheaper parts before replacing more expensive ones.'

These two heuristics may give contradictory advice in some cases, and so one might have to be more dominant than the other if they are to coexist in the same control regime.

1.3.4 Explaining solutions

The whole question of how to help a user understand the structure and function of some complex piece of software relates to the comparatively new field of *human/computer interaction*, which is emerging from an intersection of AI, engineering, psychology, and ergonomics. The contribution of expert systems researchers to date has been to place a high priority upon the accountability of consultation programs, and to show how explanations of program behavior can be systematically related to the chains of reasoning employed by such systems. Ongoing contributions include attempts to separate out the different kinds of knowledge implicit in expert performance, and attempts to make explicit and accessible the design decisions associated with the specification of consultation programs.

Explanations of expert system behavior are important for a number of reasons:

- *users* of the system need to satisfy themselves that the program's conclusions are basically correct for their particular case;
- *knowledge engineers* need some way to satisfy themselves that knowledge is being applied properly even as the prototype is being built;
- *domain experts* need to see a trace of the way in which their knowledge is being applied in order to judge whether knowledge elicitation is proceeding successfully;
- *programmers* who maintain, debug and extend knowledge-based programs must have some window onto the program's behavior above the level of the procedure call;

- *managers* of expert system technology, who may end up being responsible for a program's decisions, need to satisfy themselves that a system's mode of reasoning is applicable to their domain.

The topic of explanations sometimes goes under the name of *transparency*, meaning the ease with which one can understand what the program is doing and why. It interacts with the issue of control, mentioned in the previous section, because the steps of reasoning exhibited by the program will depend upon how it goes about its search for a solution. How best to manage the interaction between explanation and control is still a research question, which we address in Chapter 16.

Explanation is closely linked to the topic of *evaluation*, since it is by scrutinizing the outputs of a system and examining a trace of its reasoning that we decide whether or not that system is getting the right answer for the right reasons. Unless a system has a good explanation facility, an expert will be unable to assess its general performance or give advice as to how its performance could be improved. Evaluation is a difficult task that requires a certain level of commitment from both the expert and the computer scientist (see Chapters 3, 13 and 17).

BOX 1.4

The Riddle of the Picture

A well-known riddle has a man looking at a portrait and saying:

'Brothers and sisters have I none, but this man's father is my father's son.'

Who is the man in the picture? First, take a moment to solve this puzzle. Second, imagine how you would explain the solution to someone who could not work it out, without using any props, such as pencil and paper. Many people find this puzzle hard to solve, and may even find it hard to follow the solution (Smullyan, 1978).

The answer is that the man in the picture is the son of the man looking at the picture. If we use a logical representation, this can become clearer. Let Pete be the man in the picture and Luke be the man looking at the picture.

'this man's father is my father's son'
```
son(father(luke), father(pete)).
```

'brothers and sisters have I none'
```
for all X,
  if son(father(luke), X)
  then X = luke.
```

Thus son is a relation between two people, but father can be represented by a function, since everyone has a single father. Stated in this way, it becomes obvious that

```
father(pete) = luke.
```

by substitution, so Luke is looking at his son's picture.

The right representation can sometimes make problems easier to solve and solutions easier to understand. But there is still an art to choosing such representations and presenting such solutions. And explanations do not always take the form of a proof, as we shall see in Chapter 16.

1.4 Summary and chapter plan

In this section, I try to be frank about the limitations of expert systems, as well as emphasizing their strengths, so that the general reader has at least some idea of how applicable this technology might be to his or her area. Then I give an overview of the rest of the book, together with some hints about which chapters to read, depending upon your interests. Such information is also provided in the preface, but since no one (including myself) ever reads prefaces, I reproduce it here.

1.4.1 What is the state of the art?

The main question that occurs to a potential consumer of expert systems technology is 'Will it solve my problem?' and the answer is 'That depends.' The three most critical factors are the nature of the task, the availability of a certain kind of expertise, and the ability to analyze that task and that expertise in such a way that a computer program, using rather limited forms of reasoning, can work out what has to be done. The following points cover most of the ground.

Someone (your expert) must:

- be able to perform the task;
- know how they perform the task;
- be able to explain how they perform the task;
- have the time to explain how they perform the task;
- be motivated to cooperate in the enterprise.

These conditions will tend to rule out certain applications from the start. Weather prediction, for example, is not a task that anyone performs very well – not even the professionals. Speech recognition is a task that we all perform extremely well, but none of us (including linguists) have much idea how we do it, so knowledge-based methods have so far met with less success than statistical modeling. Even given a genuine expert with insight into his or her skills, your application depends crucially upon that person's ability and willingness to explain their skills in detail. These conditions may not be met. Your expert may be too inarticulate or too busy to take part in the knowledge engineering enterprise. Experts are usually in demand, and they often prefer doing what they do best to talking about it. They may be jealous of their expertise, perhaps fearing that its mechanization will threaten their livelihoods. There may be lack of commitment on the part of management to make adequate resources available to the engineers.

Even if the above conditions are met, there may be features of the task that limit the extent that the skills can be mechanized, for example:

- if the task involves complex *sensory-motor skills* beyond the scope of current technology in robotics and computer vision;
- if the task involves *commonsense reasoning* or arbitrary amounts of everyday knowledge (see Chapter 3).

It is useful to contrast the kind of knowledge required to become an expert in some field with the kind of knowledge that one needs just to get to and from work. Navigating busy streets in a vehicle requires rather more in the way of scene analysis and hand–eye coordination than the present generation of robots. But one wouldn't want to call human drivers 'experts' (certainly not in my home town of Rochester, New York).

It is also useful to consider the enormous amount of knowledge that we all possess about the world: knowledge of objects and their properties, people and their motivations, physical causality and likely courses of events – the list appears to be endless. This collection of hazy perceptions, vague intuitions and general principles certainly isn't expertise, but nonetheless we still have only the most rudimentary notions about how to impart this kind of information to computers. So any task that is not sufficiently self-contained to be encapsulated in a finite set of facts and rules is definitely beyond the start of the art.

On the other hand, problems which can be solved by the enumeration of associations between observable patterns of data and classes of events are well suited to this technology. For example, operational problems in engineering systems, such as heating, ventilation and air conditioning, can be monitored and diagnosed by rule-based systems which correlate energy consumption signatures of buildings and environmental parameters with underlying causes. Also, problems which involve constructing some object, by either selecting and fleshing out a skeletal plan, or combining primitive components, are within the state of the art. Thus, in Chapters 14 and 15, we encounter systems which configure elevator and computer systems.

1.4.2 Chapter plan of the book

Table 1.1 summarizes the topics we discussed in Section 1.3, and provides pointers to those chapters which have most to say about them. The general reader might wish to concentrate on knowledge representation and control of reasoning, since these are the core topics of expert systems. Knowledge acquisition and explanation of solutions are crucial topics also, but they relate more to the practical side of getting information into and out of a real system that will see operational use.

Chapters 2 and 3 introduce some basic concepts in expert systems. Chapter 2 contains a brief survey of those developments in artificial intelligence which created the intellectual climate in which expert systems research was conceived and conducted. Chapter 3 is also introductory in nature, in that it describes an early expert system and explains why it was built and how it works.

Chapters 3–9 cover the main *representation schemes* for encoding domain-specific knowledge in programs, in such a way that the knowledge can be applied to complex problems by a computer. We begin with a brief overview of symbolic computation and

Activity	Definition	See Chapters
Acquiring knowledge	Transfer of expertise from a person to a program	10–15, 20
Representing knowledge	Encoding expertise in a machine usable form	2–9, 21–23
Controlling reasoning	Deciding when to apply what piece of knowledge	3, 11–12, 17–19
Explaining solutions	Transfer of results from program to person	3, 5, 16, 23

Table 1.1 Summary of expert system topics and guide to chapters of this book

then proceed to explore a number of special-purpose representation languages, such as CLIPS. We also consider the use of more general-purpose object-oriented languages, such as C++, in the construction of expert systems. Finally, we address the problem of approximate reasoning, and introduce various quantitative and qualitative methods for coping with uncertainty.

Chapters 10–16 deal with the practical, engineering side of expert systems technology. We begin with the problem of *knowledge acquisition* – that is, how to elicit knowledge from a human expert and codify it before representing it using the techniques described in earlier chapters. Subsequent chapters consider a number of problem solving paradigms which have been found suitable for tasks such as diagnosis and design, and illustrate them with exemplars from the literature. These exemplars were chosen for pedagogical reasons, rather than because they were necessarily the 'best' in the field. Nevertheless, they do include some success stories of expert systems research, and there are lessons to be learned from the way in which these systems were designed and implemented.

Chapters 17–19 examine *software tools* and *architectures*. We begin by taking a critical look at the kinds of programming tool and programming environment typically provided for building expert systems. Then we describe two additional frameworks around which expert systems can be organized: *blackboard systems* and *truth maintenance systems*.

In the remaining chapters, we touch on some more advanced topics, such as *machine learning, belief networks, case-based reasoning*, and *hybrid systems*. The final chapter contains a summary of the book, recommends some topics for further study, and discusses a few outstanding problems.

BIBLIOGRAPHICAL NOTES

Early reviews of expert systems research can be found in Barr and Feigenbaum (1982), Hayes-Roth *et al.* (1983), Buchanan and Shortliffe (1984) and Waterman (1986).

Applications of expert systems technology are described in Weiss and Kulikowski (1983), Klahr and Waterman (1986), Gale (1986) and Quinlan (1987).

Business-oriented readers can consult Feigenbaum, *et al.* (1988) for a look at expert systems in industry. Many industries publish their own reviews of expert system applications, for example, the *Expert Systems Review for Business and Accounting*.

Recent texts on expert systems include Harmon and Sawyer (1990), Giarratano and Riley (1994) and Stefik (1995).

1. What are the features which distinguish an expert system from a more conventional applications program or a typical AI program? Can you think of a non-AI program that satisfies all of these features?

2. What is the difference between an expert system and a knowledge-based system?

3. Is a program that forecasts summer weather in Southern California by printing out the sentence 'Tomorrow will be just like today' an expert system or not? Assume that it represents today's weather symbolically, is easy to extend or modify, performs well, and can explain its reasoning by printing out the sentence

   'Daily variations in climatic conditions are unlikely at this time of year.'

4. Is a program that forecasts tomorrow's (say 16 June) weather by averaging the local temperature, inches of rainfall, and hours of sunshine of every 16 June since the year 1900 an expert system or not?

5. Is a World Wide Web search engine an expert system? If not, what characteristics would it have to exhibit to be considered an expert at finding useful sites?

6. Why is knowledge acquisition such a bottleneck? What solutions have been proposed?

7. Explain the notions of logical and heuristic adequacy as they relate to knowledge representation languages.

8. Consider this variant of the riddle in Box 1.4. A man is now looking at a portrait and saying:

   'Brothers and sisters have I none, but this man's *son* is my father's son.'

   Solve the riddle and construct an explanation using the notation from Box 1.4.

9. We saw in Section 1.3.4 that a good representation can sometimes make a problem easier to understand, and also make solutions easier to analyze. In the 8-Queens puzzle, the task is to place eight queens on a chess board without any one queen threatening to take another. (Queens can take other pieces along files or along diagonals.)

   One can imagine representing the state of the chess board in various ways, for example, using a 8×8 binary array, and coding for the position of a queen by placing a 1 in the right cell. However, it turns out that there is a far better representation using only a vector of length 8 that reduces the magnitude of the task. Can you think what it is?

2

An Overview of Artificial Intelligence

2.1   The Classical Period: game playing and theorem proving
2.2   The Romantic Period: computer understanding
2.3   The Modern Period: techniques and applications
Bibliographical notes
Study suggestions

What is artificial intelligence? The following definition from Barr and Feigenbaum (1981) is representative of opinion in the field.

Artificial Intelligence (AI) is the part of computer science concerned with designing intelligent computer systems, that is, systems that exhibit the characteristics we associate with intelligence in human behavior – understanding language, learning, reasoning, solving problems, and so on.

In other words, AI is concerned with programming computers to perform tasks that are presently done better by humans, because they involve such higher mental processes such as perceptual learning, memory organization and judgmental reasoning (Minsky, 1968).

Thus, writing a program to perform complicated statistical calculations would not be seen as an artificial intelligence activity, while writing a program to design experiments to test hypotheses would. Most people are not very good at doing long calculations by hand, whereas computers excel at such tasks. On the other hand, devising good experiments to test hypotheses is a skill that the research scientist derives partly from training and partly from experience. Programming a computer to perform such a task would be non-trivial.

There are differences of outlook and emphasis among researchers, however. Some incline towards the view that AI is a branch of Engineering, since it is ultimately about building intelligent artifacts, such as robots (Nilsson, 1971). Others stress the link with cognitive science: a discipline which concerns itself with the study of human information processing, and sometimes uses computers to model or simulate such processing. Still other writers are interested in the overlap with problems of philosophy associated with knowledge and consciousness.

At bottom, AI is about the emulation of human behavior: the discovery of techniques that will allow us to program machines so that they simulate or extend our mental capabilities. It is therefore hardly surprising that the discipline should be close-ly related to a wide range of other academic subject areas such as computer science, psychology, and linguistics. The fact that AI crosses a number of traditional interdis-ciplinary boundaries sometimes causes friction, but is more often a source of inspira-tion and new ideas.

As an aid to the general reader, this chapter attempts a very brief overview of arti-ficial intelligence research, insofar as it relates to the design and construction of expert systems. It also tries to explain in what way knowledge-based programming differs from both

- more conventional programming techniques; and
- the general-purpose problem solving methods devised by the pioneers of AI research.

As a rhetorical device, the history of AI from about 1950 to the present day will be broken into three periods. These periods will be characterized in terms of their domi-nant themes with respect to both which research topics were most active and what practical results were achieved. For a more general introduction to AI, the reader is referred to textbooks cited in the bibliographical notes at the end of the chapter.

2.1 The Classical Period: game playing and theorem proving

Artificial intelligence is scarcely younger than conventional computer science; the be-ginnings of AI can be seen in the first game-playing and puzzle-solving programs writ-ten shortly after World War II. Game playing and puzzle solving may seem somewhat remote from expert systems, and insufficiently serious to provide a theoretical basis for real applications. However, a rather basic notion about computer-based problem solving can be traced back to those early attempts to program computers to perform such tasks.

2.1.1 State space search

The fundamental idea that fell out of early research is called *state space search*, and it is essentially very simple. Many kinds of problem can be formulated in terms of three important ingredients:

- a *starting state* of a problem, for example the initial state of a puzzle;
- a *termination test* for detecting final states or solutions to the problem, for example a simple rule that says when the puzzle is solved;
- a *set of operations* that can be applied to change the current state of the problem, for example the moves or steps involved in solving a puzzle.

One way of thinking of this conceptual space of states is as a tree in which the states are *nodes* and the operations are *arcs*. Consider the problem of making a word from a small collection of letters in the game of Scrabble. Given some operators for arrang-ing letters, we can generate a search space.

Suppose the available letters are T, C, and A. We could decide that at each level in the tree we would add a particular letter. Each branch at a given level would correspond

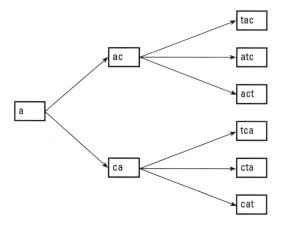

Figure 2.1 **The Scrabble search space for the letters A, C, T.**

to putting that letter in a different position in the word we are trying to assemble (see Figure 2.1).

In our example, we decided to add the letters in alphabetical order. As we generate this search space, we will sooner or later encounter a word, either 'act' or 'cat.' (Let's assume that we quit as soon as we find a word; we are not looking for a long word, or a high scoring word, as in Scrabble.)

This search space has two nice properties that not all search spaces have:

- it is finite, because there are only so many ($n!$) ways to arrange n letters;
- it does not contain any repeated nodes that might lead to loops among the arcs.

This method of generating anagrams by progressive enumeration is an instance of a simple algorithm called *generate-and-test*:

---

(1) *Generate* a new state by modifying the current state; for example, form a new configuration of letters from an existing configuration.

(2) *Test* to see if this state is a solution; for example, see if it forms a word. If so, quit, else go to (1).

The set of solutions that satisfy the termination condition of step (2) is sometimes called the *solution space*. In some puzzles, for example 8-Queens, solutions are plentiful, while in others, for example the 8-Puzzle, solutions are sparse. This is because there are many ways to arrange 8 queens on a chess board without any one queen threatening another, but the 8-Puzzle has only one solution (see Exercise 7).

There are two main variants of basic generate-and-test: *depth-first search* and *breadth-first search*. The difference between them lies in the order in which possible solutions are generated in step (1). The actual algorithms are given in Exercise 5; an informal description is given below.

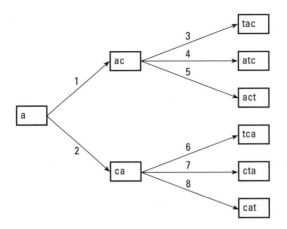

Figure 2.2 **Breadth-first search.**

At any given node, *N*, depth-first search considers the 'children' of *N*, that is, those states which result from applying operators to *N*, before considering 'siblings' of *N* (those states which were generated along with *N*, when applying operators to *N*'s 'ancestor'). In breadth-first search, it is the other way round: *N*'s siblings are checked out before expanding *N*, that is, before going on to *N*'s children. Thus, in breadth-first search, one searches layer by layer through successive levels of the search space (see Figure 2.2), whereas in depth-first search one pursues a single path at a time, returning to *N* to pick another path only if the current path fails (see Figure 2.3).

In both Figures 2.2 and 2.3, the numbers on the arcs indicate the order in which nodes might be visited. I say 'might,' because, in both cases, whether we visit 'ac' before 'ca' or vice versa will depend upon the order in which we apply our operators. In the present example, we chose to add a new letter at the end of each string first, and then progressively back the new letter up through the string, but we could have chosen differently. As a result, both methods, as instantiated here, will terminate on 'act', not 'cat'. Breadth-first search visits five nodes to achieve this, while depth-first search visits four.

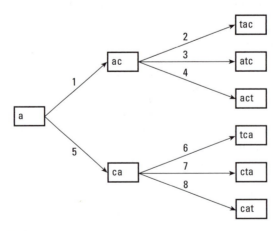

Figure 2.3 **Depth-first search.**

However, these two search methods have rather different properties.

- Breadth-first search finds the shortest solution path, if there is one. In other words, it finds the shortest path between the root node (start state) and the solution. Algorithms with this property are called *admissible*.
- Depth-first search can get there faster as long as it is guided by heuristics, that is, if it makes good decisions when choosing which path to pursue next. But depth-first search may never terminate if the search space is infinite, even if a solution exists.

It is not hard to see how the number of nodes may grow exponentially at each stage, regardless of the order in which nodes are generated. This phenomenon is usually referred to as *combinatorial explosion*, and it poses insuperable problems to programs which attempt to play games like chess by 'brute force' enumeration of all the alternatives (see Box 2.1). Since human beings are slower than computers at such enumeration tasks, and much less reliable, one can safely assume that chess grand masters do not function in this way. Rather they apply their experience, imagination, and analytic skills to the selection of both overall strategies and winning moves. We are all inclined to call such behavior 'intelligent.'

Game playing programs also work by doing search, but their search strategies are more selective than simple generate-and-test, and the algorithms are complicated by the fact that two different players take turns at moving. Highly successful programs have been written for checkers, backgammon, and chess. Such chess programs are not knowledge-based systems, but rather programs that search large numbers of board configurations selectively and efficiently, using specialized algorithms that are outside the scope of this book.

In addition to games and puzzles, another principal concern of artificial intelligence that began in the 1950s was *theorem proving*. Theorem proving involves showing that some statement in which we are interested follows logically from a set of special statements, the *axioms* (which are known, or assumed, to be true), and is therefore a *theorem*.

BOX 2.1

Combinatorial Explosion

The study of the tractability or intractability of computations is called *complexity theory*. For the uninitiated, it is only necessary to know that there are classes of problem whose solution requires resources which are an exponential function of the size of the particular problem.

For example, the time taken to find a path through a maze increases exponentially with the number of branching paths. Similarly, the time taken to find a proof for a theorem of the propositional calculus is exponential in the number of variables. Such problems are intractable in general, and called *NP-hard*; the interested reader is referred to a standard text, such as Hopcroft and Ullman (1979), for further technical details and an explanation of the terminology.

Problems that admit of polynomial time algorithms, on the other hand, are deemed tractable. For example, verifying a given path through a maze, or checking a proof of some theorem, are tractable problems. Unhappily, most of the problems that interest us in artificial intelligence can be shown to be NP-hard; hence the importance of heuristic methods.

A nice non-technical introduction to computational complexity can be found in Poundstone (1988, Chapter 9).

As an example, suppose we have the two axioms

'If a computer can go wrong, it will go wrong'

and

'My computer can go wrong'

expressed as sentences in some formal language. Then we can derive a sentence representing

'My computer will go wrong'

as a theorem, using only the inference rules of the calculus. Thus 'My computer will go wrong' follows logically from the axioms, in the sense that it cannot be false if the axioms are true. The correctness of this inference has nothing to do with computers and everything to do with the form of the statements expressed in a logical notation, such as

$$\frac{(\forall X)\ (F(X) \supset G(X))}{F(a)}$$
$$G(a)\ \{X/a\}$$

which can be read as:

'All Fs are Gs, a is an F, therefore F is a G.'

Our argument about computers is valid because it conforms to this pattern, if we substitute a for X.

As was the case with puzzles, some of the concepts and techniques developed in the field of automatic theorem proving (sometimes called *automated reasoning*) provided a starting point for students of more realistic problem solving. Thus, knowledge relevant to the solution of some problem can be represented as a set of axioms, the *theory*, and problem solving can be viewed as the process of showing that the desired solution is a *theorem* (see Chapter 8). In other words, searching for a solution among the theorems generated is analogous to traversing a state space graph, and can be considered as such.

Unfortunately, the process of generating all the theorems that follow from some set of axioms is combinatorially explosive, since one can add any theorems so derived to the axioms and use the new set of statements to derive still more theorems. Deriving solutions by theorem proving may involve computations which require more resources than can be provided by any conceivable computer, and it can be shown that some such computations may never terminate. The field of automated reasoning has enjoyed considerable success in circumventing these problems in the context of generating mathematical proofs, but these methods do not easily transfer to less formal domains.

Since most human beings are poor logical reasoners, and yet do not appear to be hampered by combinatorial difficulties, it seems unlikely that they engage in formal reasoning of this kind. Rather they appear to intersperse valid steps of inference with plausible assumptions and likely hypotheses that are largely informal. It is this kind of inference that expert systems typically attempt to model when problem solving in some real-world domain.

2.1.2 Heuristic search

Given that exhaustive search is infeasible for anything other than small search spaces, some means of guiding the search is required. A search which uses one or more items of domain-specific knowledge to traverse a state space graph is called a *heuristic search*. A heuristic is best thought of as a rule of thumb: it is not guaranteed to succeed, in the way that an algorithm or decision procedure is, but it is useful in the majority of cases.

A simple form of heuristic search is *hill climbing*. This involves giving the program an *evaluation function* which it can apply to the current state of the problem in order to obtain a rough estimate of how well things are going. It then uses this function to select the next move.

For example, a simple evaluation function for a chess-playing program might involve a straightforward comparison of material between the two players. The program then seeks to maximize this function when it applies operators, such as the moves of chess. In other words, it will select the move that results in the most favorable balance of material after the move has been executed.

A basic algorithm for hill climbing can be given as follows:

(1) From the current point in the state space, apply rules that generate a new set of possible solutions, for example, the legal moves of chess that can be made from the current state.

(2) If any state in the newly derived set is a solution, then quit with success, else take only the 'best' state from the set, make it the current state, and go to step (1).

There are well-known problems with this approach, however. To begin with, your evaluation function may not be a faithful estimate of the 'goodness' of the current state of the problem. To pursue the chess example, I may have more pieces than you, but you may be in a better position. Simple estimates based on material advantage will not capture all the subtleties of the game.

Furthermore, even if the evaluation function gives a good estimate, there are various states of play that can cause problems. For example, there may be no obvious next move, because they all appear to be equally good or bad. This is like being on a 'plateau' with no clear path towards the heights. Another problem is that of *local maxima*, which occurs when your evaluation function leads you to a peak position, from which the only way is down, while your goal is on some other, higher peak. Thus, I can take your queen, but in so doing lose the game.

Best-first search is another form of heuristic search that has better properties. As in hill climbing, we have an evaluation function that rates the nodes we encounter, but we select the next node for expansion from among *all* the nodes encountered so far, and not just from among the successors of the current node. Such algorithms are moderately complicated (see Box 2.2 for the A* search algorithm), but the general idea is that we must now keep track of all the nodes we have seen so far, and be prepared to 'take up where we left off' elsewhere if none of the successors of the current node look promising. Best-first search improves on hill climbing because it does not make irrevocable decisions based on local information. However, it is computationally more expensive, thanks to all the bookkeeping required to bear in mind nodes we have looked at but 'left behind' on unexplored paths through the search space.

BOX 2.2

The A* Algorithm

There is a well-known algorithm for best-first search, known as A* (pronounced 'A star'). The basic idea behind A* is that, for each node n that we develop, we compute the value of the function

$$f(n) = g(n) + h(n)$$

where $g(n)$ reflects the distance of n from the start node and $h(n)$ estimates the distance from n to the goal node. Thus a low value of $f(n)$ is 'good' (that is, n is on a short path to the goal), while a high value is 'bad.' The idea is to use $f(n)$ to find the cheapest path from the start to the goal.

It turns out that if $h(n)$ is a lower bound on the *actual* distance to the goal, that is, if $h(n)$ never overestimates the distance, then the A* algorithm will always find an optimal path to the goal using f(n) as its evaluation function. Algorithms with this property are called *admissible* (see Nilsson, 1980, Chapter 2 and Pearl, 1984, Chapter 2 for further discussions).

Notation
s is the start node
g is the goal node
OPEN is a list that holds unexpanded nodes
CLOSED is a list that holds expanded nodes

The algorithm
(1) OPEN := {s}.
(2) If OPEN = {}, then halt. There is no path to the goal.
(3) Remove a node n from OPEN for which $f(m) \geq f(n)$ for all other nodes m on OPEN, and place n on CLOSED.
(4) Generate the successors of n, reject all successors that contain a loop, and give each remaining node a pointer back to n.
(5) If g is among the successors of n, then halt and return the path derived by tracing pointers back from g to s.
(6) For each extant successor n' of n do the following:
    (6.1) Compute $f(n')$.
    (6.2) If n' is not on OPEN or CLOSED,
        then add it to OPEN, assign $f(n')$ to n', and set a pointer back from n' to n.
    (6.3) If n' is already on OPEN or CLOSED,
        then compare new value of $f(n') = new$ with the old value $f(n') = old$.
        If $old < new$,
        then discard the new node.
        If $new < old$,
        then substitute the new node for the old in the list,
        moving the new node to OPEN if the old node was on CLOSED.
End of algorithm

See Exercise 8 for an application of this algorithm.

Using the power of a computer to search for solutions, either exhaustively or guided by an evaluation function, is not always adequate for real applications. The search spaces associated with such tasks as understanding speech, configuring computing systems, and planning sequences of actions are too large to be traversed in a reasonable time unless constrained by more than 'local' knowledge. Many of these problems can be shown to be isomorphic with abstract problems that are known to be intractable, in the sense that the resources required to solve them are exponential in the size of the problem.

As we shall see, expert systems attempt to tackle the difficulties of search by explicitly representing *in detail* both the knowledge that experts possess about some domain and the strategies that they use to reason about what they know.

Early attempts at game playing and theorem proving are well represented by the collection of papers in Feigenbaum and Feldman (1963). I tend to think of the period that begins with the publication of Shannon's (1950) paper on chess and ends with the publication of Feigenbaum and Feldman as the 'Classical Period' of AI research. Among the most important discoveries of this period were the twin realizations that

- problems of whatever kind could, in principle, be reduced to search problems so long as they were formalizable in terms of a start state, an end state, and a set of operations for traversing a state space; but
- the search had to be guided by some representation of knowledge about the domain of the problem.

In a minority of cases, it proved possible to restrict the application of knowledge to the use of an evaluation function which was able to use features of the problem local to the current state to give the program some idea of how well it was doing. However, in the majority of cases it was felt that something more was required, such as a global problem-solving strategy, or an explicit encoding of knowledge about the objects, properties, and actions associated with the domain, or both.

2.2 The Romantic Period: computer understanding

The mid-1960s to the mid-1970s represents what I call the 'Romantic Period' in artificial intelligence research. At this time, people were very concerned with making machines 'understand', by which they usually meant the understanding of natural language, especially stories and dialogue. This endeavor drew a certain amount of scorn from one or two philosophers, who doubted that a computer program could ever be said to understand anything.

2.2.1 SHRDLU

Winograd's (1972) SHRDLU system was arguably the climax of this epoch: a program which was capable of understanding a quite substantial subset of English by representing and reasoning about a very restricted domain (a world consisting of children's toy blocks). The program exhibited understanding by modifying its 'blocks-world' representation in response to commands, and by responding to questions about both the configuration of blocks and its 'actions' upon them. Thus it could answer questions like

'What is the color of the block supporting the red pyramid?'

and derive plans for obeying commands such as

'Place the blue pyramid on the green block.'

SHRDLU was deemed to understand the sentences because it responded to them appropriately. The rationale for this view of understanding was called *procedural semantics*, the idea being that a program can be said to understand a query if it can answer the question correctly, and it can be said to understand a command if it can carry the command out. Needless to say, this is a rather operational view of understanding, that is, a view which explains understanding in terms of behavior, rather than in terms of mental operations.

Another line of inquiry attempted to root understanding in less artificial and more everyday contexts, such as visits to a doctor, or dining in a restaurant. Schank and Colby (1973) used a structure called a *script* to assemble the various elements that make up a real-world situation. Scripts can be thought of as packages for the various goals, solutions, and customs that are associated with particular events. Thus a 'restaurant script' would be activated by an 'eating' goal, be satisfied by a 'meal' solution, and would assemble intermediate knowledge about seating, menus, checks, tips, and the like. Such devices explain why certain behaviors (such as undressing in front of strangers) are deemed normal in one setting (a doctor's office) and abnormal in others (a burger bar). They also explain certain assumptions that everyone makes; for example, 'a visit to the doctor' is a visit to his office, not his home, because this is the default location for the 'doctor's visit' script.

BOX 2.3

A Restaurant Script

Scripts may be described in different notations, but they should contain certain basic ingredients: a goal that actions in the script should satisfy, preconditions for employing the script, and postconditions that will hold after the script is employed. There should also be a breakdown of key phases of a script that serve to organize the action. Here is a simple script for a visit to a restaurant.

```
Goal: Eat without having to cook.

Preconditions: Hungry, have money, restaurant open.

Postconditions: Not hungry, have less money.

Act One: Enter restaurant. Seat oneself, if no sign to the
contrary, or no host(ess). Otherwise, allow host(ess) to seat
you.

Act Two: Consult menu, order, and eat. Remember there may be
'specials.'

Act Three: Get check. Pay waiter/waitress or cashier, as
appropriate. Leave.
```

Note that there are various conventions that may differ from place to place, for example, with respect to seating, specials, and paying, that serve to guide appropriate behavior. Certain assumptions are built into this script, for example that you pay after you eat, unlike in a cafeteria. Ideally, a script would contain some backup behaviors for when certain assumptions are violated.

Scripts can be seen as viewing the problem of knowledge representation at a higher level than procedural semantics. Descriptions of meaning at the somewhat lower sentence level are hard to 'lift' to a level where whole episodes and encounters become meaningful, partly because so many of the motivations behind what people say and do are never explicitly stated. Some researchers realized that this focus upon context-free interpretation was one of the great obstacles to computer understanding, and therefore pursued a quite different path, in which formal, domain-free models of thought and language were neglected in favor of relatively informal, domain-specific patterns of reasoning. This laid the foundations for the 'neat' versus 'scruffy' dichotomy in AI which spilled over into the Modern Period (see next section).

Other researchers (for example, Newell and Simon, 1972; Anderson, 1976) attempted to model human problem-solving behavior on simple tasks, such as puzzles, word games and memory tests. The aim was to make the knowledge and strategy used by the program resemble the knowledge and strategy of the human subject as closely as possible. Empirical studies compared the performance of program and subject in an attempt to see how successful the simulation had been.

The fundamental problem with such comparative studies is that there are no direct methods for showing that a human subject and an AI program do the same thing in the same way. Thus, indirect arguments have to be employed; for example, showing that program and subject make the same kinds of errors when faced with hard problems or bad data, or showing that program and subject display similar profiles with respect to the time taken to solve different classes of problem. Simply showing that they get the same answer is obviously not enough, because there are a multitude of different strategies and encodings of knowledge that will solve the same problem.

2.2.2   Knowledge representation schemes

Regardless of whether or not these forays into cognitive science were ultimately productive for psychological theory, the new emphasis on knowledge representation proved to be extremely fruitful for computer science. Newell and Simon generated a scheme known as *production rules* (see Chapter 5) which has since become a mainstay of expert systems design and development. They also pioneered a technique known as *protocol analysis*, whereby human subjects were encouraged to think aloud as they solved problems and such protocols were later analyzed in an attempt to reveal the concepts and procedures employed. This approach can be seen as a direct precursor of some of the knowledge elicitation techniques that engineers use today. These psychological studies showed just how hard the knowledge representation problem was, but demonstrated that it could be addressed in a spirit of empirical inquiry, rather than philosophical debate.

In the Romantic Period, researchers explored a multitude of possibilities for encoding both particular facts and general principles about the world in such a way that they could be applied by a computer program in the course of its goal-directed reasoning. These involved using constructs of the following kind:

- *rules* of the form 'if these conditions hold, then apply this operator';
- various kinds of *network*, where nodes stood for concepts and arcs for relationships between them; and

- *logical formulas* for encoding facts and principles, including control information about when to draw what inferences.

Sometimes these constructs were used in combination. However, most of the programs produced at this time were essentially research vehicles. Few of them found their way into real applications.

Minsky (1968) contains a representative sample of papers from the first half of this period. All of them are interesting, but not all are convincing, from the point of view of actual achievement. Nevertheless, many of the knowledge representation schemes that we currently take for granted were developed during this time. For example, Quillian's paper gave rise to *associative nets* and *semantic networks* (see Chapter 6): a graphical formalism for encoding facts and definitions. Without this decade of imaginative exploration, which had its share of spectacular failures, it is doubtful that expert systems would exhibit the variety of functions and structures that they do today.

A representative sample of papers from the latter half of this period can be found in Winston (1975b); Minsky's paper on a knowledge representation formalism called *frames* is particularly worth reading. Also worth consulting are both volumes of Winston and Brown (1979), which summarize much of the work done at the Massachusetts Institute of Technology during the 1970s. They contain a number of important papers on such topics as natural language processing, computer vision, and robotics, which will be neglected here.

BOX 2.4

Bother with Bats and Problems with Penguins

Semantic networks are meant to encode world knowledge and word meanings in a graph-theoretic format. Thus the taxonomic tree of Figure 2.4 attempts to capture our knowledge that birds, bats, and even certain species of fish, fly. However, birds are much more typical of flying animals than bats, which are in turn more typical than the somewhat unusual flying fish. A simple tree diagram does not represent this fact.

Similarly, although most birds fly, penguins do not. Hence a penguin is not a flying animal, as Figure 2.4 suggests. One would still like to be able to say that, in general, birds fly. But how do we handle exceptions in a graph? Chapter 6 has some of the answers.

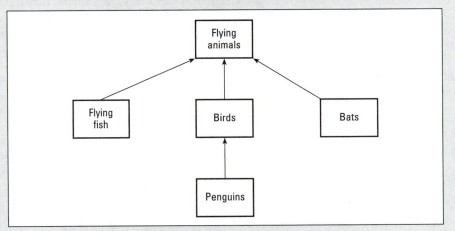

Figure 2.4 A simple taxonomic tree with exceptions.

The whole notion of 'computer understanding' is entirely problematic, of course. It is simply not clear under what conditions one would be prepared to assert that a machine understood anything. (Neither are the grounds for imputing human understanding particularly clear, for that matter.) However, even if one is unsure about what would constitute sufficient grounds for understanding, one can at least list some of the necessary grounds.

One is the ability to represent knowledge about the world, and reason using such representations. Expert systems exhibit this ability, insofar as they possess explicit representations of knowledge about some domain, and are capable of applying this knowledge to solve real problems. However, like the Winograd program, their outlook is strictly circumscribed: reliability still tends to be an inverse function of the size of the domain.

Another sign of understanding is the ability to perceive equivalences or analogies between different representations of the same situations. Expert systems score badly here, since they expect their inputs to be in a certain form, namely one that corresponds to their stored knowledge. Any deviation from the patterns they expect tends to result in breakdown or unpredictable behavior.

Finally, understanding implies an ability to learn in some non-trivial way, that is, in some non-rote fashion that requires new information to be integrated with information already possessed, perhaps in a way that modifies both. Few expert systems have demonstrated this kind of facility, although some progress towards machine learning has been made in recent years (see Chapter 20). Also, progress has been made in the design of programs which elicit knowledge from experts via an interaction at the terminal and then compile that knowledge into an applications program (see Chapter 10).

Although current expert systems fall short on some of these criteria, it is arguable that they do not have to 'understand' a domain, in the way that a human understands it, in order to solve problems (Davis, 1989). A number of well-documented systems perform as well as human experts without exhibiting the kind of understanding that the Romantic Period was all about. As Davis points out, there is no necessary connection between a particular *process* for solving a problem and the solution itself. In other words, all we require is that an expert system gets more or less the same answer as an expert, or helps an expert get the right answer. We do not demand that the system go through the same steps of reasoning as a human, or organize its domain knowledge in exactly the same way, because we are not doing psychological research.

However, we shall also see (in Chapter 11 and beyond) that subsequent attempts to use expert systems for teaching purposes led to some revisions in this point of view and introduced a greater degree of sophistication into expert system designs. Many of these advances and refinements take us closer to the nebulous goal of computer understanding. They have also generated novel insights into the human problem-solving process, and are now providing us with a more powerful collection of concepts for analyzing problem solving activity by both people and machines.

2.3 The Modern Period: techniques and applications

What I shall call the Modern Period stretches from the mid-1970s to the end of the 1980s. It contains the rise of expert systems, the so-called 'AI winter,' and ends with the resurgence of interest that accompanied the advent of the World Wide Web. At the time of writing, we are in a new Post-Modern Period that I shall not attempt to characterize here, being too close to the event. However, it is a safe bet that it will be driven largely by Internet applications involving intelligent agents and advisors that facilitate information retrieval and electronic commerce. The success or failure of AI in this period will depend largely upon the ability and willingness of researchers to forsake the traditional concerns that characterized earlier periods and address real problems in the new information environment.

2.3.1   Knowledge is power

During the Modern period, the conviction grew that the heuristic power of a problem solver lies in the explicit representation of relevant knowledge that the program can access, and not in some sophisticated inference mechanism or some complicated evaluation function. Researchers have developed techniques for encoding human knowledge in modules which can be activated by patterns (see Box 2.5). Early attempts to simulate human problem solving (for example, Newell and Simon, 1972) strove for uniformity in the encoding of knowledge and simplicity in the inference mechanism, although recent attempts have typically allowed themselves more variety, as we shall see in Chapters 11–18.

It became clear that there are advantages attached to the strategy of representing human knowledge explicitly in pattern-directed modules, instead of encoding it into an algorithm that could be implemented using more conventional programming techniques.

- The process of rendering the knowledge explicit in a piecemeal fashion seemed to be more in tune with the way that experts store and apply their knowledge. In response to requests as to how they do their job, few experts will provide a well-articulated sequence of steps that is guaranteed to terminate with success in all situations. Rather, the knowledge that they possess has to be elicited by asking what they would do in typical cases, and then probing for the exceptions.
- This method of programming allows for fast prototyping and incremental system development. If the system designer and programmer have done their jobs properly, the resultant program should be easy to modify and extend, so that errors and gaps in the knowledge can be rectified without major adjustments to the existing code. If they haven't done their jobs properly, then changes to the knowledge may well have unpredictable effects, since there may be unplanned interactions between modules of knowledge.
- Practitioners realized that a program doesn't have to solve the whole problem, or even be right all of the time, in order to be useful. An expert system can function as an intelligent assistant, which enumerates alternatives in the search for a solution, and rules out some of the less promising ones. The system can leave the final judgment, and some of the intermediate strategic decisions, to the user and still be a useful tool.

However, it was also recognized that rule-based systems are not easy to build and debug. As the knowledge base grows, rules will tend to interact in unexpected ways, by competing for attention, that is, competing to be applied to the problem. Different control regimes seem to work for some types of problem solving and not others, but evidence for this was initially anecdotal.

Experience has taught us that there are different problem solving methods that work best on particular kinds of problem. These methods – with mysterious names like 'heuristic classification,' 'hierarchical hypothesize and test,' and 'propose and revise' – typically employ different means for controlling computations. We examine such methods in detail in Chapters 11–15, where we also address the issues of representation and control raised by their deployment.

BOX 2.5

Procedural versus Declarative

In procedural programming languages, such as C, we typically do not make a physical distinction between that part of the program which contains the 'logic' and that part which manipulates the 'data.' For example, a procedure to check if a given bird species can fly might look like this:

```
char fly(char * s)
{
  char answer = 'y';
  if (strcmp(s, "penguin")==0)
  { answer = 'n'; }
  return answer;
}
```

Regardless of whether or not you understand C, it is clear that this is executable code which will be explicitly called by another part of the program, for example along the lines of

```
char c;
c = fly("penguin");
```

Imagine instead that we simply have two rules, kept in a knowledge base:

```
(defrule
  (bird (type ?X))
  =>
  (assert (yes))
)
(defrule
  (bird (type penguin))
  =>
  (assert (no))
)
```

Here, the rules (in the syntax of CLIPS) are closer to being declarations or definitions. Given a random bird, we assert that it can fly. But if we know that the bird is a penguin, we assert that it cannot fly. Of course, penguins are birds, so some other part of the expert system must decide which rule to apply to a given case. This is called the *inference engine*.

The modular nature of the rules is nonetheless apparent. No code explicitly 'calls' a rule. We shall deal with these implementation issues in detail in Chapter 5.

The Modern Period has seen the development of a number of systems that can claim a high level of performance on non-trivial tasks, for example the R1/XCON system for configuring computer systems (see Chapter 14). A number of principles have emerged which distinguish such systems from both conventional programs and earlier work in AI (see Davis, 1982). The most important of these are considered below.

- As we saw in Chapter 1, the part of the program which contains the representation of domain-specific knowledge, the *knowledge base*, is generally separate from the

BOX 2.6

Separation of Inference Engine and Knowledge Base

An expert system is usually built by assembling a knowledge base which is then interpreted by an off-the-shelf program that contains an inference engine. An empty knowledge base comes with such a program, which is typically called a *shell*. The end user of the application interacts with the shell via the inference engine, which uses the knowledge put in the knowledge base to answer questions, solve problems, or offer advice (see Figure 2.5).

The knowledge base contains both rules and various declarations. For example, in the 'Penguin' example of Box 2.5, the CLIPS knowledge base would need the declaration

```
(deftemplate bird
  (field (type SYMBOL)))
```

in addition to the rules

```
(defrule
  (bird)
  =>
  (assert (yes))
)

(defrule
  (bird (type penguin))
  =>
  (assert (no))
)
```

which states that 'bird' is a data object that may contain a 'type' field. Other declarations may influence the inference engine's behavior, as we shall see in Chapter 5.

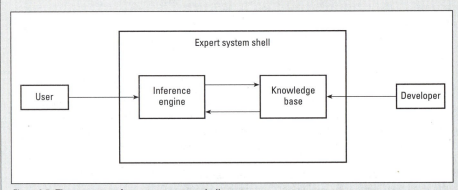

Figure 2.5 The structure of an expert system shell.

part of the program which performs the reasoning, the *inference engine*. This means that one can make at least some changes to either module without necessarily having to alter the other. Thus one might be able to add more knowledge to the knowledge base, or tune the inference engine for better performance, without having to modify code elsewhere.

- Practitioners try to use as uniform a representation of knowledge as possible. This makes the knowledge easier to encode and understand, and helps keep the inference engine simple. However, as we shall see in Chapter 11 and beyond, uniformity can sometimes pose problems if different kinds of knowledge are forced into the same formalism. Thus there is a trade-off between simplicity and requisite variety in the representation.

- Unlike more conventional problem solving programs, expert systems are expected to offer the user some kind of explanation as to how the conclusions were arrived at. Given a uniform knowledge representation and a simple inference engine, this usually involves presenting a trace of which modules of knowledge became active in which order. We shall see in Chapter 16 that such traces are often less informative than we would wish, and so stronger methods are required.

2.3.2 'AI winter' and 'AI spring'

The latter part of the Modern Period was characterized by increased self-consciousness and self-criticism. One symptom of this was the 'neat' versus 'scruffy' debate in which proponents of formal versus informal methods in AI argued their case; there was also a 'symbolic' versus 'subsymbolic' debate (see Chapter 23). It seems obvious that the job of 'neat' R&D is to build and test the foundations of a discipline, while the job of 'scruffy' R&D is to adapt, prove, and if necessary re-engineer these building blocks for use in real applications.[1]

Meanwhile, many expert systems were successfully developed for a wide range of applications, but the technology was oversold by AI companies marketing expensive software packages that ran on specialized hardware and were poorly integrated into other commercial systems. Instead of developing niche markets by solving problems that were particularly susceptible to knowledge-based approaches, large claims were made for the general efficacy of these techniques. But not all domains are well suited to AI technology, nor is AI in any form a 'magic bullet' that will serve as a substitute for sound engineering practices.

The resultant 'AI Winter' is thawing largely because the information environment is expanding at an ever-increasing rate, and it is hard to believe that AI does not contain at least part of the solution to the problems posed by the plethora of data, including text and images, that needs to be retrieved, analyzed, classified, routed, indexed, summarized, interpreted, and so forth. In a sense, the time has come for symbolic

---

[1] On the other hand, one can sensibly argue about the proportion in which these activities should figure in the discipline as a whole. If everyone is engaged in writing theoretical papers full of Greek letters, then research will not be grounded in reality, while a lack of theoretical results will encourage *ad hoc* approaches to applications.

computation, and knowledge-based systems generally, to enter the mainstream. But such approaches must also be combined with statistical and probabilistic approaches, if we are to deal with the vast amounts of information that are now available on the Internet and various commercial online services.

In the next chapter, we introduce two early AI programs, and give a simplified account of how they worked. Although the systems are now more than 20 years old, they provide such good illustrations of the basic concepts that I make no apologies for using them here. Each can be seen as a bridge between earlier programs based on state space search and the evolution of a more knowledge-based approach. This is an important transition for the student of expert systems to understand. More modern systems are described in Chapters 11–15, and especially Chapters 22 and 23, where we examine some experiments on the cutting edge of expert systems research.

BIBLIOGRAPHICAL NOTES

Rich and Knight (1991) and Winston (1992) are both good introductory texts in AI, with the latter having more depth. The various volumes of the *Handbook of Artificial Intelligence* (Barr and Feigenbaum, 1981, 1982; Cohen and Feigenbaum, 1982) are a good source of concise reference material for the beginning student, albeit somewhat out of date. Readers interested in the current state of computer understanding are recommended to consult Allen (1995) for a thorough account of basic research in natural language processing, while futuristic visions of AI from the MIT lab can be found in Winston and Shellard (1990).

The early chapters of Nilsson (1980) still provide an excellent introduction to topics in heuristic search, while Pearl (1984) is also recommended for the more mathematically minded. Some modern applications of heuristic search are collected in Rayward-Smith *et al.* (1996), while Rayward-Smith (1994) provides an up-to-date text on the subject. Heuristic search is still seen as a viable technique in a wide range of applications, for example financial planning, edge detection in computer vision, molecular design.

A* and related algorithms are still deemed worthy of study. For example, in a recent paper, Korf and Reid (1998) showed that heuristics typically improve search not by reducing the breadth of search, as is commonly supposed, but by reducing its depth. Thus, heuristics appear to work by finding shorter solution paths, rather than by lowering the branching factor.

STUDY SUGGESTIONS

1. Why isn't a statistical analysis package an AI program?

2. What, if anything, can psychology tell us about how to construct intelligent machines?

3. What do you understand by the term 'search space'? What is the search space for the game of chess?

4. What do you understand by the term 'solution space'? What is the solution space for the game of chess?

5. Here is the algorithm for depth-first search. It is written in a functional notation which renders its recursive structure apparent. Thus `dfs` is a function of three arguments: `goal`, `current` and `pending`:

continued

- `goal` is the object of the search,
- `current` is the current node (initially the start state), and
- `pending` is a list of nodes waiting to be expanded, initially empty.

In what follows, : = indicates assignment, expand is a function that generates the successors of a node, and + is a function that appends two lists, e.g.,

```
(a b c) + (d e f) = (a b c d e f).
```

`()` is the empty list, while `first` and `rest` are functions which return the head of a list and the tail of a list respectively, for example:

```
first(a b c) = a
rest(a b c) = (b c).
```

(i) Encode the following algorithm in the programming language of your choice.

```
dfs(goal, current, pending)
{
  if current = goal, then success;
  else
  {
    pending := expand(current) + pending;
    if pending = () then fail;
    else dfs(goal, first(pending), rest(pending))
  }
}
```

(ii) Write a similar algorithm for breadth-first search, and implement it. It is only necessary to change one statement in the `dfs` function.

6. Consider the 'missionaries and cannibals' puzzle, shown in Figure 2.6. This puzzle can be stated as follows.

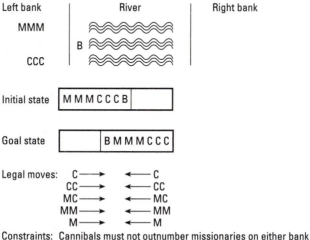

Figure 2.6 The missionaries and cannibals puzzle.

continued

There are three missionaries, three cannibals, and a boat on the left bank of a river (initial state). To solve the puzzle, you must transport all six persons to the right bank using the boat (goal state). The boat only carries two persons at a time, and at least one person must bring the boat back. Thus the legal moves are

    C->   one cannibal from left to right
    CC-> two cannibals from left to right
    MC-> one missionary and one cannibal from left to right
    MM-> two missionaries from left to right
    M->   one missionary from left to right

plus the inverse moves from right to left. However, the following complication acts as a further constraint: if the cannibals ever outnumber the missionaries on either bank, then they will naturally devour them. A solution to this problem is therefore a sequence of moves which leads from the start state to the goal state without mishap.

It is possible to solve this problem by exhaustive generate-and-test, since the underlying search space is quite small. Figure 2.7 shows how the search space can be formed by the recursive application of applicable operators, with 'loop nodes' and 'illegal nodes' clearly marked. Loop nodes are nodes where the application of an operator leads back to an earlier state, while illegal nodes are nodes that fail the anthropophagic constraint. Clearly, the node expansion function, such as `expand` in the `dfs` algorithm, should not return such nodes.

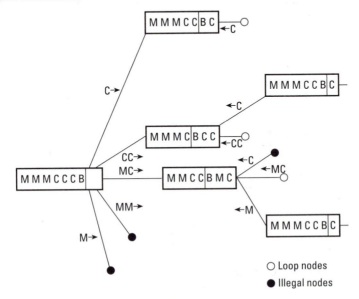

Figure 2.7 **Developing the missionaries and cannibals search space.**

continued

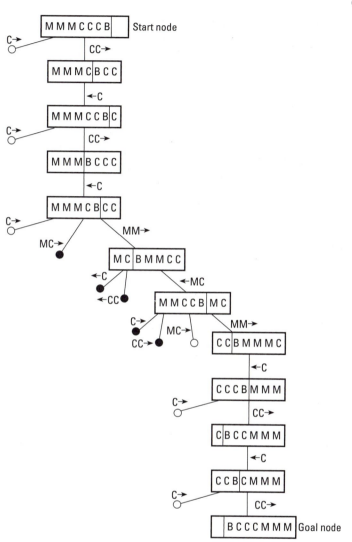

Figure 2.8 The complete search space by depth-first search.

Figure 2.8 shows the complete search space as developed by depth-first search, with moves being tried in the order in which they are listed above. The search expands 22 nodes, and the success path is 11 nodes long, so we say that the *penetrance* of the search is 11/22 = 0.5. Roughly speaking, the penetrance tells us how much unnecessary work the search algorithm has managed to avoid, so a high penetrance is good.

continued

(i) Choose a representation for the state of the river banks, and write programs which solve this problem by both depth- and breadth-first search. You might like to consult Amarel (1968) on the different ways in which this problem can be represented. You will see that considerable computational savings can be derived by using more efficient representations of states.

(ii) Attempt to improve upon the penetrance of depth-first search in Figure 2.8 by changing the order in which moves are considered at each state.

(iii) Generalize your program so that both the 'size' of the boat and the number of missionaries/cannibals are now parameters rather than being fixed. If you experiment, you will find that

- these parameters cannot be varied independently, because some combinations render the problem insoluble, and
- increasing both parameters greatly increases the size of the search space.

7. Another classic problem is that posed by the 8-puzzle. In this puzzle, one can slide eight moveable tiles up, down, left and right in a 3×3 frame. The goal is to get from some arbitrary jumbled configuration to some order state (see Figure 2.9).

Note that the specification of the legal moves can be greatly simplified if the movement of any tile is seen in terms of moving the 'blank', that is, the single empty space.

2	8	3
1	6	4
7		5

Initial state: As above (say)

Goal state:

1	2	3
8		4
7	6	5

Legal moves: Move blank up
                           down
                           left
                           right

Constraints: No diagonal moves

Figure 2.9 **The 8-puzzle.**

continued

Unlike the missionaries and cannibals problem, the 8-puzzle is not soluble in reasonable time by exhaustive search methods. This is because the puzzle has 9! possible states. Consequently, an evaluation function must be used to augment generate and test with hill climbing.

(i) Devise an evaluation function for this problem, and write a program which performs hill climbing on the underlying search space. Possible evaluation functions for states include (i) the number of tiles out of place, and (ii) the sum of the Euclidean distance of each tile from its 'home' space.

(ii) Which of the evaluation functions suggested above is the most sensitive? Can you devise a better guide for search?

(iii) How does your program perform on the 15-puzzle? (This variant consists of 15 tiles arranged in a 4 × 4 frame. It has 16! possible states.)

The 8-puzzle is well discussed in Nilsson (1980, Chapter 1).

8. Consult Box 2.2 on the A* algorithm, and then do the following.

(i) Implement A* in the language of your choice.

(ii) Use the resulting program to solve the missionaries and cannibals puzzle and the 8-puzzle. (You will need an evaluation function for the missionaries and cannibals puzzle. Use an evaluation function from Exercise 7 for the 8-puzzle.)

(iii) Finally, try the algorithm on the following cryptarithmetic puzzles (see explanation below):

BEST	SEND	DONALD	CROSS
+ MADE	+ MORE	+ GERALD	+ ROADS
MASER	MONEY	ROBERT	DANGER

Cryptarithmatic means coded arithmetic, where letters represent digits and words represent numbers. The problem is to find which digits must be substituted for the letters so that the sum is arithmetically correct. Such puzzles are discussed in many standard AI texts, for example Raphael (1976, Chapter 3).

You will need to decide how to represent the summands and their sum, what the possible 'moves' are (that is how you generate new nodes in the search space), and what are good heuristics for guiding the search.

CHAPTER

3

Knowledge Representation

In Chapter 2, we saw that researchers had, for the most part, become disillusioned with weak methods of problem solving, such as generate-and-test, and hill climbing. Various technical problems were noted with the discovery and use of evaluation functions, and it was felt that such methods undervalued domain-specific knowledge and common sense, and overvalued the notion of general intelligence. It is unlikely that expert systems as a field of research would exist today, had these attempts to develop general-purpose problem solving programs proved successful.

This chapter describes an early expert system, MYCIN, which was one of the first programs to depart from the 'general problem solving' tradition. Its design incorporates a very simple search algorithm, much simpler than A* (see Box 2.2). The program's problem solving ability derives not from this algorithm but from a *representation of knowledge* specific to its domain of operation: the treatment of blood infections.

But we begin with an explanation of the mysterious term 'representation of knowledge,' using as an example another early AI program, the STRIPS planner, which one would not consider to be an expert system. Then we describe MYCIN's knowledge representation and search algorithm and attempt to evaluate the system's performance. Finally, we compare MYCIN with STRIPS, noting the similarities and differences between the two programs, and using these differences to illustrate how expert systems technology extended AI practice in the 1970s.

3.1 The representation of knowledge: principles and techniques

In the field of expert systems, knowledge representation implies that we have some systematic way of codifying what an expert knows about some domain. However, it would be a mistake to suppose that representation is the same thing as encoding, in the sense of encryption. If one encodes a message by transposing its constituent symbols in some regular fashion, the resultant piece of code would not be a representation of the contents of the message from an artificial intelligence point of view, even if the code were machine-readable and easy to store in the memory of the machine.

For one thing, the code would preserve any lexical or structural *ambiguity* of natural language inherent in the message. Thus the message

'Visiting aunts can be a nuisance'

is just as ambiguous in its encrypted form as it is in English. Transcribing it into code does not alter the fact that it could mean either 'It is a nuisance having to visit one's aunt' or 'It is a nuisance having one's aunt to visit.'

BOX 3.1

Hammers, Vases and Theorems

One of the paradoxes of artificial intelligence is that many of the reasoning tasks that humans find easy are hard for a machine to perform and vice versa. Consider the following sentence:

'The hammer hit the vase and it broke.'

What does 'it' refer to? The answer is obvious to us, we don't even consider the sentence to be ambiguous. But how would a machine interpret such sentences in a principled way? Having 'it' refer to the last mentioned object doesn't always work, for example:

'The vase hit the wall and it broke.'

Even if one has never broken a vase, one somehow knows that the vase will be the casualty in both of these encounters. We have prior knowledge, but it isn't altogether clear how this should be represented. Nor is it obvious how this knowledge could be gathered together and organized for retrieval. Are we going to have a huge table that states, for any two objects in the universe, which is more durable?

Now consider a quite different task, that of deciding whether or not a logical formula is a theorem of the propositional calculus (see Chapter 8). For example, is

$$(p \; \& \; (q \supset r)) \supset ((s \vee p) \; \& \; (-r \supset -q))$$

a theorem or not? It turns out that it isn't, because there is a consistent assignment of truth values to the variables p, q, r, s that renders it false. It is trivial to write a program to make this kind of decision, whereas solving such problems is relatively hard for the average human.

Roughly speaking, the difference between the two problems is that the knowledge needed to solve the propositional calculus problem can be characterized by a handful of terse rules, whereas the knowledge required to interpret all sentences of the form

'the X hit the Y and it broke'

appears to be endless and admits of irritating exceptions involving plastic hammers, stone vases, paper walls, and the like. A program seems to need 'common sense' to solve this problem, whereas the logic problem requires no common sense at all.

Also, any communication of a technical nature always assumes some *prior knowledge* on the part of the addressee. Thus discourse on the subject of diagnosing digital circuitry assumes a knowledge of the basic principles governing electricity. Needless to say, a computer has no such prior knowledge, and so any representation of the technical expertise required for problem solving must be self-contained.

Finally, representation implies *organization*. A representation of knowledge should render that knowledge accessible and easy to apply via more or less natural mechanisms. Simply encoding knowledge in a machine-readable form will not accomplish this. Relevant items of knowledge should be evoked by the circumstances in which they are most likely to be used. Thus a knowledge base should be extensively indexed and content-addressable, so that any program using it can control the way in which different pieces of knowledge are activated without having to know exactly how they are stored.

Of course, whatever notational system is used, ultimately a computer must be able to store and process the corresponding codes. It turns out that this is not a very constraining requirement, however. Many representational schemes that appear to be distinct can be shown to be formally equivalent, that is, anything that can be expressed in one can be expressed in the other.

Before we get down to specific examples, let's sharpen our terminology with some quotations from a key artificial intelligence text.

A *representation* has been defined as 'a set of syntactic and semantic conventions that make it possible to describe things' (Winston, 1984). In artificial intelligence, 'things' normally means the state of some problem domain; for example, the objects in that domain, their properties, and any relationships that hold between them. A *description* 'makes use of the conventions of a representation to describe some particular thing' (Winston, 1992).

The *syntax* of a representation specifies a set of rules for combining symbols to form expressions in the representation language. It should be possible to tell whether or not an expression is well formed, that is, whether or not it could have been generated by the rules. Only well-formed expressions are obliged to have meaning.

A common syntax used in artificial intelligence is a *predicate–argument* construction of the form:

```
<sentence> ::= <predicate> (<argument>, ..., <argument>)
```

in which a k-place predicate is followed by k arguments. Thus at might be a two-place relation which takes as its first argument the name of some object and as its second argument the name of some place, such as a room, for example:

```
at(robot, roomA).
```

The *semantics* of a representation specifies how expressions so constructed should be interpreted, that is, how meaning can be derived from form. This specification is usually done by assigning meanings to individual symbols, and then inducing an assignment to the more complex expressions. Thus, given meanings for the symbols at, robot and roomA, we say that

```
at(robot, roomA)
```

means that the robot is located in Room A (rather than Room A being located at the robot).

Now problem solving typically involves reasoning about actions, as well as states of the world. As we saw in Chapter 2, problems can often be formulated in terms of an initial state, a goal state, and a set of operations that can be employed in an attempt to transform the initial state into the goal state. The question then arises as to how operations can be represented.

3.2 The STRIPS planner

The STRIPS program (Fikes and Nilsson, 1971) demonstrates one approach to this representational problem (STRIPS stands for Stanford Research Institute Problem Solver). It was intended to solve the problem of plan formation in a robot designed to move objects about in a set of interconnected rooms. STRIPS was an influential program, and its basic representation for actions is still used in some of today's planning systems.

The current state of this world of rooms and objects was represented by a set of *predicate–argument expressions* called the *world model*. Thus the set of formulas

$$W = \{\texttt{at(robot, roomA), at(box1, roomB), at(box2, roomC)}\}$$

would indicate that the robot was in Room A, and that there were two boxes, one in Room B and one in Room C.

Actions available to the robot took the form of operators upon the current world model which would add and delete certain facts. For example, executing the action

'Move the robot from Room A to Room B'

in world W would involve generating a new world model, W', from W by adding and deleting facts. `at(robot, roomA)` would be deleted and `at(robot, roomB)` would be added, to produce

$$W' = \{\texttt{at(robot, roomB), at(box1, roomB), at(box2, roomC)}\}$$

Note that this symbolic manipulation of W is in a sense distinct from whatever physical gyrations the robot would actually have to perform in order to get from Room A to Room B. As well as changing its external location, an intelligent robot must also update its internal representation of where it is. Of course, it is possible to run such a program without it being attached to a robot at all, in which case it is only performing 'imaginary' actions.

3.2.1 Operator tables and means–ends analysis

Permissible actions, such as moving from room to room and pushing objects about, were encoded in *operator tables*. Figure 3.1 shows a table entry for the push operation, where

`push(X, Y, Z)`

denotes that object X is pushed from location Y to location Z (by the robot). The X, Y and Z are variables which range over objects, unlike roomA, roomB, roomC and robot, which are names of objects and hence refer to them directly.

From a programming language point of view, X, Y and Z are like the formal parameters of a procedure definition which states that:

```
push(X, Y, Z)

Preconditions          at(robot, Y), at(X, Y)
Delete list            at(robot, Y), at(X, Y)
Add list               at(robot, Z), at(X, Z)
```

Figure 3.1 **The push operation.**

'to push any object from any place to any other place, if the following preconditions hold, then delete these formulas and add these formulas.'

From a logical point of view, the operator table can be read as a formula which states that:

'for all X, Y and Z, X has been pushed from Y to Z if the robot and X were at Y and then changed to being at Z.'

Goal statements were also represented as formulas, for example:

```
at(box1, roomA), at(box2, roomB).
```

The STRIPS program consisted of many procedures that did various jobs, for example:

- maintaining a list of goals,
- selecting a goal to work on next,
- searching for operators that are applicable to the current goal,
- matching the goal against formulas in the add list, and
- setting up precoditions as subgoals.

If this seems mysterious, consider the simple problem of getting ready to have lunch with a potential client. In order to execute this maneuver, you should have money, since you are going to be paying, and an appetite, since you might as well eat. These can be thought of as preconditions of the 'lunch' goal, which can be represented as an operator, as in Figure 3.2. After lunch, you've spent your money, and you no longer have an appetite, but hopefully you do have a client. These simple facts are reflected in the add and delete lists for this operator. However, having money is not man's natural state; it first requires a trip to a cash machine, which in turn requires transportation. Consequently, two other operators need to be invoked so that you can go to the cash machine, get money and have lunch.

This simple example is not without interesting features. Note that we assume that formulas in our world model, initially

```
at(work), have(transport)
```

remain untouched unless we explicitly delete them. Thus you continue to have transport throughout the plan, because there is no indication that you lose it, even though your car could conceivably be stolen, or you could be involved in an accident, or the trip to the cash machine could cause you to run out of gas. Similarly, the cash machine could swallow your card, or you could forget to retrieve it, or a mechanical hand could appear and snip it in two with a pair of scissors. But we assume that plan actions do not have unforeseen consequences, as far as the add and delete lists are concerned, even though we cannot prove that this is the case.

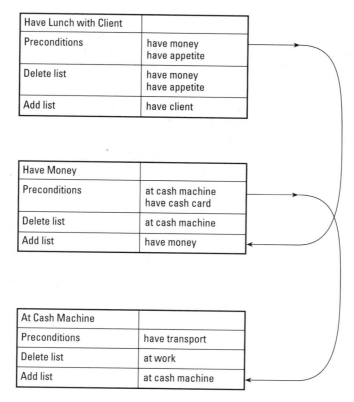

Have Lunch with Client	
Preconditions	have money have appetite
Delete list	have money have appetite
Add list	have client

Have Money	
Preconditions	at cash machine have cash card
Delete list	at cash machine
Add list	have money

At Cash Machine	
Preconditions	have transport
Delete list	at work
Add list	at cash machine

Figure 3.2 Operators associated with lunch goals and subgoals.

This strategy of reasoning backward from goals to subgoals is very common in AI programs and expert systems, as we shall see in our description of MYCIN. However, unlike our simple set of operators, there might be more than one way to get cash, or more than one form of transport that you could use. In this situation, you would need to make choices, or perform some kind of search for the best sequence of operators to achieve your ultimate goal.

Essentially, STRIPS performed a state space search of the kind described in Chapter 2, when choosing which operators to apply. Its output was a *plan*, that is, a sequence of actions that would achieve the goals, derived by tracing back through the operators it had chosen. The main difference between STRIPS and other programs was that, instead of using generate-and-test, it used another weak method, known as *means–ends analysis*, to navigate the search space of possible actions.

Think of what generate-and-test would mean in the present context. The program would simply apply all the operators that it could to the current state and then see if the current goal is achieved. But that would be madness, since the number of things that the robot could do in any given world state is large indeed, and most of them would do nothing towards the achievement of a given goal. After only a few operations, the state space would be enormous and would continue to grow exponentially with each new operation applied. A more focused approach to the problem is essential.

The basic idea behind means–ends analysis is that each operation applied should reduce the difference between the current state and the goal state. This requires that there be some measure of the 'distance' between the current state of the goal. Such a measure is rather like an evaluation function. If the current goal is

    at(box1, roomA)

and the box is in Room B, then moving the robot from Room A to Room C will do nothing towards achieving it, but moving the robot from Room A to Room B does reduce the distance between the current state and the goal, because the robot is now in a position to push the box from Room B to Room A. In a sense, the robot is reasoning backwards from the goal to subgoals that must be achieved on the way to achieving the main goal.

The way that a STRIPS-style program actually works is to read in a list of goals, such as

    at(box1, roomA), at(box2, roomB)

and then match the goals one at a time against the add lists of the operators. Thus at(box1, roomA) matches at(X, Z) in the add list of push(X, Y, Z).

Pattern matching will be discussed in more detail in Chapters 4, 5 and 8, but for now it is easy to see that there is a *substitution* of values for variables

    {X/box1, Z/roomA}

which renders at(box1, roomA) and at(X, Z) identical.

The program then sets up the preconditions as subgoals in two steps.

(1) *Instantiate* the preconditions by applying the substitution {X/box1, Z/roomA} derived from matching at(box1, roomA) with at(X, Z) to get

    at(robot, Y), at(box1, Y).

(2) *Find* the formula in the world model that represents the current position of the box, at(box1, roomB), and match it against at(box1, Y) to derive the substitution {Y/roomB} which is then applied to the part-instantiated preconditions to derive the subgoals

    at(robot, roomB), at(box1, roomB).

The first precondition now gives a desired location for the robot; the second precondition is trivially satisfied, that is, already true.

Given that the operator tables, the world model, and the goals were all represented in the same predicate–argument syntax, the program could easily determine which actions were applicable in the achievement of a given goal by a process of pattern matching and table look-up. One virtue of the operator table representation is that it is easy to tell, for any given goal, which operators will be effective in achieving it. All you have to do is look in the add lists of the operators for formulas that match the current goal, as shown in Figure 3.2.

It is also easy to see what the preconditions of the operators are, and subgoals can be derived from them by a process of matching and instantiation. So once an operation has been selected for application, its preconditions can be added to the list of goals. If more than one operator could apply to the current state of the problem, then heuristics must be applied to choose between them. For example, one could choose the operator that provided the largest reduction in the distance between the current state and the goal. Or operators in the table could be hand ordered, and the first available operator in the ordering could be applied.

This whole process of problem reduction is recursive. Subgoals may themselves be achievable by other operators, and the process of goal reduction should bottom out with operations that have no preconditions or preconditions that are trivially satisfied. We discuss other applications of means–ends analysis in Chapters 5 and 14.

3.2.2 Assessment of STRIPS representation and control

In order to see the virtues of the STRIPS representation, consider an alternative way of representing things. Suppose the current state of the world was represented by a typed array (in which cells stood for locations and entries in the cells stood for objects, say). The array representation would be more space efficient than the propositional one, but it would not permit the kinds of matching operation described above. One could, of course, express goals and operations in a compatible array-oriented language, but then several things would have been lost.

- Operators would now be array manipulation procedures that were less easy to read, write and debug than the operator tables.
- The program would be less easy to modify or develop. Suppose more locations are added or the connectivity between rooms is completely altered. The array access procedures might have to be modified by hand, because array dimensions and relationships will have changed. In STRIPS, one would only have to change the world model, which is not a program but a description.
- Suppose that, in addition to being able to reference specific boxes in goal statements, you want to have non-specific goals like 'bring *any* three boxes to Room A.' The array-oriented procedures will have to be modified substantially to achieve this extension. In a predicate–argument representation, non-specific goals can be represented by goal statements containing variables, for example:

```
at(X, roomA), at(Y, roomA), at(Z, roomA)
```

and one can use pattern matching to look for suitable boxes to bring.

STRIPS is interesting because it introduces a number of fundamental ideas in the artificial intelligence approach to problem solving.

- Problem solving is mostly *heuristic search*, and there is usually more than one way in which a search can be conducted, even in quite simple-looking problems.
- Having a *uniform representation* can facilitate search, in that it is then easier to see what operations are applicable and what the effects of applying them will be, and it is easier to write programs that reason about how to search.
- Goals can often be achieved by a process of *problem reduction*, in which we reason backwards from what we want to achieve to simpler subgoals until we reach goals that are trivial, in the sense that they can be accomplished by simple actions.

In general, a representation language, such as the predicate–argument language used by STRIPS, requires an *interpreter*, that is, a program capable of recognizing formulas in the language, such as push(box1, roomB, roomA), and realizing their meaning in terms of procedures that must be carried out. Thus the meaning of push(box1, `roomB, roomA)`, as far as the interpreter is concerned, lies in the achievement of the preconditions

```
at(robot, roomB), at(box1, roomB)
```

and the enactment of the add and delete postconditions, adding

```
at(robot, roomA), at(box1, roomA)
```

and deleting

```
at(robot, roomB), at(box1, roomB).
```

This approach to interpretation is sometimes called *procedural semantics*, because all the program knows about what a formula means is what actions it must carry out to make the formula true. As we noted in Chapter 2, this is not a very rich view of meaning, and it doesn't take us very far down the road to computer understanding. While this is undoubtedly true, procedural semantics does at least have something to say about the vital link between thought and action.

3.3 Subgoaling in MYCIN

MYCIN is a more heterogeneous program than STRIPS, consisting of many different modules. However, there is a part of MYCIN's control structure that is rather similar to that of STRIPS, namely the part that performs a quasi-diagnostic function. But the goals to be achieved are not physical goals, involving the movement of objects in space, but reasoning goals that involve the establishment of diagnostic hypotheses.

This section concentrates upon the diagnostic module of MYCIN, giving a simplified account of its function, structure and runtime behavior. We then contrast this account with the account of STRIPS, with a view to illustrating what it is that makes MYCIN an expert system, as opposed to just an AI program. We end by broaching the topic of how to evaluate expert systems: a question that we return to in Chapter 14.

3.3.1 Treating blood infections

First, we need to give a brief description of MYCIN's domain: the treatment of blood infections. This description presupposes no specialized medical knowledge on the part of the reader. But, as with any expert system, having some understanding of the domain is crucial to understanding what the program does.

An 'antimicrobial agent' is any drug designed to kill bacteria or arrest their growth. Some agents are too toxic for therapeutic purposes, and there is no single agent effective against all bacteria. The selection of therapy for bacterial infection can be viewed as a four-part decision process:

- deciding if the patient has a significant infection;
- determining the (possible) organism(s) involved;
- selecting a set of drugs that might be appropriate;
- choosing the most appropriate drug or combination of drugs.

Samples taken from the site of infection are sent to a microbiology laboratory for culture, that is, an attempt to grow organisms from the sample in a suitable medium.

Early evidence of growth may allow a report of the morphological or staining characteristics of the organism. However, even if an organism is identified, the range of drugs
it is sensitive to may be unknown or uncertain.

MYCIN is often described as a diagnostic program, but this is not so. Its purpose
is to assist a physician who is not an expert in the field of antibiotics with the treatment
of blood infections. In so doing it develops diagnostic hypotheses and weights them,
but it need not necessarily choose between them. Work on MYCIN began in 1972 as
a collaboration between the medical and AI communities at Stanford University. The
most complete single account of this work is Shortliffe (1976).

There have been a number of extensions, revisions and abstractions of MYCIN
since 1976, but the basic version has five components, as shown in Figure 3.3, where
arrows show the basic pattern of information flow between the modules.

(1) A *knowledge base* which contains factual and judgmental knowledge about the
    domain.
(2) A *dynamic patient database* containing information about a particular case.
(3) A *consultation program* which asks questions, draws conclusions, and gives ad-
    vice about a particular case based on the patient data and the static knowledge.
(4) An *explanation program* which answers questions and justifies this advice, using
    static knowledge and a trace of the program's execution.
(5) A *knowledge acquisition program* for adding new rules and changing existing ones.

The system consisting of components (1)–(3) is the problem solving part of MYCIN,
which generates hypotheses with respect to the offending organisms, and makes therapy recommendations based on these hypotheses. We shall look at each of these components, emphasizing basic design principles rather than programming detail. Rule
acquisition systems are discussed in Chapters 10–15, while explanation facilities are
discussed in Chapter 16.

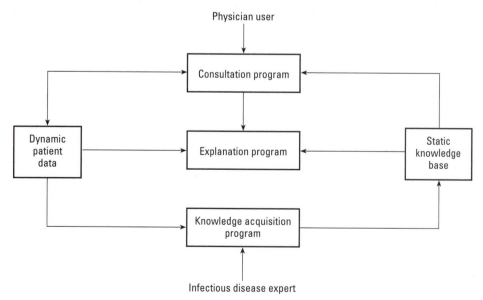

Figure 3.3 Organization of MYCIN (from Buchanan and Shortliffe, 1984).

3.3.2   MYCIN's knowledge base

MYCIN's knowledge base is organized around a set of rules of the general form

> *if* condition$_1$ *and ... and* condition$_m$ hold
> *then draw* conclusion$_1$ *and ... and* conclusion$_n$

encoded as data structures of the LISP programming language (see Chapter 4).

Figure 3.4 shows the English translation of a typical MYCIN rule for inferring the class of an organism. This translation is provided by the program itself. Such rules are called ORGRULES and they attempt to cover such organisms as streptococcus, pseudomonas, and enterobacteriaceae.

The rule says that if an isolated organism appears rod-shaped, stains in a certain way, and grows in the presence of oxygen, then it is highly likely to be in the class enterobacteriaceae. The number 0.8 is called the *tally* of the rule, which says how certain the conclusion is, given that the conditions are satisfied. The use of the tally is explained below. Each rule of this kind can be thought of as encoding a piece of human knowledge whose applicability depends only upon the context established by the conditions of the rule.

The conditions of a rule can also be satisfied with varying degrees of certainty, so the import of such rules is roughly as follows:

> *if* condition$_1$ *holds with certainty* x_1 ... *and* condition$_m$ *holds with certainty* x_m
> *then draw* conclusion$_1$ *with certainty* y_1 *and ... and* conclusion$_n$ *with certainty* y_n

where the certainty associated with each conclusion is a function of the combined certainties of the conditions and the tally, which is meant to reflect our degree of confidence in the application of the rule.

In summary, a rule is a premise–action pair; such rules are sometimes called 'productions' for purely historical reasons (see Chapter 5). *Premises* are conjunctions of conditions, and their certainty is a function of the certainty of these conditions. *Conditions* are either propositions which evaluate to truth or falsehood with some degree of certainty, for example:

> 'the organism is rod-shaped,'

or disjunctions of such conditions. *Actions* are either *conclusions* to be drawn with some appropriate degree of certainty, for example the identity of some organism, or *instructions* to be carried out, for example compiling a list of therapies.

We will explore the details of how rules are interpreted and scheduled for application in the following sections, but first we must look at MYCIN's other structures for representing medical knowledge.

```
IF     1) The stain of the organism is gramneg, and
       2) The morphology of the organism is rod, and
       3) The aerobicity of the organism is aerobic
THEN   There is strongly suggestive evidence (.8) that
       the class of the organism is enterobacteriaceae
```

Figure 3.4 A MYCIN ORGRULE for drawing the conclusion enterobacteriaceae.

In addition to rules, the knowledge base also stores facts and definitions in various forms:

- simple lists, for example the list of all organisms known to the system;
- knowledge tables, which contain records of certain clinical parameters and the values they take under various circumstances, for example the morphology (structural shape) of every bacterium known to the system;
- a classification system for clinical parameters according to the context in which they apply, for example whether they are attributes of patients or organisms.

Much of the knowledge not contained in the rules resides in the properties associated with the 65 clinical parameters known to MYCIN. For example, shape is an attribute of organisms which can take on various values, such as 'rod' and 'coccus.' Parameters are also assigned properties by the system for its own purposes. The main ones either (i) help to monitor the interaction with the user, or (ii) provide indexing which guides the application of rules.

Patient information is stored in a structure called the *context tree*, which serves to organize case data. Figure 3.5 shows a context tree representing a particular patient, PATIENT-1, with three associated cultures (samples, such as blood samples, from which organisms may be isolated) and a recent operative procedure that may need to be taken into account (for example, because drugs were involved, or because the procedure involves particular risks of infection). Associated with cultures are organisms that are suggested by laboratory data, and associated with organisms are drugs that are effective against them.

Imagine that we have the following data stored in a record structure associated with the node for ORGANISM-1:

```
GRAM  = (GRAMNEG 1.0)
MORPH = (ROD .8) (COCCUS .2)
AIR   = (AEROBIC .6)
```

with the following meaning:

- the Gram stain of ORGANISM-1 is definitely Gram negative;
- ORGANISM-1 has a rod morphology with certainty 0.8 and a coccus morphology with certainty 0.2;
- ORGANISM-1 is aerobic (grows in air) with certainty 0.6.

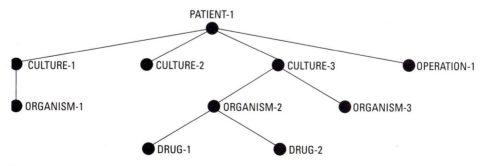

Figure 3.5 A typical MYCIN context tree (after Buchanan and Shortliffe, 1984).

Suppose now that the rule of Figure 3.4 is applied. We want to compute the certainty that all three conditions of the rule

```
IF    1) the stain of the organism is gramneg, and
      2) the morphology of the organism is rod, and
      3) the aerobicity of the organism is aerobic
THEN there is strongly suggestive evidence (0.8) that
      the class of the organism is enterobacteriaceae.
```

are satisfied by the data. The certainty of the individual conditions is 1.0, 0.8 and 0.6 respectively, and the certainty of their conjunction is taken to be the *minimum* of their individual certainties, hence 0.6.

The idea behind taking the minimum is that we are only confident in a conjunction of conditions to the extent that we are confident in its least inspiring element. This is rather like saying that a chain is only as strong as its weakest link. By an inverse argument, we argue that our confidence in a disjunction of conditions is as strong as the strongest alternative, that is, we take the maximum. This convention forms part of a style of inexact reasoning called *fuzzy logic*, which is discussed in Chapter 9.

In this case, we draw the conclusion that the class of the organism is enterobacteriaceae with a degree of certainty equal to

$$0.6 \times 0.8 = 0.48.$$

The 0.6 represents our degree of certainty in the conjoined conditions, while the 0.8 stands for our degree of certainty in the rule application. These degrees of certainty are called *certainty factors* (CFs). Thus, in the general case,

$$CF(\text{action}) = CF(\text{premise}) \times CF(\text{rule}).$$

The use of certainty factors is discussed in more detail in Chapter 9 and Chapter 21, where we revisit the whole topic of how to represent uncertainty. It turns out that the CF model is not always in agreement with the theory of probability; in other words, it is not always correct from a mathematical point of view. However, the computation of certainty factors is much more tractable than the computation of the right probabilities, and the deviation does not appear to be very great in the MYCIN application.

3.3.3 MYCIN's control structure

MYCIN has a top-level goal rule which defines the whole task of the consultation system, which is paraphrased below:

IF   1) there is an organism which requires therapy, and
      2) consideration has been given to any other organisms requiring therapy
THEN compile a list of possible therapies, and determine the best one in this
      list.

A consultation session follows a simple two-step procedure:

- create the patient context as the top node in the context tree;
- attempt to apply the goal rule to this patient context.

Applying the rule involves evaluating its premise, which involves finding out if there is indeed an organism which requires therapy. In order to find this out, it must first find out if there is indeed an organism present which is associated with a significant disease. This information can either be obtained from the user direct, or via some chain of inference based on symptoms and laboratory data provided by the user.

The consultation is essentially a search through a *tree of goals*. The top goal at the root of the tree is the action part of the goal rule, that is, the recommendation of a drug therapy. Subgoals further down the tree include determining the organism involved and seeing if it is significant. Many of these subgoals have subgoals of their own, such as finding out the stain properties and morphology of an organism. The leaves of the tree are fact goals, such as laboratory data, which cannot be deduced.

A special kind of structure, called an *AND/OR tree*, is very useful for representing the way in which goals can be expanded into subgoals by a program. The basic idea is that the root node of the tree represents the main goal, terminal nodes represent primitive actions that can be carried out, while non-terminal nodes represent subgoals that are susceptible to further analysis. There is a simple correspondence between this kind of analysis and the analysis of rule sets.

Consider the following set of condition–action rules:

```
if X has BADGE and X has GUN, then X is POLICE
if X has REVOLVER or X has PISTOL or X has RIFLE, then X has GUN
if X has SHIELD, then X has BADGE
```

We can represent this rule set in terms of a tree of goals, so long as we maintain the distinction between conjunctions and disjunctions of subgoals. Thus, in Figure 3.6, we draw an arc between the links connecting the nodes BADGE and GUN with the node POLICE, to signify that both subgoals BADGE and GUN must be satisfied in order to satisfy the goal POLICE. However, there is no arc between the links connecting RE-VOLVER and PISTOL and RIFLE with GUN, because satisfying either of these will satisfy GUN. A node such as BADGE can have a single child, SHIELD, signifying that a shield counts as a badge.

The AND/OR tree in Figure 3.6 can be thought of as a way of representing the *search space* for POLICE, by enumerating the ways in which different operators can be applied in order to establish POLICE as true.

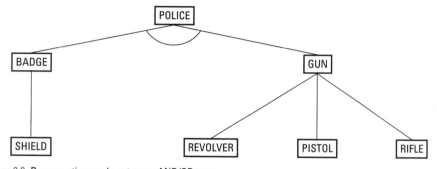

Figure 3.6 **Representing a rule set as an AND/OR tree.**

This kind of control structure is called *backward chaining*, since the program reasons backward from what it wants to prove towards the facts that it needs, rather than reasoning forward from the facts that it possesses. In this respect, MYCIN resembles STRIPS, where goals were achieved by breaking them down into subgoals to which operators could be applied. Searching for a solution by backward reasoning is generally more focused than forward chaining, as we saw earlier, since one only considers potentially relevant facts.

MYCIN's control structure uses an AND/OR tree, and is quite simple as AI programs go; there are only a few deviations from the exhaustive search methods described in Chapter 2:

(1) Each subgoal set up is always a generalized form of the original goal. So, if the subgoal is to prove the proposition that the identity of the organism is E. Coli, then the subgoal actually set up is to determine the identity of the organism. This initiates an exhaustive search on a given topic which collects all of the available evidence about organisms.

(2) Every rule relevant to the goal is used, unless one of them succeeds with certainty. If more than one rule suggest a conclusion about a parameter, such as the nature of the organism, then their results are combined (see Box 3.2). If the evidence about a hypothesis falls between -0.2 and +0.2, it is regarded as inconclusive, and the answer is treated as unknown.

(3) If the current subgoal is a leaf node, then attempt to satisfy the goal by asking the user for data. Else set up the subgoal for further inference, and go to (1).

The selection of therapy takes place after this diagnostic process has run its course. It consists of two phases: selecting candidate drugs, and then choosing a preferred drug, or combination of drugs, from this list.

Evidence Combination

In MYCIN, two or more rules might draw conclusions about a parameter with different weights of evidence. Thus one rule might conclude that the organism is E. Coli with a certainty of 0.8, while another might conclude from other data that it is E. Coli with a certainty of 0.5, or -0.8. In the case of a certainty less than zero, the evidence is actually against the hypothesis.

Let X and Y be weights derived from the application of different rules. MYCIN combines these weights using the following formula to yield the single certainty factor.

$$CF(X, Y) = \begin{cases} X + Y - XY & X, Y > 0 \\ X + Y + XY & X, Y < 0 \\ (X + Y)/(1 - \min(|X|, |Y|)) & \text{otherwise} \end{cases}$$

where $|X|$ denotes the absolute value of X.

One can see what is happening on an intuitive basis. If the two pieces of evidence both confirm (or disconfirm) the hypothesis, then confidence in the hypothesis goes up (or down). If the two pieces of evidence are in conflict, then the denominator dampens the effect.

This formula can be applied more than once, if several rules draw conclusions about the same parameter. It is commutative, so it does not matter in what order weights are combined.

```
IF the identity of the organism is pseudomonas
THEN I recommend therapy from among the following drugs:

1 - COLISTIN (.98)
2 - POLYMYXIN (.96)
3 - GENTAMICIN (.96)
4 - CARBENICILLIN (.65)
5 - SULFISOXAZOLE (.64)
```

Figure 3.7 A MYCIN therapy rule

The special goal rule at the top of the AND/OR tree does not lead to a conclusion, but instigates actions, assuming that the conditions in the premise are satisfied. At this point, MYCIN's therapy rules for selecting drug treatments come into play; they contain sensitivities information for the various organisms known to the system. A sample therapy rule is given in Figure 3.7.

The numbers associated with each drug are the probabilities that a pseudomonas will be sensitive to the indicated drug according to medical statistics. The preferred drug is selected from the list according to criteria which attempt to screen for contra-indications of the drug and minimize the number of drugs administered, in addition to maximizing sensitivity. The user can go on asking for alternative therapies until MYCIN runs out of options, so the pronouncements of the program are not definitive.

3.4 Evaluating and comparing expert systems

There are many ways in which one might evaluate or compare expert systems, but the most obvious one is in comparison with a human expert. In developing the system, expert and knowledge engineer typically work together on a set of critical examples until the program can solve them all. Evaluation then involves giving the system 'unseen' examples and seeing if its judgments agree with those of the expert.

3.4.1 Evaluation of MYCIN

As early as 1974, an initial study using the current version of MYCIN produced encouraging results. A panel of five experts in the diagnosis of infectious diseases approved 72 percent of MYCIN's recommendations on 15 real cases of bacterial infection. The main problem was not the accuracy of the diagnosis, but a lack of rules for judging the severity of the illness.

In 1979, more formal studies of an improved system showed that MYCIN's performance compared favorably with that of experts on patients with bacteremia and meningitis. The program's final conclusions on 10 real cases were compared with those of Stanford physicians, including the actual therapy administered. Eight other experts were then asked to rate the 10 therapy recommendations on each of the cases and award a mark out of 80 for each set of recommendations, without knowing which, if any, came from a computer. The results are shown in Figure 3.8.

```
Ratings by 8 experts on 10 cases
Perfect score = 80

MYCIN            52         Actual therapy     46
Faculty-1        50         Faculty-4          44
Faculty-2        48         Resident           36
Inf dis fellow   48         Faculty-5          34
Faculty-3        46         Student            24

Unacceptable therapy = 0
Equivalent or acceptable therapy = 1
```

Figure 3.8 MYCIN's performance compared with human experts.

The differences between MYCIN's score and those of Stanford experts were not significant, but its score is as good as the experts and better than the non-expert physicians.

However, MYCIN was never used in hospital wards for a number of reasons, including:

- its knowledge base is incomplete, since its 400 or so rules do not cover very much of the domain of infectious diseases;
- running it would have required more computing power than most hospitals could afford at that time;
- doctors do not relish typing at the terminal and require a much better user interface than that provided by MYCIN in 1976.

MYCIN was a research vehicle, and therefore did not set out to achieve practical application or commercial success. Nevertheless, descendants of MYCIN have seen application in hospitals (see Chapter 13 on the PUFF system). Also, the success of the 'subgoaling' approach has not been confined to medical applications (see Chapter 11 on the SACON system).

Throughout the text, we shall tend to deal with evaluation on a case-by-case basis. Expert systems, and their associated domains and tasks, are sufficiently diverse to resist generalization concerning the criteria for success. Nevertheless, we can identify a number of preconditions that are necessary for evaluation to be meaningful (see Hayes-Roth *et al.*, 1983, Chapter 8 for a discussion).

- There must be some *objective criteria* for success, otherwise we will never know whether or not the answer returned by a system is correct. In some domains, for example financial investment, there may be no criteria other than (i) the consensual opinion of a panel of experts, or (ii) actually carrying out the advice of the system and seeing if it is proved right by events. The trouble with the former is that experts may disagree on precisely those cases where their opinion would be most helpful (that is, the difficult cases); the trouble with the latter is that experimentation in the real world may be expensive or deleterious to health and safety.
- Proper *experimental procedures* must be followed. Rather than asking experts to rate a program's performance, it is better (as in the MYCIN study cited above) to run a 'blind' experiment, so that the raters do not know which solutions are generated by computer and which by humans. This design has the beneficial effect

of both removing bias and imparting a real sense of how well a program performs with respect to the human competition.

- Evaluation should be done *painstakingly* or not at all. There is no point in attempting it with insufficient time or resources. It may take longer to thoroughly test a knowledge-based program than it did to design and implement it, so a certain level of commitment is essential.

The reader should also bear in mind that expert systems may play very different roles in problem solving which require rather different standards of performance. Some systems function mostly as assistants, presenting the user with a range of possibilities. All we require of such systems is that they do not miss any solutions with respect to a given set of constraints, and get back to us in a finite time. Others generate whole solutions which the user can accept or reject. Given that their recommendations are being monitored, such systems do not have to be 100 percent right all the time in order to be useful, but they should be capable of generating alternative solutions fairly briskly.

3.4.2   Comparison with STRIPS

Returning to STRIPS, experience has shown that the simple version of the program described above does not perform well on anything other than the easiest problems. Difficulties arise under a number of circumstances; here are just two examples.

- Sometimes the world must become more disordered (with respect to the evaluation function), not less disordered, before progress towards the current goal can be made.
- When the system has multiple goals, individual goals can interact, so that achieving one goal undoes another goal.

Clearly, the STRIPS world model is 'knowledge-poor', that is, it contains very little knowledge that is specific to the domain of rooms and objects with which the robot must work; for example, the weights of objects, the height and width of door-frames. Other than the operator tables, there are no heuristics for moving objects around; for example, avoiding certain doorways as being too narrow, combining objects into loads that the robot can handle. Neither is there any notion of a preparation phase, in which objects are manipulated (for example, unstacked or ordered) prior to moving.

MYCIN's problem solving power derives from two sources: a rich set of rules which suggest hypotheses and ways of confirming them, and a database of containing information about organisms, drugs, and laboratory tests. Otherwise, its control structure is rather similar to STRIPS, and in fact simpler than that of many STRIPS variants. The main difference between the two programs is not their domain of operation but rather the extent to which they use declarative knowledge about that domain.

In Chapter 2, we noted that pioneers of expert systems research were quick to realize that giving a program a lot of domain-specific facts and rules at different levels of abstraction, and then applying rather simple rules of inference, was more beneficial than giving it a few general laws of the domain together with a general-purpose algorithm for goal-directed reasoning. Experts tend to work from first principles only when confronted with an unusual case, or an especially difficult one. Much of the time, experience enables them to 'home in' on the important aspects of the problem, and derive a solution in a relatively small number of steps.

We also noted that one way in which expert systems differ from more conventional programs is that they are generally programmed to use heuristics of various kinds to find a solution with a minimum of search. These short cuts mean that expert systems, like human experts, rarely derive their results from first principles. As a result, the chains of reasoning involved are usually both short and highly focused.

The use of heuristics also means that an expert system's reasoning will not always be *sound*; that is, it will not always consist of a chain of reliable deductions. Certain pieces of evidence crucial to drawing a definite conclusion may be missing, in which case the system must proceed on the assumption that the evidence will ultimately support the conclusion (or qualify the conclusion in some way). Also a system's reasoning may not be *complete*, in that another chain of reasoning might have found a solution that the system missed (see Chapter 8 for more formal definitions of soundness and completeness).

Thus, in addition to deciding *how to structure* the knowledge in an expert system's knowledge base, a knowledge engineer must also decide *how to use* that knowledge to derive conclusions. The design of the inference engine will usually determine both when representations of knowledge are applied and how their application is controlled. For example, at any given point in a computation, there may be more than one piece of knowledge that appears to be applicable. Furthermore, it may not be consistent to apply both of them. Thus an errand planner may have a heuristic which says

'do errands that are close together first'

and another that says

'avoid going downtown during heavy traffic.'

If the errands that are close together are also downtown, and plan execution is scheduled to begin during the rush hour, then these two pieces of knowledge give contradictory advice. It is normally the job of the inference engine to resolve conflicts of this kind.

Heuristic reasoning may seem rather slipshod, in that two heuristics can contradict each other in some circumstances, and neither may be guaranteed to work. The problem is that for the majority of tasks requiring human experience and expertise, either (i) there are no algorithmic solutions known, or (ii) it is known that the problem is computationally intractable, in that any algorithmic solution will consume resources that increase as an exponential function of the size of the problem (see Box 2.1 – Combinatorial Explosion). Thus it is the importance of domain-specific knowledge and the primacy of task-specific heuristics that have shaped the knowledge representation schemes which we shall explore in Chapters 4–8 and beyond.

BIBLIOGRAPHICAL NOTES

Planning ideas based on STRIPS still abound in the AI literature (see, for example, Givan and Dean, 1997). However, STRIPS planning has been shown to be computationally expensive; the general case is P-SPACE complete (Bylander, 1994). Nilsson (1980) provides an in-depth treatment of the original STRIPS formalism, and versions of the program are available from various university Web sites; for example, follow planning-related links from

    http://www.cs.brown.edu/research/ai

The most comprehensive reference for MYCIN is Shortliffe (1976). However, clear accounts of aspects of MYCIN can be found in Buchanan and Shortliffe (1984) and Clancey and Shortliffe (1984); the latter contains accounts of other early forays into medical expert systems. Cendrowska and Bramer (1984) describe a reconstruction and reimplementation of MYCIN that exposes many interesting details of the program.

STUDY SUGGESTIONS

1. What is an operator table? Could an operator table represent *any* action that we might want a robot to take?

2. What is a production rule? What do you think the relationship is between a set of production rules and a decision tree?

3. What is the relationship between operator tables and production rules? Are they equivalent? Could you implement one in terms of the other?

4. Imagine that a robot arm hovering over a tray of toy blocks can move a block, B, from one location, L, to another, M, using the operator table given in Figure 3.9.

```
move (B, L, M)
  Preconditions        on (B, L), clear (B), clear (M)
  Delete list          on (B, L), clear (M)
  Add list             on(B,M), clear (L), clear (tray)
```

Figure 3.9 **An operator table for** move.

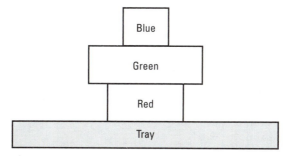

Figure 3.10 **A blocks world problem.**

continued

on(B, L) means that B is resting directly on L. L may be another block or the tray itself. Only one block can rest on another block, but by convention any number of blocks can rest upon the tray. clear(L) means that there is nothing on L.

(i) Represent the scene in Figure 3.10 using symbolic descriptions of this kind.

(ii) A robot's goal in life is to stack the blocks portrayed in Figure 3.10 into a tower, with the blue block on the red block, and the red block on the green block, with the green block resting on the tray. Thus, its final world model should contain the following representations:

on(green, tray), on(red, green), on(blue, red).

Describe a plan for achieving this goal.

(iii) Show how the database is modified as the plan is executed by the robot's operator table.

(iv) Why do we need to add the formula clear(tray) after every application of move?

(v) Can you use the operator table for move to achieve negative goals, for example, achieve the goal that the green block is not on the red block?

5. How confident can we be that a simple plan, such as that derived in the preceding exercise, is actually correct, in the sense that it is guaranteed to succeed, assuming perfect execution by the robot?

6. Can you think of types of plan that could not be generated using the simple operator table formalism as presented here?

7. Consider the MYCIN rule in Figure 3.11.

```
IF      1) The stain of the organism is gram-positive, and
        2) The morphology of the organism is coccus, and
        3) The growth conformation of the organism is chains
THEN    There is suggestive evidence (.7) that
        the identity of the organism is streptococcus
```

Figure 3.11 **A MYCIN ORGRULE for drawing the conclusion** streptococcus.

Suppose that the conditions of the rule are satisfied with the following degrees of certainty:

Condition 1: 0.8
Condition 2: 0.2
Condition 3: 0.5.

What certainty will MYCIN associate with the conclusion that the identity of the organism is streptococcus?

continued

8. Consider the pair of MYCIN rules in Figure 3.12.

```
IF      1) The site of the culture is blood, and
        2) The patient has ecthyma gangrenosum skin lesions
THEN    There is suggestive evidence (0.6) that
        the identity of the organism is pseudomonas

IF      1) The type of the infection is bacterial, and
        2) The patient has been seriously burned
THEN    There is weakly suggestive evidence (0.4) that
        the identity of the organism is pseudomonas
```

Figure 3.12 A pair of MYCIN rules for drawing the conclusion pseudomonas.

Suppose that the conditions of the first rule are satisfied with certainties 0.8 and 0.9 respectively, while the conditions of the second rule are satisfied with certainties 0.2 and 0.3 respectively. According to MYCIN's evidence combination function, what certainty will be attributed to the conclusion that the identity of the organism is pseudomonas?

9. Draw an AND/OR tree to represent the following set of fire hazard rules, along the lines of the example in Section 3.3.3.

    if FUEL and HEAT and OXYGEN, then FIRE

    if LIQUID and FLAMMABLE, then FUEL
    if SOLID and COMBUSTIBLE, then FUEL
    if GAS and COMBUSTIBLE, then FUEL

    if FLAME and OPEN, then HEAT
    if ELECTRICITY, then HEAT
    if FRICTION, then HEAT

10. Render the rules of Exercise 9 in the CLIPS syntax (see appendix).

4

Symbolic Computation[†]

Before discussing specialized languages for knowledge representation, it is worth spending some time on the more general topic of artificial intelligence programming languages. The purpose of this chapter is not to teach the reader a particular language, but rather to address a number of issues in representation and control that are pertinent to the implementation of expert systems. Interestingly, the increasing emphasis on object-oriented approaches to analysis and design (OOA and OOD) in current software engineering practice has to some extent closed the gap between AI and non-AI views of computer problem solving. Also, the new emphasis on component ware and viewing applications as consisting of interacting, relatively autonomous modules is consonant with AI approaches. As such thinking becomes widespread, we might expect AI and non-AI software tools to become more similar.

This chapter:

- explains why artificial intelligence research and applications have traditionally required particular kinds of programming languages;
- discusses ways in which these languages differ from more mainstream languages for scientific computing and data processing;
- introduces the beginning student to the central concepts of LISP: the main programming language of artificial intelligence;
- explains why LISP has not typically been chosen as a vehicle for general-purpose expert system implementation;
- explains why more specialized languages, such as CLIPS (see appendix), are often used.

There are later chapters (namely 5, 7, and 17) which discuss specialized languages, object-oriented approaches and software tools for building expert systems in more detail.

Here we are concerned primarily with programming concepts and structures that are essential to expert systems design. Further implementation details and specific techniques are discussed and exemplified in the context of particular systems in Chapters 11 through 16.

One reason for concentrating on LISP in this chapter is that later tools, such as CLIPS, follow the syntax of LISP quite closely, and contain many LISP-like constructs. However, we also introduce the PROLOG programming language in Chapter 8, when we introduce logic programming concepts. The logic-based syntax we introduced in Chapter 3 for our discussion of STRIPS is deliberately based on that of PROLOG.

4.1 Symbolic representation

The notion of a *symbol* is so pervasive in the current theory and practice of artificial intelligence that its importance is easily overlooked. It is this notion that forms the crucial link between artificial intelligence and formal systems of logic and mathematics. In the simplest possible terms, a symbol is something that stands for something else. This 'something else' is usually called the *designation* of the symbol. It is the thing that the symbol refers to or represents. The designation may be a physical object or it may be a concept, but the symbol itself is physical. Thus an occurrence of the numeral '7' is a symbol; it stands for the number 7, which is a concept.

The idea behind symbolic computation is that we want to allow symbols to stand for anything at all. Programming languages based on this paradigm provide a number of primitive data structures for associating symbols with other symbols, as well as primitive operations for manipulating symbols and their associated structures. A programmer must then specify

- *syntactic rules* for forming symbol structures out of symbols, in such a way that the resulting structures have a meaning that is a function of their constituents;
- *transformation rules* which turn symbol structures into other symbol structures.

Typically a symbolic program takes as its input one or more symbol structures, representing the initial state of some problem, and returns as its output a symbol structure, representing a terminal state or solution, that is both well formed in terms of the syntactic rules and has been derived by the application of legal transformations. *Programs in such languages are themselves symbol structures.* Thus there is no reason why some programs cannot treat other programs as data, and it turns out that this uniformity in the representation of data and programs is particularly useful in the context of artificial intelligence. But even more central is the idea that we can do more than merely write down rules for manipulating symbols; we can embody these symbols, and the rules for manipulating them, in some physical device. This leads to a very simple but powerful idea: that of the physical symbol system.

4.2 Physical symbol systems

Newell (1981) describes a physical symbol system as a machine with the following components, located in some environment:

- a *memory* containing symbol structures, which can vary in number and content over time;
- a set of *operators* for manipulating symbol structures, for example reading, writing, copying;
- a *control* for the continual interpretation of whatever symbol structure is currently active, or being attended to;
- an *input* from its environment via receptors, and an *output* to that environment via some motor component.

A *program* in a physical symbol system is just a symbol structure that is interpreted or *evaluated* in some manner that is a function of its constituent symbols and its symbolic input. The primitive programs correspond to operators for manipulating symbol structures; more complex programs describe processes composed of these operators. Control is able to tell the difference between data and programs, even though both are just symbol structures; the former are just returned, while the latter must be interpreted.

A physical symbol system resembles a general-purpose computer equipped with symbol processing software. We know that stored program computers are universal machines (roughly speaking, they can simulate the operation of any other machine), and therefore capable in principle of computing all general recursive functions (roughly, all functions computable by any machine). It is the apparent power of these physical realizations of symbol systems that has encouraged researchers to suppose that such systems are capable of intelligence.

The next section looks at the implementation and use of physical symbol systems in artificial intelligence.

BOX 4.1

A Bold Hypothesis

The Physical Symbol System Hypothesis of Newell and Simon (1976) has been stated as follows:

> 'A physical symbol system has the necessary and sufficient means for general intelligent action.'

In other words, symbolic computation is both necessary for intelligent action and sufficient for its enablement. Thus, insofar as animals, persons and machines are acting intelligently, they are performing symbolic computation of some kind. (Your cat is smarter than you think.)

Regardless of whether or not this conjecture ultimately turns out to be true, symbolic computation has become a reality, and its utility as a programming paradigm is impossible to deny.

4.3 Implementing symbol structures in LISP

Given that we want to be able to arrange physical symbols into structures, and perform operations on those structures, the question immediately arises as to what kind of structure we should use. The symbols of logic and mathematics are normally aggregated into *sets* and *sequences*. Each of these formal structures is well understood, but neither of these abstract entities is entirely suitable as a basis for a physical symbol structure.

Sets are unordered collections of elements, whereas physical symbols are forced to have location in a structure. (This location can be hidden from the programmer, to give the impression of a set, but it is nonetheless a reality of the implementation.) Sequences give terms a location, but an abstract sequence can be infinite.

A good candidate for a symbol structure is a *list*: it imparts a position to its members, but it is normally a finite physical entity. We can use a list to represent a set, of course; just as we can use various tricks to represent a sequence by extending a list indefinitely. However, the basic data structure remains ordered and finite.

4.3.1 LISP data structures

One of the first LISt Processing languages was LISP (McCarthy, 1960). This language has undergone a good deal of development over the past four decades, but the basic design has remained more or less the same. As McCarthy *et al.* (1965) point out, LISP differs from most programming languages in three important respects:

- its main data structure is the list;
- its programs are also represented by list structures; and
- its primitive operations are operations on lists.

The original choice of the list as the basic data structure for LISP was somewhat revolutionary in 1960. Today, most general-purpose languages support lists in one way or another, although the programmer is usually required to allocate and free the memory used to build a list out of linked memory cells. LISP was also revolutionary for providing automatic 'garbage collection' mechanisms, which reclaim memory automatically.

The basic building block of LISP data structures is the symbolic expression, or *S-expression*, for short. Simple S-expressions are just atomic symbols, or *atoms*: strings of (not more than some implementation-dependent number of) alphanumeric characters beginning with a letter, for example WOMBAT. An atom is represented internally as a cell in reclaimable memory. T is also a special atom that stands for 'true,' while another special atom, NIL, stands for 'false.' NIL also serves as the *empty list*.

Complex expressions are implemented as memory cells combined to form arbitrary finite tree structures, exploiting a straightforward correspondence between finite trees and S-expressions. The details are given in Box 4.2 for the mathematically-minded.

Lists are very flexible data structures, being untyped and of arbitrary length. Thus there is nothing wrong with the list

```
("a" (9) () T (? (WOMBAT)) (A . B) NIL 0.9)
```

even though it contains elements of rather different types, that is, strings, fixed and floating point numbers, atoms, booleans, dotted pairs and other lists.

However, there are some obvious disadvantages with lists which have led to other data structures being added to LISP. LISP's lists are really stacks, that is, they can only be accessed from the front. There is no notion of access by position, as in an array, or by a key, as in hash tables. So although lists are still useful as repositories for temporary data local to particular functions, large amounts of permanent data are better represented in other kinds of structure. Modern LISP provides various alternatives – including arrays, hash tables, and record-like structures – which are more efficient in terms of storage space and speed of access.

BOX 4.2

Lists and Dotted Pairs[†]

Given an operator '.' for combining cells into tree structures, the definition of an S-expression in LISP can be derived as follows.

> Any atom is an S-expression.

> If A_1 and A_2 are S-expressions, then $(A_1 \ . \ A_2)$ is an S-expression.

> If $S = (A_1 \ . \ (A_2 \ . \ (\ldots \ . \ (A_{n-1} \ . \ A_n) \ \ldots)))$ is an S-expression for some $n > 0$, then S is a list if and only if $A_n = \text{NIL}$.

By convention, if $n = 0$, then S is the empty list, NIL. This definition allows for lists of lists, as well as lists of atoms. If S_1, S_2, $\ldots$, S_n are S-expressions, then we shall represent the list

> $(S_1 \ . \ (S_2 \ . \ (\ldots \ . \ (S_n \ . \ \text{NIL}) \ \ldots)))$

as simply

> $(S_1 \ S_2 \ \ldots \ S_n)$

Thus $(A \ . \ (B \ . \ \text{NIL}))$ is a list; it represents the list $(A \ B)$, but $(A \ . \ (B \ . \ C))$ is not a list, because $C \neq \text{NIL}$.

S-expressions that are neither atoms nor lists are called *dotted pairs*. If $(A \ . \ B)$ is a dotted pair, then A is its *head*, and B its *tail*. Dotted pairs can be arbitrarily complex. Thus $((A \ . \ B) \ . \ C)$ is a dotted pair, as is $((A \ . \ B) \ . \ (C \ . \ D))$. Thanks to the correspondence between dotted pairs and lists, the notions of head and tail are defined for them too. Given that the list $(A \ B)$ is just $(A \ . \ (B \ . \ \text{NIL}))$, it should be obvious that although A is the head of $(A \ B)$, its tail is (B), not B. Finally, the tail of (B) is NIL.

4.3.2 LISP programs

We can easily get used to the idea of lists as data structures. Less familiar is the idea that a list can be a *program*, or a program statement; for example, the list

```
(+ X Y)
```

is a mathematical expression of the form

```
(<Function> <1st argument> <2nd argument>)
```

denoting the addition of two numbers. This notation, somewhat different to the

```
f(x₁, ..., xₙ)
```

notation that we are used to for functions of *n* arguments, is adopted precisely because we want the resultant expression to be a list.[1]

---

[1] We will use both notations in this chapter, depending upon whether we are writing LISP code or writing about functions in the abstract. It is worth the inconvenience of two notations to maintain this distinction, I think.

But how could this work, without causing confusion? How could a compiler or interpreter for the language know when it was dealing with data and when it was dealing with executable statements? Well, at least the following machinery is required.

- We must be able to *evaluate* expressions such as (+ X Y). To do this, we need to be able to look up some kind of function definition for +, that tells us what sequence of primitive operations to apply to the arguments in order to compute the value.
- We must be able to *define* functions in the first place, and apply their definitions to arguments (that is, actual, not formal, parameters). The mechanisms of function definition and function application are based on a logistic system, called the *lambda calculus* (see Church, 1941). Unlike first-order predicate calculus, lambda calculus is functional rather than relational; that is, the primitive notion is that of many-to-one relations, rather than many-to-many relations. Thus *father* is a functional relation, since for each person there is only one father, whereas *brother* is a more general relation, since each person may have more than one brother. We shall touch upon the relation between LISP and the lambda calculus later in this section.
- We must be able to *access* the current values of variables (or formal parameters) like X and Y. The evaluation of each S-expression is performed relative to an *environment* of variable bindings. We need to be able to save and restore these environments, as we compute the value of a complex S-expression by computing and combining the values of any sub-expressions contained therein.
- In the evaluation of complex S-expressions, which may involve both the application of more than one function and the composition of functions, we need to be able to store the *current* S-expression, that is, the one we are evaluating at a given moment. We need to be able to *copy* S-expressions pending evaluation so that we can save them during sub-computations. We also need to store intermediate results.
- Finally, we must be able to inhibit the evaluation of lists that are not program statements but merely data structures. Thus, we don't want to try to evaluate an expression such as

  ((1 2 3)(4 5 6)(7 8 9))

by looking to see if we have a definition for the non-existent function

  (1 2 3).

This is achieved by the special form QUOTE: for all x,

  (QUOTE X)

returns x. So does

  (quote X).

Modern LISP is normally case-insensitive, although it is possible, but not advisable, to configure it as case-sensitive.[2]

---

[2] CLIPS is case-sensitive, for some reason.

BOX 4.3

Functions, Evaluation and Quotation in CLIPS

There are two main ways to deal with the quotation problem. One is to have the interpreter evaluate every expression unless inhibited from doing so, for example, by QUOTE. The other is to inhibit evaluation by default, unless it is triggered by a special syntactic device. Modern LISP adopts the former convention, while CLIPS adopts the latter.

Thus we can define a CLIPS function called outside, which tells us whether or not an integer falls outside a range defined by a lower bound and an upper bound as follows:

```
(deffunction between(?lb ?value ?ub)
   (or (> ?lb ?value) (> ?value ?ub))).
```

The query prefix tells the CLIPS interpreter that expressions ?lb, ?ub, and ?value are variables that need to be evaluated.

The standard way of implementing functional languages like LISP is to use a four-stack machine, called the *SECD machine*. These four stacks keep track of partial results, values for variables, the current expression, and copies of the current state of the computation for restoration after sub-computations. Without going into details, the evaluation of an S-expression performed by such a machine implements the basic operation of function application as defined by the lambda calculus (see, for example, Henderson, 1980; Glaser *et al.*, 1984).

4.3.3 Functional application and lambda conversion†

In understanding the relationship between lambda calculus and LISP, it is useful to bear in mind Church's original distinction between a *denotation* and an *abstraction*. The expression (X * X) *denotes* a particular number; which number depends upon the value of X. However, it can also be taken as a function square(X), in which X is *bound* rather than being *free*. This function is an abstraction, because it can apply to many different values of X. To distinguish between the denotation and the abstraction, the latter is represented by

$$(\lambda X)(X * X)$$

in the lambda calculus. The lambda operator, λ, is said to bind the variable X, rather as a quantifier binds an individual variable in the predicate calculus. Thus $(\lambda X)(X * X)$ can serve as a definition of the square function:

$$square(X) = (\lambda X)(X * X).$$

Now in applying the square function to a particular number, say 3, we have to substitute the 3 for the variable X somehow, so that 3 is the value of X and evaluating (X * X) returns 9. When we apply the function definition $(\lambda X)(X * X)$ to the argument 3, we use an inference rule called *lambda conversion*. Let $(\lambda X)M$ stand for any lambda abstract, and let S(a, X, M) stand for the result of uniformly substituting a for X in M.

Lambda conversion: Replace any part $(\lambda X)M$ of a formula by S(a, X, M), provided that the bound variables of M are distinct both from X and from the free variables of a.

If we let $((\lambda X)M)(a)$ stand for the application of the function definition $(\lambda X)M$ to the argument a, then

```
((λX)(X * X))(3) = (3 * 3) = 9.
```

What has this to do with LISP? Well, the LISP definition of the square function is something like

```
(define SQUARE (LAMBDA (X) (* X X))).
```

The exact details depend upon the dialect and implementation of the language, but the intent is clear. In fact, in COMMON LISP, one would simply use the shorthand

```
(defun SQUARE (X) (* X X)).
```

Either way, the intent of the definition is to associate a function name, like SQUARE, with a lambda expression that constitutes its definition. (LAMBDA (X) (* X X)) is just a syntactic variant of $(\lambda X)(X * X)$. In fact

```
(SQUARE 3) = ((LAMBDA (X) (* X X)) 3) = ((λX)(X * X))(3) = 9
```

in any LISP at all, once SQUARE has been defined. Thus evaluating

```
((LAMBDA (X) (* X X)) 3)
```

binds X to 3 by lambda conversion, so that (* X X) now *denotes* the number 9, in Church's terminology. Remember that LAMBDA is *not* a function; it is a special operator in the lambda calculus.

The basic syntax of a LISP function call is just a list of the form

```
(<Function> <Argument> ... <Argument>).
```

This is not the most complicated syntax in the world, but together with QUOTE, LAMBDA, and the form of the conditional statement (which we shall see in a moment), that's all you need to know. People who are irrationally attached to commas, full stops, colons, semi-colons, palindromes *(if ... fi, case ... esac)* and the like may find this a bit hard to take, but having parentheses as the only delimiter has one amazing advantage. LISP programs are just LISP data structures. Thus LISP programs can read, write, and manipulate other LISP programs as if they were data.

4.3.4   List processing

LISP is a formal language that can be given a very concise description. Most LISP programs can be specified in terms of only *five* primitive operations (see Box 4.4) on S-expressions and one special form (a conditional expression). It is easy to overlook the beauty and elegance of pure LISP, because most implementations supply a host of additional operations. Modern LISP is also smothered in Fortran-like features, some of which are useful, and some of which are an abomination. (Needless to say, some are both.)

It turns out that lists are an extremely good medium for non-numeric computations such as those discussed in Chapter 2, which require that a program mount some kind of search for a solution in a space of alternatives. Lists can keep track of these alternatives, those which have already been visited, those which have yet to be visited, and so forth. Given the isomorphism between lists and rooted, ordered trees, it is natural to represent an unfolding search space using one or more lists.

BOX 4.4

LISP Primitives†

The five operations underlying LISP are the following; these are not the LISP names for them, however. LISP typically uses them as 'virtual machine code' to build more complex or flexible primitives for the user. For example, LISP has polymorphic equality predicates.

Let S be the set of S-expressions. We shall write for example,

```
E(X, Y): S × S → {T, NIL}
```

to signify that E is a function from the product of S and S to the set of truth values. Thus E is a function of two arguments, both of which are S-expressions, and its value is either T or NIL.

(1) `E(X, Y): S × S → {T, NIL}` tests if two atoms are *equal*.
(2) `A(X): S → {T, NIL}` tests if an S-expression is an *atom*.
(3) `H(X): S → S` takes the *head* of a non-atomic S-expression; if X is an atom, the result is undefined.
(4) `T(X): S → S` takes the *tail* of a non-atomic S-expression; if X is an atom, the result is undefined.
(5) `C(X, Y): S × S → S` *constructs* S-expressions; thus if A and B are S-expressions, we can form the S-expression (A . B).

Together with function composition and the conditional, these operations are sufficient for computing all general recursive functions. Function composition is the ability to make the value of one function the argument of another by nesting, for example `C(H(X), Y)`.

In fact, the system consisting of

(1) the single atom `NIL`;
(2) a conditional with an equality test of the form:

```
if E(X, NIL) then ... else ...
```

(3) the functions `H(X), T(X), C(X, Y)`

together with function composition is sufficient to represent a Turing machine (see Minsky, 1972, Chapter 10).

One can also use lists to associate one symbol with another. Thus the list

```
((alabama montgomery) (alaska juneau) (arizona phoenix) ...)
```

could encode the capitals of the 50 states. The LISP program in Figure 4.1 would then retrieve the capital of a given state from this *association list*.

```
(defun assoc (key alist)
 (cond ((null alist) NIL)
       ((eq (first (first a list)) key) (first alist))
       (T (assoc key (rest alist)))))
 )
```

Figure 4.1 The `assoc` function for processing association lists.

```
if the alist is null,
then return NIL
else
{
    if the head of the head of the alist is the key,
    then return the head of the alist,
    else return the result of calling assoc on the tail of the alist.
}
```

Figure 4.2 **A paraphrase of a simple** cond **construct using** if-then-else.

The function call

```
(assoc 'alaska '((alabama montgomery) (alaska juneau) ...))
```

would then return

```
(alaska juneau).
```

NULL is the predicate that tests for the empty list, EQ is a predicate that tests for equality between atoms, FIRST is the function that returns the head of a list and REST is a function that returns its tail (see Box 4.4).

COND is LISP's main conditional statement. In the above example, it could be paraphrased as shown in Figure 4.2.

COND can be implemented in terms of the primitive if-then-else described Box 4.4 on LISP Primitives. A COND can contain any number of embedded if-then-else clauses.

Association lists are not a very efficient means of storing data, of course, but they provide a good illustration of how recursive list processing functions work.

4.3.5 Pattern matching

At the heart of most artificial intelligence programs, there is a *pattern matcher* that somehow recognizes input lists or other structures as instances of a symbolic pattern.

We saw in Chapter 3 that facts about the world are typically represented in a predicate–argument notation. Thus

```
at(robot, room)
```

represents the fact that the robot is in the room. In LISP, this would be represented at the S-expression

```
(at robot room).
```

Now let '?' be a 'wildcard', so that

```
(at robot ?)
```

is a pattern that matches (at robot room) and any other expression of the form

```
(at robot blah)
```

where *blah* is any symbol. One can imagine writing a simple pattern matcher in LISP that would compare any two flat lists, a sample and a pattern, and return true if the sample were an instance of the pattern (Figure 4.3). (A list is said to be *flat* if it does not contain embedded sublists.) We assume that a pattern can be any finite length and can contain any number of wildcards.

Thus, the function call

```
(match '(at robot room) '(at robot ?))
```

will return T, while a call such as

```
(match '(at box room) '(at robot ?))
```

will return NIL.

Further refinements to our pattern matcher are possible. For example, we might want to have a new kind of wildcard that acts as a variable which gets assigned the value of the symbol that it matches. Thus, pattern such as

```
(at ?X ?Y)
```

should match a sample such as

```
(at robot room)
```

resulting in the substitution {?X/robot, ?Y/room}, as encountered in Chapter 3. We should also insist that assignments to variables are consistent, so that

```
(at robot room)
```

will not match the pattern

```
(at ?X ? X).
```

However, as we saw in Chapter 3, the main use of pattern matching is to show that the data in a program's world model satisfy the conditions of some rule, which the program could then apply. Thus, given a simple rule, such as one stating that anything in the room should be painted,

```
if (at ?X room)
then (paint ?X)
```

one can match a datum such as

```
(at box room)
```

with the condition

```
(at ?X room)
```

deriving the substitution {?X/box} and then apply this substitution to the conclusion of the rule, to derive

```
(paint box).
```

```
(defun match (sample pattern)
  (cond ((and (null sample) (null pattern)) T)
        ((or (null sample) (null pattern)) NIL)
        ((eq (first pattern '?))
         (match (rest sample) (rest pattern)))
        ((eq (first sample) (first pattern))
         (match (rest sample) (rest pattern)))
        (T NIL))
  )
```

Figure 4.3 A pattern matching function for flat lists.

Pattern matching is an inherently expensive operation, unless done cleverly. We shall see in Chapter 17 that fast algorithms exist for deciding which rules in a rule set have their conditions satisfied by data. Rule-based systems are no longer implemented in LISP, mostly for reasons of efficiency, but the underlying computations are nonetheless symbolic ones of the kind pioneered by list processing languages.

4.4 Why LISP isn't a knowledge representation language

One might wonder why LISP is not the answer to all our knowledge representation needs. After all, it is eminently capable of storing, manipulating and controlling the evaluation of symbol structures. It supports pattern matching, heuristic searching, and the association of one symbol with another. Doesn't LISP provide much of what we need to implement a physical symbol system for intelligent action?

4.4.1 Symbol level versus knowledge level

Certainly the *medium* of symbolic computation is well suited to the implementation of structures for representing knowledge, but the symbolic level of analysis doesn't tell you *what* those structures should be. In a perfect world, there would be a level of analysis above the symbol level which, properly understood, would constrain the set of possible representations for solving some problem. Newell (1982) calls this the *knowledge level*, and suggests that knowledge should be characterized *functionally*, in terms of what it does, rather than structurally.

It seems to follow from Newell's analysis that we cannot represent knowledge adequately without knowing what it will be used for. Perhaps that is one of the things that serves to differentiate between *facts* and *knowledge*. The fact that the Normans invaded England in the year 1066 is just a fact; but my knowledge of it can be put to various uses, such as passing History examinations, or provoking fights between Englishmen and Frenchmen. If the former is my goal, then my representation had better be linked to other facts about King Harold and King William. If the latter is my goal, then my representation ought to be linked to other inflammatory material, such as the national disgrace of British soccer violence or the bizarre driving habits of French motorists. Thus there is no 'correct' way to represent some fact, but there are more or less useful representations of knowledge of some fact.

There is nothing in the syntax or semantics of LISP that tells you how you ought to organize your knowledge. The list is a convenient, if sometimes inefficient, data structure, but it is no more a knowledge representation device than a Fortran array, and somewhat less useful than a C++ class. LISP's staying power is largely attributable to the fact that, if you are an experienced programmer, it is relatively easy to create the embedded language of your choice. But running your own language interpreter inside LISP has significant performance disadvantages. And, unless your requirements are extremely specialized, you are probably doing unnecessary work.

4.4.2 LISP and program design

There are people who like to write spaghetti code, and such people generally run amok when confronted with the wide range of features that LISP provides. Surprisingly little

BOX 4.5

Another Hypothesis

Smith (1982) advanced a Knowledge Representation Hypothesis, which states that:

> 'Every intelligent physical symbol system includes symbol structures that we as external observers can take to be a propositional account of the system's knowledge.'

Obviously, this tells us nothing about how such knowledge might actually be represented. The only clues that we, as external observers, have regarding a symbol system's representation language are the inferences that it makes. But these inferences, in and of themselves, will not uniquely determine the underlying representation scheme.

in the way of a strong programming methodology has emerged from the LISP community, although see Abelson *et al.* (1996). The fact is that the LISP culture predates the advent of structured programming by several years, and that is perhaps one reason why many AI efforts never reach industrial strength.

On the other hand, it is certainly the case that many ideas from knowledge representation have found their way into more mainstream software practices, such as object-oriented analysis and design. Some authors in the area are gracious enough to acknowledge the debt and reference the relevant literature, for example Booch (1994). This kinship is no coincidence, because the whole thrust of modern programming is away from language features and towards an approach that stresses representing the domain in a manner that hides implementation detail.

Object-oriented languages, such as C++, SmallTalk and Eiffel, provide a viable alternative for the software engineer wishing to build expert systems. There are now many class libraries to choose from that aid speedy and reliable development. In the hands of talented personnel having more than passing acquaintance with OOA/OOD techniques, such tools can be used to construct robust applications. Lisp also offers the Common Lisp Object System (CLOS), which is an excellent programming language that handles multiple inheritance far more cleanly than C++ (see Chapter 7). However, even its staunchest adherents admit that it is unlikely to gain industry acceptance any time soon.

4.5 Languages for knowledge representation

Knowledge representation and object-orientation are each based on a common view, namely that it is at least as important to model the *domain* of an application as it is to model the problem you want to solve. If you are working in a particular domain – be it engineering, publishing, or command and control – the kinds of problems that you will asked to solve will change not only between projects but during the course of a single project as concepts are refined and goals are redefined. What will remain relatively constant are the inhabitants of that domain, whether they are machines, processes, inanimate objects, or people. A machine-readable, program-manipulable representation of these entities is almost bound to find multiple application in a variety of projects, assuming that such representations are constructed with reusability in mind.

What distinguishes knowledge representation from object-orientation generally is that it attempts to represent not merely the domain of relevant entities but also a domain expert's *knowledge* of those entities, for example different ways in which they might be viewed, ordered, categorized, and manipulated in the performance of various tasks. Seen in this light, the knowledge representation question then becomes: Is it possible to codify knowledge about a domain in a manner that supports multiple applications of that knowledge to different problems in the context of different projects? The construction of application-neutral 'knowledge banks' remains some way off (see Chapter 10) but we shall encounter examples later in the book, for example in Chapters 13 and 16, where the knowledge accessed by a problem solving program is put to multiple uses within an application.

In the next three chapters, we provide an introduction to rule-based and object-oriented programming methods, often in the context of the CLIPS language, which combines the two. The reason for the continuing popularity of such tools in industry is that, however hard it may be to codify human knowledge, such epistemological difficulties are as naught when compared with the management of C++ pointers by untrained personnel. Building a rule-based system in such a language is a non-trivial exercise best left to experts.

Another reason is that crafting a knowledge-based system from scratch forces analysts and programmers to face large numbers of design decisions in a space of alternatives where there are many more ways to go wrong than to do right. Representation languages provide both a high-level program architecture and a set of low-level conventions for organizing and applying knowledge. They also incorporate syntactic and semantic primitives that have been found to be useful in the past and that make success more likely.

CLIPS is chosen as the main vehicle for illustrating rule-based systems in Chapter 5 and beyond because:

- it is relatively cheap (like so much else in life, it used to be free);
- it borrows features shamelessly from other successful tools;
- it has a fairly standard (albeit LISP-like) syntax – so go back and read all those boxes you skipped earlier in this chapter;
- it is reasonably efficient, so that programs run in a finite time;
- it is reasonably flexible, e.g., it allows foreign function calls;
- it provides some (limited) facilities for combining rules with objects.

In Chapter 6, we examine the use of structured objects such as semantic nets and frames before going on to a more thorough treatment of object-oriented programming in Chapter 7. Chapter 8 ends our examination of knowledge representation languages with a look at logic programming techniques, specifically the PROLOG language. Chapter 17 provides an overview of the main kinds of software package that are available for building expert systems, while Chapters 18 and 19 analyze some more specialized tools.

BIBLIOGRAPHICAL NOTES

Winston and Horn (1988) is one of the more accessible LISP textbooks, as is Graham (1994). Charniak, *et al.* (1987) is also worth consulting for a more detailed look at how to implement advanced AI techniques.

Two excellent LISP-based texts are Norvig (1992), which focuses on Common LISP case studies, and Russell and Norvig (1995), which concentrates on AI programming in LISP.

Bratko (1990) provides a thorough introduction to AI programming in PROLOG, while Sterling and Shapiro (1994) is another good PROLOG text.

STUDY SUGGESTIONS

1. What is a symbol, as used in AI? Is a symbol different from a picture or a word?

2. What is the Physical Symbol System hypothesis? Do you think that it is plausible?

3. Let L be the list

   ```
   (a (b) c ((d) e (f)) g).
   ```

   What is the value of the following function composition?

   ```
   first(first(rest(rest(rest(L)))))).
   ```

   Write the above expression in LISP syntax.

4. The function f is defined by

   ```
   f(X Y) = (λX)(if Y = 0 then 1, else X * f(X, Y - 1)).
   ```

   What is the value of the following function application?

   ```
   f(2 3).
   ```

   Write the function definition give above in LISP syntax.

5. Extend the pattern matcher in Figure 4.3 so that it handles arbitrarily embedded lists. Thus, it should be capable of matching the sample

   ```
   (lisp (a functional language) (invented by (john mccarthy)))
   ```

   with the pattern

   ```
   (lisp (a ? language) (invented by (? mccarthy)))
   ```

   but not the pattern

   ```
   (lisp (a ? language) (invented by (mary ?)).
   ```

continued

6. Extend the pattern matcher in Figure 4.3 so that it returns a substitution of values for variables that would render sample and pattern identical. Pattern variables now have the form

   `(? variable-name),`

   so that a pattern like

   `(at (? X) (? Y))`

   should match a sample such as

   `(at robot room)`

   returning the substitution

   `((X robot) (Y room))`

   as a list. You can assume that the sample list is flat.

7. Combine the programs from Exercises 5 and 6 so that the pattern matcher now both handles embedded samples and produces a substitution. Thus the sample

   `(lisp (a functional language) (invented by (john mccarthy)))`

   should match

   `(lisp (a (? type) language) (invented by ((? name) mccarthy)))`

   to return the substitution

   `((type functional) (name john)).`

5

Rule-Based Systems

It is probably an axiom of artificial intelligence, and modern psychology, that intelligent behavior is rule-governed. Even in the world at large, people have a tendency to associate intelligence with regularities in behavior, and we often explain behavior by appeal to such regularities. Take the example of speaking one's native language. We all behave as if we have complete knowledge of the rules of English, although we don't, of course. (Anyone who did could write it all down and enjoy a dazzling career in Linguistics.)

The point is that intelligent behavior, such as using a language appropriately, appears to be executed in a way that is respectful of rules, even if intelligent agents don't know precisely what the rules are. In artificial intelligence, rules play a rather more direct role in the production of behavior. We say that an agent behaves in the way that he does because he possesses a representation of rules relevant to the generation of the behavior in question.[1]

Production rules are a formalism which saw some use in automata theory, formal grammars, and the design of programming languages, before being pressed into the service of psychological modeling (Newell and Simon, 1972) and expert systems (Buchanan and Feigenbaum, 1978). In the expert systems literature, they are sometimes called condition–action rules or situation–action rules. This is because they are usually used to encode empirical associations between patterns of data presented to the system and actions that the system should perform as a consequence.

---

[1] Over the past 15 years, advocates of connectionist methods have argued for the use of *neural networks* to model behavior (see Chapter 23 for an outline of connectionist theory). Such networks avoid the explicit encoding of rules in favor of a more distributed representation of knowledge in terms of strengths of association among connected nodes. Thus the opening statements of this chapter are somewhat controversial, although at the time of writing connectionist models of problem solving are less advanced than rule-based approaches.

Thus production rules serve precisely the function that we discussed above: they are intended as generative rules of behavior. Given some set of inputs, the rules (interpreted in a particular way) determine what the output should be. In expert system applications, such rules normally determine how the symbol structures that represent the current state of the problem should be manipulated in order to bring the representation closer to a solution.

5.1 Canonical systems†

Productions are really grammar rules for manipulating strings of symbols, sometimes called *rewrite rules*. Post (1943) studied the properties of rule systems based on productions, which he called *canonical systems*. A canonical system is a kind of formal system based on

- an *alphabet A* for making strings;
- some strings that are taken as *axioms*; and
- a set of *productions* of the form:

$$\alpha_1\$_1 ... \alpha_m\$_m \rightarrow \beta_1\$'_1 ... \beta_n\$'_n$$

where

(i) each α_i and β_i is a fixed string
(ii) α_1 and α_m are often null
(iii) some or all of the α_i or β_i may be null
(iv) each $\$_i$ is a variable string which can be null
(v) each $\$_i$ is replaced by a certain $\$'_i$.

The definition of a canonical system is best understood with the aid of an example. Let A be the alphabet $\{a, b, c\}$ and let the axioms be

$a, b, c, aa, bb, cc.$

Then the following productions generate all and only the palindromes based on this alphabet, starting from the axioms.

(P1) $\$ \rightarrow a\$a$
(P2) $\$ \rightarrow b\$b$
(P3) $\$ \rightarrow c\$c.$

Furthermore, in this case we can trace the rule applications that must have given rise to a particular palindrome. Thus *bacab* must have been generated by applying **P1** to the axiom *c* and then applying **P2** to the result. In other words, given *c* as an axiom, we can derive *aca* as a *theorem*, and so add this to the axioms. From *aca*, we can then derive the further theorem *bacab*. Note that this set of productions is not *commutative*; that is, if we apply the same rules starting with a particular input but in a different order, then we get a different result. Applying **P2** then **P1** to *c* would give us *abcba*.

Canonical systems may seem rather trivial at first sight; all they do is rewrite one string of symbols into another. But there is a sense in which all calculi of logic and mathematics are just sets of rules that tell you how to manipulate symbols. It is easy to forget this, because the symbols of logic and arithmetic often have some meaning for us, unlike strings such as *abcba*.

BOX 5.1

The Meaning of Productions

Given a production rule of the form

$$\alpha_1 \$_1 \ldots \alpha_m \$_m \rightarrow \beta_1 \$'_1 \ldots \beta_n \$'_n$$

$\alpha_1 \$_1 \ldots \alpha_m \$_m$ is sometimes called the *antecedent* of the rule and $\beta_1 \$'_1 \ldots \beta_n \$'_n$ the *consequent*, by analogy with conditional statements of propositional logic (see Chapter 8). The conditional operator, usually written as '⊃', is featured in statements of the form

$$p \supset q$$

which have the interpretation, 'if *p*, then *q*', as in 'if you fall in the river, then you will get wet.'

However, it is not a good idea to confuse '→' with '⊃', because of the imperative or permissive flavor of '→'. It is telling you to do something, or that you can do something, rather than what logically follows.

Put another way, a rule of the form $X \rightarrow Y$ says that you can write, generate or *produce* the consequent *Y*, given the antecedent *X*. It does not say that, given *X*, *Y* is an inescapable consequence, as with our 'river' example. Rewrite rules are called 'productions' in linguistic theory, because a rule such as

$$S \rightarrow NP + VP$$

has the interpretation: 'one way of producing a sentence is to take a noun phrase and add a verb phrase to it.'

It turns out that any formal system can be realized as a canonical system (see, for example, Minsky, 1972, Ch.12). Actually, there is a trivial proviso that says that a system may need to help itself to the letters of an auxiliary alphabet to use as a kind of punctuation in complex proofs. Thus the ability to scan a string of symbols, dissect and rearrange it (perhaps adding and deleting symbols) is all the machinery that is required to verify proofs in some formal system or to carry out *any* effective procedure.

5.2 Production systems for problem solving

Production rules in the service of expert systems differ from productions as rewrite rules in certain superficial respects, but the fundamental principles and formal properties remain the same. For example, we are not interested in the grammar of symbol structures *per se*, as we were in the palindrome example. Rather we are interested in taking a representation of some problem and transforming it until it satisfies some criterion that says: 'This is a solution to the problem.'

5.2.1 The syntax of rules

Nowadays, production rules are usually implemented as rules that manipulate symbol structures such as lists or vectors, rather than strings of symbols. This is largely due to the influence of languages such as LISP and the data structures that they provide. (Early implementations used the string-manipulation language SNOBOL for its pattern matching capabilities.)

Thus the alphabet of canonical systems is replaced by a vocabulary of symbols or atoms, and a rather simple grammar for forming symbol structures. The vocabulary normally consists of three sets:

- a set N of names of objects in the domain;
- a set P of property names that impute attributes to objects; and
- a set V of values that these attributes can take.

In practice, N and V may overlap.

The grammar typically used is that of *object–attribute–value* triples. If $v \in N$, $\pi \in P$ and $\varpi \in V$, then (v, π, ϖ) is such a triple; for example:

(ORGANISM-1, morphology, rod)

would represent that a particular organism has a rod-like shape.

This syntax is often generalized, so that instead of having a number of triples for some object v in order to represent the various attribute–value pairs

$$(\pi_1, \varpi_1), ..., (\pi_n, \varpi_n)$$

associated with n, we combine them into a vector of the form

$$(v, \pi_1, \varpi_1, ..., \pi_n, \varpi_n).$$

In CLIPS, the fact that a particular organism had a rod morphology and grew in air would be represented by the vector

```
(organism-1 (morphology rod) (aerobicity aerobic)).
```

We shall use this syntax going forward, since we will be looking at CLIPS in more detail later on.

Once we have a vocabulary of symbols and a grammar for generating symbol structures, we can encode the initial state of some problem we are interested in. This representation corresponds to the axioms of a canonical system; these are the symbol structures that we are going to progressively rewrite in a series of rule applications.

Finally, we come to the rules themselves. These are no longer string manipulation rules, as in the palindrome example, but rules whose antecedents match against symbol structures and whose consequents contain special operators which manipulate those symbol structures. The details will become clear in the next section, where we consider the computational mechanism for applying such rules.

A *production system* consists of a *rule set* (sometimes called *production memory*), a *rule interpreter* that decides when to apply which rules, and a *working memory* that holds the data, goal statements and intermediate results that make up the current state of the problem. The working memory is the central data structure which is examined and modified by productions. The rules are triggered by this data, and the rule interpreter controls the activation and selection of rules at each cycle.

Schematically, rules in a production system have the general form:

$$P_1, ..., P_m \rightarrow Q_1, ..., Q_n$$

with the reading

if *premises* P_1 and ... and P_m are true,
then perform *actions* Q_1 and ... and Q_n.

```
(defrule diagnosis
   (patient (name Jones) (organism organism-1))
   (organism (name organism-1) (morphology rod)
            (aerobicity aerobic))
   =>
   (assert
      (organism
         (name organism-1)
         (identity enterobacteriaceae)
         (confidence 0.8)))
```

Figure 5.1 **A CLIPS rule in the style of a MYCIN ORGRULE.**

The premises are sometimes called 'conditions,' and the actions 'conclusions,' since one kind of action is to conclude, if certain conditions are met, that a particular proposition is true or probable, as we saw in Chapter 3. Another piece of terminology is that the premise is sometimes called the 'left-hand side' of the rule, while the action is called the 'right-hand side', for obvious reasons.

Premises are usually represented by object–attribute–value vectors such as

```
(organism-1 (morphology rod) (aerobicity aerobic)).
```

which states that a particular organism is rod-shaped and grows in air.

One can imagine a rule that includes this condition, for example the rule given in Figure 5.1. This rule is in the syntax of the CLIPS programming language, where rules have the general form

```
(defrule <rule-name>
   <premise₁>
   ...
   <premiseₘ>
   =>
   <action₁>
   ...
   <actionₙ>)
```

Premises are patterns that are meant to match vectors in working memory. Actions, like (assert ...) in the above example, *modify* working memory; for example:

```
(assert
   (organism
      (name organism-1)
      (identity e-coli)
      (confidence 0.8)))
```

adds the new vector

```
(organism (name organism-1) (identity e-coli) (confidence 0.8))
```

to working memory.

```
(defrule diagnosis
    (patient (name ?pat) (organism ?org))
    (organism (name ?org) (morphology rod) (aerobicity aerobic))
       =>
    (assert
       (organism
          (name ?org)
          (identity enterobacteriaceae)
          (confidence 0.8))))
```

Figure 5.2 **A CLIPS rule with pattern variables.**

Thus our `diagnosis` rule signifies that: if a particular patient is associated with a particular organism which has certain properties, then we can hazard a guess as to what kind of organism it is. This is not a very general rule, since it only applies to the patient Jones and organism-1. Presumably there is nothing special about Jones such that he requires his very own production rule. More likely, we want to make a statement that applies to any patient and any organism. The name field of the patient vector need not even appear in such a rule.

The desire to make general statements requires that we introduce variables which do not denote particular objects or values, but can be seen as 'place holders' that will match against suitable values and become bound to them. In the rule shown in Figure 5.2, the variables are those symbols preceded by the query '?'. Note that the variable `?pat` does not appear in the conclusion of the rule, and so the use of the name field in the premise is really redundant.

As one might expect, all occurrences of a given variable in the premises must be instantiated to the same value when the rule is interpreted.

5.2.2 The working memory

The basic function of the working memory (WM) is to hold data in the form of object–attribute–value vectors. These data are used by the interpreter to activate the rules, in the sense that the presence or absence of data elements in the working memory will 'trigger' some rules by satisfying the patterns in their premises. An example will make this clear.

If working memory contains the following vectors

```
(patient (name Jones) (age 40) (organism organism-1))
(organism (name organism-1) (morphology rod) (aerobicity aero-
bic))
```

then at the next cycle the interpreter will look to see which rules in production memory have conditions which are capable of being satisfied.

If a condition contains no variables, then it is satisfied just in case an identical expression is present in working memory. If a condition contains one or more variables, that is, if it is a pattern, then it is satisfied just in case there exists an expression in working memory with an attribute–value pair which matches it in a way that is consistent with the way in which other conditions in the same rule have already been matched.

In the simplest case, a match is just an assignment of constants to variables which, if applied as a substitution, would make the pattern identical to that part of the expression that it matched against.

Thus,

```
(patient (name Jones) (age 40) (organism organism-1))
```

satisfies the premise

```
(patient (name ?pat) (organism ?org))
```

with substitution: Jones for ?pat and organism-1 for ?org.

Note that we can disregard attribute–value pairs, like (Age 40), which are not mentioned in the premise. The other premise is also satisfied by other vectors without the aid of pattern matching, so

```
(organism
    (name organism-1)
    (identity enterobacteriaceae)
    (confidence 0.8))
```

is added to working memory.

Since the value of ?pat is not important to the conclusion, we could have used plain '?' instead, which matches without creating a variable binding. '?' is simply a wildcard that matches anything. Or, as noted above, we could have omitted the name field from the patient premise altogether, since

```
(patient (name Jones) (organism organism-1))
```

also satisfies the simpler premise

```
(patient (organism ?org)).
```

Let's examine the CLIPS rule set in Figure 5.3, together with an initial working memory full of vectors. This example is based on the STRIPS planner we examined in Chapter 3. The following program consists of three kinds of statement:

- *declarations*, or templates, which say what working memory vectors should look like;
- *fact definitions*, which give the initial state of the problem;
- *production rules*, which describe how to transform the problem state.

Lines preceded by ';;' are comments.

This is a complete CLIPS program that will run under CLIPS 6.0. We do not need to specify any particular conflict resolution strategy, because the default strategy will work for this example (see Section 5.3). Type it in carefully, and try it out! All you have to do is:

- load the program into CLIPS
- type (reset)
- then type (run).

Check out the watch command to see what's happening as rules fire. See Box 5.2 for a trace of the program running and an explanation of its output.

```
;; TEMPLATES

;; A 'goal' is a vector with four properties:
;; an action to be performed
;; an object that the action should be performed on
;; a location that you start from
;; a location that you move to.
(deftemplate goal
 (field action (type SYMBOL))
 (field object (type SYMBOL))
 (field from (type SYMBOL))
 (field to (type SYMBOL))
)

;; 'in' records when an object is in a location.
(deftemplate in
 (field object (type SYMBOL))
 (field location (type SYMBOL))
)

;; FACTS

;; 'deffacts' is a function that enters a bunch of statements into
;; working memory whenever the system is reset (reinitialized).
;; Here, the initial state of the world is a robot in Room A,
;; a box in Room B, and a goal to push the box to Room A.
(deffacts world
 (in (object robot) (location RoomA))
 (in (object box) (location RoomB))
 (goal (action push) (object box) (from RoomB) (to RoomA))
)

;; RULES

;; This rule says 'stop when a goal has been achieved.'
(defrule stop
 (goal (object ?X) (to ?Y))
 (in (object ?X) (location ?Y))
 =>
 (halt)
)

;; If the robot isn't at the location where the object to be
;; acted upon resides, then move the robot there.
(defrule move
 (goal (object ?X) (from ?Y))
 (in (object ?X) (location ?Y))
 ?robot-position <- (in (object robot) (location ?Z&~?Y))
 =>
 (modify ?robot-position (location ?Y))
)
```

continued

```
;; If the robot is in the right place, then move both robot and
;; object to the destination location.
(defrule push
  (goal (object ?X) (from ?Y) (to ?Z))
  ?object-position <- (in (object ?X) (location ?Y))
  ?robot-position <- (in (object robot) (location ?Y))
  =>
  (modify ?robot-position (location ?Z))
  (modify ?object-position (location ?Z))
)
```

Figure 5.3 **A CLIPS** rule set for a simple STRIPS problem.

BOX 5.2

A Trace of the STRIPS Program[†]

Running the program with the trace on will yield the following output. The reset command initializes working memory while the run command actually runs the program. In the trace, lines beginning with '==>' show additions to working memory, while lines beginning with '<==' show deletions. Lines beginning with 'FIRE' show rule firings. Ignore the other annotations for now.

```
(reset)
==> f-0  (initial-fact)
==> f-1  (in (object robot) (location RoomA))
==> f-2  (in (object box) (location RoomB))
==> f-3  (goal (action push) (object box) (from RoomB) (to RoomA))
CLIPS> (run)
FIRE 1 move: f-3,f-2,f-1
<== f-1  (in (object robot) (location RoomA))
==> f-4  (in (object robot) (location RoomB))
FIRE 2 push: f-3,f-2,f-4
<== f-4  (in (object robot) (location RoomB))
==> f-5  (in (object robot) (location RoomA))
<== f-2  (in (object box) (location RoomB))
==> f-6  (in (object box) (location RoomA))
FIRE 3 stop: f-3,f-6
[PRCCODE4] Execution halted during the actions of defrule stop.
CLIPS> (reset)
<== f-0  (initial-fact)
<== f-3  (goal (action push) (object box) (from RoomB) (to RoomA))
<== f-5  (in (object robot) (location RoomA))
<== f-6  (in (object box) (location RoomA))
CLIPS>
```

Note that the program was halted by the 'stop' rule. The final reset shows the contents of working memory being cleared away, with the robot having pushed the box from Room B to Room A. I did this reset just so these contents would show up in the trace.

5.3 Controlling the behavior of the interpreter

The interpreter for a set of production rules can be described in terms of the *recognize–act* cycle, which consists of the following sequence of steps.

(1) *Match* the premise patterns of rules against elements in working memory.
(2) If there is more than one rule that could fire, then *choose* one to apply; this step is called *conflict resolution*.
(3) *Apply* the rule, perhaps adding a new item to working memory or deleting an old one, and then go to step (1).

Usually, a 'start-up' element is inserted into the working memory at the beginning of the computation to get the cycle going. In CLIPS, this start-up element is the vector

```
(initial-fact).
```

The computation halts if there is a cycle in which no rules become active, or if the action of a fired rule contains an explicit command to halt.[2]

In step (2), the system has a set of pairs consisting of rules and the variable bindings derived from pattern matching; these pairs are called *instantiations*. Conflict resolution corresponds to the system 'making up its mind' which rule to fire. Of course, it is possible to design a rule set such that, for all configurations of data, only one rule is ever eligible to fire. Such rule sets are called *deterministic*, that is, you can always determine the 'right' rule to fire at any point in the computation. Most of the rule sets in which we are interested from an expert systems point of view will be *non-deterministic*, that is, there may often be more than one piece of knowledge that might apply at any given time.

Controlling the behavior of rule-based systems can pose non-trivial problems. There are two general approaches to this: *global control* and *local control*. Global control regimes tend to be domain-independent, in that the strategy employed does not use domain knowledge to any significant extent. All of the conflict resolution strategies listed in the next section are examples of global control, since they apply across the board in all applications. Such strategies are usually 'hard-coded' into the interpreter, as in CLIPS, and therefore difficult for programmers to change.

Local control regimes tend to be domain-dependent, in that special rules are required which use domain knowledge to reason about control. Such rules are sometimes called *meta-rules* (see Section 5.3.3), because they reason about which (object-level) rule to fire, rather than reasoning about objects or relationships in the domain. Local techniques are usually 'soft-coded' in the sense that the programmer can write explicit rules to create particular effects, as in MYCIN.

5.3.1 Conflict resolution

As we have seen, production systems typically interpose a decision-making step between pattern matching and rule application. After matching, we can form a list of all

---

[2] Note that we didn't use (initial-fact) in the STRIPS program, but we did use the explicit (halt) command. If we had simply retracted the goal statement, then the program would also have halted, since all rules require that there be a goal.

rules that have their conditions satisfied by working memory elements. This set of rules is sometimes called the *conflict set*; in CLIPS it is called the *agenda*.

Conflict resolution will normally select a single rule to fire from the conflict set. The conflict resolution strategy has a marked effect upon the behavior of a production system, so most software packages such as CLIPS provide more than one option. This is done in the hope that the programmer will find a strategy that suits the current problem.

Conflict resolution strategies are usually combinations of different basic mechanisms, each of which have different properties. Good performance from an expert system depends on certain key properties of the control regime, such as *sensitivity* and *stability*. Sensitivity means responding quickly to changes in the environment reflected in working memory, while stability means showing some kind of continuity in the line of reasoning (McDermott and Forgy, 1978; Brownston *et al.*, 1985, Chapter 7).

Conflict resolution mechanisms vary from system to system, but three are very popular.

- *Refractoriness*. A rule should not be allowed to fire more than once on the same data. The obvious way of implementing this is to discard from the conflict set instantiations which have been executed before. A weaker version only deletes the instantiation which fired during the last cycle. The latter is used specifically to prevent loops. If a loop is what you want, there is sometimes a 'refresh' function that will allow you to explicitly override refractoriness whenever you wish.
- *Recency*. Working memory elements are time-tagged in CLIPS, so that you can tell at which cycle an item of data was added to working memory. The recency strategy ranks instantiations in terms of the recency of the elements that took part in the pattern matching. Thus rules which use more recent data are preferred to rules which match against data which has been loitering in working memory for some time. The idea is to follow the 'leading edge' of the computation, if possible, rather than doubling back to take another look at old data. Such doubling back may, of course, occur if the current line of reasoning fails.
- *Specificity*. Instantiations which are derived from more specific rules, that is, rules which have a greater number of conditions and are therefore more difficult to satisfy, are preferred to more general rules with fewer conditions. The idea is that more specific rules are 'better' because they take more of the data into account. This strategy can be used to deal with exceptions to general rules.

Without conflict resolution, a production system would have no simple methods for dealing with non-determinism, handling exceptions or focusing attention on a particular line of reasoning. In other words, the representation would lack *heuristic power*, in that the behavior of such a program could be very hard to control, even if the knowledge it represented were essentially correct.

CLIPS uses the mechanisms of refractoriness, recency and specificity, and more, to good effect (see Box 5.3). In addition, it allows the user to attach a *salience* property to each rule, which is used in sorting the agenda into salience classes (see Box 5.5). Roughly speaking, the agenda is sorted by salience and then other conflict resolution mechanisms, such as those described above, are used to sort rules of equal salience.

BOX 5.3

Conflict Resolution in CLIPS[†]

This box describes some of the conflict resolution strategies used by CLIPS. For ease of expression, we shall speak of sorting 'rules,' whereas in fact we are interested in ordering rule instantiations, that is a rule that has been activated by data, and is therefore accompanied by a substitution of values for variables.

The *depth strategy*. This is a recency strategy that places rules activated by new data above rules of the same salience activated by old data in working memory. It is so called because it tends to promote a depth-first search of the problem space, in which the data derived from the last rule application stand a good chance of triggering the next rule. This is the default strategy in CLIPS 6.0.

The *breadth strategy*. Rules activated by new data are placed below all rules of the same salience on the agenda. This tends to promote a breadth-first search of the problem space, since all the rules that can fire at a given stage of problem solving will tend to fire before the data so derived triggers other rules.

The *simplicity strategy*. This is a specificity strategy for sorting with salience classes, in which newly-activated rules (rules activated by new data) are placed above all activations of rules with the same or higher specificity. Specificity is computed by counting the number of tests that are performed in the conditions of a rule.

The *complexity strategy*. Like simplicity, except that rules are placed above other rules with the same or lower specificity.

The *LEX strategy*. First LEX applies refraction, eliminating from the conflict set all instantiations that have previously fired. Remaining rules within a salience class are then sorted with respect to the recency of the data that matched their condition elements. If two instantiations have the same recency, then the most specific wins.

The *MEA strategy*. MEA applies refraction, but then sorts rules within a salience class with respect to the recency of the datum that matched their first condition element only. If this produces a clear winner, the corresponding rule is fired, otherwise, we apply the recency and specificity stages of LEX.

MEA stands for 'Means–Ends Analysis,' which is an early AI technique for backward reasoning. The idea is that MEA should be used in conjunction with special goal tokens in working memory which guide the reasoning and which match against the first condition element of selected rules. We shall see an extended example of this technique in Chapter 14.

LEX and MEA were the only two strategies originally provided by the earlier OPS5 language.[3] LEX is a good general-purpose strategy that keeps the computation moving along the leading edge of recently derived data. MEA is more specialized and is often used in planning and other constructive tasks, where some additional control needs to be exerted, but see Figure 5.4 in the next section for a trivial example.

5.3.2 Forward and backward chaining

At the global level of control, production rules can be driven forward or backward. We can chain forward from conditions that we know to be true towards problem

---

[3] OPS5 stands for 'Official Production System, Version 5,' and was the most well-known member of a family of rule-based languages developed at Carnegie-Mellon University. Many OPS5 features found their way into CLIPS, including the LEX and MEA conflict resolution strategies. We examine an application of OPS5 in Chapter 14.

states which those conditions allow us to establish, or we can chain backward from a goal state towards the conditions necessary for its establishment. This is rather like the difference between forward and backward strategies in theorem proving (see Chapter 8).

CLIPS is essentially a *forward chaining* system, while we saw in Chapter 3 that the production rules of MYCIN were mostly *backward chaining*. In CLIPS, we always match the left-hand sides of rules against working memory, and then perform the manipulation described by the right-hand side of the instantiation that emerges victorious from conflict resolution. In MYCIN, it is the right-hand side of a rule which drives the reasoning; thus if we wish to establish the identity of an organism, we find all the rules that draw conclusions about organisms in their right-hand sides, and then see which, if any, of them have conditions that can be satisfied by data.

Perhaps the easiest way to think of this forward and backward distinction is in terms of grammar rules, like those given in Section 8.1. As we saw earlier, we can use rules like

(P1) $\$ \rightarrow a\$a$
(P2) $\$ \rightarrow b\$b$
(P3) $\$ \rightarrow c\$c$

in two distinct ways.

Firstly, we can use them to *generate* palindromes. Given any start symbol from the alphabet, any sequence of rule applications will result in a palindrome; thus the sequence of rule applications **P1, P1, P3, P2, P3** to the start symbol c generates, in order, the strings

aca, aacaa, caacaac, bcaacaacb, cbcaacaacbc.

This is an example of forward chaining, since we match c, and each successive string generated, against the left-hand side of a rule, and detach the instantiated right-hand side.

Secondly, we can use the rules to *recognize* palindromes. We saw earlier that, given a string like *bacab*, we can trace the sequence of rule applications that led to its construction. *bacab* matches against the right-hand side of **P2**; we sometimes say that the right-hand side of **P2** 'accepts' *bacab*. The instantiated left-hand side of **P2** is *aca*, which matches the right-hand side of **P1**. The instantiated left-hand side of **P1** is just the axiom c, and therefore our recognition procedure terminates with success. Thus we have verified that *bacab* is indeed a palindrome. This is an example of backward chaining, since we match each substring of *bacab*, including *bacab* itself, against the right-hand side of a rule, and detach the instantiated left-hand side. Given a string like *acbcb*, there is no rule whose right-hand side accepts *acbcb*, and so it cannot be a palindrome.

In the theorem proving literature, forward chaining is typically associated with 'bottom-up' reasoning, that is, reasoning from facts to goals, while backward chaining is associated with 'top-down' reasoning from goals to facts. However, these terms are not, strictly speaking, synonymous where production systems are concerned. For example, it is possible for a forward chaining production system to perform top-down reasoning, if it is informed by a local control regime, such as an explicit ordering on goals.

In the next example, shown in Figure 5.4, we see how a simple program for stacking blocks into a tower switches between two tasks:

- finding the next block to pick up; and
- building a tower with the block.

The templates define a block as a data object having color, size and location. If a block's position isn't specified, then we assume it is on a heap of blocks that we are going to use to build a tower. The template 'on' simply provides a way of recording that one block (the 'upper' one) is directly on top of another block (the 'lower' one). The 'goal' template allows us to say what phase of the problem solving we are in, finding or building.

```
;; CONFLICT RESOLUTION STRATEGY

    (declare (strategy mea))

;; TEMPLATES

;; A block has color, size and location.
(deftemplate block
  (field color (type SYMBOL))
  (field size (type INTEGER))
  (field place (type SYMBOL) (default heap))
)

;; The upper block is directly on the lower block.
(deftemplate on
  (field upper (type SYMBOL))
  (field lower (type SYMBOL))
  (field place (type SYMBOL) (default heap))
)

;; The current goal is to 'find' or to 'build.'
(deftemplate goal
  (field task (type SYMBOL))
)

;; INITIALIZATION
;; There are three blocks of different colors and sizes.
;; They will be assumed to be on the heap.
(deffacts the-facts
  (block (color red) (size 10))
  (block (color yellow) (size 20))
  (block (color blue) (size 30))
)

;; PRODUCTION RULES
;; Set the first goal: finding the first block.
(defrule begin
  (initial-fact)
  =>
  (assert (goal (task find)))
)
```

continued

```
;; Pick up the largest block on the heap.
(defrule pick-up
  ?my-goal <- (goal (task find))
  ?my-block <- (block (size ?S1) (place heap))
  (not (block (color ?C2) (size ?S2&:(> ?S2 ?S1)) (place heap)))
  =>
  (modify ?my-block (place hand))
  (modify ?my-goal (task build))
)

;; Place the first block as the foundation of the tower.
;; It is not on any other block.
(defrule place-first
  ?my-goal <- (goal (task build))
  ?my-block <- (block (place hand))
  (not (block (place tower)))
  =>
  (modify ?my-block (place tower))
  (modify ?my-goal (task find))
)

;; Place subsequent blocks on the uppermost block of the tower.
(defrule put-down
  ?my-goal <- (goal (task build))
  ?my-block <- (block (color ?C0) (place hand))
  (block (color ?C1) (place tower))
  (not (on (upper ?C2) (lower ?C1) (place tower)))
  =>
  (modify ?my-block (place tower))
  (assert (on (upper ?C0) (lower ?C1) (place tower)))
  (modify ?my-goal (task find))
)

;; Stop when there are no more blocks in the heap.
(defrule stop
  ?my-goal <- (goal (task find))
  (not (block (place heap)))
  =>
  (retract ?my-goal)
)
```

Figure 5.4 **A CLIPS rule set for stacking blocks.**

Note that the order in which these rules are listed is immaterial. In the STRIPS program, the termination rule was at the top of the rule set, whereas here it is at the bottom. It makes no difference. See Box 5.4 for a trace of the block-stacking program's execution and an explanation of its output.

BOX 5.4

A Trace of the Block Stacking Program[†]

Running the program with the trace on will yield the following output.

```
CLIPS> (reset)
==> f-0    (initial-fact)
==> f-1    (block (color red) (size 10) (place heap))
==> f-2    (block (color yellow) (size 20) (place heap))
==> f-3    (block (color blue) (size 30) (place heap))
CLIPS> (run)
FIRE 1 begin: f-0
==> f-4    (goal (task find))
FIRE 2 pick-up: f-4,f-3,
<== f-3    (block (color blue) (size 30) (place heap))
==> f-5    (block (color blue) (size 30) (place hand))
<== f-4    (goal (task find))
==> f-6    (goal (task build))
FIRE 3 place-first: f-6,f-5,
<== f-5    (block (color blue) (size 30) (place hand))
==> f-7    (block (color blue) (size 30) (place tower))
<== f-6    (goal (task build))
==> f-8    (goal (task find))
FIRE 4 pick-up: f-8,f-2,
<== f-2    (block (color yellow) (size 20) (place heap))
==> f-9    (block (color yellow) (size 20) (place hand))
<== f-8    (goal (task find))
==> f-10   (goal (task build))
FIRE 5 put-down: f-10,f-9,f-7,
<== f-9    (block (color yellow) (size 20) (place hand))
==> f-11   (block (color yellow) (size 20) (place tower))
==> f-12   (on (upper yellow) (lower blue) (place tower))
<== f-10   (goal (task build))
==> f-13   (goal (task find))
FIRE 6 pick-up: f-13,f-1,
<== f-1    (block (color red) (size 10) (place heap))
==> f-14   (block (color red) (size 10) (place hand))
<== f-13   (goal (task find))
==> f-15   (goal (task build))
FIRE 7 put-down: f-15,f-14,f-11,
<== f-14   (block (color red) (size 10) (place hand))
==> f-16   (block (color red) (size 10) (place tower))
==> f-17   (on (upper red) (lower yellow) (place tower))
<== f-15   (goal (task build))
==> f-18   (goal (task find))
FIRE 8 stop: f-18,
<== f-18   (goal (task find))
CLIPS> (reset)
<== f-0    (initial-fact)
<== f-7    (block (color blue) (size 30) (place tower))
<== f-11   (block (color yellow) (size 20) (place tower))
<== f-12   (on (upper yellow) (lower blue) (place tower))
```

```
                                                              continued
<== f-16    (block (color red) (size 10) (place tower))
<== f-17    (on (upper red) (lower yellow) (place tower))
```

Note the manipulation of goal tokens as they are added and deleted by rules. The final reset shows the contents of working memory as they are cleared away, with the red block on the yellow block which is on the blue block, forming a tower.

The point of this example is that the reasoning strategy of this program is top-down, even though the rules are forward chaining on data, and hence operating bottom-up. We achieve this effect by manipulating goal tokens. In this case, (initial-fact) stands for our top-level goal, to build a tower. This goal has two subgoals, finding and placing blocks, represented by the tokens

```
(goal (task find))
```

and

```
(goal (task build)).
```

When there are no more blocks to be placed, the main goal has been achieved. We did this rather informally, using (initial-fact) to simplify the code, but the principle still applies.

Thus it is sometimes necessary to draw a distinction between the directionality of the *chaining* and the directionality of the actual *reasoning*. These two activities are really on different levels of analysis. Obviously, the chaining implements the reasoning and not vice versa, but the reasoning strategy *controls* the chaining, in this case by manipulating goal tokens. We will see a much more sophisticated example of this method in Chapter 14, when we look at the real-world system R1/XCON.

Such distinctions highlight a common problem in talking about the way in which AI programs work. Most complex systems, whether they are pieces of software, physical devices, or some combination of the two, can be understood at various levels of description, as Newell (1982) noted. To adopt Newell's terminology, chaining is a phenomenon of the symbol level, where we are only interested in 'left-hand sides' and 'right-hand sides' of rules, whereas reasoning is something that occurs at the knowledge level, where we can distinguish between facts and tasks.

It was stated earlier that most production rule sets of interest in artificial intelligence applications are non-deterministic. When forward chaining, there may be more than one rule whose conditions are satisfied by data, while when backward chaining there may be more than one rule that can help establish a goal. Thus control issues are crucial, regardless of the direction in which the rules chain, and a production system that is ill-controlled may produce spurious conclusions, or no conclusions at all (due to looping or premature termination).

We saw in Chapter 3 that an *AND-OR tree* is a useful device for representing the search space associated with a set of production rules. Nodes in the tree correspond to states of working memory, while branches correspond to possible rule applications. The tree diagram is typically laid out in a backward chaining style, with the main goal at the top, the subgoals in the middle, and the data at the terminal nodes.

Thus the *root node* of the tree is the start state of the problem, while the *leaf nodes* contain candidate solutions. Non-terminal nodes, on the other hand, will be of two kinds: AND nodes and OR nodes. AND nodes correspond to rule applications which rewrite a goal as a conjunction of subgoals, while OR nodes correspond to alternative rule applications. Thus, in the terminology introduced in Chapter 2, the possible rule applications generate a *search space* and determine its underlying structure.

Rule-based programming does not abolish combinatorial explosion, since the AND/OR tree for any problem may branch exponentially. But, in practical applications, it is hoped that the conflict resolution strategy employed by the interpreter will tend to choose a rule that leads to a reasonable solution. In the next section, we review a more strong-arm approach to the control of search.

5.3.3 Rules and meta-rules[†]

The code for each production rule is meant to be self-contained, in that all necessary context for rule activation is provided only by the premises. There is no way for one rule to call another, as if rules were procedures. Rule R at cycle C_i may facilitate the subsequent firing of rule R' at cycle C_i+_1, but only via the changes that it makes to the contents of working memory.

Sometimes you might want to use knowledge in deciding which rules to fire, instead of following the conflict resolution strategy. So some production system interpreters allow the programmer to write *meta-rules*, which reason about which rules should be considered for firing, or should ultimately be fired. (CLIPS is not one of these.)

Meta-rules are distinguished from ordinary rules in that their role is to *direct* the reasoning required to solve the problem, rather than to actually *perform* that reasoning. This distinction between different levels of reasoning is often referred to as the distinction between *meta-level* and *object-level*. Thus, one might have meta-rules which reason about which (problem solving) rule to apply next, thereby performing conflict resolution, or enhancing an existing conflict resolution strategy.

For example, MYCIN's production rules are indexed by the clinical parameters appearing in their action parts. Thus it is easy to retrieve for consideration all of the rules which might apply in determining the value of a given parameter. This information is used by meta-rules which, instead of applying to subgoals, apply to the rules which apply to subgoals. Given that we wish to achieve subgoal G, say finding the identity of an organism, there may be as many as 30 rules which could apply. Meta-rules are used to prune and order the list of rules applicable at any one point.

Figure 5.5 shows a sample pruning rule for MYCIN, taken from Buchanan and Shortliffe (1984, Chapter 28).

METARULE001
IF: 1) the culture was not obtained from a sterile source, and
        2) there are rules which mention in their premise a previous organism,
        which may be the same as the current organism
THEN: it is definite (1.0) that each of them is not going to be useful.

Figure 5.5 An English rendition of a MYCIN pruning rule.

METARULE002
IF: 1) the infection is a pelvic-abscess, and
        2) there are rules which mention in their premise enterobacteriaceae, and
        3) there are rules which mention in their premise gram-positive rods,
THEN: there is suggestive evidence (0.4) that the former should be done
        before the latter.

Figure 5.6 A MYCIN meta-rule encoding strategic knowledge.

It states that when trying to identify organisms from a non-sterile site, rules which base their identification on other organisms found at that site are not applicable. Other meta-rules are there to reorder relevant domain rules, and they encode strategic knowledge of the kind 'try this before trying that,' for example the rule in Figure 5.6.

Note that meta-rules also admit of uncertainty, since their conclusions may be qualified by a certainty factor that is less than 1. Thus we find that our basic pattern of reasoning at the meta-level is that same as at the object-level. It is simply that meta-rules reason about the object-level rules, while the object-level rules reason about the domain itself.

Finally, Figure 5.7 shows an example of a very general meta-rule, since it refers to general problem solving strategy, rather than specific medical knowledge.

Meta-rules can be either relatively domain-specific or domain-free, although the former is more usual. A domain-specific meta-rule is one that encodes a particular piece of strategic knowledge about the domain; for example, in medical diagnosis, one might wish to encode the fact that special groups of patients, such as alcoholics or people suffering from burns, are especially prone to particular kinds of infection, and write meta-rules which point the program in the direction of the rules which seem most applicable to such cases. A relatively domain-free meta-rule might be one which advises the program to consider rules which generate small search spaces before rules that generate larger ones.

However, it is important not to be misled by this distinction, as a lot depends upon the level of abstraction at which the knowledge is expressed. For example, a meta-rule such as

> if x is an alcoholic, then consider rules for determining this disease before rules for determining that disease

could be abstracted along the lines of

> if x is some reason for believing that y is of category z, and there are special rules associated with category z, then apply those rules before trying other applicable rules.

METARULE003
IF: 1) there are rules which do not mention the current goal in their premise,
and   2) there are rules which mention the current goal in their premise
THEN: it is definite (1.0) that the former should be done before the latter.

Figure 5.7 A MYCIN meta-rule for encoding preferences among rules.

The latter is less domain-dependant, insofar as it could be applied to a greater variety of problems. A particular domain-specific application of this principle, such as the example concerning alcoholics, could be regarded as an instantiation of a more general meta-rule. At the present time, there is considerable interest in the possibility of identifying abstract problem-solving principles capable of being applied in different domains (see Chapters 11, 12 and 17).

We shall return to the topic of meta-level reasoning in Chapters 12, 15, 18 and 23. For now, we shall simply observe that it is a powerful idea, but one that should be applied selectively. If a program spends too much time thinking about how it should proceed, then it will not achieve its goals in a timely fashion.

BOX 5.5

Salience in CLIPS: The Penguin Flies Again (or Not)

CLIPS does not provide any mechanism for defining meta-rules. The main mechanism for exerting influence over the preferential selection of rule instantiations for firing is the salience property. This gives selected rules an additional chance of being selected during conflict resolution.

For example, given the 'penguin' example from Chapter 2, we could ensure that the 'penguin' rule fires in preference to the more general 'bird' rule by giving it greater salience, as follows:

```
(defrule
   (bird (type ?X))
      =>
   (assert (yes))
)

(defrule
   (declare (salience 100))
   (bird (type penguin))
   =>
   (assert (no))
)
```

By default, rules have a salience of 0. They can be upweighted by being given a positive number, or downweighted with a negative number (see Appendix).

The above solution may not be theoretically satisfying (or ideologically sound) as a general solution to the problem of reasoning with assumptions, but it will serve for many practical applications.

BIBLIOGRAPHICAL NOTES

An excellent introduction to rule-based approaches to AI problems can be found in Nilsson (1980). Davis and King (1977) do a good job of summarizing the strengths and weaknesses of production systems as a programming paradigm; this early treatment is in many ways more detailed than later analyses. An account of recent attempts to parallelize production systems can be found in Schmolze (1991).

The appendix is provided for readers who are interested in trying their hands at programming with production systems. It contains an introduction to the rule-based language CLIPS, which has been widely used in expert systems applications. The intention is to illustrate some of the concepts introduced in the text, rather than to impart an encyclopedic knowledge of the language. For more details of production rule coding strategies, the interested reader is referred to Brownston *et al.* (1985).

STUDY SUGGESTIONS

1. What do you understand by the term 'conflict resolution'?

2. Let A be the alphabet $\{a, b\}$ and let the axioms be

    ab, ba.

    Describe the strings that would be generated by the following productions

    (**P1**) $\$a \rightarrow \$ab$
    (**P2**) $\$b \rightarrow \$ba$.

3. Let A be the alphabet $\{a, b\}$ and let the axioms be

    aa, bb.

    Write a set of two production rules that will generate all strings of the form

    $aa, bb, aabb, bbaa, aabbaa, bbaabb, aabbaabb, bbaabbaa$, etc.

4. Write a CLIPS program to perform syllogistic reasoning. A syllogism is an argument based on a simple pattern, such as

    All As are Bs
    <u>All Bs are Cs</u>
    All As are Cs

    All As are Bs
    <u>Some As are Cs</u>
    All Cs are Bs

    All As are Bs
    <u>No Cs are Bs</u>
    No Cs are As

continued

These arguments can easily be drawn using Venn diagrams. You can model them in CLIPS with three corresponding rules.

Here is the only template you will need. It says that a statement consists of a quantifier (all, some, or no), and two sets.

```
(deftemplate statement
  (field quantifier (type SYMBOL))
  (field set1 (type SYMBOL))
  (field set2 (type SYMBOL))
)
```

Thus, 'All As are Bs' would be represented by the statement

```
(statement (quantifier all) (set1 As) (set2 Bs))
```

Here are some facts to test the program on.

```
(deffacts the-facts
  (statement (quantifier all) (set1 puppies) (set2 dogs))
  (statement (quantifier all) (set1 dogs) (set2 mammals))
  (statement (quantifier all) (set1 mammals) (set2 animals))
  (statement (quantifier no) (set1 sea-creatures) (set2 dogs))
  (statement (quantifier some) (set1 sea-creatures)
             (set2 mammals))
)
```

5. Examine the CLIPS program for diagnosing causes of abdominal pain (Figure 5.8). (Hypochondriacs should be aware that these rules are merely copied from a textbook, and do not have the weight of a true diagnosis.)

```
;; TEMPLATES

;; A 'sign' is a symptom associated with a site in an organ or
;; appendage, e.g., a pain in the upper right abdomen.
(deftemplate sign
  (field symptom (type SYMBOL))
  (field organ (type SYMBOL) (default NIL))
  (field site (type SYMBOL) (default NIL))
)


;; A 'diagnosis' identifies a disorder with some organ.
;; The organ may not be specified or may be assumed.
(deftemplate diagnosis
  (field disorder (type SYMBOL))
  (field organ (type SYMBOL) (default NIL))
)
```

continued

```
;; FACTS
;; Some sample symptoms
(deffacts the-facts
 (sign (symptom pain) (organ abdomen) (site lower))
 (sign (symptom poor-appetite))
 (sign (symptom weight-loss))
)

;; RULES
;; If recurrent pain in upper abdomen & poor appetite & weight
;; loss then stomach tumor.
(defrule stomach-tumor
 (sign (symptom pain) (organ abdomen) (site upper))
 (sign (symptom poor-appetite))
 (sign (symptom weight-loss))
 =>
 (assert (diagnosis (disorder tumor) (organ stomach)))
)

;; If recurrent pain in lower abdomen & diarrhea & nausea & no
;; fever then inflammation of large intestine.
(defrule inflammation1
 (sign (symptom pain) (organ abdomen) (site lower))
 (sign (symptom diarrhea))
 (sign (symptom nausea))
 (not (sign fever))
 =>
 (assert (diagnosis (disorder inflammation)
                    (organ large-intestine)))
)

;; If recurrent pain in lower abdomen & recurrent diarrhea & fever
;; then inflammation of large intestine.
(defrule inflammation2
 (sign (symptom pain) (organ abdomen) (site lower))
 (sign (symptom diarrhea))
 (sign (symptom fever))
 =>
 (assert (diagnosis (disorder inflammation)
                    (organ large-intestine)))
)

;; If recurrent pain in upper right abdomen & no fever
;; then gallstones.

(defrule gallstones
 (sign (symptom pain) (organ abdomen) (site upper-right))
```

continued

```
=>
(assert (diagnosis (disorder gallstones)
                   (organ gallbladder)))
)
;; If recurrent pain in upper right abdomen & vomiting & fever
;; then gallbladder inflamation.
(defrule gallbladder
 (sign (symptom pain) (organ abdomen) (site upper-right))
 (sign (symptom vomiting))
 (sign (symptom fever))
 =>
 (assert (diagnosis (disorder inflammation)
                    (organ gallbladder)))
)
```

Figure 5.8 **A CLIPS** rule set for diagnosing abdominal disorders

This program has one obvious limitation. All the symptoms must be present in the initial state of the working memory for a diagnosis to ensue. Yet patients will typically mention only the most distressing symptoms first, such as pain, and may not mention other symptoms, such as swollen ankles, right away.

Modify the program so that it asks about missing symptoms. The easiest way to do this is to add rules that have as their sole condition a pain symptom, such as

```
(sign (symptom pain) (organ abdomen) (site lower))
```

and whose actions put questions to be asked into working memory. You will then need a rule to ask those questions and place the right sign vectors in working memory, depending upon the answer received. Here is a template for the 'question' datatype.

```
;; A 'question' asks about a symptom in some organ and has an
;; answer.
(deftemplate question
 (field symptom (type SYMBOL))
 (field organ (type SYMBOL) (default NIL))
 (field answer (type SYMBOL) (default NIL))
 )
```

Thus both patterns in production rules and the working memory elements they match against must conform to this template.

6. What do you see as being the limitations of the 'salience' approach to the Penguin Problem in Box 5.5?

6

Associative Nets and Frame Systems

I shall follow Nilsson (1982) in using the generic term *structured object* to refer to any representational scheme whose fundamental building blocks are analogical to the nodes and arcs of graph theory or the slots and fillers of record structures. I shall systematically contrast this kind of representation with schemes which have been derived either from the rewrite rules of formal grammars or the well-formed formulas of various logics. Structured object representations are essentially ways of grouping information in a more or less natural way, and providing equally natural access paths.

We saw in the last chapter that production rules are a good representation for linking the state of some problem with actions that could be taken to move towards a solution. However, sometimes 'what to do when' isn't the only focus of interest; sometimes it is the properties and interrelationships of complex objects in the domain that determine the solution to a problem. It is not very convenient to represent knowledge about such objects and events and arbitrary relationships (such as type–subtype, part–whole, before–after and so on) in the rather limited format of rewrite rules and working memory elements.

In this chapter and the next, we explore more suitable representations for structural knowledge, paying attention to some of the difficulties that researchers and practitioners have encountered. The formalisms studied in this chapter are all based on various kinds of graph, with nodes that may hold information in the form of records, and links which stand for important relationships between these entities. The following chapter concentrates on object-oriented approaches to knowledge representation, which bring a particular design methodology and programming style to bear upon the problem.

6.1   Graphs, trees and networks

The terminology of graph theory has been imported into artificial intelligence and computer science to describe certain kinds of abstract data structure. The following

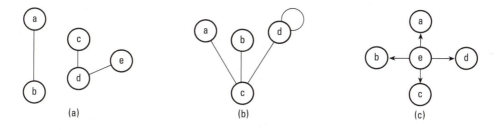

Figure 6.1 **Some graph structures: (a) a simple graph; (b) a connected graph with a self-loop; and (c) a simple digraph that is also a tree.**

definitions are phrased in such a way as to reflect their current usage in describing structured objects, rather than their original definitions in their home discipline.

All of the definitions assume that there exist two kinds of primitive entity, *nodes* and *links*. The nodes are the sources and destinations of links, and they usually have labels to distinguish them. The links may or may not have labels, depending upon whether or not there is more than one kind of link. Nodes are sometimes called 'vertices' and links are sometimes called 'edges' or 'arcs,' which is the standard graph-theoretic terminology.

Definition 6.1 **If *N* is a set of nodes, then a *general graph*, *G*, is any subset of *N* × *N*. If the order of the pairs in *N* × *N* is material, then *G* is also a *digraph*, or directed graph.**

Note from Figure 6.1 that a graph need not be connected. If we outlaw self-loops in a graph, by adding the restriction that the pairs must contain distinct nodes, then the result is a *simple graph* (or simple digraph). If we outlaw circuits as well, that is, paths through the graph which begin and end with the same node, then G is a *forest*.

Definition 6.2 **If *G* is a simple graph on *n* nodes with *n* − 1 links and no circuits, then *G* is also a *tree*.**

In other words, a tree is a connected forest. It is usual to designate one of the nodes as the 'root' of the tree, for example node *e* in the digraph of Figure 6.1 (c). The rest of the nodes form a loop-free, branching structure consisting of successors of the root. Nodes with no successors are called *terminals*, or 'leaves,' of the tree, while the others are *non-terminals*.

In graph theory, a *network* is simply a weighted digraph, that is, a directed graph with numerical labels associated with links. These labels normally indicate the cost of traversing the link, or the distance between links, as in a road map. In AI, the labels on links can stand for anything at all; they signify arbitrary relations between nodes.

The following definition of a network is probably closer to current AI practice than the original graph-theoretic one.

Definition 6.3 **If *L* is a set of labeled links and *N* is a set of nodes as before, then a *network* is any subset of *N* × *L* × *N*, where the order of the triples is material.**

Links in networks are almost always directed, since the relations that labeled links stand for need not be symmetric.

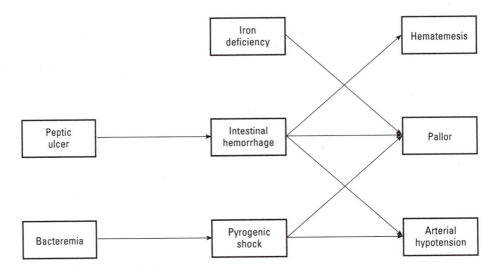

Figure 6.2 **Portion of a causal network, adapted from Pople (1982).**

Simple graphs are useful for analogical representations of spatial and temporal relationships. They are also used to represent more abstract relationships, like causal connections between medical disorders (see Figure 6.2). Accessing such information involves graph search, for which various algorithms are already available (see, for example, Pearl, 1984).

Trees, on the other hand, are useful for representing classification hierarchies and discrimination nets. For example, one might wish to classify different kinds of disease according to organ location (see Figure 6.3). The resulting tree would have the set of all diseases as its root node, and the successors of this node would be nodes standing

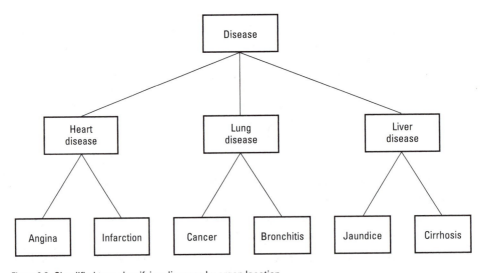

Figure 6.3 Simplified tree classifying diseases by organ location.

for such categories as heart disease, liver disease, kidney disease, and so on. Each of these nodes could have successors which specialize their ancestor node in different ways, and so on. Terminal nodes might stand for actual diseases that one can diagnose and treat, for example a liver disease like cirrhosis.

Semantic nets (somewhat misleadingly named) are a kind of network commonly used to structure more general kinds of information. These are constellations of nodes and links in which the nodes stand for concepts and the links stand for relationships between them. They got their name because they were originally employed to represent the meaning of natural language expressions.

Figure 6.4 shows fragments of a semantic net. The first fragment represents the verb *give*, showing that it has three associated roles: a donor, a recipient, and an object that is given. The node labels at the end of these links state what kind of entity is allowed to fill the role in question. Thus the donor and the recipient are typically persons, while that which is given is normally a thing.

The second fragment shows an instance of giving, which we shall call *give-256*, in which John gives Mary a copy of the book *War and Peace*. This can be seen to be a valid instance of *give*, since the fillers for the roles obey the restrictions on the appropriate nodes. We assume that *mary* and *john* are both instances of *person*, and that 'war & peace' is an instance of a class such as *book*, which is a kind of *thing*.

Similarly, *give-256* would normally be connected to *give* by a link which signifies that this particular act of giving is an instance of the general concept of giving. This special link is often called the 'ISA' link. It is used to attach specific instances, which normally represent data, to the concepts in the network.

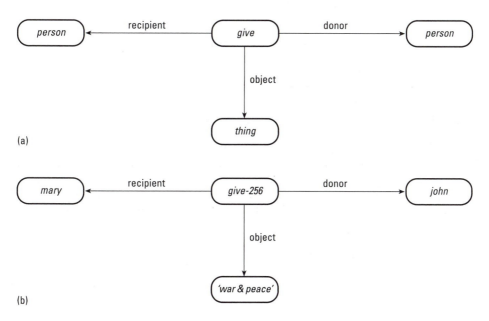

Figure 6.4 Fragments of a semantic network, (a) representing the verb 'to give,' (b) representing an instance of giving.

The term *associative nets* is better for our purposes, being more neutral with regard to what the network is used for. The use of some form of network for the modeling of domain-specific objects and relationships is becoming more and more widespread in expert systems, so it is worth looking at their underlying assumptions in more detail.

6.2 The rise of associative networks

The systematic use of networks for knowledge representation begins with Quillian's (1968) work on language understanding. Quillian questioned the notion that our ability to understand language can be characterized, even in principle, by a set of basic rules. He suggested that text understanding involved 'the creation of some mental symbolic representation,' which led to a concern with how the meanings of words might be stored so that a computer could make human-like use of them. Quillian was not the first to stress the importance of general knowledge in language understanding; this had already been discovered by the machine translation community. However, he was among the first to suggest that human memory could be modeled by a network of nodes representing concepts and relations, and propose a processing model for memory retrieval.

If we want more robust programs, and ones that remain reliable in the face of modifications, then a program should be able to make reasonable assumptions where knowledge is missing and monitor the integrity of its own knowledge. This in turn places a constraint on the representation of knowledge employed: the knowledge should be organized in a way that facilitates integrity checking. The kinds of knowledge structure explored in this chapter are relevant to these goals.

6.2.1 The type–token distinction and cognitive economy

There are two aspects of Quillian's memory model that are particularly relevant to subsequent semantic net systems, and so I shall emphasize these at the expense of other features.

Firstly, there is a *type–token* distinction made between concept nodes. The type node for a concept is connected to a configuration of tokens of other concept nodes which constitute its definition. This is rather like a dictionary, in which each entry is defined in terms of other entries, which are defined elsewhere in a similar fashion. Thus the meaning of token nodes is derived with reference to the corresponding type node, just as, in order to understand a word used in a dictionary definition, you may need to refer to the entry for that word. Localization of this kind aids the construction and maintenance of representations of knowledge.

For example, one might choose to define the meaning of 'machine' as an assembly of connected components which transmit force to perform work. This would require connecting the type node for 'machine' to tokens representing 'assembly,' 'components' and so on. However, in addition to links within this definitional plane, there will be paths to other tokens, such as those standing for 'typewriter' and 'office,' which represent knowledge to the effect that typewriters are a kind of machine for office use.

Another interesting feature of the memory model is usually referred to as *cognitive economy*. Thus, if we know that a machine is an assembly of interconnected parts, and we know that a typewriter is a machine, then we can deduce that a typewriter is an assembly. It doesn't make sense to store this information explicitly by attaching it to the type node for 'typewriter.' If we allow 'typewriter' to have the property of being an assembly by virtue of its standing in a certain relation to 'machine,' we can save some storage space and still get the information that we need, so long as we can draw the right inference.

This convention, known today as the *inheritance of properties*, is extremely widespread in knowledge representation schemes which employ any kind of structured object. As we shall see later in this chapter, a number of extra features have been added to this facility in later years, but the basic idea remains the same. Inheritance of properties is a particularly clear example of the storage space versus processing speed trade-off that the designers of knowledge representation schemes need to consider. However, we shall see that it poses a number of non-trivial problems, particularly if we allow exceptions, that is token nodes that do not inherit all the properties of their type. Furthermore, although meaning is still localized within the network, for a given node, bits and pieces of its definition may be distributed here and there among its type nodes. In our example, only part of the meaning of 'typewriter' is now stored at the type node for typewriter; the rest of it is with the 'machine' node.

Thus, in addition to the space/speed trade-off, there is also a trade-off between the space saved by modularizing definitions and the intelligibility of those definitions from the user's point of view. However, if this idea is correctly implemented, a program will always know how to retrieve and assemble the definition of a given concept. The main advantage is that we can store an arbitrary amount of semantic information at a node, for example ranges for the values of properties that tokens of a type must possess. This is simply not practical in a formalism like production systems, where exhaustive checking of the consistency of working memory would have to be performed either by special rules representing integrity constraints or by the problem solving rules themselves. Either way, this activity would consume computational resources needed for problem solving, and it would be hampered by the unstructured nature of the working memory.

6.2.2   Assessing the adequacy of associative nets

The basic information retrieval operation in the processing model which goes with Quillian's memory model can be described as an intersection search by *spreading activation*. The idea is that if you want to know whether or not a typewriter is a machine, then 'activation' of some kind will spread out in all directions from both the 'machine' type node and the 'typewriter' type node. At some point, these ripples of spreading activation will intersect, establishing that there is indeed a relationship between these two concepts, since there is a path from each to the other. Spreading activation was typically implemented by passing markers along labeled links. We shall encounter this rather simple but powerful idea again in Chapter 23, when we discuss neural networks.

It is interesting to note that Quillian's ideas enjoyed only a limited success as a psychological model of human memory organization and functioning. Collins and Quillian (1969) tested the model by measuring the time that human subjects took to answer questions about category membership and properties of concepts, and found that response time did increase with the number of assumed nodes involved in the intersection search. However, this result only held for positive responses. There were indications in the data that negative responses would cause trouble for the theory, and subsequent experiments by other researchers showed that this was indeed the case.

These results do not detract from Quillian's contribution to research in knowledge representation, however. His work anticipated a decade of research into network-based formalisms for conceptual encoding. Although modern associative nets differ substantially from the original conception in their overall structure, and are often employed to ends other than natural language understanding, many of the basic principles derive from the ideas described above.

Nevertheless, a number of problems have dogged network representations. During the 1970s, various critiques of net-based formalisms were published, of which the most influential was probably that of Woods (1975). Using nodes and links to represent concepts and relations may sound straightforward, but experience has shown that it is strewn with pitfalls for the unwary.

- Network architects were not always scrupulous in the way in which they assigned meanings to nodes. Thus, faced with a type node labeled 'typewriter,' it was often unclear as to whether it stood for the concept of a typewriter, or the class of all typewriters, or a typical typewriter. Similarly, token nodes were open to many interpretations, such as a particular typewriter, an indefinite singular typewriter, an arbitrary typewriter, and so on. Different interpretations support rather different sets of inferences, and so these are not idle distinctions.
- Reducing inference to intersection search does not abolish the problems associated with the combinatorial explosion noted in Chapter 2. Hence it was felt that a memory organization in terms of constellations of nodes, with spreading activation as the main retrieval process, resulted in a system whose behavior was insufficiently constrained. For example, negative responses to queries seemed to involve extravagant amounts of search, since it is only after the activation has spread as far as it will go that you can be sure that two concepts do not in fact stand in the hypothesized relation.

Thus it was realized that early associative network formalisms were lacking in two respects: logical and heuristic adequacy.

- Nets were logically inadequate because they could not make many of the distinctions that logic can make, for example between a particular typewriter, at least one unspecified typewriter, all typewriters, no typewriters, and so on. The meaning of nodes and links was often inextricably bound up with the retrieval and inference capabilities of the system. This confounding of semantics with details of implementation resulted from the fact that nets were meant to represent, retrieve and draw inferences about knowledge using a uniform set of associative mechanisms; understandably, the distinctions between these three functions sometimes got blurred.
- Nets were heuristically inadequate because searches for information were not themselves knowledge based. In other words, there was no knowledge in such systems which told you how to search for the knowledge that you wanted to find.

These two shortcomings interacted in unpleasant ways; for example, if you were unable to represent negation or exclusive alternation (logical inadequacy), this led to gaps in your knowledge as to when you could safely terminate a failed search (heuristic inadequacy).

Various formalisms and mechanisms were proposed to deal with these problems (but few of them were widely adopted). For example, many network systems were enriched so that they were closer to various logics in their expressive power, thus making it possible to represent some of the distinctions described earlier (for example, Schubert, 1976). Others were given enhanced heuristic power by attaching procedures to nodes which could be executed whenever the nodes became active (for example, Levesque and Mylopoulos, 1979). Nevertheless, the basic organization of the memory in terms of nodes and links remained the same, even in cases where extra structures, such as 'supernodes' standing for partitions of nodes, were added (for example, Hendrix, 1979). The resulting systems were often unwieldy, and the original simplicity was sometimes lost with not much gain in capability.

6.3 Representing typical objects and situations

This section reviews a somewhat simpler mechanism, called a *frame system*, for representing real-world knowledge in a way that attempts to integrate

- declarative notions about objects and events and their properties, and
- procedural notions about how to retrieve information and achieve goals,

thereby overcoming some of the problems associated with semantic networks.

6.3.1 Introduction to frame concepts

One of the intuitions behind frame system theory was that conceptual encoding in the human brain is not much concerned with strictly defining the properties that entities must possess in order to be considered exemplars of some category. Many of the categories that we use are not sharply defined, being based on rather vague concepts (see Chapter 9). Humans seem to be more concerned with the salient properties associated with just those objects which are somehow typical of their class.

Such objects have been called 'prototypical objects' or *prototypes*. Thus a prototypical bird, like a sparrow, can fly, and so we tend to think of this as being a property of birds, even though there are birds, such as the penguin, which cannot fly. There is a sense in which a sparrow is a better exemplar of the bird category than a penguin, because it is more typical of the class. Nevertheless, the existence of exceptional birds, such as the penguin, forces us to qualify generalizations such as 'birds fly.'

Even with mathematical objects, such as polygons, one suspects that we have well-developed notions of typicality. Given the three quadrilaterals in Figure 6.5, there can be little doubt that typicality increases as we proceed from left to right. Quadrilaterals with obtuse inner angles are somehow less typical than convex quadrilaterals, possibly because we are used to correlating area with perimeter, and this correlation makes more sense where angles are more or less equal.

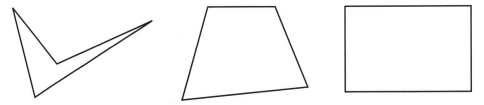

Figure 6.5 **Typicality among quadrilaterals.**

Frame systems attempt to reason about classes of objects by using prototypical representations of knowledge which hold good for the majority of cases, but which may need to be deformed in some way to capture the complexities of the real world. Thus if I know nothing about the area of a more or less rectangular plot of land, but I know the length of the sides, then I may estimate the area, assuming that the angles are more or less equal. To the extent that I am wrong in this assumption, I will overestimate the area, but this state of affairs is typical of heuristic devices.

In practical problem solving, exceptions to rules abound and there are often rather fuzzy boundaries between classes. Frame systems are useful because they provide a way of structuring the heuristic knowledge associated with the application of rules and the classification of objects. Instead of being peppered here and there in the code of an applications program, or gathered together into a pool of meta-rules, heuristics are distributed among the kinds of object that they apply to, and exist at levels of control in a hierarchy of such objects.

6.3.2 Complex nodes in a network

Minsky (1975) described frames as 'data structures for representing stereotyped situations' to which are attached various kinds of information, including what kinds of object or event to expect in that situation, and how to use the information in the frame. The idea is to use a single data structure as a focus for all the knowledge that might be useful about a given class of objects or events, rather than distributing that knowledge among smaller structures, like logical formulas or production rules. Such knowledge will either be contained in the data structure itself, or it will be accessible from the structure (for example, if it is stored in some other, related structure).

Thus a frame is essentially a way of bundling both declarative and procedural knowledge about some entity into a record structure, consisting of *slots* and *fillers*. The slots are like fields in a record, while the fillers are like values stored in those fields. However, frames differ from familiar structures, like Pascal records, in a number of significant respects, as we shall see.

A frame has a special slot filled by the name of the entity that it stands for, and the other slots are filled with the values of various common attributes associated with the object. Attached to such slots, there may also be procedures, which are called whenever a slot is accessed or updated. The idea is that problem solving computations occur largely as a side effect of the flow of data in and out of a frame.

A frame can be thought of as a complex node in a special kind of associative network. Frames are typically arranged in a loose hierarchy (or heterarchy) in which frames 'lower down' the network can inherit values for slots from frames 'higher up'. (A heterarchy is a 'tangled hierarchy,' that is, an acyclic graph in which nodes can have more than one predecessor.)

The fundamental idea is that properties and procedures associated with frames in the properties of nodes high up in the frame system are more or less fixed, insofar as they represent things which are typically true about the entity of interest, whereas frames in the lower levels have slots that must be filled with more contingent information. If such information is absent, due to incomplete knowledge of the prevailing state of affairs, then slot values for lower frames can be inherited from global values in frames higher up the hierarchy. Otherwise, local values supplied lower down are allowed to overwrite the heuristic information held higher up.

The main link types in a frame system are between instances and classes and between classes and superclasses. Thus the `Computer` node would stand in a class–superclass relationship to the node `Machine`, while the node `sol2`, representing a particular computer (one of my department's Sun servers), would stand in an instance–class relationship to the `Computer` node. Properties and relationships that would normally be encoded by labeled links between nodes in a typical semantic network are now encoded using the slot–filler representation. In addition, slots can have all sorts of extra information attached to them, for example, procedures for computing a value for the slot in the absence of one, procedures for updating the value of one slot when another slot is updated, restrictions upon the values that a slot can take, and so on.

6.3.3 Defaults and demons

Let's imagine that we are real estate agents, and our job is to estimate the price of plots of land as they come on the market, even if we do not have all the information that we need to set an exact price. We are so eager to make money and get deals rolling that we are prepared to make assumptions about plots we haven't even seen on the basis of incomplete descriptions. Most plots are convex quadrilaterals, so our price estimates are based on this assumption, unless we have information to the contrary.

Suppose that Figure 6.6 encodes knowledge about planar geometry for reasoning about such plots. Each node in the hierarchy consists of a record structure with the following format

```
NAME:
Number of Sides:
Length of Sides:
Size of Angles:
Area:
Price:
```

We could leave the slots of the `Polygon` record blank, because there is nothing we can say about the sides and angles of a typical polygon. However, we might hazard a default value of 4 for the slot `Number of sides`, since plots of land are typically four-sided. The force of this assignment would mean that all plots of land not known to have a number of sides other than 4 would be treated as if they had four sides, for the sake of argument.

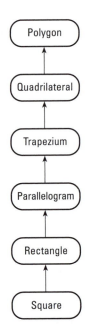

Figure 6.6 A hierarchical representation for geometric figures.

We cannot fill the Area slot, but we know how to compute the area of a polygon given other information, since any n-sided polygon can be divided into $n - 2$ triangles whose areas can be summed. We can encode this as a procedure which, given the requisite information, computes the value and places it in the slot. We attach this procedure to the slot itself. Procedures which are attached to data structures and are triggered by queries or updates are sometimes called *demons*. Those which compute values on demand are called *IF-NEEDED* demons.

It would also be useful to have a demon which computed the price of a plot once the area was known. This can be implemented as an *IF-ADDED* demon attached to the Area slot, so that if the value of this slot is added (or updated), then the price is automatically (re)computed and placed in the Price slot. We may want to recompute the price if extra information becomes available that allows us to make a better estimate of the area. Looking further down the hierarchy, we can obviously fill in the Number of Sides slot of Quadrilateral; the value of this slot really is 4. This value will be inherited by each successor frame in the hierarchy. We can compute the area and price of a four-sided plot in the same manner as any other polygon, so we allow Quadrilateral to inherit these procedures from Polygon.

Nothing else is known about quadrilaterals in the general case, but we might like to be able to estimate the area of a four-sided plot of land if we know the length of its sides, even if we don't know the angles. A reasonable heuristic would be to multiply the average of one pair of opposing sides with the average of the other pair. If the plot is not convex, then we may overcharge the client, but that has never broken a realtor's heart, as far as I know.

BOX 6.1

Implementing Frames and Inheritance in CLIPS

CLIPS does not explicitly support semantic nets or frames, but one can easily use CLIPS' `defclass` construct to define frame-like structures. (We will explore `defclass` further in the next chapter, since it is really a construct from object-oriented programming.) Thus the following definitions could represent the geometric hierarchy in Figure 6.6.

```
(defclass polygon (is-a USER))

(defclass quadrilateral (is-a polygon))

(defclass trapezium (is-a quadrilateral))

(defclass parallelogram (is-a trapezium))

(defclass rectangle (is-a trapezium))

(defclass square (is-a rectangle))
```

Note that polygon is defined as a subclass of the class USER, which is the class of all user-defined classes. The 'is-a' relationship, which figures in all frame languages, is obviously *transitive*, a square is a rectangle, but a square is also a trapezium, and so on. The relationship is also *anti-symmetric*, that is, if a square is a rectangle, then a rectangle is not a square.

If we now wish to encode the fact that most polygons are assumed to have four sides, some extra machinery is called for. We need to change the definitions of `polygon` and `quadrilateral` as follows:

```
(defclass polygon (is-a USER)
  (role abstract)
  (slot no-of-sides (default 4)))

(defclass quadrilateral (is-a polygon)
  (role concrete))
```

`polygon` is declared to be an *abstract* class, that is, one that will not generate any instances. `quadrilateral`, and its subclasses, are *concrete* classes, which can generate instances. The `no-of-sides` slot of `polygon` is assigned a default value, 4, in accordance with our intuition that most plots of land are four-sided. This value can now be inherited by all the subclasses of `polygon`. In the jargon of frame systems, `(default 4)` is a *facet* of the slot `no-of-sides`.

We can now define a demon, using the `defmessage-handler` construct provided by CLIPS. (We explore `defmessage-handler` in more detail in the next chapter.)

```
(defmessage-handler polygon sides ()
  ?self:no-of-sides)
```

This demon is associated with the `polygon` class and simply accesses the `no-of-sides` slot of the callee. For example, suppose we define a particular square plot of land, called `square-one`.

```
(definstances geometry
  (square-one of square))
```

and initialize the system with a `(reset)`. We can then activate the demon by sending the message

```
(send [square-one] sides)
```

continued

and receive the result

    4

back from the CLIPS interpreter. Note that the expression `?self:no-of-sides` was evaluated in the context of square-one, the callee or recipient of the message. `?self` is a variable that gets bound to the callee, while the `':'` infix operator accesses a particular slot.

This heuristic could be encoded in an IF-NEEDED procedure attached to the area slot of Quadrilateral which does one of three things:

- it calls the corresponding IF-NEEDED demon associated with Polygon if there is side and angle information available to enable the exact computation of the area;
- it uses the heuristic approach if only side information is available;
- if no information is available, it does nothing, but 'watches' for incoming information.

Each of Trapezium, Parallelogram, Rectangle and Square inherit the value of Quadrilateral's Number of Sides slot. However, in each case, we can do a rather better job on the area calculation; for example, the area of a trapezium is the height multiplied by the average of the parallel sides. Rectangle and Square can both inherit Parallelogram's procedure, which multiplies the base by the height.

The point of this simple example is that the use of defaults and demons renders frame systems more useful than ordinary record structures. Of course, we could have a ordinary Pascal-type record structure and then write Pascal procedures that answer queries based on the records and similar heuristics, but the frame system is in many ways a neater solution. Data, definitions and procedures are packaged up together in modules which can share data and procedures by inheritance mechanisms.

6.3.4 Multiple inheritance and ambiguity

Frame systems extend and regularize the notion of inheritance found in Quillian's work in a couple of respects. It is often convenient to allow a frame to inherit information from more than one ancestor in the frame system. Thus the organization of frames becomes more like a lattice than a tree, since a node can have more than one predecessor, although a single root node is typically retained.

Such an arrangement is shown in Figure 6.7. The new frame Regular Polygon cuts across the initial classification of polygons in terms of the number of sides to introduce another attribute, regularity. It is useful to allow Equilateral Triangle and Square to inherit certain information directly from this node, instead of having to encode it more than once elsewhere. For example, we know that the inner angles of regular polygons are equal, and Regular Polygon is the best place to store this information, in accordance with the criterion of cognitive economy.

This arrangement causes no problems as long as the information contained in alternative inheritance paths is not in conflict. But consider the example shown in

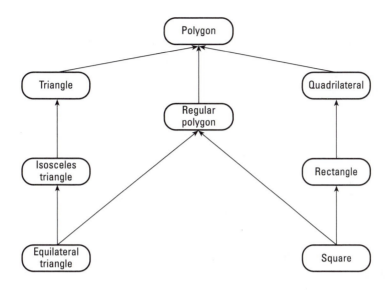

Figure 6.7 A heterarchical representation for geometric figures.

in Figure 6.8. (This is a great favorite in the literature; it is often called the 'Nixon diamond' for reasons that will become apparent.)

Suppose that we assume by default that Quakers are Pacifists (so the quaker frame has true in its pacifism slot) and that Republicans are not (so the republican frame has false in its pacifism slot). Remember that this does not rule out pistol-packing Quakers or Republicans who are Doves. It simply means that, in the absence of further information about an individual Quaker or Republican, we make the corresponding assumption.

But what can we say about a Republican Quaker, such as former US President Richard Nixon? (In the absence of any further information, that is.) Is he a pacifist or not? In other words, where should republican quaker inherit the value of its pacifism slot from, assuming that the value is not defined locally?

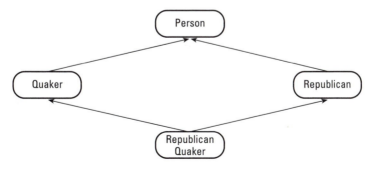

Figure 6.8 A recipe for conflicting defaults among frames.

In the above example, the defaults are in conflict, and so we cannot decide about Nixon's pacifism using just information in the heterarchy. Some inheritance systems would draw no conclusion here, because the evidence is in conflict; such reasoners are called *skeptical* (for example, Horty *et al.*, 1987). Other systems recognize the ambiguity and allow multiple alternative conclusions to be drawn; such reasoners are called *credulous* (for example, Touretzky, 1986).

Whatever theoretical position we adopt, we have to be careful to allow for this kind of eventuality when implementing a frame system. For example, we might argue that a peaceful Republican is less exceptional than a Quaker who supports military action, and either order the search of the ancestors accordingly or simply set the `pacifism` slot of `republican quaker` to `true`. Alternatively, we might attach an IF-NEEDED demon to the `pacifism` slot of `republican quaker` which uses special knowledge to resolve the ambiguity. Thus Republican Quakers might be deemed non-pacifist by default in election year in accordance with party guidelines; otherwise they revert to their natural inclinations and are pacifist by default.

It should be pointed out that inheritance networks are simpler than frame systems, since nodes in the network need not contain the paraphernalia of slots or attached procedures. All that is required to generate ambiguities of the kind noted above is a set of nodes {A, B, C, ...} structured into an acyclic graph by two kinds of link: positive links which denote that *A is a B*, and negative links which denote that *A is not a B*. Thus we could have represented the Nixon problem of Figure 6.8 as the network of Figure 6.9, where `pacifist` is a node in its own right, and the negative link between `republican` and `pacifist` is shown by a crossed through arrow.

A related aspect of multiple inheritance networks is that we can look at nodes from different perspectives. It is often useful to distinguish between the properties that a node inherits from different inheritance paths. Thus, the human brain can be considered as having certain properties, for example localization of function, by virtue of the fact that it is a complicated piece of electrical circuitry. Yet it has other properties, for example global states such as sleep, by virtue of the fact that brain circuitry is suspended in an electrochemical soup. Looking at complex objects in different ways is often helpful to understanding.

It is clear that in a heterarchical system, the potential for rich interconnections is that much greater than in a strict hierarchy. Higher-level nodes may share lower-level successors, indicating an indirect (and often analogical) relationship between them,

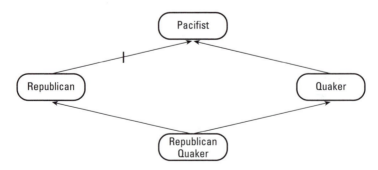

Figure 6.9 **The Nixon problem as an inheritance network.**

for example the relationship that holds between an equilateral triangle and a square. However, in frame systems the values of slots in a frame can also be pointers to other frames (see the CENTAUR system in Chapter 13), thereby yielding yet other dimensions along which frames can be structured.

6.3.5 Comparing nets and frames

In summary, the majority of associative networks failed to provide a satisfactory answer to the following questions:

- What do nodes and links really stand for?
- How can we process the stored information efficiently?

Frames are typical of more recent approaches to structured object representations which attempt to provide answers to both of these questions. They attempt to clarify the semantics of nodes and links by sharpening the type–token distinction and using only a small number of links. They attempt to solve the problem of efficient processing by attaching procedures to nodes which know how to compute values of variables in response to queries and how to update values of variables in response to assertions.

The use of frames as data structures for storing expectations about typical objects and events has become quite widespread in artificial intelligence applications (see Chapters 13 and 16); most software tools for building expert systems provide such facilities in one form or another (see Chapters 17 and 18). In many cases, we wish to score frames representing hypotheses according to how well they account for data, such as a collections of symptoms or other observations. A match between data and the slot values of a frame provides evidence for the hypothesis represented by the frame, as well as generating expectations concerning what other data to look for, for example additional symptoms whose presence or absence would confirm or disconfirm the hypothesis in question (see Chapter 13).

Of course, some form of external program or interface is required to get the frame system to do useful work. Although individual frames may contain procedures attached to their slots, this local code is insufficient to organize a whole computation. Some form of interpreter is needed which handles information requests and decides at what point the goal of the query has been achieved. For this reason, frames are mostly used in conjunction with other representations, such as production rules. In the next chapter, we review a style of programming which to some extent liberates structured objects from the need for external control, by allowing objects to pass messages to each other, thereby initiating more complex computations.

BIBLIOGRAPHICAL NOTES

Both Bobrow and Collins (1975) and Findler (1979) contain papers that are representative of the heyday of associative networks. Minsky's paper in Winston (1975) is essential for a proper understanding of the origin of various frame concepts, such as typicality and default values. The related notions of *script theory* are also worth pursuing in Schank and Abelson (1977).

Touretzky (1986) discusses some of the theoretical issues involved in inheritance networks, and provides a sound procedure for reasoning about exceptions. Later papers worth chasing up include Touretzky *et al.* (1987), Horty *et al.* (1987) and Selman and Levesque (1989). The latter paper shows that Touretzky's procedure is NP-hard, that is, it is computationally intractable for large, richly connected networks.

More recently, Thomason (1992) provides an overview of modern path-based inheritance, while two papers by Yen *et al.* (1991a, 1991b) describe the integration of inheritance concepts into rule-based expert systems.

STUDY SUGGESTIONS

1. Read the paper by Hayes in Brachman and Levesque (1985). Are frames no more than an implementation device for a subset of predicate logic, or do they capture genuinely extralogical aspects of human reasoning?

2. Ambiguities such as those found in the Nixon problem can be cascaded to produce even more puzzling examples. The one in Figure 6.10 is taken from Touretzky *et al.* (1987). Read the paper and then answer the questions.

   (i) What would a credulous reasoner conclude about a Republican Quaker's attitude towards the army?
   (ii) What would a skeptical reasoner conclude?

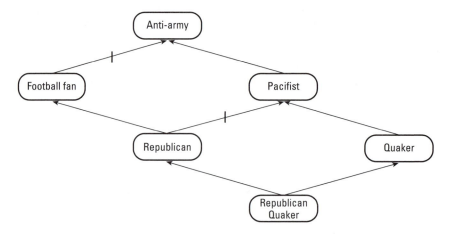

Figure 6.10 An inheritance network with cascaded ambiguity.

continued

3. The inheritance example in Figures 6.11 and 6.12 are also taken from Touretzky *et al.* (1987). They show two topologically identical inheritance networks, which differ only in the labels assigned to nodes. The first shows that royal elephants are exceptional, because they are elephants that are not gray, while the second shows that chaplains are exceptional, because they are men who do not drink beer.

   (i) Touretzky's reasoner would conclude in both cases that multiple interpretations are possible. Do you agree or disagree, and what are your reasons?

   (ii) Sandewall (1986) argues that the correct interpretation for Figure 6.11 is to allow the direct path from `royal elephant` to `gray thing` to dominate the indirect path via `elephant`. What are your intuitions here?

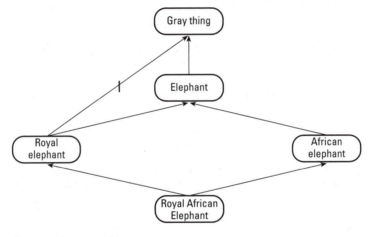

Figure 6.11 The royal elephant problem.

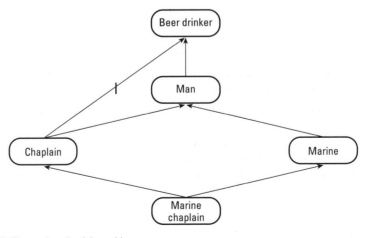

Figure 6.12 The marine chaplain problem.

continued

(iii) For Touretzky, the example of Figure 6.12 shows that changing the node labels can change one's intuitions about how inheritance should proceed. He argues that concluding that a marine chaplain is not a beer drinker (as Sandewall's approach would advocate) is less appealing than the elephant example. The reasons that Touretzky advances for his judgment are:

- that neither chaplains nor marines are typical men, and are very different from each other, so it is hard to decide what a marine chaplain would be like; and
- that although we know that chaplains abstain, we know nothing about the rate of beer drinking among marines, which might be high and include marine chaplains.

With whom do you agree, or are there arguments for both sides?

4. Refer to the CLIPS example in Box 6.1. Write a message handler for the class square that will compute the area of an instance such as square-one, and then assign it to a slot in the instance.

To do this, you must first add to the class definition for square.

```
(defclass square (is-a rectangle)
  (slot length-of-side (create-accessor write))
  (slot area (create-accessor write)))
```

square now has two slots, one for the length of its sides and the other for its area. The create-accessor facet says that we want slot access functions to be created automatically by CLIPS. As a result, the functions put-area and put-length-of-side will now be magically defined, so we can use them in message handlers.

Secondly, you must modify the specification of the instance square-one, so that it specifies the length of its sides:

```
(definstances geometry
  (square-one of square
    (length-of-side 10)))
```

Now write a message handler that uses put-area to assign the right value to the area slot of square-one.

5. The solution proposed in the previous exercise is fine for squares, but does not solve the problem of how to compute the areas of other regular quadrilaterals in the is-a hierarchy: rectangles, parallelograms and trapeziums. Now that you know how to create slots and message handlers, elaborate the original CLIPS frame system so that it solves this problem. You want to be able to send any instance of any class below quadrilateral the message area and have it fill in its area slot with a value that depends upon slot values representing such quantities as the length of its sides, height, and so on, and a formula embodied in the message handler.

continued

Confine your attention to regular quadrilaterals, so that you do not need to worry about angles. Try to make your solution as uniform and general as possible, for example, so that different classes of quadrilateral are represented and respond to the area message in a similar manner. Remember that subclasses can inherit both slots and message handlers from their superclasses.

7

Object-Oriented Programming

Many experimental knowledge representation languages have been produced in the past 20 years, and most of them are object-oriented. As with frames, the fundamental organizing principle in such schemes is the packaging of both data and procedures into structures related by some form of inheritance mechanism (see Chapter 6). They differ from the formalisms described in the last chapter in that procedures can be inherited (and combined) as well as data, and such objects communicate directly with each other via a special message-passing protocol.

First we take a brief look at a precursor of some of today's software tools, a system called KRL (standing for a Knowledge Representation Language), with a view to understanding why these tools developed as they did. Then we see how some of the difficulties associated with this style of programming were handled in the evolution of AI systems: such as Flavors, LOOPS and the more recent Common LISP Object System (CLOS). Finally, we describe the object-oriented functionality provided by CLIPS, and discuss the pros and cons of using a more general-purpose object-oriented language, such as C++.

This chapter revisits some of the topics addressed in the previous chapter, such as inheritance, in rather more depth. Regardless of the language under discussion, all examples are provided in either COOL (the CLIPS Object-Oriented Language) or C++. In a few sections, the level of technical detail with respect to particular tools or programming languages may be more than some readers want, so these are marked with a dagger. Other examples involving code are in boxes which can be skimmed or skipped without compromising one's understanding of the issues.

7.1 Prototypes, perspectives and procedural attachment

KRL (Bobrow and Winograd, 1977) was a self-conscious attempt to integrate much of what had been learned from earlier work on structured objects into a single system that was both theoretically defensible and of practical utility. The building blocks of the representation were called 'conceptual objects' and were similar to Minsky's frames in that they stood for prototypes and their associated properties. Their basic idea is well described by the following quotation from their 1977 paper (p. 5):

> ... to explore the consequences of an object-centered factorization of knowledge, rather than the more common factorization in which knowledge is structured as a set of facts, each referring to one or more objects.

This orientation led to a declarative, description-based language, in which conceptual objects are viewed, not in isolation, but from the perspective of other prototypical objects. The fundamental intuition is that the properties of an object that appear relevant, interesting and so on are a function of how you perceive the object and for what purpose. Thus, if you have to play a piano at a concert, you are interested in the quality of the sound and whether or not it is in tune, whereas if you have to carry a piano upstairs, you are interested only in its size and weight, and you couldn't care less about its musical properties!

Seen in this light, description can be viewed as a process of comparison, in which one specifies a new entity by saying in what way it is similar to, but different from, existing objects. Thus a van is very like a car except that it has no seats or windows in the rear. This is a rather holistic view of representation, rather than a reductionist one. In other words, a complete constellation of concepts can be defined in terms of each other, rather than in terms of some smaller set of primitive ideas. The trouble with the use of primitives in semantic representations is that no one can ever agree on which are the primitive concepts, or how they should be combined to form more complex ideas (although see, for example, Schank, 1975 and Schank and Abelson, 1977 for attempts in this direction).

The procedural apect of KRL also constituted a departure from more conventional programming methods, in that general procedures (as opposed to demons hovering over slots) were attached to classes of data object. Bobrow and Winograd integrated this kind of procedural attachment with the underlying frame structure, and made it possible for subclasses to inherit procedures as well as data from their associated superclasses. This turned out to be a rather liberating idea.

The intuition behind the inheritance of procedures is that it is useful to be able to program in terms of *generic operations* whose implementation details can be defined differently for different classes of objects. Just as abstract data types allow the programmer to forget about the details of how data are actually stored in the machine, so generic operations allow one to forget about how operations on such data objects are actually implemented. An example will help make this clear.

Suppose you are Commander-in-Chief of a combined forces operation. You have at your disposal tanks, ships, and aircraft, awaiting your order to attack. When you ask different units to attack, they will respond in totally different ways – aircraft may drop bombs, ships may fire missiles, and so on. However, underlying this variety of attack-

BOX 7.1

Procedures and Objects

Figure 7.1 attempts to portray the main difference between procedure- and object-oriented programming.

The gray ellipses in the left-hand diagram are procedures, some of which have direct access to data records in a file or database. The black ellipse represents the top-level function, for example, the 'main' function in C. This function calls other functions which ultimately call the slave functions that perform data I/O.

In the right-hand diagram, objects contain both data and procedures, and are arranged in one or more hierarchical structures, such as trees or lattices. The heavily-outlined object represents the most abstract class. Instances of these objects communicate and share data by passing messages to each other in a manner that is orthogonal to the inheritance hierarchy.

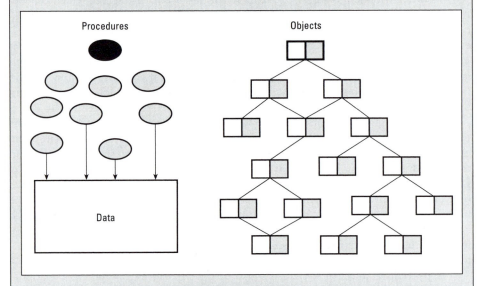

Figure 7.1 A graphical view of the difference between procedure- and object-oriented programming styles. Clear boxes represent data, while filled boxes represent procedures.

ing behavior implemented in terms of various lethal devices being unleashed, is a very general concept, namely that of offensive action. As Commander-in-Chief, you are only interested in a particular level of description; you want implementation decisions about which buttons to press, and so forth, to be made locally in the units themselves.

To return to KRL, the idea behind an object-centered organization of procedures was to try to learn from studies of human information processing how more natural-istic styles of reasoning might be programmed. In particular, it was assumed that the control of inference would be done locally, in contrast with the more global regimes associated with both production systems and automatic theorem proving. In other words, as well as knowing how to implement generic operations, classes of objects would also know *when to invoke* the various procedures to which they had access.

KRL had other features of interest, such as scheduling agendas and process frameworks, which are less central to the present discussion, although they were equally influential. Lehnert and Wilks' (1979) critique of KRL is also worth a look, as is Bobrow and Winograd's (1979) reply. KRL was really a vehicle for research into the theoretical foundations of knowledge representation; next we look at two systems with a more practical orientation.

7.2 LOOPS and Flavors

The object-oriented style of programming (OOP) is particularly suited to problems that require detailed representations of real-world objects and dynamic relationships between them. The classic application is simulation, achieved by mapping the components of a complex system onto data structures armed with procedures which govern their behavior. The first language recognizably in this tradition was probably Small-Talk (Goldberg and Robson, 1983), which saw some of its first applications in office systems which support the 'desktop metaphor,' where icons on the screen represent familiar pieces of office equipment.

The AI languages LOOPS and Flavors were both object-oriented extensions to LISP. Although they are no longer in widespread use, their features were widely copied in later knowledge representation languages, including the current Common Lisp Object System (CLOS) and CLIPS. We review the main attributes of these languages briefly here to expose some of the complexities associated with this style of programming.

7.2.1 Message passing

The central notion of OOP is that the whole program is built around a set of objects, each of which has a set of operations defined over it. Instead of representing such objects in terms of passive data structures, object-oriented systems permit representational units a more active role, in which they are capable of interacting with other units by *passing messages*. The resultant emphasis is therefore less upon the design of a global control structure that will invoke procedures in the ordinary way than upon the specification of the objects themselves, the roles that they perform, and the communication protocol between them. This protocol is essentially an *interface* between objects. For another object, or an arbitrary piece of code, to interact with an object, it must use this interface of function calls.

Objects have their own internal representations of data, like the slots of a frame, and their own mechanisms for updating and using the information so encoded. In addition to interface functions, they are armed with private procedures, which are usually local implementations of generic operations. In addition to data passed as arguments, these procedures can reference local variables whose values are the fillers of the structure's slots.

Suppose we define an object to stand for the class `ship` and associate with it the properties `x-velocity` and `y-velocity`, these being its velocities in a two-dimensional space. We can now create an instance of `ship`, called 'Titanic', at the same time instantiating the `x-velocity` and `y-velocity` slots of the new instance with initial values. This isn't very different from the way we created instances of frame objects in the previous chapter.

But suppose we want to define a procedure, called speed, to calculate the speed of a ship, using the values of these properties and the formula

$$\sqrt{(\text{x-velocity}^2 + \text{y-velocity}^2)}$$

We want such a procedure to belong to the abstract data type representing ships. (In the parlance of SmallTalk speed is therefore a *method* of the class ship; C++ would say that speed is a *member function* of ship.)

The idea is that as well as encoding declarative knowledge about ships, that is, attributes commonly associated with the prototypical ships, we are also able to encode procedural knowledge, that is, methods for using declarative knowledge to solve problems. To invoke this procedure to calculate the speed of a particular ship, such as the Titanic, we send a message to the object titanic which causes an appropriate implementation of the speed operation to be executed in the context of the data values associated with this object. titanic is an instance of the class ship, and so it inherits the speed procedure from ship.

BOX 7.2

The Titanic Example

Here is a CLIPS implementation of the 'Titanic' example used in the text.
First we define 'ship' as a class with slots x-velocity and y-velocity.

```
(defclass ship
    (is-a INITIAL-OBJECT)
    (slot x-velocity (create-accessor read-write))
    (slot y-velocity (create-accessor read-write))
)
```

Then we create an instance of ship, called the Titanic. This is most easily done by using the function definstances, which takes any number of instance definitions as its arguments. These instances will be initialized whenever you reset the CLIPS interpreter.

```
(definstances ships
    (titanic of ship
        (x-velocity 12)
        (y-velocity 10)
    )
)
```

Finally, we define a message handler for the class of ships, so that all instances know how to calculate their speed. Note that the ?self:x-velocity incantation evaluates to the instance's private value for this datum.

```
(defmessage-handler ship speed ()
    (sqrt
        (+
            (* ?self:x-velocity ?self:x-velocity)
            (* ?self:y-velocity ?self:y-velocity)))
)
```

If you type these constructs into a file, load it into CLIPS, and then type

```
(send [titanic] speed)
```

the value of the Titanic's speed will be returned.

This seems very straightforward, but as a way of life it only works if a couple of conventions are observed.

Firstly, programs designed in this way must institute and observe a *protocol* or 'contract' between objects, such that each object only communicates with others in a well understood way. In other words, the interface between such units must be properly designed and then strictly adhered to. The best way to see this is by example.

In order to find out the x-position of the Titanic, the program must send a well-formed request to the object `titanic`, saying 'tell me your x-position.' How the x-position is actually stored and retrieved is that object's business and nobody else's. Neither objects in other classes nor any non-object-oriented parts of the overall applications program need to know this. Indeed, the actual access mechanism should be hidden from them, in case they use these mechanisms directly instead of going through the object itself. The convention is usually called *encapsulation*.

Secondly, it is clearly redundant to define separate methods for calculating the speeds of different classes of object moving in the same coordinate system. The method defined above for ships will do just as well for any object traveling in a similar coordinate system, since calculating the speed of such objects constitutes a *generic operation*. Therefore it makes sense to associate this method with a superordinate class, like `mode of transport` or `weapon platform`, and have instances of subclasses like `ship` and `tank` inherit this method from higher up the class structure.

This is little more than cognitive economy, or inheritance of properties, extended to the procedural side of things. Performing a generic operation is thus assimilated into the message-passing paradigm, with both the name of the operation and the arguments to the operation being transmitted according to the protocols defined. Sending a message is not the same thing as procedure invocation, because it gets things done without the caller having to know which method will be employed, or where it will be inherited from. All the caller knows is the name of the generic operation and the arguments to that operation. The data object that is the recipient of the message determines which function is actually used.

7.2.2 The method combination problem

The simple picture that we painted above is complicated somewhat if we wish to avail ourselves of multiple inheritance. As we pointed out in Chapter 6, this can lead to problems of ambiguity, not to mention philosophical hair-splitting, in the inheritance of properties. The additional question that arises in the context of an object-oriented system is how to combine *behaviors* that are inherited from different parents, given that inheritance is now a part of the procedural side of things.

This problem was first addressed in detail by an OOP language called Flavors, which supported both multiple inheritance and method combination (Cannon, 1982). Flavors allowed objects to have more than one parent, and therefore to inherit procedures as well as data from more than one place. Thus the organizing principle is not a hierarchy of objects, but a heterarchy of the kind seen in the last chapter, and is therefore represented by a lattice rather than a tree. Why would you want to do this? Consider the following example (taken from Cannon's paper).

The window-oriented display of AI workstations is often implemented in the object-centered style. That is to say, windows on the screen are represented internally

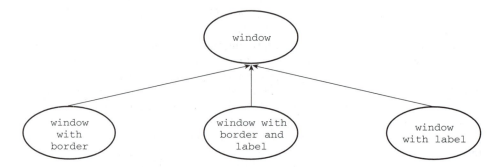

Figure 7.2 A hierarchical solution to the window problem.

as LISP objects, which record both properties of windows, such as length, breadth and position, and procedures for opening, closing and drawing windows. These windows come in a variety of designs – with and without borders, with and without labels, and so on.

Thus the class `window with border` is a subclass of the class `window`, and so is `window with label`. In a hierarchical system, these would each be disjoint subclasses of the same superordinate class. They would inherit certain methods, such as `refresh` from the `window` class, and have more specialized methods of their own, for drawing borders or labels, as appropriate.

What happens if you want a bordered window with a label? This new class, representing `window with border and label`, could be treated as a subclass of `window` in a hierarchical system, disjoint from either the `window with border` or `window with label` subclasses, which would be its siblings in the tree structure (see Figure 7.2). However, this would be wasteful, as well as counter-intuitive. What we really want is to mix two existing 'flavors' of window to get a new flavor. We would like this new kind of window to inherit from both its parents, `window with label` and `window with border`, and combine the properties and methods so derived in the right way (see Figure 7.3).

The question is: how do you achieve multiple inheritance of procedures, so that the resultant mix of behavior does what you want? The problem falls into two parts:

- finding suitable methods higher up the lattice; and
- combining them to get the desired effect.

One mechanism that works well is to have *before* and *after* code that is executed on either side of the main method. Thus, in the example of the windows given above, you could compose a method for drawing a window with border and label by having instances of the mixed class inherit the `refresh` method from `window` itself, via either parent, and then inherit more specialized after methods from each of its parents. The combined method would then consist of executing the more general method from `window` first, and then executing both the 'border' and 'label' specializations afterwards (in that order) to get a labeled, bordered window. Order is important because otherwise the border will mask the label.

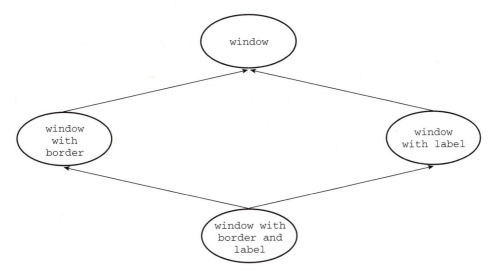

Figure 7.3 A heterarchical representation of the window problem.

7.2.3 Metaclasses[†]

LOOPS differed from Flavors in that it provided *metaclasses*, that is, classes that have other classes as members. Metaclasses originally surfaced in the SmallTalk system, early implementations of which had the single metaclass Class, whose members were all the classes in the system (including itself). In later implementations of SmallTalk, a metaclass is created automatically every time a new class is created, and the class automatically becomes an instance of that metaclass. Metaclasses in SmallTalk-80 are not themselves instances of metaclasses, but belong to the single metaclass, Metaclass. We shall refer to classes that are not metaclasses as 'object classes.'

The purpose of metaclasses is to support the creation and initialization of instances. Usually, we send messages to instances, not classes, and instances inherit their behaviors from their (object) classes. Occasionally, we want to send messages directly to classes, for example, the message that says 'make an instance of yourself with these properties.' Classes inherit their behaviors from their metaclasses, giving a pleasing uniformity to the system as a whole. (Ordinarily, we do not send messages to metaclasses but, if we did, they would inherit their behaviors from the metaclass Metaclass, to which they all belong, including Metaclass itself.)

LOOPS did not create a metaclass for every class, but had a simpler class structure of the kind shown in Figure 7.4. Ellipsoidal nodes stand for object- and metaclasses, while rectangular nodes stand for instances of object classes. The thinner arrows denote the relation 'A is a subclass of B,' while the thicker arrows denote the relation 'A is an instance of B.'

LOOPS provided three standard metaclasses: Object, Class and MetaClass. The thinner arrows of Figure 7.4 show that Object is a superclass of Class, and that Class is a superclass of MetaClass. In other words, some objects are classes and some classes are metaclasses. In addition, Object is a member of Class, Class is a member of MetaClass, and MetaClass is a member of itself. Thus Object is the root of

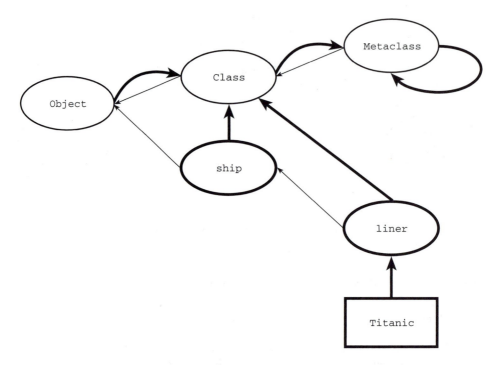

Figure 7.4 **The class structure of LOOPS.**

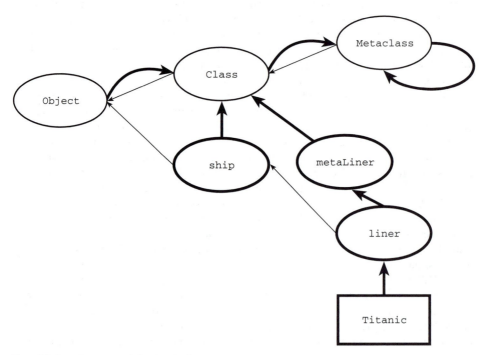

Figure 7.5 **Inserting a user-defined metaclass.**

the class hierarchy (having no superclasses), and MetaClass is the root of the instance hierarchy (having no class other than itself).

Nodes with thicker outlines, such as ship and liner, are meant to be typical user-defined classes. Note that all such classes are members of Class, from which they inherit their behavior. Thus to create the instance Titanic, we send a new message to liner, which inherits its new behavior from Class. Titanic inherits its behavior via liner, of course.

Making some objects metaclasses has the advantage that certain kinds of structure and behavior can be programmed into an object-oriented system as defaults at the highest level. Thus, instances of object classes such as liner will normally be created in a standard way but, if we wish to override this behavior, we have only to interpose a user-defined metaclass (say metaliner) between liner and class that introduces the required modification (as in Figure 7.5). Thus the LOOPS class structure combined power and flexibility in a principled way.

7.3 CLIPS and the Common LISP Object System (CLOS)

The future of LISP appears to lie with Common LISP: a 1980s attempt to standardize the LISP language and prevent the proliferation of dialects. Similarly, the future of object-oriented programming in LISP lies with the Common LISP Object System (CLOS), which has been adopted as part of the standardization process. This section attempts to do no more than show how CLOS and CLIPS combine and extend ideas found in Flavors and LOOPS, such as multiple inheritance, method combination, and metaclass structure.

The CLIPS object-oriented language, COOL, is closely modeled on CLOS, as we shall see in the examples below.

7.3.1 Multiple inheritance in CLOS and CLIPS

Multiple inheritance is handled more or less as it was in LOOPS. The order in which the direct superclasses of a class are listed in the definition of that class determine the order in which those superclasses will be consulted in the search for data or procedures. This convention, together with the rule that a class always takes precedence over any of its superclasses, ensures that it is always possible to compile an unambiguous *class precedence list* for a given class.

Let us consider the CLIPS statements in Figure 7.6, representing the 'Nixon Diamond' that we met in Chapter 6. These state that person is a user-defined class, that a Quaker is a person, a Republican is a person, and a Republican Quaker is both a Republican and a Quaker. USER is simply a system-defined class. It is also an *abstract* class, in that it exists for inheritance purposes and not to have instances. Hence, if we wish to create instances of any class derived from USER, we have to declare that class to be 'concrete', as we have done with republican-quaker.

The class precedence list of republican-quaker is

```
(republican-quaker republican quaker person)
```

We compute this by simply tracing the superclasses of republican-quaker up the lattice of definitions, observing the precedence among superclasses implicit in the is-a slots.

```
(defclass person
  (is-a USER)
)

(defclass quaker
  (is-a person)
)

(defclass republican
  (is-a person)
)

(defclass republican-quaker
  (is-a republican quaker)
  (role concrete)
)
```

Figure 7.6 **CLIPS classes for the 'Nixon diamond.'**

The significance of the class precedence list becomes apparent when we define message handlers for these classes. Let quaker and republican have their customary dove- and hawk-like behaviors, as follows:

```
(defmessage-handler quaker speak ()
  (printout t crlf "Peace")
)
(defmessage-handler republican speak ()
  (printout t crlf "War")
)
```

Let us also create an instance of republican-quaker.

```
(definstances people
  (richard of republican-quaker))
```

If we load these constructs into CLIPS and reset, we can then send a message to Richard, asking him to speak, as follows:

```
(send [richard] speak)
```

and obtain the answer

```
War
```

Richard's hawk-like behavior dominates, because republican takes precedence over quaker in the class precedence list of republican-quaker. Had republican-quaker been defined as

```
(defclass republican-quaker
  (is-a quaker republican)
  (role concrete)
)
```

then the dove-like behavior would have dominated. Adding

```
(defmessage-handler person speak ()
  (printout t crlf "Beer!")
)
```

to the program would not affect Richard's behavior, since this implementation of the speak method is masked by more specific implementations. Thus, in resolving potential ambiguities, all subclasses of person must be consulted before person or any of its superclasses are consulted. This is sometimes called the *up-to-the-131joins* convention, for obvious reasons.

The data slots in COOL classes are also provided with *facets*, that is, properties which govern their runtime accessibility and behavior. For example, there is a 'visibility' facet, which determines which other classes can gain access to a slot. A value of 'private' means that only message handlers of that class may access the data, whereas a value of 'public' means that message handlers of sub- and super-classes may too.

Other facets provide such facilities as:

- the automatic definition of accessor and assignment functions[1] in the style of Flavors;
- the storage of data as either local to an instance, or shared by all instances of the class, in the style of C++'s static data members.

7.3.2 Method combination in CLOS and CLIPS

Flavors and LOOPS adopted rather different solutions to the problem of how to combine behaviors. In Flavors, the basic mechanism was to use before and after methods, while in LOOPS super-sending was a trick for invoking additional or alternative code. (Flavors had a variety of additional mechanisms which are to some extent regularized in CLOS, as we shall see.)

CLOS supports both before and after methods and a form of super-sending. As usual, there is a primary method which does most of the work of a generic function, such as refresh in the window example. As in Flavors, *before methods* can be used to set up the computation performed by the primary method, while *after methods* can be used to clean up, or add finishing touches.

In addition, CLOS supplies a kind of method called an *around method*, which provides a way of wrapping a layer of code around the core framework of before, primary and after methods. This is for situations where the core framework doesn't do the right thing; for example, when you want the before method to set a local variable to be used in the computation performed by the primary method, or when you want to wrap the primary method up in a special control structure. In the core framework, before and after methods are executed for their side effects; the value of a method invocation is the value returned by the primary method, unconstrained by any external control structures.

The most specific around method associated with a message is called before calling the appropriate before, primary or after methods. The core framework is invoked by evaluating the system function call-next-method in the body of the around method. This is rather like super-sending in LOOPS; Flavors used special (not to say weird) methods called *wrappers* and *whoppers* to similar effect.

---

[1] This was true of CLIPS 5.0. It is no longer true of CLIPS 6.0. Such functions must now be explicitly defined, possibly for reasons of efficiency.

BOX 7.3

Making People More Polite

Given message handlers for the `quaker` and `republican` classes as before, we can make their pronouncements more polite by defining an *after method* for `person`, which executes after whichever primary method is chosen for the speak operation.

```
(defmessage-handler quaker speak ()
    (printout t crlf "Peace"))

(defmessage-handler republican speak ()
    (printout t crlf "War"))

(defmessage-handler person speak after ()
    (printout t ", please" t crlf))
```

An expression such as

```
(send [richard] speak)
```

will now yield

```
War, please
```

Message handlers are primary by default, so we don't need to write

```
(defmessage-handler republican speak primary ()
    (printout t crlf "War"))
```

although this does no harm and is probably good form.

Standard method combination in CLOS (and CLIPS) is summarized in Figure 7.7.

CLOS supplies a variety of additional method combination types, as well as the ability for users to create their own types. For example, *or combination* returns the value of the first method component to return non-nil. Users can create their own combining functions using logical, arithmetical and list operators.

It should be pointed out that standard method combination is probably adequate for 90 percent of a programmer's needs. Nevertheless, it is nice to have strong-arm techniques available for tricky computations. It seems that CLOS has struck a good balance between the unbridled power of the original Flavors and the rather limited facilities provided by LOOPS.

Finally, it is worth mentioning that method definition in CLOS is in some ways more powerful than Flavors or LOOPS. As before, methods are effectively generic functions, whose applicability depends upon a specialized parameter which states the class of the first message argument. They are called just like LISP functions (that is, there is no 'sending' function, as in LOOPS), with the recipient of the message as the first argument, and the rest of the arguments as normal parameters to the function.

However, there are also *multi-methods*, which allow the behavior to depend upon the class of more than one argument. For example, people from different cultures not only eat different foods but eat them in different ways. Thus Japanese eat more fish than Americans, but they also eat more raw fish. Thus the `prepare-meal` method should be sensitive to both the nationality of the message recipient and the type of dish proposed; that is, in

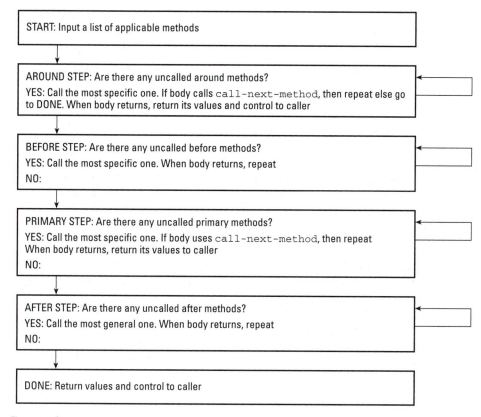

Figure 7.7 Standard method combination in CLOS and CLIPS (after Keene, 1989).

```
(prepare-meal X Y)
```

the implementation of `prepare-meal` might depend on both the class of X (the cook) and the class of Y (the dish). CLIPS provides a similar mechanism via *generic functions* (see Chapter 17).

7.3.3 Metaclasses in CLOS and CLIPS[†]

In CLOS, classes and metaclasses are better integrated with the LISP environment than was the case in LOOPS. In fact, every LISP object is an instance of a class. For example, there is a class `array` corresponding to the COMMON LISP data type array.

CLOS provides three basic metaclasses:

- `standard-class`. This is the default class of any class object defined by the user using the primitive function `defclass`. Thus

```
(defclass father (man parent)
  (:name)
```

```
(:occupation)
(:documentation "The class of male parents"))
```

defines the ordinary class father, with superclasses man and parent, slot specifiers for the name and occupation of instances of the class, and a little documentation. Most user-defined classes will be of this kind.

- built-in-class. This is the class of class objects that are implemented in some special way; for example, some of the classes might correspond to COMMON LISP data types. Many system-defined classes are of this kind.
- structure-class. This is the class of class objects defined using defstruct rather than defclass. defstruct is a COMMON LISP function which creates frame-like objects consisting of slots and fillers with automatically defined access functions, but it does not support multiple inheritance. Occasionally, LISP programmers with existing LISP programs may wish to use defstruct to implement extant data objects.

There are also classes which contain objects representing methods, but we shall not delve any deeper into the details of this side of CLOS. The functionality associated with basic metaclasses like standard-class is meant to be adequate for most applications. However, as in LOOPS, one has the option of specializing standard-class to obtain more exotic behaviors. In particular, one can use *meta-object protocols* to redefine the generic dispatch algorithm, thereby customizing inheritance mechanisms for particular applications. This kind of facility goes way beyond what is provided by a language such as C++, but it also goes beyond the needs and capabilities of most users.

The COOL language embedded in CLIPS has 17 system classes, and some of these function as metaclasses. The upper level of the class structure is represented in Figure 7.8.

All user-defined classes are meant to be derived from User, which serves many of the functions of a metaclass, in that it incorporates all the basic message handlers for initializing and deleting objects. However, it is not a metaclass, because user-defined classes are specializations of it, not instances. Initial-Object is a default instance that gets created when definstances is executed; it is rather like initial-fact in this regard (see Chapter 5).

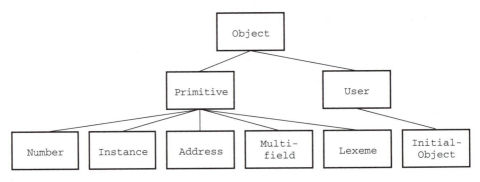

Figure 7.8 Top two levels of COOL class hierarchy.

`Primitive` and its subclasses implement basic data objects, such as numbers, symbols and strings, as well as addresses and instances of objects, and their fields. All the classes in Figure 7.8, except `Initial-Object`, are abstract classes. One cannot create instances of them; they exist solely to define the class structure of generic operations and data types.

7.4 Multiple inheritance in C++

C++ is like CLOS, in that it takes an existing programming language, in this case C rather than LISP, and embeds an object-oriented facility within it, while preserving the full functionality of the host language. However, leaving the host language to one side, the main differences between C++ and CLOS concern the implementation of inheritance, particularly multiple inheritance. The treatment of multiple inheritance in C++ runs somewhat counter to the intuitions we have developed in this chapter and the last, and therefore merits some discussion.

In C++, generic operations are implemented as *virtual functions*. The virtual functions of a class, *X*, are those functions which can be overridden in a class derived from *X*. The function may be defined for the class *X*, having a null or non-null body of code, or it may be *pure virtual*, that is, have no function body associated with it at all. (Classes having one or more pure virtual functions are called *abstract base classes*, and are not allowed to have any instances.) Either way, the 'virtual' keyword tells the compiler that this operation can be bound late, that is, that a little work may be required to figure out what implementation should be used at runtime.

What we have been calling methods are implemented as non-virtual member functions – functions which execute actual code and which are not meant to be overridden in subclasses. This is in contrast with languages such as CLOS, where more or less all the functions of a superclass are overridable, or modifiable via method combination. Consequently, there are a number of syntactic niceties in C++ which are inessential in the more freewheeling world of CLOS; for example, continuing to declare virtual functions as virtual as you move down the class hierarchy until such time as you provide an implementation.

Where single inheritance alone is concerned, method invocation is now a relatively straightforward affair, in which the instances of a class obtain the equivalent of

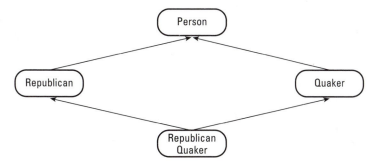

Figure 7.9 **The 'Nixon diamond' revisited.**

message handlers from the class hierarchy in the usual way. One refinement is that C++ distinguishes between public and private inheritance. Roughly speaking, *public inheritance* is the 'is a' relationship that we are used to from our discussion of frames, where the class–subclass relationship means 'a kind of.' *Private inheritance* is more an 'implemented in terms of' relationships that is meant to be hidden from the public interface to an object. This useful distinction is somewhat lost in CLOS, where every class–subclass relationship appears to carry semantic significance.

When we move to multiple inheritance, things look very different. Because C++ has no notion of class precedence, even the simplest 'diamond' heterarchy, as described in Chapter 6, can lead to ambiguity, depending upon how member functions are distributed and how base classes are declared. Given classes Person, Quaker, Republican, and Republican_Quaker, arranged as before in Figure 7.9, we have a situation that requires a little thought.

```
// Class heterarchy to demonstrate the Nixon diamond problem

#include <iostream.h>

class Person
{
public:
  Person() {};
  virtual ~Person() {};
  virtual void speak() = 0;
};

class Republican : public Person
{
public:
  Republican() {};
  virtual ~Republican() {};
  virtual void speak() { cout << "War"; }
};

class Quaker : public Person
{
public:
  Quaker() {};
  virtual ~Quaker() {};
  virtual void speak() { cout << "Peace"; }
};

class Republican_Quaker : public Republican, public Quaker
{
public:
  Republican_Quaker() {};
  virtual ~Republican_Quaker() {};
};
```

Figure 7.10 nixon.h: The Nixon diamond in C++ (Version 1).

Consider the C++ class declarations in the `nixon.h` file of Figure 7.10. Now let Richard be a Republican Quaker, as in the following 'main' program:

```
#include "nixon.h"

void main()
{
  Republican_Quaker richard;
  richard.speak();
}
```

As things stand, the C++ compiler will detect that the member function call `rich-`
`ard.speak()` contains an ambiguous reference. This is intuitive enough, since we cannot tell whether Richard should say 'War' or 'Peace.'

If we supply a 'speak' member function for `Republican_Quaker`, for example, by making the Quaker impulses prevail, then we can make the problem go away in two ways, either

```
void S::speak() { cout << "Peace"; }
```

or

```
void S::speak() { Quaker::speak(); }
```

```
class Person
{
public:
  Person() {};
  virtual ~Person() {};
  virtual void speak() { cout << "Beer"; }
};

class Republican : public Person
{
public:
  Republican() {};
  virtual ~Republican() {};
};

class Quaker : public Person
{
public:
  Quaker() {};
  virtual ~Quaker() {};
};

class Republican_Quaker : public Republican, public Quaker
{
public:
  Republican_Quaker() {};
  virtual ~Republican_Quaker() {};
};
```

Figure 7.11 **The Nixon diamond in C++ (Version 2).**

The first simply overrides both of the inherited implementations, while the second explicitly invokes just one of them.

However, seemingly innocent changes to this file will cause things to go awry. Suppose we decide to simplify everything by removing the 'speak' member functions from all classes except `Person`, as shown in Figure 7.11.

The compiler will complain of an ambiguous reference to 'speak,' even though it appears to be defined in only one place. This is because, as things stand, the compiler creates two copies of `Person`, one for each path through the inheritance lattice, which results in a name collision. To disambiguate, we have to declare `Person` to be a *virtual base class* of both `Republican` and `Quaker`, so that these derived classes will point to a single superclass object (see Figure 7.12).

Making `Person` a virtual base class of both `Republican` and `Quaker` has other advantages. Suppose that we wish Republican Quakers to follow the Quaker impulse towards peace, but we wish all other persons to be indifferent, by inheriting the default behavior associated with the `Person` class. Then, as long as `Person` is a virtual base class, we can make `Quaker::speak()` dominate `Person::speak()` for Republican Quakers (see Figure 7.13).

```
class Person
{
public:
  Person() {};
  virtual ~Person() {};
  virtual void speak() { cout << "Beer"; }
};

class Republican : virtual public Person
{
public:
  Republican() {};
  virtual ~Republican() {};
};

class Quaker : virtual public Person
{
public:
  Quaker() {};
  virtual ~Quaker() {};
};

class Republican_Quaker : public Republican, public Quaker
{
public:
  Republican_Quaker() {};
  virtual ~Republican_Quaker() {};
};
```

Figure 7.12 The Nixon diamond in C++ (Version 3).

```
class Person
{
public:
  Person() {};
  virtual ~Person() {};
  virtual void speak() { cout << "Beer"; }
};

class Republican : virtual public Person
{
public:
  Republican() {};
  virtual ~Republican() {};
};

class Quaker : virtual public Person
{
public:
  Quaker() {};
  virtual ~Quaker() {};
  virtual void speak() { cout << "Peace"; }
};

class Republican_Quaker : public Republican, public Quaker
{
public:
  Republican_Quaker() {};
  virtual ~Republican_Quaker() {};
};
```

Figure 7.13 **The Nixon diamond in C++ (Version 4).**

It is a stated goal of C++ (Stroustrup, 1997) that multiple inheritance be implemented in such a way that it costs little more than single inheritance and resolves ambiguities at compile time. This is in marked contrast with SmallTalk implementations, where ambiguities are typically resolved at runtime. It is also somewhat different to the CLOS approach, where class precedence lists are used to resolve ambiguities, and where name collisions are automatically resolved by assuming that base classes with the same name are identical.

The price you pay for more efficient programs is that you have to understand rather more about the way in which inheritance is actually implemented in C++. In this respect, C++ is like C, where you are somewhat closer to the machine than you are in LISP, in that you directly manipulate memory addresses, perform your own space allocation, return memory to the heap, and so on. Which culture you prefer is largely a matter of taste and upbringing, although some technical and economic considerations should also be taken into account. If efficiency is at a premium, the more control you have over the allocation of resources the better, and there are a number of good diagnostic tools on the market that will help you detect memory 'leaks' and bad pointer references. If development time is at a premium, then the less time spent fooling around with resource allocation the better, regardless of what tools are available.

In summary, C++ can provide an object-oriented vehicle for expert systems development. If a production-rule interpreter is required, one can either write one's own (a non-trivial undertaking), or use a commercially available library which embeds a production rule interpreter inside a C++ environment. As long as sufficient care is taken with the treatment of multiple inheritance, the user can enjoy the many benefits of C++, such as static type checking, the distinction between public and private inheritance, and the many uses of 'const' to protect data objects from unwanted modification.

7.5 Object-oriented analysis and design for expert systems

The philosophy and techniques of object-oriented programming have a great deal to offer the designers of expert systems.

- The philosophy of representing our knowledge of the world in terms of interacting objects and agents provides an appropriate framework for many classes of problem, particularly those (like planning and scheduling) which have a strong simulation component.
- The techniques of procedure and data abstraction encourage AI programmers to think about the kinds of object and behavior that are relevant to the problem, instead of becoming engrossed in the implementation of functions and data objects at too early a stage in the design.
- There is a growing literature on object-oriented analysis and design which is relevant to the design of expert systems modules.

However, it is interesting to note that the limitations of object-oriented technology have become apparent in recent years.

- An overly literal interpretation of objects as faithful representations of real-world objects can be both confusing and limiting; objects are still primarily computational devices.
- Inheritance of behaviors can lead to implementation problems, as we saw in the 'Window' example; some new object-oriented schemes only allow inheritance of interfaces.
- In large systems, it can be limiting if a class only has one interface; new component technologies, such as COM, allow more than one interface (Chappell, 1996).

In a perfect world, one would like to be able to develop systems, especially expert systems, incrementally by only ever adding code. The examples given in this chapter should convince the reader that this is not always possible, even within the object-oriented framework, just as it was not possible in the net- or rule-based frameworks of Chapters 5 and 6. Adding new modules of knowledge of whatever kind often has unanticipated side effects, whether it involves rules in competition or ambiguous patterns of inheritance, and we shall see that these problems recur in the logic programming paradigm of Chapter 8.

Thus it is obvious that object-oriented methods do not solve all our problems; they still leave the expert system designer with plenty of difficult decisions to make. However, the object-centered paradigm makes it easier to think about certain kinds of design decision, and facilitates implementation once those decisions have been made. This seems to be all that one can legitimately ask of current software technology.

BIBLIOGRAPHICAL NOTES

For a general review of object-oriented computing, covering both concepts and implementations, the papers in Peterson (1987) are recommended. A more specialized review of object-oriented systems in artificial intelligence can be found in Stefik and Bobrow (1986). Keene (1989) provides a very clear account of CLOS.

Meyers' (1995, 1997) books cannot be too highly recommended for their lucid treatment of practical C++ programming, while Booch (1994) provides a valuable perspective on object-oriented thinking.

STUDY SUGGESTIONS

1. What features differentiate an object-oriented programming language from a more conventional procedural language?

2. What is the difference between a concrete and an abstract class?

3. Why does a multiple inheritance hierarchy take the form of a lattice?

4. What is method combination, and why is it problematical?

5. What is a metaclass, and why is it a useful construct?

6. What do you understand by the phrase 'class precedence list'?

7. Consult the class lattice in Figure 7.14.
   Use the `defclass` construct of CLIPS to define this class lattice. observing the following orders among the 'is-a' lists of classes with multiple superclasses.

   ```
   wkg-man: (man worker)
   father: (parent man)
   wkg-woman: (worker woman)
   mother: (parent woman)
   wkg-father: (wkg-man father)
   wkg-mother: (mother wkg-woman)
   ```

   Start with the class `person`, as follows:

   ```
   (defclass person
     (is-a USER)
     (role concrete))
   ```

   What are the class precedence lists of `wkg-father` and `wkg-mother`?

continued

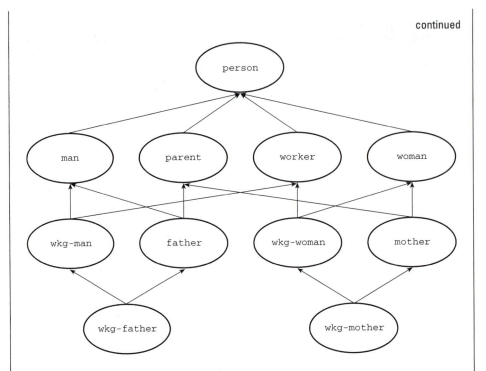

Figure 7.14 **The class lattice for Exercise 7.**

8. Suppose that man, parent, worker and woman in Figure 7.14 have the
    following breakfast preferences:

    ```
    man: donut
    woman: croissant
    parent: fruit
    worker: bacon
    ```

    Encode these preferences in message handlers, so that recipients of the
    breakfast message in a given class simply return the appropriate symbol
    indicating their preference.

    Now create the following instances:

    • Joan is a working mother;
    • Jim is a working man;

    and send each of them a message, for example:

    ```
    (send [joan] breakfast).
    ```

    How do Joan and Jim respond to the breakfast message? Why do they
    respond as they do?

8

Logic Programming

Since the late 1970s, there has been a significant trend towards the use of 'formal methods' in artificial intelligence research, that is, methods that derive from mathematical logic, rather than more intuitive or heuristic methods, such as those employed by MYCIN, say. To understand what this means, it is necessary to explain a little (but not too much) about logical languages, and then relate their properties to the kinds of reasoning that expert systems typically have to support.

8.1 Formal languages

Mathematical logic is a *formal language*, in that one can say, for any sequence of symbols, whether or not it conforms to the rules for constructing expressions of the language (*formulas*). Formal languages are usually contrasted with natural languages, such as French and English, where grammatical rules are imprecise. In saying that a logic is a *calculus* with syntactic rules of deduction, one is saying (roughly speaking) that the inferences sanctioned depend solely upon the external form of expressions in the language, and not upon any extraneous ideas or intuitions.

Automated reasoning refers to the behavior of any computer program which draws inferences in a law-like way. (Thus a program which effectively tossed a coin to decide on whether one formula followed from a set of other formulas would not be deemed an automated reasoner.) However, much of the literature is actually given over to automated *deduction*, since that is what we understand best.

In automated reasoning, one often aims for maximum uniformity and standardization in the representation of formulas, unlike the various notations found in logic texts. The main syntactic schemes employed are *conjunctive normal form* (CNF), full *clausal form*, and the *Horn clause* subset of the clausal form. We shall see that these representations simplify the inference procedure considerably – but first let us look at the elements of the propositional and predicate calculi.

8.1.1 Propositional calculus

Propositional calculus is the logic of unanalyzed propositions in which *propositional constants* can be thought of as standing for particular simple expressions, like 'Socrates is a man' and 'Socrates is mortal.' I shall use lower case letters in the range p, q, r, ... (possibly with subscripts) as propositional constants. These constants are sometimes called atomic formulas, or *atoms*.

The following are all the syntactic rules you need for constructing well-formed formulas (*wffs*) of the propositional calculus. In these rules, Greek lower case letters such as ψ and ϕ are *propositional variables*, and stand not for particular atomic expressions, but for any simple or compound proposition. Propositional constants like p, q, and so on are part of the propositional *language* that we use when we apply the *calculus* of propositional variables to actual problems.

> **(S.ψ)** If ψ is atomic, then ψ is a wff.
> **(S.¬)** if ψ is a wff, then so is ¬ψ.
> **(S.$\vee$)** if ψ and ϕ are wffs, then so is ($\psi \vee \phi$).

¬ψ is read as 'not ψ,' and ($\psi \vee \phi$) is read as the disjunction 'ψ or ϕ (or both).' We can introduce the other logical constants – '$\wedge$' (conjunction), '$\supset$' (implication, or the conditional), '$\equiv$' (equivalence, or the biconditional) – as abbreviations:

> ($\psi \wedge \phi$), read as 'ψ and ϕ', is defined as ¬(¬$\psi \vee$ ¬ϕ).
> ($\psi \supset \phi$), read as 'ψ implies ϕ', is defined as (¬$\psi \vee \phi$).
> ($\psi \equiv \phi$), read as 'ψ is equivalent to ϕ', is defined as ($\psi \supset \phi$) $\wedge$ ($\phi \supset \psi$).

In the CNF of the propositional calculus, conditionals and biconditionals are eliminated in favor of disjunction and negation, by expanding their abbreviations. Then negation is driven in, so that it governs only atomic formulas (propositions containing no logical operators), using the following equivalences (known as 'De Morgan's laws'):

> ¬($\psi \wedge \phi$) becomes (¬$\psi \vee$ ¬ϕ)
> ¬($\psi \vee \phi$) becomes (¬$\psi \wedge$ ¬ϕ)
> ¬¬ψ becomes ψ

Finally disjunction is distributed over conjunction, using the following equivalence:

> ($\zeta \vee (\psi \wedge \phi)$) becomes (($\zeta \vee \psi$) $\wedge$ ($\zeta \vee \phi$))

It is customary to reduce the nesting of parentheses by making $\wedge$ and $\vee$ operators of variable *arity* (that is, allowing occurrences of them to govern any number of operands) using the following equivalences. Both the disjunction sign and the conjunction sign can now be dropped without ambiguity, and the resulting expression treated as an implicit conjunction of disjunctions. An example will make this clear.

$$\neg(p \lor q) \supset (\neg p \land \neg q)$$
$$\neg\neg(p \lor q) \lor (\neg p \land \neg q) \qquad \text{eliminating } \supset$$
$$(p \lor q) \lor (\neg p \land \neg q) \qquad \text{driving } \neg \text{ in}$$
$$(\neg p \lor (p \lor q)) \land (\neg q \lor (p \lor q)) \qquad \text{distributing } \land \text{ over } \lor$$
$$\{\{\neg p, p, q\}, \{\neg q, p, q\}\} \qquad \text{dropping } \land \text{ and } \lor$$

Expressions within inner brackets are either atomic formulas (*atoms*) or negated atomic formulas. Such expressions are called *literals*, and from a logical point of view their order is immaterial, hence the use of the curly brackets from set theory. Literals in the same clause are implicitly disjoined, while clauses within outer brackets are implicitly conjoined.

Clausal form is very similar to CNF, except that the positive and negative literals in each disjunction tend to be grouped together on different sides of an arrow and the negation symbols are dropped. Thus

$$\{\{\neg p, p, q\}, \{\neg q, p, q\}\}$$

from the above example would become the two clauses

$$p, q \leftarrow p$$
$$p, q \leftarrow q$$

where positive literals go to the left of the arrow, and negative literals go to the right. Most people agree that this is more readable (for humans) than CNF. A little thought will convince you that

$$\leftarrow p$$

is equivalent to $\neg p$, and that

$$p \leftarrow$$

is equivalent to plain p.

More precisely, a clause is an expression of the form

$$p_1, ..., p_m \leftarrow q_1, ..., q_n$$

where $p_1, ..., p_m \leftarrow q_1, ..., q_n$ are atomic formulas, with $m \geq 0$ and $n \geq 0$. The $p_1, ..., p_m$ are the disjoined *conclusions* of the clause, while the $q_1, ..., q_n$ are the conjoined *conditions*.

8.1.2 The predicate calculus[†]

The propositional calculus has its limitations, however. You can't deal properly with general statements of the form 'All men are mortal.' Of course, you can let a propositional constant, like p, stand for such a statement, and you can let q stand for 'Socrates is a man,' but you can't derive 'Socrates is mortal' from $(p \land q)$.

To do this, you need to analyze propositions into *predicates* and *arguments*, *quantifiers* and *variables of quantification* (rather as we did in the STRIPS example of Chapter 3). Predicate logic provides syntactic rules for performing this analysis, semantic rules which interpret expressions so formed, and a proof theory which allows us to derive valid formulas using syntactic rules of deduction. Predicates stand for properties, like 'being a man,' and relationships, like 'being taller than.'

Arguments can be (i) individual constants, like *plato*, or (ii) function-argument compositions, like *AUTHOR-OF(republic)*, which stand for entities in some universe of objects that we are interested in, or (iii) individual variables of quantification which range over such a universe. Special operators called *quantifiers* are used to bind such variables and delimit their scope. The standard quantifiers are the universal, $\forall$, and the existential, $\exists$, which can be read as 'all' and 'some' respectively.

Here are the syntactic rules of the first-order predicate calculus:

(S.α) Any constant symbol or variable is a term,
and if Γ_k is a k-place function symbol,
and $\alpha_1, ..., \alpha_k$ are terms,
then $\Gamma_k(\alpha_1, ..., \alpha_k)$ is a term.

(S.Ψ) If Ψ_k is a k-place predicate symbol,
and $\alpha_1, ..., \alpha_k$ are terms,
then $\Psi_k(\alpha_1, ..., \alpha_k)$ is a wff.

(S.$\neg$) and (S.$\vee$) from the propositional calculus.

(S.$\forall$) If ψ is a wff and χ is a variable, then $(\forall\chi)\psi$ is a wff.

As before, we use variables like Ψ (to stand for arbitrary predicates), Γ (to stand for arbitrary functions), α (to stand for arbitrary terms) and χ (to stand for arbitrary variables). Actual names, function symbols and predicates, like *plato*, *AUTHOR-OF*, and *PHILOSOPHER*, are elements of a *first-order language*, that is, an application or instantiation of the calculus.

We can introduce the existential quantifier, $\exists$, as an abbreviation in terms of the universal quantifier, $\forall$:

$(\exists\chi)\psi$ is defined as $\neg(\forall\chi)\neg\psi$.

The expression $(\exists X)(PHILOSOPHER(X))$ is read as the sentence 'Something is a philosopher,' while the expression $(\forall X)(PHILOSOPHER(X))$ is read as 'Everything is a philosopher.' The expression $PHILOSOPHER(X)$ is well formed, but it is not a sentence, since the occurrence of the variable X is unbound by any quantifier. Formulas in which all occurrences of all variables are bound are called *closed formulas*.

As in the propositional calculus, predicate calculus expressions can be put into normal form, although we need to extend the rules of syntactic transformation. The sequence of rule applications is now as follows. For any expression:

(1) Eliminate biconditionals and then conditionals.
(2) Drive negation in, using De Morgan's Laws and the equivalence between $(\exists\chi)\psi$ and $\neg(\forall\chi)\neg\psi$ (and hence between $(\forall\chi)\psi$ and $\neg(\exists\chi)\neg\psi$).
(3) Standardize variables apart. For example, in

$(\exists X)(PHILOSOPHER(X)) \;\&\; (\exists X)(ATHLETE(X))$

it is sensible to give variables bound in the scope of different occurrences of quantifiers different names. Otherwise, when the quantifiers are eliminated, logically distinct variables might end up with the same name. Then, in the above example, one might end up deriving

$(\exists X)(PHILOSOPHER(X) \;\&\; ATHLETE(X))$

which does not follow from the original formula.

(4) Eliminate existential quantifiers. Existential variables which occur outside of the scope of any universal quantifier can be replaced by arbitrary names (called Skolem constants), while existential variables which occur inside the scope of one or more universal quantifiers must be replaced by Skolem functions, whose arguments are the universally bound variables within whose scope the existential occurs. A Skolem function is just an arbitrary function name that says 'the value of this variable is some function of the values assigned to the universal variables in whose scope it lies.'

(5) Convert to prenex form. In this step, the remaining quantifiers (all of them universal) are moved to the 'front' of the expression, so that we are left with a list of universally quantified variables followed by a 'matrix' in which no quantifiers occur.

BOX 8.1

Robots and Rooms Revisited

We have already encountered a simplified form of predicate calculus in Chapter 3, where an expression such as

```
at(robot, roomA)
```

denoted that our robot was in Room A. `robot` and `roomA` are constants that denote particular entities. But what does

```
at(X, roomA)
```

mean, where `X` is a variable? That something is in Room A? If so, the variable has existential import. That everything is in Room A? If so, the variable has universal import. It easy to confuse these usages in the absence of a set of rules.

The rules of the predicate calculus cited in this section provide a consistent interpretation to expressions that contain variables.

Thus, the clause

```
at(X, roomA) ← at(X, box1)
```

is interpreted as

for all X, X is at Room A if X is at box1

and so the variable has universal import.

Similarly the clause

```
at(X, roomA) ←
```

is interpreted as

for all X, X is at Room A.

But the clause

```
← at(X, roomA)
```

is interpreted as

for all X, X is not at Room A.

In other words, it is not the case that some X is at Room A, so the variable has existential import.

(6) Distribute disjunction over conjunction.
(7) Drop the universal quantifiers. All free variables are now implicitly universally quantified variables. The existentials are either constants or functions of universal variables.
(8) Drop the conjunction signs, as before, leaving a set of clauses.
(9) Rename variables again, so that the same variable does not appear in different clauses.

We can now convert to clausal form, with positive literals on the left of the arrow, and negative literals on the right. If a clause of the form

$$p_1, ..., p_m \leftarrow q_1, ..., q_n$$

contains variables $x_1, ..., x_k$, then the correct interpretation is

for all $x_1, ..., x_k$
   p_1 or ... or p_m is true
   if q_1 and ... and q_n are true

If $n = 0$, that is, if there are no conditions specified, then the correct interpretation is an unconditional statement to the effect that

for all $x_1, ..., x_k$
   p_1 or ... or p_m is true.

If $m = 0$, that is, if there are no conclusions specified, then the correct interpretation is the following denial

for all $x_1, ..., x_k$
   it is not the case that q_1 and ... and q_n are true.

If $m = n = 0$, then we have the empty clause, whose correct interpretation is always falsity.

8.2 The PROLOG language

The *Horn clause subset* of first-order logic is just like the full clausal form of logic, except that you are allowed one atom at most in the conclusion. Thus a Horn clause rule will have the general form

$$p \leftarrow q_1, ..., q_n.$$

Write this as

```
p :- q₁, ..., qₙ.
```

(not forgetting the period at the end) and you have a clause in the syntax of the PRO-LOG language for logic programming, with the intended interpretation:

for all values of variables occurring in the clause,
   p is true if $q_1, ..., q_n$ are true.

Thus ': -' can be read as 'if' and commas can be read as 'and.'

```
on(a, b).

on(b, c).

above(X, Y) :- on(X, Y).

above(X, Y) :- on(Z, Y), above(X, Z).
```

Figure 8.1 A simple PROLOG program featuring the 'on' relation.

PROLOG is an unusual language in which programs consist mostly of logical formulas, and running a program consists mainly of a particular kind of theorem proving. A clause of the form

```
p :- q₁, ..., qₙ.
```

can be viewed as a procedure. Such a procedure is invoked as follows.

(1) A goal literal successfully matches (or *unifies*) with p, which is called the *head* of the clause.
(2) The *tail* of the clause, q_1, ..., q_n, is instantiated with the substitution of values for variables (or *unifier*) derived from this match.
(3) The instantiated clauses in the tail are then set up as subgoals that can invoke other procedures.

Thus pattern-matching (or *unification*) serves the function of parameter passing in more conventional languages.

For example, consider the PROLOG clauses in Figure 8.1. Imagine that a and b are blocks in a blocks world. The first two clauses state that a is on b and b is on c. The third clause states that x is above y if x is on y. The fourth clause states that x is above y if there is some other block z on top of y, and x is above z.

It is clear that we ought to be able to derive the goal above(a, c) from this set of clauses. We shall see exactly how in Section 8.3.2, but the derivation involves invoking the two procedures for above, and using the two on clauses to terminate the proof.

8.3 Resolution refutation†

PROLOG employs the 'problem-solving interpretation of Horn clauses' described in, for example, Kowalski (1979, pages 88–9). The fundamental theorem-proving method that PROLOG relies upon is called *resolution refutation*, and is fully described in Robinson (1979). This section attempts to impart no more than the basic ideas and the rationale behind the method.

8.3.1 The resolution principle

It was mentioned earlier that we simplify the syntax of calculi so that we can reduce the number of inference rules that we need to prove theorems. Instead of the dozen or more rules found in most methods for doing proofs by hand, automatic theorem provers for clausal forms typically use only a *single* rule of inference: the *resolution principle*, first described by Robinson (1965).

Consider the following example from the propositional calculus. From now on, I shall use upper case letters in the range P, Q, R, ... to denote particular clauses, using ψ, ϕ, and ζ (possibly with subscripts) for propositional variables, as before.

If ψ and ϕ are any two clauses which have been transformed into CNF, and

$$\psi = \{\psi_1, ..., \psi_i, ..., \psi_m\} \text{ and}$$
$$\phi = \{\phi_1, ..., \phi_j, ..., \phi_n\} \text{ and}$$
$$\psi_i = \neg\phi_j \text{ for } 1 \leq i \leq m, 1 \leq j \leq n$$

then a new clause, ζ, can be derived from the union of ψ' and ϕ' where

$$\psi' = \psi - \{\psi_i\} \text{ and}$$
$$\phi' = \phi - \{\phi_j\}.$$

$\zeta = \psi' \cup \phi'$ is the *resolvent* of the resolution step, and ψ and ϕ are its *parent clauses*. We sometimes say that ψ and ϕ 'clash' on the pair of *complementary literals*, ψ_i and ϕ_j.

Resolution is very powerful because it subsumes many other inference rules, as can be seen if we express more conventional rules in CNF.

In Figure 8.2, the left-hand column cites the name of the inference rule, the middle column shows how it commonly appears in logic texts, with expressions above the line being premise schemas, while the expression below the line is the conclusion schema. The right-hand column shows the rules with their premises and conclusions in clausal form. You can see from this column that each of the five rules cited above is just an instance of resolution!

Notice in the rule *Reductio* that a contradiction, normally denoted by $\perp$, gives the empty clause, $\{\}$, signifying that the premises are inconsistent. Considered as a 'state description' of some world, we say that the premises are *unsatisfiable* – roughly speaking, there can be no such world. The significance of this will become apparent shortly.

Inference rule	Usual form	CNF
Modus ponens:	$\dfrac{\psi \supset \phi,\ \psi}{\phi}$	$\{\neg\psi, \phi\}, \{\psi\}$ $\{\phi\}$
Modus tollens:	$\dfrac{\psi \supset \phi,\ \neg\phi}{\neg\psi}$	$\{\neg\psi, \phi\}, \{\neg\phi\}$ $\{\neg\psi\}$
Chaining:	$\dfrac{\psi \supset \phi, \phi \supset \zeta}{\psi \supset \zeta}$	$\{\neg\psi, \phi\}, \{\neg\phi, \zeta\}$ $\{\neg\psi, \zeta\}$
Merging:	$\dfrac{\psi \supset \phi, \neg\psi \supset \phi}{\phi}$	$\{\psi, \phi\}, \{\neg\psi, \phi\}$ $\{\phi\}$
Reductio:	$\dfrac{\psi, \neg\psi}{\perp}$	$\{\neg\psi\} \{\psi\}$ $\{\}$

Figure 8.2 The generality of resolution.

For the moment, suffice it to say that the theorem prover at the heart of many AI programs, and AI programming languages such as PROLOG, is a *resolution refutation system*. In order to prove that *p* follows from some state description (or *theory*) *T*, you assume ¬*p* and then attempt to derive a contradiction from its conjunction with *T*. If you succeed in doing this, then you are justified in asserting *p*, otherwise you aren't.

Resolution in the predicate calculus requires additional machinery because of the presence of variables. The basic pattern-matching operation in resolution theorem proving is called *unification* (see, for example, Nilsson, 1980 for details of the algorithm). When matching complementary literals, we look for a substitution of terms for variables that makes two expressions identical.

For example,

RUNS-FASTER-THAN(*X*, *zeno*)

and

RUNS-FASTER-THAN(*tortoise*, *Y*)

have the following substitution that renders them identical: {*X*/*tortoise*, *Y*/*zeno*}. This substitution is called a *unifier*. We want to compute the most general such substitution; roughly speaking, the one that binds as few variables as possible.

8.3.2 Proof search in resolution systems

Resolution is a rule of inference that allows you to derive new wffs from old. However, the logistic system described so far doesn't tell you how to do proofs. This section explores the strategic aspects of theorem proving.

Let *p* represent 'Socrates is a man' and *q* represent 'Socrates is mortal.' Let our theory be

$$T = \{\{\neg p, q\}, \{p\}\}.$$

Thus we hold that if Socrates is a man implies that Socrates is mortal, and that Socrates is a man. {*q*} is derivable from *T* in a single step of resolution equivalent to *modus ponens*.

{¬*p*, *q*} and {*p*} clash on the pair of complementary literals *p* and ¬*p*, and {*q*} is the resolvent. Thus *T* *logically implies* *q*, written *T* ⊢ *q*. We are therefore entitled to add {*q*} to *T* to derive the theory *T'* = {{¬*p*, *q*}, {*p*}, {*q*}}.

Many proofs will require more than one inference step, of course. For example, let *T* be

$$\{\{\neg p, q\}, \{\neg q, \neg r\}, \{p\}\}$$

where *p* and *q* are as before and *r* represents 'Socrates is a god.' If we want to show that *T* ⊢ ¬*r*, then we require two steps of resolution:

$$\frac{\{\neg p, q\}, \{p\}}{\{q\}}$$

$$\frac{\{\neg q, \neg r\}, \{q\}}{\{\neg r\}}$$

Notice that in the first step we used two clauses from the original set T, but that in the second step we used a resolvent $\{q\}$ that we had added to T, in order to complete the proof. Notice also, that we could have done the proof a different way, for example

$$\frac{\{\neg p, q\}, \{\neg q, \neg r\}}{\{\neg p, \neg r\}}$$

$$\frac{\{\neg p, \neg r\}, \{p\}}{\{\neg r\}}$$

which results in a different resolvent being added to T. A number of problems arise in connection with this.

- If T is very large to begin with, it is conceivable that there might be many ways to derive a particular formula in which we are interested (our *goal*). Obviously, we would prefer the shorter proofs, if we can get them without too much search.
- T may support all kinds of inferences which have nothing to do with the proof of our goal. Yet how can we know in advance which inferences will lead to the goal?
- The whole process has a built-in potential for combinatorial explosion. T grows with each inference step, giving us more and more options. Some of these options may lead to circularity.

The pattern of reasoning we have followed so far is usually referred to as *forward reasoning*. That is to say, you start from what you know and reason in the direction of what you are trying to prove. One way of tackling some of the problems listed above is to reason backward from the goal towards the evidence you need.

Suppose you want to derive $\{q\}$ from some set of clauses

$T = \{..., \{\neg p, q\}, ...\}$.

It seems sensible to comb the set looking for clauses that have q as a literal, and then try to resolve the other literals away (if there are any). However $\{q\}$ doesn't clash with, for example, $\{\neg p, q\}$, since the pair of literals q and q aren't complementary.

If q is a goal, then *resolution refutation* works by adding the *negation* of the goal to T, and then trying to show that $T' = T \cup \{\neg q\}$ is inconsistent. Assuming that T was consistent in the first place, if T' is inconsistent, it must be because $T \vdash q$. (If T isn't consistent, then q is a trivial consequence of T.)

Let's consider this in more detail. First we negate the goal to derive $\{\neg q\}$, and then we attempt to resolve $\{\neg q\}$ with another clause in T'. There are only three possibilities.

- There is no clause containing q in T, in which case the proof fails.
- T contains $\{q\}$, in which case the proof is immediate, since from $\{\neg q\}$ and $\{q\}$ we can derive the empty clause $\{\}$, signifying contradiction.
- T contains a clause $\{..., q, ...\}$ that resolves with $\{\neg q\}$ to generate a clause, which contains the remaining literals, all of which need to be resolved away if we are to demonstrate the contradiction.

These remaining literals can be thought of as *subgoals* that need to be solved if we are to solve our main goal. This is clearly a *backward reasoning* strategy; as such it resembles subgoaling in MYCIN (see Chapter 3).

As an example, let T be $\{\{\neg p, q\}, \{\neg q, \neg r\}, \{p\}\}$ as before. If we want to show that $T \vdash \neg r$, then we negate $\neg r$ to derive our goal statement $\{r\}$, and then add this to T. The search for a contradiction proceeds as follows:

$$\frac{\{\neg q, \neg r\}, \{r\}}{\{\neg q\}}$$

$$\frac{\{\neg p, q\}, \{\neg q\}}{\{\neg p\}}$$

$$\frac{\{\neg p\}, \{p\}}{\{\}}$$

This method of proving theorems is called resolution refutation because it uses the resolution rule of inference, but adopts a refutation strategy. The use of resolution in backward reasoning is characteristic of the *modus tollens* of natural deduction systems, just as its use in forward reasoning is characteristic of *modus ponens* (see Figure 8.2).

To return to our earlier PROLOG example, Figure 8.3 shows a resolution refutation proof of `above(a, c)`, laid out as a *proof tree*. By convention, we draw the tree upside down, and each branch of the tree connects two 'parent' clauses containing complementary literals with a clause that is generated from them by a single step of resolution. We write all goals on the right hand side of a ':-', since they are implicitly negated (refer back to Section 8.1.2 if this seems mysterious). Goals are listed on the left of the tree, while clauses from the database are listed on the right.

The root of the tree is the empty clause, signifying that our proof search has been successful. Adding the negative clause `:- above(a, c)` to our theory results in an inconsistency. Therefore, we are entitled to conclude that `above(a, c)` is a logical consequence of the theory.

Note the role that unification plays in this proof. The goal `above(a, c)` unifies with the clause head `above(X, Y)` with substitution

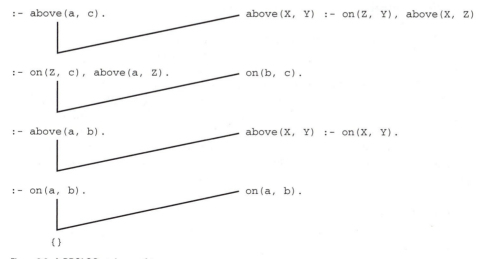

Figure 8.3 **A PROLOG-style proof tree.**

```
{X/a, Y/c}
```

where X/a can be read as 'X gets the value a.' This substitution is then applied to the clause tail

```
on(Z, Y), above(X, Z).
```

to derive the subgoals

```
on(Z, c), above(a, Z).
```

The next subgoal, on(Z, c), unifies with on(b, c) with substitution {Z/b}. This substitution is then applied to the remaining subgoal, which becomes above(a, b), and so on, until we derive the empty clause.

The main advantage of resolution refutation is that reasoning backward from what you are trying to prove serves to focus the search for a solution, since inferences drawn are at least potentially relevant to the goal. Also, seeing the production of resolvents as the generation of subgoals is intuitively satisfying. However, it doesn't solve all the problems noted above. For example, it doesn't guarantee that you will find shorter proofs rather than longer ones. Neither does it abolish the combinatorial explosion inherent in the proof-generation process that we discussed in Chapter 2, although the 'attention-focusing' effect of goal-directed reasoning obviously prevents totally irrelevant inferences from being generated and added to the set of clauses.

In the next two sections, we look at the evolution of *procedural deduction systems*: reasoning systems which use procedures to

- add extra control features to guide proof search; and
- represent knowledge that does not lend itself to a purely declarative characterization.

These developments are instructive, because they demonstrate the departures from standard logic and additional machinery that are normally required to get a theorem prover to do useful work from an AI point of view.

8.4 Procedural deduction in PLANNER

PLANNER (Hewitt, 1972) was one of the first designs for an AI programming language based on the idea of an extended theorem prover. The full conception was never realized, but a significant subset of the language, called Micro-PLANNER, was implemented and saw application in planning and question-answering applications, notably the SHRDLU program described in Chapter 2. Here we shall confine our discussion to those aspects of PLANNER which impinge on knowledge representation issues (rather than, say, issues of programming language design).

PLANNER modeled the state of some universe of discourse in terms of an associative database containing both *assertions* and *theorems* which functioned as procedures. Assertions were LISP-like predicate-argument lists, such as

```
(BLOCK B1)
(ON B1 TABLE)
```

while 'theorems' were really patterns which enabled inferences to be drawn. Thus a theorem along the lines of

```
(ANTE (BLOCK X) (ASSERT (ON X TABLE)))
```

is really a procedure which says 'if X is asserted to be a block, then also assert that X is on the table.' So if (BLOCK B1) is asserted, then (ON B1 TABLE) will be asserted too. The function ASSERT adds its instantiated argument to the database.

The above is an example of an *antecedent theorem*, so called because we are only interested in reasoning from the antecedent to the consequent (by analogy with *modus ponens*) and not from the negation of the consequent to the negation of the antecedent (by analogy with *modus tollens*). We say that such a theorem is really a procedure because it contains control information; indeed, it functions rather like a demon in a frame system (as described in Chapter 6).

PLANNER also provided a second kind of procedure, called a *consequent theorem*, such as

```
(CONSE (MORTAL X) (GOAL (MAN X))).
```

This procedure effectively says 'to show that X is mortal, show that X is a man.' Thus if (MORTAL SOCRATES) is a goal to be proved, then (MAN SOCRATES) will be set up as a subgoal. The function GOAL initiates a search of the database for its instantiated argument. However, one cannot use this theorem to go from the assertion of (MAN SOC-RATES) to the assertion of (MORTAL SOCRATES).

Consequent theorems can also manipulate the database. For example, to put block B1 (whose surface is clear) on another block B2 (whose surface is clear), we need to find the surface that B1 is already on, delete the old assertion to this effect, and then make the new assertion that B1 is on B2.

```
(CONSE (ON X Y)
       (GOAL (CLEAR X)) (GOAL (CLEAR Y))
       (ERASE (ON X Z)) (ASSERT (ON X Y)))
```

Given the goal (ON B1 B2), so long as B1 and B2 are clear, PLANNER will perform the desired manipulations of the database. Consequent theorems therefore provide a mechanism for implementing STRIPS-like operators for planning applications (see Chapter 3).

The reader can see from this sketch that, in PLANNER, control information was represented explicitly in the database of procedures, rather than being concealed in the strategic component of the theorem prover, as in resolution refutation systems. The power of this approach is that we can decide when certain classes of inferences are to be drawn. We can also model changes of state in a reasonably efficient way.

One problem with procedural deduction relates to the concept of completeness. A proof system is *complete* if all tautologies, that is, trivially true statements such as $(p \lor \neg p)$, can be derived as theorems. This is clearly not the case for PLANNER; we noticed that we could not generate (MORTAL SOCRATES) from a database containing

```
(MAN SOCRATES)

(CONSE (MORTAL X) (GOAL (MAN X))).
```

Arguably this is the kind of price you pay if you want to mix control information with propositional representations. Unfortunately, PLANNER was not *that* much more efficient than a resolution theorem prover. This was because its control information is rather short-sighted. There is no overall strategy for satisfying a goal, just a collection of theorems whose local decisions may or may not add up to the desired effect.

Also, there was no facility in PLANNER for reasoning about control, for example by using meta-rules of the kind described in Chapter 5.

The next section shows how a later system attempted to address the problem of how to perform *meta-level inference* in a principled way.

8.5 PROLOG and MBASE

We saw earlier that we can render a proposition such as

'If a philosopher beats someone in a race, then that person will admire him'

in first-order predicate calculus, for example

$$(\forall X)(\forall Y)(PHILOSOPHER(X) \wedge BEATS(X, Y) \supset ADMIRE(Y, X))$$

and that such a formula could be rendered in conjunctive normal form as follows:

$$\{ADMIRE(Y, X), \neg BEATS(X, Y), \neg PHILOSOPHER(X)\}.$$

We also saw that if we write this as

```
admire(Y, X) :- philosopher(X), beats(X, Y).
```

with the single positive literal on the left side of the `:-` operator, and the negative literals on the right side, then we have a Horn clause statement in the syntax of the logic programming language PROLOG. In what follows, we explore the problem of how to control the application of such rules.

8.5.1 PROLOG's search rules

A statement such as

```
admire(Y, X) :- philosopher(X), beats(X, Y).
```

is rather like a consequent theorem in PLANNER. Given the query 'who admires whom?', which can be represented by the clause

```
:- admire(V, W).
```

the statement says that 'to show that Y admires X, show that X is a philosopher, and then show that X beats Y.'

A goal that unifies with `admire(Y, X)` can be construed as a *procedure invocation*, and the unifier can be considered as a mechanism for passing actual parameters to the other literals, which constitute the body of the procedure. It does not matter if these 'parameters' are themselves variables, as in the present example. The subgoals in the body are ordered; this is called PROLOG's *left–right search rule*.

As with PLANNER, and earlier resolution-based systems, the goal is easily attained if the database contains just the assertions

```
philosopher(zeno).
beats(zeno, achilles).
```

and we get the answer

```
admire(achilles, zeno).
```

If the database contains other relevant information, then the program may have to *backtrack* before achieving its goal. Backtracking is where we undo the variable bindings achieved by a subgoal because those bindings have caused a later subgoal to fail, and look for new bindings. If the database contained just the additional clause

```
philosopher(socrates).
```

then if we find this formula before we find

```
philosopher(zeno).
```

then the next subgoal

```
beats(socrates, W)
```

will fail, and we have to look for another philosopher. The amount of work that the theorem prover typically has to do to achieve a goal like `admire(V, W)` depends on what else the database contains.

Suppose the database knows of 100 philosophers apart from Zeno; that is it contains another 100 statements of the form `philosopher(X)` for some `X` other than `zeno`. Then it is an unfortunate fact of life that in the worst case the program will backtrack 100 times between the two subgoals before it demonstrates the goal. If the order of the subgoals were exchanged, then the program would succeed without backtracking with this database, but would perform less well in the context of a database where we have only one philosopher but a lot of races going on.

Alternatively, the database may contain other rules which interact with our statement about admiration. For example, 'X beats Y' might be deemed a transitive relation, in which case we might have the rule

```
beats(X, Y) :- beats(X, Z), beats(Z, Y).
```

or we might define a philosopher as someone who loses at least one footrace to a tortoise:

```
philosopher(X) :- beats(Y, X), tortoise(Y).
```

The presence of such rules will greatly complicate the search space and multiply opportunities for backtracking.

We now describe an extension to PROLOG, called MBASE, which was used to implement a knowledge-based system called MECHO for solving high school problems in Newtonian mechanics.

8.5.2 Explicit search control in MBASE

One obvious way of controlling the search when trying to prove a goal is to order the clauses in the database carefully. PROLOG searches the database from top to bottom when looking for facts or rules to unify with the goal; this is called the *top-down computation rule*. We can sometimes take advantage of this convention to keep proofs short.

- *Particular facts* (that is, ground atoms) should appear before rules that have the corresponding predicate as a goal, to minimize the cost of rule invocation, for example

```
beats(achilles, zeno).
```

should appear before

```
beats(X, Y) :- beats(X, Z), beats(Z, Y).
```

- *Exceptions* to general rules should also appear earlier in the database than the rules to which they constitute exceptions. Thus

```
flies(X) :- penguin(X), !, fail.
```

should appear before

```
flies(X) :- bird(X).
```

The `fail` literal is a way of expressing negation in PROLOG: it's a subgoal that always fails. The `!` literal, called 'cut,' is PROLOG's way of saying 'if you fail back to this point, then fail back to the last procedure call.' This *cut and fail* combination is a very common means of controlling backtracking. It prevents the interpreter from pursuing a depth-first search for all possible solutions. Unfortunately, this convention can also make the flow of control hard to understand (see Exercise 1). Note also that the database is now inconsistent, from a purely logical point of view.

- *Default assumptions* can be implemented by asserting non-ground clauses at the bottom of the knowledge base. For example, a clause of the form

```
pacifist(X) :- quaker(X).
```

should appear after all clauses of the form

```
pacifist(nixon) :- !, fail.
```

if we want Quakers to be pacifists by default, that is, unless we have information to the contrary.

In summary, clauses in the knowledge base are typically ordered so that special cases occur first, for example particular facts and exceptions, then come general cases, in the form of inference rules, and finally defaults, which can be assumed if they can't be proven one way or the other.

MBASE used all these devices, but in addition it provided facilities for controlling depth of search; one could call a literal to three different depths:

- A *database call* (DBC) involves restricting the search to ground literals in the database and thereby avoiding rule applications. This facility was achieved by the simple expedient of wrapping ground literals in the predicate DBC, thus the fact that `b1` was a block would be represented by the clause

```
DBC(block(b1)).
```

Subgoals of the form DBC(P) for some clause P were then effectively database only calls. This is for cases where PROLOG would try too hard.

The cut and fail combination described above can also be used in conjunction with DBC as a 'trap' to stop silly searches for goals that cannot be satisfied, such as trying to prove that a block is in two places at once, for example

```
at(Block, Place1) :-
  DBC(at(Block, Place2)),
  different(Place1, Place2), !, fail.
```

Note that without the use of the DBC predicate in the procedure body, the program would quickly go into a loop.

- An *inference call* (DBINF) applies rules in the usual way, using PROLOG's top-down and left-right search conventions.
- A *creative call* (CC) generates place-holders for intermediate unknowns and pursues the computation where an inference call would fail and give up. This is useful for mathematical computations in which we do not have values for all the variables in an equation, but we keep the variables around because we may be able to eliminate some of them later on. So, in some applications, we actually want to try harder than PROLOG.

The use of cut and fail to encode negation, exhibited above in the 'penguin' example, is usually regularized by defining not as a proper procedure, along the lines of

```
not(P) :- call(P), !, fail.

not(P).
```

call is a special PROLOG system predicate which evaluates a goal passed in as a parameter. The idea is that, if the call succeeds, then the not goal fails, and the cut disables backtracking. Otherwise, we fall through to the second clause, and the not goal succeeds straightforwardly.

Some of the problems of completeness associated with PLANNER can also be present in PROLOG. Thus the use of cut and fail to encode negation, as shown above, can sacrifice completeness and consistency. There are various different ways in which negation can be incorporated into Horn clause logic, but the conditions under which they have desirable properties are rather restricted (see Shepherdson, 1984, 1985).

However, it was found that the global control mechanisms described so far were still insufficient to guide computations to a successful conclusion. The problem was that they were only based on knowledge local to the current state of the computation. MBASE addressed the problem of how to supply local control by two further mechanisms – schemata and meta-predicates – to which we now turn.

The associative mechanisms employed by MECHO are called 'schemata,' and they are mainly used to encode general knowledge about such things as pulley systems, for example

```
sysinfo(pullsys,
    [Pull, Str, P1, P2],
    [pulley, string, solid, solid]
    [  supports(Pull, Str),
       attached(Str, P1),
       attached(Str, P2) ]).
```

sysinfo is a predicate which takes four arguments, each of which is like the slot of a *frame* (see Chapter 6):

- the first argument, pullsys, says that this schema is meant to represent a typical pulley system, so this is the name slot;
- the second argument, [Pull, Str, P1, P2], is simply a list of the parts of a pulley system: a pulley, a string, and two particles;
- the third argument, [pulley, string, solid, solid], contains type information about these components;
- the fourth argument contains a list of relationships that hold between these components.

Note that there is nothing very propositional about such representations, for example the way in which type information is represented by an implicit mapping between two lists. Neither is obtaining such information deduction, in any interesting sense, even though it involves resolution theorem proving. It is far more like accessing information in a frame (except that it is unlikely to be as efficient).

The cueing of schemata is only one of the ways in which MECHO attempts to package the background information that the program needs in order to solve such problems. Various additional kinds of structure are also needed which say which formulas to use to solve for which quantities. Thus

```
kind(a1, accel, relaccel(...)).
```

states that a1 is a quantity of type accel, which is defined in the relaccel assertion, that is, in the context of relative acceleration, while

```
relates(accel, [resolve, constaccel, relaccel]).
```

states that the formulas called resolve, constaccel, and relaccel contain variables of type accel, and can therefore be used to solve for acceleration. This is the kind of extra indexing that the type–token distinction of an associative network would supply. Here it has to be represented in logic, using structures that are not typically found in the first-order predicate calculus.

Finally, there are *meta-predicates*, whose role is to select the inference method most suited to the solution of a particular goal. Consider the following example:

```
solve(U, Expr1, Ans) :-
    occur(U, Expr1, 2),
    collect(U, Expr1, Expr2),
    isolate(U, Expr2, Ans).
```

This procedure states that Ans is an equation that solves for unknown U in the expression Expr1 if

- Expr1 contains two occurrences of U;
- Expr2 is Expr1 with these two collected together;
- Ans is Expr2 with U isolated on the left-hand side.

Meta-predicates like solve are really plans that serve to structure a computation, in this case putting an equation into a form such that it can be used to solve for an unknown. Like meta-rules in production systems, they can be used to reason about how reasoning should be performed. Together with facilities for packaging information and extra indexing, such extensions to PROLOG made it possible to harness a theorem prover for the purposes of complex problem solving. Without such devices, one doubts whether much useful work could have been done.

Some of the examples from MECHO suggest that programming in logic is just like programming in any other language, in that the purity of the original conception and design can quickly become muddied by implementation requirements. However, for applications which involve reasoning over a large set of structured facts, for example, descriptions of circuits, mechanical devices, and other systems governed by physical laws, PROLOG is often an excellent vehicle. PROLOG can also be used as a host language for commonsense theories about time, space, causality, permissions and obligations, and so on, where there are general principles that admit of a declarative representation and where very little search is required.

We shall see in Chapter 23 that despite these problems PROLOG, and associated logic programming concepts, find application in two other research areas which are of interest to expert systems, namely *explanation-based generalization*, which supports a form of machine learning, and *meta-level inference*, where a program reasons about its own behavior.

BOX 8.2

Tractability and Decidability

It is worth pointing out that although there is an effective procedure for the decision problem in the propositional calculus, this problem can be shown to be intractable in general, because in the worst case it is exponential in the number of propositional constants involved. However, the predicate calculus is not even decidable, so long as we have predicates of arity greater than one; that is, we cannot always tell whether a formula is a theorem of the calculus or not. The details of this result are well beyond the scope of this text, but its immediate consequences are two-fold.

- No proof procedure for the predicate calculus is guaranteed to terminate if we try to show that an arbitrary formula follows from a theory. If the formula *does* follow, then the procedure *will* ultimately terminate with success, but if it does not, the procedure may *never* terminate. By reason of this asymmetry, predicate logic is *semi-decidable*.
- In the general case, it is impossible to show that an arbitrary predicate calculus theory is consistent, *even in principle*. This astonishing result was proved by Gödel in 1931, and it has had tremendous repercussions throughout the fields of logic and mathematics. For example, it can be shown that any formalization of arithmetic (for example, Peano's axioms) will either be incomplete or inconsistent, and any proof of consistency must resort to principles extraneous to the theory.

Gödel's result bears directly upon the use of logic as a basis for representing knowledge. If we wish to formalize expertise in some complex domain using the full expressive power of predicate logic, we will have to live with the fact that it will be impossible to demonstrate that our formalization is consistent, and that some of our deductions based on this representation of knowledge may never terminate. This is a rather sobering thought. We have already gotten used to the idea that certain computations will always take too long on even the most powerful machines, and that heuristics will be required to cut the cost. But Gödel's result says that certain computations *cannot* be carried out, even in infinite time and using infinite resources. In such cases, heuristic methods are our *only* resort, and these will usually compromise either soundness or completeness or both.

BIBLIOGRAPHICAL NOTES

A clear technical introduction to the proof theory of mathematical logic can be found in Andrews (1986). Readers are also recommended to consult Quine (1979), which is the revised edition of his 1940 classic *Mathematical Logic*. For a thorough introduction to automated reasoning, it is still hard to improve on Robinson (1979).

A gentler introduction, with an emphasis on artificial intelligence, is Genesereth and Nilsson (1987, Chapters 1–5). In addition, the paper by Hayes and Michie (1984) provides an accessible discussion of mathematical logic in the context of AI. Ginsberg (1993) is a more recent AI text with an emphasis on the logical point of view.

STUDY SUGGESTIONS

1. Translate the following statements into predicate logic.
   (i) Every student uses some computer, and at least one computer is used by every student. (Use only the predicates *STUDENT, COMPUTER,* and *USES.*)
   (ii) Every year, some male students fail every exam, but every female student passes some exam. (Use only the predicates *STUDENT, MALE, FEMALE, PASSES, EXAM, YEAR.*)
   (iii) Every man loves some woman who loves another man. (Use only the predicates *MAN, WOMAN, LOVES,* and =.)
   (iv) No two philosophers have the same favorite book. (Use only the predicates *PHILOSOPHER, BOOK, LIKES,* and =.)

2. Put the sentences of Exercise 1 into clausal form.

3. How worthwhile is it to translate the following quotations into predicate logic? Identify the difficulties involved in representing the author's intention in each case.
   (i) No man is an island. (John Donne)
   (ii) The man who lives everywhere lives nowhere. (Tacitus)
   (iii) The past is a foreign country; they do things differently there. (L.P. Hartley)
   (iv) A man of the highest virtue does not keep to virtue, and that is why he has virtue. (Lao Tzu)

4. Consider the clausal formula

   ```
   shaves(X, X), shaves(barber, X) ←
   ```

   which says that one shaves oneself or the barber shaves one.
   (i) Show that

   ```
   shaves(barber, barber) ←
   ```

   follows from this formula using backward reasoning.

continued

(ii) Demonstrate the same result by forward reasoning.

(iii) What do you understand by the following clause in this context?

```
← shaves(Y, Y), shaves(barber, Y)
```

(iv) Show that the following clauses are inconsistent by using them to derive the empty clause.

```
shaves(X, X), shaves(barber, X) ←
← shaves(Y, Y), shaves(barber, Y)
```

5. Here is a simple fault-finding problem.

> 'If an engine misfires and the spark at the plugs is intermittent, then the ignition leads are loose or the battery leads are loose. My engine misfires. The spark at my plugs is intermittent. My ignition leads are not loose.'

(i) Translate these sentences into formulas of predicate logic.

(ii) Put the formulas into conjunctive normal form.

(iii) Show that 'My battery leads are loose' follows as a logical consequence of the set of sentences using forward reasoning. Then repeat the process using backward reasoning.

6. Suppose that our goal is `:- bachelor(fred)`.

(i) What would the following PROLOG program conclude about Fred's marital status?

```
man(fred).
man(george).
wife(george, georgina).
bachelor(X) :- not(wife(X, Y)).
not(P) :- call(P), !, fail.
not(P).
```

(ii) What would the following program conclude?

```
man(fred).
man(george).
wife(george, georgina).
bachelor(X) :- not(wife(X, Y)).
wife(X, Y) :- !, fail.
wife(fred, freda).
```

7. Suppose that our goal is `:- enemy(fred)`.

(i) What would the following MBASE program conclude about Fred?

```
DBC(friend(george)).
republican(fred).
enemy(X) :- not(DBC(friend(X))).
```

continued

```
friend(X) :- republican(X).

not(P) :- call(P), !, fail.

not(P).
```

(ii) What would the following MBASE program conclude?

```
DBC(friend(george)).

enemy(X) :- not(DBC(friend(X))).

friend(X) :- not(communist(X)).

not(P) :- call(P), !, fail.

not(P).
```

8. Here is a PROLOG program that identifies a small subset of those persons who are designated as peace officers in the State of New York. You might like to type this in and play with it.

Then try adding a new rule which captures the following case:

> 'Constables of a village, provided that such a designation is not inconsistent with local law.'

Data for testing this rule is included in the FACTS section.

```
/* RULES for identifying Peace Officers */

/* The sheriff and deputy sheriffs of NYC */

po(X) :-
  (sheriff(X) ; deputy(X)),
  jurisdiction(X, nyc).

/* Officers of Westchester county public safety services
   appointed after 1982 who perform functions
   previously performed by a Westchester county sheriff
   on or prior to such date */

po(X) :-
  safetyOfficer(X),
  jurisdiction(X, westchester),
  appointed(X, Date),
  Date > 1982.

/* FACTS */

/* Wayne, Doug, Ken, and Pete are fictitious characters, of
course. */

sheriff(wayne).
jurisdiction(wayne, nyc).

deputy(doug).
jurisdiction(doug, nyc).
```

continued

```
constable(ken).
jurisdiction(ken, naples).
village(naples).
ruledOut(constable, naples).

safetyOfficer(pete).
jurisdiction(pete, westchester).
appointed(pete, 1990).
```

9. Try adding another rule to the program in Exercise 8, based on the following definition.

> 'A sworn officer of the water supply police employed by the City of New York and acting outside said city, appointed to protect the sources, works, and transmission of water supplied to the city of New York, and to protect persons on or in the vicinity of such water sources.'

What is the crucial part of the definition, given that you are not going to represent it all?

10. Rewrite the program in Exercise 8 in CLIPS. Compare and contrast the two programs.

9 Representing Uncertainty

Unlike game playing, puzzle solving and theorem proving, many applications often require a problem solver to reason with imperfect information. In this chapter, we introduce a number of basic ideas to do with the measurement of uncertainty and methods of inexact reasoning. In Chapters 11–15, we will see various different methods in action. But here the emphasis will be upon theoretical issues in the representation of uncertainty and the reason why AI researchers have deemed it necessary to experiment with a number of different formalisms. In Chapter 21, we return to the topic of uncertainty at a more advanced level, treating it in greater depth and describing some recent work. However, for many readers, this chapter may suffice.

9.1 Sources of uncertainty

There are many different sources of uncertainty in problem solving, but most of them can be attributed to either *imperfect domain knowledge* or *imperfect case data*.

Thus the theory of the domain may be *vague* or *incomplete*. Such domain theories typically use concepts which are not precisely defined, and deal with phenomena that are imperfectly understood. Consider the concept of schizophrenia in the diagnosis of mental illness, which studies have shown to be applied rather differently in different parts of the world.

Incompleteness necessitates the employment of rules of thumb which (unlike scientific laws) may not always give the correct result, even on simple cases. Having incomplete knowledge also means that the effects of actions are not always predictable; for example, therapies using new drugs frequently have unexpected outcomes. Finally, even if the domain theory is complete, an expert may find it profitable to employ heuristic methods in preference to exact methods, owing to the inherent complexity of the domain. Thus fault repair of electronic devices by swapping boards until the device works is often preferable to exhaustive circuit analysis in search of the actual fault.

In addition to problems with the domain theory, case data may be *imprecise* or *unreliable*. Sensors have only finite resolving power and less than 100 percent reliability; reports may be ambiguous or inaccurate; evidence may be missing or in conflict. We shall say that data is partial when answers to relevant questions are not available. Even when answers are available in principle, they may not be available in practice. Thus although it may be possible to gain additional information about a patient by means of surgery or expensive tests, considerations of cost and risk rule out such procedures in all but extreme cases. We shall say that data is *approximate* when answers are available but these are of variable precision; for example, it may be possible to second guess some costly or high risk procedures with more acceptable methods which give less accurate results. Finally, even if complete and exact data are available in principle, the situation may render exact methods inappropriate. Thus the decision about whether or not to shut down an ailing nuclear power station should not always wait upon a full analysis of all the facts.

In summary, experts employ inexact methods for two reasons:

- exact methods are *not known*; and
- exact methods are known but are *impractical*, owing to lack of data, or problems with collecting the data (for example, cost and risk), or difficulties with processing the data within the time constraints set by the problem (for example, where there is danger to life).

There is broad agreement among artificial intelligence researchers that inexact methods are important in many expert systems applications; however, there is less agreement concerning what form these methods should take. Until recently, opinion tended to follow McCarthy and Hayes (1969), who felt that probability theory was epistemologically inadequate to the task of representing uncertainty. They argued that

- it is not altogether clear how to deal with the interaction of probabilities with quantifiers (see Chapter 8); and
- the assignment of probabilities to events requires information that is simply not available.

Other researchers have criticized probabilistic approaches on the following additional grounds:

- it has little to say about inherently imprecise notions, such as the quantifiers 'most' and 'few', or vague terms, such as 'tall' and 'old';
- the application of probability theory requires 'too many numbers,' and forces engineers to be too precise about quantities they cannot hope to estimate;
- probabilities are expensive to update, leading to intractable computations.

These sentiments led to the exploration of alternative formalisms for handling uncertainty, such as *fuzzy logic* and *belief functions*, for many expert systems applications. Fuzzy logic is described later in this chapter, while the theory of belief functions (also called the Dempster–Shafer theory of evidence) is outlined in Chapter 21. However, advocates of probability theory have staged a rather effective counterattack in recent years, and so we shall present the basic concepts of the theory and its main rivals in this chapter, and review further developments in the later chapter.

9.2 Expert systems and probability theory

In this section, we look more closely at some of the problems involved in taking a probabilistic approach to the management of uncertainty. We begin with a brief elementary account of conditional probability, and consider why probabilistic approaches have not been very attractive to expert systems researchers. Then we explain the certainty factors approach of MYCIN (mentioned in Chapter 3) in a little more detail, and compare its results with those of probability theory.

9.2.1 Conditional probability

The *conditional probability* of d given s is simply the probability that d occurs if s occurs, for example the probability that a patient really is suffering from disease d if he or she complains only of symptom s.

In traditional probability theory, the conditional probability of d given s is computed using the following formula:

$$P(d \mid s) = \frac{P(d \wedge s)}{P(s)}. \qquad (9.1)$$

Thus conditional probability is defined in terms of joint events; it is the ratio between the probability of the joint occurrence of d and s and the probability of s. Now it follows from formula (9.1) that

$$P(d \wedge s) = P(s \mid d)P(d)$$

and if we divide both sides by $P(s)$ and substitute using (9.1), we derive the simplest form of *Bayes' Rule* – sometimes called the inversion formula, because it defines $P(d \mid s)$ in terms of $P(s \mid d)$.

$$P(d \mid s) = \frac{P(s \mid d)P(d)}{P(s)} \qquad (9.2)$$

$P(d)$ is the *prior probability* of d, that is, the probability prior to the discovery of s. $P(d \mid s)$ is the posterior probability, that is, the probability once we have discovered s.

For the purposes of knowledge-based systems, formula (9.2) is much more useful than (9.1), as we shall see.

Given that a patient has a disturbing symptom, such as chest pain, one would like to know the probability of this being due to something potentially serious – for example, myocardial infarction (heart attack), acute pericarditis (inflammation of chest cavity) – or something less serious, such as indigestion. However, to calculate the probability

$$P(myocardial\ infarction \mid chest\ pain)$$

using (9.1), one would need to know (or estimate) how many people in the world were suffering from the disease, how many complained of the symptom, and how many were both suffering from the disease and complaining of the symptom. Such information is usually unavailable, particularly for

$$P(myocardial\ infarction \wedge chest\ pain).$$

Thus the definition is not much use at it stands, because the practicing clinician will not have the data that this form of reasoning requires.

The difficulty of obtaining these numbers has caused many AI writers and researchers to dismiss probabilistic approaches to uncertainty (see, for example, Charniak and McDermott, 1985, Chapter 8). In this dismissal, they have been aided and abetted by much of the literature on probability, which can be described as *frequentist* or *objectivist*. It gives the impression that

- probability is about *long-run relative frequencies* of events, and so the numbers needed to model inexact reasoning must be derived from objective empirical investigation, for example, medical records; and
- what one really needs is a *joint distribution function*, that is, a function which assigns probabilities to every elementary event or state of affairs that one might be interested in.

However, there is a body of opinion in AI and elsewhere (for example, Pearl, 1982; Cheeseman, 1985) that these fundamental assumptions are questionable from the point of view of practical applications. There is also a *subjectivist* view of probability that allows us to work with estimates of joint occurrences rather than actual frequencies. This outlook links the probability of a compound event to the strength of a person's belief that it will indeed occur, as evidenced by their willingness to place bets upon its occurrence.

Thus doctors may not know, or be able to calculate, what proportion of chest pain patients have had heart attacks, but they will have some consistent notion of how many heart attack patients have chest pain, and therefore be able to give an estimate of

$P(chest\ pain \mid myocardial\ infarction)$.

The subjectivist view of probability is strongly associated with Bayes' Rule, for the following reason. Given a reasonable estimate of $P(s \mid d)$, for symptom s and disease d, one can then use (9.2) to calculate $P(d \mid s)$. Medical statistics should enable an estimate of $P(d)$, while a doctor's own records could provide an estimate of $P(s)$.

The computation of $P(d \mid s)$ is not too problematic in the single symptom case, that is, when reasoning about some set of diseases, D, and some set of symptoms, S, and limiting ourselves to calculating, for each disease in D, the conditional probability that a patient is suffering from D given that he complains of a *single* symptom in S. Nevertheless, given m diseases in D and n symptoms in S, we require $mn + m + n$ probabilities. This will not be a small number for a reasonable set of diagnostic categories, such as the 2000 or more that clinicians actually use, and the wide range of signs and symptoms that people present with.

But the situation gets considerably more complicated if one attempts to take more than one symptom into account when performing the diagnosis.

The more general form of Bayes' Rule,

$$P(d \mid s_1 \wedge \ldots \wedge s_k) = \frac{P(s_1 \wedge \ldots \wedge s_k \mid d)P(d)}{P(s_1 \wedge \ldots \wedge s_k)} \tag{9.3}$$

requires $(mn)^k + m + n^k$ probabilities, which is a very large number for even modest values of k. These probabilities are required because, in order to compute $P(s_1 \wedge \ldots \wedge s_k)$ in the general case, we must compute

$$P(s_1 \mid s_2 \wedge \ldots \wedge s_k)P(s_2 \mid s_3 \wedge \ldots \wedge s_k)\ldots P(s_k).$$

However, a simplification is possible if you can assume that certain symptoms are *independent* of each other, that is, if for any pair of symptoms, s_i and s_j,

$$P(s_i) = P(s_i \mid s_j)$$

because then it follows that

$$P(s_i \wedge s_j) = P(s_i)P(s_j).$$

If all the symptoms are independent, then (9.3) does not require that the expert supply any more probabilities than in the single symptom scenario.

Even where this is not the case, we can sometimes assume *conditional independence*; that is, that a pair of symptoms, s_i and s_j, are independent once we have some additional evidence or background knowledge, E, so that

$$P(s_i \mid s_j, E) = P(s_i \mid E).$$

For example, if my car has a flat tire and the lights don't work, I am safe in assuming that these symptoms are independent, because there are no direct or indirect causal connections between them. On the other hand, if my car won't start and the lights don't work, I would be foolish to assume that these symptoms are independent, since there are common faults, such as a flat battery, that would cause them both. My degree of belief in faulty lights is increased if my car won't start, so I check the lights, not the tires. Keeping track of such dependencies in a program, and updating belief values accordingly, turns out to be intractable in the most general case (Cooper, 1990).

Thus probability theory leaves us with the following problem, which is best stated in terms of a trade-off:

- *either* we assume that data are independent, in which case we need fewer numbers and have simpler computations but sacrifice accuracy on the altar of convenience;
- *or* we somehow track down dependencies among data, quantify them, and pay the computational price of propagating belief updates.

In Chapter 19, we review symbolic methods for keeping track of dependencies among data, while in Chapter 21, we describe some new numerical methods for modeling probablistic dependencies. But next we turn to alternative approaches that have been used by expert systems builders in an effort to circumvent these problems. We also examine critiques of these approaches, both here and in Chapter 21, where some advanced topics are discussed.

9.2.2 Certainty factors

If we return to MYCIN's use of certainty factors (CFs), previously outlined in Chapter 3, we are now in a position to see how its treatment of uncertainty deviates from probability theory.

In a perfect world, one would like to be able to calculate $P(d_i \mid E)$, where d_i is the *i*th diagnostic category and E is all the evidence you need, using only conditional probabilities $P(d_i \mid s_j)$, where s_j is the *j*th clinical observation. We have seen that Bayes' Rule provides a convenient means of doing this only if

- all the $P(s_j \mid d_i)$ are available; and

- independence assumptions make the computation of the joint probabilities of symptom sets feasible.

The alternative explored by MYCIN was to use a rule-based approach, in which statements which link evidence to hypotheses are expressed as decision criteria, along the lines of

IF: the patient has signs and symptoms $s_1 \wedge ... \wedge s_k$, and
          certain background conditions $t_1 \wedge ... \wedge t_m$ hold
THEN: conclude that the patient has disease d_i, with certainty τ

τ is a tally in the range $[-1, +1]$. $\tau = 1$ means that the conclusion is certain to be true if the conditions are completely satisfied, while $\tau = -1$ means that the conclusion is certain to be false under the same conditions. Otherwise, a positive value for τ denotes that the conditions constitute suggestive evidence for the conclusion d_i, while a negative value denotes that the conditions are evidence against d_i.

The idea was to use production rules of this kind in an attempt to approximate the calculation of $P(d_i \mid s_1 \wedge ... \wedge s_k)$, and provide a scheme for accumulating evidence that reflected the reasoning process of an expert. As we saw in Chapter 3, the application of such a rule results in the association of a degree of certainty with the conclusion, given by

$$\text{CF}(d_i, s_1 \wedge ... \wedge s_k \wedge t_1 \wedge ... \wedge t_m)$$
$$= \tau \times \min(\text{CF}(s_1), ..., \text{CF}(s_k), \text{CF}(t_1), ..., \text{CF}(t_m)).$$

The extra conditions $t_1 \wedge ... \wedge t_m$ represent background knowledge that serves to constrain the application of the rule. It is often the case that such conditions are binary tests that evaluate to truth or falsity, so their CF equals either +1 or −1, and only the signs and symptoms $s_1 \wedge ... \wedge s_k$ contribute to a non-trivial CF for the conclusion. Their function is to test for conditions under which the rule definitely should or should not be applied. For example, a rule that links abdominal pain to possible pregnancy should only apply to female patients.

Buchanan and Shortliffe (1984, Chapter 11) argue that a rigorous application of Bayes' Rule would not have produced accurate probabilities in any case, since the conditional probabilities used would have been subjective. As we have already seen, this is the primary argument used against the employment of Bayesian inference. However, it assumes an objective interpretation of probabilities; that is, it assumes that the 'right' numbers are out there somewhere, but we can't get at them and, since we can't get at them, there is no point in applying Bayesian methods. In some ways, this is a curious argument, because any knowledge engineering enterprise is surely seeking to represent an expert's knowledge of the world (imperfect though it may be), rather than create a veridical model of the world. Also, from a theoretical point of view, it seems more sensible to apply a mathematically correct formalism to (albeit imperfect) data than a formalism that is mathematically incorrect, since this can only compound any problems with the data.

However, as Pearl (1988, p. 5) points out, there is a striking difference between the rule-based approach and that of probability theory which conveys an enormous practical advantage upon Shortliffe's method. The computation of the certainty associated with a conclusion is entirely *modular*; that is, we don't need to consider any information that is not contained in the rule. Thus we don't care about the certainties of any other propositions, and we don't care how the current certainties of the conditions of the rule were derived.

This property is often assumed in expert systems, even though it does not often hold in general. In practice, it would mean that rule premises had to be logically independent for all rules dealing with a particular parameter. With respect to MYCIN, Shortliffe advised that dependent pieces of evidence should be grouped into single rather than multiple rules (see, for example, Buchanan and Shortliffe, 1984, p. 229).

Thus, given a dependency between two pieces of evidence, E_1 and E_2, the recommendation is that they should be combined into a single rule

if E_1 and E_2, then H with certainty τ

rather than two separate rules of the form

if E_1, then H with certainty τ
if E_2, then H with certainty τ.

This is because, according to probability theory, $P(H \mid E_1, E_2)$ cannot be a simple function of $P(H \mid E_1)$ and $P(H \mid E_2)$.

Statements of conditional probability are obviously not modular in this sense. The statement

$P(B \mid A) = \tau$

does not sanction the inference $P(B) = \tau$ in the presence of A, unless A is *the only thing we know*. If, in addition to A, we acquire extra knowledge E, then we need to compute $P(B \mid A, E)$ before we can say anything about $P(B)$. This degree of context-sensitivity forms the basis of a very powerful inference mechanism but, as we have already discovered in Chapter 8, inferential power usually means computational cost.

9.2.3 Certainty factors versus conditional probabilities

Adams (1976) showed that the CF associated with a hypothesis by MYCIN does not correspond to the probability of the hypothesis given the evidence, if you adopt a simple probability model based on Bayes' Rule. This may not sound too bad, as CFs are only used to rank hypotheses. However, Adams also showed that it is possible for two hypotheses to be ranked in reverse order to their respective probabilities by the use of certainty factors; it is worth looking at this in a bit more detail.

The expert's subjective probability that hypothesis h is correct, $P(h)$, can be taken to reflect the expert's degree of belief in h at a given time. If we now complicate matters, by adding fresh supporting evidence e, such that $P(h \mid e) > P(h)$, then the increase in the expert's degree of belief in d is given by:

$$MB(h, e) = \frac{P(h \mid e) - P(h)}{1 - P(h)}$$

where MB stands for Measure of Belief.

If, on the other hand, e constitutes evidence against h, such that $P(h \mid e) < P(h)$, then the increase in the expert's degree of disbelief is given by:

$$MD(h, e) = \frac{P(h) - P(h \mid e)}{P(h)}$$

where MD stands for Measure of Disbelief.

However, as Adams points out, degrees of belief in a hypothesis derived from the consideration of different pieces of evidence cannot be chosen independently. If some piece of evidence is an absolute diagnostic indicator for a particular illness, that is, if all patients with symptom s_1 have disease d_i, then no other piece of evidence has any diagnostic value. In other words, if there are two pieces of evidence, s_1 and s_2, and

$$P(d_i \mid s_1) = P(d_i \mid s_1 \wedge s_2) = 1$$

then

$$P(d_i \mid s_2) = P(d_i).$$

Adams also criticizes the treatment of conjoined hypotheses. The MYCIN model assumes that our belief in a joint hypothesis $d_1 \wedge d_2$ is as great as our belief in the weakest hypothesis, while our degree of disbelief should be as great as that associated with the strongest hypothesis. But this treatment makes strong assumptions regarding the independence of d_1 and d_2. Suppose d_1 and d_2 are not independent, but mutually exclusive alternatives. Then $P(d_1 \wedge d_2 \mid e) = 0$, for any evidence e, regardless of our degree of belief (or disbelief) in d_1 or d_2.

Buchanan and Shortliffe (1984, p. 249) describe the certainty factor as an artifact for combining degrees of belief and disbelief into a single number. It is simply the difference between the measures of belief and disbelief, according to the formula

$$CF(h, e_a \wedge e_f) = MB(h, e_f) - MD(h, e_a),$$

where e_f is the evidence for h and e_a is the evidence against h. However, this is not equivalent to the computation of the conditional probability of h given $e_a \wedge e_f$ that one would derive from Bayes' Rule:

$$P(h \mid e_a \wedge e_f) = \frac{P(e_a \wedge e_f \mid h)P(h)}{P(e_a \wedge e_f)}.$$

Thus, although changes in belief brought about by rule applications can be related to subjective probabilities in a fairly direct way, the certainty factor is a composite number. Its main uses are

- to guide the program in its reasoning;
- to cause the current goal to be deemed unpromising and pruned from the search space if its CF falls in the range $[+0.2, -0.2]$;
- to rank hypotheses after all the evidence has been considered.

However, Adams shows that in some circumstances this ranking will depart from that produced by the application of probability theory. The example that he gives is the following.

Let d_1 and d_2 be two hypotheses, and let e be a body of evidence that tends to confirm both of them. Let the prior probabilities be such that

$$P(d_1) \geq P(d_2) \text{ and}$$

$$P(d_1 \mid e) > P(d_2 \mid e).$$

In other words, d_1 has a higher subjective probability than d_2 to begin with, and this superiority remains after the consideration of the evidence. Under these circumstances, it is possible that $CF(d_1, e) < CF(d_2, e)$.

Suppose that

$P(d_1) = 0.8$
$P(d_2) = 0.2$
$P(d_1 \mid e) = 0.9$
$P(d_2 \mid e) = 0.8.$

Then the increase in belief in d_1 is given by

$$\frac{0.9 - 0.8}{0.2} = 0.5$$

while the increase in belief in d_2 is given by

$$\frac{0.8 - 0.2}{0.8} = 0.75$$

so $CF(d_1, e) < CF(d_2, e)$ even though $P(d_1 \mid e) > P(d_2 \mid e)$.

Adams describes this as an 'undesirable feature' of certainty factors. To avoid it, all prior probabilities would have to be equal; one can easily see that the effect in the above example is due to the fact that the evidence favored d_2, even though d_1 triumphed in the end, due to a superior prior probability. However, such an equality would be at variance with the way in which diagnosticians reason, given the widely differing frequencies of occurrence associated with different diseases, and hence the widely different subjective probabilities that a diagnostician would provide for them.

The chaining of rules in MYCIN also causes some theoretical problems. The combination functions employed appear to be based on the assumption that if some evidence, e, implies an intermediate hypothesis, h, with probability $P(h \mid e)$, and h implies a final diagnostic category, d, with probability $P(d \mid h)$, then

$$P(d \mid e) = P(d \mid h)P(h \mid e).$$

This transitive relation across chains of reasoning seems acceptable at first sight, but it is not true in general, because the populations associated with these categories have to be nested in the manner of Figure 9.1 for this inference to be valid.

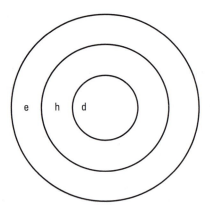

Figure 9.1 Populations validating $P(d \mid e) = P(d \mid h)P(h \mid e)$.

Adams concludes that the empirical success of MYCIN, and other systems which use the same combination functions, may be due to the fact that the chains of reasoning are short and the hypotheses involved are simple. He argues that these shortcomings in MYCIN illustrate the difficulty of creating a useful and internally consistent system of inexact reasoning that is not simply a subset of probability theory. Thus the careful comparison of such systems with the standard theory can be beneficial in showing exactly where the differences and possible difficulties lie, as we shall see in Chapter 21.

Other criticisms of MYCIN (for example, Horvitz and Heckerman, 1986) have centered around the use of certainty factors as measures of change in belief, when they were actually elicited from experts as degrees of absolute belief. In attaching CFs to rules, experts responded to the question 'On a scale of 1 to 10, how much certainty do you affix to this conclusion?'. But the evidence combination function employed by MYCIN treats CFs as belief updates, and this results in values which are inconsistent with Bayes' theorem.

9.3 Vagueness and possibility

Apart from certainty factors, there are a number of other alternatives to probability theory in the literature, notably fuzzy logic and belief functions. We shall deal with belief functions in Chapter 21, which delves deeper into some of the theoretical issues. In this section, we review fuzzy logic, and see why it has often been preferred to probability theory for expert systems applications.

9.3.1 Fuzzy sets

The knowledge that an expert uses in interpreting some signal, or perceiving a symptom as a manifestation of a particular disorder, is usually based on relationships between classes of data and classes of hypothesis, rather than individual data and hypotheses. Most forms of problem solving involve some kind of data classification: signals, symptoms and the like are seen as instances of more general categories. However, such categories may not be sharply defined. Thus class membership may be difficult to assess; a datum may exhibit some of the properties of the class but not others, or may exhibit properties only to a certain degree. *Fuzzy set theory* (Zadeh, 1965) is a formalism for reasoning about such phenomena, and it forms the basis of both *fuzzy logic* (Zadeh, 1975) and *possibility theory* (Zadeh, 1978).

Classical set theory is based on two-valued logic. Expressions of the form $a \in A$, where a is a constant denoting an individual and A denotes a set of individuals, are either true or false. Since the advent of fuzzy sets, classical sets are sometimes called *crisp*. The crispness of set theory poses a problem when we deal with concepts that are not sharply defined.

Consider the concept denoted by the word 'fast' as applied to an automobile. Given the vagueness of the concept, how do we characterize the set of fast cars? In set theory, we can describe a set A either by enumeration (listing the members of A) or by providing a characteristic function, f, such that for any X in the universe of discourse,

$f(X)$ = true if and only if $X \in A$.

Thus we could characterize the set of cars capable of more than 150 mph by the function

$$GT150(X) = \begin{cases} true \text{ if } CAR(X) \text{ and } TOP\text{-}SPEED(X) > 150 \\ false \text{ otherwise} \end{cases}$$

The set so defined is often written as

$$\{X \in CAR \mid TOP\text{-}SPEED(X) > 150\},$$

that is, those members of the set *CAR* such that their top speed is over 150 mph.

But what of the set of fast cars? Intuitively, the situation is more like that depicted in Figure 9.2, where the boundaries of the set are unclear, and membership appears to be graded in some way. Rather than being an all-or-none member of the set, individual cars appear to be more or less typical of the associated concept.

One way round the problem might be to provide an operational definition of 'fast' for practical purposes by introducing an artificial boundary to the set; for example, every car with a top speed of over 150 mph is fast, and all other cars are not in the set. However, as well as violating our intuitions, such rigid definitions might have a detrimental effect upon our ability to act. If it is my ambition to own a fast car but I am presented with a limited choice, then a car that will do 140 is still a better proposition that one which will only do 100.

Elements of a fuzzy set are members of that set *to a degree*. A fuzzy set is therefore a function, f, from an appropriate domain to the interval $[0, 1]$, where $f(X) = 0$ denotes that X is not a member of the set, $f(X) = 1$ denotes that X is definitely a member, and all other values denote degrees of membership. In the car example, we need a function from the domain of top speeds; thus we might have $f_{FAST}(80) = 0$, $f_{FAST}(180) = 1$, and some histogram of monotonically increasing values between the two, constructed over intervals of 5 or 10 mph. Thus the set of fast cars could be characterized by the function

$$f_{FAST\text{-}CAR}(X) = f_{FAST}(TOP\text{-}SPEED(X))$$

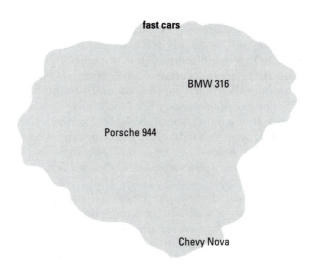

Figure 9.2 The fuzzy set of fast cars.

from the domain of cars, yielding a set of ordered pairs of the form (*make, degree*), for example

FAST-CAR = {(*Porsche-944*, 0.9), (*BMW-316*, 0.5), (*Chevy-Nova*, 0.1)}.

9.3.2 Fuzzy logic

Just as classical set theory is governed by a two-valued logic, fuzzy set theory can be related to a many-valued logic in which propositions such as *FAST-CAR(Porsche-944)* have a value which is a real number between 0 and 1. The question then arises as to how to compute the truth values of compound statements involving vague concepts, such as

¬*FAST-CAR(Chevrolet-Nova)*.

In the case of negation, if F is a fuzzy predicate, then

$$\neg F(X) = 1 - F(X)$$

by analogy with probability theory. However, in its treatment of conjunction and disjunction, fuzzy logic departs from probability theory in significant ways. Consider the sentence

'Porsche 944 is a fast, pretentious car.'

In classical logic, the proposition

FAST-CAR(*Porsche-944*) ∧ PRETENTIOUS-CAR(*Porsche-944*)

is true if and only if both conjuncts are true. In fuzzy logic, the convention is that if F and G are fuzzy predicates, then

$$f(_F \wedge {_G})(X) = \min(f_F(X), f_G(X)),$$

as we saw in Chapter 3, when computing the certainty of conjunctions of conditions for MYCIN's production rules.

Thus if

FAST-CAR(*Porsche-944*) = 0.9
PRETENTIOUS-CAR(*Porsche-944*) = 0.7

then

FAST-CAR(*Porsche-944*) ∧ PRETENTIOUS-CAR(*Porsche-944*) = 0.7.

But consider the statement

FAST-CAR(*Porsche-944*) ∧ ¬*FAST-CAR(Porsche-944)*.

The probability of this statement is 0, since

P(*FAST-CAR(Porsche-944)* | ¬*FAST-CAR(Porsche-944)*) = 0,

but it is easy to see that in fuzzy logic its value is 0.1. What does this mean? Fuzzy logicians would regard this as representing the Porsche's degree of membership in the fuzzy set of medium performance cars, which are both fast and not fast to some degree.

The main difference between the two approaches is that a probability is normally regarded as an approximation to something more precise. There is a 50 percent chance that a fair coin will come down heads, but the coin, when tossed, will come down 100 percent heads or 100 percent tails. In the 'fast car' example, the intended meaning of

FAST-CAR(Porsche-944) = 0.9

is not that a Porsche really is 100 percent fast or 100 percent not fast but we are only 90 percent sure that it is fast. The uncertainty is inherent in the vagueness of the concept. Thus it seems reasonable to suppose that there remains a degree to which it is not fast, for example it is slow by comparison with a Formula 1 racing car.

Fuzzy logic deals with disjunction by taking the maximum value of the disjuncts; thus

$$f_{(F/G)}(X) = \max(f_F(X), f_G(X))$$

for fuzzy categories F and G. This is similarly in contrast with probability theory, where

$$P(A \lor B) = P(A) + P(B) - P(A \land B).$$

Consider the following propositions and their values in fuzzy logic with reference to the fuzzy set FAST-CAR, given above.

FAST-CAR(Porsche-944) $\lor$ ¬FAST-CAR(Porsche-944) = 0.9
FAST-CAR(BMW-316) $\lor$ ¬FAST-CAR(BMW-316) = 0.5
FAST-CAR(Chevrolet-Nova) $\lor$ ¬FAST-CAR(Chevrolet-Nova) = 0.9.

In probability theory, the value of each of these propositions would be 1. Fuzzy logicians would explain that the high values accorded to Porsche and Chevrolet are due to the fact that their degree of membership in the fuzzy set FAST-CAR is extreme. The fuzzy concept 'fast or not fast' therefore applies to them, whereas the more medium performance BMW is neither one thing nor the other, and therefore gets a lower value.

The max and min operators are commutative, associative and mutually distributive. Like the operators of standard logic, they obey the principle of *compositionality*; that is, the values of compound expressions are computed from the values of their component expressions and nothing else. This is in contrast with the laws of probability, where conditional probabilities must be taken into account when computing conjunction and disjunction.

9.3.3 Possibility theory

Fuzzy logic deals with situations where the question that we pose and the relevant knowledge that we possess both contain vague concepts. However, vagueness is not the only source of uncertainty. Sometimes we are simply unsure of the facts. If I say: 'It is possible that John is in Paris,' there is nothing vague about the concepts of John and Paris. The uncertainty is about whether or not John really is in Paris.

Possibility theory is a species of fuzzy logic for dealing with precise questions on the basis of imprecise knowledge. Here we shall content ourselves with no more than a brief introduction. The best way to proceed is by example.

Suppose that an urn contains 10 balls, but all we know is that several of them are red. What is the probability of drawing a red ball at random?

Now we cannot compute an answer directly from the knowledge that several balls are red. Nevertheless, for each value, X, of $P(RED)$ in the range $[0, 1]$, we can compute the possibility that $P(RED) = X$, as follows.

Firstly, we define 'several' as a fuzzy set, for example

$$f_{SEVERAL} = \{(3, 0.2), (4, 0.6), (5, 1.0), (6, 1.0), (7, 0.6), (8, 0.3)\}.$$

For example, $(3, 0.2) \in f_{SEVERAL}$ denotes that 3 out of 10 barely qualifies as several out of 10, while $(5, 1), (6, 1) \in f_{SEVERAL}$ denotes that 5 and 6 out of 10 are excellent candidates for 'severalhood.' Note that neither 1 nor 10 is a member of the fuzzy set, since 'several' normally implies 'more than one' and 'not all.' Fuzzy sets whose domains are numbers are called *fuzzy numbers*. f_{FEW} and f_{MOST} could be defined as fuzzy numbers in an analogous way.

The possibility distribution for $P(RED)$ is now given by

$$f_{P(RED)} = SEVERAL/10$$

which evaluates to

$$\{(0.3, 0.2), (0.4, 0.6), (0.5, 1.0), (0.6, 1.0), (0.7, 0.6), (0.8, 0.3)\},$$

where $(0.3, 0.2) \in f_{P(RED)}$ denotes that there is a 20 percent chance that $P(RED) = 0.3$. We can regard $f_{P(RED)}$ as a *fuzzy probability*.

Given that almost anything can be the domain of function, it is natural to think about fuzzy truth values. We frequently talk of statements being 'very true' or 'partly true,' in addition to plain 'true.' Thus one can imagine a fuzzy set

$$f_{TRUE}: [0, 1] \rightarrow [0, 1],$$

where both the domain and range of the function f_{TRUE} are the possible truth values of fuzzy logic. Hence we could have

$$TRUE(FAST\text{-}CAR(Porsche\text{-}944)) = 1$$

even though $FAST\text{-}CAR(Porsche\text{-}944) = 0.9$, so long as $(0.9, 1.0) \in f_{TRUE}$. This would mean that we take any proposition with a value of 0.9 as being true, or 'true enough.' Thus we are sure that a Porsche is a fast car, even though there are faster cars on the market.

9.4 The uncertain state of uncertainty

The great advantage of fuzzy logic for expert systems appears to be the compositionality of its logical operators.

We have seen that, given a MYCIN-style rule of the form

IF: the patient has signs and symptoms $s_1 \wedge ... \wedge s_k$, and
          certain other conditions $t_1 \wedge ... \wedge t_m$ hold
THEN: conclude that the patient has disease d_j, with certainty τ

the evaluation the conjoined conditions $s_1 \wedge ... \wedge s_k$ according to the axioms of probability theory involves the computation of

$$P(s_1 \mid s_2 \wedge ... \wedge s_k)P(s_2 \mid s_3 \wedge ... \wedge s_k)...P(s_k),$$

thus requiring $k - 1$ probabilities over and above those required for the s_i, in the worst case.

We have also seen that MYCIN interprets conjunction as a fuzzy operator, computing $\min(s_1 \wedge ... \wedge s_k)$, and that this can lead to results which run counter to probability theory. Empirical studies comparing different methods for handling uncertainty commonly used in AI have discovered further examples of error, in which methods based on fuzzy logic perform less reliably than Bayesian approaches (see, for example, Wise and Henrion, 1986).

On the other hand, it is worth pointing out that human beings do not appear to be reliable Bayesian reasoners. The research of Kahneman and Tversky (1972) showed that people are apt to discount prior odds and accord more weight to recently presented evidence. Other research suggests that people are over-confident in their judgments (see for example, papers in Kahneman *et al.*, 1982) and have a poor understanding of sampling theory (Tversky and Kahneman, 1974).

Part of the charm of fuzzy logic is that it seems to be grounded in our use of language. Thus terms such as 'fast,' 'few,' 'true' are given an interpretation that is in accordance with our everyday intuitions. This simplifies the knowledge engineering process, in that judgments can be elicited from human experts and translated directly into the appropriate fuzzy functions. However, it is by no means clear that the inference rules defined over such interpretations are appropriate for arbitrary expert systems applications. After all, our everyday use of language need not be bound by strict mathematical constraints, while higher standards of formality and precision may be required for some problem solving applications.

We shall return to these topics later in the book, particularly in Chapter 21. The present chapter provides no more than a basic grounding in the concept of uncertainty and uncovers a few theoretical problems. But the reader can see, even from this brief review, that we still have a way to go before we understand all the issues involved in choosing a representation for uncertainty.

BIBLIOGRAPHICAL NOTES

Part 4 of Buchanan and Shortliffe (1984) contains a coherent account of MYCIN's certainty factors and why they were preferred to alternative treatments. It also reproduces Adams' critical paper. Mamdani and Gaines (1981) is a book of papers by some of the pioneers who sought to apply fuzzy logic to substantive problems. Sanford (1987) contains an easy to read but interesting review of psychological research into probabilistic judgments.

Recent papers on applications of fuzzy logic can be found in Baldwin (1996), Dubois *et al.* (1996), and Jamshidi *et al.* (1997). Walker and Nguyen (1996) provides a first course in fuzzy logic, while Yager and Filev (1994) combines an introduction to fuzzy concepts with applications to modeling and control. McNeill and Freiberger (1993) is a highly readable history of fuzzy thought for the general reader, rich in both anecdote and insight.

1. What is the probability of drawing a court card (king, queen or jack) from a full deck of cards?
2. What is the probability of throwing better than three on each of two successive throws of a fair dice?
3. Suppose that the probability that an engine will fail on a three-engined aircraft is 0.01. What is the probability that all three engines will fail, if the failure of each of the three engines is independent of the failure of the other two engines?
4. What is the probability that all three engines in Exercise 3 will fail, if the independence assumption does not hold, but we have the following conditional probabilities?

    P(*engine1 fails* | *engine2 fails* ∨ *engine3 fails*) = 0.4
    P(*engine2 fails* | *engine1 fails* ∨ *engine3 fails*) = 0.3
    P(*engine3 fails* | *engine1 fails* ∨ *engine2 fails*) = 0.2

    P(*engine1 fails* | *engine2 fails* ∧ *engine3 fails*) = 0.9
    P(*engine2 fails* | *engine1 fails* ∧ *engine3 fails*) = 0.8
    P(*engine3 fails* | *engine1 fails* ∧ *engine2 fails*) = 0.7

5. Given that P(*three engines fail* | *sabotage*) = 0.9, and the probability of any one engine failing is 0.01 as before, use the probabilities in Exercise 4 to compute the probability that the airplane was sabotaged if all three of its engines fail.
6. Explain the difference between the frequentist and subjectivist interpretations of probability.
7. Why don't all expert systems use Bayes' Rule to compute the degrees of certainty associated with conclusions?
8. What problems might arise from a pair of MYCIN rules such as the following? What is it about MYCIN's control structure that exacerbates the situation?

    if *E1*, then *H* with certainty +0.5
    if *E1* and *E2*, then *H* with certainty −0.5.

    How could these rules be rewritten to avoid such problems?
9. Suppose that 'few' is defined as the fuzzy set:

    f_{FEW} = {(3, 0.8), (4, 0.7), (5, 0.6), (6, 0.5), (7, 0.4), (8, 0.3)}.

    If an urn contains 15 balls, but all we know is that few of them are blue, what is the probability of drawing a blue ball at random?
10. Suppose that 'abnormal marks out of ten' is defined as the fuzzy set:

    $f_{ABNORMAL}$ = { (0, 1.0), (1, 0.9), (2, 0.7), (3, 0.5), (4, 0.3), (5, 0.1),
          (6, 0.1), (7, 0.3), (8, 0.5), (9, 0.9), (10, 0.9)},

    and 'high marks out of ten' is defined as the fuzzy set:

    f_{HIGH} = { (0, 0), (1, 0), (2, 0), (3, 0.1), (4, 0.2), (5, 0.3)
          (6, 0.4), (7, 0.6), (8, 0.7), (9, 0.8), (10, 1.0)},

    Derive the composite function 'abnormally high marks out of ten.'

10 Knowledge Acquisition

In Chapter 1, we cited Buchanan's definition of *knowledge acquisition* as

> the transfer and transformation of potential problem solving expertise from some knowledge source to a program.

Knowledge acquisition is a generic term, as it is neutral with respect to how the transfer of knowledge is achieved. For example, it could be achieved by a computer program that learns to associate symptom sets with diagnostic categories by processing a large body of case data. The term *knowledge elicitation*, on the other hand, often implies that the transfer is accomplished by a series of interviews between a domain expert and a knowledge engineer who then writes a computer program representing the knowledge (or gets someone else to write it).

However, the term could also be applied to the interaction between an expert and a program whose purpose is

- to elicit knowledge from experts in some systematic way, for example, by presenting them with sample problems and eliciting solutions;
- to store the knowledge so obtained in some intermediate representation; and
- to compile the knowledge from the intermediate representation into a runnable form, such as production rules.

The use of such programs is advantageous because it is less labor intensive, and because it accomplishes the transfer of knowledge from the expert to a prototype in a single step.

In this chapter, we shall examine the knowledge elicitation problem in more detail, looking at both theoretical analyses and practical approaches. Section 10.1 suggests ways in which knowledge acquisition can be broken down into different stages of activity or levels of analysis. Section 10.2 reviews some early work on automated knowledge elicitation, which focused on the syntax of rules, and Section 10.3 compares this with later developments, which focus more upon the semantics of the domain.

10.1 Theoretical analyses of knowledge acquisition

We mentioned in Chapter 1 that knowledge elicitation interviews generate between two and five 'production rule equivalents' per day. The reasons why productivity is so poor include

- the technical nature of specialist fields requires the non-specialist knowledge engineer to learn something about the domain before communication can be productive;
- the fact that experts tend to think less in terms of general principles and more in terms of typical objects and commonly occurring events; and
- the search for a good notation for expressing domain knowledge, and a good framework for fitting it all together, is itself a hard problem, even before one gets down to the business of representing the knowledge in a computer.

As with any difficult task, it is beneficial to try to break the process of knowledge acquisition down into subtasks that are easier to understand and simpler to carry out.

10.1.1 Stages of knowledge acquisition

Buchanan *et al.* (1983) offer an analysis of knowledge acquisition in terms of a process model of how to construct an expert system (see Figure 10.1); it is worth summarizing these stages here.

(1) *Identification.* Identify the class of problems that the system will be expected to solve, including the data that the system will work with, and the criteria that solutions must meet. Identify the resources available for the project, in terms of expertise, manpower, time constraints, computing facilities and money.

(2) *Conceptualization.* Uncover the key concepts and the relationships between them. This should include a characterization of the different kinds of data, the flow of information and the underlying structure of the domain, in terms of causal, spatio-temporal, or part–whole relationships, and so on.

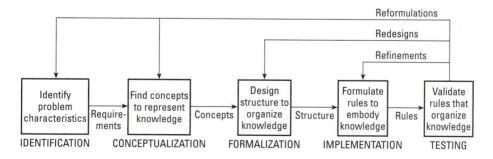

Figure 10.1 Stages of knowledge acquisition.

(3) *Formalization.* Try to understand the nature of the underlying search space, and the character of the search that will have to be conducted. Important issues include the certainty and completeness of the information, and other constraints upon the logical interpretation of the data, such as time dependency, and the reliability and consistency of different data sources.

(4) *Implementation.* In turning a formalization of knowledge into a runnable program, one is primarily concerned with the specification of control and the details of information flow. Rules will have to be expressed in some executable form under a chosen control regime, while decisions must be made about data structures and the degree of independence between different modules of the program.

(5) *Testing.* The evaluation of expert systems is far from being an exact science, but it is clear that the task can be made easier if one is able to run the program on a large and representative sample of test cases. Common sources of error are rules which are either missing, incomplete or wholly incorrect, while competition between related rules can cause unexpected bugs.

As Figure 10.1 suggests, the primary consideration in designing an expert system is the class of problems that you want the system to solve. It is a mistake to begin either with a particular conceptual analysis of the domain or with a particular organization of knowledge in mind. This is because one suspects that the way in which we represent concepts to ourselves and the way in which we organize our ideas depend to some significant extent upon our current needs and purposes.

10.1.2 Different levels in the analysis of knowledge

The distinction drawn between identification, conceptualization, and formalization can also be found in the work of Wielinga *et al.* (1992) who have developed a modeling approach to knowledge engineering within a framework called KADS. The authors argue that a knowledge-based system is not a container filled with knowledge extracted from an expert but an 'operational model' that exhibits some desired behavior and impacts real-world phenomena. Knowledge acquisition involves not just eliciting domain knowledge but also interpreting the elicited data with respect to some conceptual framework and formalizing these conceptualizations in such a way that a program can actually use the knowledge.

The KADS framework is founded on five basic principles, as follows:

(1) The introduction of multiple models as a means to cope with the complexity of the knowledge engineering process.

(2) The KADS four-layer framework for modeling the required expertise.

(3) The reusability of generic model components as templates supporting top-down knowledge acquisition.

(4) The process of differentiating simple models into more complex ones.

(5) The importance of structure-preserving transformation of models of expertise into design and implementation.

Here we shall concentrate on the first two principles.

The motivation behind the KADS framework is primarily the management of complexity. Today's knowledge engineer is faced with a large space of methods, techniques and tools which could be used to build an expert system. However, he or she is also faced with three invariant issues, namely

- *defining the problem* that the expert system is meant to solve;
- *defining the function* that the expert system will fulfill with respect to that problem; and
- *defining the tasks* that must be performed in order to fulfill that function.

The first principle of KADS is that a framework should provide multiple partial models to help answer these questions, for example:

- an *organizational model* of the 'socio-economic environment' in which the system will have to function, for example, financial services, health care;
- an *application model* of the problem to be solved and the function to be fulfilled, for example, diagnosis, job-shop scheduling;
- a *task model* which shows how the function is fulfilled by breaking the desired behavior down into component tasks, for example, gathering income data, generating disease hypotheses.

The mapping between this terminology and that of Buchanan is not exact, but clearly the organization and application models incorporate aspects of the 'identification stage,' as described in the previous section.

The original KADS approach breaks the 'conceptualization stage' down into two parts: a *model of cooperation or communication* and a *model of expertise*. The former is responsible for decomposing the problem solving behavior into primitive tasks and then distributing these tasks across agents, whether human or mechanical. The latter corresponds to what one normally means by knowledge elicitation, namely an analysis of the different kinds of knowledge that an expert brings to the problem solving process.

Finally, there is the *design model*, which suggests computational techniques and representational mechanisms that could be used to realize the specification derived from the previous models.

The above analysis seems to blur the distinction between the stages of conceptualization and formalization somewhat, although one could argue that formalization is simply a more detailed specification of the concepts and relations identified in the

Knowledge category	Organisation	Knowledge types
Strategic	Strategies	Plans, meta-rules
Task	Tasks	Goals Control terms Task structures
Inference	Inference structure	Knowledge source Metaclass Domain view
Domain	Domain theory	Concept Property Relations

Figure 10.2 **The KADS four-layer view of knowledge.**

earlier stage. The design model takes us part way to implementation, but still leaves us with something less than a runnable program.

In earlier writings, Wielinga and Breuker (1986) made a slightly different set of distinctions between these levels of analysis, which now appear to overlap with the models proposed in KADS-II, but are nonetheless worth articulating.

- *Knowledge conceptualization* aims at the formal description of knowledge in terms of primitive concepts and conceptual relations.
- *Epistemological analysis* is concerned to uncover the structural properties of the conceptual knowledge, such as taxonomic relations.
- *Logical analysis* is concerned with knowledge about how to perform reasoning tasks in the domain.
- *Implementational analysis* deals with the mechanisms upon which other levels of analysis are based.

The first three levels are now incorporated in the KADS model of expertise, whereas the concerns of the implementational level overlap the design model. The KADS 'four-layer' view follows Clancey (1985) in differentiating between different kinds of knowledge according the roles that they play in problem solving (see Chapter 11). In

BOX 10.1

CommonKADS and KACTUS

The future of KADS appears to lie with CommonKADS (Breuker and van de Velde, 1994), a knowledge engineering workbench that contains model editors for each of the KADS models and various tools and components to speed expert system development. It includes a new *lifecycle model* for project managers which helps to generate plans and assign tasks. Other models have been added since the original conception of KADS, for example, the *agent model*, which describes the expert system itself, its users, and related computer systems.

KADS has also spawned its own ontologies and methodologies for the construction of large, reusable knowledge bases, in the related KACTUS initiative (Wielinga and Schreiber, 1994). (KACTUS stands for Knowledge about Complex Technical Systems for Multiple Use.) This project addresses the problem of making knowledge shareable over different applications so that it can be reused.

Wielinga and his colleagues put forward a number of design principles to form the basis of a methodology for constructing sharable knowledge bases. One is the clean separation of domain and control knowledge; another is the development of distinct domain ontologies, that is, models of the entities in a domain and the relations that hold between them. These two concerns form recurrent themes in the modern expert systems literature, and are to some extent a reaction against methodologies that were driven more by programming technologies, such as the production rule formalism.

Of course, there is an assumption operating here to the effect that the kind of pencil-and-paper analysis advocated by KADS can be successfully performed without commitment to an implementation paradigm. Not everyone would agree that this is possible. How do you know that a KADS model is correct until you implement it and test it? How do you prove that a knowledge base is reusable, other than by reusing it in the context of another implemented system? One reason that production rules have proved so popular is that they provide an analysis tool embedded in an implementation vehicle which permits an incremental cycle of analysis, development and testing.

particular, domain knowledge is now subordinated to higher levels of knowledge, such as knowledge of how to reason in a domain, knowledge of what tasks need to be performed, and strategies for getting those tasks done.

Figure 10.2 shows these different knowledge levels. The strategic level controls the execution of tasks which apply inference methods appropriate to the domain to use domain knowledge to solve problems. We shall explore this kind of differentiation of knowledge further in the next chapter.

For now, suffice it to say that this view complicates the rather simple picture of expert systems architecture we have so far contented ourselves with. In particular, it suggests that even within the traditional 'knowledge base plus inference engine' architecture, there may be tasks and strategies implicit in both the way the domain knowledge is structured and the way the inference engine is implemented. We shall see that making these tasks and strategies explicit is a central part of both knowledge acquisition and expert system design.

10.1.3 Ontological analysis

Another knowledge-level analysis for expert problem solving is called *ontological analysis* (Alexander *et al.*, 1986). This approach describes systems in terms of entities, relations between them, and transformations between entities that occur during the performance of some task. The authors use three main categories for structuring domain knowledge:

- the *static ontology*, which consists of domain entities, together with their properties and relations;
- the *dynamic ontology*, which defines the states that occur in problem solving, and the manner in which one state may be transformed into another;
- the *epistemic ontology*, which describes the knowledge that guides and constrains state transformations.

There is some obvious overlap here with the *knowledge conceptualization* and *epistemological analysis* levels of Wielinga and Breuker's framework. However, there is less of a correspondence with lower levels, such as the *logical* and *implementational* analyses. Ontological analysis assumes that the problem under study can be reduced to a search problem, but does not focus upon the method of search; we shall see an application of this approach in the OPAL system, described in Section 10.3.2 below.

These analyses may seem rather abstract, but they are valuable because they help to structure an ill-structured task. Anyone who has attempted to elicit knowledge from an expert knows how hard it is to find a suitable framework around which the knowledge can be organized. Too often, people say 'let's use frames!' or 'let's use rules!' as if that takes care of the whole issue, when they should be deferring the choice of implementation vehicle until they have understood both the nature of the knowledge and the key inferences that will have to be drawn in order to solve problems.

10.2 Expert system shells

Early expert systems were built 'from scratch,' in the sense that the architects either used the primitive data and control structures of an existing programming language to represent knowledge and control its application, or implemented a special-purpose rule or frame language in an existing programming language, as a prelude to representing knowledge in that special-purpose language.

These special-purpose languages typically had two different kinds of facility:

- *modules*, such as rules or frames, for representing knowledge; and
- an *interpreter* which controlled when such modules became active.

The modules, taken together, constituted the knowledge base of the expert system, while the interpreter constituted the inference engine. In some cases, it was clear that these components were reusable, in the sense that they would serve as a basis for other applications of expert system technology. Since such programs were often abstractions of existing expert systems, they became known as expert system *shells*.

10.2.1 EMYCIN as architecture and abstraction

For example, EMYCIN (van Melle, 1981) was a domain-independent framework for constructing and running consultation programs. Its name stands for 'Empty' MYCIN (or 'Essential' MYCIN), since it can be thought of as the MYCIN system minus its domain-specific medical knowledge. However, it was more than just an abstraction of MYCIN, since it offered a number of software tools to help expert system architects build and debug performance programs.

EMYCIN provided a number of features which have since become widespread in expert system shells:

- An abbreviated rule language, which is neither LISP nor the subset of English used by MYCIN, but an ALGOL-like notation, as in Figure 10.3, which is easier to read than LISP and more concise than the English subset used by MYCIN.
- An indexing scheme for rules, which also organizes them into groups, based on the parameters that they reference. Thus MYCIN had CULRULES that applied to cultures, ORGRULES that applied to organisms, and so on.
- A backward-chaining control structure like MYCIN's, which unfolds an AND–OR tree, the leaves of which are data that can be looked up in tables or requested of the user.
- An interface between the final consultation program and the end user, which handled all communications between the program and the user (for example, the program's requests for data and provision of solutions; the user's provision of data and requests for explanations).
- An interface between the system designer and the evolving consultation program, providing tools for displaying, editing and partitioning rules, editing knowledge held in tables, and running rule sets on sets of problems.

As part of its interface with the system designer, EMYCIN included a program called TEIRESIAS (Davis, 1980b). As we shall see in the next subsection, this was a 'knowledge editor' devised to help with the development and maintenance of large knowledge bases. TEIRESIAS concentrated on the syntax of the production rules in an evolving expert system, for example making sure that new rules referenced medical parameters referenced in similar, extant rules. However, TEIRESIAS had no knowledge of either the domain of application or the problem solving strategy to be employed by the system under construction.

IF: composition = (list of metals) and
         error < 5 and
         nd-stress > .5 and
         cycles > 10000
THEN: ss-stress = fatigue

IF: 1) the material composing the substructure is one of the metals, and
         2) the analysis error (in percent) that is tolerable is less than 5, and
         3) the non-dimensional stress of the substructure is greater than 0.5, and
         4) the number of cycles the loading is to be applied is less than 10000
THEN: it is definite (1.0) that fatigue is one of the stress behavior phenomena
         in the substructure

Figure 10.3 An EMYCIN rule in the Abbreviated Rule Language from SACON.

This turns out to be both a strength and a weakness. The strength of the method lies in its generality; such a syntactic analysis can be applied to rules in almost any domain. The weakness lies in the fact that it places a considerable burden on both the expert and knowledge engineer: they are the sole repositories of all the background knowledge about the domain upon which the decision rules are based. In other words, they alone are responsible for ensuring that the rules make sense at any level deeper than that of syntactic conformity. Nevertheless, TEIRESIAS contained many innovations which are worth looking at in more detail. We treat knowledge elicitation programs that delve deeper into the semantics of the domain in Section 10.3.

10.2.2 Maintaining and debugging knowledge bases in TEIRESIAS

Experts know more about their fields than they realize, or can put into words spontaneously. It is not very helpful to ask them general, open-ended questions like

'What do you know about blood infections?'

in an attempt to uncover this knowledge. A better approach, adopted by TEIRESIAS, is to let them bring their expertise to bear upon some sample problem that will elicit the required knowledge.

Given an initial rule set, representing a prototype expert system, TEIRESIAS runs the rules on stored problems and invites the expert to critique the result. New rules, or rule modifications, proposed by the expert are monitored for consistency and coherence using *rule models*. These are essentially generalizations about the kinds of rules that are found in the performance program.

For example, MYCIN's rules for attempting to establish the identity of an organism almost invariably have conditions in their premises which mention the parameters for culture site and infection type. So, if the expert wishes to add a new rule of this kind, it seems reasonable for the system to expect this rule to reference these parameters. If they are not referenced, it can at least point this out to the user, and give him the option of doing something about it.

Another rule model might note that the rules referencing culture site and infection type in their premises also mention the portal of entry of the organism as another of their conditions. Again, the system can prompt the user for this information if it not provided by the new rule. Further, it can probably deduce which portal of entry is usually associated with the other clinical parameters found in the rule, and fix the bug itself.

Rule models are really a kind of *meta-rule* (see Chapter 5), in that they make general statements about rules, instead of statements about objects in the domain of application. In particular, TEIRESIAS has meta-rules which refer to the attributes of object-level rules, instead of referring to other rules direct. Such rules might suggest that, in some circumstances, it is better to investigate certain parameters before trying to trace others when fixing a bug in the rule set.

Facilities also exist for helping an expert add a new instance of a data type. Errors that commonly occur with this task are giving the new instance the wrong structure, and not integrating the new instance properly into the system. For example, if one wishes to introduce a new clinical parameter to MYCIN, that parameter should inherit the structure of attributes associated with other parameters of that context type, and values for those attributes should fall within the allowed ranges.

A data abstraction used to guide the creation of instances is called a *schema*. Schemas (or schemata) are descriptions of data types, just as data types are generalizations about data. As such, they can be organized into a hierarchy, where each schema inherits the attributes associated with its superordinate, and has additional attributes of its own.

Creating a new instance then involves tracing a path from the root of the schema hierarchy to the schema representing the appropriate data type. At each level, there will be attributes which need to be instantiated, until the instance is completely described. Relations between schemas will indicate updating tasks that the system might need to perform.

TEIRESIAS therefore distinguishes between three levels of generality:

- *domain-specific* knowledge about data objects;
- *representation-specific* knowledge about data types;
- *representation-independent* knowledge about declarations.

In summary, an expert can use TEIRESIAS to communicate with an expert system like MYCIN, to find out what the performance program is doing and why. Given that the program is incomplete, and prone to error, one can then ask the question 'What do you know that the program doesn't know?'. Faced with a specific problem to solve, experts can focus their attention upon assigning credit or blame to individual rules, debugging old rules and adding new ones.

TEIRESIAS used a number of facilities for monitoring the behavior of a rule set, provided by the shell EMYCIN.

- EXPLAIN. After each consultation, a terse explanation is provided which tells the user how the conclusion was reached. Each rule that was activated is printed along with the cumulative certainty factor of its conclusion.
- TEST. In this mode, the expert can compare the results of the current run of the program with stored correct results and explore the discrepancies. EMYCIN has a question–answer facility that can be used to ask why new values were concluded, and why correct ones weren't concluded.
- REVIEW. The expert can review system conclusions about a stored library of cases. This helps monitor the effects of alterations in the rule set, since the debugging

effort may well introduce new bugs. Batch runs between debugging sessions can be used to see if alterations to improve performance on some cases degrade performance on others.

It should be stressed that there is no well-understood or widely accepted methodology for incrementally extending knowledge bases in the manner of REVIEW. However, some work has been done on evaluating individual rules (for example, Langlotz *et al.*, 1986) and optimizing rule sets (for example, Wilkins and Buchanan, 1986). This work is reviewed in Chapter 20.

In summary, EMYCIN was an attempt to generalize the MYCIN architecture to other domains, and experience with the tool showed that it was more suited to some problems than others. This raised the question of why this should be the case, that is, what features of a problem made it more or less amenable to an EMYCIN solution. Was it something about the subject area? Was it something about the style of reasoning, or the size of the problem?

We shall defer further discussion of these questions to Chapters 11 and 12, but the key point to be made here is that EMYCIN and similar experiments got people thinking about these issues. In particular, researchers were interested in classifying problems, such as medical diagnosis, route planning, sonar interpretation, and so on, as a prelude to associating solution methods with these classes. In other words, researchers began to invent taxonomies to describe problems with a view to being able to prescribe problem solving methods. This, in turn, led to an association between problem types and knowledge acquisition methods. The knowledge required to diagnose a disease or troubleshoot an electrical device is very different from the knowledge required to construct a health plan or configure a computer system, and may need to be elicited in a quite different way.

10.3 Knowledge acquisition methods

Having examined the theoretical underpinnings of knowledge acquisition and some early tools, we continue this chapter with two more recent case studies which form an interesting contrast. One involves knowledge acquisition for troubleshooting a telephone company switching system, and the other involves planning therapeutic regimes for cancer patients. The two projects dealt with the issues of knowledge acquisition and knowledge representation in rather different ways, largely as a consequence of both the task at hand and the way that the task was approached.

10.3.1 Knowledge elicitation by interview in COMPASS

A telephone company 'switch' is not simple device, but an extremely complex system whose circuitry may occupy a large part of a building. The goals of switch maintenance are to minimize the number of calls that have to be rerouted owing to bad connections and ensure that faults are repaired quickly to maintain the redundancy of the system. Bad connections are caused by some failure in the electrical path through the switch that connects two telephone lines.

GTE's COMPASS (Prerau, 1990) is an expert system which examines error messages derived from the switch's self-test routines, which look for open circuits, shorts, lag time in the operation of components, and so forth. The causes of a switch problem can only be identified by looking at a series of such messages and bringing significant expertise to bear. COMPASS can suggest the running of additional tests, or the replacement of a particular component, such as a relay or circuit card.

Skilled maintenance personnel were scarce, yet many such error logs had to be analyzed, so there was clearly a case for trying to capture the expertise of a top expert in a computer program. Such an expert was procured and troubleshooting knowledge was elicited through a series of interviews. The expert would describe a problem solving heuristic, and the knowledge engineer would formulate it into an if-then rule expressed in English (see Figure 10.4). This formalization was then examined by the expert to see if it corresponded with his intuitions and experience. If this was not the case, the knowledge engineer would reformulate the rule until it was acceptable.

Such rules were typically implemented by one or more production rules in the KEE language (see Chapter 17), although sometimes a KEE frame or a LISP procedure was deemed more appropriate. The English rules were accumulated in a 'knowledge document' that then became part of the project documentation. This document contained the rules in an amplified form which spelled out the thinking behind the rule.

Hand simulation formed an important part of the knowledge acquisition process, because it was found to be easier to troubleshoot the rules with pencil and paper, at least in the first instance, than to implement the rules and be constantly changing them. In the early stages of development, there may not be enough knowledge formalized to warrant an implementation, or it may be the case that the rules are still in a state of flux. It may also be the case that implementors have not yet caught up with the knowledge that has been elicited so far.

Thus the knowledge acquisition cycle employed in COMPASS had the following form:

(1) Elicit knowledge from the expert.
(2) Document the elicited knowledge.
(3) Test the new knowledge as follows:
   - Have the expert analyze a new set of data.
   - Analyze the same data in a hand simulation using the documented knowledge.
   - Compare the results of the expert's opinion with the hand simulation.
   - If the results differ, then find the rules or procedures that generated the discrepancy, and return to (1) to elicit more knowledge from the expert to resolve the problem, else exit loop.

IF   There exists a BC Dual Expansion One PGA Dominant Problem, and
        The number of messages is five or more
THEN The fault is in the PGA of the indicated expansion (.5), and
        The fault is in the PGA of the silent expansion (.3), and
        The fault is in the IGA (.1), and
        The fault is in the Backplane (.1)

Figure 10.4 **The English form of a COMPASS rule (from Prerau, 1990).**

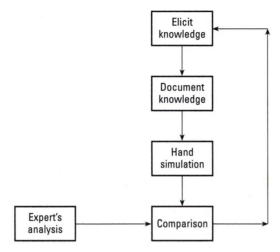

Figure 10.5 **Knowledge acquisition cycle in COMPASS (from Prerau, 1990).**

This *elicit–document–test* cycle is represented graphically in Figure 10.5.

After implementation began in earnest, the COMPASS project switched to a cycle that interposed implementation between documentation and test. Testing now involved running the program on new data and comparing the results with the pronouncements of the expert. The comparison phase is now more complicated, because in addition to conceptual errors in the formulation of the rule, there are also a range of possible errors in the implementation – everything from minor bugs to incorrect heuristics.

Prerau notes that as the knowledge elicitation progressed, experts became adept in presenting their knowledge in a manner that was closer to the rule formalism, just as knowledge engineers acquired more expertise in the domain. Such 'meeting of minds' is a good sign, and if it doesn't occur to some extent this is probably a bad sign for any project. The use of hand simulation as a test technique probably facilitated this joint understanding.

By 1990, COMPASS had been deployed in GTE telephone companies, as an aid to the maintenance of a particular kind of switching system serving half a million customers. The system's success was due in no small measure to the painstaking knowledge elicitation process outlined above. Also, the architects of the system took the knowledge acquisition problem into account when selecting the domain; that is, they chose an application for which they knew that expertise was both available and acknowledged as a valuable commodity.

10.3.2 Automating knowledge elicitation in OPAL

The COMPASS project is a good example of a conventional knowledge acquisition method, that of the structured interview, well executed and meticulously documented. Such a methodology has its roots in the protocol analyses of Newell and Simon, which we described in Chapter 2. In this section, we look at a project, called OPAL, that departed from this established practice in two important respects.

- It attempted to automate some part of the elicitation process by extracting knowledge from experts during an interactive session with a computer program.
- It attempted to use knowledge acquisition strategies which were guided by knowledge of the domain.

We saw that TEIRESIAS concentrated on identifying errors in an existing rule set, drawing the knowledge engineer's attention to faulty or missing rules, and allowing him to test the performance of the modified set. TEIRESIAS did not use any knowledge of the domain of application as a basis for constructing the initial rule set, or monitoring changes to the rule set as it evolved. By contrast, OPAL attempts to conceal from the user much of the detail of how knowledge is represented and deployed, and sets out to elicit knowledge from an expert directly by an 'interview' session conducted at the terminal. OPAL is not a general-purpose program, however; it uses knowledge about a particular domain of application (cancer therapy) to elicit treatment plans from which decision rules can be generated.

10.3.3 A graphical interface to a domain model

OPAL expedites knowledge elicitation for the expert system ONCOCIN (Shortliffe *et al.*, 1981), which constructs treatment plans for cancer patients. Its interest lies in its use of a model of the domain to acquire knowledge directly from an expert via a graphical interface. The notion of a *domain model* can be explained in terms of the different kinds of knowledge that experts possess.

In order to gain knowledge of a domain, whether it be a game like chess or a substantive field of technical expertise, there are certain prerequisites, or previous experiences that one must possess. In chess, one must understand what a game is, what it means to win a game, and so forth. In medical diagnosis, the basic concepts of patient, disease, test, and so on, must be understood. This kind of background knowledge is sometimes called *deep knowledge* in the expert systems literature, and is contrasted with *shallow knowledge*, which consists of more *ad hoc* linking of stimulus and response.

Thus, a chess program which simply chooses legal moves at random has no deep knowledge of the game, whereas a program which knows the values of pieces and various board positions has at least some deep knowledge. Similarly, a diagnostic program that does no more than map symptoms to disease candidates is somewhat shallow compared with a program that attempts to construct a coherent explanation of all the symptoms in terms of some small number of commonly co-occurring disorders. Persons who understand the basic principles of chess or clinical diagnosis can typically build on that foundation to improve their skills, whereas persons without this grounding have a harder time improving their performance.

OPAL is a knowledge elicitation program that has some knowledge of the domain of cancer therapy, which it then leverages to acquire more knowledge from a human expert. It also uses domain knowledge to translate the information acquired at the terminal into executable code, such as production rules and finite state tables. This combination of incremental knowledge acquisition followed by knowledge compilation is both interesting and attractive as a methodology for building expert systems. The basic idea can be represented by Figure 10.6, where a human expert concentrates on refining and extending the domain model, which is then compiled into a program

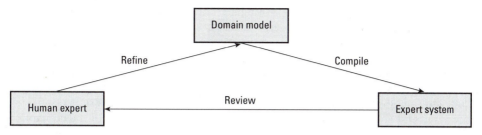

Figure 10.6 Knowledge acquisition using a domain model.

containing procedures and productions. The behavior of this program is then routed back to the expert for review, suggesting further development of the model.

In order to understand how OPAL actually works, it is necessary to say a little bit about the domain. Cancer treatments are called *protocols*, and these specify combinations of drugs given over a period of time, together with laboratory tests and (sometimes) radiation therapy. ONCOCIN derives therapy recommendations from a knowledge base of cancer protocols, stored as skeletal plans. The program works by first *selecting* a suitable protocol, and then instantiating it by filling in details of drugs, routes of administration, and so on. This problem solving method is sometimes called *plan refinement*.

The ONCOCIN expert system employs three different representations of knowledge in suggesting therapies.

- a *hierarchy of objects*, representing protocols and their components, such as drugs;
- *production rules*, which are linked to frames and which conclude the values of medical parameters during plan refinement;
- *finite state tables* (explained below) which represent sequences of therapies to be administered over time.

Entering a new protocol into ONCOCIN therefore involves creating a hierarchy which represents its components, linking suitable production rules to the new objects, and filling in a finite state table that specifies the order in which component treatments should be administered. OPAL achieves the entry of a new protocol by eliciting knowledge via a graphical interface, encoding the knowledge in an intermediate representation, and finally translating this representation into the format used by ONCOCIN, generating the appropriate production rules. The intermediate encoding and the ultimate steps of translation and generation are facilitated by OPAL's model of the cancer therapy domain, to which we now turn.

OPAL's domain model has four main aspects, and it was derived using ontological analysis, as outlined in Section 10.1.3.

- *Entities and relationships*. Entities are therapeutic elements, such as drugs, which form part of the static ontology of the domain. Much of the domain knowledge is structured around the attributes of various alternative drugs, such as dosages and routes of administration. The relationships between therapeutic elements are compositional, in the sense that they hold between levels of specificity in treatment plans. Thus a drug may be part of a chemotherapy, and a chemotherapy may be part of a protocol.

- *Domain actions.* Given the compositional relationships, refining a plan to administer can proceed by invoking plans to administer the component drugs. In other words, the process of plan refinement is implicit in the hierarchical organization of domain entities. Thus the domain model in OPAL is able to concentrate upon the task, rather than the search method employed. However, component plans may need to be modified to suit individual patients, for example by altering dosage, or substituting one drug for another. Concepts such as altered dosage and drug substitution form part of the dynamic ontology of the domain.
- *Domain predicates.* These concern conditions under which plan modification is considered, and include such things as the results of laboratory tests and symptoms exhibited by the patient (for example, drug toxicity). This knowledge forms part of the epistemic ontology of the domain, that is, it is the knowledge which guides and constrains domain actions. At the implementation level, rules which modify treatments are predicated on such conditions; these predicates appear in the 'left-hand sides' of ONCOCIN production rules. Such a rule is attached to an object in the planning hierarchy so that it applies only in the context of a particular drug in a particular chemotherapy in a particular protocol.
- *Procedural knowledge.* Because treatment plans are administered over time, knowledge about the way in which protocols can be carried out forms an essential part of the domain model. This knowledge enables OPAL to elicit the information that will eventually reside in the finite state tables that describe possible sequences of therapies, and it forms another part of the epistemic ontology. At the implementation level, OPAL uses a special programming language to describe such procedures, enabling an expert to create complex algorithms by manipulating icons.

OPAL uses this domain model to elicit and display knowledge about treatment plans via a variety of visual representations, such as: icons that stand for elements of plans; graphical forms to be filled with information about drugs; and a visual language for representing the procedural aspects of treatment.

Entities and relationships are entered via graphical forms in which the user normally selects items to be entered into the blanks from a menu of alternatives. These forms are then turned into frames, where the blanks are slots and the items of information elicited are slot values (or fillers). This new object is then automatically linked to other objects in the hierarchy; for example, drugs are linked to the chemotherapies of which they are components.

Domain actions are also entered by form-filling. Here the forms stand for skeletal plans, such as administering combinations of drugs, and available actions (such as *attentuate dose*, *delay dose*, and so on) can be selected from menus. This approach is feasible because the list of possible actions is fairly small. Unlike TEIRESIAS, OPAL does not require users to concern themselves with details of implementation, such as which medical parameters are referenced by such actions in the internal workings of ONCOCIN. All relevant information concerning medical parameters, such as platelet counts and white blood cell counts, is attached to the forms. Like the domain actions, the domain predicates are limited in number, so OPAL can display predefined lists containing laboratory tests known to the system when eliciting information about how a protocol should be modified in the light of different test results. The translation into expressions that evaluate ONCOCIN parameters is concealed from the user.

The acquisition of procedural knowledge is facilitated by a *visual programming language*. The graphical interface allows the user to create icons standing for plan elements, and arrange them into a graph structure. By positioning these elements and drawing connections between them, the user can create charts which mimic the control flow of conventional programming languages.

These programs are ultimately converted into *finite state tables* (which should be familiar to computer scientists). In general, such tables say, for any given state of some process or machine and any new input, what new state the process should go into, and what outputs should be generated as a function of the transition. In the present context, the states are treatment plans, and inputs and outputs are medical data.

10.3.4 Efficacy of OPAL and related efforts

Musen *et al.* note that knowledge acquisition posed considerable problems in developing the original prototype of ONCOCIN. It took two years and about 800 hours of an expert's time to encode the protocols for lymph node cancer, and adding additional protocols took months at a time. The rationale for developing OPAL was to speed up the acquisition process by reducing the dependence upon the knowledge engineer as the transcriber and translator of expertise.

Using OPAL, specifications of new protocols can be entered in a matter of days, with about three dozen new protocols being entered during the first year. Clearly it is the incorporation of domain assumptions into OPAL which makes the form-filling approach effective. Needless to say, outlining these assumptions itself involves a knowledge engineering effort. Yet once that investment has been made, subsequent knowledge elicitation is greatly facilitated. The success of OPAL illustrates the benefit of viewing domain knowledge at different levels of abstraction instead of focusing solely on implementation details.

The technique of eliciting domain knowledge from an expert by an interview conducted at the terminal is a feature of many acquisition systems, which use something analogous to form-filling to read information into structured objects like frames, for example, ETS (Boose, 1986) and Student (Gale, 1986). However, not all such systems have the graphical sophistication of OPAL, and not all compile such knowledge directly into decision rules. On the other hand, knowledge elicitation in OPAL is made easier by the highly structured and stylized nature of cancer therapy plans, as the authors themselves acknowledge.

Experience with OPAL led to a more general-purpose system called PROTEGE (Musen *et al.*, 1995) which is not confined to the cancer therapy domain. The current incarnation, PROTEGE-II, is a suite of tools for creating domain ontologies and generating OPAL-like knowledge acquisition programs for particular applications. Thus, as with the progress from MYCIN to EMYCIN, generality was achieved by abstraction from a successful application, rather than by designing a general tool from scratch.

10.4 Knowledge-based knowledge acquisition

We shall return to the theme of knowledge acquisition again in later chapters, since it is crucial to practical expert systems development. We shall see that many of the lessons learned from trying to extend expert systems technology in various directions have application to the knowledge acquisition problem. Specifically,

- attempts to use expert systems as a basis for intelligent tutoring systems have led to a deeper understanding of the different kinds of knowledge that experts deploy in problem solving; and
- attempts to build generic expert system tools like EMYCIN have posed interesting problems concerning how to help developers with the task of encoding knowledge from some arbitrary domain into frame or production rule format.

Such endeavors have required researchers to examine the role of domain knowledge and domain inference more closely, particularly with respect to the different styles of reasoning that are appropriate to different domains.

Looking ahead slightly, what seems to be clear is that knowledge acquisition is greatly facilitated by being itself knowledge based. In other words, a knowledge elicitation program needs some knowledge of a domain or a problem area in order to acquire new knowledge effectively, just as knowledge engineers need to have some knowledge of a domain before they can communicate effectively with an expert.

Perhaps this result is not surprising, given the lessons of knowledge-based approaches to problem solving. Knowledge elicitation is a substantial problem in itself, and there is no reason to suppose that there is a single general method that will be effective in all domains, any more than there is reason to suppose that there are general problem solving methods that will always be effective. The knowledge that one needs in order to acquire more knowledge can be viewed as a form of meta-knowledge. It is mostly knowledge about *structure* and *strategy*, involving information about ways of classifying phenomena (such as diseases) and ways of deciding between alternative courses of action (such as therapies). Not surprisingly, this is also the kind of knowledge needed to explain solutions (as we shall see in Chapter 16).

Knowledge elicitation by interview based on a domain model is not the last word in automated approaches to acquisition. In later chapters we shall consider two further approaches:

- acquisition strategies organized around a particular problem solving method, and
- unsupervised machine learning of rules by induction over a set of examples.

We shall deal with acquisition strategies based on problem solving methods as we deal with the methods themselves throughout the next five chapters. We shall become familiar with a number of different methods, with mysterious names like 'heuristic classification,' 'Match,' 'propose and apply,' and 'propose and revise.' Each of these methods appears to be effective in rather different circumstances and requires a different knowledge acquisition strategy.

We defer a discussion of machine learning until Chapter 20, since it is something of an advanced topic for an introductory text.

BIBLIOGRAPHICAL NOTES

Van Melle (1981) gives a detailed account of the systems-development aids in the EMYCIN framework. Boose and Gaines (1988) contains a representative sample of research papers on knowledge acquisition, including a paper on OPAL. Also included in the collection is Boose and Bradshaw's (1987) account of ETS and AQUINAS. Panoramic views of knowledge acquisition strategies in the 1980s, with extensive bibliographies, can be found in Boose (1989) and Neale (1988). Extended descriptions of PROTEGE-II can be found in Eriksson *et al.*, (1995) and Tu *et al.* (1995).

CommonKADS is becoming a *de facto* standard for European expert systems development in the 1990s, and experimentation with KADS has also taken place in the US (for example, Linster and Musen, 1992). Linster and Musen used CommonKADS to model the cancer therapy task performed by the ONCOCIN expert system. Worked examples of the CommonKADS design model can be found in a number of recent papers (for example, Kingston, 1995; Kingston *et al.*, 1995; Kingston, 1997).

STUDY SUGGESTIONS

1. Troubleshooting guides and shop manuals are available for many devices on the market, and these can provide material for a knowledge elicitation exercise in the absence of a tame expert.

   For example, one shop manual for the Colt .45 automatic pistol contains six dense pages of troubleshooting tips backed up with extensive amplification of key concepts in the text. The (somewhat cryptic) tips are organized in a chart along the lines of:

Where?	What?	Check for	Remark
Firing pin	Binds	Straightness	Replace as needed
Ejector	Erratic ejection	Recoil spring binding	Install long guide
Extractor	Vectors shell overhead	Bottom angle	Dress as needed

   Understanding such charts require a little knowledge acquisition with respect to the functioning of the device and the various causes and effects associated with malfunctions. Thus

   - a crooked firing pin will tend to get trapped in its tunnel causing misfires, and must therefore be replaced;
   - a recoil spring that binds inside the slide is probably buckling, which could be helped by replacing the standard short spring guide with a full-length one;
   - an extractor set at the wrong angle will throw spent shell cases back at you instead of off to the right, but this can be fixed by fitting and polishing the bottom of the extractor.

continued

Ontological analysis is a systematic way to effect this familiarization. Attempting to write diagnostic rules before fully understanding the device is a recipe for disaster.

(i) Choose your own domain, and then develop a rough ontology for it, in terms of:

- *key entities and relationships*, such as parts and part–whole relationships;
- *domain predicates*, such as erratic, straight, binding;
- *domain actions*, such as replacing, dressing, installing, and so on;

as explained in Section 10.3.

(ii) Take this further, by considering

- how fine grained the part-whole analysis needs to be;
- how domain predicates might be used to partition the space of fault symptoms; and
- what logical relationships hold among domain actions, for example, the similarity between replacing and installing (one contains the other as a subaction).

2. Implement a simple rule-based system in CLIPS which gives advice about troubleshooting the device you chose for the last exercise. Use the following program fragment as a guide for how this might be done.

```
;; ##############################################
;; # Troubleshooting a Smith & Wesson revolver #
;; ##############################################
;; REVOLVER CLASS identifying significant parts
(defclass revolver
   (is-a INITIAL-OBJECT)
   (slot barrel (create-accessor read-write))
   (slot barrel-pin (create-accessor read-write))
   (slot cyl-stop (create-accessor read-write))
   (slot cyl (create-accessor read-write))
   (slot handspring (create-accessor read-write))
)

;; REVOLVER INSTANCE to test the program with.
;; Specifies parts and part numbers.
(definstances guns
  (M19 of revolver
   (barrel 4499)
   (barrel-pin 5431)
   (cyl-stop 5869)
   (cyl 5436)
   (handspring 5022))
)

;; METHOD for returning the part number of a revolver part
(defmessage-handler revolver part-no (?part)
   (dynamic-get ?part))
```

continued

```
;; USEFUL FUNCTIONS

;; Prompts the user for input.
(deffunction prompt ()
   (printout t crlf "USER> "))

;; Prints a parts list, but the rules only cover barrel problems.
(deffunction parts-list ()
  (printout t crlf
   "barrel cylinder ejector trigger hammer firing-pin cylinder-
    stop cylinder-hand yoke frame sideplate rear-sight front-
    sight"
  crlf))

;; Elicits a choice from a list.
(deffunction choose-list ()
   (printout t crlf "Please choose from the following list: "
   crlf))

;; The rules only deal with Model 19 revolvers.
(deffunction kind-list ()
   (printout t crlf
    "M10 M12 M13 M14 M15 M16 M17 M18 M19" crlf)
)

;; PROBLEM SOLVING TEMPLATES

;; A problem involves a part, a symptom, a possible implicated
;; subpart and may have an associated check or test that can
;; be performed.
(deftemplate problem
   (field part (type SYMBOL) (default nil))
   (field symptom (type SYMBOL) (default nil))
   (field subpart (type SYMBOL) (default nil))
   (field check (type SYMBOL) (default nil))
)

;; A repair involves a part, an action upon that part,
;; a possible subpart, a check to be performed, and
;; an explanatory remark for the user.
(deftemplate repair
   (field part (type SYMBOL) (default nil))
   (field action (type SYMBOL) (default nil))
   (field subpart (type SYMBOL) (default nil))
   (field check (type SYMBOL) (default nil))
   (field remark (type STRING) (default ""))
)

;; ****************
;; PRODUCTION RULES
;; ****************

;; START rule:
```

continued

```
;; IF: we are at the start of the computation
;; THEN: determine the affected part and create problem tem-
   plate
(defrule start
  ?start-token <- (initial-fact)
  =>
  (retract ?start-token)
  (printout t crlf
  "What part of the gun are you having problems with?" crlf)
  (choose-list)
  (parts-list)
  (prompt)
  (bind ?part (read))
  (assert (problem (part ?part)))
)

;; FINISH rule:
;; IF: Problem is fixed
;; THEN: Halt.
(defrule finish
  (repair (check done) (remark ?rem&~""))
  =>
  (printout t crlf ?rem crlf)
  (printout t crlf "Glad to be of service!" crlf)
  (halt)
)

;; CHECK-REPAIR rule:
;; IF: We have a solution less drastic than replacement
;; THEN: Inform the user and mark problem as repaired
(defrule check-repair
  ?rep <- (repair
      (part ?part)
      (action ?action&~replace)
      (subpart ?sub&~nil&~?part))
  (problem (part ?part) (symptom ?sym))
  =>
  (printout t crlf
  "If you " ?action " the " ?sub " that should "
  "fix the " ?sym " problem with the " ?part crlf)
  (modify ?rep (check done))
)

;; CHECK-REPLACE rule:
;; IF: The solution requires replacement of the part
;; THEN: Inform the user and mark problem as fixed,
;; adding an empty model vector to the working memory
;; to prompt elicitation of what model the gun is.
(defrule check-replace
  (repair (part ?part) (action replace))
  (not (model ?mod&~nil))
```

continued

```
    ?prob <- (problem (part ?part) (symptom ?sym))
    =>
    (printout t crlf
    "You have to replace the " ?part
    " to fix the " ?sym " problem" crlf)
    (assert (model nil))
)

;; REPLACE rule
;; IF: User needs to replace a part
;; THEN: Find out the model of the gun.
(defrule replace
   ?rep <- (repair (action replace))
   ?mod <- (model nil)
   =>
   (printout t crlf "What model of revolver do you have?" crlf)
   (kind-list)
   (prompt)
   (bind ?answer (read))
   (retract ?mod)
   (assert (model ?answer))
   (modify ?rep (check part-no))
)

;; PART-NO rule
;; IF: User needs to replace a part
;; THEN: Find the part number by sending a message to the ob-
ject
   ;; representing the actual model of the gun.
(defrule part-no
   (model ?mod&~nil)
   ?rep <- (repair (part ?part) (action replace) (check part-no))
   =>
   (bind ?no (send (symbol-to-instance-name ?mod) part-no
   ?part))
   (printout t crlf
   "The part number of the " ?mod " " ?part " is " ?no crlf)
   (modify ?rep (check done))
)

;; BARREL rules
;; BARREL-SYMPTOM rule
;; IF: Recent problem part has no symptom
;; THEN: Elicit the symptom.
(defrule barrel-symptom
   ?prob <- (problem (part barrel) (symptom nil) (subpart nil))
   =>
   (printout t crlf "Is there a problem inside the barrel?" crlf)
   (prompt)
   (bind ?answer (read))
   (if (eq ?answer yes)
```

continued

```
  then (modify ?prob (subpart bore))
  )
)

;; BARREL-INSIDE rule
;; IF: There is a problem inside the barrel
;; THEN: Ask the user what it is (offering help).
(defrule barrel-inside
  ?prob <- (problem (part barrel) (symptom nil) (subpart bore))
  =>
  (printout t crlf "What is the problem inside the barrel?" crlf)
  (choose-list)
  (printout t crlf "  leading rust jam" crlf)
  (prompt)
  (bind ?answer (read))
  (modify ?prob (symptom ?answer))
)

;; BARREL-RUST rule
;; IF: There is rust inside the barrel
;; THEN: Check for pits.
(defrule barrel-rust
  ?prob <- (problem (part barrel) (symptom rust))
  =>
  (printout t crlf
  "Are there pits on the inside of the barrel?" crlf)
  (prompt)
  (bind ?answer (read))
  (if (eq ?answer yes)
  then
    (assert
    (repair
      (action replace)
      (part barrel)
      (subpart bore)
    (remark "Please consult your local dealer")))
  else
    (assert
      (repair
      (action clean)
      (part barrel)
      (subpart bore)
    (remark "Gun should be kept clean and dry")))
  )
)

;; BARREL-LEADING rule
;; IF: There is leading inside the barrel
;; THEN: Check for wrong ammunition
(defrule barrel-leading
```

continued

```
  ?prob <- (problem (part barrel) (symptom leading) (check
  nil))
  =>
  (modify ?prob (check ammo))
  (printout t crlf "You may be using the wrong ammunition" crlf)
)

;; BARREL-LEADING-CHECK rule
;; IF: There is leading inside the barrel
;; THEN: Check for wrong ammunition.
(defrule barrel-leading-check
  ?prob <- (problem (part barrel) (symptom leading) (check am-
  mo))
  =>
  (assert (repair (part barrel) (action clean) (subpart bore)
    (remark "Use Lewis Lead Remover")))
)
```

Feel free to use the ancillary functions provided and copy some of the structure of the rule set, but choose another application and use the knowledge you acquired in the previous exercise.

3. Think of a major purchase you are interested in, and do a rough specification of what you are looking for. For example, you might want to buy a new car, but this is not a well-defined problem unless you also specify how much money you want to spend, the primary purpose of the vehicle, makes and models you are definitely not interested in, and so on. A wide variety of goods, from houses to hi-fis, work for this kind of exercise.
   Then further refine the specification as follows.
   (i) List the key concepts and relationships involved in the problem. In the car example, these would obviously include such things as makes and models of cars, their various properties, such as engine size and fuel consumption, and their relationship to key factors in your 'lifestyle,' for example amount of driving you do, whether or not you have a horse or a dog or a boat, and so on.
   (ii) Find some way of formally representing these concepts and relationships. For example, makes and models of cars could be collected under various classes, such as sedan, sports, station wagon, and so on, in an object-oriented design. However, there may be more than one dimension along which concepts can be grouped and differentiated, in which case you will be forced to cope with aspects of multiple inheritance.
   (iii) Priorities among properties may also be important, as well as some means of resolving conflicts. If you want a powerful car, but at the same time low fuel consumption, how will you effect a compromise?

4. Implement a simple advice-giving program in CLIPS that helps a user step through the important stages of decision making in the problem you chose for the last exercise. This means deciding how the representation of concepts and relationships will be realized in data structures. You will also have to design a

continued

control regime that respects both the structure of the search space (for example, the way that cars are classified) and any mechanisms for prioritizing properties or resolving conflicts (for example, deciding what to do when faced with incompatible demands).

5. To what extent do you think it is possible to design an expert system without knowing how it will be implemented? Conversely, what dangers do you see in deciding too early how an expert system will be implemented?

11

Heuristic Classification (I)

11.1 Classifications of expert system tasks
11.2 Classification problem solving
11.3 Classification versus construction
Bibliographical notes
Study suggestions

In Chapter 10, we saw that the inference engine and knowledge representation of a successful expert systems application could often form the basis of another application. Thus the EMYCIN architecture, derived from MYCIN, was used as a vehicle for a number of other systems. However, the designers and implementors of EMYCIN never claimed that it would be suitable for arbitrary applications.

In this chapter, we shall ask a number of rather difficult questions about the various problem solving methods that are available to expert systems practitioners, and the kinds of application that they are most suitable for. In a perfect world, we would like answers to the following questions:

- Can we attempt a *classification of expert systems applications* on the basis of easily identifiable features of the task or the domain?
- Can we identify a well-differentiated *set of problem solving methods* which are relevant to classes of expert system applications?
- Can we specify what *styles of representation and inference* are most suitable for a given problem solving method?

The answers that we shall give are based on the best of current thinking on these topics, but they are hardly definitive or complete. Needless to say, these questions are of great theoretical and practical interest. If expert systems technology is to have a firm basis in theory, we must understand why the technology works (and sometimes doesn't work). On the practical side, helping expert system builders to make the right design decisions would do much to prevent the frustration and disillusion that often accompany bad choices.

The plan of this chapter is as follows.

- First, we take a critical look at classifications of expert system tasks that have been suggested in the literature.

- Then we examine an analysis of a particular problem solving method, known as *heuristic classification*, which appears to characterize the behavior of a large number of expert systems which perform tasks such as diagnosis and data interpretation.
- Finally, we contrast heuristic classification with other problem solving methods, which appear to succeed on tasks where heuristic classification is unsuitable.

Such a contrast will set the stage for the further exploration of different problem solving methods in Chapters 12–15. These methods will be exemplified by expert systems performing different tasks in different domains, chosen mostly because they are well documented in the literature. Proceeding in this fashion, we will attempt to identify which common knowledge representation schemes and inference mechanisms appear to be suited to which tasks. Further exploration of more exotic schemes and mechanisms will be deferred to Chapters 18, 22 and 23.

11.1 Classifications of expert system tasks

Hayes-Roth *et al.* (1983) offer a classification of expert systems which reflects the different kinds of task that can be addressed by expert systems technology. Their classification scheme has received some criticism over the years, largely because it appears to mix up different dimensions, and because the categories employed are not mutually exclusive. Nevertheless, we describe the categories briefly here to provide a starting point for our discussion, since their scheme has not been substantially improved upon by anyone else.

- *Interpretation systems* infer situation descriptions from observations or sensor data. Typical tasks include signal understanding and chemical structure elucidation.
- *Prediction systems* infer likely consequences from situations or events. Typical tasks include weather forecasting and financial forecasting.
- *Diagnosis systems* infer system faults from symptom data. This category includes a broad spectrum of tasks in medical, mechanical and electronic domains.
- *Design systems* develop configurations of objects that satisfy certain constraints. Typical tasks include circuit design and producing optimal arrangements of machinery in a confined space.
- *Planning systems* generate sequences of actions that achieve stated goals. Most typical tasks are planning robot motions and route planning.
- *Monitoring systems* study observations of system behavior over time to guard against deviations that threaten stated goals. Typical applications involve air traffic control and monitoring of power stations.
- *Debugging systems* generate remedies for system faults. Typical applications involve computer-aided instruction and aids to computer programmers.
- *Repair systems* generate and administer remedies for system faults. Typical applications involve avionics systems and computer networks.
- *Instruction systems* diagnose and treat students' misconceptions concerning some domain.
- *Control systems* govern the behavior of a system by anticipating problems, planning solutions and monitoring the necessary actions. Typical tasks involve battle management and mission control.

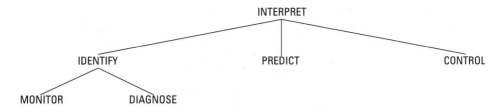

Figure 11.1 Generic operations for analyzing a system (adapted from Clancey, 1985).

As noted above, this classification has a number of shortcomings. Reichgelt and van Harmelen (1986) argue that some of the categories seem to overlap with, or include others; for example, *planning* can be seen as a special case of *design*, namely the design of actions (as Hayes-Roth *et al.* (1983) point out). Similarly, Clancey (1985) asks 'Is automatic programming a *planning* problem or a *design* problem?'. There are also obvious overlaps among debugging, repair, monitoring, and instruction systems.

Clancey proposes an alternative analysis in terms of *generic operations* upon a system. Instead of attempting to categorize problem solving programs directly in terms of the kind of problem that they set out to solve, one can ask what kinds of operation such a program can perform with respect to a real-world (mechanical, electrical or biological) system. Such systems might include manufacturing machinery, VLSI chips, or the organs of human respiration.[1]

Clancey distinguishes between *synthetic* operations that *construct* a system and *analytic* operations that *interpret* a system. These very general concepts can be specialized, resulting in a hierarchical analysis of the kinds of operation that a program can be called upon to perform. The hierarchies for interpretation and construction are shown in Figures 11.1 and 11.2 respectively.

Looking at Figure 11.1, we can see how the different kinds of INTERPRET operation relate to the notion of a system. Given input–output pairs, the IDENTIFY operation tells us what kind of system we are dealing with. Given a known system, PREDICT tells us what outputs to expect for a class of given inputs. CONTROL, on the other hand, takes a known system and determines inputs which achieve a desired output. Thus the three specializations of INTERPRET cover all the possibilities in which one member of the set {*input, output, system*} is an unknown quantity. IDENTIFY can be further specialized for faulty systems. The MONITOR operation detects discrepant behavior, while DIAGNOSE explains it.

Looking at Figure 11.2, the CONSTRUCT operation can be specialized three ways. SPECIFY states the constraints that any system design must satisfy. DESIGN generates an arrangement of parts which satisfies those constraints, while ASSEMBLE realizes the design by putting the parts together. The DESIGN process can itself be specialized in two ways. CONFIGURE concentrates on the actual structure of the system, while PLAN concentrates on how that structure will be assembled.

---

[1] There is a possible source of confusion here, since we also use the term 'system' to denote suites of programs. The kind of system that Clancey is talking about here is obviously distinct from the expert system itself. By the general term 'system' we usually intend some complex arrangement of interacting objects, existing in some environment and engaged in some process, involving the exchange of energy and information with that environment.

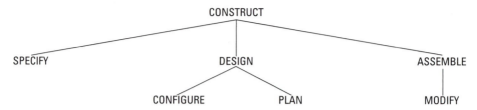

Figure 11.2 Generic operations for synthesizing a system (adapted from Clancey, 1985).

It is worth looking back at the categories proposed by Hayes-Roth *et al.* to see how they fit in with Clancey's analysis.

- *Interpretation* is now a generic category that covers any task which involves describing a working system. *Prediction* and *control* are now varieties of interpretation task.
- *Monitoring* and *diagnosis* are now varieties of identification task, which is itself a kind of interpretation task. *Debugging* is assimilated into *diagnosis*, although it also includes a modification task (to put things right).
- *Design* remains a basic category, but *instruction* is assimilated into a modify operation, as is *repair*. *Planning* is now a specialization of *design*.

As we observed earlier, our interest in classifying expert system tasks is not purely theoretical. Ideally, we would like to map problem solving methods onto tasks, in such a way that we can say, for any given task, which methods are most appropriate. Clancey's contribution to this topic was the identification of a particular problem solving method, heuristic classification, and it is to this method that we now turn. We study this method simply because it is well understood, and because it can be used to characterize the behavior of a number of systems that we have studied in earlier chapters. It is safe to say that there are other methods currently being used that we understand less well, as well as methods that are waiting to be discovered.

11.2 Classification problem solving

Classification is a problem common to many domains. For example, in botany and zoology, experts are interested in placing new species in a taxonomy of existing plant or animal types. The classes involved usually have a hierarchical organization, in which subclasses possess the discriminating features of their superclasses, and classes which are 'siblings' in the hierarchy are mutually exclusive with respect to the presence or absence of some set of features.

11.2.1 Heuristic matching

Clancey argues that the essential characteristic of classification is that the expert *selects* a category from a set of possible solutions which has already been enumerated. In simple problems, the salient features of an object are sufficient for its classification, so the match between data and category is immediate. For more complex problems, the salient features may be insufficient to identify the correct branch and level in the

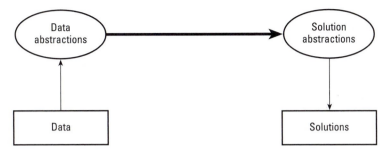

Figure 11.3 Inference structure of heuristic classification (after Clancey, 1985).

hierarchy. In this case, we may resort to what Clancey calls heuristic classification: a *non-hierarchical* association between data and category requiring intermediate inferences, possibly involving concepts in *another* taxonomy. This is best understood schematically, as in Figure 11.3.

Figure 11.3 shows the three basic steps in heuristic classification: data abstraction, matching data abstractions to solution abstractions (the heavy arrow), and solution refinement. We shall consider each of these in turn.

- *Data abstraction*. It is often useful to abstract from the data of a particular case. Thus, when diagnosing illness, the important fact may not be so much that the patient has a body temperature of 105.6 degrees, but that the patient's temperature is above normal. Usually we want to reason in terms of temperature ranges, not continuous values.
- *Heuristic match*. Although the match between the raw data of a particular case and the final diagnosis is hard to perform, it is often easier to perform a match between data abstractions and broad classes of illness. Thus high body temperature indicates fever, suggesting infection. Data 'trigger' hypotheses, but only at a relatively high level of abstraction. This matching process is heuristic because the map from data to hypotheses may not be one-to-one at any level, and there may well be exceptions to general rules. Observing data that fit the data abstraction merely makes solutions that fit the solution abstraction more likely.
- *Solution refinement*. Having identified a solution abstraction which narrows the solution space, we still need to identify and rank candidate solutions in that space. This may require further reasoning, for example about the actual data values, or it may require the gathering of further data. Either way, the goal is to rule out some of the competing hypotheses in the solution space and rate those that remain.

Clancey differentiates between three varieties of data abstraction.

- *Definitional*. This involves essential features of a class of objects, and therefore resembles the taxonomic approach of botany and zoology.
- *Qualititative*. This involves abstracting over quantitative measures, as in the example of body temperature, given above.
- *Generalization*. This involves abstraction in a hierarchy; for example, immunosuppressed patients are compromised hosts.

Figure 11.4 illustrates heuristic classification in the context of the MYCIN program discussed in Chapter 3.

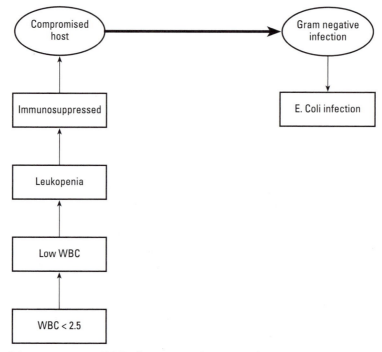

Figure 11.4 Inference structure of MYCIN (adapted from Clancey, 1985).

Thus the original datum concerning the patient's white blood cell count can be qualitatively abstracted as a low count which defines the condition of Leukopenia (that is, lack of leukocytes). Leukopenia is a kind of immunosuppression (that is, an impairment of the body's ability to defend itself against infection), while an immuno-suppressed patient is a kind of 'compromised host' (that is, someone more liable to infection than normal). The generic category compromised host suggests a gram-negative infection (that is, infection involving a particular class of bacteria), while the details of the case suggest the organism E. Coli.

In MYCIN's case, the match between data and solution abstractions performed by production rules, and the heuristic nature of this match is represented by the certainty factor. This can be thought of as a measure of how strong the correspondence encoded by the rule is deemed to be. Other rules will refine the match, thereby adjusting the certainty factor.

11.2.2 The generality of heuristic classification

The interesting thing about Clancey's analysis is that it identifies a wide range of expert systems in different domains which appear to function in more or less the same way. His paper applies this analysis to a number of systems other than MYCIN, including the following.

The SACON program (Bennett *et al.*, 1978) advises engineers concerning the use of a software package (MARC), which uses finite-element analysis to simulate the mechanical behavior of objects, for example, metal fatigue in bridges. MARC is a powerful and complex program that offers users a lot of options; SACON's role is to help MARC users set up the kind of simulation that they want. The output of SACON is an *analysis strategy*, which is inferred from load and substructure descriptions supplied by the user.

SACON has knowledge of over 30 classes of analysis. In identifying the type most suitable for a user's problem, it employs two steps of heuristic matching similar to those described by Clancey. The first step involves choosing a mathematical model for estimating stress and deflection under various conditions, based on the input data about loadings and structure geometries. The second step involves choosing an analysis strategy based on the worst-case stress and deflection behaviors derived from the chosen model.

Both steps involve selection from a set of alternatives and heuristic match between abstractions. There is no solution refinement step, however, because the second step only identifies useful classes of MARC program, although the analysis strategy does come with recommendations about specific features provided by MARC. Unlike MYCIN, there is no qualification of the match by certainty factors: SACON's conservative use of worst-case behaviors allows for categorical recommendations, even though the match is inexact.

As Clancey points out, many expert systems perform more than one of the generic operations outlined in Figures 11.1 and 11.2. Thus MYCIN's therapy recommendations involve *monitoring* the patient's state, *diagnosing* the disease category, *identifying* the bacteria, and *modifying* the state of the patient (or the state of the organism). SACON, on the other hand, *identifies* types of structure, *predicts* how such structures will behave in terms of a mathematical model and then *identifies* appropriate analyses.

Another program that Clancey analyzes is SOPHIE (Brown *et al.*, 1982), which troubleshoots electronic circuits. The main purpose of this program was as a research vehicle for ideas about computer-assisted learning, but its problem solving modules were capable of classifying an electronic circuit in terms of the component that caused the faulty behavior. Thus its pre-enumerated solution space contains descriptions of valid and faulty input–output pairs.

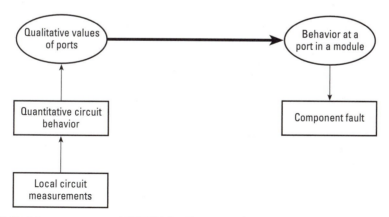

Figure 11.5 The inference structure of SOPHIE (after Clancey, 1985).

Figure 11.5 shows how we can see SOPHIE's inference structure as an instance of heuristic classification. Measurements taken at various points in an electronic circuit allow SOPHIE to make quantitative statements about circuit behavior, such as the voltage across two points. The program can then turn these into qualitative statements about behavior, such as 'high voltage,' which can be heuristically mapped to faults at the level of the module. Solution refinement then consists in deciding which components of the module are faulty. Thus, in terms of the task analysis of Figure 11.1, SOPHIE can be seen to MONITOR the state of a circuit and DIAGNOSE faulty modules and components.

The COMPASS system described in the last chapter also uses a form of heuristic classification as part of its problem decomposition. When analyzing faults in a telephone company switch, the program first clusters error messages into groups in a data abstraction step that detects commonalities among certain messages. This is necessary because no single message is sufficient to identify a fault, and it is possible because there are heuristics which match such commonalities to faults. But there is also a refinement stage which addresses ambiguities that remain after clustering, as well as later routines which order and merge suggested maintenance actions. Without the abstraction implicit in message clustering, the matching of messages to faults would probably be impossible, while without the subsequent refinement stage, the system's recommendations would be less focused and reliable.

Clancey's analysis is worthwhile because it addresses some of the questions we posed at the beginning of this chapter. In particular it identifies a generic problem-solving method which seems to be applicable across a number of different domains. In the next section, we attempt to sharpen the distinction between heuristic classification and other methods by identifying a class of problems for which heuristic classification is not well suited.

However, before we leave the topic of classification *per se*, it is worth noting that Clancey's is not the only analysis of the generic aspects of expert-level problem solving. For example, Chandrasekaran (1986) has put forward the notion of a *generic task*, which is essentially a task specification which includes:

- a description of various forms of domain knowledge and their organization for the task in hand, and
- a family of control regimes relevant to performing the task.

Examples of such tasks include: hierarchical classification, hypothesis matching or assessment, and knowledge-directed information passing, each of which are described briefly below.

Hierarchical classification involves selecting an explanatory hypothesis from a hierarchically organized space of alternatives, and then refining that hypothesis to account for data. The hypotheses could be disease categories or equipment malfunctions, for example. Each such hypothesis is capable of being suggested by data, but requires some form of test before it can be firmly established, and may need to be modified to account for many of the facts of a case. We shall look at expert systems that perform such generic tasks in Chapter 13, and again in Chapter 16.

Hypothesis matching is about the weighing of evidence concerning the goodness of fit between a hypothesis and data, including such considerations as the prior probability of the hypothesis, how far a hypothesis accounts for data, what competing hypotheses are available, and so on. MYCIN's confidence factors can be viewed as providing a mechanism for this kind of generic task. We will examine some of these issues in detail in Chapter 12.

Knowledge-directed information passing is exemplified by the drawing of inferences which are not classificatory but nonetheless necessary for expert behavior. For example, a doctor may infer that a patient who has recently had surgery received

Defining Assault Weapons

The term 'assault weapon' is often applied to a wide range of military-style, high-capacity, semi-automatic firearms. Precisely defining what an assault weapon is, and how it differs from a sporting firearm, has turned out to be difficult in practice. Yet this is a task that many federal, state and local lawmakers have taken on, and it provides a good example of heuristic classification.

The definition used by the City of Rochester, New York, Ordnance No. 93-62, addresses the problem in five parts:

- Parts 1–3 specify the general properties of such firearms.
- Part 4 simply lists specific US and foreign-made firearms that qualify as assault weapons.
- Part 5 specifies types of firearm that are *not* deemed to be assault weapons.

Parts 1–3 can be seen as performing *data abstraction*, as in the opening sentence:

'Any centerfire rifle or shotgun which employs the force of expanding gases from a discharging cartridge to chamber a fresh round after each single pull of the trigger, and which is loaded or capable of being loaded with a combination of more than six (6) cartridges in the ammunition feeding device and chamber combined.'

This covers most semi-automatic rifles and shotguns with magazines greater than five rounds.

Part 4 simply lists 17 firearms, some of which seem to be covered by the general case and some of which, like the Cobray M11, are not. The Cobray is a semi-automatic pistol capable of taking a 30-round magazine. This part is obviously meant to capture special cases not covered by the rules in Parts 1–3.

Part 5 can be viewed as a *solution refinement* stage, in which certain firearms caught by the generalizations in Parts 1–3 are exempted, for example:

'Manually operated bolt-action weapons, lever-action weapons, slide-action weapons or single-shot weapons.'

The above exception appears to allow slide-action shotguns with pistol grips, even though there is a clause in Part (3) which identifies as an assault weapon:

'Any stockless pistol grip shotgun.'

This inconsistency in the rules is presumably handled by allowing the exception in Part 5 to override this clause, even if the gun can hold more than five rounds, as such guns are routinely sold in the city.

See Exercise 4 for a CLIPS rule set based on this problem.

anesthesia, and this could be relevant to the formation of a diagnosis. This kind of inference uses background knowledge of the domain, rather than the primary diagnostic kinds of rules that we associate with a medical expert system. We discuss the differentiation of different kinds of knowledge further in Chapter 12.

Thus one difference between Chandrasekaran and Clancey's approach is that the former attempts to break problem solving down into a smaller set of abstractions than the latter. Clancey assimilates hypothesis matching into heuristic classification, whereas Chandrasekaran points out that the evaluation of hypotheses can be considered as a generic task in its own right, outside of such a context. This raises the thorny problem of what is the right 'grain-size' for these abstractions, and what criteria we should choose to select our level of granularity. These considerations are well beyond the scope of an introductory text. However, potential expert system designers need to be aware of the many different ways in which one can think about these issues, and then allowed to determine which approach best meets their needs.

11.3 Classification versus construction

The distinguishing feature of heuristic classification is that the solution set can be enumerated in advance. Thus, in the diagnostic phase of MYCIN, the program selects from a fixed set of offending organisms. However, in many tasks, solutions are *constructed* rather than selected, for example, MYCIN's therapy program, which recommends some combination of antibiotics at various dosages. In theory, one could compile an enormous table of drug–dosage combinations, but such an approach doesn't make much sense.

Constructing a solution to a problem normally involves having some model of the structure and behavior of the complex object one is trying to build. This model must contain knowledge concerning constraints that the finished product must satisfy. These will include

(1) constraints upon the *configuration* of solution components;
(2) constraints upon the *inputs and outputs* of any processes, and
(3) constraints upon any *interactions* between (1) and (2).

For example, in generating a plan for a robot to attain some goal, there will be constraints which rule out certain actions, or sequences of actions. There will be *physical constraints* that state how objects can be handled or placed, in terms of the inputs and outputs of handling and placing actions. (In Chapter 3, these were called pre- and post-conditions.) These constraints will partially determine *temporal constraints* upon how handling and placing actions can be strung together; that is, they determine the configuration of solution components. We also need to pay attention to constraints upon interactions between such components. Thus, if our goal is to decorate a house in a single day, then we should probably paint the upstairs rooms first.

Typically, such problems do not lend themselves to a solution in terms of heuristic classification. The space of possible sequences of actions for open-ended planning tasks is essentially infinite, so there is no way that all such sequences could be prestored for selection. The order in which things are done is also important in other constructive tasks, such as assembly and configuration. Unlike classification, construction problems involve permutations of possible solution elements, as well as the possibilities themselves. This usually militates against merely selecting and refining a solution by heuristic matching.

Nevertheless, it is important to maintain Clancey's distinction between the *task* and the problem solving *method* used to perform it. All diagnostic tasks are not classification problems, because we may need to create new classes of faults or modify existing ones, as we gain experience with a new device. Similarly, it may be possible for a domain-specific planner to select from a library of plans or plan skeletons, as we saw in our discussion of ONCOCIN in Chapter 10. It all depends on how constrained the problem solving situation is. Even an obvious construction task, like building a new house, can be approached in more than one way. At one extreme, one could employ an architect to design the house from scratch (construction method); at the other extreme, one could merely select a design from a catalog (classification method).

Clancey claimed that his work had the following implications for expert systems research:

- It provides a framework for decomposing problems into operations in such a way that they can be more easily classified.
- Understanding a method like heuristic classification can be seen as a prelude to specifying a special knowledge engineering tool for that purpose.
- It provides a basis for choosing applications; for example, if a problem appears to be amenable to heuristic classification, there is good reason to believe that it can be solved by expert systems technology.

In the next chapter, we shall see how tasks, methods and tools can be related using high-level concepts such as construction and heuristic classification. In particular, we shall be interested to see the implications of such analyses for automated knowledge elicitation. It turns out that knowledge-based knowledge acquisition gains in power if programs for interviewing an expert know something about the problem solving method to be employed, as well as knowing something about the domain.

BIBLIOGRAPHICAL NOTES

In addition to references cited in the text, there is an early taxonomy of problem solving types due to Chandrasekaran (1983). Theoretical work on generic tasks was linked to a project known as MDX (Chandrasekaran, 1984), which investigates diagnostic problem solving in the domain of liver disease. For an exposition of the generic task approach, with commentators and discussion, see Chandrasekaran (1988).

Clancey's work on heuristic classification grew out of an interest in intelligent tutoring systems, which (unlike early 'teaching machines') use a representation of expert knowledge for the purposes of automated instruction. A full account of this work can be found in Clancey (1987a), while a shorter tutorial on the main theoretical issues can be found in Clancey (1987b). A prototype shell designed specifically for heuristic classification problems, called HERACLES, is described in Clancey (1987c), while more recent systems such as MINERVA and ODYSSEUS (Wilkins, 1990) are discussed in Chapter 23.

Heuristic classification has been rolled into KADS (Schreiber *et al.*, 1993) as an abstract model of expertise. The first stage in KADS is to perform an analysis of the system to be built, and the first stage of this analysis is typically to select or develop such a model (see Chapter 10). There are now KADS models for other generic tasks, such as monitoring, assessment, configuration, modeling, and design.

STUDY SUGGESTIONS

1. Study Hayes-Roth's classification of expert system tasks.
   (i) Are there any additional kinds of task that you can think of which are not well covered by this scheme?
   (ii) Where would an expert system that gave legal advice fit into this scheme, that is, a system which advised clients concerning their rights under the law, and advised various courses of action, such as litigation?

2. Study Clancey's task analysis (given in Figures 11.1 and 11.2).

   (i) Where would a computer dating system fit into this analysis?
   (ii) Can you think of ways of extending or embellishing this analysis? For example, are there different kinds of CONTROL task?

3. Are the following tasks primarily classification tasks, construction tasks, or a mixture of the two?

   (i) Deciding what courses to take at college.
   (ii) Deciding on and organizing a vacation.
   (iii) Changing one's vacation plans because of unforeseen circumstances.
   (iv) Preparing your tax return.

4. Here is a partly constructed CLIPS rule set which attempts to mirror the definition of an assault weapon (see Box 11.1). I have left some rules for you to implement.

```
;; DECLARATIONS

(deftemplate gun
  (field name (type SYMBOL))
  (field class (type SYMBOL))
  (field action (type SYMBOL))
```

continued

```
    (field caliber (type FLOAT))
    (field capacity (type INTEGER))
    (field feature (type SYMBOL))
  )
  (deftemplate assault-weapon
    (field name (type SYMBOL))
  )

  ;; FACTS

  ;; Only the Heckler & Kock Model 91 and the Benelli qualify as an
  ;; assault weapon, given the initial rule set.

  (deffacts guns
    (gun (name Browning22) (class rifle) (action semi) (caliber .22)
         (capacity 11))
    (gun (name CobrayM11) (class pistol) (action semi) (caliber 9.0)
         (capacity 30))
    (gun (name HK91) (class rifle) (action semi) (caliber .308)
         (capacity 20))
    (gun (name Glock17) (class pistol) (action semi) (caliber 9.0)
         (capacity 17))
    (gun (name Mossberg500) (class shotgun) (action slide)
         (caliber .410) (capacity 5) (feature pistol-grip))
    (gun (name BenelliSuper90) (class shotgun) (action semi)
         (caliber 12.0) (capacity 5) (feature barrel-shroud))
  )

  ;; RULES

  ;; The general case

  ;; Any semi-automatic rifle or shotgun with a capacity of
  ;; more than 5 rounds
  (defrule Part1
   (gun (name ?N) (class ?C&rifle|shotgun) (action semi)
        (capacity ?X&:(> ?X 5)))
   =>
   (assert (assault-weapon (name ?N)))
  )

  ;; Any semi-automatic rifle or shotgun with an offending
    feature
  (defrule Part2
    (gun (name ?N) (class ?C&rifle|shotgun) (action semi)
       (feature ?F&flash-suppressor|barrel-shroud|night-scope))
      =>
    (assert (assault-weapon (name ?N)))
  )

  ;; Any pistol-grip shotgun
```

continued

```
;; Insert a rule called pistol-grip here.

;; Specific cases

;; A Cobray M11 is an assault weapon.
;; Insert a rule called cobray here.

;; Exceptions

;; No rimfire rifle is an assault weapon
(defrule rimfire
  ?except <- (gun (name ?N) (class rifle) (caliber .22))
  ?mistake <- (assault-weapon (name ?N))
  =>
  (retract ?mistake)
  (retract ?except)
)

;; No slide-action shotgun is an assault weapon.
;; Insert a rule called slide here.
```

If you extend the rule set, as indicated above, it will also catch the Cobray M11 as a special case. When you add the 'pistol-grip' rule, you should catch the Mossberg, and when you add the refinement rule about slide-action shotguns, the Mossberg should escape the definition.

5. What follows is an outline of a Wine Advisor in CLIPS (after a Teknowledge OPS5 program by Rand Waltzman). This program takes as input the kind of meal that one is having, and returns suggestions as to which wines might be suitable. It works by heuristic classification, since it assumes a rough mapping between gross features of the meal (for example meat or fish, kind of sauce, and so on) and broad classes of wine (such as color, body, and sweetness).

(i) Your task is to flesh out the rule base and make certain design decisions about how to organize the knowledge about food and wine, how to handle uncertainty, how to move between various stages of the reasoning. The program contains comments to help you understand what is going on and to suggest ways in which you might extend the program. Consult the appendix for guidance, (and go easy on the knowledge acquisition).

```
;; TEMPLATES

(deftemplate wine
  (field property (type SYMBOL))
  (field is (type SYMBOL))
  (field cert (type FLOAT))
)

(deftemplate meal
  (field property (type SYMBOL))
  (field is (type SYMBOL))
)
```

continued

```
(deftemplate decision
  (field re (type SYMBOL))
  (field is (type SYMBOL))
)

;; FACTS

(deffacts the-facts
  (task dish)
)
; Production rules of the form

; (defrule <rulename> <RHS> => <LHS>).

;; RULES THAT FIND OUT ABOUT THE DISH.

; This corresponds to the data abstraction stage.

; dish-type is the rule invoked first because its calling
; pattern is put into WM by the fact list when CLIPS is reset.

(defrule dish-type
  (initial-fact)
  (task dish)
  =>
  (printout
     t crlf
     "Is the main dish of the meal MEAT, FISH or POULTRY?"
     t crlf)
  (assert (meal (property dish-type) (is (read))))
)

; meat finds out more about the dish, if it is meat.

(defrule meat
  (task dish)
  (meal (property dish-type) (is meat))
  =>
  (printout
     t crlf
     "What kind of meat? for example STEAK, VEAL, LAMB"
     t crlf)
  (assert (meal (property meat-type) (is (read))))
)

; You can write a similar rule for fish distinguishing, e.g.
; wet fish from shell fish; also a rule for poultry.

;; RULES THAT SUGGEST WINE PROPERTIES

; This is the heuristic matching stage.

; steak is an example of a meat rule which suggests wine
; properties.
```

continued

```
(defrule steak
  ?task <- (task dish)
  (meal (property meat-type) (is steak))
  =>
  (assert (wine (property color) (is red) (cert 1.0)))
  (assert (wine (property body) (is full) (cert 1.0)))
  (assert (wine (property flavor) (is dry) (cert 0.7)))
  (assert (wine (property flavor) (is sweet) (cert 0.2)))
  (retract ?task)
  (assert (task attributes))
)

; You can write similar rules for lamb, veal, etc.
; We remove the dish task once we know what the dish is.
; Then we set up the task of deciding upon wine attributes.

; You should have default rules for meat, fish and poultry,
; which catch any cases, such as alligator, that you have not
; anticipated.

;; RULES THAT HANDLE CERTAINTIES

; If there are two structures in WM with the same value for
; the same attribute but with different certainties then
; attribute-update creates a third structure with a new
; value and deletes the other two.

; The formula for computing the new CF is
;    cf = cf1 + cf2(1 - cf1)

(defrule attribute-update
  (task attributes)
  ?wine1 <- (wine (property ?attribute) (is ?value) (cert
  ?cert1))
  ?wine2 <- (wine (property ?attribute) (is ?value) (cert
  ?cert2))
  (<> ?cert1 ?cert2)
  =>
  (bind ?newcert (+ ?cert1 (* ?cert2 (- 1 ?cert1))))
  (assert (wine (property ?attribute) (is ?value) (cert
  ?newcert)))
  (retract ?wine1)
  (retract ?wine2)
)

; Write a rule called preference, which is only invoked if there
  is
; more than one possible value for an attribute in working
; memory. The rule should ask the user's preference and change
; the certainty of the relevant attribute-value combination to
; unity, deleting theother values from working memory.

; Write a rule called choose-value which fires if there are two
; structures in working memory which carry different values
```

continued

```
; under the same attribute. The rule should choose the
; structure with the greater CF and delete the other.

; Write a rule called unique, which fires if there is only one
; candidate value for an attribute, and declares the attribute
; done.

; Write a rule called unity, which fires if a particular value
; is definite (has CF = 1) and declares the attribute done.

; If all the attributes of the wine are done then report them.

(defrule all-attributes-done
  ?task <- (task attributes)
  ?col <- (color done)
  ?bod <- (body done)
  ?fla <- (flavor done)
  (wine (property color) (is ?colour))
  (wine (property body) (is ?body))
  (wine (property flavor) (is ?flavor))
  =>
  (printout
    t crlf
    "Try a " ?flavor " " ?color " wine with a " ?body " body"
    t crlf)
  (retract ?col)
  (retract ?bod)
  (retract ?fla)
  (retract ?task)
  (assert (task brand))
)

; RULES FOR THE WINE

; Select a wine, given an attribute-value description.

; This corresponds to the solution refinement stage.
; Generate all the candidates before you offer selections to
; the user.

; Write a rule called go-choose which selects the highest
; scoring wine when no other rules will fire to propose any
; more wines.

; soave is a sample wine rule. Write as many as you like.

(defrule soave
  (task brand)
  (wine (property color) (is white))
  (wine (property flavor) (is dry) (cert ?cert1))
  (wine (property body) (is fine) (cert ?cert2))
  =>
  (assert
```

continued

```
      (wine (property brand) (is soave) (cert (min ?cert1
      ?cert2)))))
)

; RULES FOR PRESENTING SELECTIONS

; The user responds to these by typing 'yes' or 'no'.

; Write a rule called selection which finds the highest scoring
; wine and offers it to the user.

; Write a rule called rejection which deals with a negative
; response to the current suggestion.
; acceptance ends the session on the correct obsequious note.

(defrule acceptance
  (task choice)
  (decision (re ?candidate) (is yes))
  =>
  (printout t crlf "Sir/Madam has impeccable taste" t crlf)
  (halt)
)
```

(ii) How easy would it be to change the search strategy, for example to generate candidate wines in rough order of 'goodness' and offer them to the user as they appear, rather than generating all possible candidates first?

12 Heuristic Classification (II)

12.1 Mapping tools to tasks
12.2 Heuristic classification in MUD and MORE
12.3 Making strategy more explicit
Bibliographical notes
Study suggestions

In this chapter, we continue to develop the distinction between classification and construction tasks outlined in Chapter 11. The emphasis will be on problem solving methods, including different kinds of knowledge representation and inference engine. In particular, we shall

- look more closely at the kinds of software tool that are most suitable for constructing systems that use method of heuristic classification;
- examine a more up-to-date example of heuristic classification than MYCIN and its EMYCIN derivatives; and
- see how an automated knowledge elicitation system for this example can benefit from the possession of knowledge concerning the problem solving method to be employed.

We focus on heuristic classification as a problem solving method because it appears to be relatively well understood. In the next several chapters, we shall examine other methods, which can be profitably compared and contrasted with heuristic classification. However, here our concern is to examine the *process* of choosing an expert system building tool, and a knowledge acquisition tool, given that a problem solving method has been selected.

12.1 Mapping tools to tasks

Clancey (1985) notes that, although rule-based languages such as EMYCIN omit many of the refinements of his model of heuristic classification, they have provided a good programming tool for classification tasks, such as diagnosis. Thus neither MYCIN nor EMYCIN-based systems contained a specific taxonomy of symptoms or disorders, as Clancey recommends, but the fact that solutions are enumerated in advance means that backward chaining can be employed to reason from solution abstractions to relevant data via data abstractions which are implicit in the rules. The fact that productions in the rule set are indexed in terms of the medical parameters that they cite renders this goal-directed strategy easy to implement.

Other features of MYCIN that we have already observed are:

- the rejection of backtracking in favor of destructive modification of working memory; and
- the exhaustive nature of the basic search strategy (apart from various heuristic devices, such as pruning branches of the tree when certainty falls below a certain level).

These two features are closely related. We never need to backtrack because we pursue multiple lines of evidence independently and rank hypotheses at the end. If the search were not more or less exhaustive, some form of backtracking would be required in the course of best-first search, as we saw in Chapter 2. Backtracking is extremely expensive, because old states of the computation must be saved in case we decide to return to them. On large search spaces, the memory consumed will typically affect performance, for example, by forcing paging. On the other hand, it can also be expensive to fire every rule that will fire, so not all systems do this. Many take a hill-climbing approach (see Section 2.1.2) in which a rule application counts as an irrevocable decision. Some rather localized backtracking may be required, however (see Chapter 14 and the appendix).

In constructive problem solving, such a simple control regime is seldom appropriate. Design and configuration problems typically present a problem solver with many alternative ways to proceed, not all of which turn out well. In many cases, there are no good evaluation functions that one can employ to guide search, because the suitability of a solution is not dependent upon isolated features of a design, but rather more global properties that are only discernible in the finished product. For example, when arranging furniture in a room, there are certain *constraints* that one might wish to satisfy; for example, desk by the window, bookcase by the desk, sofa opposite the television, and so on. However, a proposed solution can satisfy such constraints while failing to satisfy other more global properties, for example allowing a clear path across the room, or having the furniture evenly distributed.

We shall see in Chapters 14 and 15 how additional strategies for controlling search are typically required by constructive tasks. These include

- *least commitment*, that is, deferring decisions that constrain future choices for as long as possible;
- *propose and revise*, that is, attempting to fix constraint violations as you go along; and
- various forms of *backtracking* which undo some recent decisions and restart from a particular choice point.

Mapping such methods to types of task is still something of a research issue.

Nevertheless, the identification of a level of task analysis that is grounded in problem solving methods, such as heuristic classification, is essential to the task of choosing software tools to do the job. This level appears to be situated between the 'higher' conceptual and epistemological levels that we met in Chapter 10, and the 'lower' logical or implementational levels. Without it, we appear to lack useful generalizations that link task types to inference structures and representation languages.

12.2 Heuristic classification in MUD and MORE

In this section, we examine some of the consequences of Clancey's analysis for knowledge acquisition. First we review an expert system for drilling problems (MUD) that uses the method of heuristic classification to good effect. Then we describe a knowledge elicitation prototype (called MORE) for this system which links acquisition strategies to the problem solving method employed.

As in MYCIN, MUD's knowledge acquisition process is mostly concerned with the mapping between solutions and data. However, other kinds of knowledge, for example hierarchical relationships between data and solution abstractions, heuristics for unfolding the search space, and so forth, tended to be only implicitly represented in MYCIN's rules. The 'MUD and MORE' approach makes this knowledge more explicit since, like OPAL (see Chapter 10), it uses an intermediate representation that serves as a model of the domain.

12.2.1 A model of the drilling fluid domain

The MUD system (Kahn and McDermott, 1984) assists an engineer in maintaining drilling fluid at installations such as oil rigs. It does this by diagnosing problems with the fluid, based on a description of its properties, and suggesting various causes and remedies. Changes in the fluid, such as sudden increase in viscosity during drilling, can be caused by a variety of factors, such as high temperature or pressure, or a wrong mix of chemical additives.

MUD is implemented in the production rule language OPS5 (a forebear of CLIPS), and its rules map changes in fluid properties (data abstractions) to possible causes of these changes (solution abstractions). The following rule, given in an English translation, is typical:

```
IF:    (1) there is a decrease in density of the fluid, and
       (2) there is an increase in viscosity (of the fluid),
THEN:  moderately (7) suspect that there has been an influx of
       water.
```

The numbers in parentheses are certainty factors; these are combined in the manner of MYCIN (see Chapter 3). Thus, in order to determine the likelihood of an influx of water, each rule that could contribute evidence for or against this hypothesis is considered. Measures of belief and disbelief are derived as described in Chapter 9, and the certainty in the hypothesis is the difference between these two measures.

Kahn's experience was that experts often found it difficult to provide the necessary rules for the heuristic classification approach. The rule format did not always correspond to the way in which they thought about their knowledge or communicated it amongst themselves. Experts sometimes have problems assigning certainty factors to new rules, and typically like to review rules that they have already written, for the purposes of comparison. Often experts use the certainty factors to produce a partial ordering with respect to a particular conclusion. Buchanan and Shortliffe (1984, Chapter 7) also found that experts sometimes need to know details of the control regime and the propagation of certainty factors in order to write effective rules.

In building heuristic classification programs like MUD and MYCIN, rule writing and refinement is essentially a six-step process:

(1) The expert tells the knowledge engineer what rules to add or modify.
(2) The knowledge engineer makes changes to the knowledge base.
(3) The knowledge engineer runs one or more old cases for consistency checking.
(4) If any problems arise with old cases, the knowledge engineer discusses them with the expert, and then goes to Step 1.
(5) The expert runs the modified system on new cases.
(6) If no problems are discovered, then the process halts, else we return to Step 1.

As we saw in Section 10.2, the architects of MYCIN kept this basic framework, but attempted to improve the efficiency of some of the steps with various tools, for example the abbreviated rule language and explanation facility of EMYCIN, and a library of test cases for running in batch mode.

Kahn and his coworkers (Kahn *et al.*, 1985; Kahn, 1988) took a different route in the construction of the MORE system: a knowledge elicitation program which uses both knowledge of the domain and knowledge of the problem solving strategy to flesh out the MUD knowledge base. Like OPAL, MORE has a domain model incorporating important relationships between domain concepts. It uses this knowledge to guide the interview with the expert, recognize errors in the assignment of confidence factors, and generate rules that perform heuristic classification.

A domain model for MORE has the following ingredients:

- *symptoms* that we may observe during diagnosis and seek to explain;
- *attributes* that serve to further discriminate symptoms, for example rapid increase or decrease in some property;
- events that are possible causes of symptoms and therefore serve as *hypotheses*;
- *background conditions* which make symptoms more or less likely given the occurrence of a hypothetical cause, and conditions which make hypotheses more or less likely;

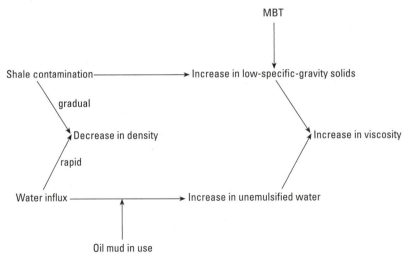

Figure 12.1 A fragment of a MORE model of the MUD domain (adapted from Kahn (op cit. 1998).

- *tests* that can be used to determine the presence or absence of any such background conditions;
- *test conditions* that have a bearing upon the accuracy of the tests.

This knowledge is organized into a network that makes explicit the connection between causes and symptoms, as well as the connection between conditions and the states or events that they facilitate or inhibit. Figure 12.1 shows a network fragment from the MUD domain.

Shale contamination and *water influx* are hypotheses which between them cause the four symptoms *decrease in density, increase in low-specific-gravity-solids, increase in unemulsified water* and *increase in viscosity*, which are all properties of the drilling fluid caused by contamination. Note that causal links can be qualified by the degree of onset of the symptom. *MBT* is the methylene blue test for the increase of solids in the fluid, while *oil mud in use* is a background condition that has a bearing on the causal connection between the influx of water and the increase in unemulsified water.

BOX 2.1

Knee-deep in MUD

Here is a rendering of some diagnostic rules for the MUD domain based on Figure 12.1 and implemented as a CLIPS program. If you run it, and answer both questions in the affirmative, it should conclude that both shale contamination and water influx are possible explanations of the data. Answering 'no' to one of the questions will cause one hypothesis to win over the other.

```
;; TEMPLATES

(deftemplate symptom
  (field datum (type SYMBOL))
  (field change (type SYMBOL))
  (field degree (type SYMBOL) (default NIL))
)

(deftemplate hypothesis
  (field object (type SYMBOL))
  (field event (type SYMBOL))
  (field status (type SYMBOL) (default NIL))
)

(deftemplate testing
  (field name (type SYMBOL))
  (field for (type SYMBOL))
  (field status (type SYMBOL) (default NIL))
)

;; FACTS

(deffacts mud
  (symptom (datum viscosity) (change increase))
  (symptom (datum density) (change decrease) (degree gradual))
  (testing (name MBT) (for low-SG-solids))
  (testing (name oil-mud) (for unemulsified-water))
)
```

continued

```
;; RULES

;; Rules that reason backward from viscosity.
(defrule viscosity
  (symptom (datum viscosity) (change increase))
  =>
  (assert (hypothesis (object low-SG-solids) (event increase)))
  (assert (hypothesis (object unemulsified-water)
                      (event increase)))
)

;; Rules that reason backward from changes in density.
(defrule density
  (symptom (datum density) (change decrease) (degree gradual))
  =>
  (assert (hypothesis (object shale) (event contamination)))
)

(defrule density
  (symptom (datum density) (change decrease) (degree rapid))
  =>
  (assert (hypothesis (object water) (event influx)))
)

;; Evidence for shale contamination.
(defrule shale
  ?effect <- (hypothesis (object low-SG-solids) (event increase)
                         (status yes))
  =>
  (assert (hypothesis (object shale) (event contamination)
                      (status yes)))
  (modify ?effect (status done))
)

;; Evidence for water influx.
(defrule water
  ?effect <- (hypothesis (object unemulsified-water)
                         (event increase) (status yes))
  =>
  (assert (hypothesis (object water) (event influx) (status yes)))
  (modify ?effect (status done))
)

;; Find a test for a hypothesis.
(defrule peek-test
  (hypothesis (object ?obj) (event ?change))
  ?operator <- (testing (name ?name) (for ?obj) (status NIL))
  =>
  (printout t crlf "Is there " ?obj " " ?change " according to
   the " ?name " test? ")
  (modify ?operator (status (read)))
)
```

continued

```
;; Apply test result to hypothesis.
(defrule poke-test
  ?cause <- (hypothesis (object ?obj) (event ?change))
  ?operator <- (testing (name ?name) (for ?obj) (status yes))
  =>
  (modify ?cause (status yes))
  (modify ?operator (status done))
)

;; Print out active hypotheses.
(defrule show-and-tell
  (hypothesis (object ?obj) (event ?ev) (status yes))
  =>
  (printout t crlf ?obj " " ?ev " is a possibility" t crlf)
)
```

12.2.2 Knowledge acquisition strategies

Kahn and his colleagues attacked the knowledge elicitation problem from two directions. On the one hand, they noted the interview techniques used by knowledge engineers in the construction of the MUD system. On the other hand, they analyzed these techniques in terms of the problem solving method of heuristic classification used by MUD. As a result, they identified eight knowledge acquisition strategies, which are worth summarizing below. Each of these strategies is used by the MORE program to elicit knowledge for confirming or ruling out hypotheses during diagnosis.

- *Differentiation.* Seek symptoms that distinguish between hypotheses, for example symptoms that have only one cause. Such one-to-one mappings between symptom and disorder are called *pathognomic* associations in the medical literature.
- *Frequency conditionalization.* Determine any background conditions that make a particular hypothesis more or less likely. In decision-theoretic approaches to diagnosis, the degree of evidential support lent by a symptom to a disorder should depend upon the prior probability of the disorder.
- *Symptom distinction.* Identify special properties of symptoms that indicate the underlying cause. Thus, in Figure 12.1, we see that a rapid decrease in the density of the drilling fluid suggests an influx of water, rather than shale contamination.
- *Symptom conditionalization.* Find out the conditions under which different symptoms might be expected to manifest themselves, given a particular disorder. Such conditions set up expectations which may serve to rule out hypotheses if they are not confirmed.
- *Path division.* Attempt to uncover intermediate events between a hypothesized disorder and an expected symptom, which have a higher conditional probability of occurrence than the symptom itself. Failing to observe such intermediate events constitutes stronger evidence against a hypothesis than failing to observe the symptom.
- *Path differentiation.* As in path division, elaborate causal pathways between disorder and symptom. Here the motivation is to discover intermediate events that will allow us to differentiate between disorders which have similar symptoms.

- *Test differentiation*. Determine the degree of confidence to be placed in test results. Evidence is normally the result of tests which have varying degrees of reliability.
- *Test conditionalization*. Determine the background conditions that affect the reliability of tests. Such information has a bearing upon the significance of observations in particular cases.

MORE begins by eliciting from an expert some basic information concerning diagnosable disorders and observable symptoms. Then it evokes knowledge acquisition strategies selectively, based upon its current state of knowledge. It is worth looking at MORE's knowledge representation in more detail, in order to understand the conditions under which the different strategies are deployed.

The MORE domain requires three kinds of production rule:

- *Diagnostic rules*. These perform the heuristic mapping between symptoms and hypotheses typically found in systems like MYCIN, ONCOCIN, and MUD.
- *Symptom confidence rules*. These qualify the data abstraction implicit in the symptom space with estimates of test reliability under different background conditions.
- *Hypothesis expectancy rules*. These qualify the solution abstraction implicit in the hypothesis space with estimates of the prior probability of hypotheses under different background conditions.

MUD's diagnostic rules differ from MYCIN's in that they have *two* confidence factors associated with them: a positive and a negative one. The positive factor represents the degree of support for the conclusion when the rule's conditions are satisfied, while the negative factor represents the amount of disbelief in the conclusion when the rule's condition is not satisfied. Symptom confidence and hypothesis expectancy rules only use one confidence factor. For symptom confidence rules, the value represents the degree of change in the system's confidence in an observation. For hypothesis expectancy rules, the value represents degree of change in the expected likelihood of a hypothesis, given the rule's conditions.

MORE maintains both an *event model* and a *rule model*. The event model consists of symptoms, hypotheses and conditions, connected together by links, as in Figure 12.1. This representation is used to generate the required production rules, rather as OPAL generates rules from its domain model.

More precisely, MORE generates whole *families* of diagnostic rules, one for each diagnostic hypothesis. For example, MORE might generate the following diagnostic rule directly from the MUD event model:

```
If there is an increase in chlorides          [rule 1]
Then there is salt contamination.
```

However, this rule is too general. It needs qualifying, for example by the strategy of symptom distinction, which identifies the effect of background conditions upon the significance of a symptom. The following rule might therefore be added to the *salt contamination* rule family:

```
If there is an increase in chlorides          [rule 2]
and the drilling fluid is undersaturated
Then there is salt contamination.
```

MORE manages its rule families in the following way. When it learns of a new condition relevant to a hypothesis, it creates a new, single-condition rule and adds it to the rule family for that hypothesis. If this condition is relevant to other rules already in the rule family, then this condition will be added to those rules. (If the new condition does not manifest itself with other conditions in a rule, then that rule is not modified.) Rules to which a new condition has been added are called *constituent rules*; these are discussed further in the following section on confidence factors.

Symptom distinction is an example of a strategy which serves to refine existing diagnostic rule families. It is called into play when a family contains no rules with extreme positive confidence factors. The initial rule given above is too general to be given a high confidence factor and, since it is the only rule in the rule family, symptom distinction is called upon to refine the rule. Eventually, rules like `rule1`, whose conditions are subsumed by those of other rules, are eliminated from the family. This can be seen as enforcing (in advance) the preference for more specific rules found in most conflict resolution strategies.

Symptom conditionalization, on the other hand, is evoked when there are no rules in a family that have extreme *negative* confidence factors. In this case, MORE attempts to elicit background conditions that make a symptom more or less likely, given the hypothesis. Knowledge of conditions that increase the likelihood of a symptom allows the problem solver to rule out a hypothesis if a strongly suggested symptom does not occur.

Other strategies – such as differentiation, path differentiation and path division – serve to create *new* rule families. The differentiation strategy is pursued when MORE discovers a pair of hypotheses, H_1 and H_2, which have no *differentiating symptom*; that is there is no symptom in the event model which is linked to H_1 but not to H_2, and are therefore, for all practical purposes, in the same family. MORE elicits such a symptom, and adds it to the event model with appropriate links. This more elaborate event model will then be used to generate a distinct rule family for each of H_1 and H_2.

The path differentiation strategy is selected when a symptom in the event model is linked to two different hypotheses. MORE elicits from the expert an intermediate event that causes the symptom, and is caused by one hypothesis but not the other. Observing such an event will help discriminate between the competing explanations of the symptom, and so a rule family is created for it.

The path division strategy is evoked when a rule family is found to lack a rule which associates a high negative confidence factor with failure to observe a symptom of that family's hypothesis. MORE then seeks an intermediate event which is caused by the hypothesis. Failure to observe such an event will constitute stronger evidence against the hypothesis than failure to observe the symptom, and so a rule family is created for it.

The remaining strategies – frequency conditionalization, test differentiation and test conditionalization – are pursued when a rule family lacks a rule with either a high or a low positive or negative confidence factor. In such a situation, the rules are not informative enough to solve the classification problem. Eliciting information about (i) new tests and test conditions, and (ii) estimates concerning the prior probabilities of hypotheses under various background conditions, will tend to either increase or reduce the confidence factors of heuristic rules mapping symptoms to hypotheses. Information of the first kind is ultimately turned into symptom confidence rules, while information of the second kind is turned into hypothesis expectancy rules.

12.2.3 Confidence factors in MORE

We mentioned earlier that experts often have problems assigning certainty factors to rules, and like to review rules that they have already written, for the purposes of comparison. They are obviously striving for some notion of consistency in both the degree of significance that they accord to different pieces of evidence and the strength of the association between evidence and hypotheses. The question then arises as to how experts can best be helped with this task.

MORE entertains expectations about the assignment of confidence factors to rules. If the values assigned to rules violate any of these expectations, MORE cautions the knowledge engineer, and explains the inconsistency. The user then has the option of modifying one of the 'conflicting' confidence factors.

MORE's expectations concerning confidence factors are as follows.

Suppose that a disorder D leads to a symptom, S_1, and S_1 leads to another symptom, S_2. Then MORE expects that the negative confidence factor associated with the rule that maps S_1 to D will be greater than or equal to the negative confidence factor associated with the rule that maps S_2 to D. In Figure 12.2, we expect that $C1 \geq C_2$, where C_1 weights the association between S_1 and D, and C_2 weights the association between S_2 and D.

The intuitive idea behind this expectation is that failure to observe S_1 is stronger evidence against D than failure to observe S_2, all other things being equal. Referring back to Figure 12.1, the negative association between *water influx* and *increase in unemulsified water* should be greater than that between *water influx* and *increase in viscosity*.

The diagnostic significance of a symptom is an inverse function of the number of hypotheses that could account for that symptom. In Figure 12.3, MORE expects that $C_1 > C_2$, because S_1 is only caused by D_1, whereas S_2 could be caused by other disorders.

MORE has expectations regarding the relative values of confidence factors associated with rules in the same rule family. (Recall that rule families are formed by rules which draw conclusions about the same hypothesis.) For example, when we add to a rule family a symptom condition which increases the conditional likelihood of the symptom, this should result in rules which have greater negative confidence factors than their constituent rules. (Recall that constituent rules are the extant rules to which the new condition was added.) The rationale behind this expectation is that the more we anticipate a particular symptom, given a particular hypothesis, the greater our shift towards disbelief in the hypothesis if that symptom is not observed.

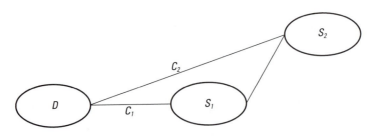

Figure 12.2 **Negative confidence factors in causal chains.**

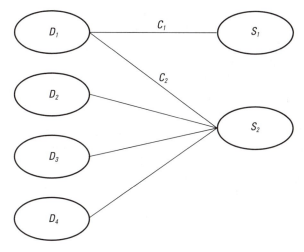

Figure 12.3 **Positive confidence factors where there are many causes.**

Each of these expectations attempts to enforce certain qualitative notions of consistency upon the assignment of confidence factors to rules within a family. The notion of a rule family is crucial here, as it was in the implementation of MYCIN, where rules were also grouped according to the parameters that they updated.

12.2.4 Evaluating MORE

In his thesis, Shortliffe (1976) acknowledged the need for a knowledge elicitation mechanism to help the expert with problems such as consistency and independence in assigning weights to MYCIN production rules. Buchanan and Shortliffe (1984, Chapter 10, Section 5) reprint a number of memos which discuss some salient issues. These are also worth reading because they discuss the question of how easy it is to add rules to the rule set and modify existing rules.

MORE clearly goes some way towards helping to enforce notions of consistency which are both intuitively reasonable and easy to understand. However, MORE does not address the problem of independence that Shortliffe raised. We saw in Chapter 6 that the application of Bayes' theorem requires that evidences be independent if we are to combine weights of evidence using a simple multiplication scheme.

Shortliffe suggested that dependent pieces of evidence should be grouped into single rather than multiple rules, and treated as a 'super symptom' whose weight approximates that of the conjunction of individual symptoms. MORE does not appear to enforce this preference, although it has some of the necessary information in the event model, given that the latter encodes causal relationships. Such empirical studies as have been performed confirm that confidence factors diverge most widely from probabilities when independence assumptions are violated (for example, Shortliffe and Buchanan, *op.cit.*, Chapter 11, Section 5).

Kahn acknowledges a number of other problems with the MORE prototype.

- Users would have preferred MORE to infer rule weights somehow from the event model, and ask far fewer questions in general.

- Concepts such as *hypothesis* and *symptom* were not familiar to domain experts in factory-floor applications, whose knowledge appeared to be encoded in troubleshooting procedures for dealing with different kinds of breakdown.
- A conventional alphanumeric interface to the system was judged to be 'completely inadequate' even for the purposes of experimenting with the prototype.

The last point shows how important the man–machine interface to an expert system is. Unless users can easily understand what they see on the screen, and search effectively for the information that they need, they will not understand what the system is doing. Development and debugging is greatly enhanced by the use of mouse- and window-oriented graphic displays which enable a user to interleave the activities of browsing, editing, and executing programs.

Another problem was that MORE was implemented in OPS5, and so the event model had to be coded in terms of complex vectors held in working memory. Such a representation is not well suited to the encoding of causal knowledge, and so the event model was hard to build, modify, and maintain. With the benefit of hindsight, we can see that a structured object representation (see Chapter 6) should have been used.

Since MORE, a number of programs have been written which set out to elicit knowledge for expert systems that do heuristic classification, and we shall encounter one of these programs (TDE) in the next chapter.

12.3 Making strategy more explicit

When heuristic knowledge has been encoded as an initial set of production rules, the knowledge engineer's task is far from over. Both researchers and practitioners have come to realize that the subsequent development of a knowledge base is at least as difficult as creating that first version. Problems attach to both the task of managing a large set of rules and the task of further refining those rules to ensure their correct behavior.

Software tools such as MORE, with their associated methodologies, are certainly part of the answer to these problems. But some aspects of these problems seem to be inherent in the rule-based approach, and require a rethinking of the ways in which rule sets are organized. In this section, we attempt a review of current thinking on such matters.

12.3.1 Lessons of the GUIDON project

Clancey (1983) presents a critique of the use of unstructured sets of production rules in expert systems, largely based upon his experience in attempting to adapt MYCIN for teaching purposes in the GUIDON project (see, for example, Clancey 1987a). His main argument is that the uniform '*if … then*' syntax of production rules hides the fact that such rules often perform very different functions and are correspondingly constructed in different ways. Certain structural and strategic decisions about the representation of domain knowledge are therefore implicit in the rules, and therefore not explicitly represented anywhere.

We have already seen that production rules of the general form

$$P_1, \ldots, P_m \rightarrow Q_1, \ldots, Q_n$$

have an informal reading along the lines of

```
if premises P₁ and ... and Pₘ are true,
then perform actions Q₁ and ... and Qₙ.
```

Now the order of the P_i is immaterial with respect to this declarative reading, since $P_1 \wedge P_2$ is entirely equivalent to $P_2 \wedge P_1$ in any standard logic. However, the order of the P_i is material to the procedural interpretation of such rules, just as it is material in logic programming. Different orderings of conjuncts will produce quite different search spaces which will be traversed in different ways, as we saw in Chapter 8. Similarly, the order in which rules for a goal are tried will affect the order in which subgoals are generated. Making sure that conflict resolution tries the most 'likely' rules first can save search effort in the majority of cases.

The problem is that the criteria for rule and clause ordering are only *implicit* in the rule set. Knowledge about which rules to try first and the best order for considering conjuncts is really meta-knowledge, that is, knowledge about how to apply knowledge. There is little doubt that such knowledge is a crucial aspect of expertise that is difficult to capture and codify.

Clancey argues that rule-based systems require an epistemological framework which somehow makes sense of the domain-specific knowledge one is seeking to represent. In other words, inference rules relevant to some problem domain are often implicitly embedded in knowledge of a more abstract kind. The best way to explain this is to use Clancey's own example; look at the rule in Figure 12.4.

The ordering of the conjuncts in this rule is extremely significant. Obviously one needs to establish a hypothesis concerning the nature of the infection (1) before one can decide whether or not the evidence for it is circumstantial (2). Bacterial meningitis is a subclass distinct from viral meningitis, and so (3) can be seen as a refinement of (1). Finally, the decision to delay the test at (4) is probably a strategic one. Making this the first clause would alter the shape of the search space, perhaps causing subsequent tests to be pruned if this one failed.

Knowledge representation means making knowledge explicit, but production systems leave a number of general principles for controlling search implicit. This is probably why adding and deleting rules or conditions often has unexpected effects. A purely declarative reading of the rules leads us to expect one outcome, but their procedural interpretation determines another outcome.

```
   IF:     1) The infection is meningitis,
           2) Only circumstantial evidence is available,
           3) The type of infection is bacterial,
           4) The patient is receiving corticosteroids,

   THEN: There is evidence that the organisms involved are
               e.coli (.4)
               klebsiella-pneumoniae (.2) or
               pseudomonas-aeruginosa (.1).
```

Figure 12.4 A simplified version of MYCIN rule no. 543.

Clancey offers a rather attractive analysis of the different kinds of knowledge that make up the epistemological framework of a rule-based system. The main components are described as structural knowledge, strategic knowledge, and support knowledge. It is worth considering each of these in turn.

- *Structural knowledge* consists of the different levels of abstraction through which one can view the knowledge domain. Taxonomy is perhaps the most obvious example of a source of knowledge which is not normally represented explicitly in production rules. The knowledge that meningitis is an infection which can be either acute or chronic, bacterial or viral, and so on, is implicit in many of the premises.
- *Strategic knowledge* is knowledge about how to approach a problem by choosing an ordering on methods and subgoals which minimizes effort in the search for a solution. For example, the rule of thumb that compromised hosts (for example, alcoholics) are likely to have an unusual etiology can lead the expert to focus upon less common causes of infection first. Such knowledge typically interacts with structural knowledge, for example such a heuristic might be linked to bacterial meningitis, rather than viral.
- *Support knowledge* is typically knowledge involving a causal model of the domain of discourse which explains why certain contingencies typically hold. Thus, the MYCIN rule which links steroid use with gram-negative rod organisms causing bacterial meningitis has as its rationale the fact that steroids impair the immuno-response system. Again, such knowledge makes contact with structural knowledge concerning the classification of diseases and the classification of organisms.

It should be clear that much of this background knowledge does not lend itself to being explicitly represented by production rules. Structural knowledge is best represented by complex data objects, such as frames, while some kinds of control information may be inherently procedural. Support knowledge may be relegated to the documentation of the program, but it must be accessible to the explanation program. Forcing these different kinds of knowledge into the same format can have a deleterious effect upon the clarity and utility of the representation, in spite of the ingenious things that one can do with rule and conjunct orderings. As in all forms of programming, the need for excessive 'cleverness' in the code is usually a sign of inferior program design.

12.3.2 NEOMYCIN's task structure

The lessons of GUIDON led Clancey to develop a more complex model of diagnostic behavior called NEOMYCIN: a consultation system whose medical knowledge base was used in a new tutoring program, called GUIDON2. NEOMYCIN can be contrasted with MYCIN in two main ways:

- The reasoning procedure that the program uses is more clearly separated from the content of the production rules, as discussed in the previous section on GUIDON.
- The reasoning procedure can work both *forwards* from findings, such as signs and symptoms associated with the chief complaint, and *backwards* from hypotheses suggested by such findings.

Thus, the flow of information and control within the program is more independent of the product rules and their interpreter than was the case in MYCIN, which tended to perform an exhaustive, top-down search. MYCIN asked questions and collected information when it ran out of rules that it could apply in order to deduce some fact. In this respect, it resembled the rather simplistic 'query the user' facility sometimes used in logic programming, in which the interactive user of the program is allowed to enter facts that help complete a proof. By contrast, NEOMYCIN's control structure can best be described as a variety of hypothesize and test, in which findings suggest an initial hypothesis which is evaluated against its competitors. Consequently, the questions asked are dictated by a desire to decide between alternatives, rather than being merely the collection of data to enable a single line of reasoning to succeed or fail.

Clancey argues that NEOMYCIN is a better model of human diagnostic behavior than MYCIN, in that it incorporates more of the stages of reasoning actually observed in physicians.

For example, clinicians will usually attempt to determine the range of possible diseases that the patient could be suffering from, with a view to eventually limiting the scope of the investigation. For Clancey, this behavior is part of 'establishing the hypothesis space.' One reasoning strategy employed here is called 'group and differentiate,' that is, given a diagnostic hypothesis suggested by data, a clinician will then first gather together all the hypotheses that would account for the sign or symptom and then attempt to divide them into those that could apply in the present case and those which can be ruled out.

NEOMYCIN's diagnostic strategy is represented by a tree of tasks, with CONSULT as the top-level task, and subtasks such as IDENTIFY PROBLEM and COLLECT INFORMATION. It is this hierarchy of tasks that determines the flow of control, rather than an implicit hierarchy of rule concepts traversed by backward chaining. In addition to 'group and differentiate,' there are two other tasks that help establish the hypothesis space: 'explore and refine,' which involves pursuing a particular hypothesis, and 'ask general questions' which serves to introduce any special considerations; for example, is the patient pregnant, or has the patient had surgery recently?

Both the 'group and differentiate' and the 'explore and refine' tasks take place in the context of a complex hierarchy of disorders. 'Group and differentiate' involves examining those parts of the hierarchy above the current focus or hypothesis to look for competing hypotheses. 'Explore and refine' involves examining parts of the hierarchy below the current focus, in order the refine the diagnosis.

We shall examine the whole process of hypothesize and test in a hierarchy of alternatives in the next chapter. What is significant here is the principle of representing a program's reasoning strategy explicitly in a task structure. Although Clancey's motivation for this work was primarily the construction of intelligent tutoring systems, his work had implications for the architecture of expert systems generally.

Regardless of whether one agrees with every aspect of this analysis, its effect has been the levitate the perspective of expert system researchers and designers. Just as expert system tasks demand some form of ontological analysis to clarify the objects and relationships in the domain, so do they also require an epistemological analysis of the kinds of knowledge that experts possess about how to solve problems in that domain. This knowledge, and the reasoning steps in which it is applied, are typically too diverse to be captured in a single formalism (such as rules) and implemented under a simple control regime (such as backward chaining).

One way of looking at the problem of building expert systems (and programs generally) is to ask where you want the complexity to be. There is generally a trade-off between having a sufficiently rich design which permits a relatively clean implementation versus having an overly simple design which then requires much cleverness at the code level to make it work. This is an instance of the 'no free lunch' principle as applied to software development; work skimped at one level will have to be made up elsewhere.

BIBLIOGRAPHICAL NOTES

MOLE (Eshelman and McDermott, 1986; Eshelman *et al.*, 1987; Eshelman, 1988) is another interesting expert system shell for classification problem solving. It is rather more sophisticated, and perhaps harder to understand, than MORE, so we do not review it here. Briefly, it distinguishes between *covering knowledge* (knowledge that maps data to hypotheses) and *differentiating knowledge* (knowledge that allows one to choose between competing hypotheses), and uses this distinction to structure the processes of knowledge elicitation and knowledge base refinement.

Further discussion on the topics of heuristic classification and the epistemological underpinnings of rule-based systems can be found in Clancey (1993a, 1993b) respectively.

STUDY SUGGESTIONS

1. Why don't rule-based systems backtrack much?
2. What are the six main steps in building a knowledge-based system?
3. What is the difference between frequency conditionalization and symptom conditionalization in MORE?
4. MORE's hypothesis expectancy rules are said to 'qualify the solution abstraction implicit in the hypothesis space.' What does this mean?
5. What is the significance of background conditions in a MORE model?
6. What is the difference between an event model and a rule model in MORE?
7. What is wrong with the assignment of certainty factors shown in Figure 12.5? D is a disorder, and S_1, S_2, and S_3 are symptoms.

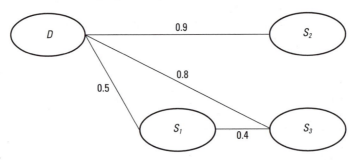

Figure 12.5

continued

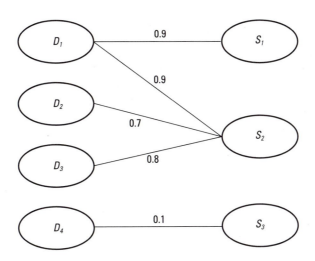

Figure 12.6

8. What is wrong with the picture in Figure 12.6? D_1–D_4 are disorders, while S_1–S_3 are symptoms.
9. Take the CLIPS program in Box 12.1 and build on it as follows.
   (i) Add new rules to the effect that

```
If there is an increase in chlorides
and the drilling fluid is undersaturated
Then there is salt contamination.

If there is salt contamination
Then there is an increase in viscosity.
```

   (ii) Assign certainty factors to arcs that link nodes in the causal diagram of Figure 12.1. Include certainty factors that link tests to test results. Do this in a way that respects the constraints outlined in Section 12.2.3. These certainty factors can all be positive.
   (iii) Then alter the template definitions so that both hypotheses and tests can have certainties associated with them.
   (iv) Finally, alter the rules, so that certainties are propagated as hypotheses are generated and tests are done. Combine certainties using the formula:

$$Z = X + Y - XY,$$

   where Z is the new certainty factor derived from the old certainties, X and Y. Thus if we conclude

```
increase in low-specific-gravity solids
```

   from both an increase in viscosity (with certainty X) and the methylene blue test (with certainty Y), then we use the formula to compute our current certainty in the hypothesis (Z), given that both pieces of evidence are operative.

continued

(v) Run and debug the program, checking out all the different ways the questions could be answered.

10. The following diagnostic model is taken from the *Owners Workshop Manual* for the BMW 320.

(i) Represent the following knowledge about automotive troubleshooting as a MORE-style domain model in the manner of Figure 12.1. In the first instance, just draw the graph.

Symptom	Causes
● Engine fails to turn	
No current at starter motor	Flat battery
	Loose battery leads
	Defective starter solenoid
	Engine earth strap disconnected
Current at starter motor	Jammed starter motor drive pinion
	Defective starter motor
● Engine turns but won't start	
No spark at spark plug	Ignition leads damp or wet
	Distributor cap damp or wet
	Dirty contact breaker points
	Incorrectly set contact breaker points
	Faulty condenser (early models)
	Defective ignition switch
	Faulty coil (early models)
No fuel at carburetor jets	No petrol in tank
	Vapor lock in fuel line (hot climate or high altitude)
	Blocked needle float chamber valve
	Blocked jets
	Faulty fuel pump
● Engine stalls and will not restart	
Carburetor flooding	Too much choke
	Float damaged
	Float lever incorrectly adjusted
No fuel at carburetor jets	No petrol in tank
	Petrol tank breather choked
	Obstruction in carburetor
	Water in fuel system

Remarks in parentheses under 'Causes' should be treated as MORE background conditions.

(ii) Put these diagnostics into a production rule format to build a CLIPS program. Background conditions should give rise to questions for the user.

13 Hierarchical Hypothesize and Test

In this chapter, we consider three systems that employ a method that combines aspects of both heuristic classification and constructive problem solving, known as *hierarchical hypothesize and test*. As in heuristic classification, one is still interested in the mapping between data abstractions and solution abstractions, but there is the added complication that solution elements so derived may need to be combined into a *composite hypothesis* in order to explain all the data. A classic example is differential diagnosis, where a patient presents with a variety of signs and symptoms, and the clinician's job is to postulate the presence of one or more disease processes that account for them all.

Admitting composite hypotheses complicates matters considerably, and calls for a structuring of the search space to make it more manageable. Hierarchical hypothesize and test attacks this problem by reasoning with an explicit taxonomic representation of the space of hypotheses; this is usually a tree whose leaves are solution elements. Not surprisingly, the knowledge representation is normally based upon structured objects organized in a hierarchy, and the pattern of hypothesis activation is guided by this organization, as well as by some overall control regime.

The CENTAUR system (Aikins, 1983) is considered first, because it is well documented and easy to understand. Then we consider another system, called INTERNIST (Pople, 1977), which is large and complex enough to address many of the problems associated with this approach. Finally, we examine a more recent system, called TEST (Kahn *et al.*, 1987), which shows that the hierarchical strategy also has some implications for knowledge elicitation.

13.1 Managing complexity

In a system like MYCIN, which deals with only a fraction of a small branch of medicine (the blood infections), exhaustive depth-first search with pruning may be an acceptable way for a machine to approach the problem of checking out alternatives.

But what if you were interested in the whole of internal medicine? The number of distinct diseases that a clinician is likely to encounter is not huge (estimates vary between two and ten thousand diagnostic categories), yet it is not unknown for a patient to be suffering from ten or more concurrent diseases. As Pople pointed out, in the worst case, an exhaustive backward-chaining program would need to consider about 10^{40} diagnostic categories!

When the solution space is potentially very large, hierarchical hypothesize and test is extremely beneficial. The search space can then be thought of as a tree which represents a taxonomy of solution types, with nodes higher up standing for 'vaguer' solutions than nodes lower down, and with terminal nodes standing for actual solutions. The process of refining hypotheses is now very much easier, because the structure of the solution space can be used to derive focusing and scheduling heuristics, as we shall see.

Figure 13.1 shows a portion of the disease hierarchy used by the CENTAUR system. The root node is PULMONARY-DISEASE, and all other nodes represent kinds of pulmonary disease (that is, lung disease). The immediate successors stand for subtypes of lung disease, such as an obstructive defect, while leaf nodes stand for kinds of obstructive defect which can be diagnosed and treated.

Of course, if one were representing the whole of internal medicine in this manner, the tree would be very large indeed. In INTERNIST, the tree is organized around the various organ systems, for example lungs, liver, heart, and so on. Although the hierarchical organization aids search, it does not abolish the problem of finding the best explanation of a set of case data, given that disease hypotheses may need to be combined to cover all the signs and symptoms.

This variation of hypothesize and test is particularly useful in cases where:

- the association between evidence and hypotheses which correspond to solutions is weak or noisy, but the association between initial data and 'non-terminal' hypotheses is reasonably good, and there exist methods for refining hypotheses and discriminating between them once they have been established;
- a fully expanded set of rules might be highly redundant, owing to a large number of shared conditions associated with many of the conclusions, or else might obscure some important structural principles implicit in the domain;

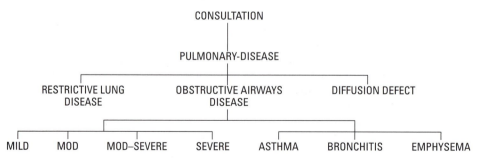

Figure 13.1 A hierarchical representation of lung diseases.

BOX 13.1

Swinging through the Trees

A simple algorithm for hierarchical hypothesize and test (HAT) can be sketched as follows. We assume a tree of hypotheses which are capable of being evoked by data. These hypotheses suggest other data that we could collect.

The HAT algorithm
(1) read in initial data;
(2) for each evoked hypothesis, give it a score which reflects what proportion of the data it accounts for;
(3) determine the best scoring node, n;
(4) if n is a terminal node, then quit, else partition the whole hypothesis space into two sets, K and L, where K contains the successors of n, and L puts n's competitors on hold;
(5) gather more data that will discriminate between the hypotheses in K, and rate them;
(6) let k be the best scoring node in K and l be the best node in L;
(7) if k scores better than l, then let n be k, else let n be l;
(8) go to (4).

End of HAT algorithm

- one is interested in explicitly representing and manipulating the space of hypotheses which are competing at any one time, rather than pursuing competing hypotheses independently;
- the conditions are not equally easy to establish, either computationally or according to other criteria such as cost or risk, and so the process of evidence gathering must itself be represented and reasoned about;
- multiple solutions and partial solutions may be possible or acceptable, for example a patient may be suffering from more than one disease, or knowing the general class of disease or the principal alternative diseases may be sufficient for some form of treatment.

The general approach used in CENTAUR involves seeing how well some (possibly idealized) representation of a hypothetical disease actually fits the facts. Nodes in CENTAUR's disease tree are activated by data, instantiated and scored on the basis of how much of the data they account for and how well they predict other data points. High-scoring nodes are placed on an agenda, to be followed up. Roughly speaking, following up means seeing how well each of the node's successors explains the data. In this way, the program converges on a set of high-scoring terminal nodes which constitute good hypotheses.

13.2 Structured objects in CENTAUR

In order to explain how CENTAUR works, it will help if we first summarize the domain of application. CENTAUR reconstructs a medical expert system called PUFF (Kunz *et al.*, 1978; Aikins *et al.*, 1984), originally implemented in EMYCIN. PUFF's task is to interpret measurements gained from certain tests of pulmonary function (that is, the working of the lungs). Typical measurements are the amount of gas in the lungs, and the rates of flow of gases into and out of the lungs. The purpose of the tests is to determine if the patient shows signs of lung disease, and gauge the severity of his or her condition.

13.2.1 The structure of prototypes

The basic idea in CENTAUR is that frame-like structures provide an explicit representation of the context in which production rules do their reasoning. This allows one to separate strategic knowledge about how to control the reasoning from situational knowledge about what can be inferred from what set of facts. In theory, this allows inferential knowledge to be put to different uses in different contexts, with gains in both economy and coherence for the knowledge representation.

Thus production rules can be conceived of as simply one kind of value for a particular kind of slot in a frame. Associating rules with slots in frames provides one mechanism for organizing rules into what appear to be natural groupings. The other slots in a given frame provide the explicit context in which its rules are applied.

The frame-like structures used in CENTAUR are *prototypes*, *components* and *facts*. Of the 24 prototypes, 21 represent disease patterns in pulmonary function, one represents knowledge common to all such diseases, while the other two represent relatively domain-free knowledge about how to run a consultation and how to review the evidence. Thus knowledge is organized around the diagnostic categories themselves, rather than this organization being implicit in a set of unstructured rules.

Prototypes in CENTAUR contain both object- and meta-level knowledge. They are arranged in a network, a portion of which is reproduced in Figure 13.1. At the top of the hierarchy is the CONSULTATION prototype, which effectively controls the way in which the consultation develops through various stages, such as initial data entry and the triggering of hypotheses. Then there is a layer of prototypes which represent different pathological states, such as RESTRICTIVE LUNG DISEASE and OBSTRUCTIVE AIRWAYS DISEASE. Finally, diseases are specialized according to their subtypes and degree of severity. Thus OBSTRUCTIVE AIRWAYS DISEASE can be categorized as MILD, MODERATE, MODERATELY SEVERE or SEVERE, while its subtypes are ASTHMA, BRONCHITIS and EMPHYSEMA.

Each prototype has slots for a number of components, which point to subframes of knowledge at the object level. Thus, associated with each pulmonary disease prototype, there are slots which represent lung tests, each of which is a frame-like structure in its own right, with its own internal structure. For example, the OAD (Obstructive Airways Disease) frame has 13 components, each with its associated name, range of plausible values, and importance measure. In addition, a component frame often contains a special slot, called 'inference rules,' which holds a set of production rules for inferring a value for that component. If no such rule set is provided, or if the rule set fails to return a value, then the system questions the user. This provision of a rule set is rather like procedural attachment: the main differences are the stylized syntax in which rules are written and the gain in modularity over the use of general procedures. Conventional procedural attachment can involve arbitrarily complex pieces of LISP code which are hard to understand and modify.

The facts that the program works with are frames with six slots, containing information about the name of the parameter, its value, the degree of certainty, its source, classification and justification.

As well as domain-specific knowledge, prototypes contain *control slots*, meta-level knowledge about how to reason with these knowledge structures. The slots hold LISP clauses for:

- instantiating a prototype, by specifying a set of components for which values should be determined;
- reacting to its confirmation or disconfirmation, by specifying the set of prototypes to be explored next;
- printing statements that summarize the final conclusion.

Each control slot can be considered as the consequent part of a rule whose condition is that the situation must match that described by the prototype.

13.2.2 Rules embedded in prototypes

The reader will remember that it is the prototype components which represent the majority of the domain-specific object-level knowledge, since it is these structures which contain information about the tests which can be used to diagnose a particular pulmonary disease. These components are the values of slots in the disease prototypes, but they have their own internal structure and are therefore prototypes in their own right. Thus, in addition to having production rules embedded in prototypes, it is true to say that there are also prototypes embedded in other prototypes. This introduces another dimension of organization in the arrangement of prototypes in addition to the hierarchical one explicitly represented in terms of types and subtypes of disease. Data structures which can be embedded in themselves in this way are often called 'recursive.'

There are five different kinds of rules used by CENTAUR:

- *Inference rules*. These are associated with components representing clinical parameters, and specify ways in which their values might be determined.
- *Triggering rules*. These are antecedent rules associated with clinical parameters which serve to advance prototypes as hypotheses with some degree of certainty.
- *Fact-residual rules*. After a conclusion has been reached, in the form of a set of confirmed prototypes, these rules attempt to account for any case data that has been left out.
- *Refinement rules*. These suggest further tests, and their execution returns a final set of prototypes with an indication of which ones account for which facts.
- *Summary rules*. These have actions which cause the information in prototypes to be translated into English and printed.

Other slots include those for general bookkeeping, for example name of the author, source of the information, and those which record the circumstances under which the prototype was evoked for explanatory purposes.

CENTAUR's rules are therefore classified according to their function. In the EMYCIN implementation of PUFF, all rules are classified as inference rules, even though many of them do other things, for example summarizing evidence and setting default values. Also, since CENTAUR rules are the values of slots, their context of application is made explicit. For example, in the EMYCIN implementation of PUFF, rules for inferring the values of clinical parameters are indexed according to which parameter features in the conclusion, or action, side of the rules, as is the case in the original MYCIN program. In CENTAUR, rules for inferring a particular parameter are stored in a slot value in the prototype component representing that parameter, and only applied within in the context of that prototype, that is, when that prototype is active.

We shall see in Chapter 18 that this 'distributed' approach to the organization of production rules is taken even further in what are called *blackboard systems*. However, CENTAUR illustrates many of the benefits of associating rules with a context of application. As well as being good software engineering, this way of structuring heuristic knowledge also aids the construction of explanations (see Chapter 16).

13.3 Model-based reasoning in INTERNIST

INTERNIST is a program which sets out to model the actual steps of diagnostic reasoning performed by human clinicians. Typically, a pattern of symptoms will evoke one or more hypotheses about what could be wrong with the patient, and these in turn give rise to expectations concerning the presence or absence of other symptoms. Further observations may lead to some hypotheses being discarded or confirmed, or they may lead to new hypotheses being entertained. The initial setting up of hypotheses is *data-driven*, in the sense that a particular manifestation will trigger a number of conjectures. The subsequent gathering of new data in an attempt to support or refute a hypothesis is *model-driven*, in the sense that it is based upon stereotypical or schematic ideas about the way in which different diseases manifest themselves.

In many reasoning tasks, including medical diagnosis, one cannot always reason directly towards one's goal (whether in a forward or a backward direction). This is because the clinician often begins with insufficient information to even formulate the problem properly. For example, he may not have enough information to delineate the space of possible diseases, or the signs and symptoms may point in more than one direction (after all, people are quite capable of suffering from more than one disease).

INTERNIST has to distinguish between a set of mutually exclusive disease hypotheses to arrive at a diagnosis. If a patient is suffering from more than one disease, then the program must find a set of diseases that account for some or all of the symptoms. It does this by considering the most likely hypothesis first, noting the symptoms covered, and then proceeding to the next likely hypothesis and so on, until all the symptoms have been accounted for.

13.3.1 Representing knowledge in a disease tree

Pople describes diagnostic inference as a four-step judgmental process, along the following lines.

(1) Clinical observations must be able to suggest candidate diseases capable of causing them.
(2) These hypothesized candidates should then generate expectations with regard to what other findings might co-occur.
(3) There needs to be some method for choosing between hypotheses on the basis of available evidence.
(4) It must be possible to group hypotheses into mutually exclusive subsets, so that the acceptance of one subset means rejection of another, otherwise you would never be able to rule anything out.

The key lies in the bidirectional relationship between diseases and their associated signs and symptoms. INTERNIST considers this link as two separate relations, evocation and manifestation, as follows.

- The EVOKE relation accounts for the way in which a manifestation can suggest the presence of a disease.
- The MANIFEST relation describes the way in which a disease can manifest itself via signs and symptoms.

INTERNIST's medical knowledge is held in the *disease tree*: a hierarchical classification of disease types. The root node in this tree stands for all known diseases, non-terminals stand for *disease areas*, for example lung disease, liver disease, while terminals stand for *disease entities*, that is, actual diseases one can diagnose and treat. This is a static data structure, separate from the main body of the program, rather like MYCIN's knowledge tables. The difference is that they play a far more active role in directing the reasoning of the program.

The INTERNIST knowledge base is constructed in the following way.

(1) The basic structure of the hierarchy is determined initially by dividing the 'root' of the disease tree into general areas of internal medicine, such as heart disease, liver disease and so on.

(2) At the next level, subcategories are introduced which group together disease areas which are similar with respect to pattern of development (pathogenesis) and mode of clinical presentation (signs, symptoms and so on).

(3) Further subdivision of these subcategories goes on until one reaches the level of 'disease entities,' that is to say, individual diseases which can be diagnosed as such.

(4) Then data are collected concerning the association between disease entities and their manifestations, including (i) a list of all the manifestations associated with a particular disease, (ii) an estimate of the likelihood that the disease is the cause of the manifestation, and (iii) an estimate of the frequency with which patients suffering from the disease will exhibit each manifestation.

(5) A list of associated manifestations $(M_1, ..., M_n)$ is attached to the representation of each disease entity, D, along with an evoking factor which estimates the likelihood $L(D, M_i)$ and a frequency factor which estimates $L(M_i, D)$, both factors being on a scale of 0–5.

(6) As well as signs, symptoms and test results associated with some disease, D, there may be other diseases which are themselves manifestations of D, that is diseases caused by the original disease, D, and such causal links are also coded in the EVOKE and MANIFEST relationships.

(7) Once all this information has been attached to the nodes representing the disease entities (which can be thought of as the 'leaves' or terminal nodes of the disease tree), there is a program which will turn the tree into a generalization hierarchy, that is to say, a tree structure in which non-terminal or 'branch' nodes share only those properties held in common by all of their successors.

(8) Finally, data about individual manifestations are entered. The most important properties of manifestations are their TYPE (for example, sign, symptom, laboratory finding, and so on) and IMPORT (an index on a 1–5 scale of how important a manifestation is).

Steps (1)–(3) create the 'superstructure' of the knowledge base, by determining its basic shape, for example the range of categories and the levels of analysis within each category. Steps (4)–(6) correspond to the entry of basic medical knowledge into the database, represented in a manner that is convenient for the consultation program to use. The estimates of likelihood and frequency allow the consultation program to 'weigh the evidence' for and against a particular hypothesis.

At step (7), the program simply computes manifestations for non-terminal nodes representing disease areas by intersecting the manifestations of successor nodes. Consequently, all manifestations associated with a particular non-terminal are also associated with every terminal or non-terminal node directly or indirectly below it in the hierarchy. For example, jaundice is a manifestation associated with particular kinds of liver disease, such as the various forms of hepatitis.

The reasoning behind this generalization procedure is as follows. It was pointed out earlier that the space of diagnostic categories for patients suffering from multiple diseases was extremely large. Because of this, conventional search methods such as depth-first search could not be expected to perform well on realistic cases. What is needed is some way of pruning this search space, or focusing the attention of the program on particular areas of the space, in such a way as to facilitate a speedy diagnosis.

The search problem would not be so acute, even in the case of multiple diseases, if there were more direct and reliable associations between diseases and their manifestations, such that the presence of a particular manifestation were sufficient to allow a clinician to conclude the presence of a particular disease. Such relations are termed 'pathognomonic,' and they do actually occur. Unfortunately it is rare for a sign or symptom to be pathognomonic in this sense; it is a property more likely to be associated with findings which come from either expensive laboratory techniques or surgical procedures that one would not recommend as a matter of routine.

However, it is possible to establish quite robust associations between common manifestations and whole areas of disease at higher levels of a disease hierarchy. Thus jaundice suggests a liver problem, while bloody sputum suggests a lung problem. INTERNIST uses such associations to 'constrict' the search space, with the intention of homing in on the correct diagnostic category at a certain level of abstraction, before proceeding to the business of arriving at the right diagnosis at the level of disease entities.

The *constrictors* of a case, in Pople's terminology, are findings which cue the setting up of hypotheses within broad categories of the disease hierarchy. However, constriction is a heuristic device; it is not guaranteed to succeed. At higher levels of the hierarchy, while some manifestations are uniquely associated with disease areas, other are only predominant, that is, they could be explained by other areas. This situation deteriorates as you go further down the hierarchy, of course.

Hence, Step (7) is taken so that the consultation program can begin to make a differential diagnosis at a fairly high level in the hierarchy, using a generalization of the pathognomonic concept. This means that whole classes of diagnoses can be ruled out before going on to make an individual diagnosis. This is one of the mechanisms which make possible the use of the attention-focusing heuristics.

Step (8) elaborates upon the properties of the manifestations themselves, as a further aid to the strategic level of diagnostic reasoning. For example, the TYPE property indicates how expensive it is to test for a manifestation, and how dangerous such a test might be for the patient, so that cheaper and safer manifestations can be followed up first. The IMPORT property indicates whether or not one can afford to ignore a particular manifestation in the context of a particular disease. Note that steps (5) and (8) represent a fairly informal method of handling uncertainty. Nevertheless, we shall see that the problems with INTERNIST were not due to any imprecision or lack of rigor in this area; rather they derived from an imperfect formulation of the hypothesis space.

Finally, note how the hierarchical structure suggests strategies for eliciting knowledge from experts. Although this task was not automated in the building of INTERNIST, we shall see in Section 13.4 how a knowledge elicitation tool can be constructed which exploits such a representation.

13.3.2 Focusing attention in INTERNIST

An INTERNIST consultation proceeds in the following way. At the start of a session, the user enters a list of manifestations. Each of these evokes one or more nodes in the disease tree.

The program creates a *disease model* for each such node, consisting of four lists:

(1) observed manifestations not associated with the disease;
(2) observed manifestations consistent with the disease;
(3) manifestations not yet observed but which are always associated with the disease;
(4) manifestations not yet observed but which are consistent with the disease.

Disease models receive positive scores for manifestations they explain and negative scores for ones they fail to explain. Both kinds of score are weighted by IMPORT, and a model gets a bonus if it is causally related to a disease that has already been confirmed. The disease models are then divided into two sets, depending upon how they relate to the most highly rated model. One partition contains the top-ranked model and all those diseases which are mutually exclusive to it, that is, its evoked 'sibling' nodes in the tree. The other contains all those diseases which are complementary to it, that is, evoked nodes in other disease areas (see Figure 13.2).

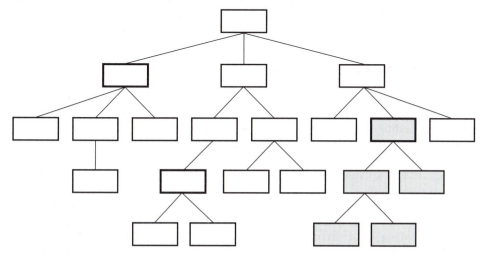

Figure 13.2 Partitioned disease tree with evoked nodes (heavy outline) and top scorer with successors (gray fill).

Partitioning involves the concept of *dominance* in the following sense. Disease model D_1 dominates model D_2 if the observed manifestations not explained by D_1 (or any part-diagnosis done so far) are a subset of those not explained by D_2. Given a top-ranked model, D_0, each member D_i of the evoked models list is compared with D_0. If D_0 either dominates it, or is dominated by it, then D_i is grouped with D_0 on the list of 'considered' hypotheses. Otherwise its consideration is deferred for the moment.

The rationale behind this kind of partitioning is that the set of models being considered at any one time can be treated as mutually exclusive alternatives. This is because, for any D_i and D_j in the set, the diagnosis consisting of D_i and D_j would add little or nothing to the explanatory power of either D_i or D_j on their own. Deferred models will be processed in similar fashion once the current problem of deciding between the models associated with D_0 has been resolved; partitioning will begin again with a new D_0, the model of best fit from among the deferred models.

After the initial input, some nodes will have been evoked and others not. The problem for the program is to transform the tree from this starting state to a solution state. A solution state consists of a tree with evoked terminal nodes which account for all of the symptoms.

Having partitioned the disease models, the program uses a number of alternative strategies, depending upon how many hypotheses it is entertaining.

- If there are more than four hypotheses, it adopts a refutation strategy (RULEOUT mode), and tries to eliminate as many as possible, asking questions about symptoms that strongly indicate the presence of candidate diseases.
- If there are between two and four possibilities, it adopts a differentiation strategy (DISCRIMINATE mode), asking questions that will help decide between candidate diseases.
- If there is only one candidate, it adopts a verification strategy (PURSUING mode), asking questions that will confirm the presence of the disease.

This whole process is iterative. Responses to queries asked in any of these modes are processed in much the same way as the original input of manifestations by the user. Thus new nodes are evoked, old nodes are updated, models are ranked and partitioned, and a (possibly new) mode is selected resulting in further questions being asked.

13.3.3 Practical and theoretical problems with INTERNIST

In summary, the INTERNIST program worked like this. During the initial input phase, patient data could be entered in any order and any amount. Each positive finding evoked a differential diagnostic task that might involve both disease areas (that is, non-terminal nodes standing for classes of disease) and disease entities (that is, terminal nodes standing for actual diseases one can diagnose and treat). Hypotheses were given credit for explaining important manifestations observed so far; they were penalized when manifestations were expected but not found in the patient. Given a ranked list of hypotheses, two disease entities were considered to be in competition if their conjunction explained no more of the data than each would explain separately. Having determined a set of alternatives in this way, the program had formulated a differential diagnostic task. The set containing the highest scoring hypothesis and its competitors then became the current focus of the problem solver.

However, it should be stressed that INTERNIST did not actually employ a simple hierarchical hypothesize and test algorithm of the general form outlined in Section 13.1. This was because symptoms which evoked a particular non-terminal node might also be significant for other nodes in the disease tree. Thus the program could not assume that the disease that the patient was actually suffering from must therefore be found among the successors of the non-terminal node. So although cholestasis accounts for symptoms of jaundice, other diseases, quite unrelated to cholestasis in the disease tree, might also exhibit such symptoms, for example, alcoholic hepatitis. Thus, although the basic idea of the disease tree is that nodes which are close to each other in the hierarchy are those which have symptoms in common, the program must often gather hypotheses from further afield when postulating a differential diagnostic task.

This departure, although necessary, caused problems. Pople (1982) later expressed dissatisfaction with INTERNIST's performance on the grounds that sometimes important patient data were disregarded by the program's control heuristics, because of a preponderance of less important findings. Since the search for a solution did not converge in quite the same way as the algorithm outlined earlier, this tended to prolong interactive sessions on difficult cases, because the program would initially set up inappropriate diagnostic tasks. Thus clinical evidence from multiple organ systems might point in different directions when considered separately, misleading the program. An experienced physician would probably integrate the data at an earlier stage to converge on a key hypothesis. Thus the simple control scheme which made the program's behavior so robust was really too simple as a model of how clinicians actually reason.

So although hierarchical hypothesize and test worked well in the application of CENTAUR to PUFF, some problems arise in scaling up to a larger domain. The method did not fail, because the INTERNIST program was still able to solve difficult problems. However, users could see that it was sometimes taking a circuitous route to the solution.

Pople concluded that the basic strategy of hierarchical hypothesize and test needed to be augmented by new knowledge structures which represent what a clinician knows about well-structured sets of alternatives. It seemed that INTERNIST still did not contain enough different kinds of knowledge concerning which disease entities are in genuine competition with each other, what strategy to employ once the differential has been constructed, and what are useful criteria for ruling hypotheses in or out. In Clancey's terminology (see Chapter 12), there were structural and strategic aspects of medical problem solving which were not represented or rendered explicit in either the organization of the hypothesis space or the inference procedure which constructed and solved differential diagnostic tasks.

13.4 TDE as knowledge engineering workbench

TDE (Kahn *et al.* 1987) is a development environment for an expert system tool called TEST (Pepper and Kahn, 1987) which is primarily intended for solving classification problems, such as diagnosis. (TEST stands for Troubleshooting Expert System Tool, and TDE stands for TEST Development Environment.) However, these programs differ from both the MYCIN/EMYCIN approach (see Chapter 10) and that of MUD/MORE (see Chapter 12), in a number of important respects.

- The primary unit of representation is the structured object, rather than the production rule. (TDE was implemented in a frame-based language called Knowledge Craft.)
- Objects represent concepts that more closely resemble the way that troubleshooters think about equipment. Thus abstract notions such as *hypothesis* and *symptom* are replaced by more concrete notions, such as *failure mode* and *test procedure* (which are explained below).
- Users organize their knowledge by manipulating icons in a high-resolution, bit-mapped interface. (As we saw in Chapter 10, OPAL also uses graphical representations to good effect.)
- The representation of knowledge has a strong procedural aspect, for example it associates test procedures with failure modes, in addition to computing degrees of belief in hypotheses as a function of the symptoms observed.

The failure mode is perhaps the most important concept in TEST and TDE: it denotes any deviation of the unit under test, whether a total breakdown or the malfunctioning of a small component. Thus, in the domain of car maintenance, 'failure to start' would be an obvious failure mode, but so would 'flat battery.' In a more traditional expert systems analysis, one would have to decide whether 'flat battery' was a hypothesis that accounted for data or a datum in itself. This distinction does not seem to be as central to TEST as it is to MUD and MYCIN. The other concepts around which knowledge is organized are

- procedures for the test and repair of failures; and
- explicit causal relationships among failures.

Failure modes are organized into a tree, with the root node typically representing device breakdown and the leaf nodes representing the failure of individual components. Non-terminal nodes represent failures of function within the device, for example 'lights not working.' Many levels of such failures are possible between total breakdown and component failures.

As with CENTAUR and INTERNIST, this tree of disorders is the primary structure of a TEST knowledge base. A secondary level of structure is provided by procedures for performing tests and repairs, as well as various kinds of rule, which represent procedural knowledge associated with failure modes, for example what measurements to make to confirm a failure, how to fix a failure, and how to search for component failures that account for a failure mode. Finally, there is a tertiary layer of declarative knowledge provided by various attributes associated with failure modes, which describe such things as important properties of components and relationships between them.

Although TEST's knowledge base is not structured around the traditional concepts of symptom and hypothesis, what TEST does is still recognizable as a form of heuristic classification. Failure modes higher up the tree represent data abstractions, while those lower down represent solution abstractions (see Figure 13.3). The task that TEST performs is to construct a causal chain from high-level failure modes, such as 'failure to start,' to lower-level modes, such as 'battery flat.' The mapping between data and solution abstractions consists of *due-to* and *always-leads-to* relations between failure modes in the tree. The heuristic aspect is encoded by attaching rules to nodes in the tree, which guide the search for lower-level modes

TDE is a relatively new system, which makes a recognizable attempt to improve on aspects of MORE. It is not possible to attempt to evaluate the prototype at the time of writing, although certain trends in the design are obvious. For example, it is clear that the graphical interface gives users more freedom in how they go about building the knowledge base than MORE did. However, novices have the option of being led by interrogation techniques, which encourage them to elaborate the tripartite structure of the knowledge base in the order that the three layers are described above. It is possible to move between 'guided' and 'unguided' modes of interaction with the system.

Comparing TDE and MORE, once can see that there is more than one way that one can go about the business of designing tools for eliciting and structuring knowledge, even within a given problem solving method, such as heuristic classification. There is a lot that we still do not know about how to compare and contrast such approaches for the purposes of evaluation. Nevertheless, prototypes such as MORE and TDE are essential data points in this empirical enterprise, for the problem of knowledge elicitation will not be solved by theorizing alone, however inspired.

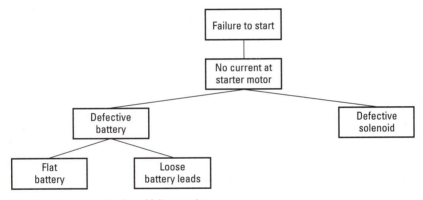

Figure 13.3 Hierarchical organization of failure modes.

BIBLIOGRAPHICAL NOTES

Pople (1982) gives a thorough account of INTERNIST and related research efforts. However, not all of the ideas expressed in this paper have been implemented or pursued. The CENTAUR architecture has been successfully applied to domains other than medicine, for example the REX program, which advises a statistician on the analysis of regression problems (Gale, 1986). Gale (1987) describes a knowledge elicitation program called Student, created for the REX domain, which has some similarities with the OPAL system outlined in Chapter 10, in that it is knowledge-based, rather than being based on a particular problem solving strategy.

Musen et al. (1995) describe a reconstruction of INTERNIST using a toolkit called PROTEGE, (Musen, 1989; Rothenfluh et al., 1994). PROTEGE is like CommonKADS insofar as it represents both a methodology and a suite of programs for building and maintaining expert systems. It combines an OPAL-like ontological framework with a reusable problem solving method to generate a domain-specific knowledge acquisition tool (Puerta et al., 1994).

1. What is a *prototype* in CENTAUR? What function does a prototype serve?

2. What are the advantages of CENTAUR's mixed knowledge representation?

3. What is a *disease model* in INTERNIST? Explain the concept of *dominance* as it relates to disease models in INTERNIST.

4. What problems did INTERNIST encounter, and how do these relate to Clancey's analysis of different kinds of knowledge?

5. This exercise requires a little background about pulmonary function test interpretation, but no previous medical knowledge is required to understand the simplified story I am going to give here. (Such that I know of this subject I owe to Drs Jeremy Wyatt and Patricia Tweedale. Any errors of fact or emphasis are obviously my fault, but they need not affect the validity of the exercise.)

    Some important medical parameters in diagnosing respiratory defects are as follows:

    - FEV1. Forced Expiratory Volume in 1 second, measured in litres. The associated test measures the amount of air you can expel from your lungs in a single second. It is an index of elasticity (and hence health) of lung tissue.
    - IFEV1. This is the increment in FEV1 following the administration of a bronchodilator: a drug that helps your tubes relax.
    - FVC. Forced Vital Capacity, that is how much air your lungs can take in if you force them.
    - IFVC signifies the increase in FVC after bronchodilator.
    - TLC. Total Lung Capacity.
    - RV. Residual Volume, that is the amount of air left in the lungs after expiration.
    - RATIO1 = FEV1/FVC.
    - RATIO2 = FEV1/FVC after bronchodilator.

    In the specification I shall give below, the variable PRED will stand for the predicted value of any of the above parameters; context will make the parameter clear. (The predicted value of a medical parameter depends largely upon the gender of the patient.) Expressions such as

    ```
    80% < RATIO1 < 100% (PRED-2SD)
    ```

    signify that RATIO1 is between 80 and 100 percent of the predicted value less two standard deviations from the mean value for the parameter in the relevant population.

    RTB stands for Response To Bronchodilation.

    (i) Design frames for each of the following respiratory defects and their associated medical parameters, organizing them into a hierarchy along the lines of CENTAUR (see Figure 13.1), under the root note PULMONARY DISEASE.

continued

AIRWAYS OBSTRUCTION
```
present if:
  RATIO1 < PRED-2SD
no RTB if:
  RATIO2 < PRED-2SD
good RTB if:
  RATIO2 > PRED-2SD
```

SLIGHT AIRWAYS OBSTRUCTION
```
present if:
  80% < RATIO1 < 100% of (PRED-2SD)
no RTB if:
  IFEV1 < FEV1/10
  IFVC < FVC/10
good RTB if:
  FEV1 > (PRED-2SD)/4
  FEV1/3 < IFEV1
```

MODERATE AIRWAYS OBSTRUCTION
```
present if:
  55% < RATIO1 < 80% of (PRED-2SD)
```

SEVERE AIRWAYS OBSTRUCTION
```
present if:
  RATIO ≤ 55% of PRED-2SD
```

RESTRICTIVE DEFECT
```
present if:
  RV < PRED+2SD
  TLC ≤ 80% of PRED-2SD
  RATIO1 > 80% of PRED-2SD
```

EARLY RESTRICTIVE DEFECT
```
present if:
  TLC < PRED-2SD
  RATIO1 > PRED-2SD
```

MILD RESTRICTIVE DEFECT
```
present if:
  RATIO1 > PRED-2SD
  80% < TLC < 100% of PRED-2SD
```

MODERATE RESTRICTIVE DEFECT
```
present if:
  RATIO1 > PRED-2SD
  60% < TLC < 80% of PRED-2SD
```

SEVERE RESTRICTIVE DEFECT
```
present if:
  RATIO1 > PRED-2SD
  TLC < 60% of PRED-2SD
```

continued

You will need procedures to capture the diagnostic knowledge associated with them.

Each frame needs to have slots which hold the predicted value of a parameter, together with the necessary standard deviation values. Thus the slot PRED-RATIO1 could hold the expected value for the parameter RATIO1, while the slot SD-RATIO1 could hold the standard deviation of this parameter. Clearly, for the purposes of this exercise, it does not matter what these values are. All your procedures need to do is reference the relevant slots.

For example, SEVERE-RESTRICTIVE-DEFECT could be a frame/object with a LISP procedure/method called PRESENT, defined along the lines of

```
SEVERE-RESTRICTIVE-DEFECT.PRESENT
  (and(> RATIO1 (- PRED-RATIO1 (* SD-RATIO1 2)))
      (< TLC (/ (* 6 (- PRED-TLC (* SD-TLC 2))) 10)))
```

which returns T if the relevant conditions are met.

(ii) Encode the diagnostic knowledge associated with these frames in production rules instead of procedures. As with the procedures, assume that rules can reference slot values in a straightforward manner.

6. Design and implement a simple knowledge elicitation program that allows a user to declare a fault in some device and list possible causes of that fault. For example, in the automobile domain, the program should be able to elicit a TDE-style failure mode, such as 'engine does not turn,' refine it with tests, such as 'is there current at the starter motor?', and associate possible causes with each refinement.

Thus 'no current at starter motor' is explicable by causes such as 'defective battery' and 'defective starter solenoid.' Nodes such as 'defective battery' are amenable to further refinement, for example 'flat battery' or 'loose battery leads.' The program should store all this information in a tree structure, such as that described in Section 13.4.

7. Test the program from Exercise 6, either on yourself, or better on someone other than yourself who is knowledgeable about the domain. If you are not yourself knowledgeable, and cannot find an expert, get the knowledge you need from some source. For example, troubleshooting knowledge about cars can be gleaned from workshop manuals, as in Exercise 10 of Chapter 12.

14 Constructive Problem Solving (I)

At the end of Chapter 11, we noted that the distinguishing feature of constructive problem solving was that solutions have to be built out of more primitive components. We contrasted this with classification problem solving, where solutions can be selected from some fixed set. The next two chapters describe artificial intelligence techniques that have been found useful for constructive problem solving, and illustrate these techniques with examples from the literature.

When we speak of constructing a solution to some problem, we imply that there is a space of solution elements that we can *select* from, and that there are rules that help us *combine* such elements. A simple example would be deciding what to wear to the office. There are certain (written or unwritten) rules in most places of work which tell you what is acceptable work attire. Your daily task is to assemble an outfit which (i) meets these requirements, and (ii) doesn't look too bad.[1]

Even if there are no selection rules handed down from on high, you probably wouldn't combine sneakers with a suit. One way to think about such constructive tasks is in terms of *constraints*. The trick is to build a solution that satisfies some overall test of goodness, and does not violate any specific rules that outlaw certain selections or combinations of elements.

14.1 Motivation and overview

Typical tasks which require constructive problem solving are planning, design, and certain kinds of diagnosis.

---

[1] If you are an engineer, then traditionally (ii) need not apply.

- In planning, the solution elements are actions, and solutions are sequences of actions that achieve goals. Constraints are provided by the laws of time and space, for example, you can't be in two places at once.
- In design, the solution elements are components, and solutions are combinations of components which form a complex object that satisfies certain physical constraints on materials, or certain aesthetic considerations.
- In the diagnosis of multiple disorders, the solution elements are disorders, and solutions are sets of disorders which cover the symptoms in a parsimonious way. Thus, one constraint might be that we don't want to account for symptoms many times over by diagnosing more diseases than we need.

In each of these cases, it is infeasible to fix the solution set in advance. There are too many different ways in which actions can be ordered, components can be assembled, and faults can co-occur. Furthermore, actions can interfere with each other, components compete for space and connections, while disorders may interact in various ways, for example via causal relationships.

Relatively simple versions of each of these tasks can be solved by classification. For example, we saw in Chapter 10 that ONCOCIN planned cancer therapies by selecting from a library of skeletal plans which only needed to be instantiated appropriately before being proposed as solutions. Nevertheless, more complex problems require the ability to construct and revise plans more flexibly from primitive actions.

As we noted in Chapter 2, the naive approach to tasks such as planning runs into problems of computational complexity, because the size of the search space is an exponential function of the number of solution elements. This does not present too much difficulty if solutions are plentiful and we are not too fussy about the quality of the solution. Unguided search may find a satisfactory solution in a reasonable time. But if we want a near optimal solution to a complex problem, then unguided search is doomed to failure, on even the most powerful computers. What is required is knowledge that can be used to constrict the solution space and focus the search upon combinations of elements that make good solutions.[2]

In the next section, we look at a system that uses a problem solving method called *Match*. The Match method is useful when there is sufficient domain knowledge to recognize the right thing to do at any given point in the computation. It permits a 'propose and apply' approach to problem solving, in which the emphasis is upon selecting the right operator to extend partial solutions. In Chapter 15, we shall see that this approach will not work for all constructive problems. However, when applicable, it is more flexible than consulting a library of partial solutions.

14.2 A case study: R1/XCON

R1 (McDermott, 1980, 1981, 1982a) was one of the success stories of expert systems in the 1980s. It is a program that configures VAX computer systems by first checking that the order is complete and then determining the spatial arrangement of components.

---

[2] This is where AI approaches to constructive problem solving differ from other approaches, such as combinatorial optimization, from Operations Research.

The commercial version of the system, developed by a collaboration between Carnegie-Mellon University and Digital Equipment Corporation, is called XCON; we shall sometimes distinguish the two when discussing the historical development of the program.

XCON began life configuring VAX-11/780 systems in Digital's Salem, New Hampshire, plant and then its expertise was expanded to include other product lines, such as the 11/750 and beyond. The project is interesting because it shows what a relatively weak problem solving method can achieve if you have enough domain knowledge of the right kind. Its story also illustrates the way in which a commercial system grows, how that growth can best be managed, and how a system is ultimately integrated into a production environment.

R1's task is not trivial. Computer systems typically consist of 50–150 components, the main ones being the central processor, memory control units, unibus and massbus interfaces, all connected to a synchronous backplane. The buses can support a wide range of peripheral devices – for example, tape drives, disk drives, printers – giving rise to a wide variety of different system configurations.

Given an order, R1 has to decide on both a combination of components that completes the specification and what their spatial arrangement should be. Deciding whether or not a configuration is complete is difficult, because it requires knowledge of individual components and their relationships. Deciding on a spatial arrangement is difficult, because there are many *constraints* that need to be taken into account. For example, assigning unibus modules to the backplanes involves taking into account features such as the amperage available on the backplane and the interrupt priority of the modules. This configuration task is therefore a classic construction problem that requires considerable expertise.

14.2.1 Components and constraints

Although both R1 and MYCIN are production rule programs, they differ substantially in a number of important respects. One difference is that MYCIN takes a *hypothesis-driven* approach to problem solving; that is, it begins with some goal (producing a diagnosis) and then proceeds to generate subgoals, the conjoined solution of which solve the original goal (see Chapter 3). R1's approach is largely *data-driven*; it begins with a set of components and tries to produce a configuration within the constraints imposed by the properties of these components and relationships between them. The program is implemented in OPS5, a forerunner of the rule-based language used in CLIPS.

R1 needs two kinds of knowledge:

- knowledge about *components*, for example voltage, amperage, pinning-type, number of ports and so on; plus
- knowledge about *constraints*, that is, rules for forming partial configurations of equipment and then extending them successfully.

Component knowledge is stored in a database, which is separate from both the production memory of the production system and the working memory of transient data elements. The database is therefore a static data structure, while the working memory is dynamic. Unlike the production memory, the database does not consist of pattern-directed modules, but of more conventional record structures which state, for each component, its class and type plus a set of attribute–value pairs. Consider the example in Figure 14.1, which describes an RK611* disk controller.

```
RK611*
    CLASS:                  UNIBUS MODULE
    TYPE:                   DISK DRIVE
    SUPPORTED:              YES
    PRIORITY LEVEL:         BUFFERED NPR
    TRANSFER RATE:          212

    ...
```

Figure 14.1 **Partial record structure for RK611* disk controller.**

Constraint knowledge is provided by each of the rules in R1's production memory. The left-hand sides recognize situations in which partial configurations can be extended, while the right-hand sides perform those extensions. The working memory starts off empty and ends containing the configuration. Components are represented in working memory by component tokens implemented as the usual attribute–value vectors. R1 can perform five actions in accessing the component database: it can generate a new token, find a token, find a substitute for a specific token, retrieve the attributes associated with an existing token, and retrieve a template for filling out.

As well as component tokens, the working memory contains elements that represent partial configurations of equipment, the results of various computations, and symbols which indicate what the current task is (see Figure 14.2).

A significant portion of R1's 10 000 rules deal with the problem of what to do next, rather than encoding either component knowledge or configuration operators. This *domain-specific control knowledge* allows R1 to make good decisions about how to start and extend assemblies without having to do extensive search. As we shall see, R1 does not typically need to backtrack over bad decisions by undoing partial configurations in favor of new ones.

This control knowledge is less concerned with the precise order in which individual rules fire than with the activation of groups of rules that correspond to recognizable subtasks of the overall configuration task. Such knowledge allows R1's problem solving to be driven by the consequences of recently fired rules, so that it is always following the 'leading edge' of the computation. As we shall see in the next section, there are aspects of OPS5's conflict resolution strategy that facilitate this.

```
DISTRIBUTE-MB-DEVICES-3

IF:  the most current active context is distributing massbus devices
&    there is a single port disk drive that has not been assigned to a massbus
&    there are no unassigned dual port disk drives
&    the number of devices that each massbus should support is known
&    there is a massbus that has been assigned at least one disk drive and that should support additional
     disk drives
&    the type of cable needed to connect the disk drive to the previous device on the disk drive is known

THEN: assign the disk drive to the massbus
```

Figure 14.2 **An English translation of an R1 rule, from Forgy (1982).**

14.2.2 Using contexts to impose task structure

In addition to information about components and constraints, R1's working memory contains symbol structures which specify the current context of the computation. This helps to break the configuration task down into subtasks which, as we noted in the last section, roughly correspond to the activations of rule groupings. Moreover, these subtasks can be arranged into a hierarchy with temporal relationships between them, thereby imposing a plan-like structure on the configuration task.

In other words, the main task, say 'configure this order for a VAX-11/780', can be analyzed into subtasks, like 'check that the order is correct' and 'arrange the components of the (possibly corrected) order.' Performing these two tasks constitutes performing the main task; however, they should obviously be performed in the order stated. It wouldn't make sense to configure the components in the order, and then check that the order was correct afterwards.

Thus R1 analyzes the configuration task into six immediate subtasks, each involving subtasks of their own:

(1) Check the order, inserting any omissions and correcting any mistakes.
(2) Configure the CPU, arranging components in the CPU and CPU expansion cabinets.
(3) Configure the unibus modules, putting boxes into the expansion cabinets and then putting the modules into the boxes.
(4) Configure the paneling, assigning panels to cabinets and associating panels with unibus modules and the devices they serve.
(5) Generate a floor plan, grouping components that must be closer together and then laying the devices out in the right order.
(6) Do the cabling, specifying what cables are to be used to connect devices and then determining the distances between pairs of components.

Such hierarchies can be thought of as being either *determinate* or *indeterminate* with respect to the ordering of subtasks. If there is a fixed order within the subtasks at every depth, then we say that the task analysis is determinate, since the sequence of tasks is completely determined. If there is some latitude with respect to the ordering between some subtasks at some levels, then the task analysis is indeterminate.

Parts of R1's task analysis are determinate, in that some of the tasks are always performed in the same order. This simplification is achieved as follows. Many of R1's rules serve mainly to manipulate context symbols: those working memory elements that tell the program where it has got to in the task hierarchy. Some rules recognize when a new subtask needs to be initiated; these add context symbols to working memory. Others recognize when a subtask has been completed; these remove context symbols from working memory. All other rules contain condition elements that are sensitive to context symbols, so that they only fire when their context is 'active,' that is, when the requisite symbols are the 'recent' context symbols in working memory. In order to understand this, it is necessary to understand the conflict resolution strategy employed by R1.

Each context symbol contains a context name, for example 'assign-power-supply,' a symbol which states whether the context is active or not, and a time tag which indicates how recently the context was made active. The rules that recognize when a new subtask should be set up do this on the basis of the current state of the partial config-uration. Rules which have the appropriate context symbol in their conditions will now receive preferential treatment during the recognize–act cycle.

It is customary to put patterns which recognize context among the first condi-tions in the left-hand side of productions, so that the pattern matcher fails quickly on rules that lack the right context recognizers. Also, the conflict resolution strate-gy used by R1, which is called MEA (see Chapter 5 and Box 14.1), stresses the first condition of a rule when evaluating rule instantiations for possible execution. Rules which deactivate contexts are simply rules whose left-hand side is composed solely of context symbols. Such a rule will only fire when all the other rules sensitive to that context have fired or failed. This is a use of the *specificity* strategy, and the way it is employed here ensures that R1 does all it can within a particular context before leaving it.

The basic specificity heuristic works as follows. If there are two rules in the conflict set, Rule 1 and Rule 2, and Rule 2's conditions are a subset of Rule 1's, then Rule 1 will be preferred over Rule 2. Another way of looking at this is to regard Rule 2 as more 'general' than Rule 1; it acts as a default which catches cases for which Rule 1 is too specific. Rule 1 might deal with an exception to Rule 2, in which extra factors need to be taken into account.

In OPS5 (and CLIPS), specificity is a little more sophisticated than this. The infer-ence engine creates a partial order of rule instantiations based on the number of tests that occur in the conditions of the corresponding rules, that is, relational tests against constants or variables that must be satisfied for the match to succeed. The instantia-tions with the greatest number of tests dominate. In any event, when used as part of the MEA conflict resolution strategy, specificity helps ensure that that rules fire in co-herent groups which accomplish a subtask in some context, instead of lapsing into more of a 'shotgun' approach.

McDermott's justification for this use of contexts is not so much that it is somehow essential to the task of configuring a computer system. Rather, he argues that it reflects the way in which human experts actually approach the task. However, it is worth pointing out that R1 has no real knowledge of the properties of the contexts it deals with. Context names are just symbols, unlike components, say, which have all kinds of attributes and values associated with them. Consequently, R1 cannot reason about contexts in the same way that it can reason about components or constraints; it simply recognizes when a new context is needed and when it has done all it can in a particular context. This seems to be all the task requires.

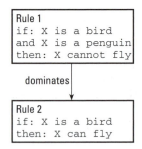

Figure 14.3 An example of specificity; Rule 1 dominates Rule 2.

BOX 14.1

LEX and MEA Revisited

In Chapter 5, we mentioned the conflict resolution strategies LEX and MEA, which are now offered by CLIPS. Here we outline MEA in more detail, since it is the OPS5 strategy used by R1/XCON.

As we saw in Section 3.2.1, *means–ends analysis* is an abstract control regime for reasoning backward from some goal to select operators or rules that reduce the distance between the current state of some problem and this goal. It easy to see how one might implement such a control regime in the context of a backward-chaining production system, such as that employed by MYCIN (see Section 3.3), where one starts with a top-level goal. In a forward-chaining system, such as OPS5 or CLIPS, the MEA conflict resolution strategy is a somewhat weaker regime which enables a program to walk through an implicit tree of goals, which are represented by special tokens in working memory.

The MEA algorithm is a simple five-step process, as outlined below. Recall that the *conflict set* is the set of rule instantiations that are activated at any given cycle of the computation; an *instantiation* is a rule together with the variable bindings that it derived from the pattern match.

(1) Discard from the conflict set any instantiations that have already fired at any previous cycle. If the set is now empty, then halt.
(2) Compare the recencies of working memory elements (WMEs) that match the *first condition elements* of the instantiations. Instantiations that use the most recent WMEs dominate. If there is a single such instantiation, then it is selected for firing at the process halts. Otherwise, if there are instantiations that tie for first place, retain them, and discard the rest, moving on to step (3).
(3) Order the instantiations on the basis of the recency of WMEs associated with the other condition elements. If one instantiation dominates, then select it for firing and halt, else discard all but the highest scoring and move on to step (4).
(4) If no single instantiation dominates with respect to recency, then compare the specificity of the conditions in the remaining rules. The instantiation whose conditions involve the most tests on working memory dominates, and is selected for firing, else, if there is no such rule, discard all but the highest scoring and move on to step (5).
(5) Make an arbitrary selection from among the remaining instantiations for one to fire and halt.

MEA is therefore a strategy that combines refractoriness, recency and specificity into a single algorithm. LEX is like MEA, except that step (2) is missing, and the comparison of step (3) now applies to all condition elements of an instantiation and their associated WMEs. The first condition elements referred to in step (2) are typically task tokens in working memory (see Chapter 5 for example programs that manipulate such tokens).

14.2.3 Reasoning with constraints: the Match method

To illustrate the use of constraints by R1, let us consider Subtask 3: the configuration of the unibus modules in their boxes and cabinets.

The main trouble with 'bin packing' problems of this kind is that there is usually no way of pruning the search space, because there is no suitable evaluation function for partial configurations. In other words, there is no formula that you can apply which will allow you to say that one partial configuration is better than some other partial solution. A system of functional and spatial relationships is a complex whole, and it succeeds or fails as such. It is not possible to tell in advance, by looking at some solution fragment, whether or not it will lead to a complete and acceptable solution, unless there are regularities in the system, for example various kinds of symmetry, which introduce redundancy.

In the context of Subtask 3, there are certain constraints that can be used to inform the search for a solution:

- Each unibus module requires a backplane slot of the right pinning type.
- Each backplane in a box must be positioned so that its modules draw power from only one set of regulators.
- Regulators can only supply a certain amount of power, regardless of the number of slots available on the backplane.
- If a module needs panel space, the space must be in the cabinet that contains the module.
- Some modules may require supporting modules, either in the same backplane or in the same box.
- There is an optimal sequence for modules on the unibus, in terms of their interrupt priority and transfer rate, and so modules should be positioned as close to that sequence as possible.

Obviously there is a limited amount of box space. As a result, you can't tell whether or not a module's configuration is acceptable until all the modules are on the unibuses. Sometimes R1 has to generate more than one candidate solution before an acceptable one is found.

Although R1 may have several attempts at a particular task, as in the above example, it never backtracks. In other words, it never makes a decision which it later has to go back and undo. At any point in the problem solving process, it has enough knowledge to recognize what to do – this cuts down on trial and error search. Backtracking is computationally expensive, especially in terms of run-time storage, as well as making the behavior of programs hard to understand.

The basic problem solving method used by R1 is called, rather confusingly, 'Match.' All pattern-directed inference systems use matching to some extent, of course, but Match with a big 'M' is more than this. A program using Match 'recognizes' what to do at any given point in its execution, rather than generating candidate solutions and then trying them out as in the generate-and-test paradigm used by expert systems like DENDRAL (see Chapter 20).

We don't usually think of matching as being search; pattern-matching is normally a process whereby search is initiated, continued or terminated. For example, matching often determines whether or not an operator is applicable, or whether a solution has been found. However, Match can be considered as a search technique in which you look for an exemplar which instantiates some 'form,' a form being a symbolic expression containing variables. An example of a form would be the left-hand side of a production rule: a symbol structure made up of one or more patterns which may share variables. The search space for Match is then 'the space of all instantiations of the variables in a form' (McDermott, 1982a, p. 54), with each state in the space a partially instantiated form.

It is the form that embodies the domain-specific knowledge about constraint satisfaction, and it is the Match method which applies this knowledge to particular problems. However, McDermott lists two conditions which must be satisfied if this rather 'weaker' notion of search is to be successful in finding the solution to some problem:

- The *correspondence condition*. It must be possible to determine the value that a variable can take on 'locally,' that is using only such information as is ready to hand at the point of correspondence when you compare the exemplar with the pattern. In the case of R1, 'ready to hand' information is that information which is available from the current context. Decisions must not depend upon information that will only become available in 'daughter' and 'sister' contexts elsewhere in the hierarchy. This is not to say that contexts should be independent; merely that subsequent matches do not affect what has already been matched.
- The *propagation condition*. When an operator is applied, this should only affect aspects of the solution which have not yet been determined. In other words, there should be no 'retroactive' effects of decisions; decisions must be partially ordered. This condition is so called because the consequences of our decisions should propagate in one direction only: from a particular context to its 'daughter' and (as yet unvisited) 'sister' contexts, and not to its ancestors (or 'aunties').

McDermott divides R1's rules into three broad categories, depending upon the role they play in the Match method.

(1) *Operator rules* create and extend partial configurations.
(2) *Sequencing rules* determine the order in which decisions are made, mostly by manipulating contexts.
(3) *Information-gathering rules* access the database of components or perform various computations for the benefit of the other rules.

It was noted earlier that the use of contexts in configuration had a certain psychological justification, in that human experts tended to approach the problem in this way, but no attempt was made to justify contexts by saying that they were somehow 'necessary' from a formal or computational point of view. With regard to Match, the situation is somewhat reversed. Humans frequently depart from the Match method, in that they tend to use a form of heuristic search that involves some backtracking. However, the computational advantages of Match are considerable, and there are practical reasons for supposing that heuristic search is not a good method for programming a solution to this problem, such as the inherent inefficiency of unnecessary backtracking.

14.3 Elicitation, evaluation and extensibility

In this section, we shall look at the problems of evaluation and extensibility, as well as knowledge elicitation. XCON's progress is rather better documented in this regard than most systems. Clearly, these three issues are linked, in that the quality of the knowledge determines performance, while the nature of the knowledge determines how difficult extensibility is. XCON's knowledge elicitation problem is made harder by the sheer diversity of the knowledge required to perform the task. However, a more penetrating analysis of the problem solving method employed can facilitate knowledge elicitation, just as we saw in Chapters 11, 12 and 13.

14.3.1 Knowledge elicitation in R1/XCON

McDermott (1982a) has a number of interesting observations to make about the initial phases of knowledge elicitation for R1.

- The experts had a reasonably clear idea of the regular decomposition of the main task into subtasks, and the temporal relationships *between* these subtasks.
- *Within* subtasks, however, their behavior is driven more by exceptions than regularities, for example 'when performing subtask *S*, do *X*, unless *Y*.' Humans are not very good at recalling these exceptional circumstances on demand; that is, they are driven by events.

This regularity of relations between tasks but irregularity within tasks is dealt with in the OPS5 implementation by the use of contexts and special cases. Refinement of rules and contexts provides a modular way of correcting erroneous behavior during the initial stages of program development. However, McDermott (1988) points out that different kinds of knowledge were not always well differentiated within subtasks. In particular, two classes of knowledge tended to be confounded in the rules:

- knowledge about the different ways in which partial configurations could be extended; and
- knowledge about which competing extensions to select for actual execution.

Bachant (1988) joins Clancey (1983) and others in arguing for a more principled approach to this problem in which control is realized by explicit means. She notes that conflict resolution acts at too low a level to relate to the task itself, although it can obviously be used to effect decomposition into tasks, as we have seen. In a new methodology called RIME (which stands for 'R1's Implicit Made Explicit'), Bachant tries to strike a balance between over-controlling and under-controlling sequences of actions. Over-controlling involves over-specifying the order in which tasks are executed, and is typical of conventional sequential programming languages. Under-controlling is typical of the data-driven style of pattern-directed inference systems, where modules compete for the attention of the interpreter.

Bachant identifies the basic problem solving method of R1 as *propose-and-apply*, which can be analyzed into the following steps:

(1) *Initialize-Goal.* This step creates a control element for the current task, removing any obsolete control elements for completed tasks.
(2) *Propose-Operator.* This step suggests plausible courses of action, rejecting those that are obviously inappropriate.
(3) *Prune-Operator.* This step eliminates operators according to global criteria, such as a predefined preference order.
(4) *Eliminate-Operator.* This step performs a pairwise comparison between any competing operators that remain and favors one over the other.
(5) *Select-One-Operator.* This step examines the results of steps (2)–(4) and chooses just one operator.
(6) *Apply-Operator.* This step applies an operator to the current problem state, extending a partial configuration.
(7) *Evaluate-Goal.* This step looks to see if the goal has been achieved at the end of the cycle, terminating on success or failure, and iterating otherwise.

So what is the difference between Match and propose-and-apply? From Bachant's analysis, we can see that R1 used the weak problem solving method (Match) to implement a stronger, knowledge-based method (propose-and-apply). This is analogous to the use that heuristic classification (strong method) makes of subgoaling (weak method) in MYCIN.

More recently, McDermott (1988) has used the phrase 'role-limiting methods' to describe these stronger methods that are constructed over weak methods. Such methods are characterized by the kinds of control knowledge that they use to identify, select, and evaluate candidate actions that the system could perform. The assumption is that there are groups of tasks whose individual use of control knowledge can be seen to exhibit a strong family resemblance, and is therefore not very task-specific.

Role-limiting methods are thus defined as 'methods that strongly guide knowledge collection and encoding.' Although such a definition is far from precise, the idea is that a method is role-limiting if the control knowledge it typically uses is not tied too closely to the details of the task. One could argue that heuristic classification, as used in MYCIN, represented such a method, if one confined one's attention to MYCIN's use of production rules.

However, it is also true that certain parts of an expert system may contain control knowledge that is less abstract, in that it is intimately connected with the properties of domain objects and the relations that hold between them. McDermott cites the R1/XCON rules listed in Figure 14.4 as examples. They belong to a particular module of the system, in which the task is to determine the next device to configure.

The first rule could perhaps be generalized if we knew why we prefer doing the RA60 first, but the second seems to be hopelessly dependent upon a host of details to do with the relationships that exist between devices, cabinets and drives. Furthermore, these relationships appear to inhabit different levels of abstraction, from the most contingent and specific, for example, 'bundled with a cabinet,' to the more general and possibly subjective, for example, concerning what is 'desirable.' As McDermott points out, the kinds of consideration encoded in such rules will change from product to product, and therefore cannot be generalized as they stand.

If two of the candidate actions are
   to configure an RA60 drive,
   to configure another type of drive that uses the same cabinet type,
Then prefer configuring the RA60 next.

If two of the candidate actions are
   to configure a rackmountable device whose subtype is not RV20A or RV20B,
   to configure a different rackmountable device whose subtype is not RV20A or RV20B,
and no cabinet has been selected,
and the second device is not bundled with an available cabinet,
and there is an available cabinet or tape drive in which the devices can be placed,
and it is desirable to place the first device in the cabinet before the second device,
Then prefer configuring the first device.

Figure 14.4 **Two R1 rules.**

14.3.2 The evaluation and extension of R1/XCON

As mentioned in Chapter 3, evaluation is a difficult issue to address; it is even difficult to discuss. Expectations regarding expert system performance are often hazy. The program must run in a reasonable time and be able to deal with a collection of 'typical' cases, perhaps those cases used to elicit the knowledge from the domain expert. However, it is wishful thinking to suppose that one can devise some test or series of tests that will tell you when an expert system has reached some imaginary peak of performance.

In domains lacking the structure of formal systems like mathematics and logic, it is unlikely that you will ever be able to 'prove' that your expert system is indeed an expert in any rational sense. The evidence must be empirical, and yet the range of possible situations that your program might encounter will be vast in any non-trivial application. Even though XCON has to date processed tens of thousands of orders, it has only seen a small fraction of the space of possible orders it might receive.

McDermott reports that, in the early days of R1, it was predicted that the program would have to be 90 percent correct in its configurations before it began to be useful. R1 took three years to reach this goal, but experience showed that the prediction was in error. The program was able to assist with configuration before it reached this criterion, because it did no worse than its human predecessors. The configuration task is such that no single individual is entrusted to perform it alone; individuals typically lack both the knowledge and the time to take total responsibility for an order. So there was already sufficient redundancy in the system for R1 to usefully contribute its two cents' worth.

Is comparison with a human expert the criterion? This is a more difficult question than it sounds. In addition to the problem of finding a suitable set of test cases, there is the problem of making the right comparison. The configuration task is usually performed by technical editors; however, R1 does the job at a lower level of detail than this human expert, taking in aspects of the role of the technician who physically assembles the system. So should we compare R1 with the technical editor plus the technician? Well, it's not really that simple either: R1 doesn't really assemble the system, of course, so it's operating rather differently from the man who actually manipulates the components, and is therefore able to experiment with them directly. Surely this isn't comparing like with like?

In addition to adding new knowledge for the purpose of debugging old knowledge, there are three other reasons for extending a knowledge base.

(1) You might want to add new knowledge about a wider class of data, for example configuring new types of machine.
(2) You might want to add new knowledge and introduce new subtasks which 'flesh out' the main task, for example being more sophisticated about the placement of panels.
(3) You might want to extend the definition of the main task, for example asking R1 to configure multiple CPU orders.

When is the extensibility task complete? Judging from the experience with R1, the answer may be – never. The domain of computer systems is constantly changing; this means new components with new properties capable of entering into new relationships with each other, and so both the database and the production memory will be in a more or less constant state of flux. Furthermore, the system will always present the evaluation process with a moving target, making an already difficult task even more difficult.

The experience with XCON is that incremental development leads naturally to redundancy and *ad hoc* solutions. In other words, unless vigorously opposed, the amount of disorder in the program will always increase. Rebuilding a system from scratch is expensive in terms of time, money and effort, but the investment can be worthwhile if it makes the program easier to extend. There are no easy answers here. The educated expert system builder should be aware of the issues and make such decisions on a case-by-case basis. The reader is referred to Box 14.2 for a brief discussion of how the architects of XCON resolved this issue.

In the next chapter, we look at two systems which set out to solve constructive problems requiring a rather more complex control strategy. Problems arise because, in some applications, the correspondence condition discussed in Section 14.2.3 is not met. In other words, we cannot always determine locally what the next step should be, because the current state of the computation is underconstrained. In such situations, we can try to make decisions in such a way as to keep our options open, or we can be prepared to undo decisions if they later turn out to violate constraints. We shall see that such strategies can complicate the situation considerably, but that we can often use domain knowledge to manage that complexity.

BOX 14.2

Reimplementation of XCON

XCON was reimplemented using the RIME methodology during 1986 and 1987. R1's top-down refinement of the computation into tasks (now called *problem spaces*) has been retained, but rules are now classified according to the steps that they perform in the propose-and-apply method. Each problem space represents a relatively independent subtask, and is specified in terms of three things:

- a control structure that describes the kind of problem solving that will go on in that space;
- knowledge which decides what problem space should be active at any given time; and
- operators which manipulate objects in a given space, once it becomes active.

Thus there are Propose-Operator rules, Prune-Operator rules, and so on, for problem spaces, thereby regularizing R1's original representation of knowledge. However, the main utility of this framework is that it allows for a more systematic approach to knowledge elicitation. In particular, it helps with the problem of eliciting knowledge within subtasks noted by McDermott.

Reviewing R1/XCON some years later, McDermott (1993) claimed that three valuable lessons were learned from this research and development effort:

- R1 demonstrated the importance of domain-specific control knowledge – the fact that, given enough knowledge about what to do next, a program can perform a complex task by recognizing the right action to perform based on local information.
- A production system provides a good implementation vehicle for refining and extending an expert system's knowledge, particularly where there are ordering constraints among subtasks, and when only a subset of all possible task actions are relevant to a particular task instance. When these circumstances prevail, adding new rules to accomplish new tasks is less likely to interfere with old rules that perform old tasks.
- To be useful and gain acceptance, a system has to do more than just correctly perform a task. Integrating a program like R1 into the production process is crucial for success, but this involves dealing with an extant infrastructure of organizations, workflows, and personnel, some of which may be indifferent or antagonistic to change.

continued

Thus, in the case of XCON, the reimplementation appears to have been worthwhile. This may not be the case for every application, however. For smaller, less ambitious expert systems, the old adage 'If it ain't broke, don't fix it' may apply.

BIBLIOGRAPHICAL NOTES

R1/XCON's progress has been well documented, although there seems to be no single source that tells you all the details of its development. McDermott and Bachant (1984) is not a bad starting point, if what you want is an overview to supplement this chapter. Another interesting system which came from the collaboration between Carnegie-Mellon and Digital Equipment was XSEL: an OPS5 program which helps a salesperson select components for a VAX computer system and assists with floor layout (McDermott, 1982b, 1984).

Musen (1992) provides a useful analysis of the strengths and weaknesses of role-limiting methods, such as 'propose and revise,' and is therefore worth reading after McDermott's (1988) paper. Studer *et al.* (1998) discuss both role-limiting methods and generic tasks, illustrating these concepts with examples from CommonKADS and PROTEGE-II.

STUDY SUGGESTIONS

1. Why are planning and design problems not always amenable to being solved by classification methods? Under what conditions *can* they be solved by classification?

2. What is the Match method? What is the 'correspondence condition' that must hold for this method to be applicable?

3. What is the 'specificity' conflict resolution strategy, and how does R1 use it?

4. Describe in detail R1's use of contexts. Does R1 'understand' its problem solving strategy of top-down refinement; for example, would the program be able to reason about its own strategy?

5. What is a 'problem space' in the RIME methodology, and what function do such spaces serve?

6. What are the advantages in reimplementing XCON so that its propose-and-apply strategy is more explicit?

7. Consider automating the following configuration task, which is just complicated enough to be interesting, but not as complex as configuring a computer system.
   Specification. The user is a budding electric guitarist who wants to replace his current gear with a stage set-up consisting of a new guitar, amplifier and effects pedals. The task of the expert system is to help the user choose a combination of makes and models of such equipment that will achieve the desired effect.

continued

Data and knowledge. Data supplied to the system might include values for the following parameters:

- Kinds of music that the user intends to play (for example, jazz, blues, rock, and so on)
- Style of playing (for example rhythm or lead, two-hand tapping, string bending, sliding, and so on)
- Tonal preferences (for example 'fat' sound versus a thinner sound, 'sweet' tone versus a more acerbic tone, degree of sustain, and so on)
- 'Guitar heroes' of user (for example Clapton, Beck, Page, van Halen, Vai, and so on)
- Amount of money available for each major item.

Find your local guitar player (there's at least one in every class) and elicit this knowledge from him or her. Look upon this primarily as a design exercise, rather than an implementation exercise.

Task analysis. Use the same kind of task analysis that we observed in R1, that is, break tasks down into subtasks. The AND/OR tree of Figure 14.5 should serve as a reasonable starting point. Either try to develop your system to a uniform depth in this tree, or else specialize, for example in guitars or in amps.

Traversal of the task tree by the program can be deterministic and proceed top–down and left–right. The most important single decision is the guitar, so complete that subtask before moving on to the amplifier, since it will have implications for other choices. Naturally, you have to determine the make and model before considering what strings to use and whether or not to bother with custom pickups.

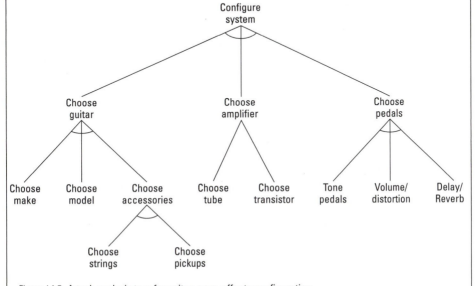

Figure 14.5 A task analysis tree for guitar–amp–effects configuration.

continued

Amplifiers fall into two main categories, depending on whether they use tubes (valves) or transistors. Each can be used with any kind of guitar, but certain kinds of music, coupled with certain choices of guitar and style of playing, indicate one kind of amp over another. Another dimension upon which amplifiers differ is whether or not they offer built-in effects, such as reverb and chorus. This will have implications for the pedal requirements, since there is no point in duplicating the capabilities of the amplifier without special reason.

Pedal choices depend very much upon the kind of music to be played. Some players use no pedals, other use them sparingly, while still others use many different combinations of sound effects. Options include distortion (the 'dirty' sound of heavy rock and metal), delay (pronounced echo effects), reverb (more subtle echo effects), and so on.

15 Constructive Problem Solving (II)

15.1 Construction strategies
15.2 An architecture for planning and meta-planning
15.3 Eliciting, representing and applying design knowledge
15.4 Summary of constructive problem solving
Bibliographical notes
Study suggestions

In the last chapter, we examined a constructive problem solver that never needed to undo design decisions. However, not all construction problems can be tackled in this way, because it is not always the case that we have enough domain knowledge to make the right decision at each step as we build the solution. In this chapter, we explore both *least commitment* and *propose and revise* strategies with the aid of examples, and review some more knowledge acquisition tools for constructive problem solving.

15.1 Construction strategies

Imagine that you are arranging furniture in a room. The goal is to devise an arrangement that satisfies the physical constraints supplied by the dimensions of room (in terms of floorspace, width of alcoves, and so on) and the dimensions of the furniture, plus a set of preferences (for example, desk by the window, sofa opposite the TV, and so on). Most likely, having taken some measurements and identified a number of possible locations for different items, you would 'anchor' one or two important pieces at suitable sites and then see if you could complete the arrangement in a satisfactory way.

If you are lucky, your first complete arrangement will work out, and you might well decide to keep things that way, rather than continue the search for an even better solution. But it is just as likely that some proposed extensions to the partial arrangement will violate physical constraints or preferences. However, when this happens, you will not necessarily backtrack all, or even some, of the way to Square One. Rather, you will discover a fix, such as swapping the locations of two items, which does not violate the constraint. A good fix is one that undoes as little of your previous work as possible.

As mentioned earlier, construction problems are hard, because there is often no way of telling in advance whether a partial construct will work out. If one is arranging furniture, designing an electrical circuit, or planning a series of errands, then one had better be prepared to rearrange, redesign or replan. The general, bottom-up strategy that we use for small problems appears to be something like the following.

(1) If possible, begin with a partial arrangement that satisfies the constraints. Otherwise begin at the very beginning.
(2) If the arrangement is complete, then halt. Otherwise perform a 'promising' extension to the current arrangement.
(3) If the new arrangement violates a constraint, then propose a fix which generates a new arrangement by undoing as little of the previous steps as possible.
(4) Go to Step (2).

This strategy is impossibly general, of course, but it has a few interesting features, even at this level of vagueness. Firstly, whenever possible, start with something other than nothing. Thus, if you are planning some sequence of actions, start with a partial plan, extensions of which have worked in the past. It is not too fanciful to suggest that humans have a 'library' of skeletal plans for accomplishing common tasks. Secondly, 'promising' extensions are often those which leave your options open. For example, when planning actions, a good heuristic is to select as your next action the one that least constrains the order and timing of the remaining actions. This is usually called a *least commitment* strategy. Thirdly, fixes do not necessarily involve chronological backtracking, that is, undoing the last thing you did. Placing the desk may have obscured the TV, but maybe the TV is in the wrong place, in the sense you will have to move it anyway if anything resembling the current plan is to work out.

For complex arrangements, it might seem that the search space is very large, and therefore that the problem is intractable. However, an arrangement task can often be simplified by considering it at different degrees of detail. For example, consider the problem of designing a house for a plot of land; in particular, consider the problem of room layout. As Rosenman *et al.* (1987) point out, configurations of rooms can be described at various levels of abstraction, for example:

- in terms of *adjacencies*, for example, Room A is next to Room B;
- in terms of *orientations*, for example, Room A is north of Room B; and
- in terms of *coordinates* which precisely determine the spatial relationship between Rooms A and B.

At the highest level of abstraction, deciding that certain rooms need to be adjacent (for example, kitchen and dining room, main bathroom and master bedroom) constrains the search space in a manner that produces exponential savings. At the next level down, deciding that the living room should face south for sunshine and that the kitchen should face north for coolness places constraints upon the orientation of the dining room. Once adjacencies and orientations are established, we then need heuristics for allocating space to rooms and resolving conflicts over space allocation, for example, by committing space to the most important rooms first, and then splitting the remainder between less important rooms.

This hierarchical approach to problem solving is well known in the planning community, where the successors of the STRIPS program, such as NOAH (Sacerdoti, 1974) and NONLIN (Tate, 1977), sought to simplify the search space by:

- viewing actions at higher levels of abstraction that group whole sequences of actions into larger units;
- solving the planning problem in terms of a partial order of these units; and then
- filling in the details at successively lower levels of abstraction until the plan is fully specified.

This is a top-down approach to problem solving, and as such it resembles the task–subtask organization of the R1 program that we studied in the last chapter. However, it may sometimes be the case that (unlike R1) we need to remake decisions within a level of abstraction. This is the *revise* part of propose and revise. In really hard problems, we may even need to remake decisions at a higher level of abstraction, and then return to the current level. Clearly, we would like to avoid this if possible, hence the emphasis on generating good proposals while at the same time keeping one's options open.

In Section 15.2, we begin by looking at the MOLGEN system (Stefik, 1981a, 1981b) for planning experiments in molecular genetics; we shall de-emphasize the rather specialized domain here as much as possible. This system is a good example of the multi-layered approach to construction problems with a least commitment strategy, and it demonstrates the kind of organizational complexity that hard problems require. In Section 15.3, we look at a bottom-up problem solver called VT (Marcus *et al.*, 1988) for designing elevator systems using a 'propose and revise' strategy, and then focus upon an associated knowledge acquisition tool called SALT (Marcus, 1988b) which helps elicit design knowledge.

15.2 An architecture for planning and meta-planning

MOLGEN is a multiple-layered system, in which each layer acts as a level of control for the layer beneath it. This kind of organization is sometimes called *meta-level architecture*. The idea is that, in addition to the 'first-level' representation of the domain problem, there are higher levels which represent such things as possible actions upon domain objects, and criteria for selecting and combining those actions.

In MOLGEN, the various layers of control are called *planning spaces*. The program uses three such spaces, each with its own objects and operators, which communicate with each other via message-passing protocols (see Chapter 7). Their organization is shown schematically in Figure 15.1, with sample operators listed on the left-hand side of the box representing each space. The interpreter is MOLGEN's outermost control loop; it creates and executes strategies. As we shall see, these strategies implement a kind of meta-level reasoning, which controls the way in which the program addresses the basic design problem of planning experiments.

Beginning at the bottom, the *laboratory space* is the domain space which contains knowledge about the objects and operations of a laboratory. The objects are things that can be manipulated by operations that a laboratory technician can perform, such as sorting objects, merging two objects, and so on. We shall not say much about this layer of the program here; interested readers are referred to the original paper.

The *design space* contains knowledge about plans, in the form of classes of operators for

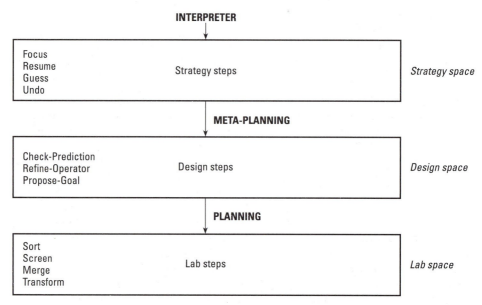

Figure 15.1 **MOLGEN's planning spaces (after Stefik, 1981b).**

- checking predictions and finding unusual features of objects (*comparison* operators);
- proposing goals and operations and predicting results (*temporal-extension* operators); and
- refining plan steps in accordance with constraints (*specialization* operators).

Thus *Propose-Goal* is a temporal-extension operator which sets goals for laboratory steps to achieve. *Check-Prediction* is a comparison operator which compares the predicted results of performing a laboratory step with the current goal. *Refine-Operator* is a specialization operator which replaces abstract steps in a laboratory operation with more specific ones in a form of plan refinement.

Operators have priorities preassociated with them. In general, comparison operators tend to outrank temporal-extension operators, which tend to outrank specialization operators. This ranking reflects the overall least commitment strategy, since it is obviously less 'committing' to perform comparisons and make predictions than it is to refine plan steps. In MOLGEN's domain, the expertise being modeled by these operators is that of someone who designs experiments, but the general principles involved in their organization would apply to many other constructive domains.

The following three operations on constraints are important in MOLGEN, and relevant to most applications of constructive problem solving.

- *Constraint formulation* creates constraints that limit the solution space. An example in the room layout domain would be deciding that the kitchen and dining-room must be adjacent.
- *Constraint propagation* passes information between subproblems which are almost, but not quite, independent of each other. Thus resolving the layout of the

upstairs and downstairs of a house are nearly independent subproblems, but they interact along some dimensions, for example, stairs and plumbing.

- *Constraint satisfaction* pools constraints from subproblems as the details of the design are worked out. Thus our house design might juggle the upstairs and downstairs arrangements to simplify the plumbing problem.

It is useful to characterize operations in terms of the constraints that currently act upon them. For example, if the problem is what to do on Saturday night, and the current operation is 'Go to the cinema,' then we say that the operation is *underconstrained* so long as there is more than one film showing in town. In general, an operation is underconstrained if there is not enough information available to realize it in terms of more detailed steps. On the other hand, the operation 'Go to a horror film' is overconstrained if there are no such films showing in town. In general, an operation is *overconstrained* if an attempt to execute it violates a constraint.

The *strategy space* reasons about the plan steps in the design space, using heuristics and a least commitment approach. Thus the design operators create and schedule domain steps, while strategy operators create and schedule design steps. Since the design steps constitute a planning activity, we shall refer to the strategy as *meta-planning*. In other words, at the strategy level, MOLGEN reasons about (or plans) how it is going to do its planning at the design level. Here we shall concentrate upon the strategy operators, and their deployment in a least commitment cycle that sometimes resorts to heuristics.

MOLGEN's strategy space consists of the following strategy operators; these are described in terms of the messages that they pass to entities in the design space below.

- *Focus* sends a message to each design operator, telling it to 'find tasks' that it could perform to elaborate the current plan. Proposed operations are then put on an agenda in an order of priority determined by the rank of the operator. Not all of them will be executable: some will be underconstrained or overconstrained. *Focus* goes through its agenda executing such tasks as can be executed, sending out the 'find tasks' message after each successful execution, suspending underconstrained tasks, and only relinquishing control to the *Undo* operator when an overconstrained task is encountered.
- *Resume* is like *Focus*, except that it looks for suspended steps to restart, rather than creating new tasks.
- *Guess* is invoked when all the pending design steps are underconstrained. This represents a situation where there is no obvious best next step in the least commitment approach, and one can only use heuristics to guess what to do next. *Guess* sends each suspended step a message, asking it to estimate the utility of its various options, and then executes the one with the highest rating.
- *Undo* is invoked when the plan has become overconstrained. This represents a situation where the least commitment approach has failed and bad guesses have led the planner to a dead end, that is, to a state from which it cannot proceed, because the plan cannot be elaborated by a pending design step without violating a constraint. *Undo* as implemented in MOLGEN is fairly primitive: it looks for a 'guessed' step whose output is an input to the pending step and tells it to remove its effects from the plan.

This use of an agenda is more flexible than that described in the summary of IN-TERNIST and CENTAUR in Chapter 13. Although all three systems make the crucial separation between posting a task for execution and actually executing it, only MOL-GEN's architecture allows for the case where tasks may interact in non-trivial ways. As Stefik points out, if these interactions are not reasoned about explicitly at higher levels in a program, they tend to surface in confusing ways at lower levels. Of course, multi-layered architectures must ultimately simplify the problem, if we are to justify their employment. Thus, the kinds of task performed by higher levels must get simpler and simpler, until the top-level interpreter is responsible for only trivial tasks, such as executing the task on the top of its agenda.

As noted earlier, a weakness of MOLGEN is that it is sometimes forced to guess when developing a plan, but has no very sophisticated method for backtracking. In other words, MOLGEN is better at proposing than revising, and does not always recover from bad guesses. The next section describes a system which solves problems in the propose and revise paradigm using a single architectural level but has a better revision process.

Running Errands (Least Commitment Strategy)

The following CLIPS program schedules an errand by first fixing its start time as early as possible, and then fixing its end time, if a suitable start time has been found. It prioritizes tasks and tries to keep its options open for as long as possible. However, it is not able to recover from bad decisions, either by backtracking or fixing a partial schedule that will not work out.

```
;; TEMPLATES

;; An errand has a name, an interval in which it must start,
;; defined by earliest and latest, a duration, a priority
;; (low number is high priority), and a symbol that says
;; whether it not it has been scheduled.
(deftemplate errand
  (field name (type SYMBOL))
  (field earliest (type INTEGER) (default 0))
  (field latest (type INTEGER) (default 0))
  (field duration (type INTEGER) (default 100))
  (field priority (type INTEGER) (default 0))
  (field done (type SYMBOL) (default no))
)

;; A schedule item has a task, which is the name of an errand,
;; start and finish times, a priority, and a status that says
;; whether or not it has been completely specified.
(deftemplate schedule
  (field task (type SYMBOL))
  (field start (type INTEGER) (default 0))
  (field finish (type INTEGER) (default 0))
  (field priority (type INTEGER) (default 0))
  (field status (type INTEGER) (default 0))
)
```

continued

```
;; The goal template is used to control the behavior of the
;; program by enforcing a certain order in which goals are
;; achieved. Start times of errands are fixed first, then end
;; times are filled in.
(deftemplate goal
  (field subgoal (type SYMBOL)))

;; FACTS

(deffacts the-facts
  (goal (subgoal start))
  (errand (name hospital)
    (earliest 1030) (latest 1030) (duration 200) (priority 1))
  (errand (name doctor)
    (earliest 1430) (latest 1530) (duration 200) (priority 1))
  (errand (name lunch)
    (earliest 1130) (latest 1430) (duration 100) (priority 2))
  (errand (name guitar-shop)
    (earliest 1000) (latest 1700) (duration 100) (priority 3))
  (errand (name haircut)
    (earliest 900) (latest 1700) (duration 30) (priority 4))
  (errand (name groceries)
    (earliest 900) (latest 1800) (duration 130) (priority 5))
  (errand (name dentist)
    (earliest 900) (latest 1600) (duration 100) (priority 2))
)

;; FUNCTIONS

;; Does start time S occur in the interval [T, T+D]?
;; Note that no two tasks can start at the same time.
(deffunction overlap1 (?s ?t ?d)
  (and (<= ?t ?s) (< ?s (+ ?t ?d))))

;; Does end time S occur in the interval [T, T+D]?
;; Note that since we assume instant transition from
;; one task to another, Task A can start on B's end time.
(deffunction overlap2 (?s ?t ?d)
  (and (< ?t ?s) (< ?s (+ ?t ?d))))

;; Clumsy addition for times represented as integers according to
;; the 24-hour clock, for example,, 900, 1030, etc. We assume that
;; all times are already rounded to ten-minute intervals.
(deffunction +t (?X ?Y)
  (bind ?T (+ ?X ?Y))
  (if
    (or (= (- ?T 60) (* (div (- ?T 60) 100) 100))
        (= (- ?T 70) (* (div (- ?T 70) 100) 100))
        (= (- ?T 80) (* (div (- ?T 80) 100) 100))
        (= (- ?T 90) (* (div (- ?T 90) 100) 100)))
    then (+ ?T 40)
    else ?T))
```

continued

```
;; RULES

;; Certain tasks have to performed at a fixed time, so we anchor
;; them right away.
(defrule fixed
  (declare (salience 80))
  (goal (subgoal start))
  ?E <- (errand (name ?N)
  (earliest ?T) (latest ?T) (duration ?D) (priority ?P) (done no))
  (not (schedule (start ?U1&:(overlap1 ?U1 ?T ?D))))
  (not (schedule (finish ?U2&:(overlap2 ?U2 ?T ?D))))
  =>
  (printout t crlf "Fixing start and end of " ?N t crlf)
  (modify ?E (done finish))
  (assert (schedule (task ?N)
    (start ?T) (finish (+t ?T ?D)) (priority ?P)))
)

;; Next we schedule highest priority task at its earliest time,
;; if we can do so without clashing with any fixed task.
(defrule priority1
  (declare (salience 50))
  (goal (subgoal start))
  ?E <- (errand (name ?N) (earliest ?T) (duration ?D) (priority
  ?P))
  (not (errand (priority ?Q&:(< ?Q ?P)) (done no)))
  (not (schedule (start ?U1&:(overlap1 ?U1 ?T ?D))))
  (not (schedule (finish ?U2&:(overlap2 ?U2 ?T ?D))))
  =>
  (printout t crlf "Fixing start of " ?N t crlf)
  (modify ?E (done start))
  (assert (schedule (task ?N) (start ?T) (priority ?P)))
)

;; Next we advance the earliest time of any task that cannot be
;; started at its earliest time, because such a start would lead
;; it to overlap with the start of a scheduled task.
(defrule priority2
  (declare (salience 60))
  (goal (subgoal start))
  ?E <- (errand (name ?N)
        (earliest ?T) (duration ?D) (priority ?P) (done no))
  (not (errand (priority ?Q&:(< ?Q ?P)) (done no)))
  (schedule (task ?M) (start ?U&:(overlap1 ?U ?T ?D)))
  (errand (name ?M&~?N) (duration ?C))
  =>
  (printout t crlf ?N " overlaps with start of " ?M t crlf)
  (modify ?E (earliest (+t ?U ?C)))
)
```

continued

```
;; We also advance the earliest time of any task that cannot be
;; started at its earliest time, because such a start would lead
;; it to overlap with the end of a scheduled task.
(defrule priority3
  (declare (salience 60))
  (goal (subgoal start))
  ?E <- (errand (name ?N) (earliest ?T) (priority ?P) (done no))
  (errand (name ?M&~?N) (duration ?C))
  (schedule (task ?M) (start ?U&:(overlap1 ?T ?U ?C)))
  =>
  (printout t crlf ?N " overlaps with end of " ?M t crlf)
  (modify ?E (earliest (+t ?U ?C)))
)

;; We also advance the earliest time of any task that cannot be
;; started at its earliest time, because such a start would lead
;; it to begin and end within the scope of a scheduled task.
(defrule priority4
  (declare (salience 60))
  (goal (subgoal start))
  ?E <- (errand (name ?N)
        (earliest ?T) (duration ?D) (priority ?P) (done no))
  (errand (name ?M&~?N) (duration ?C))
  (schedule (task ?M)
    (start ?U&:(<= ?U ?T)) (finish ?F&:(<= (+ ?T ?D) ?F)))
  =>
  (printout t crlf ?N " would occur during " ?M t crlf)
  (modify ?E (earliest (+t ?U ?C)))
)

;; We change the goal to establishing the finish times of tasks.
(defrule change-goal
  ?G <- (goal (subgoal start))
  =>
  (modify ?G (subgoal finish))
)

;; A task's finish time is its start time plus its duration.
(defrule endpoint
  (goal (subgoal finish))
  (errand (name ?N) (latest ?L) (duration ?D))
  ?S <- (schedule (task ?N) (start ?T&:(<= ?T ?L)) (finish 0))
  =>
  (printout t crlf "Fixing end of " ?N t crlf)
  (modify ?S (finish (+t ?T ?D)))
)

;; The goal is now to report the plan.
(defrule unfinish
  ?G <- (goal (subgoal finish))
  =>
```

continued

```
    (modify ?G (subgoal report))
)

;; Tasks are printed out in chronological order.
(defrule scheduled
  (declare (salience 10))
  (goal (subgoal report))
  ?S <- (schedule (task ?N) (start ?T1) (finish ?T2&~0)
                  (status 0))
  (not (schedule (start ?T3&:(< ?T3 ?T1)) (status 0)))
  =>
  (printout t crlf ?N " from " ?T1 " till " ?T2 t crlf)
  (modify ?S (status 1))
)

;; Certain tasks may be left over.
(defrule unscheduled
  (goal (subgoal report))
  ?S <- (schedule (task ?N) (finish 0) (status 0))
  =>
  (printout t crlf ?N " not scheduled." t crlf)
  (modify ?S (status 1))
)
```

The program will happily schedule the facts given above in the `deffacts` statement. See Exercise 4 below for hints as to how to break this program by giving it a set of tasks that it cannot schedule, even though a good schedule exists.

15.3 Eliciting, representing and applying design knowledge

VT (Marcus *et al.*, 1988) is an expert system for designing elevator systems that was generated using the knowledge acquisition system SALT (Marcus, 1988b). In the next section, we concentrate upon the VT program itself, and its domain-dependent approach to guessing and revising, known as *knowledge-based backtracking*. The following section focuses upon the elicitation and representation of design knowledge in SALT.

15.3.1 Knowledge-based backtracking in VT

The VT (Vertical Transportation) program is used by Westinghouse Elevator to custom-design elevator systems: a task that it performs unaided, although it can be run in interactive mode. The input to VT consists of a set of important parameters and their values, such as required speed, carrying capacity, dimensions of existing shafts. Its output is a selection of appropriate equipment and a layout in the shaft that meets safety and performance requirements.

VT works by generating an approximate design and then refining it, dealing with constraint violations along the way. The first phase forward chains rules which take as data either values of the initial parameter set or values of parameters computed by

```
IF:     values are available for the parameters
        DOOR-OPENING, PLATFORM-WIDTH and OPENING-WIDTH,
        and DOOR-OPENING = CENTER
THEN:   CAR-JAMB-RETURN = (PLATFORM-WIDTH - OPENING-WIDTH)/2.
```

Figure 15.2 A VT rule for a design extension, freely adapted from Marcus (1988b).

other procedures. A typical rule (confusingly called a PROCEDURE in VT) might be as shown in Figure 15.2.

This whole phase is data-driven: any design step can be taken as soon as it has enough information. However, unlike the rule shown in Figure 15.2, some of these initial steps will be underconstrained and, in the absence of fully constrained steps, they will be allowed to make guesses and propose extensions based on partial information. In other words, the correspondence condition we met in the last chapter will not always hold, but the problem solver proceeds anyway on the assumption that subsequent constraint violations can be fixed.

As the design is extended, VT keeps track of which values contributed to each derived value at each step by means of a *dependency network*. This kind of data structure is described in more detail in Chapter 19, but it is simply a directed acyclic graph. The nodes represent values computed for important parameters, such as CAR-JAMB-RETURN, while the links represent rule applications. Nodes and links are created as rules are fired, so that the program can keep track of its reasoning and subsequently identify decisions that contribute to constraint violations. Such decisions become potential backtrack points in the revision process.

Constraint violations are detected by *demons* (see Chapter 6): when enough is known to compute the effect on a value of the values that constrain it, the comparison is made. Potential fixes have preference ratings and are tried in order; an example of a fix is given in Figure 15.3. The dependency network is then used to propagate the changes made by the selected fix through the parameter values.

Figure 15.3 shows a rule that proposes two alternative fixes for excessive pressure on the hoist cables: one that reduces the grip on the cables and one that increases the number of cables. The former is preferred, but if this fails to reduce the pressure enough, or interacts with another fix, then the latter will be tried. The latter has a lower rating, because changing the number of cables in the hoist has a knock-on effect upon other equipment sizes.

We say that two constraints are *antagonistic* if complying with one constraint aggravates another. To return to our cinema example, if two people want to go to the movies together, and one is bored by anything but horror films while the other dislikes the sight of blood, then we have a recipe for conflict. Gratifying either person will involve upsetting the other.

```
IF:     there has been a violation of MAXIMUM-MACHINE-GROOVE-PRESSURE
THEN:   try a downgrade for MACHINE-GROOVE-MODEL (1)
        try an increase of HOIST-CABLE-QUANTITY (4).
```

Figure 15.3 A rule that proposes two alternative fixes for a constraint violation, freely adapted from Marcus *et al.* (1988).

Thus the problem of revision is complicated by the fact that fixes can interact. As we saw above, changing the number of cables in the hoist can affect constraints on other equipment; for example, there comes a point where you have to upgrade the elevator model. VT's knowledge base contains 37 chains of interacting fixes, and three of these contain antagonistic constraints. For example, the constraint antagonistic to MAXIMUM-MACHINE-GROOVE-PRESSURE is MAXIMUM-TRACTION-RATIO. Reducing pressure on the hoist cables can result in an increased traction ratio, while reducing the traction ratio can increase pressure on the cables.

If antagonistic constraints are violated simultaneously, one can conceive of a situation in which attempts to resolve one constraint aggravate the other constraint and vice versa, leading to an endless loop if the level of aggravation amounts to a violation. VT deals with this problem by treating the violation of antagonistic constraints as a special case. When a demon detects a violation in one of an antagonistic pair, it checks to see if the other has been violated. If it has, the demon resets each parameter value implicated in the violation to the last value that it had before the violation of *either* constraint, thereby undoing all fix attempts so far. Then it tries combinations of potential fixes in the following order:

(1) fixes that help both violations;
(2) fixes that help one but do not aggravate the other;
(3) fixes that help one but do aggravate the other.

In the third case, VT tries to fix the most important constraint first. Thus VT can be contrasted with MOLGEN in that it puts more effort into the revise part of the propose and revise strategy, whereas MOLGEN concentrates on managing its least commitment policy.

VT is implemented in OPS5 and its rule base consists of about 3000 rules. Published data are available on rule firings and CPU time per run: rule firings range between 2500 and 11 500, while CPU time on a VAX 11/780 with 20 Mb of memory ranges between 7 and 20 minutes. It is interesting to note that about 2000 of VT's rules are domain-specific ones generated by the SALT acquisition system (to which we now turn); the other 1000 handle input-output, explanation and control.

15.3.2 Acquiring propose and revise knowledge in SALT

The SALT system associated with VT assumes a *propose and revise* problem solving strategy, and uses this assumption to impose structure upon the process of knowledge acquisition. One method is to collect knowledge which fills particular roles within the problem solving strategy. Identifying these roles, and understanding the relationships between them, turns out to be crucial to successful knowledge acquisition.

Domain knowledge is seen as performing one of three roles in any propose and revise system under construction; these are listed below with their SALT names in parentheses:

(1) knowledge which proposes an extension to the current design (PROPOSE-A-DESIGN-EXTENSION);
(2) knowledge which identifies constraints upon design extensions (IDENTIFY-A-CONSTRAINT); and
(3) knowledge about how to repair constraint violations (PROPOSE-A-FIX).

SALT is an automatic system which acquires knowledge under each of these headings by interacting with an expert, and then compiles this knowledge into production rules to generate a domain-specific knowledge base. This knowledge base can then be coupled with an interpreter in a problem solving *shell* (see Chapter 10) to create an expert system. SALT retains the original knowledge it acquired in a declarative form, which can be updated and recompiled as necessary.

The intermediate representation that SALT uses is a dependency network. Each node in the net is the name of a value, and can represent an input (such as TYPE-OF-LOADING), a design parameter (such as PLATFORM-WIDTH), or a constraint (such as MAXIMUM-MACHINE-GROOVE-PRESSURE). There are three kinds of directed links in the network:

- *contributes-to* links A to B if the value of A is used to compute the value of B;
- *constrains* links A to B if A is a constraint that restricts the value of a design parameter B;
- *suggests-revision-of* links A to B if A is a constraint, and a violation of A suggests a change to the current value of B.

The user of SALT can enter knowledge in any order, but each piece of knowledge must be either a PROCEDURE (for extending the design), a CONSTRAINT (for restricting the value of a design parameter) or a FIX (for repairing a constraint violation). There are schemas for each kind of knowledge, and the three kinds correspond to the three knowledge roles outlined above in an obvious way. Once a role has been chosen for elaboration, SALT will prompt the user for all the knowledge required by the role.

A PROCEDURE must be supplied for every design parameter that figures in a completed design, and should try to take into account all considerations relevant to that par-ameter's value. Where parameters are underconstrained, some preference between alternative values should be supplied. Thus the completed schema for computing the parameter CAR-JAMB-RETURN (as featured in Figure 15.2) might look as in Figure 15.4. A CONSTRAINT is intended to capture interactions between parameter values which are not captured by the knowledge encoded in PROCEDUREs, but which need to be checked before a solution can be deemed complete. A FIX suggests revisions that can be tried in the light of a constraint violation, and involves changing one or more pa-rameter values. Figure 15.5 shows a completed SALT schema for a fix to the violation of the constraint MAXIMUM-MACHINE-GROOVE-PRESSURE.

Given the stylized nature of the schemas, it is not hard to see how they could be automatically compiled into production rules. However, SALT does more than merely translate these schemata; it also analyzes how the different pieces of knowledge fit together. To get the most out of SALT's analytic abilities, the user should enter FIXes last, so that the implications of each fix can be analyzed for the whole knowledge base.

1.	Name:	CAR-JAMB-RETURN
2.	Precondition:	DOOR-OPENING = CENTER
3.	Procedure	CALCULATION
4.	Formula	(PLATFORM-WIDTH – OPENING WIDTH) / 2
5.	Justification	CENTER-OPENING DOORS LOOK BEST WHEN CENTERED ON THE PLATFORM

Figure 15.4 A filled-out PROCEDURE schema for CAR-JAMB-RETURN.

Constraint Name:	MAXIMUM-MACHINE-GROOVE-PRESSURE
Value to Change:	HOIST-CABLE-QUANTITY
Change Type:	INCREASE
Step Type:	BY-STEP
Step Size:	1
Preference Rating:	4
Preference Reason:	CHANGES MINOR EQUIPMENT SIZING

Figure 15.5 A FIX for MAXIMUM-MACHINE-GROOVE-PRESSURE violation.

SALT derives each link in the dependency network from a piece of knowledge supplied by the user. Thus it can work out that PLATFORM-WIDTH *contributes-to* CAR-JAMB-RETURN from the PROCEDURE that links these parameters. Similarly, the *constrains* and *suggests-revision-of* links can be derived from the declaration of CONSTRAINTS and FIXes respectively.

The task of the generated expert system is to find a path through the network and assign values at each node, in such a way that all constraints have been checked and satisfied, so that the network can settle into a stable state. It is the job of the compiler to proceduralize these paths, but also to determine compilability by confirming that there is indeed a unique and complete path for a set of inputs. Much of this work involves checking that the preconditions associated with PROCEDUREs do not interact in detrimental ways. For example, if preconditions overlap for a set of inputs, then this may affect path uniqueness, whereas if there are gaps in the preconditions, then some inputs may not result in the generation of a complete path. SALT also detects loops among PROCEDUREs, which would prevent the system from converging on a solution.

15.4 Summary of constructive problem solving

We have seen that some construction problems can be sufficiently constrained by domain knowledge to all but eliminate trial and error. Thus, in configuring a computer system, R1 never had to guess at the best next step in elaborating the current state of the problem, or go back and undo an extension to a previous partial solution. In this situation, an overall strategy of top-down refinement may be all that is required to control the bottom-up search for an acceptable arrangement of solution elements. Since you never need to look back, there is no need to keep a history of previous decisions. Neither is there any need to keep track of dependencies between decisions.

Yet many construction problems will remain insufficiently constrained by domain knowledge, either because

- the available knowledge is incomplete, or
- many near-optimal solutions are possible.

Incompleteness indicates that the problem solver should follow a least commitment strategy and be prepared to make a guess at the best extension to the current partial solution. Since guesses may turn out wrong, the program must be able to detect conflicts among constraints and either (i) backtrack and try again or (ii) propose a fix for the conflict. However conflicts are resolved, some mechanism for recording previous decisions and dependencies between them is essential; we shall return to this topic in Chapter 19.

If there are many near-optimal solutions, then the program may wish to simply adopt the first solution that it finds which meets some minimum set of requirements. Pursuing the search for an optimal or best-scoring solution will normally incur prohibitive computational cost. Design and configuration problems are often defined over extremely large, if not infinite, search spaces, and this is one of the features that distinguishes them from the classification problems that we reviewed in Chapters 11 and 12.

It is clear that problems of scale can affect construction problems more dramatically than classification problems. Even if we examine toy problems, such as the 'Queens' problem outlined in Chapter 1, it is evident that methods that work well for four queens or eight queens will not work at all for 100 queens or 1000 queens. Classification is a problem that is often amenable to a 'divide and conquer' strategy, particularly if the space of target categories can be arranged hierarchically, as we saw in Chapter 13.

By the same token, there are many real tasks, such as robot planning and job shop scheduling, which involve combinatorial problems that resist solution by the most sophisticated algorithms and which do not lend themselves to 'divide and conquer' approaches. This is partly because, in many cases, there are no good metrics that tell you whether or not a particular solution fragment will form part of a total solution. A plan has to work as a whole; its goodness is not a straightforward function of the goodness of its individual steps. Also, for many problems, the 'plan library' approach of ONCOCIN (see Chapter 10) does not provide sufficient power or flexibility, either because there is no natural organization of useful plans into a library of skeletons, or because the environment in which planning has to be done is too dynamic to permit the anticipation of all possible responses.

Knowledge-based methods offer a viable alternative to algorithmic approaches in those cases where there is sufficient domain expertise to drive a propose-and-refine or propose-and-fix approach. But these methods require some rather special control machinery in the context of construction problems, and also some special machinery for tracking program decisions. We return to this topic at a more advanced level in the following chapters.

In Chapter 18, we explore a system that attempts to identify the three-dimensional structure of proteins in solution. The combinatorics of considering all possible arrangements of molecules obviously prohibits the use of exhaustive search or backtracking, so the program employs a special architecture for multiple knowledge bases that supports a number of control heuristics for traversing the solution space. This architecture, called a *blackboard system*, provides powerful mechanisms for implementing strategies such as successive refinement of partial solutions and the repair of faulty solutions.

In Chapter 19, we examine truth maintenance systems – a mechanism for recording decisions in a manner that facilitates intelligent backtracking. In those cases where backtracking is unavoidable, one would at least like to be able to identify the choice point that caused the computation to go astray, rather than to backtrack chronologically through alternative rule applications. Or, alternatively, one might like to develop certain lines of reasoning in parallel for a while, before choosing between them.

BIBLIOGRAPHICAL NOTES

Many standard texts contain good chapters on planning, for example, Nilsson (1980), Genesereth and Nilsson (1987), and Charniak and McDermott (1985). See Sacerdoti (1974) for an early work on least commitment planning. See also Brown and Chandrasekaran (1989) and Coyne (1988) for descriptions of research into design problem solving.

A good recent text on planning is Dean and Wellman (1991) which combines AI, control theory and decision theory to provide a well-rounded view of the field. On the research side, IEEE has published proceedings of its *AI Simulation and Planning in High Autonomy Systems Conference* (1991, 1992). These contain papers on a broad range of constructive applications from fault modeling and diagnosis to planning and intelligent control.

The EXPECT system (Gil and Paris, 1994) is a role-limiting knowledge acquisition tool that has been applied to the building of 'propose and revise' expert systems, such as VT. Like PROTEGE (see Chapter 10), it separates declarative domain knowledge from problem solving knowledge, but focuses on constraint satisfaction problems. Such problems are specified with a set of constraints and a state, and constraints can have fixes, as in VT.

STUDY SUGGESTIONS

1. Explain 'least commitment strategy,' and contrast it with 'propose and revise.'

2. Try to list as many tasks as you can think of which
   (i) are amenable to solution by least commitment alone, and
   (ii) are not amenable to solution by least commitment alone.
   Think of everyday tasks, such as planning a shopping expedition. What properties distinguish the two classes of tasks?

3. Explain the terms 'meta-level architecture' and 'metaplanning.'

4. Examine the program in Box 15.1. Can you think of a way of modifying the data supplied by the `deffacts` statement to break the program, so that it won't find a schedule where one exists? (Hint: Try manipulating only the priorities of the tasks.)

5. The errand program in Box 15.1 fails to schedule all the tasks given in the following `deffacts` statement, even though it is possible to find a schedule that meets the constraints.

```
(deffacts the-facts
  (goal (subgoal start))
  (errand (name hospital)
    (earliest 1030) (latest 1030) (duration 200) (priority
1))

  (errand (name doctor)
    (earliest 1430) (latest 1530) (duration 200) (priority
1))

  (errand (name lunch)
    (earliest 1130) (latest 1430) (duration 100) (priority
2))

  (errand (name guitar-shop)
    (earliest 1000) (latest 1700) (duration 100) (priority
2))

  (errand (name haircut)
    (earliest 900) (latest 1700) (duration 30) (priority 2))
```

continued

```
    (errand (name groceries)
      (earliest 900) (latest 1800) (duration 130) (priority 2))
    (errand (name bank)
      (earliest 930) (latest 1530) (duration 30) (priority 2))
    (errand (name dentist)
      (earliest 900) (latest 1600) (duration 100) (priority 1))
  )
```

Why?

6. Figure 15.6 shows an additional rule for the errand program which solves the problem noted in Question 4 above. When a clash is detected between a task that must take place at a fixed time and another task, the second task is rescheduled. When a clash between 'unfixed' tasks is detected, these rules reschedule the one with the lower priority.

```
;; Move any task scheduled to clash with a more constrained task
;; so that it starts when the more constrained task would end.
;; A more constrained task is a task that is scheduled to start
;; closer to its latest possible start time.
(defrule clash
  (declare (salience 100))
  (goal (subgoal fix))
  ?S <- (schedule (task ?M) (start ?M1))
  (errand (name ?M) (duration ?C) (earliest ?E1) (latest ?L1))
  (schedule
      (task ?N&~?M)
      (start ?N1&:(and (<= ?M1 ?N1) (< ?N1 (+ ?M1 ?C)))))
  (errand (name ?N) (duration ?D) (earliest ?E2)
      (latest ?L2&:(< (- ?L2 ?E2) (- ?L1 ?E1))))
  =>
  (printout t crlf ?M " clashes with " ?N t crlf)
  (modify ?S (start (+t ?N1 ?D)))
  )
```

Figure 15.6 A rule for resolving schedule clashes.

Thus the clash rule says 'reschedule the least constrained task in the event of a clash.' This rule will fire as many times as it likes under the control of the 'fix' subgoal. The 'start' and 'finish' rules, that is, the rules governed by the 'start' and 'finish' subgoals, remain the same.

Your job is to write three control rules that will allow these new rules to be added to the rule set and produce the right behavior. The control rules break down as follows:

(i) Write a rule called **fixstart** which fires when all the other rules within

```
    (goal (subgoal start))
```

continued

their premises have failed to fix the start of an errand. This rule simply asserts a schedule vector for the task, and fixes its start time to be the current value of the errand's **latest** slot.

(ii) Change the existing rule **unstart** so that it changes the subgoal in the goal statement from 'start' to 'fix,' instead of from 'start' to 'finish.'

(iii) Write a rule called **unfix** which changes the subgoal in the goal statement from 'fix' to 'finish.'

Then, do the following.

(iv) Test the program and ensure that it solves the problem for the given set of facts.

(v) Finally, the heuristic embodied in the clash rule is not failsafe. Devise a new set of facts that breaks this program, that is, a set of facts for which the program fails to find a schedule when one exists.

7. So far there is nothing particularly knowledge based about our planning program, since it does not apply any constraints over and above the obvious temporal ones. So let's add two rules which apply a domain-specific constraint, namely that in order to avail oneself of a service, or buy an item, one must have money. Hence, the trip to the bank must be scheduled before all such tasks.

(i) Add a field called **kind** to the errand template, so that you can put one of the following three symbols into that field for each errand fact in deffacts:

- goods
- service
- visit.

Thus the bank and medical tasks can be deemed visits, while haircut and lunch are services, and groceries and guitar-shopping involve goods.

(ii) Interpose a new problem solving phase called **tune** between the 'start' and 'fix' subgoals, so that we apply domain constraints before fixing clashes. You will need to change and extend the rules for manipulating goal tokens.

(iii) Add a rule called **money**, which only fires when

```
(goal (subgoal tune))
```

is in working memory. The money rule should recognize the situation where a task that needs money is scheduled to start before the trip to the bank. It should then move that task so that it starts after the trip to the bank. The 'fix' rules can then resolve any conflicts that this causes.

(iv) Test your program on the following collection of facts.

```
(deffacts the-facts
  (goal (subgoal start))
  (errand (name hospital) (kind visit)
    (earliest 930) (latest 930) (duration 200) (priority 1))
  (errand (name lunch) (kind service)
    (earliest 1130) (latest 1430) (duration 100) (priority 2))
  (errand (name guitar-shop) (kind goods)
```

continued

```
        (earliest 1000) (latest 1700) (duration 100) (priority 3))
      (errand (name haircut) (kind service)
        (earliest 0900) (latest 1700) (duration 30) (priority 4))
      (errand (name groceries) (kind goods)
        (earliest 0900) (latest 1800) (duration 130) (priority 5))
      (errand (name bank) (kind visit)
        (earliest 0930) (latest 1530) (duration 30) (priority 2))
  )
```

8. How easy did you find the incremental program development steps of
   Exercises 4–7? What are the pros and cons of this style of programming?

16 Designing for Explanation

There are two compelling reasons for the requirement that expert systems should be 'transparent,' that is, able to explain their reasoning and justify their conclusions in a manner that is intelligible to users.

- The *clients* of automatic advice need to be convinced that the reasoning behind a conclusion is substantially correct, and that the solution proposed is appropriate to their particular case.
- The *engineers* of an expert system need to be able to satisfy themselves that the mechanisms employed in the derivation of a conclusion are functioning according to specification.

In this chapter, we begin with a short survey of early work on explanations. Then we discuss in detail how better explanations for clients were generated in the CENTAUR system, which we met in Chapter 13. Finally, we discuss a particular line of research, the Explainable Expert Systems project, which concentrated on transparency from a knowledge engineer's point of view, and linked it to methods of knowledge elicitation.

16.1 Rule-based explanation

Such progress as has been made in the generation of explanations can be summed up briefly in the following way. The pioneering efforts of Stanford researchers in the 1960s and 1970s provided little more than high-level trace facilities in the first instance, although these were subsequently augmented by a range of debugging tools. This level of software engineering was satisfactory for a research vehicle, such as MYCIN, but left a lot to be desired for commercial systems. More recent efforts have concentrated on making more explicit certain issues to do with the control of inference and the underlying architecture. We review these efforts in detail in this section and the next.

It has also been recognized that automatic explanation requires access to a *domain model*, just as automatic knowledge elicitation does (see Section 10.3.1). In other words, just as a program needs a modicum of domain knowledge in order to acquire more knowledge, so a program needs access to a representation of deep knowledge about the domain in order to explain its own behavior, instead of merely reporting what it has done. Such knowledge is essential to bridge the gap between the low-level implementation detail (for example, what rules the system fired) and the higher-level strategy that the system was pursuing (for example, attempting to choose between competing hypotheses).

The implications of this idea have been increasingly explored over the past 10 years, and we review some recent research in Section 16.3. The reader will see that there is indeed an intimate connection between the problems of knowledge elicitation and explanation, in that the way that knowledge is acquired and compiled has a marked effect upon the way in which it can subsequently be used to explain system output. Work in this area has also received a boost from improvements in the technology supporting graphical user interfaces, which now support audio, video and the like, although this technology does not itself solve the problem of what explanatory material to present to the user and how to present it.

16.1.1 MYCIN's explanation system

The explanation module of the MYCIN system (see Chapter 3) was automatically invoked at the end of every consultation. To explain how the value of a particular medical parameter was established, the module retrieved the list of rules that were successfully applied and printed them, along with the conclusions drawn. It also allowed the user to interrogate the system about the consultation, and ask more general questions.

Thus all question-answering facilities were based upon the system's ability to:

- display the rule invoked at any point in the consultation;
- record rule invocations and associate them with specific events, such as questions asked and conclusions drawn;
- use rule indexing to retrieve particular rules in answer to queries.

As mentioned in Chapter 3, a consultation with a backward chaining expert system involves a search through a tree of goals (see Figure 16.1). Consequently, inquiries during a consultation fall into two types:

- those that ask WHY a particular question was put;
- and those that ask HOW a particular conclusion was reached.

To answer a WHY question, one must look up the tree to see what higher goals the system is trying to achieve. To answer a HOW question, one must look down the tree to see what subgoals were satisfied to achieve the goal. Thus the explanation process can be considered as a kind of tree traversal, and is thereby reduced to a search problem.

The fact that MYCIN keeps track of the goal–subgoal structure of the computation enables it to answer questions such as

'Why do you ask if the stain of the organism is Gram negative?'

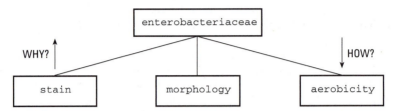

Figure 16.1 Answering questions in a MYCIN-style tree of goals.

It can simply cite the production rule which states that Gram negative staining, in conjunction with various other conditions, would suggest that the class of the organism was enterobacteriaceae, and that the current goal was to identify the organism.

MYCIN also maintains a record of the decisions it makes, and uses this record to explain and justify its decisions in response to HOW questions like

> 'What made you think that Organism-1 might be a proteus?'

In reply, MYCIN cites the rules that it applied, its degree of certainty in that decision, and the last question asked. General questions can also be asked; these reference the rules without considering the state of the dynamic database with respect to a particular patient. An example might be

> 'What do you prescribe for pseudomonas infections?'

The reply could simply cite the therapy rules that mention the organism pseudomonas.

However, the user cannot access the static knowledge contained in simple lists and knowledge tables, because these other sources of knowledge lack the uniform format of the production rules. Also, the mechanisms for creating the therapy lists and choosing the preferred drug are complex LISP functions which the user cannot inspect, and probably would not understand if he could. Finally, the order in which rules are considered for application, and the order in which the conditions of premises are considered are not aspects of the system which the user is able to question.

Thus, although WHY and HOW questions appear to provide a neat and intuitively satisfying basis for finding out what a backward chaining rule-based consultation program is doing, one must bear in mind that this approach does not cover every aspect of system function, and that a trace of rule applications will not be easy to follow if the chains of reasoning are at all long. (It just so happens that MYCIN's chains are typically not long, because the search space is relatively shallow.) Arguably, such traces tell the client more than he wants to know, although their level of detail may be useful for the knowledge engineer.

With respect to *forward* chaining systems, a mere trace of the rules applied so far is even less meaningful, because we are not in a position to know, at any given point of the computation, where the system's line of reasoning is headed, although the application of structuring techniques, such as R1's use of means–ends analysis (see Chapter 14), helps provide the missing goal structure.

16.1.2 Explanation in MYCIN derivatives: EMYCIN and NEOMYCIN

It is well known that the problems associated with understanding, monitoring and correcting the behavior of an expert system multiply as the knowledge base increases in size (Davis, 1980b). For example, it becomes more difficult to ensure that 'new' rules are consistent with 'old' ones, and to understand the flow of control in situations where large numbers of applicable rules may be in competition for the attention of the interpreter. Not much work has been done on how to monitor rule bases as they are extended in order to detect conflict or redundancy, although see Suwa *et al.* (1982) for one approach to this problem.

EMYCIN (van Melle 1981) developed and elaborated MYCIN's facilities to some extent. Thus EXPLAIN, TEST and REVIEW commands were provided as debugging aids for the knowledge engineer (see Chapter 10). As in MYCIN, EXPLAIN worked by printing each rule that contributed to the conclusion, together with

(1) the certainty factor that resulted from the successful application of the rule;
(2) the 'tally' value associated with the evaluation of the premises of the rule; and
(3) the last question asked by the system before the conclusion was drawn.

The use of meta-rules in MYCIN and EMYCIN, which was intended to make some of the control choices explicit, opened the door to reasoning about problem solving strategy, in addition to reasoning at the object level of the domain. It then became feasible to think about meta-level reasoning in the context of explanations, such that explanations of what had been inferred could be augmented by an account of why certain inferences had been drawn in preference to others.

Two rational reconstructions of the early Stanford work were begun at the end of the 1970s. One was the NEOMYCIN system (Clancey and Letsinger, 1984; Clancey, 1987c), which represented an attempt to take a more abstract approach to MYCIN-style medical problem solving, based on epistemological and psychological considerations. The focus of attention was on what kinds of knowledge clinicians actually used in routine diagnosis, and what their reasoning processes were like. Thus NEOMYCIN was much more concerned with the simulation of human problem solving (or *cognitive modeling*) than MYCIN had been. No one had ever claimed that clinicians actually reasoned in the way that MYCIN did – all that mattered were the results.

This novel approach had implications for the explanation facilities. In NEOMYCIN, there was an emphasis on *strategic explanation*, in which one tried to make clear the overall plans and methods used in attaining a goal, instead of merely citing the rules employed (Hasling *et al.*, 1984). In other words, the program was expected to have some explicit representation of the problem solving process, as well as domain knowledge. Rather as in INTERNIST, the collection and interpretation of data was focused by the current set of hypotheses (the *differential*: a term derived from the basic task of differential diagnosis). To understand the behavior of the program, in terms of the questions it asks and the flow of control, the user needs to have some access to the diagnostic strategies that the program is using.

NEOMYCIN had the following basic organization:

METARULE397

IF: There are two items on the differential that differ in some disease process feature
THEN: Ask a question that differentiates between these two kinds of processes.

Figure 16.2 A NEOMYCIN meta-rule.

- Strategic knowledge was separated out from the medical knowledge and encoded in meta-rules.
- Diseases were organized taxonomically, as in INTERNIST, so that there was some explicit representation of the hypothesis space.
- Both of the above kinds of knowledge were kept separate from the rules that encode various kinds of association between data and hypotheses.

Thus the basic approach is still based on heuristic classification (see Chapters 11 and 12), but the mixed representation scheme structures and controls the use of domain rules, simplifying them in the process. In addition, the domain rules are themselves differentiated into four classes:

- *Causal rules* connect symptoms and diseases via a network of symptom and disease categories.
- *Trigger rules* associate data with hypotheses, enabling a kind of forward reasoning. When such a rule fires, the relevant hypothesis is placed in the differential.
- *Data/hypothesis rules* also associate data with hypotheses, but they only work on hypotheses already in the differential.
- *Screening rules* encode such things as restrictions on data, for example 'if the patient is male, then discount the possibility of pregnancy.'

The meta-rule shown in Figure 16.2 encodes a general strategy of looking for data that differentiates between two current hypotheses, for example, data that are predicted by one hypotheses but not the other.

Thus, in NEOMYCIN, the execution of meta-rules replaces the MYCIN-style global control regime of backward chaining. The flow of control depends entirely upon which meta-rules get executed. This is a rather more radical use of meta-rules than was found in MYCIN, where meta-rules merely served to occasionally order or prune domain rules that were being considered for application.

An ordered set of meta-rules for performing some task can be considered as a meta-level architecture, where tasks and subtasks correspond to meta-level goals and subgoals. Meta-rules are methods for achieving abstract goals, such as 'generate questions,' while domain-level rules ask particular questions. Rather than eliciting or reasoning about specific pieces of information, meta-rules encode general strategies for manipulating information.

METARULE073

IF: There is a datum that can be requested that is a characterizing feature of the recent finding that
        is currently being considered
THEN: Find out about the datum.

Figure 16.3 Another NEOMYCIN meta-rule.

Thus, in addition to rules that elicit particular data from the user, there is a NEO-MYCIN meta-rule which guides the asking of questions, as shown in Figure 16.3. Such a rule can then be cited as an explanation of why a particular question was asked. In MYCIN, this strategy of finding out about data associated with a recent finding was implicit in the architecture.

The other attempt at a reconstruction of MYCIN begun at the end of the 1970s was the CENTAUR system (Aikins, 1983). This program (described in Chapter 13) experimented with a mixed representation of knowledge in the reimplementation of the PUFF expert system for pulmonary function test interpretation. Its architecture combined frames (see Chapter 6) and production rules (see Chapter 5) in an interesting way that it made it easier to generate explanations.

16.2 Frame-based explanation

We have seen that it is not a simple matter to generate coherent explanations from traces of rule activity alone. Rules specify their own context of application in a somewhat minimal way by containing only those conditions sufficient to make the rule worth activating. There need not be any indication of what high-level tasks the rule is meant to accomplish; for example, whether it asserts a hypothesis, discriminates between competing hypotheses, gathers data from the user, and so on.

Consequently, researchers and developers in the 1980s sought to combine production rules with frames which supply some of this extra context. Such frames represented important relationships between data and hypotheses not encoded in the rules, as well as storing explanatory text. In the 1990s, with the advent of multimedia, frames also came to store pointers to images, such as schematics, and entire electronic manuals, as we shall see in Section 16.2.2.

16.2.1 Explanation in CENTAUR

The original implementation of PUFF in EMYCIN (see, for example, Aikins *et al.*, 1984) performed satisfactorily, in terms of solving the problems posed to it, but the knowledge representation was found to be deficient in a number of other respects.

- It was difficult to represent typical patterns of data or typical classes of patient.
- Adding or modifying rules to encode additional knowledge or refine existing knowledge frequently had unexpected effects.
- Changing the order in which information was requested from the user proved to be difficult, since the requests were automatically generated as the interpreter fired the rules.
- Generating clear explanations presented problems, since little more than a trace of rule activations was available.

Aikins argued, as Clancey had done, that the very modularity and uniformity of production rules, which had been cited as positive features, had their negative aspect. Most rule sets contain implicit groupings, either using various kinds of indexing concealed in the interpreter (for example, the ORGRULES and PATRULES of MYCIN, which related to organisms and patients respectively), or having conditions and actions that manipulate goal tokens in working memory. This organization is often hierarchical, owing to the taxonomic organization of hypotheses (in classification tasks), or the decomposition of goals into subgoals (in constructive tasks). Many of the problems cited above can be traced to the failure to differentiate between different kinds of knowledge, which may need to be represented and applied in different ways. As we saw in Chapter 13, CENTAUR attempted to combine the strengths of rule- and frame-based programming in a way that compensated for some of the weaknesses of the individual paradigms.

From an explanation point of view, CENTAUR emphasized the *context* in which reasoning was done, as well as the *stage-dependent* nature of expert-level problem solving. In order to understand why a particular question was asked, one needed to understand not merely the rule that fired but also the active hypothesis that was being considered. Thus Aikins shares some of Clancey's concerns, although her approach is a little less ambitious, since it stops short of an attempt at cognitive modeling.

A run of the CENTAUR consultation program consists of an interpreter executing an agenda of tasks, rather than a chaining together of rules. A primary use for the agenda is to provide an explanation of why the system behaved as it did in the course of the consultation. Consequently, each task entry contains information about both the source of the task and the reason that the task was scheduled.

The source of the task will be an active prototype (that is, one that is a good match for the case data) or another task. Tasks are added to the agenda either by prototype control slots or in the course of executing tasks already on the agenda. The reasons are generated from the name of the prototype and the name of the control slot responsible for setting up the task.

During program execution, a prototype is always in one of three states:

- *inactive*, that is, not being considered as a hypothesis;
- *potentially relevant*, that is, suggested by data values;
- *active*, that is, selected from the above and placed on the hypothesis list.

Disease prototypes represent hypotheses. The hypothesis list is simply a list of prototypes paired with their certainty factors, ordered in decreasing order of certainty. Two other lists keep track of confirmed and disconfirmed prototypes.

The key events in a CENTAUR consultation are

- entering the initial data;
- triggering the prototypes using antecedent rules;
- scoring the prototypes and selecting one to be 'current';
- using known facts to fill in the current prototype;
- testing the match between the facts and the expected values;
- accounting for data left over by the initial diagnosis;
- refining the diagnosis accordingly;
- summarizing and printing the results.

Thus the consultation proceeds in *stages*, rather as a normal consultation might. As a session begins, the CONSULTATION prototype is selected as the current prototype, and the empty agenda is given two tasks: to FILL-IN and then to CONFIRM the current prototype, courtesy of the TO-FILL-IN and IF-CONFIRMED control slots in the CONSULTATION prototype. The TO-FILL-IN slot of the prototype actually contains

```
CONSULTATION
-------------

TO-FILL-IN:
Ask for the TRACING-LEVEL for the CONSULTATION
Ask for the AGENDA-PRINTING for the CONSULTATION
Ask for the STRATEGY for the CONSULTATION

IF-CONFIRMED:
Set the confirmation threshold to 0
Set the percentage of filled-in slots necessary to confirm the prototype to .75
Set the default procedure for filling in slots to fill in slots in decreasing order of their importance
measures
Determine the domain of the consultation
Select the current best prototype
Fill in the prototype
Apply tasks in the if-confirmed slot
Mark facts that are accounted for by the prototype
Apply the refinement rules associated with the confirmed prototypes Apply the summary rules
associated with the confirmed prototypes Execute actions associated with the confirmed prototypes
```

Figure 16.4 Unfolding of tasks in CENTAUR.

three tasks, each of which sets a variable for the consultation: the TRACING-LEVEL governs the amount of detail in the trace, AGENDA-PRINTING determines whether or not tasks are printed as they are added to the agenda or executed, and STRATEGY can take on the values CONFIRMATION (select the best match and attempt to confirm it), ELIMINATION (select the worst match and attempt to eliminate it), or FIXED-ORDER (use a predetermined order for evaluating hypotheses).

The first three tasks in the IF-CONFIRMED slot set other variables which control the consultation, such as setting the percentage of a prototype's slots that have to be filled in before that prototype can be considered confirmed. This allows the knowledge engineer to experiment with variations on the basic control regime, and possibly tune the system for different domains. The rest of the IF-CONFIRMED tasks control the stages of the consultation, as can be seen from the listing of the CONSULTATION prototype reproduced in Figure 16.4.

Once the domain of the consultation has been determined (in the present context this is pulmonary function), PULMONARY-DISEASE becomes the next current prototype, and it elicits the initial data from the user by asking a series of questions, as shown in Figure 16.5. In each exchange, the numbered line is a prompt printed by the program; acronyms on this line stand for laboratory data. The line prefixed by '**' is the user's data entry response. Any comment that follows in square brackets is a message from the system, alerting the user to the fact that a prototype has been matched. Acronyms on this line stand for disease prototypes.

It can be seen from this transcript that data values trigger prototypes even as they are being entered. For example, the lines

6) FEV1/FVC ratio:
** 40
[Trigger for OAD and CM900]

```
--------PATIENT-7--------
1) Patient's identifying number:
** 7446
2) referral diagnosis:
** ASTHMA
[Trigger for ASTHMA and CM900]
3) RV/RV-predicted:
** 261
4) TLC (body box) observed/predicted:
** 139
5) FVC/FVC-predicted:
** 81
[Trigger for NORMAL and CM500]
6) FEV1/FVC ratio:
** 40
 [Trigger for OAD and CM900]
7) the DLCO/DLCO-predicted:
** 117
[Trigger for NORMAL and CM700]
8) Change in FEV1 (after dilation)
** 31
9) MMF/MMF-predicted:
 ** 12
[Trigger for OAD and CM900]
10) The slope F5025:
** 9
[Trigger for OAD and CM900]
```

Figure 16.5 Questions and triggers in CENTAUR.

indicate that the FEV1/FVC ratio of 40 activates the OAD (Obstructive Airways Disease) prototype with a certainty measure of 900. (FEV1 stands for the Forced Expiratory Volume in one second, that is the volume of air expelled in one second during a forced breathing out, starting with the lungs full of air, while FVC stands for Forced Vital Capacity, that is, the volume of air expired during a rapid forced breathing out, starting with the lungs full of air and ending with whatever residual volume of air is left in the lungs after full expiration.)

Certainty measures range from -1000 to 1000 for computational convenience, and they indicate how sure the system is that the prototype cited matches the data for a particular case. They are therefore a measure of how well the actual values provided by the user fit into the prototypical or expected values stored in the slots of a prototype, and it is used to select the current best hypothesis. These measures are similar to the certainty factors found in MYCIN and EMYCIN, and the algorithm for combining more than one measure is the same. (Note that these values are not explained. Thus the algorithm for combining certainties is a 'black box' as far as the user is concerned.)

Figure 16.5 illustrates that the user can see immediately what is the impact of the input data upon the disease prototypes. In a system that is wholly rule based, it is usually the case that data which activate the rule that 'wins' in the conflict resolution are the only data that appear in the trace. Thus one is left wondering what effect, if any, the other data might have had.

```
Hypothesis: ASTHMA, CM: 900, Reason: RDX was ASTHMA
Hypothesis: NORMAL, CM: 500, Reason: FVC was 81
Hypothesis: OAD, CM: 900, Reason: FEV1/FVC was 40
Hypothesis: NORMAL, CM: 700, Reason: DLCO was 117
Hypothesis: OAD, CM: 900, Reason: MMF was 12
Hypothesis: OAD, CM: 900, Reason: F5025 was 9

More specific hypotheses chosen: NORMAL, OAD
[New prototypes being filled in... NORMAL, OAD]
```

Figure 16.6 **Summary of triggered prototypes.**

After the initial data has been elicited, a summary of the triggered prototypes is printed out for inspection, as shown in Figure 16.6. NORMAL and OAD will be considered next, since these are immediate successors of the PULMONARY-DISEASE prototype. Consideration of the ASTHMA hypothesis will be deferred, because ASTHMA is a subtype of OAD, and is therefore considered after OAD in the overall strategy of top-down refinement. The hierarchical structure of the hypotheses space makes this overall strategy extremely clear and comprehensible to the user. In a system that is wholly rule based, the user might need to understand the conflict resolution strategy (for example, specificity) before understanding why some hypotheses are evaluated before others.

Notice that not all of the data values entered were responsible for triggering a prototype, and that more than one prototype has been triggered. In other words, some data values did not suggest any initial hypotheses, while some values suggested OAD, and others suggested normality. As the new prototypes for NORMAL and OAD are filled in, data values such as TLC (Total Lung Capacity), which did not activate any prototypes, will be considered in the context of active hypotheses, and may cause their certainty measures to be altered. Thus, the TLC value of 139 casts doubt upon the hypothesis of normality, as shown in Figure 16.7. Data values which fall outside the range of expected values stored in the slots of a prototype will tend to lower the certainty measure associated with that prototype.

Figure 16.7 shows that, although NORMAL was suggested as a hypothesis by two of the original test results, five other test results militate against this hypothesis being correct, and its certainty measure is reduced accordingly. All this can be gleaned from the trace. The hypothesis list is then constructed and ordered, with OAD as the current best prototype:

Hypothesis List: (OAD 999) (NORMAL –699)
I am testing the hypothesis that there is Obstructive Airways Disease.

```
!Surprise value! 261 for RV in NORMAL, CM: 700
!Surprise value! 139 for TLC in NORMAL, CM: 400
!Surprise value! 40 for FEV1/FVC in NORMAL, CM: –176
!Surprise value! 12 for MMF in NORMAL, CM: –499
!Surprise value! 9 for F5025 in NORMAL, CM: –699
```

Figure 16.7 **CENTAUR reporting unexpected data values.**

```
[Refinement rules being applied...]
20) The number of pack-years of smoking:
** 17
21) The number of years ago that the patient stopped smoking:
** 0
22) The degree of dyspnea:
** NONE
```

Figure 16.8 The application of refinement rules.

Eventually, the system will confirm the hypothesis that the patient is indeed suffering from OAD, that the degree of OAD is severe, and that the subtype of OAD is asthma. The consultation now moves into the refinement stage, which causes further questions to be asked, such as the degree of dyspnea (shortness of breath). This stage is instigated by the application of refinement rules, which are stored with the relevant prototypes (see Figure 16.8).

Now summary rules associated with the confirmed prototypes are executed, as shown in Figure 16.9. These merely summarize the information that has been gained in the process of filling in the prototype, and require no further interaction with the user. The printing out of findings is done by the ACTIONS slot of the relevant prototype.

The printing of the final conclusions is performed by the ACTIONS slot of the PULMONARY-DISEASE prototype, as in Figure 16.10.

The stage-dependent behavior of the program makes the program's output particularly easy to understand. At every stage of the process, it is clear what CENTAUR is trying to achieve, and which prototypes are active. This makes both debugging the program and understanding its conclusions easier than would be the case without the additional structure provided by the hierarchical frame system.

To summarize, Aikins argued that to understand a consultation, in terms of both the direction that it takes and the results that it returns, a user must be able to understand:

- the questions being asked;
- the reasons for asking them;
- the justification for intermediate conclusions.

```
[Actions slot of OAD being executed...]
Conclusions: the findings about the diagnosis of obstructive airways disease are as follows:
Elevated lung volumes indicate overinflation.
The RV/TLC ratio is increased, suggesting a severe degree of air trapping. Forced Vital Capacity is normal
but the FEV1/FVC ratio is reduced, suggesting airway obstruction of a severe degree.
Low mid-expiratory flow is consistent with severe airway obstruction. Obstruction is indicated by
curvature of the flow-volume loop which is of a severe degree.
Following bronchodilation, expired flow shows excellent improvement as indicated by the change in the
FEV1.
Following bronchodilation, expired flow shows excellent improvement as indicated by the change in the
MMF.
Reversibility of airway obstruction is confirmed by improvement in airway resistance following
bronchodilation.
```

Figure 16.9 Applying the summary rules.

[Action slot of PULMONARY-DISEASE being executed...]
-----Prototype Summary-----
-----Obstructive Airways Disease-----
Obstructive Airways Disease was suggested by the following findings
The fev1/fvc ratio of PATIENT-7: 40
The mmf/mmf-predicted ratio of PATIENT-7: 12
The f5025 of PATIENT-7: 9
In addition, Obstructive Airways Disease is consistent with
The tlc/tlc-predicted ratio of PATIENT-7: 139
The rv/rv-predicted ratio of PATIENT-7: 261
The f25 of PATIENT-7: 45
The severity of coughing of PATIENT-7: NONE
The degree of sputum production of PATIENT-7: NONE
The Obstructive Airways Disease accounts for the following findings:
The referral diagnosis of PATIENT-7
The fev1/fvc ratio of PATIENT-7
The f25 of PATIENT-7
The severity of coughing of PATIENT-7
The degree of sputum production of PATIENT-7

All facts have been accounted for by the confirmed prototypes.
Conclusions: Smoking probably exacerbates the severity of the patient's airway obstruction.
Discontinuation of smoking should help relieve the symptoms. Good response to bronchodilators is
consistent with an asthmatic condition, and their continued use is indicated. The high diffusing capacity
is consistent with asthma. Pulmonary Function Diagnosis: Severe Obstructive Airways Disease
Asthmatic type. Consultation finished.

Figure 16.10 CENTAUR's final conclusions.

Aikins argued that there were four principal shortcomings associated with the kinds of explanation generated by EMYCIN:

- The user needs to be able to follow the backward chaining of rules, and one suspects that this mode of reasoning is not typically employed by humans.
- The knowledge in the rules may not be complete, or may not be specified at a level of detail that makes rule applications easy to follow.
- Knowledge about context and control is not distinguished from knowledge about the content of the domain, that is, no clear demarcation between meta and object level.
- Each rule application only explains the most recent question, with no broader context being supplied.

CENTAUR asks questions of the user if it fails to deduce some piece of information it needs from its rules, or if it needs a value for a parameter that is explicitly labeled 'ask-first.' Questions asked of the system by the user include the 'HOW' and 'WHY' of EMYCIN, but with a stage-dependent interpretation. Thus, a WHY question asked in the context of a particular prototype during the diagnostic stage will be interpreted as 'why are you considering this prototype?'. In the review stage, however, such a question would be interpreted as 'why was this prototype confirmed?'. CENTAUR always displays the current prototype, so that the context of the question and answer is clear.

CENTAUR's final interpretation consists of a list of confirmed prototypes, accompanied by a good deal of additional information, including:

- findings that suggest each prototype (the trigger values);
- findings consistent with each prototype (the plausible values);
- findings inconsistent with each prototype (error or surprise values);
- findings not accounted for by any prototype (residual facts).

Any test results not accounted for by any prototype on the confirmed list are listed, together with any other prototypes that might account for them. This helps to track down both possible errors in the tests and possible bugs in the knowledge base. Finally, a statement of conclusions and final diagnosis is presented along with a list of those prototypes which were disconfirmed during the consultation.

Like Clancey's work, this case study demonstrates that the task of explanation should not be relegated to some relatively independent module of an expert system. The issue of explanation has implications for many different aspects of representation and control which permeate the entire program. Thus the moral of the story is that explanation capabilities must be designed for in the system as a whole, if they are to be effective.

16.2.2 Multimedia interfaces for explanation

The topics of user interface design and multimedia presentation will not be dealt with in great detail here; the interested reader is referred to references in the bibliography section. In this section, we focus upon the ways in which expert system researchers and developers are going beyond conventional text-based explanation facilities, and examine some of the issues that they confront. We shall consider higher-level design issues, such as how to coordinate different media in the service of explanation, at the expense of lower-level, 'look and feel' issues.

One obvious way to supplement frame-based explanations is to enhance them with relevant images. Thus the JETA system (Abu-Hakima *et al.*, 1993) improves on CENTAUR's text-based interface by supporting explanations with diagrams, such as schematics and graphs. JETA's architecture features a three-level frame system in

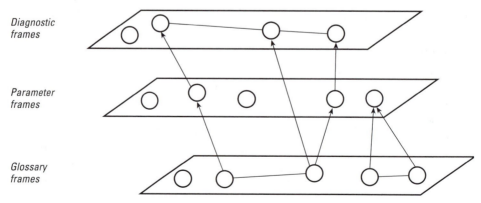

Diagnostic frames

Parameter frames

Glossary frames

Figure 16.11 JETA's three-layer frame system.

which CENTAUR-like frames for representing diagnostic information and parameters of interest are supported by 'glossary frames' which include hypertext markers. Glossary frames provide explanation and help material to the other frames in the domain of jet engine troubleshooting. The integration of this material with the underlying knowledge representation and reasoning seems to be fairly loose (see Figure 16.11).

The COMET[1] research vehicle (Feiner and McKeown, 1991) attempts a fuller integration between the explanation facility and the underlying expert system, in that pictures and text and not 'canned' but are generated from three knowledge bases:

- a frame system of domain objects and actions;
- a diagnostic rule base;
- a geometric knowledge base needed for graphical layout.

COMET's domain is that of field maintenance and repair for a military radio. It can both impart instructions for how to perform some procedure, and provide an explanation for a diagnostic repair that needs to be carried out. The idea is to be able to coordinate graphical output with the text to illustrate key aspects of these procedures and repairs.

For example, to check the transceiver's remote I/O module, one must perform or observe the following actions or events:

(1) Press the BATT/CALL button on the front panel.
(2) Key the rt (receiver-transmitter), using the handset or the intercom 'push-to-talk' switch.
(3) Check the display for 'CALL.'

These instructions to the user can be realized by coordinating a voice-over (V) and an animation sequence (A), as shown in Figure 16.12.

Such an explanation of how to check the module both helps the user locate the requisite parts of the device and makes the timing of the various actions easier to follow. To generate such displays requires both a *content planner*, which determines what information to include in what media, and a representation of temporal relationships between actions. The plans are rather like the *scripts* we encountered in Section 2.1, while the representation of time draws upon work in temporal logic (Allen, 1983).

V: Press and hold the BATT/CALL button.
A: *Closeup of keyboard and display, with inset of button.*

V: While holding it, key the rt.
A: *Zoom out to include handset, keyboard and display.*

V: Simultaneously, check the display.
A: *Highlight display.*

Figure 16.12 Example of integrating test and graphics in temporal display.

---

[1] COMET stands for Coordinated Multimedia Explanation Testbed.

In the next section, we take a closer look at this planning aspect of explanation as part of a larger framework for generating explanations. For now, we merely note that the ability to use multimedia as part of explanations raised as many questions as it provides solutions; for example, what to present, how to coordinate different media, how much initiate to allow the user to exercise, and so on. The underlying problems of how best to plan, generate and evaluate the effectiveness of explanations all remain.

16.3 Explanation and automatic programming[†]

This section looks at a rather radical approach to explanation, in which explanation knowledge is represented explicitly and kept separate from the knowledge needed to solve problems in the domain. Nevertheless, these two kinds of knowledge are correlated, as we saw earlier in the context of MYCIN and NEOMYCIN via a number of domain principles. Some problems with explanation arise because various design decisions and control heuristics, which are vital to the system's operation, are implicit in the architecture and therefore not available for the explanation facility to reason about or present to the user.

This section describes two research systems, XPLAIN and PEA, which set out to explore this problem within a particular framework, which became known as the 'Explainable Expert Systems' (EES) project.

16.3.1 Automatic programming in XPLAIN

Swartout (1983) began by agreeing with Clancey and Aikins that providing traces of rule activations may describe program behavior, but they cannot be said to justify it. This is because although the justification is part of the knowledge used to design and implement the program, this knowledge is nowhere represented explicitly in the code. In other words, the 'knowing how' of the system (the principles of reasoning in the domain) is typically confounded with the 'knowing that' (the model of the domain that the system reasons with).

The idea behind Swartout's XPLAIN system is a simple but powerful one which links the two processes of designing an expert system and obtaining coherent explanations from it. One way to design an expert consultation program is to specify the domain model and the domain principles, and then invoke an automatic programmer upon this specification to generate the performance program. The process of integrating the prescriptive and descriptive aspects of the specification into the final system is recorded and used to produce explanations of the system's behavior.

The domain model contains facts about the domain of application, such as causal paths and taxonomies. This concept corresponds quite closely to what Clancey would call 'structural knowledge' (see Chapter 12), that is, the kind of knowledge that underlies situation/action rules of the usual kind. The domain principles include methods and heuristics, which are usually either hard-coded into the interpreter or given to the interpreter as meta-rules. This corresponds quite closely to what Clancey would call 'strategic knowledge.' Swartout argues convincingly, as Clancey does, that separating out these different kinds of knowledge has positive effects upon aspects of system performance other than the explanation facility, such as modifiability.

Swartout collected observational data on the kinds of questions that medical students and fellows asked when they ran the Digitalis Therapy Advisor. Three kinds of question were identified:

- Questions about the methods employed by the program, for example how it calculates values for certain parameters.
- Justifications of program behavior, for example why certain adjustments to therapy are recommended.
- Explanation of system questions, when there is some doubt about what kind of answer the system wants or expects.

The first type is the kind of question that most expert systems can answer without difficulty. All that is required is that the program be able to produce an English description of the code that is executed. The second type requires something more: the ability to represent and reference the medical knowledge underlying the code. The third type requires something else again: the ability to represent the user's understanding of the terminology in a question and resolve any conflicts between that understanding and the intended meaning. XPLAIN concentrates upon the second type of question.

The automatic programming approach adopted in the XPLAIN system can be seen as a way of combining both the specification and implementation phases of constructing an expert system. The idea is that the specification of the domain model should be entirely declarative, since the program may want to use the same piece of knowledge in different ways. The domain principles are used to refine the goal structure associated with the task in a recursive manner until there are methods associated with each of the bottom-level steps that the program has to perform.

The kind of control exercised by domain principles is rather stronger than MYCIN's use of meta-rules, since the former does more than merely order or prune the application of domain-specific rules. The integration of the program fragments thus generated is a complex process that need not concern us here, since we are more interested in the principle of deriving explanations from declarative representations of domain knowledge. However, potential interactions between program actions have to be resolved, using knowledge that is also derived from the domain model and the domain principles.

16.3.2 The Explainable Expert Systems project

Swartout draws attention to the problem of 'computer artifacts' in previous explanation systems. These artifacts are aspects of the computation which derive not from the underlying domain model or the domain principles but from the simple fact that parts of the program are nothing more than low-level algorithms which are implemented so that the computer will run the consultation. Such computational artifacts are of no interest to physicians, and users are unlikely to understand either how they work or why they are necessary.

The ideas behind the XPLAIN system have since been generalized into an approach to expert systems design called the Explainable Expert Systems paradigm (Neches *et al.*, 1985; Moore, 1995). As we have seen, these ideas are compatible with the drive to differentiate and render explicit different kinds of domain knowledge, but they also

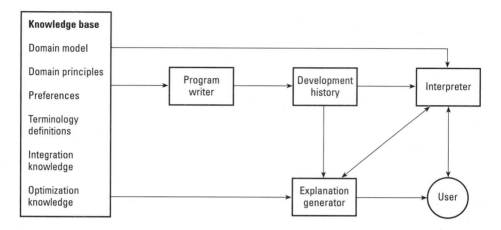

Figure 16.13 Global view of the EES framework, adapted from Neches *et al.* (1985).

include the crucial insight that many of the ultimate grounds for justification reside in the system development process. In the absence of formal machinery for recording and subsequently deploying these decisions, such information is typically lost in the implementation phase.

Figure 16.13 gives a global view of the EES framework. Note that the left-hand box containing the domain model and domain principles also contains other kinds of knowledge. For example, definitions of domain terminology are separated out from the domain model and principles; they had been a part of the principles in XPLAIN. Trade-offs are another kind of knowledge associated with domain principles, which indicate pros and cons of selecting a particular strategy to achieve a goal, while preferences are used to set priorities on goals based on their associated trade-offs. Integration knowledge is used to resolve conflicts between principles at the time that the automatic programmer is run, while optimization knowledge is concerned with the efficient execution of the expert system derived by the programmer. These ancillary sources of knowledge are a good illustration of kinds of meta-knowledge that go beyond the pruning and ordering of object-level rules at execution time that one associates with earlier expert system paradigms.

The specification of an EES system's knowledge base is represented in a semantic network formalism (see Chapter 9) called NIKL (Moser, 1983), which is a descendant of KL-ONE (Brachman and Schmolze, 1985). Like KL-ONE, NIKL builds constellations of concepts, which have an internal structure consisting slots (or roles), and which are capable of entering into relations (or links) with other concepts. NIKL also contains a *classifier* which, given an existing network and a new concept with a particular structure, can place the concept at the correct location in a taxonomy.

For example, given nodes representing ANIMAL, DOG, and RABID-ANIMAL, the classifier will take the new concept RABID-DOG, create a new node for it, and correctly locate this node as a descendent of DOG and RABID-ANIMAL in the hierarchy. It does this by reasoning about the features and properties of RABID-DOG (see the example in Figure 16.14). This facility is useful when a large domain model is being built incrementally.

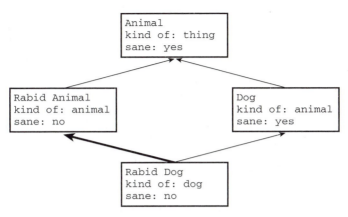

Figure 16.14 How a classifier fits a new class into a hierarchy. DOG inherits sanity from ANIMAL, but RABID-DOG is specified as an insane dog, so the system reasons that it is also an instance of RABID-ANIMAL.

Neches describes an application of the EES framework for building a Program Enhancement Advisor (PEA), which attempts to advise a programmer about ways of improving the readability of his code. The NIKL concepts in this domain are code transformations, such as changing a LISP COND (see Chapter 4) into an IF-THEN-ELSE. The IF-THEN-ELSE concept is a kind of the KEYWORD CONSTRUCT concept which is, in turn, a kind of the concept EASY-TO-READ CONSTRUCT. Thus, the program might advise the user to replace

```
(COND ((ATOM X) X) (T (CAR X)))
```

by the more readable

```
(IF (ATOM X) THEN X ELSE (CAR X)).
```

Problem solving knowledge is represented in NIKL too, in terms of plans and goals organized into a hierarchy. Plans and goals are related; each plan has a 'capability description' which describes what the plan can achieve. NIKL also stores terminological knowledge which is used by the program writer, for example, to gather together instances of concepts.

As in the XPLAIN system, the program writer works by top-down refinement, expanding goals into subgoals. Thus the main goal in PEA, *achieve enhanced program*, is refined into subgoals, such as *enhance readability* and *enhance maintainability*. This is an example of what the authors call 'user directed dynamic refinement,' since which kind of enhancement is performed by the resultant system is determined by the knowledge engineer's input. If *enhance readability* is chosen, then this goal will automatically be subject to goal/subgoal refinement, for example, into scanning the program for transformation opportunities, confirming them with the user, and ultimately performing them. A portion of the PEA design history which reflects this feature is shown in Figure 16.15.

The authors of EES claim the following advantages for their approach.

- It is easy to express high-level strategies of the kind that are only implicit in the majority of expert systems, and show how they are refined into lower-level strategies.

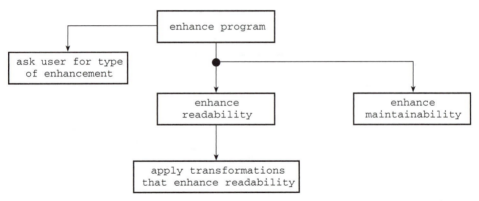

Figure 16.15 **Fragment of PEA design history showing decomposition of** *enhance program* **goal contingent upon user input (adapted from Moore, 1995).**

- Separation of different kinds of knowledge makes a system more modular and easier to modify than first-generation expert systems.
- The automatic classification of new knowledge in a language like NIKL eases system development, since the knowledge engineer need not worry quite so much about how new knowledge should be structured.

16.3.3 Text plans and user models in PEA

Having the kind of explicit goal structure and knowledge separation that EES supports seems to be a necessary condition for providing better explanations, as we saw with NEOMYCIN. But another requirement is that there be some plan for generating explanations. Moore (1995) rejects the use of scripts[2] in EES for the following reasons.

- Scripts can be used to encode explanation patterns, but they do not encode more subjective things, like what is the intention behind an assertion or question.
- Scripts are too rigid to allow opportunistic assertions and questions in response to user input.

Moore opted instead for plan operators which set out to achieve communicative goals, such as having the user believe a statement, or motivating an action in terms of a goal. Like the plan operators which were encountered in Chapter 3, each rule has a list of

---

To achieve the state in which the hearer is persuaded to do an act
IF
        The act is a step in achieving some goal(s) of the hearer, and
        The goals are the most specific along any refinement path
THEN
        Motivate the act in terms of those goals.

Figure 16.16 **English paraphrase of a sample plan operator.**

---

[2] In the context of discourse planning, scripts are often called 'schemas' or 'schemata.'

Have user replace COND with IF
↓
Persuade user to replace COND with IF
↓
Motivate user by showing that the replacement improves readability
↓
Have user believe that there is a difference between COND and IF wrt readability

Figure 16.17 Illustrative goal–subgoal reduction in text planning.

conditions that must be true for the operator to have the desired effect. Figure 16.16 shows an English paraphrase of a plan operator for persuading a user to perform some action, for example, changing some LISP construct in the PEA domain.

Such an operator is quite general, in that it need not apply only to the PEA domain. However, the act that gets instantiated will obviously depend upon the domain, and the goals of the hearer within the PEA domain will depend upon whether readability, maintainability, or some other goal, such as efficiency, is the user's primary concern. As with STRIPS and other planners, the chaining of these rules leads to a goal–subgoal reduction, such as that sketched in Figure 16.17.

There then needs to be a means of detecting when such goals and subgoals are satisfied, for example when the user agrees that IF is a more readable construct than COND in LISP for simple conditional statements. Thus it is necessary to build a model of the user's beliefs and preferences incrementally, and then consult this model to see if conditions for using a particular plan operator are satisfied. Roughly speaking, this is not much different from the way that STRIPS consulted a world model (see Chapter 3) when deciding whether or not it could push a box from one room to another. The additional complexity comes in representing beliefs, preferences, and so on, so that they can be reasoned about.

PEA builds individual user models based on a user stereotype, which represents the knowledge assumed to be common to all users. For example, in the LISP programming domain of PEA, the following set of statements represents what a typical user is assumed to know:

```
(COMPETENT USER (DO USER REPLACE))
(KNOW-ABOUT USER (CONCEPT PROGRAM))
(KNOW-ABOUT USER (CONCEPT LISP-FUNCTION))
(KNOW-ABOUT USER (CONCEPT S-EXPR))
(KNOW-ABOUT USER (CONCEPT READABILITY))
(KNOW-ABOUT USER (CONCEPT MAINTAINABILITY))
```

These LISP expressions[3] state that the user is able to use an editor to replace one expression with another, understands what a program and a LISP function are, and so on. But PEA can also infer what a particular user knows by observing his or her behavior, or looking at his or her code. For example, it can sweep through a user's code, see what LISP functions are used, and update that user's model. It can also record

---

[3] As well as being *about* LISP, PEA is implemented *in* LISP.

when the user agrees with some statement that it has made. In this way, it can know whether or not a communicative goal has been achieved.

In summary, the planner behind PEA has communicative goals which it seeks to satisfy, if necessary by changing a user's beliefs. This level of complexity is necessary if the system is to 'follow up' on explanations that it has presented, for example, if the user does not understand or agree. The rather fine grain analysis explicitly represented by the goal–subgoal reduction in Figure 16.17 is necessary if communication failure is to be recorded or diagnosed. Did the top-level goal fail because the user disagreed, or because the user did not understand? The system's next move depends on being able to make these distinctions.

16.4 Explanation facilities and future research

We saw in Chapter 13 how INTERNIST used hierarchical hypothesize and test as a technique for factoring a large solution space and building very large knowledge bases. However, a hierarchical approach to problem solving has other advantages, including transparency of program behavior and flexibility of control. These properties were illustrated in this chapter by a case study of the CENTAUR system, which uses (i) a frame hierarchy to supply the problem solving context in which production rules operate, and (ii) an agenda of tasks to control the order in which hypotheses are explored.

The EES project is a good example of a particular methodology for knowledge engineering, that is, specification followed by compilation. However, it is not altogether clear how this methodology allows one to mix different control strategies (as one can in CENTAUR, say); presumably the domain principles must be ordered or structured in some way. The main problem associated with such an approach is that it results in a large development history and requires a very powerful program writer, as Neches *et al.* (1985) point out in their discussion. The alternative strategy, making the interpreter more complex by giving it powerful control primitives, cuts the development history and simplifies the program writer but buries control decisions in the interpreter's code. Having the program writer produce both the interpreter and the code sounds interesting. This would effect an even greater separation between control knowledge and domain knowledge, but would presumably pose more integration problems.

As you can see, automating explanations is a hard problem, and the treatment given above is not meant to be exhaustive. However, it is intended to cover the main concerns and activities of researchers who are interested in both developing a methodology for building expert systems and improving the quality of explanations they produce. The critical issues appear to be:

(1) the differentiation of different kinds of knowledge;
(2) the explicit rendition of strategic and structural knowledge that tends to be hidden in program code;
(3) the modeling of individual users' knowledge or levels of skill.

We have concentrated upon issues (1) and (2) here, and treated (3) in a more cursory fashion, since it is still very much a research topic. A typical approach involves classifying users along some dimension of expertise, and then attaching various interaction modes to these classes. For example, users lacking in domain knowledge might need to have key concepts explained to them and be kept away from 'powerful' system commands, while users who are domain experts but who have never used the system before might be more interested in learning such commands and not need the explanation of concepts. User modeling is a difficult research area; there are few simple solutions to the problem of how best to maintain a representation of some user's understanding of a domain or a system.

BIBLIOGRAPHICAL NOTES

The interested reader is referred to Sleeman and Brown (1982) for early papers which address the topic of user modeling, and Polson and Richardson (1988) for a later selection of papers. A representative sample of recent papers on the topic of user interfaces can be found in Maybury (1993). Moore and Paris (1993) and Moore *et al.* (1996) follow up on the topics of text planning and discourse generation raised by the EES project and the PEA system.

In addition to NIKL, another popular descriptive language for knowledge acquisition and explanation generation is LOOM (MacGregor, 1991). Every concept or class can have a definition that describes the set of objects that belong to that class, as well as describing how its slots can be filled and how it relates to other classes. LOOM uses these definitions to produce a subsumption hierarchy that organizes all the concepts according to their class–subclass relationship.

STUDY SUGGESTIONS

1. What is wrong with simply providing the user with a trace of which rules have fired as an explanation of a program's reasoning?

2. Why is explanation often easier in a rule-based system if we distinguish between different kinds of rules?

3. How can frames help in the construction of explanations? Why do we combine them with rules?

4. Here is another version of the 'assault weapon' program from Chapter 11. In this version, we want to elicit information from a user about a particular firearm, and then explain to him or her why that firearm is, or is not, an assault weapon, according to the rules. Let's approach this in two parts: acquiring the details and explaining the result.

   (i) Write the missing rules in the program below

```
;; DECLARATIONS

(deftemplate gun
    (field make (type SYMBOL))
    (field model (type SYMBOL))
    (field class (type SYMBOL) (default NIL))
    (field action (type SYMBOL) (default NIL))
    (field caliber (type FLOAT) (default 0.0)))
```

continued

```
    (field capacity (type INTEGER) (default 0))
    (field features (type SYMBOL) (default NIL))
)
(deftemplate assault-weapon
  (field make (type SYMBOL))
  (field model (type SYMBOL))
)

;; RULES

;; The general case

;; Any semi-automatic rifle or shotgun with a capacity
;; of more than 5 rounds
(defrule Part1
  (gun (make ?M) (model ?N) (class ?C&rifle|shotgun)
       (action semi) (capacity ?X&:(> ?X 5)))
  =>
  (assert (assault-weapon (make ?M) (model ?N)))
)

;; Write a rule called make-and-model which elicits this
;; information from the user and creates the right attribute
;; values for the gun vector in working memory. Use the
;; following rule as a model.
(defrule class-and-action
  ?G <- (gun (action NIL))
  =>
  (printout t crlf
   "Please enter the class of the gun" t crlf
   "for example shotgun, rifle, pistol" t crlf
   "CLASS: ")
  (bind ?class (read))
  (printout t crlf
   "Please enter the action type of the gun" t crlf
   "for example bolt, slide, lever, semi, revolver ..." t crlf
   "ACTION: ")
  (bind ?action (read))
  (modify ?G (class ?class) (action ?action))
)

;; Write a rule called capacity that determines the capacity
;; of the gun, that is, how many rounds of ammunition it can
;; hold. You can use the caliber rule given below as a model.
(defrule caliber
  ?G <- (gun (caliber 0.0))
  =>
  (printout
    t crlf
    "Please enter the caliber of the gun" t crlf
    "CALIBER: ")
```

continued

```
  (modify ?G (caliber (read)))
)

;; Any semi-automatic rifle or shotgun with an offending
;; feature
(defrule Part2
  (gun (make ?M) (model ?N) (class ?C&rifle|shotgun) (action
  semi)
    (features ?F&flash-suppressor|barrel-shroud|night-
    scope))
  =>
  (assert (assault-weapon (make ?M) (model ?N)))
)

;; Write a rule called pistol-grip-shotgun which
;; designates any shotgun with a pistol grip as being an
;; assault weapon.

;; Write rules which query the user about offending
;; features. Not all features make sense for all kinds of
;; guns, for example, pistols do not typically have barrel-
;; shrouds, so your rule for that feature should reflect
;; this.

;; Specific cases which we know with certainty to be
;; assault weapons because they are listed as such in the
;; ordnance.

;; A Cobray M11 is an assault weapon.
(defrule cobray
  (declare (salience 20))
  (gun (make cobray) (model M11) (class pistol))
  =>
  (assert (assault-weapon (make cobray) (model M11)))
)

;; Exceptions

;; No rimfire rifle is an assault weapon.
(defrule rimfire
  (declare (salience 10))
  ?except <- (gun (make ?M) (model ?N) (class rifle)
  (caliber .22))
  ?mistake <- (assault-weapon (model ?N))
  =>
  (printout
    t crlf
    "The " ?M " " ?N " is definitely not an assault weapon."
    t crlf)
  (retract ?mistake)
  (retract ?except)
)
```

continued

```
;; Write a similar rule called slide-action which
;; disqualifies any slide action shotgun from being an
;; assault weapon.

;; Now we need some rules to print out the result.

;; Write a rule called probably-is which recognizes that the
;; gun is probably an assault weapon and prints a message
;; to that effect. You can use the following rule as a model,
;; which covers the case of no evidence to the effect that
;; the gun is an assault weapon.

;; Identify gun as probably not an assault weapon and halt.
;; The salience of this rule is set low so that it only fires
;; if no other rule will fire.
(defrule probably-is-not
  (declare (salience -20))
  (gun (make ?M) (model ?N))
  (not (assault-weapon (make ?M) (model ?N)))
  =>
  (printout
    t crlf
    "The " ?M " " ?N " is probably not an assault weapon."
    t crlf)
  (halt)
)
```

(ii) Now we need to address the problem of explaining the system's pronouncements. First we need to record the *justification* for each decision implicit in the rules, and then we need to cite the relevant section of the definition of an assault weapon. The actual definition for identifying such weapons falls into five parts:

(1) A general description of a high-capacity semi-automatic firearm.
(2) A list of offending features, such as a flash suppressor.
(3) 'Any stockless pistol grip shotgun.'
(4) A list of disapproved makes and models, both foreign and US made.
(5) A list of mitigating features that disqualify a gun as an assault weapon.

The justification for a positive identification will be based on Parts 1–4, while a negative identification will either be based on Part 5 or the failure of Parts 1–4 to apply.

One way to implement all this is to add two new fields to the **assault-weapon** vector, as follows:

```
(deftemplate assault-weapon
  (field make (type SYMBOL))
  (field model (type SYMBOL))
  (field just (type SYMBOL) (default NIL))
  (field part (type INTEGER) (default 0))
)
```

continued

The rules that assert this vector will now fill in these attributes appropriately, for example,

```
(defrule Part1
   (gun (make ?M) (model ?N)
        (class ?C&rifle|shotgun)
        (action semi) (capacity ?X&:(> ?X 5)))
  =>
    (assert
      (assault-weapon (make ?M) (model ?N)
      (just capacity) (part 1)))
  )
```

This rule states that the justification for designating a rifle or shotgun as an assault weapon is its capacity, as stipulated under Part 1 of the definition.

To complete the program, do the following.

- Modify the rule **Part2** appropriately in a similar fashion, so that the offending feature becomes the justification.
- Then modify the **cobray** rule to reflect its basis in the definition, so that the attribute 'model' is the justification.
- Similarly, modify the **pistol-grip-shotgun** rule you wrote in part (i) of this question.
- Change the rules **rimfire, slide-action** and **probably-is**, for example by adding patterns that detect the 'just' and 'part' fields, and/ or add new rules to do a case analysis on these attributes.

You might use a standard form of words in the printout statement of each of these rules, such as

'The *MAKE MODEL* is (not) an assault weapon under Part *NUMBER* of the definition because of its *FEATURE*'

where terms in capitals are supplied by the values of variables assigned in the pattern match.

17

Tools for Building Expert Systems

17.1 Overview of expert systems tools
17.2 Expert system shells
17.3 High-level programming languages
17.4 Potential implementation problems
17.5 More maxims on expert system development
Bibliographical notes
Study suggestions

This chapter is not meant to be a comprehensive, up-to-the-minute consumer guide to commercially available knowledge engineering environments. The intention is rather to outline the functionality of typical software tools which are now being used to construct expert systems, and capture the flavor of the current debate concerning what the tools of the future ought to be like. Although we have already met some of the toolkits to be discussed in this chapter, and considered a number of knowledge representation schemes from a theoretical point of view, this chapter makes a systematic attempt to categorize such tools according to the ways in which they are typically used and to assess their practical utility.

As in earlier chapters, most programming examples will be provided in the CLIPS language, although illustrative code from other languages will also appear, as appropriate. We defer the discussion of more complex or specialized tools, such as blackboard systems and truth maintenance systems, to Chapters 18 and 19 respectively. Here the emphasis is upon the mainstream facilities for representation and control which most expert system tools provide.

17.1 Overview of expert system tools

Expert system tools are all designed to support *prototyping*. In the parlance of software engineering (see, for example, Schach, 1993), a prototype is

'a working model that is functionally equivalent to a subset of the product.'

The idea is to develop, early in the project, a 'proof of concept' program which can be critiqued by experts or users and which solves some non-trivial part of the problem.

This is done mostly as a means of refining system requirements and convincing oneself that the problem is indeed tractable before substantial amounts of money are spent.

The initial prototype is then thrown away and a period of development ensues, in which the basic approach validated by the prototype is reimplemented and filled out so that it solves the whole problem. This is normally done in a succession of 'builds' that incorporate additional functionality into the program in an 'implement, integrate and test' cycle. These successive builds may or may not form the basis of actual releases to the client, depending upon how acceptable a partial system is to end users.

Thus expert systems development is often a mix of the rapid prototyping and incremental models of software engineering, rather than the more conventional 'waterfall' model, in which requirements lead to specifications, planning, design, implementation, and integration, with feedback loops between adjacent stages. The fact that a prototype has been built and approved generally reduces the amount of replanning, redesign, and so on, that needs to be performed. One drawback of the incremental model in more conventional programming paradigms is the problem of integrating new functionality with the earlier version. Expert systems development environments aim to solve this problem by using modular representations of knowledge of the kind we encountered in Chapters 5–8. Such tools can be classified according to the nature and variety of representational schemes that they support, and the kinds of other building blocks that they provide.

The majority of software tools for building expert systems seem to fall into four broad categories:

(1) *Expert system shells*, which are essentially abstractions over one or more applications programs. As we saw in Chapter 10, among the first of these was EMYCIN, which provided the production rule interpreter of MYCIN, together with all the ancillary data structures, such as knowledge tables, and their associated indexing mechanisms. A nicer rule language was provided to improve readability, and there was also software for maintaining a library of cases and monitoring the system's conclusions with respect to them. More recent descendants of EMYCIN are S.1 and M.4, fairly sophisticated shells which combine the basic backward chaining mechanism of EMYCIN with frame-like data structures and extra control facilities, for example, for simulating forward chaining.

(2) *High-level programming languages*, which to some extent conceal their implementation details, thereby freeing the programmer from low-level considerations of efficiency in the storage, access and manipulation of data. The OPS5 rule language (see Chapters 5 and 14) is a good example of such a language; it is easy to learn and yet less constraining than a typical shell. Such languages have not usually been well packaged in the past, since most were research tools (and therefore available at low cost) rather than commercial products.

(3) *Multiple-paradigm programming environments*, which provide a set of software modules that allow the user to mix a number of different styles of artificial intelligence programming. Among the first was a research tool called LOOPS (see Chapter 7), which combined object- and rule-based representations. This architecture gave rise to a number of commercial products in the second half of the 1980s, of which KEE, KnowledgeCraft and ART were perhaps the most notable. They provided the skilled user with a range of options that is potentially very large indeed, and set the standard for later tools, such as KAPPA (see below) and CLIPS.

However, they are a little harder to learn than (2), since they contain more than a single uniform package, such as a rules language.

(4) *Additional modules* for performing specific tasks within a problem solving architecture. A good example of this kind of module is the dependency network used by VT (see Chapter 15) to keep track of which values of design variables depend upon values determined by earlier decisions. These networks can also be used to propagate updates brought about by changing data or assumptions, in which case they are called *Truth Maintenance Systems* (see Chapter 19).

It is worth saying a little more about each of these in turn, and trying to decide what their strengths and weaknesses are.

17.2 Expert system shells

Shells are intended to allow non-programmers to take advantage of the efforts of programmers who have solved a problem similar to their own. Thus the EMYCIN tool (van Melle, 1981) allowed the MYCIN architecture to be applied to another medical domain, for example pulmonary function test interpretation in PUFF, as well as a number of non-medical applications, for example the structural analysis program SACON. However, as we pointed out in Chapter 11, we need to consider more deeply the question of when this kind of technology transfer is appropriate.

17.2.1 Matching shells to tasks

It is clear that all shells are not suited to all tasks. Van Melle was among the first to point out that EMYCIN was *not* a general-purpose problem solving architecture. Rather, he suggested that EMYCIN was suitable for deductive approaches to diagnostic problems, where large amounts of data are available and it is possible to enumerate the solution space of diagnostic categories in advance. Clancey has since dubbed these 'heuristic classification' problems (see Chapters 11 and 12). The approach appeared to be less well suited to what van Melle called 'formation problems,' which involve the piecing together of a complex whole that must satisfy some set of constraints. We have called these 'construction problems' (see Chapters 14 and 15).

Unfortunately, it is difficult to be rigorous in one's recommendations concerning what shell should be used for what problem. This is because we do not have very clear ideas concerning how the broad range of expert system tasks should be classified (although see for example Hayes-Roth *et al.*, 1983; Chandrasekaran, 1984 for attempts in this direction). One feels that distinctions such as that between diagnostic and formation problems, though intuitively appealing, are not quite right. Many problems can be solved in different ways, for example INTERNIST's approach to diagnosis shares many features of constructive problem solving (see Chapter 13), and really hard problems often require a mixed approach for their solution.

We shall have more to say about the general problem of selecting an expert system tool in Section 17.4 below. With respect to shells, the majority of commercial products initially provided the user with facilities that are only adequate for small search spaces, for example exhaustive backward chaining with limited control facilities. Modern shells such as M.4 are claimed to be applicable to a wider range of problems, because they support a wider range of features for representation and control, such as simulation of forward chaining, procedures, message passing, and so forth.

17.2.2 Shells and inflexibility

The advantageous simplicity of the knowledge representation language associated with most shells also has a number of disadvantages, as noted by Aikins (1983) in her critique of the EMYCIN implementation of PUFF.

- The production rule formalism employed by EMYCIN made it difficult to distinguish different kinds of knowledge, for example heuristic knowledge, control knowledge, knowledge about expected values for parameters. We saw in Chapter 12 that the ability to differentiate knowledge types has been advocated by other authors for reasons of understandability.
- The relatively unstructured rule set employed by EMYCIN made the acquisition of new knowledge difficult, since adding a rule to the set involved making changes elsewhere in the system, for example to knowledge tables containing information about medical parameters. This was, of course, one of the problems that the TEIRESIAS system (see Chapter 10) set out to solve.
- The exhaustive backward chaining employed by EMYCIN as its major mode of inference, involving both meta- and object-level rules, made the generation of comprehensible explanations quite difficult. As Clancey (1983) pointed out, programming decisions about the order and number of clauses in a rule could have profound effects upon the way the search space unfolds (see Chapter 12).

Other criticisms voiced by Aikins concerned not only the particular implementation of PUFF in EMYCIN, but the functionality of rule-based systems generally, and hence other shells which use production rules as the main representation language. A good deal of expertise consists of knowledge about typical patterns of data; typical in the sense of being either frequently occurring or idealized in some way. Experts can recognize familiar patterns of data with ease, and are capable of classifying possibly noisy and incomplete patterns in terms of a set of prototypical ideals. They also have valuable intuitions about what constitutes a relevant, interesting or surprising data value, and such clues contribute to decisions about what to do next when trying to solve some problem. None of this is very easy to represent using condition–action rules alone, unless one allows the formalism to become arbitrarily complex, which vitiates one of the advantages of using production rules in the first place.

A final criticism of shells concerns the handling of uncertainty. A shell like M.4 comes complete with a particular formalism such as certainty factors for performing inexact reasoning. However, most if not all of the formalisms employed by these shells are either inconsistent with probability theory or have properties that are simply hard to analyze. While a pragmatic justification can often be given for a particular treatment of uncertainty in the context of a particular application, for example Shortliffe's rationale for using certainty factors in MYCIN, it is a more dangerous enterprise to adopt such a treatment simply because it comes with the shell one is using.

Modern shells are more flexible than earlier offerings in at least one respect, in that they are better integrated into commercial computing environments and have superior user interfaces. Thus M.4 runs on PCs under a widely used operating system with database integration and hooks to C, Visual BASIC, and Visual C++. A customizable user interface is provided, with a MYCIN-style explanation facility for answering WHY questions.

17.3 High-level programming languages

High-level languages give programmers a fast prototyping tool, so that more flexible designs can be explored and evaluated at relatively low cost in terms of time and effort. Typically, the runtime and buildtime interfaces are closer together, so that code can be run and tested incrementally, as it is written. The user interface will typically not be as 'friendly' as that provided by a shell, but a fluent programmer will nonetheless be able to make rapid progress.

Production rule languages, object-oriented programming languages, and procedural deduction systems usually provide the expert system builder with a few more degrees of freedom than a shell with regard to the details of such things as the specification of control and the handling of uncertainty. As noted above, shells normally come with a particular control regime, for example backward chaining, and a particular approach to inexact reasoning, for example certainty factors, hard-wired into the program. This added flexibility is particularly important in the development of experimental system designs, where one is not exactly sure in advance what mechanisms will be required to solve the domain problem.

17.3.1 Constraints of production rule languages

In fairness, high-level languages typically impose their own constraints. Thus the dynamic memory of OPS5 programs is limited to vectors in working memory; this rules out recursive data structures, such as graphs or trees. The architects of the MORE system (see Chapter 12) found this a serious limitation (Kahn, 1988). Certain kinds of control flow, such as recursion and iteration, are also hard to engineer. Arguably, this is the price you pay for the comparative simplicity of OPS5 code, and the efficiency with which it can be executed.

Early production systems spent over 90 percent of their time doing pattern matching. However, Forgy (1982) noticed that there were several possible sources of inefficiency in naive approaches to this process. The *Rete match algorithm*, designed by Forgy and used by the OPS family of production rule languages, is based on two fundamental insights:

- The left-hand sides of productions in working memory often share conditions, and naive approaches will tend to match these conditions against working memory N times for N occurrences. This is an example of *within-cycle iteration*.
- Working memory is only modified a little each time, yet naive approaches tend to match all the patterns against all the working memory elements for each cycle. This is an example of *between-cycle iteration*.

The algorithm reduces the overhead of within-cycle iteration on productions by using a tree-structured sorting network. The patterns in the left-hand sides of the productions are compiled into this network, and the match algorithm computes the conflict set for a given cycle by processing this network. The between-cycle iteration on working memory is eliminated by processing a set of tokens that indicate which patterns match which working memory elements, and then simply updating this set when working memory changes. The absence of any control process other than the reflect–act cycle (see Chapter 5) makes the resultant conflict set easy to process. Conflict resolution simply applies an algorithm to the set, without regard for any other aspect of the current computational context.

Clearly, any attempt to introduce recursive data structures would greatly complicate the matching process. Similarly, any attempt to complicate the control regime would mean that conflict resolution would have to take extra information into account. The point is that such languages always face a trade-off between expressive power and efficiency of execution, and it is arguable that OPS5 has this trade-off just about right. Later tools, such as KEE, CLIPS and KAPPA, all adopt the OPS5 approach to rule syntax and rule activation. Each uses a version of the RETE algorithm to generate the conflict set.

The solution to the shortcomings of rule-based programming is not to complicate such languages (thereby diluting their strengths), but rather to combine them with other programming paradigms which allow recursion in data and control. Thus, combining rules and frames, and allowing the conditions of a rule to match against the slots of frames, provides a pleasing solution to the data problem (see Chapter 13). Similarly, embedding rule sets in a larger computational framework, involving agendas and multiple knowledge sources, provides a basis for solving the control problem (see Chapter 18).

17.3.2 Evaluating object-oriented approaches

As we noted in Chapter 12, the rule-based format is well suited to the expression of knowledge of the form

under conditions C_1, ..., C_n, perform action A

but is less well suited to describing complex objects and the relationships between them. Object-oriented programming languages provide programmers with an alternative framework for organizing knowledge in terms of declarative representations of domain objects. The procedural side of the problem solver is factored with respect to these objects, which are armed with their own procedures and which communicate with each other via message-passing protocols.

Another pleasing aspect of object-oriented programming is that it is a rather more analogical style of knowledge representation than that found in systems based on predicate calculus or production rules. Instead of knowledge about a domain object being scattered among the many rules or axioms that reference it, the knowledge is collected in one place, which is a representation of the object itself. This chunking is virtual, in the sense that not all of the information about an object will necessarily be stored in the corresponding computational object, but it remains true that to issue a command or request to an object, one deals directly with that representation by sending a message to it.

There are many real systems in the world where the exchange of energy and information between components can be represented by message passing among computational objects, and this link with simulation technology is one that has benefits for artificial intelligence generally and expert systems in particular (see, for example, McArthur *et al.*, 1986). It is arguable that simulation is a powerful tool for model-based problem solving, and that, in the context of complex systems, such patterns of reasoning are sometimes easier to understand than those associated with a more conventional rule-based approach to inference. Object-oriented programming is also a useful way of integrating symbolic computation with computing environments based around graphical objects such as menus and icons. Although the provision of such devices does not solve the problem of transparency in expert systems, it does provide the programmer with tools for constructing better displays (see, for example, Richer and Clancey, 1985).

However, this does not mean that it is always easy to decide what the computational objects in the object-oriented program should represent. In the early object-oriented languages, where the principal application was the writing of software to perform simulations, this was less of a problem. Computational objects stood for classes or instances of the real objects in whose behavior one was interested. Thus, simulating the behavior of a production line would involve creating computational objects that represented the configuration of machines, while messages represented the exchange of information, energy and partly assembled products. The programmer's task is made relatively easy, because there is a comprehensible mapping from computational objects to objects in the world.

In many expert systems applications, one might need the computational objects to stand for far more abstract entities, if this style of programming is actually to be used to solve the problem. Hence objects might stand for facts and goals, sets of rules or individual hypotheses. It is then much less easy to decide what kinds of messages such entities should exchange, and what the meaning of those messages might be.

A lot depends on the level at which this kind of behavior is going on. If objects are just the low-level implementation vehicle for getting a particular pattern of reasoning, then this need have no epistemological consequences at all. It is simply a feature of the host programming language for your expert system application, and the objects may well remain hidden from view. If, on the other hand, the objects are visible to both the expert during system development and the user during system performance, then the appropriateness of this mapping between abstract and computational objects needs to be established.

17.3.3 Logic programming for expert systems

In their criticisms of early expert systems tools, such as EMYCIN, a number of researchers and practitioners suggested that logic programming might provide an alternative approach to the construction of knowledge-based systems (for example, Kowalski, 1982). Thus Clarke and McCabe (1982) suggest that a production system such as MYCIN could easily be reconstructed in PROLOG. Rules would be represented by Horn clauses (see Chapter 8) in which the head (positive) literal would stand for the conclusion to be drawn and the other (negative) literals would stand for the conditions.

PROLOG's built-in control regime approximates the backward chaining of MYCIN-style systems. Knowledge tables and other data could be represented by assertions. Recursive data structures, such as graphs and trees, can be created by PRO-LOG using clauses that contain complex terms. Programmers could develop their own handling of uncertainty, perhaps using certainty factors.

On the practical side, PROLOG gives you several useful things for free:

- an *indexed database* containing clauses which can be used to represent rules, procedures or data;
- *pattern matching* in the form of most general unification which allows both the datum and the pattern to contain variables and returns a substitution which would render them identical;
- a *control strategy* (depth-first search) with a top-down search rule (clauses nearer the 'top' of the database are accessed first) and a left–right computation rule (subgoals are processed in the left-to-right order in which they are listed).

It is certainly quite easy to emulate a backward-chaining production system in PROLOG; it is also possible to write a simple interpreter for forward chaining without very much effort. Either way, the ground literals function as the working memory, while the non-ground clauses function as rules. Modification of working memory is achieved by `assert` and `retract` operations which add or remove formulas from the database. It is less easy to mimic the local flow of control associated with frame systems, although we saw some examples of how this effect can be achieved in Chapter 11, by packaging procedures and data together. We also saw ways of handling defaults and exceptions, although these take you outside of standard logic, and seem to be no more principled than other (less formal) solutions.

Nevertheless, successful applications of logic programming, such as the MECHO program (described in Chapter 11), usually exhibit a number of explicit departures from the syntax of the first-order predicate calculus and its procedural interpretation in standard PROLOG. As in PLANNER, the architects' avowed intention was to work towards a computational logic for natural reasoning which contained control primitives. Some of the syntactic and semantic limitations found in MECHO and PLANNER are still common in today's logic-based systems, for example:

- Functions and equality are often deliberately avoided. Intermediate unknowns are represented by specially generated constant symbols, rather than functions. The equality axioms are combinatorially explosive and computationally intractable, and therefore cannot be used directly.
- Objects are usually assumed to have unique names. Along with the banishment of function symbols, this helps side-step the whole problem of deciding whether or not two entities described by different terms are distinct. For example, a route planner could waste time and effort deciding that the west end of one road was the east end of another.
- The program is assumed to have complete information about the domain. Thus all the relevant objects are deemed to be known to the system, as are all the relationships between them. If some proposition cannot be proven, then it is assumed to be false.

In summary, logic programming languages give the knowledge engineer facilities for quantification and pattern matching which are generally more powerful than those afforded by production rule interpreters and semantic nets. Although there certainly exist rule and net systems which offer the power of first-order logic, such capabilities are usually purchased at the price of greatly complicating the original formalism. However, the power of logic-based systems is not purchased without price: theorem proving with full unification is computationally expensive in terms of both memory and CPU.

17.3.4 Multiple-paradigm programming environments

Multiple-paradigm programming environments allow skilled programmers to experiment with novel problem solving architectures by selecting and combining different software modules. In the absence of a single universal knowledge representation language suitable for arbitrary expert systems applications, practitioners may wish to avail themselves of more than one representational scheme, particularly when prototyping. Although there is no well-articulated theory of hybrid reasoning systems, experience with different schemes of representation and inference has shown that all have their weaknesses; thus the strategy of mixing schemes attempts to play as far as possible to their strengths.

We have already suggested that production rules provide a readable representation language for encoding empirical associations between conditions and actions, or observations and hypotheses, but they are less well suited to the encoding of arbitrary relations between domain entities, including such important relations as set/element and set/subset. Structured objects, such as frames, provide a flexible format for storing and accessing descriptions of domain entities, but the application of such knowledge is typically performed by arbitrary LISP code which can be hard to analyze. The rationale behind early attempts to marry the rule- and frame-based styles was the replacement of the procedural obscurity of demonic attachments with the clarity of productions, while setting production rules in a context which provided for a richer representation of data than that afforded by working memory.

LOOPS (Bobrow and Stefik, 1983) was the first AI programming environment to mix four programming paradigms within a message-passing architecture:

- *Procedure-oriented programming.* The basic LISP paradigm in which procedures are (for the most part) active and data are (for the most part) passive, even though LISP procedures are themselves data objects, that is, lists. Procedures are allowed to side-effect data objects, that is, permanently change their public value.
- *Rule-oriented programming.* Like the above, except that condition–action rules play the role of procedures. In LOOPS, sets of rules were themselves objects, capable of being nested recursively so that the 'action' part of a rule could invoke a subordinate rule set. Rule sets had control annotations attached to them which performed a rather primitive form of conflict resolution.
- *Object-oriented programming.* Structured objects have the characteristics of both program and data, and side effects are normally local to objects, and only allowed through the 'proper channels' of the right protocol. Messages result in data values being broadcast or reset, but all data manipulation is done locally by the callee. How values are stored, modified or computed is no business of the caller.
- *Data-oriented programming.* Data access and data update trigger procedures, so that things happen as a side effect of patterns in the data and the actions of other

procedures on data. Variables which hold data values and have procedures attached to them, such as the slots in a frame, are often called *active values*. This style of programming is particularly useful in certain domains, such as simulation, where changes in data values need to be propagated across data structures.

Different modules supporting different programming styles attain varying degrees of integration within the central object-oriented paradigm of such systems. Normally, both the conditions in production rules and logic clauses can be made to trigger on the slot values of structured objects, while rule actions may modify slot values. This is the style of integration currently provided by CLIPS.

KEE and LOOPS went further by allowing the behavior of an object to be described in terms of a set of production rules, rather as Aikins did in CENTAUR (see Chapters 13 and 16). KEE, and other environments such as Knowledge Craft, also added a query language in the PROLOG style to the paradigms listed above. KAPPA-PC, the current incarnation of KEE, provides the programmer with a very wide range of options in combining rules, objects, and procedures, via the KAPPA Application Language, KAL, which includes a KAL to C compiler.

BOX 17.1

CLIPS as Multiple-Paradigm Programming Environment

In addition to a production rule interpreter of the kind described in Chapter 5, CLIPS provides:

- a LISP-like syntax for defining *standard functions* (see Chapter 4);
- *generic functions*, which are rather like CLOS's multi-methods (see Chapter 7), and
- an embedded object-oriented language, called COOL, which includes a *message-passing* capability not unlike that of CLOS.

The standard functions can be called from the right-hand side of rules, and are executed as if they were actions of the rule. They can be executed for their side effect, or they can return a value, which can be saved using the assignment operator. They use the same syntax for variables as the CLIPS rule language; for example, we could define the function over integers called `between(X, Y, Z)` to test if $X \leq Y \leq Z$ as follows:

```
(deffunction between(?lb ?value ?ub)
   (and (<= ?lb ?value) (<= ?value ?ub))).
```

Generic functions are like overloaded operators in C++, in that they provide different methods for getting things done for different sequences, or *signatures*, of argument types. Thus, the code

```
(defmethod + ((?a STRING) (?b STRING)) (str-cat ?a ?b))
```

extends the '+' operator to perform concatenation on a pair of string arguments, so that

```
(+ "dog" "fish")
```

returns the string

```
"dogfish".
```

Such a function can mix restricted and unrestricted parameters, and the restrictions can involve data types at any level of generality, for example, numbers, integers, positive integers, and so on.

continued

Generic functions are evaluated under the auspices of a *generic dispatch* algorithm, which assembles a ranked list of applicable methods. The associated methods are then called in an order dictated by their parameter restrictions, with the methods having the most specific restrictions being called first. The algorithm also obeys any explicit control statements in the method body, such as 'call-next-method,' or 'override-next-method.'

Message passing uses a 'send' mechanism, as in SmallTalk and LOOPS, and requires that the programmer provide different message handlers for different classes. Message dispatch is very similar to CLOS, with primary, around, before and after handler types.

It is also possible to call external C functions from within CLIPS, although this is somewhat messy to do. CLIPS can also be run as an embedded application, in the sense that a CLIPS program can be compiled and linked with another C program, which then calls the CLIPS program as a subroutine. These options make CLIPS a very flexible tool for incorporating AI functionality into a module of a larger software system.

17.3.5 Additional modules

Facilities coming under the heading of additional modules are useful software tools which run in conjunction with an applications program. Generally, they perform some specialized function in an 'off the shelf' fashion that does not require either real programming in the host language or significant customization of the module. One example was KEE's Simkit: a software package for integrating simulation techniques with expert systems.

Another facility provided by KEE and ART was a mechanism for maintaining many different reasoning *contexts*. Roughly speaking, contexts are generated by branches in the search space where more than one operator is applicable. Consider the scenario in Figure 17.1, where we have two rules, each of which has its conditions satisfied by data in the current context of the computation.

In most production systems, the conflict resolution strategy will pick one of these rules to fire. However, in some applications it might be advantageous to 'split' the current context into two separate contexts, one in which we apply `Rule1` and one in which we apply `Rule2` (see Figure 17.2). These two contexts will differ in that different conclusions will have been drawn; however, we may allow them to inherit information from their parent context. Thus, in each of the two contexts, today will still be Monday and the weather will still be fine.

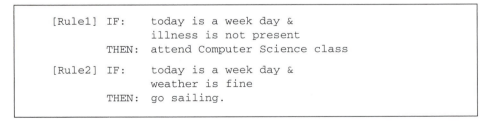

```
[Rule1]  IF:    today is a week day &
                illness is not present
         THEN:  attend Computer Science class

[Rule2]  IF:    today is a week day &
                weather is fine
         THEN:  go sailing.
```

Figure 17.1 Two applicable operators.

We can now pursue the computation separately in each context, possibly branching again to generate new contexts. In this way, we may end by generating multiple solutions to the current problem, essentially by simulating different ways in which we might proceed, instead of making irrevocable control decisions.

However, there may come a point where a context can be deemed a failure, for example if it violates a constraint. Thus, in our example, the subsequent derivation of exam failure by an application of the rule

```
[Rule3] IF:   not attend Computer Science class
        THEN: fail Computer Science exam
```

might cause us to abandon the line of reasoning generated by `Rule2`. The corresponding context is then said to be *poisoned*. Typically, it is deleted, together with all ancestor contexts between itself and the choice point that gave rise to it, assuming that these are not also ancestors of other, extant contexts. Thus the contexts shown in dark outline in Figure 17.2 would disappear, leaving a single line of reasoning in which we attend our CS class.

Contexts therefore correspond to alternative decisions or assumptions made at different points in a computation. The problem of maintaining different assumption sets, and dependencies between them, is sufficiently difficult and sufficiently central to non-trivial applications to have developed its own literature, which goes under the headings of *truth maintenance*, or *reason maintenance*. This topic is discussed in some detail in Chapter 19, where alternative computational mechanisms are explored.

The trend towards 'add-on' modules is likely to continue as users demand additional facilities and the ability to interface to other kinds of software. In real applications, expert systems are rarely self-contained. They often require access to databases or robot arms, and receive data from signal processors or statistical packages.

So far we have done no more than attempt a survey of the main types of expert system tool that are currently available, without going into detail about individual systems. In the next section, we concentrate upon the problems involved in selecting, learning to use, and actually deploying current tools. We shall see that many problems can arise in each of these phases, but that some of them are avoidable.

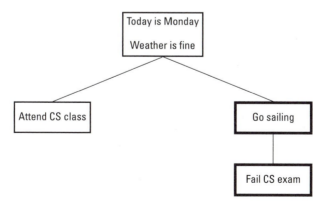

Figure 17.2 **An example of multiple contexts.**

BOX 17.2

Reasoning in Contexts

Here is some CLIPS code that implements the example in this section. We distinguish between facts, such as 'weather is sunny,' and acts, such as 'skip class.' These facts and acts hold in contexts, instead of holding globally.

```
;; Templates

;; A fact is a subject with some property.
;; The world field says what context we are in.
(deftemplate fact
  (field subj (type SYMBOL))
  (field attr (type SYMBOL))
  (field world (type INTEGER))
)

;; An act is an action with an object.
;; The world field says what context we are in.
(deftemplate act
  (field action (type SYMBOL))
  (field object (type SYMBOL))
  (field world (type INTEGER))
)

;; A context is just a numbered world
;; with a status that is either OK or NG (no good).
(deftemplate context
  (field id (type INTEGER))
  (field status (type SYMBOL))
)

;; Initial world model
(deffacts model
  (context (id 1) (status OK))
  (fact (subj weather) (attr sunny) (world 1))
)

;; Rules

;; If it isn't raining,
;; then create a new context in which you skip class.
(defrule skip
  (fact (subj weather) (attr ?W&~rainy) (world ?C))
  =>
  (assert (act (action skip) (object class) (world (+ ?C 1))))
  (assert (context (id (+ ?C 1)) (status OK)))
)

;; If you skip class, then you fail the exam.
(defrule fail
  (act (action skip) (object class) (world ?W))
  =>
  (assert (act (action fail) (object exam) (world ?W)))
)
```

continued

```
;; If a context contains failure, then mark it no good.
(defrule poison
  (act (action fail) (world ?W))
  ?C <- (context (id ?W) (status OK))
  =>
  (modify ?C (status NG))
)
```

Once a context is marked no good, we can do whatever we want with it, for example delete all its facts and acts (see Exercise 8).

17.4 Potential implementation problems

Many difficulties arise in the implementation phase of building an expert system, although there has been very little systematic study of these problems. Such discussion as there is tends to be anecdotal, although we shall also examine some published reports of experiences and experiments. This section aims to give the reader some idea of

- common pitfalls and how to avoid them;
- how to select a knowledge engineering tool;
- how hard such tools are to learn and use.

Some of what follows may be controversial, but an attempt has been made to reflect a broad range of opinions.

17.4.1 Common pitfalls and how to avoid them

As an example of the anecdotal approach, Waterman (1986, Chapter 19) lists the following pitfalls, and suggests ways of avoiding them.

- The expert's domain knowledge gets inextricably entwined with the rest of the program. In particular, it is impossible to separate it from general knowledge about search and problem solving. Waterman suggests that a rule-based organization can help achieve this, although we have seen from the comments of Clancey and Aikins that this is not always so.
- After extracting and representing hundreds of rules from an expert, the resultant knowledge base can still be radically incomplete and fail to solve simple problems, because fundamental concepts are missing or ill-represented. Waterman suggests that incremental development will help identify such problems early on. He advises testing at all phases of development, although we have seen that some knowledge engineering tools make this easier for you than others.
- The development environment does not provide built-in explanation facilities, and adding such facilities to the completed system turns out to be non-trivial. Waterman suggests designing transparency in from the very beginning. This is good advice because, if there is no 'window' into what the program is doing, even the programmers will have a hard time understanding what is going on.
- The system contains a very large number of highly specific rules which slow execution and make the system unwieldy. Waterman recommends collapsing the

smaller rules into more general ones, where possible. Yet, as we saw in Section 17.2, there is generally an inverse trade-off between having rules that are powerful and rules whose justification and behavior is easy to understand.

In the next three sections, we seek to answer three important but difficult questions that arise from this list:

- how can one select the 'right' software tool?;
- how easy to use are these tools *really*?; and
- what constitutes good programming style in such environments?

The answers are not easy to find, but everyone involved in expert system construction should care about these issues, and will be forced to think about them from time to time. My approach will be partly anecdotal, partly based on appeals to authority, and partly based on such relevant studies and surveys as have been performed. The chapter ends with some useful maxims from the literature.

17.4.2 Selecting a software tool

Hayes-Roth *et al.* (1983, Chapter 1) propose some very general issues to consider when selecting an expert system building tool.

- *Generality.* Pick a tool with only the generality necessary to solve the problem. Thus, if you do not need complicated control facilities, there is no point in using them. Using features that you do not need is almost bound to cost you more in terms of money, personnel time and computational overhead.
- *Selection.* Let the problem characteristics determine the tool selected, rather than extraneous considerations, such as what software is ready to hand. Fortunately, the authors have something more to say on this topic in their Chapter 4, in terms of a classification of problem types, as we shall see below.
- *Speed.* When development time is critical, choose a tool with built-in facilities for explanation and a good user interface. Building interfaces is time-consuming, as well as being moderately tedious.
- *Testing.* Test the tool early on by building a small prototype. This is undoubtedly good advice, although the problem of determining the degree of scale-up one can expect remains unaddressed.

The critical question of problem characteristics is discussed in Stefik *et al.* (1983). They suggest a framework for analyzing problems, mostly based on properties of the underlying search space. The main points are discussed below. My treatment is generalized to some extent, in that the authors distinguish 11 cases to my four. However, the basic principles remain the same.

(1) *Small solution space with reliable data and knowledge.* Suppose that there are not too many alternatives to consider when looking for a solution and you are certain that your data are rules are correct. Then it is possible to pursue a single line of reasoning exhaustively, backtracking where necessary, in order to find a solution. Thus there may well be an 'off the shelf' expert systems shell that will do what you want. One suspects that this approach works best if you want what is called a *satisficing* solution, rather than an optimal one, that is a solution that

is 'good enough' rather than 'the best.' Bear in mind that anything that involves combining solution elements, for example in a consistent or optimal manner, may cause combinatorial explosion, even if the elements themselves are easy to find.

(2) *Unreliable data or knowledge.* If data or knowledge are unreliable, then it will usually be necessary to combine information from diverse sources and employ some form of inexact reasoning. The authors wisely refrain from making specific recommendations, but the main candidates are certainty factors (see Chapter 3) and fuzzy logic (see Chapter 9). For a discussion of other alternatives, such as belief functions and Bayesian belief updating, see Chapter 21.

(3) *Large but factorable solution space.* One finds two senses of the word 'factorable' in the literature, and they are not identical. A search space is said to be factorable if there exist 'pruning rules' that will reduce the size of the space early in the computation (Stefik *et al.*, 1983, p. 99). However, a search space is also factorable if it can be decomposed into independent components which can then be processed separately (Nilsson, 1980, p. 37), perhaps by different rule sets or different partitions of the same rule set. This is normally achieved by breaking the main problem down into non-interacting subproblems. The success of the main goal is then dependent upon the success of a conjunction of more or less independent subgoals, and if any of these fails, then the whole computation fails without more ado. In either event, hierarchical generate-and-test is a reasonable method to employ, because you will be able to (i) rule out large numbers of possibilities by pruning and/ or (ii) decompose the solution space with respect to subproblems.

(4) *Large, non-factorable solution space.* The solution space may not be factorable in either of the above senses. Many design problems are like this: partial solutions can only be evaluated in the global context of the whole design. One never knows whether one has succeeded or not until the last piece of the puzzle falls into place. A common method for dealing with large search spaces is to consider the space at various levels of abstraction, that is, descriptions of the space at different degrees of detail. Solving problems in this way corresponds to what is sometimes called 'top-down refinement' (see Chapter 14). One then achieves some high-level goal by achieving subgoals at lower (more detailed) levels of problem specification. The idea is to try to do away with expensive backtracking over levels, but this only works if there is no significant interaction between subproblems. As we saw in Chapter 15, a least commitment strategy supplemented by guessing can be effective here, but it also helps to have domain-specific knowledge about how to resolve anticipated conflicts.

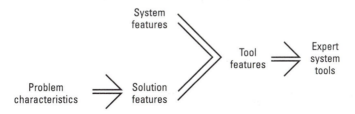

Figure 17.3 **Basis for selection of an expert system tool.**

Hayes-Roth *et al.* (1983) represent the selection problem in terms of the diagram shown in Figure 17.3. Problem characteristics suggest solution features, as in points 1–4 listed above. These are then combined with desired system features – such as production rules, forward reasoning, or explanation facilities – to suggest desirable tool features, which in turn suggest which tools might be appropriate. It has to be said that this is not as easy as it looks, but there is little doubt that this approach is more rational than most, and it is one that most system architects follow.

For example, the project team for the COMPASS expert system described in Chapter 10 list the following reasons for choosing the KEE knowledge engineering environment. They felt that

- it offered more programming paradigms than other tools;
- it had better user interface and editing facilities;
- it was better supported and was more portable than competing systems.

The team chose to use a COTS (commercial off-the-shelf) tool, rather than develop their own system, partly because they did not want to have to maintain a suite of in-house programs.

Other factors that should be taken into account in such a decision are availability of training in the use of the tool, vendor stability and track record, and, of course, price.

17.4.3 How easy is it to use these tools?

One of the 'selling points' of software tools for building expert systems, and the cause of much controversy, is the claim that many of them can be used by non-programmers, or at least by programmers with no previous grounding in artificial intelligence techniques. In this section, we attempt a critical evaluation of such claims, citing studies and surveys as appropriate. The available evidence suggests that using a typical tool is not much easier than learning a new programming language, and that even experienced programmers make the kinds of mistake committed by beginning students of conventional programming.

Ward and Sleeman (1987) monitored experienced programmers learning to use the S.1 expert systems shell (Teknowledge, 1985), which was a derivative of EMYCIN and an ancestor of M.4. S.1 knowledge bases contain many different kinds of object: control statements, classes, class types, production rules, value hierarchies and functions. Thus, in extending EMYCIN with the addition of desirable features for representation and control, the architects of S.1 also complicated the system to some considerable extent. This is also true of M.4 (see Box 17.3).

The S.1 shell had four modes of operation:

- knowledge base preparation, that is, editing;
- knowledge base consultation, that is, running the program;
- loading break, that is, a load or compile time error;
- consultation break, that is, a runtime error.

The programmers had difficulty navigating between these four modes, even though they were experienced in the usual process of creating a file, compiling it, running it, and recovering from errors. The error messages were no more helpful than those associated with conventional programming languages; that is, they were unable to distinguish between locus of error and the point in the execution of the code where the error manifested itself. Given the incremental nature of knowledge-base development, and exhortations by authorities which endorse such a strategy, the process of moving between these modes ought to be made as easy as possible, since the programmer is likely to have to perform the iteration even more times than in a more conventional programming task.

The study also found that if programmers stuck to the simplest possible model of computation – in which they input data, asked the system to determine the value of some parameter using a small knowledge base of rules and then display the result – then there were few problems in deciding how to represent things and how to control search. As matters grew complicated – for example with the size of the knowledge base, the uncertain nature of the knowledge, or more complex control regimes – careful thought was needed on strategic matters. Ward and Sleeman concluded that although learning to use S.1 seems to be no more difficult than learning a new programming language, such as Pascal, it is not any easier either.

Their judgment is that claims made to the effect that personnel with no previous programming experience can easily learn to use such tools appear to be 'quite unjustified.' My own experience of supervising post-graduate students using a range of such tools (some simpler than S.1, and some more complex) is entirely in accord with their findings and conclusions: even good programmers have problems and do not always produce sensible code, as we shall see in the next section.

On a more general note, Robinson *et al.* (1987) point out that selecting an expert system tool is a hard problem, because

- many of the more sophisticated tools are quite expensive, which prohibits speculative purchase;
- the time necessary to understand these systems by the average consumer prohibits a detailed evaluation of competing systems;
- manufacturers' terminology and notation is very diverse, even in the description of standard AI techniques, so it is hard to figure out just what is being offered.

There is a sense in which the last problem is just a special case of the general problem of software standardization. Programs of whatever kind are difficult to compare without extensive study. In the sector of AI tools, this problem has been compounded by the novelty of the technology.

BOX 17.3

Rules and Procedures in M.4

M.4's main knowledge representation is backward chaining production rules in an EMYCIN syntax (see Chapter 11). Thus the following rule selects a bolt of a certain size, given that some constraints concerning length, diameter and thread pitch can be satisfied. Upper case expressions denote variables.

```
if    recommended type = bolt and
      recommended length = LENGTH and
      recommended diameter = DIAMETER and
      recommended thread_pitch = PITCH and
      fastener(bolt, LENGTH, DIAMETER, PITCH) = BOLT
then  recommended fastener = BOLT
```

continued

Forward chaining is simulated by the constructs whenfound and whencached, which function rather like demons (see Chapter 6). For example, whencached enables some action to be taken when a new datum is instantiated. This action will typically involve calling a procedure, and is far less uniform or constrained than an action in the right-hand side of a CLIPS rule, for example,

```
whencached(sensor_reading(SENSOR, TIME) = SIGNATURE) =
  ((signature_type(SIGNATURE) = jet or
    signature_type(SIGNATURE = prop) and
  TIME - 1 = PREVIOUS and
  cached(sensor_reading)OTHER, PREVIOUS) = SIGNATURE) and
  neighbor(SENSOR) = OTHER and
  location(SENSOR) = LOC and
  do(set plane_detected(LOC, TIME))).
```

which asserts that an airplane has been detected at a particular location at time TIME whenever a sensor reading at time TIME exhibits the signature of a jet or propeller and can be associated with a similar reading by some neighboring sensor during the previous time period. How readable is this, and how far does it provide a genuine forward chaining facility?

Procedures in M.4 have a C- or Pascal-like appearance, for example,

```
procedure(determine_and_display_recs(FAULT)) =
{
  find_recommendations(FAULT);
  LIST := listof(recommendations(FAULT));
  COUNT := 1;
  while (LIST == [ITEM | REST])
  {
    display([COUNT, ". ", ITEM, nl]);
    COUNT := COUNT + 1;
    LIST := REST;
  };
}.
```

although the construction

```
LIST == [ITEM | REST]
```

is lifted from PROLOG, and splits the list LIST into its head, ITEM, and tail, REST. Readers can decide for themselves whether they would want to learn yet another procedural language of this kind.

17.4.4 What is good programming style?

In more conventional styles of programming, there exist notions of what constitutes good programming practice. Furthermore, whole books have been written which deal with aspects of program design, programming style and efficiency considerations. Even if some of these topics are controversial (for example, what is good style?), such texts, together with word of mouth from more experienced programmers, help the novice learn his or her trade.

Such is less routinely the case in the context of AI programming in general, and knowledge engineering in particular. For many years, LISP primers contained horrendous programs that would make any 'structured programming' enthusiast shudder with horror. Sample programs were often peppered with non-standard flow of control, cavalier use of dynamic variable binding, and the careless manipulation of data structures such as property lists. This situation has improved dramatically in recent years – compare Winston and Horn (1984) with Winston and Horn (1981), for example. Nevertheless, writing good LISP code is a skill that not many people acquire, and many famous AI programs contain the most appalling examples of bad programming practice.

The fact that it has taken 25 years for something resembling a good LISP programming style to become widespread does not augur well for the new languages, tools and environments that are currently emerging. It is pretty unclear to me what constitutes good KEE style, for example, and I have seen knowledge engineers who have years of experience in structured languages run amok when faced with a mix of procedural attachment, combined methods and active values! None of this is intended as a serious criticism of KEE (which I have unfairly singled out as the target of these comments), rather it is a sad fact of life that powerful tools require equally strong methodologies for their application if they are to serve our purposes. Perhaps we can take comfort from the example of OPS5. It only took five years or so for a definitive text (Brownston *et al.*, 1985) to appear telling prospective knowledge programmers how to write effective OPS5 code.

17.5 More maxims on expert system development

So as not to end this chapter on a depressing note, I include some selected maxims on how to build expert systems from Buchanan *et al.* (1983). If expert system builders all followed Buchanan's advice, they could save themselves a good deal of unnecessary grief. Prerau (1990) is also an excellent source of maxims on every aspect of expert systems development.

Some projects are doomed from the outset and quickly turn into 'death marches.' Here are some hints on how to avoid common pitfalls that occur at the very beginning of an expert systems application.

- Select a task that is neither too difficult nor too hard for human experts.
- Define the task very clearly.
- Decide early how you will evaluate the system.

It is particularly important to draw a line around what the system will be expected to achieve; better still, state explicitly what the system will *not* be expected to do. It is better to have a reliable system that performs some fraction of a real task properly than an unreliable system that does most of the task correctly sometimes. Of course, reliability can only be ascertained if you have some criteria for judging the success of the system.

- Work intensively with a core set of representative problems, and keep a library of cases presented to the system.
- Separate domain-specific knowledge from general problem solving knowledge, and aim for simplicity in the inference engine.

Make sure that your problems are representative, and either write or obtain some code that makes the running of examples easy. Software that logs a problem solving session, including user inputs, is very useful if your system is highly interactive. We have already covered the issue of separating different kinds of knowledge in Chapters 10, 11 and 16.

The authors also have good advice on rule writing:

- If a rule looks big, it is.
- If several rules are very similar, look for an underlying domain concept.

As in conventional programming, small is usually beautiful as far as chunks of code are concerned, and redundancy is usually a sign that a simplifying abstraction is possible.

Prerau also has many good suggestions concerning the implementation phase of an expert system, for example,

- Group rules into rule sets.

COMPASS partitioned its rules into 18 KEE knowledge bases. Only seven of these actually perform a problem solving function that corresponded to an expert's analysis procedures. The remainder provide support functions, or gather and provide data. Demons (see Chapter 6) were used to expand the functionality of KEE rules, for example, by passing messages to objects (see Exercise 5 below). Message passing also provided an important control facility for harnessing procedural knowledge.

- Adopt a set of programming-style conventions that give the program a uniform look.

As mentioned earlier, many programmers forget to write structured code when granted the variety of constructs and representation schemes provided by a multiple-paradigm programming language. One way of avoiding *ad hoc* design is to try to implement similar functions in a similar way throughout the program, and to have such code actually look the same, so that a programmer can recognize that a particular technique is being employed that he or she has seen before, elsewhere in the program. This should be especially true within individual knowledge bases.

- Sacrifice some program efficiency to attain better readability and maintainability, unless speed of program execution is a paramount concern.

Programmers will sometimes vie with each other to produce 'terse' code, which is generally unreadable. There is no virtue in doing this in the average expert systems application. The speed of most interactive advice-giving systems is bounded by the time taken up with user responses at the terminal and database access.

On the subject of prototyping, Buchanan *et al.* suggest building a Mark I system as soon as a typical example is well understood. However, the real nugget of pure gold is the following piece of advice: when building the Mark II system:

- Throw away the Mark I system!

Many projects have foundered because programmers or system designers became irrationally attached to the first implementation of their ideas. This raises again the important question of when to stop elaborating and debugging Mark I: programmers often indulge in obsessional behavior when building systems, 'perfecting' code that ought to be thrown away. Mark II should always build on the experience of Mark I, but only rarely on its actual code.

- The process of building an expert system is inherently experimental.

This maxim is still true today, at least to some extent. People who believe that expert systems can be built by unskilled personnel following some simple recipe are headed for a disappointment. One can always tell persons who have suffered from this experience, because they complain loud and long that AI has 'failed to deliver the goods.' Building a successful application requires the persistence and patience of a skilled programmer, as well as a genuine expert and a certain level of commitment from management.

BIBLIOGRAPHICAL NOTES

Waterman (1986, Chapters 27–28) provides a catalog of early expert systems tools; unfortunately, such material quickly becomes out of date. A critical comparison of some knowledge engineering environments of the 1980s can be found in Laurent *et al.* (1986). Harmon and Hall (1993) provides a survey of modern software development tools and methodologies, including rule-based, case-based and object-oriented systems.

Readers may care to compare for themselves the offerings of such companies as Intellicorp, Teknowledge, and Inference Corp, by browsing their Web pages. There are also FAQs (files of Frequently Asked Questions) relating to various AI newsgroups, including one on expert system shells. The ftp sites of these FAQs can be found at

```
http://hps.elte.hu/ai-faq.html
```

However, the information contained in them is not guaranteed to be especially current or complete.

STUDY SUGGESTIONS

1. Compare and contrast the use of shells, high-level programming languages, and multiple paradigm programming environments for both classification and construction tasks.

2. Why do we sometimes want to reason in different contexts, and why are some contexts eventually poisoned?

3. To what extent should the final system be based upon an initial prototype?

4. Critique the expert systems tool with which you are most familiar. To be thorough, your evaluation ought to involve
   (i) detailing features of the tool that you like, and saying in what ways they make programming easier;
   (ii) detailing features that you dislike, and saying precisely how they conspire to make programming more difficult than it needs to be; and
   (iii) identifying additional features that you wish the tool supported

   Under (iii), try to distinguish between those features which could easily be added to the tool and those which would incur substantial redesign or loss of efficiency.

continued

5. Devise some knowledge engineering maxims of your own, based on your experience so far, for example with the exercises from previous chapters. (Variations on Murphy's Law don't count.)

6. Document your own progress in learning to use an expert systems tool. Try to classify any difficulties that you have. For example, you might begin by differentiating between the following kinds of problem:

   - *Mode problems*. Finding your way around the user interface, for example editor, debugger, interpreter, and so on.
   - *Syntactic problems*. Putting all the parentheses, semicolons, and so on in the right place.
   - *Conceptual problems*. Difficulties in understanding procedural or declarative constructs of the tool, for example demons, contexts, and so on.

7. This exercise illustrates the integration of rules and objects supported by CLIPS. The primary mechanism for communication between rules and objects is for a rule's conclusion to contain an action which sends a message to an instance of a class.

   For example, suppose that an expert system which is advising a user about the purchase of a guitar wishes to have the object representing that model print out the contents of its slots. Then we might have a rule such as the following:

   ```
   (defrule describe-guitar
     (option ?guitar)
     =>
     (send (symbol-to-instance-name ?guitar) show)
   )
   ```

   show could then be a method of the class guitar which displays the slot contents of an instance in a suitable format. For example, given a class definition, such as

   ```
   (defclass guitar (is-a USER)
     (slot make)
     (slot model)
     (slot wood)
     (slot pickups))
   ```

   one could define show as

   ```
   (defmessage-handler guitar show ()
     (printout t
       "The " ?self:make " " ?self:model " is a "
       ?self:wood " guitar with " ?self:pickups " pickups")
   )
   ```

   Given an instance, such as

   ```
   (GibSG of guitar
   ```

continued

```
(make gibson)
(model SG)
(wood mahogany)
(pickups humbucking)
)
```

show would then print out

```
"The Gibson SG is a mahogany guitar with humbucking pickups."
```

Incorporate such a facility into one of the advice-giving programs you wrote as part of an earlier exercise, such as Chapter 14, Exercise 7, or Chapter 16, Exercise 4.

8. Write a pair of rules which delete all the acts and facts associated with the poisoned context in the 'skip class' example of Section 17.3.5. Why do you need two rules?

18 Blackboard Architectures

Blackboard systems are a more recent phenomenon than frames or production rules which provide the basis for an abstract architecture of great power and generality. They can emulate both forward- and backward- chaining reasoning systems, as well as being able to combine these forms of reasoning opportunistically. In addition, the blackboard model of problem solving encourages the hierarchical organization of both domain knowledge and the space of partial and complete solutions. It is therefore well suited to construction problems in which the problem space is large but factorable along some number of dimensions. Successful applications of the blackboard approach have included data interpretation (for example, image understanding, speech recognition), analysis and synthesis of complex compounds (for example, protein structures) and planning.

However, blackboard systems are neither easy to implement nor computationally inexpensive to run. In this chapter, we shall

- outline the fundamental structure of a blackboard system;
- review a number of non-trivial blackboard applications; and
- discuss issues of implementation and efficiency.

We shall see that blackboard systems combine many of the different knowledge representation schemes that we have encountered so far, but that they do so in a more tightly integrated fashion than most multiple-paradigm programming environments.

18.1 The blackboard metaphor

The basic idea behind a blackboard system is often presented in the following way (see, for example, Corkhill, 1991).

- Imagine a group of human experts seated next to a classroom blackboard trying to solve some problem.
- Each expert is a specialist in some area relevant to the problem's solution.
- The problem and initial data are written on the blackboard.
- Experts watch the blackboard to see if they can make a contribution to solving the problem.
- When an expert feels that he (or she) has a contribution to make, he (or she) will perform some computation and record the results on the blackboard.
- This new result may then enable another expert to make a contribution.
- This process halts when the problem has been solved.

One can imagine this as an effective problem solving method, if certain conventions hold, namely:

- Experts must all use the same language, although the blackboard might allow a variety of notational schemes to be used.
- There must be some protocol for scheduling who goes to the blackboard if more than one expert reaches for the chalk.

These conventions are just our old friends, *representation* and *control*, familiar from earlier chapters.

The basic organization of a blackboard system as a computational device is as follows. Domain knowledge is partitioned into independent *knowledge sources* (KSs) which run under a *scheduler*, while solutions are built up on a global data structure, the *blackboard*. Thus instead of representing 'how-to' knowledge in a single rule set, such knowledge is encoded in a suite of programs. Each of these knowledge sources may be a rule set in its own right, or the suite may contain diverse programs that mix rules with procedures.

The blackboard now serves the function rather like that of a production system's working memory, except that its structure is much more complex. Typically, the blackboard is partitioned into different *levels* of description with respect to the solution space, each corresponding to a different amount of detail or analysis. Levels usually contain more complex data structures than working memory vectors, such as object hierarchies or recursive graphs. In modern systems, there may even be more than one blackboard.

Knowledge sources trigger on blackboard objects, but their instantiations may not be executed at once. Instead, *knowledge source activation records* (KSARs) are normally placed on an agenda pending selection by the scheduler. Knowledge sources only communicate via the blackboard, and thus cannot transmit data to each other or invoke each other directly. This is rather like the convention in production systems that forbids individual rules from calling each other directly: everything must be done through working memory.

This chapter reviews earlier work on blackboard systems and assesses recent attempts to use the blackboard model of problem solving as a basis for constructing general-purpose tools for building expert systems. The basic principles are illustrated with examples, but the emphasis is upon architectural issues rather than the details of individual systems or applications. The final section briefly reviews recent attempts to deploy parallelism in the search for efficient implementations of blackboard systems.

18.2 HEARSAY, AGE and OPM

The blackboard architecture grew out of an attempt to build a speech understanding system called HEARSAY (Erman *et al.*, 1980). Programming a computer to understand speech is an extremely hard problem, and one that requires

- complex signal processing,
- some mapping from physical events in the speech waveform to symbolic units in a natural language, and
- a search through a very large space of possible interpretations which combine these different units of analysis.

A dominant way of thinking about the speech problem is in terms of various levels of description, beginning from the physical domain of acoustic signals which are recorded and processed to yield outputs such as sound spectra, and progressing through increasingly rarefied strata of linguistic abstraction, such as phonemes, syllables, morphemes, words, phrases and sentences.

18.2.1 Motivation for HEARSAY-II architecture

The intuition behind the genesis of blackboard systems was that there is a distinct body of knowledge associated with each of these levels of analysis, for example knowledge about signals, phonemics, lexical knowledge, knowledge of grammar, semantics, and knowledge about the universe of discourse. No single body of knowledge is sufficient in isolation to solve the problem; for example, even if the signal processing preserves all the important features of the original waveform, and even if we can build a machine which perfectly decodes the output of signal processing into phonemes, we still won't be able to tell the difference between expressions such as

I scream
ice cream

or

please let us know
please lettuce no
pleas letter snow

without additional information. Thus, although each body of knowledge is important, and can be considered and codified (more or less) without reference to the others, automatic (or human) speech understanding requires their cooperation.

The key problem that has to be addressed in speech understanding is the management of uncertainty, since

- the data is inherently noisy, incomplete and variable (both between and within speakers);
- the mapping between levels is inherently ambiguous, for example, the mapping between phonemic and lexical levels in the 'I scream/ice cream' example;
- the role of both linguistic and extralinguistic context is crucial: the interpretation elements that surround a given segment of speech make alternative interpretations of that segment more or less likely.

More traditional approaches to speech recognition use statistical models from communication theory to encode transition probabilities between segments, but a more knowledge-based approach requires a rethinking of uncertainty handling.

Erman *et al.* (1980) list the following requirements for a knowledge-based approach to speech understanding to be effective:

(1) At least one possible sequence of operations (partial solutions) must lead to a correct interpretation. In other words, the 'bits' that form the correct interpretation must be in the hypothesis space somewhere.
(2) The procedure for scoring interpretations should rank the correct interpretation higher than all the competing complete interpretations. In other words, the correct interpretation of an utterance should outrank all other interpretations that span the utterance.
(3) The computational cost of finding the correct interpretation must satisfy some externally specified limit in terms of space and time requirements. Thus a speech understander that takes several days to comprehend a single utterance, and requires many gigabytes of storage to do it, would not be deemed successful.

The central problem in speech understanding appears to be that requirements (1) and (3) are in serious conflict. In order to make sure that the right bits are somewhere in the space of partial interpretations, we usually have to be extremely generous at the hypothesis generation stage. This results in a combinatorial explosion of solution elements that render the search for the best spanning interpretation completely intractable for large vocabularies without extremely good heuristics for extending partial interpretations. Thus getting the scoring procedure of requirement (2) right is essential for success.

18.2.2 HEARSAY's use of knowledge sources

HEARSAY-II used diverse knowledge sources (KSs) to generate, combine and extend possible interpretations of speech segments, while the blackboard was used to store these interpretations at different levels of abstraction.

Each KS can be thought of as a condition–action pair, even though it was not be implemented as a production rule: conditions and actions were actually arbitrary procedures. The flow of control also differs from production systems in the following way. Instead of the interpreter checking to see if the conditions of knowledge sources are satisfied at each point in a recognize–act cycle, knowledge sources declare their activation conditions in advance, in terms of what kinds of data modification will trigger them. This results in an interrupt-driven polling action that is more efficient than the recognize–act of production systems: it more closely resembles the use of demons in frame systems, where control flow is governed by data update.

In general, knowledge sources are linked to levels on the blackboard in the following way. KS conditions will be satisfied by data modifications on a particular level, and KS actions will also write to a particular level (not necessarily the same as its data level). In HEARSAY-II, KSs were mostly organized so that they recognized data at a particular level of linguistic analysis and their actions operated on the next level up. Thus one knowledge source might be activated by data on the syllable level and post-lexical hypotheses on the word level.

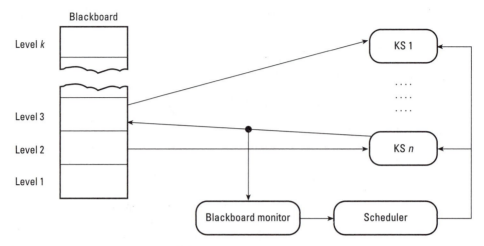

Figure 18.1 Simplified schematic of the HEARSAY-II architecture.

A schematic diagram of the HEARSAY-II architecture, simplified from Erman *et al.*, shows the basic architecture of the system (see Figure 18.1). Arrows from blackboard levels to KSs denote the triggering of KS conditions, while arrows from KSs to levels denote the output of KS actions. Arrows that impinge upon the action arrows and connect them to the blackboard monitor record modifications to blackboard levels that act as triggers for other KSs and cause them to be scheduled.

Further details of the HEARSAY program are not really relevant to our discussion. The most important thing to note about the architecture is that it does not dictate a particular control regime, such as top-down or bottom-up strategies. Thus, in the speech domain, one could proceed top-down, by hypothesizing a word and then gathering phonemic evidence for it, or else bottom-up, by assembling phoneme hypotheses into words. The monitor and the scheduler decide which KSs to activate, and this decision can be made as domain-free or domain-specific as you like. Ordinarily, KS activations are scored on the basis of how well their conditions fit the data, rather as the CENTAUR system scored tasks in Chapter 13.

18.2.3 HEARSAY-III: an abstract architecture

HEARSAY-III (Erman *et al.*, 1983) was an abstraction over the earlier HEARSAY systems, rather as EMYCIN was over MYCIN. In addition to the usual blackboard and knowledge source structures, HEARSAY-III had an underlying relational database for managing blackboard objects, and a scheduling blackboard which, together with scheduling knowledge sources, facilitated the selection of KSARs (KS activation records).

The database language was AP3 (Goldman, 1978), and it served a variety of functions in HEARSAY-III.

- Blackboard units are typed AP3 *objects*, in the object-oriented sense (see Chapter 7). This helps regularize the representation of both data and partial solutions.

- Knowledge source triggers are implemented using AP3 pattern-directed *demons* (see Chapter 6). This regularizes the procedural side of things in the manner of frame systems.
- Database *contexts* (see Section 17.3.5) are supported by AP3, and the conditions for poisoning contexts are expressed as AP3 constraints. Contexts can be used to support alternative ways of continuing a computation, for example when a program is forced to guess, or to support hypothetical reasoning.

Knowledge sources consist of a *trigger*, some *immediate code*, and a *body*. When the trigger pattern is matched, an activation record is created and the immediate code is executed. The body is not executed unless the KSAR is later selected by the scheduler. HEARSAY-III provides a default 'base scheduler' which performs the simplest scheduling operations, such as taking the next KSAR off the agenda and executing it. The user is intended to write scheduling KSs which match against changes on either the domain or the scheduling blackboards, and whose actions assign and modify ratings of KSARs.

The main strength of HEARSAY-III was its loosely-knit control regime, which allowed the user great freedom in representing and applying heuristics for the selection of KSARs, and its regularization of blackboard data objects. The main weakness was the lack of a knowledge representation language within the knowledge sources themselves. The intermediate code and the body of a KS were simply arbitrary pieces of LISP code, as in HEARSAY-II. Many of the features of HEARSAY-III were carried over into the ART expert system tool mentioned in Chapter 17. ART's inference engine has a proper production rule language that supports both forward and backward chaining.

18.2.4 Abstraction in AGE and OPM

AGE (Nii and Aiello, 1979) is a collection of tools and partial frameworks for building expert systems. A 'framework' in AGE is a configuration of components, such as the backward-chaining EMYCIN framework or the blackboard framework. A knowledge source in the blackboard framework of AGE was a set of production rules wrapped in a local context that specified a rule evaluation strategy, for example, *single-hit* (fire one rule only), or *multiple-hit* (fire as many rules as will fire).

AGE's blackboard objects, and the relationships that hold between them, are represented in UNITS (Stefik, 1979), a forerunner of the KEE system described in Chapter 17. Rule actions can post changes, either to UNITS or to the hypothesis structure where the solution is progressively built up. These changes can be actual, expected or desired, as follows.

- Actual changes are *events*, to be posted on an event-list on the blackboard after the changes have been made. These events drive forward-chaining production rules in an event-driven strategy, generating new events until some termination condition is met.
- Expected changes are *expectations* derived from some model, and these are posted on the expectation-list. Given a situation where initial data values suggest hypotheses, rules in a model-driven system post expectations whose fulfillment or non-fulfillment would count as evidence for or against a hypothesis.

- Desired changes are *goals*, and they are posted on the goal-list. The associated behavior is that of a backward-chaining goal-driven system like EMYCIN, where production rules perform subgoaling until conditions for concluding hypotheses are satisfied (or not) by data.

Aiello (1983) describes three implementations of PUFF, one using each of these control strategies, largely to demonstrate the space of possibilities created by such an architecture.

OPM (Hayes-Roth, 1985) is a blackboard control system for multi-task planning which integrates domain and control problem solving in a single control loop with no pre-programmed control biases. Actions are chosen by reconciling independent decisions concerning what actions are desirable and what actions are feasible by integrating multiple control heuristics of various grain-size and importance.

OPM's application was errand planning, and the program used four global data structures:

(1) A *blackboard* split into five panels:
- meta-plan (planning goals);
- plan abstraction (planning decisions);
- knowledge base (cache of observations and computations);
- plan (chosen actions); and
- executive (choosing KSARs to execute the actions).
(2) An *event list* for recording blackboard changes.
(3) A *map* showing the locations of the errands.
(4) An *agenda* for KSARs.

Knowledge sources had both a trigger to determine its relevance to a given node in the blackboard (the 'focus node') and a test which determined whether or not the KSAR was actually applicable at the time of execution. When scheduling, KSARs were preferred which affected the current focus, that is, the most recently added or updated node on the blackboard. Such 'focus decisions' drew on the information stored on the executive panel of the blackboard.

Although OPM was intended as a tool for the simulation of human problem solving, it also has clear advantages from a systems engineering point of view. The ability to factor control knowledge into heterogeneous knowledge sources and then reason about their recommendations represents a powerful tool for constructing meta-level architectures. The next section explores the further development of this methodology in the BB* blackboard environment for building knowledge-based systems.

18.3 The blackboard environment BB*

Hayes-Roth *et al.* (1988) describe a blackboard environment in which the three levels of applications program, task framework and abstract architecture are sharply differentiated and yet tightly integrated. The emphasis is upon intelligent systems which are capable of reasoning about their actions, using knowledge of the events and states that can occur, the actions they can perform, and the relationships that hold among actions, events and states. The authors describe an environment, BB*, which allows the combination of different task- and domain-specific modules under a generic blackboard architecture, BB1.

18.3.1 Architecture, framework and application

At the most abstract level, an *architecture* comprises a set of basic knowledge structures (representing actions, events, states, and so on) and a mechanism for choosing and executing actions. This kind of knowledge is not only domain-free; it is also independent of both task and problem solving method. The idea is that the architecture should be capable of supporting a wide variety of different tasks in different domains (just as the human cognitive architecture is, whatever it may be). General capabilities, such as reasoning about control, the ability to learn and explain, should also be incorporated at this level.

A *framework* is a set of intermediate knowledge structures representing actions, events, and so on relevant to a particular task, such as diagnosing faults in a system or constructing a system that meets some constraints. These structures contain knowledge which addresses a particular class of problems in a particular way. Such methods should be applicable to more than one domain, just as humans are able to form and execute plans in a variety of different contexts by using only a relatively small number of strategies. The ACCORD knowledge base (see Section 18.3.2) for solving arrangement problems by the method of assembly is an example of such a framework.

At the most specific level, an *application* is a set of knowledge structures that instantiate particular actions, events, and so on to solve a particular class of problems by a particular method in a particular domain. Examples of applications undertaken in the BB* environment include the PROTEAN system for deriving protein structure from constraints (Hayes-Roth *et al.*, 1986) and the SIGHTPLAN system for laying out the facilities of a construction site (Tommelein *et al.*, 1987).

18.3.2 BB1 and ACCORD as architecture and framework

These points will be illustrated with reference to the BB1 architecture, with a particular emphasis upon reasoning about control (see Johnson and Hayes-Roth, 1986). The framework under discussion will be the ACCORD knowledge base for solving a class of arrangement problems, and the application will be the PROTEAN system for deriving protein structure.

As in other blackboard systems, BB1 knowledge sources (KSs) are first triggered by events on their associated input level of the blackboard, creating knowledge source activation records (KSARs). These part-instantiations are not executed immediately, but kept on an agenda pending their selection and the satisfaction of their preconditions, which are typically properties of blackboard objects. However, in addition to domain KSs and a domain blackboard, BB1 also has control KSs and a control blackboard. A scheduler sequences the execution of both domain and control KSARs on an agenda in accordance with a control plan which develops dynamically on the control blackboard. The execution of a KSAR posts changes on its output blackboard level, thereby triggering other KSs.

Thus BB1 executes the following basic cycle.

(1) *Interpret* the action of the next KSAR.
(2) *Update* the agenda with KSARs triggered by that action and rate all KSARs against the current control plan.
(3) *Schedule* the highest-rated KSAR.

ACCORD is a language for representing knowledge underlying the performance of arrangement tasks by the method of assembling components so that they satisfy a set of constraints (as opposed to, say, refining a prototypical arrangement). This method does not entail a particular control regime, but it does require that a number of control decisions be made somehow, such as how to construct and compose partial arrangements. The basic representational device that ACCORD uses is a concept hierarchy of types, individuals and instances; it therefore fulfills roughly the same role as AP3 fulfilled for HEARSAY-III, except that it is more specifically oriented towards arrangement problems.

The types define generic concepts and roles, rather as semantic networks do, by ISA links (see Chapter 6). Individuals exemplify particular concepts without instantiating them. For example, the first element in a sequence of entities of type T exemplifies T but does not instantiate it, since we do not say which particular object is the first in the sequence. Instances instantiate individuals (not concepts) in particular contexts, for example in a particular sequence, and play particular roles in those contexts, for example the 'anchor' of a partial arrangement (see below). Concepts can have attributes, and enter into relations with other concepts. These are inheritable along ISA links, although it is also possible to define new inheritance paths.

The framework provides skeletal branches of a hierarchy for the objects to be arranged, the contexts in which they must be arranged, and the constraints that need to be satisfied. For example, ACCORD represents domain-independent arrangement roles, such as `arrangement`, `partial-arrangement` and `included-object`, with an `includes` relation between them. An important kind of `included-object` is an anchor, that is an object that has been assigned a fixed location to define the local context of a partial arrangement, while an `anchoree` is an `included-object` that has at least one constraint with an `anchor`.

18.3.3 PROTEAN: application as framework instantiation

PROTEAN (Hayes-Roth et al., 1986) is a system intended to identify the three-dimensional structure of proteins in solution. The combinatorics of considering all possible conformations prohibit the use of exhaustive search, and so the program employs a number of different techniques to traverse the solution space. In combination, these provide a powerful mechanism for implementing a strategy of successive refinement with an evolving control plan which leaves room for opportunistic focusing.

- PROTEAN combines both local and global constraints on allowable structural hypotheses. Local constraints give some indication of the proximity of constituent atoms in the molecule, while global constraints include such things as the molecule's overall size and shape.
- PROTEAN adopts a 'divide and conquer' approach by defining partial solutions that incorporate different subsets of a protein's structure and different subsets of constraints, instead of trying to apply all the constraints to the whole molecule. Having applied constraints within overlapping partial solutions, it then applies constraints between them.
- PROTEAN reasons bidirectionally across a four-level solution blackboard. The different levels of abstraction are: the molecule level, the solid level of helices, sheets and coils, the superatom level of peptides and side chains in amino acids, and the

Knowledge source	Behavior
Generic BB1 control knowledge sources	
Initialize-Focus	Identifies the initial focus prescribed by a newly recorded strategy
Terminate-Focus	Changes the status of a focus to inoperative once its goal has been satisfied
Domain-specific control knowledge sources	
Create-Best-Anchor-Space	Records the create-best-anchor-space focus
Prefer-Long-Anchors	Records a heuristic that gives higher ratings to KSARs that operate on long anchors
Domain-specific problem-solving knowledge sources	
Activate-Anchor-Space	Chooses a particular anchor at the solid level to be the anchor of a partial solution
Add-Anchoree-to-Anchor-Space	Chooses a particular solid-anchor to be an anchoree in an existing anchor space

Figure 18.2 **Some of PROTEAN's control and domain knowledge sources (after Hayes-Roth *et al.*, 1986).**

atom level about individual atomic constituents. When reasoning top-down, it uses structural hypotheses at one level to focus on positioning structures at a lower level; when reasoning bottom-up, it uses hypotheses at one level to restrict the position of structures at a higher level.

- PROTEAN also factors control knowledge into different levels of abstraction. At the highest level, that of strategy, a particular problem solving strategy is developed, which involves establishing the longest and most constraining helix as the anchor, and then positioning all other solid level structures relative to it. At the intermediate focus level, PROTEAN records the individual steps necessary to carry out the overall strategy, so that the program always knows where it is in the sequential execution of a strategy. The lowest heuristic level incorporates preferences for rating KSARs; for example, prefer KSARs that operate on long anchors.

Examples of PROTEAN's domain and control knowledge sources can be found in Figure 18.2.

PROTEAN is interesting because it shows how domain-independent task-related reasoning can be combined with domain-dependent knowledge about constraints in the BB1 architecture. Opportunistic focusing is integrated with hierarchical planning as the control plan unfolds. This occurs when control KSs triggered by partial solution states insert focus decisions which typically serve to restrict the space of possible locations. In other words, when the global strategy of successive refinement fails to narrow the solution space sufficiently, a control KS may cut in and introduce a particular focus with a particular set of constraints. Satisfying the opportunistic focus will then restrict the legal locations at which hierarchical plan foci can be satisfied.

18.3.4 Integrating different reasoning strategies

Johnson and Hayes-Roth (1986) show how goal-directed reasoning can be integrated with both hierarchical planning and opportunistic focusing in the context of PROTEAN. Goal-directed reasoning is required where instrumental action is needed so that other desirable actions may be performed. Thus KSARs which represent desirable actions, but which have unsatisfied preconditions, can give rise to subgoals to perform actions which cause those preconditions to be satisfied (and so on, recursively).

The authors differentiate goal knowledge by distinguishing between the desire to

(1) *perform an action*, such as executing a KSAR, because it is intrinsically desirable, for example because it satisfies a focus;
(2) *promote a state*, because it enables a desirable KSAR to have its preconditions satisfied, and hence become executable;
(3) *cause an event*, because it will trigger a KSAR which has a desirable action.

Goals of type (1) are simply actions which satisfy foci. Goals of type (2) are relevant when no executable KSAR rates highly against a current focus. In this case, BB1 has a generic control KS called Enable-Priority-Action, which is triggered whenever a desirable KSAR has unsatisfied preconditions. Execution of an Enable-Priority-Action KSAR results in a goal-directed focus being posted for each unsatisfied precondition, which promotes the corresponding state. Goals of type (3) are relevant when no KSAR on the agenda has the potential to perform a desirable action. A control KS for this situation would need to identify KSs capable of performing the desired action and post goal-directed foci to cause the corresponding events.

The authors show how opportunistic focusing and goal-directed reasoning can work together to satisfy hierarchical foci by restricting legal locations and removing obstacles to desirable actions. For example, yoking two helices together in a partial arrangement, using a set of constraints between solids, is a desirable action. However, before yoking can take place, both helices must be anchored in the arrangement (even though yoking actions are preferred to anchoring ones). Posting a goal which promotes the anchoring of an unanchored helix capable of being yoked enables the need for that specific anchoring action to be taken into account when rating KSARs at the next cycle. Goal-directed foci can therefore coexist with opportunistic foci, and interact with them in a well-understood way.

The relationships between the various modules that make up the relevant configuration of the BB* environment are both interesting and instructive. PROTEAN's domain-specific knowledge is layered upon the ACCORD framework for solving arrangement problems by the assembly method; that is, PROTEAN instantiates knowledge structures in ACCORD. The ACCORD framework is itself layered upon the BB1 architecture, in that its concept network, role vocabulary and type hierarchy become BB1's blackboard representation language.

18.3.5 Summarizing BB*

BB* is a complex architecture, but it does appear to have certain advantages over simpler systems.

- It successfully separates domain and control knowledge, inasmuch as it is possible to vary the control knowledge sources while holding the task and domain instantiations of the framework constant. Generic control KSs can be held constant over different task and domain instantiations, although domain control KSs are rather more constrained by the domain KSs, since many of them are intended to rate domain KSARs.
- It differentiates between different kinds of both domain and control knowledge. Domain knowledge in ACCORD is factored in terms of knowledge about actions, events and states, as well as knowledge about objects, arrangements and the roles that objects can play in arrangements. Terminological knowledge is also represented in terms of a task-specific network of assembly verbs. Control knowledge is factored into strategies, foci and heuristics, as described above, while foci can be factored further into categories such as hierarchical, opportunistic and goal-directed.
- It provides a basis for explaining system behavior in terms of control plans. Thus it is possible to explain why PROTEAN prefers one KSAR over another in terms of the current foci and the rating heuristics. Recounting control decisions can be complicated, although BB1's ExAct explanation package uses graphical devices to good effect.
- The use of languages such as ACCORD augments BB1's LISP-based representation facilities with a higher-level programming language which is more concise and uniform. This promotes analyzability from the knowledge engineering point of view. The fact that this language is also interpretable renders the knowledge so represented accessible to other modules, such as ExAct.
- Modules are now reusable, in that system builders can select and combine existing modules as a basis for constructing new systems. Thus the SIGHTPLAN configuration of BB* shares modules such as ACCORD and Generic-KS with the PROTEAN configuration. This benefit derives from the uniformity of style and content imposed upon modules within a given level.

Building skeletal systems in BB* can be seen as a way of providing some of the structure associated with expert system shells without the attendant inflexibility of such tools. Thus Hayes-Roth *et al.* (1987) suggest that a *shell* level can be interposed between the framework and application levels, by specializing particular frameworks so that they are tailored for particular tasks and/or domains. This would involve augmenting a representation language like ACCORD with prototypical knowledge sources appropriate for subclasses of tasks, for example assembly-arrangement problems of a particular kind. As with earlier Stanford work, the theoretical interest and practical utility of this approach derive from the discovery of useful levels of abstraction from which to view successful applications of AI technology to particular problems. In the next two sections, we describe attempts to cut the computational cost of running blackboard systems, which can be much higher than simple production systems.

18.4 Efficiency and flexibility in blackboard frameworks: GBB and Erasmus

The power and generality of blackboard systems does not come without price. Explicit reasoning about control and sophisticated scheduling of tasks must incur some computational overhead. Of course, the use of control knowledge sources is intended to focus search, and hence save cycles in the long run (see, for example, Reynolds, 1988). In this section and the next, we look at various issues in the implementation of blackboard systems, together with techniques for achieving efficiency. This section concentrates upon sequential implementations, while the next section looks at attempts to exploit parallelism.

18.4.1 Blackboard retrieval in GBB

The blackboard itself acts as an associative memory for the knowledge sources. The amount of processing devoted to performing blackboard manipulations forms a significant part of a system's overhead, so efficient representations and algorithms are required for both accessing and adding information. Although measurements are not widely available, early systems, such as Hearsay-II, appear to have spent about half their CPU cycles on blackboard interaction, as compared with knowledge source processing.

Early systems attempted to reduce blackboard search by partitioning the blackboard into levels or panes, so that a given knowledge source need only examine a fraction of the whole data structure. Here we examine a modern system, called GBB, which is currently a commercial offering and which represents the state of the art in blackboard implementation. GBB stands for Generic Blackboard Builder.

GBB's partitions are called *spaces*, and they are further structured into *dimensions*, accessed using dimensional index attributes. Thus blackboard units live in spaces and have their attributes indexed in various ways for fast retrieval. An index is really a key, in the database sense, although such a key can be quite complex, as we shall see below.

The dimensions used to structure a space are either *ordered*, for example, with respect to numbers in some interval, or *enumerated*, according to a set of non-numeric labels. Indexes can be *scalar*, consisting of a single, atomic value, or *composite*, consisting of a set or series of values. An ordered dimension with a scalar index type would have indices representing points or numeric ranges, while a composite index type will contain indices that are either sets of labels, or a series that is ordered according to some other dimension, such as time.

At each cycle, we want to find units in a particular blackboard space which match the trigger of a KS. This trigger will typically be a pattern, rather like the left-hand side of a production rule, but one which references blackboard units, rather than vectors in working memory. Using dimensions, the retrieval of a unit from a blackboard space is a four-step process:

(1) *Primary retrieval.* Select the set of all units in the space that might satisfy the pattern. Each space has a unit mapping which says how units are stored in that space. They could be stored in simple lists, for example, although this would not be very efficient. Units with ordered indexes can be stored in 'buckets' which are essentially ranges of the index, while units with enumerated indexes can be stored in hash tables.

(2) *Before-filter filtering*. Apply predicates to units in this candidate set prior to pattern matching. Since primary retrieval is deliberately inclusive, it is convenient to be able to apply arbitrary tests to screen out some of the candidates.

(3) *Pattern-based filtering*. Compare each unit to the pattern to see if it satisfies the pattern's constraints. Each pattern specifies a match criterion which says whether a candidate unit must exactly match the pattern, contain the pattern, overlap with the pattern, and so on. Since patterns can contain indexed elements, there must be rules which say how you match pattern elements of scalar, set and series index types with units of these various types.

(4) *After-filter filtering*. Apply more filter predicates to each unit. Like before-filter filtering, this is an optional stage at which further tests can be applied to narrow the space of candidate matches.

The details of how all this is implemented are fairly complex, and need not be covered here. But it is clear that blackboard systems introduce another level of complexity over that associated with purely rule- or object-based representations. To help users of such tools cope with this complexity, various frameworks have been offered which allow easy configuration of blackboard modules, as we shall see in the next subsection.

18.4.2 Blackboard configuration in Erasmus

Blackboard systems have the potential to be highly modular, in that blackboard data structures, the nature of knowledge sources, and the overall control regime could be varied semi-independently. Thus there are many ways that one could represent blackboard units, for example, as objects in various object-oriented systems, and there are many possible formats for knowledge sources, such as production rules, LISP code, and so on. The details of how KSs are invoked by pattern matching, how they are scheduled for execution, and so forth, are also potentially customizable, as we have seen in earlier sections.

Following on from BB1 and GBB came the Erasmus system, which was built at Boeing after some experience with a blackboard tool called BBB (the Boeing Blackboard System). BBB was based on BB1, and used KEE object units to represent blackboard objects (see Chapter 17). The idea behind Erasmus was that it should be possible to adapt a tool to the demands of an application, instead of developers having to work with the limitations or preferences of the tool. Specifically, Erasmus was a reimplementation of BBB in the light of the following design goals (Baum *et al.*, 1989).

(1) The system should be configurable.
(2) The performance of the system should be maximized within a given configuration.
(3) The system should be extensible.
(4) The system should support multiple representation schemes for blackboard objects.

The Boeing group found that some of their applications were a good fit with the BB1-style approach, while others found the representation and control of BBB constraining. For example, the Phred system, which generated manufacturing process plans for airplane parts, required two extensions to BBB.

- The developers added machinery to support problem solving phases of the kind described in Chapter 13.
- In some of these phases, it was convenient and more efficient to allow the scheduler to trigger more than one KSAR for execution.

Similarly, their Cockpit Information Manager system required the ability to find objects on the blackboard with a high degree of efficiency based on pattern matching. The implementation of blackboard objects as KEE units did not meet the performance goals of this system, although GBB would have provided that functionality. As we saw in the last subsection, GBB uses special indexing methods to enable fast retrieval from the blackboard.

Erasmus has been presented as a 'blackboard system generator.' However, another way of describing it is as a configurable *architecture*, if we wish to use the terminology that we introduced earlier in this chapter. Different configurations of the architecture make it more or less suitable for different classes of *application*, and could therefore be said to result in different *frameworks*.

The generator provides the following four configuration options.

(1) *Blackboard options*. The user can choose from four different blackboard representations, including GBB and KEE.
(2) *KS structure options*. Knowledge sources are implemented as *flavors* (see Chapter 7) and KSARs are flavor instances. The user has various options in the specification of *preconditions* for knowledge source activation, *obviation conditions* for deleting a KSAR, problem solving phases, and so on.
(3) *Control options*. The user can choose a BB1-style control regime of foci and strategies, or one that is driven wholly by heuristics in which KSAR priorities are just weighted sums.
(4) *Runtime options*. These include an explanation facility, a trace mechanism for monitoring the system's operation, and various interactive tools for debugging and tuning an application.

Thus the highly modular architecture of blackboard systems lends itself to a large number of configuration and customization options. The exploitation of these options in systems such as Erasmus can be seen as a logical extension of the abstraction-oriented development path from MYCIN to EMYCIN to NEOMYCIN and beyond. Blackboard systems can also form part of a hybrid application with non-blackboard components; we will see an example of this in Chapter 22.

18.5 Concurrency and parallelism in CAGE and POLIGON

The question arises as to whether it is possible to exploit the parallelism that appears to be inherent in the underlying architecture, where independent knowledge sources communicate via a global data structure. It is clear that parallelism could be introduced into a blackboard architecture at various levels of granularity, for example:

(1) knowledge source activation;
(2) evaluation of triggers and preconditions within a knowledge source; and
(3) execution of KSAR actions.

However, although (1) seems to be an inherently parallel process, (2) and (3) may contain serializing steps. For example, the preconditions of different rules may share variables, while actions may need to be sequenced in order to achieve the desired effect.

The Advanced Architectures Project at Stanford University has generated two prototype blackboard architectures that exploit parallelism in rather different ways. A brief summary of these systems is attempted below; more details can be found in Nii *et al.* (1988).

The CAGE system (Aiello, 1986) – essentially a concurrent version of the AGE blackboard tool described in Section 18.2.4 – is targeted on a shared memory system with a smaller number of processors. Programming language constructs are introduced to support parallelism at the discretion of the applications programmer. The parallelism is therefore relatively coarse-grained to avoid performance decrement due to memory contention and bandwidth limitations in the connections between processor and memory.

Three sources of concurrency were identified as part of the CAGE project:

- *Knowledge source concurrency.* KSs could work on different parts of the blackboard at the same time, or else in a pipeline fashion, where different operations are applied to different segments of data that move through the pipeline in a sequence.
- *Rule concurrency.* Rules could be executed in parallel. Conditions of different rules could be evaluated independently, and then actions could be carried out, either in parallel or serially, on a rule-by-rule basis.
- *Clause concurrency.* Individual conditions in a rule could be evaluated concurrently.

In CAGE, KSs could be executed in parallel, with or without synchronization. Roughly speaking, synchronization is where the outputs of a set of parallel steps are buffered until all processes have completed. Thus, with synchronization, the results of executing KSs would not be posted on the blackboard until all KSs had fired. The user could further specify whether the action parts of different rules were to be executed serially or in parallel. Finally, CAGE allowed evaluation of condition predicates in parallel and action parts in parallel within a single rule.

Experiments with CAGE gave disappointing results. Only a two-fold speed-up was achieved on eight processors with KS concurrency and synchronization, the benefit leveling off after four processors. Even without synchronization, the speed-up on eight processors was less than fourfold. Clearly, the central control mechanism presented a bottleneck, whether KSs were synchronized or not. Attempts to exploit concurrency at the rule level resulted in only a fivefold speed-up on 16 processors.

The POLIGON system (Rice, 1986) was designed from scratch for distributed-memory, multi-processor hardware, with a large number of processor/memory units enjoying high bandwidth communication. It was intended to run with a high degree of fine-grain parallelism as its default behavior. Thus knowledge sources were executed as data became available (as in data-flow architectures), instead of being polled by a central control module.

Experiments with POLIGON yielded an order of magnitude speed-up with 32 processors. This was a somewhat more encouraging result. It was found that POLIGON's performance held up as the amount of data and the number of rule firings per cycle increased.

The main focus of interest here was the comparison of these two approaches from the point of view of both programmability and performance. It would appear that concurrent processing of knowledge sources does not lead to gains if control remains centralized (as in CAGE), but decentralizing control (as in POLIGON) decreases programmability. Thus, it is clear that the task of exploiting parallelism in blackboard architectures is by no means straightforward, and such architectures should only be used where the task warrants both the additional complexity and the computational overhead.

BIBLIOGRAPHICAL NOTES

The review papers by Nii (1986a, 1986b) are recommended as a good starting point. A useful collection of research papers on blackboard systems can be found in Englemore and Morgan (1988). Unfortunately, the index is a little thin, so the book is not designed for dipping into. From an expert systems point of view, the following chapters are particularly worth reading. Chapters 5 and 6 cover some early applications not treated here. Chapter 12 gives a good account of AGE, and Chapter 26 briefly describes the implementation of GBB.

Other papers on GBB and Erasmus can be found in Jagannathan et al. (1989). The Advanced Architectures Project of which CAGE and POLIGON form a part is well described in Rice (1989). Its bibliography of project publications will prove useful to any reader wishing to follow up on parallel blackboard systems.

Craig (1995) is a good introductory text on blackboard systems, containing a range of exercises and projects. Carver and Lesser's (1994) paper provides an introduction to blackboard architecture and a discussion of the way in which control issues have evolved in recent years.

STUDY SUGGESTIONS

1. What is a knowledge source?

2. Compare and contrast blackboard architectures with production systems. Under what conditions is the additional complexity of a blackboard system justified?

3. How does a blackboard system differ from a multiple-paradigm programming environment of the kind described in Chapter 17?

4. Distinguish between the concepts of *architecture*, *framework*, and *application* in the context of blackboard systems.

5. Distinguish between a *space*, a *dimension* and an *index* in the context of the GBB framework.

6. Read Nii et al. (1988) and write a concise summary of CAGE and POLIGON which highlights (i) the important differences between them in terms of the design decisions they incorporate, and (ii) the advantages and disadvantages that attach to those decisions.

7. Specify a simple blackboard system to solve the errand planning problem of Chapter 15. Think of the different knowledge sources you might need, for example for initially scheduling errands, for revising the schedule when conflicts arise, and for finally checking that the schedule works.

continued

8. Think of a task that would merit a blackboard-style approach and design knowledge sources to solve it. For example, when investigating scuba-related deaths, the authorities tend to focus on a number of different aspects of the situation, which could be represented as distinct knowledge sources. These include the following considerations:

Environmental conditions
- Water conditions
- Adverse currents
- Potential for entrapment
- Danger from boats
- Danger from marine life

Equipment malfunctions
- Operation
- Proper use
- Maintenance

Diver profiles
- Experience and training
- Psychological problems
- Chemical problems, for example, drugs
- Physical illness

In your chosen application, think of how you would control the application of knowledge. Will knowledge sources be allowed to act independently, for example, by posting messages on the blackboard at any time, or will the knowledge sources apply in stages?

For example, in the scuba investigation, we might want to check out equipment faults first, before proceeding to environmental conditions and then more speculative aspects, such as diver psychology. However, certain kinds of equipment misuse might suggest diver inexperience, thereby triggering another knowledge source. Specify and justify the control regime for your application.

19 Truth Maintenance Systems

It has long been felt that a program should not be allowed to perform arbitrary manipulations upon its representation of the world. Typically, beliefs influence each other, and there are constraints that any set of beliefs must satisfy. If such influences and constraints are ignored, the representation may become incoherent. Mechanisms for keeping track of dependencies and detecting inconsistency are referred to as *truth maintenance systems* (TMSs), sometimes called *reason maintenance systems* (RMSs).

This chapter attempts a review of the computational mechanisms that have been employed to keep track of dependencies between data representing such things as states, actions and assumptions. We shall begin with relatively simple systems and progress towards more complicated ones. Where possible, the mathematical foundations will be neglected in favor of less formal accounts of what these systems do, why they work, and what you might use them for.

19.1 Keeping track of dependencies

In Chapter 15, we saw that it was convenient for the expert system VT to maintain a *dependency network* to record dependencies between design decisions. In this network, nodes represented the assignment of values to design parameters, while the two main kinds of link between nodes were the *contributes-to* link and the *constrains* link. Node A *contributes-to* Node B if the value at A appears in the computation of the value at B, while Node A *constrains* B if the value at A forbids B to take on certain values. In what follows, we shall simplify the discussion by using a little notation, in which upper case letters stand for nodes and lower case letters stand for the values assigned at nodes. Thus the value assigned at node A at any one time will be denoted by a.

19.1.1 Relaxation in networks

The main uses of links in a dependency network are

- to propagate values from node to node, and
- to detect contradictions among the values assigned to nodes.

For example, given a network containing nodes A and M, where A holds the value of the acceleration of some particle and M holds the value of its mass, then both A and M would contribute to the node F, which represents the force acting on the particle. Furthermore, given the familiar formula $f = ma$, A and M now constrain F as well as contributing to it, since once a and m are known, f is determined. So if $a = 2$ and $m = 3$, we can set f equal to 6 (given some assumptions about units, friction, and so on). If we already have $f = 7$, then we know that the network is in a state of contradiction.

$f = ma$ acts as a constraint on the network in the above example. If all the constraints in a network of relations are satisfied, then we say that the network is *relaxed*. Thus, in Figure 19.1:

- network (i) is not relaxed, because we have not concluded the value for node F;
- network (ii) is relaxed; and
- network (iii) is inconsistent.

Strictly speaking, the term relaxation applies to networks, not theories. But a network is just a way of representing a theory; thus network (i) can be seen as representing the theory

$f = ma$
$m = 3$
$a = 2,$

in which $f = ma$ still functions as a constraint, while network (ii) represents the theory

$f = ma$
$m = 3$
$a = 2$
$f = 6,$

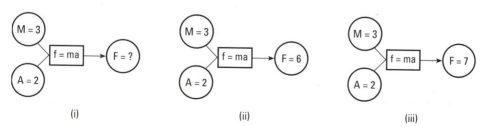

Figure 19.1 Constraint networks in which circles stand for nodes and rectangles label links connecting them.

which is 'relaxed' with respect to the $f = ma$ constraint, and network (iii) represents the inconsistent theory

$f = ma$
$m = 3$
$a = 2$
$f = 7.$

We shall switch between talking about networks and talking about theories as appropriate, using the neutral word 'representation' when we do not wish to distinguish the way that facts and constraints are implemented.

19.1.2 Belief revision

Programs of all kinds often need to maintain and update their representation of the world in the course of solving some problem (for example, the STRIPS planner, discussed in Chapter 3). However, there are a number of different ways in which one can perform the revision, depending upon how sophisticated one wants to be. The following four approaches can be found in the literature.

(1) *Monotonic revisions.* The simplest case involves assimilating new facts and computing any important consequences, thereby relaxing the representation. Such a revision is called 'monotonic' because the set of beliefs always increases. Deciding what is 'important' is not always easy, but one can readily see that deriving q from p and $(p \supset q)$ is more likely to be important than deriving $(q \vee p)$ from q.

(2) *Nonmonotonic revisions.* Sometimes we also want to retract beliefs, and this may undercut conclusions that we have already drawn. If I see you driving a Mercedes, I may conclude that you own it and therefore that you are rich. But if I subsequently learn that you stole the car, then as well as retracting my belief that you own it, I may also want to retract my belief that you are rich.

(3) *Nonmonotonic justifications.* A further complication arises if a program assumes that certain things are true if there is no evidence to the contrary. For example, a program might assume that all students are poor, unless there is specific evidence of wealth. Here it is *absence* of information to the contrary that constitutes a justification for holding a belief, rather than *positive* information that something is the case.

(4) *Hypothetical reasoning.* A program might want to entertain certain assumptions and then see what follows from them, perhaps as a prelude to entertaining some of these assumptions as actual beliefs. This involves reasoning about alternative *possible worlds*: states of the world that may or may not resemble the actual world. Keeping track of multiple theories of this kind, and keeping them distinct from each other, requires a certain amount of organization over and above that required by representations based on a single theory.

Case (1) is fairly trivial: we just add the new information to the theory, plus any additional facts that we derive by relaxing the new theory with respect to the constraints. In the next section, we look at a simple technique for performing truth maintenance that corresponds to case (2), where both kinds of revision are allowed. Sections 19.3 and 19.4 review cases (3) and (4).

BOX 19.1

Recording Support Information

It is easy to illustrate the simple recording of dependencies among data in a forward chaining production system, such as CLIPS. If we imagine that there are just two kinds of statements in working memory – implications, such as 'P implies Q,' and atoms such as 'P', 'Q' – then we could record dependencies among working memory elements as inferences are drawn. Literals will have a support field, where we record which statements were used to derive them. Some literals will have no support, being assumptions provided by the initial state of working memory using deffacts, and we encode this by giving them a support of –1. Both literals and implications have numbered identifiers, so we can keep track of them in support lists.

```
;; Templates

;; A literal is an atomic proposition, "P".
  (deftemplate literal
    (field id (type INTEGER))
    (field atom (type SYMBOL))
    (multifield support (type INTEGER) (default -1))
)

;; A condition is an implication of the form
;; "P implies Q", where "P" is the left-hand side
;; and "Q" is the right-hand side.
(deftemplate conditional
    (field id (type INTEGER))
    (multifield lhs (type SYMBOL))
    (multifield rhs (type SYMBOL))
)

;; We need an index in working memory, so we can assign
;; identifiers to newly derived propositions.
(deftemplate index
    (field no (type INTEGER))
)

;; Initial world model
(deffacts model
    (conditional (id 0) (lhs P) (rhs Q))
    (literal (id 1) (atom P) (status in))
)

;; Rules
;; Set the index to whatever the next identifier should be
;; given the numbered statements that we already have.
(defrule init
  ?F <- (initial-fact)
  (literal (id ?N))
  (not (literal (id ?M&:(> ?M ?N))))
  =>
  (assert (index (no (+ ?N 1))))
  (retract ?F)
)
```

continued

```
;; Apply modus ponens, so we derive "Q" from "P" and "P implies Q"
;; making the identifiers for "P" and "P implies Q" the support
;; of "Q".
(defrule mp
  ?I <- (index (no ?N))
  (conditional (id ?C) (lhs $?X) (rhs $?Y))
  (literal (id ?A) (atom $?X) (status in))
  (not (literal (atom $?Y) (status in)))
  =>
  (assert (literal (id ?N) (atom $?Y) (status in) (support ?C ?A)))
  (modify ?I (no (+ ?N 1)))
)
```

This primitive program only deals with simple conditionals and atomic statements. For example, we can't derive 'not P' from 'P implies Q' and 'not Q' using *modus tollens* (see Chapter 8). Remedy this in Exercise 8 below.

19.2 Revising propositional theories

McAllester's (1980) TMS was not the first, but it is perhaps the easiest to explain. The method assumes an assertional database (hereafter DB) in which formulas (the premises) can be designated 'true,' 'false' or 'unknown' by the user. Thus the underlying logic is three-valued, unlike the classical two-valued calculus that we studied in Chapter 8. The system represents assertions by nodes, which hold the appropriate truth values.

The constraints enforced by the TMS on the contents of DB must satisfy are the fundamental axioms of propositional logic. For example,

$$\neg(\psi \wedge \neg\psi)$$

is an axiom which states that no proposition ψ can be both true and false simultaneously. (Note that ψ is a *metavariable* that stands for any proposition whatever.) Like most TMSs, McAllester's deals only with formulas that do not contain quantifiers, for example $DEAD(fred)$ can be in the theory, but not $(\forall X)(DEAD(X))$. This restriction exists mainly because it is not always possible to ascertain the consistency of a first-order theory, as pointed out in Chapter 8.

The TMS fulfills four main functions with respect to DB:

(1) It performs a variety of propositional deduction which McAllester calls *propositional constraint propagation*.
(2) It generates *justifications* for the assignment of a truth value to a proposition, when that assignment is arrived at via constraint propagation (as opposed to being assigned by the user). Thus, if we conclude that q is true because p and $(p \supset q)$ are true, then p and $(p \supset q)$ form part of the justification for q.
(3) It *updates* DB whenever propositions are removed. Thus if we conclude that q is true because p and $(p \supset q)$ are true, and we later retract p, then we must dismantle the justification $\{p, (p \supset q)\}$ for q, and we should also retract q, unless it can be rederived from other propositions that remain in DB.

(4) It is capable of tracking down the premises responsible for contradictions by a method called *dependency-directed backtracking*. The user is then invited to retract one of the 'guilty' premises, thereby dismantling the justification for the contradiction.

Given p and $(\neg p \vee q)$ as premises, constraint propagation allows the TMS to derive q. It then builds the support structure shown in Figure 19.2. Each node in the network is a frame (see Chapter 6) with a number of slots, including one that holds the name of the node, one that holds its truth value, and one that holds a pointer to its justification. A justification is another frame that contains a table of supporting propositions and their truth values. Thus, in Figure 19.2, the truth of the node labeled q is justified by the fact that the node representing $(\neg p \vee q)$ is marked as true, as is the node labeled p. Note that nodes representing premises, such as p, have no pointers to justifications, since they are true by fiat.

If it later turns out that q is inconsistent with other contents of DB, then the support structure will track down its justifications. The user is then given the option of retracting either p or $(p \supset q)$. It is important that support structures be *well founded*, that is, no node must appear in its own justification, otherwise the process of tracing justifications will be circular and fail to terminate.

Propositional constraint propagation is not a complete inference procedure in the sense of Chapter 8, but it is sound, and it does allow a range of useful inferences to be drawn when assertions are added to DB. Note that all assertions are either premises or justified by the presence of another assertion. In the next section, we review a rather more ambitious TMS, which allows the absence of information as a justification for an assertion.

19.3 Nonmonotonic justifications†

Doyle's (1979) approach to truth maintenance is based on a different inference procedure to McAllester's, and has a rather different philosophical outlook. This approach is intended to model aspects of commonsense reasoning, such as *defaults*. Roughly

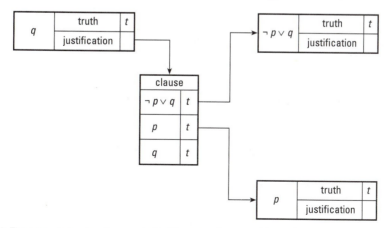

Figure 19.2 The support structure for q as derived from premises p and $(\neg p \vee q)$.

speaking, in addition to holding beliefs because of positive evidence for them, we are also allowed to hold beliefs as *reasoned assumptions*, that is, because we have no evidence against them.

A justification (or *reason*, in Doyle's terminology) for a belief, P, is now an ordered pair of sets of beliefs, which we shall represent by the pair (IN_P, OUT_P). IN_P is a conventional justification of the form used by McAllester; it contains propositions whose truth contributes to the truth of P. OUT_P, on the other hand, is a *nonmonotonic justification*; it contains propositions whose presence in the belief set would deny P. Such a justification is nonmonotonic because the simple act of accumulating more beliefs could cause us to retract P; this is not the case in McAllester's system.

For example, a reason for p might be

$$(\{\}, \{\neg p\})$$

signifying that we are allowed to assume p so long as it is not already believed to be false. A reason for q might be

$$(\{p\}, \{r\})$$

signifying that we are allowed to believe q so long as p is *in* (the current set of beliefs) and r is out (that is, not believed). Note that reasons can interact, as in the above example. If $\neg p$ is *out*, then p becomes *in*, so q becomes *in* too, as long as r is *out*.

Such reasons are called *SL-justifications* (SL stands for 'support-list'). The general rule for SL-justifications is that a belief P is in the current set of beliefs only if each belief in IN_P is *in* and each belief in OUT_P is *out*. Doyle suggests other kinds of justification in his paper, but we shall not deal with them here.

The dual structure of justifications in Doyle's system can be used to distinguish three different kinds of beliefs with respect to a belief set B:

(1) *Premises*, that is, propositions that are believed without any justification at all. Set-theoretically, the premises are given by

$$\{P \in B \mid IN_P = OUT_P = \emptyset\};$$

(2) *Deductions*, that is, propositions which are the conclusions of normal monotonic deductions, given by

$$\{P \in B \mid IN_P \neq \emptyset \text{ and } OUT_P = \emptyset\};$$

(3) *Assumptions*, that is, propositions which are held to be true because there is no evidence against them, given by

$$\{P \in B \mid OUT_P \neq \emptyset\}.$$

As in McAllester's system, each belief is represented by a node. The TMS can perform the following functions:

- create nodes;
- add or retract justifications from the set of justifications that govern dependencies between nodes; and
- mark a node as a contradiction.

When the TMS makes a contradiction node *in*, dependency-directed backtracking is invoked to identify the assumptions whose retraction would make the contradiction node *out*.

Unlike McAllester, Doyle's logic is really *four*-valued rather than three-valued. The four truth values are best represented by the sets, {}, {*true*}, {*false*}, {*true, false*}, which denote interdeterminacy, truth, falsity and contradiction respectively. Of course, the truth maintenance process described below is meant to eliminate contradiction from the belief set, so nodes have the valuation {*true, false*} only temporarily.

Doyle uses the following terminology for nodes, which will be useful in outlining the truth maintenance process.

- The *antecedents* of a node are the nodes listed in its *IN* and *OUT* lists.
- The set of *foundations* of a node is just the transitive closure of its antecedents, that is, the node's antecedents, the antecedents' antecedents, and so on.
- The *consequences* of a node are the nodes which mention that node in their *IN* and *OUT* lists.
- The set of *repercussions* of a node is just the transitive closure of its consequences.

The following is a simplified sketch of Doyle's algorithm which uses only SL-justifications. The event which triggers the truth maintenance process is the adding of a justification to a node. If the node is already in, then only minor bookkeeping is required, otherwise both the node and its repercussions must be updated.

(1) Add the new justification to the node's justification set, and add the node to the set of consequences of each of the nodes mentioned in the justification.
(2) Check the consequences of the node. If there are none, then change the node from out to in, construct its *IN* and *OUT* list, and halt. Otherwise, make a list *L* containing the node and its repercussions, record the *in-out* status of each of these nodes, mark each node with the temporary status of *nil*, and proceed to Step (3).
(3) For each node *N* in *L*, try to find a well-founded valid justification that will make it *in*. If none can be found, then mark the node as *out*. Either way, propagate any change in *N*'s status to its consequences. (*Comment*. A justification is *valid* if each node in its *IN* list is *in* and each node in its *OUT* list is *out*, and it is *well founded* if it is not circular. For example, the justifications $(\{\neg P\}, \{\})$ and $(\{\}, \{P\})$ would both be circular if applied to *P*. The first states that *P* is in only if $\neg P$ is in, while the second states that *P* is in only if *P* is out. Each justification leads to a contradiction if it is adopted as a reason for *P*.)
(4) If any node in *L* is *in* and marked as a contradiction, then call the dependency-directed backtracking procedure. If truth maintenance (Steps 1–3) occurs during backtracking, then repeat this step until no contradictions remain to be resolved.
(5) Compare the current support-status of each node in *L* with its recorded status, and alert the user to changes in status.

Both Doyle's and McAllester's systems can be thought of as representing a more sophisticated approach to the problem of maintaining a coherent world model that we encountered in discussing the STRIPS system (see Chapter 3). Both TMSs perform updates on a world model by propagating the analogs of ADD and DELETE operations through a dependency network. If a contradiction occurs, then the user must retract something from the support of the contradiction, so that consistency is restored.

BOX 19.2

A Pair of Conflicting Statements

This CLIPS program implements a simple nonmonotonic TMS for atomic statements. A literal is an atomic proposition, such as 'P', whose status is either in or out of the TMS. The inlist says what statements have to be in for the statement to be in, while the outlist says what statements have to be out for the statement to be in. As before, empty support lists have a default value of -1.

```
;; Templates

(deftemplate literal
   (field id (type INTEGER))
   (field atom (type SYMBOL))
   (field status (type SYMBOL) (default unk))
   (multifield inlist (type INTEGER) (default -1))
   (multifield outlist (type INTEGER) (default -1))
)

;; Initial world model

(deffacts model
   (literal (id 0) (atom P) (status in) (outlist 1))
   (literal (id 1) (atom Q) (status in) (outlist 0))
)

;; Rules

;; If a statement in the outlist of a statement S goes out
;; and S has an empty inlist
;; then S comes in.
(defrule in
   (literal (id ?A) (status out))
   ?F <- (literal (status out) (inlist -1) (outlist ?A))
   =>
   (modify ?F (status in))
)

;; If a statement in the outlist of a statement S comes in
;; then S goes out.
;; Note that in this rule we don't care about S's inlist.
(defrule out
   (literal (id ?A) (status in))
   ?F <- (literal (status in) (outlist ?A))
   =>
   (modify ?F (status out))
)

;; This rule invites the user to 'out' a statement
;; so that the conflicting pair flip in and out.
(defrule deny
   (declare (salience -10))
   ?L <- (literal (atom ?X) (status in) (inlist -1))
   =>
   (printout t crlf "Deny " ?X "? ")
```

continued

```
    (bind ?ans (read))
    (if (eq ?ans yes) then (modify ?L (status out)))
    )
```

What happens when you run this program? What happens when you reply 'yes' to the question posed by the deny rule? What happens when you reply 'no'?

19.4 Maintaining multiple contexts

Each TMS we have met so far concentrates on maintaining a single, consistent world model. However, sometimes it is convenient to perform reasoning in the context of different hypothetical worlds, which may or may not resemble the way the world actually is (see Chapter 17). For example, in doing diagnosis, it is often worthwhile to assume that a certain fault has occurred and then make predictions on the basis of this assumption and see if they are backed up by evidence. This strategy is particularly useful if there are a large number of hypotheses competing to account for the observations, with the possibility that a composite hypothesis may be required to cover all of them. Another domain of application might be arrangement problems, where the hypothetical worlds represent different ways of arranging objects to satisfy a set of constraints.

19.4.1 Assumption-based truth maintenance

In an *assumption-based* TMS (ATMS), the program maintains a number of different contexts, referred to as *environments* (de Kleer, 1986). An environment is best thought of as a view of the world characterized by a set of *assumptions*. Thus the environment characterized by the empty set of assumptions corresponds to the world model of earlier programs. All other environments model hypothetical worlds. These worlds are typically consistent with the world model, but extend it on the basis of various assumptions.

The environments of an ATMS can be arranged in a lattice, since the making of assumptions is an incremental thing. Thus, in Figure 19.3, our world model is such that our car won't start and it has no lights. At the next level up the lattice are hypothetical worlds in which we assume that something is wrong with the car, such as a flat battery. At higher levels, we can combine these assumptions. Note that, as we go up the lattice, hypothetical worlds get more and more specific, in the sense that we know more and more about them.

It will not always be the case that we can pool assumptions arbitrarily. For example, we cannot combine the assumption sets $\{p, q\}$ and $\{\neg p, r\}$ without getting a contradiction. Furthermore, although assumption sets may not be obviously antagonistic, as in the above example, certain combinations may give rise to a contradiction in the presence of other information.

Suppose our world model of faulty cars contains information to the effect that a car cannot be both out of gas and have a flooded carburetor. Then we can deduce that the carburetor is not flooded in the environment in which we assume that we are out

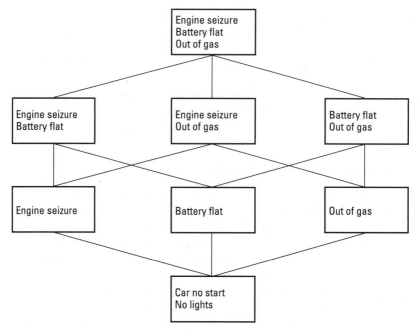

Figure 19.3 **An environment lattice.**

of gas, and we can deduce that we are not out of gas in the environment where the carburetor is flooded. Such consequences form what is known as the *context* of an environment: the set of propositions derivable from the assumptions and the facts of the world model. Thus we can have a situation as in Figure 19.4, where the environment formed by the join of two assumption sets is ruled out because its context is inconsistent. Such contexts are called *nogoods*.

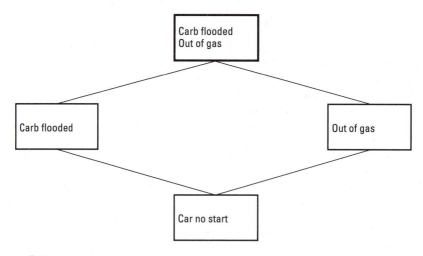

Figure 19.4 **Environment lattice with nogood.**

The above example illustrates the obvious fact that we are only allowed to extend our theory of the world in a manner that respects some body of background knowledge about the way the world is. Put another way, there are dependencies between the individual assumptions that we might make and, as in justification-based truth maintenance, these dependencies must be recorded and enforced.

In ATMS, these dependencies are called *justifications*. This terminology is slightly confusing, since the role of justifications in ATMS is rather different from that in TMS. In TMS, justifications are constructed by the program as a by-product of constraint propagation, and associated with nodes in a dependency network which stand for propositions.

In ATMS, justifications are part of the input to the program. The ATMS then constructs, for each propositional node, a *label* which lists the interesting environments that proposition holds in. We shall see what 'interesting' means shortly, but first let us look at an example.

In Figure 19.4, the proposition that the car is not out of gas holds in the environment where we assume that the carburetor is flooded, given a justification which says something like

'if the carburetor is flooded, then the car is not out of gas.'

Now this proposition also holds in the nogood, but this environment is not consistent, so *every* proposition holds in it. (Any proposition at all follows from a contradiction in classical logic.) Such an environment is not very interesting, so we do not put it in the label.

Suppose we also have a justification that says

'if the plugs are wet, then the car is not out of gas.'

Then the proposition that the car is not out of gas holds in the environment characterized by the assumption that the plugs are wet, as in Figure 19.5, so we would also include this environment in the label. The label of our proposition now contains two

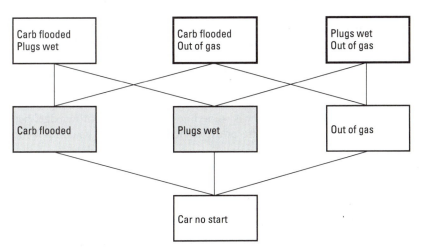

Figure 19.5 Environment lattice showing nogoods (dark border) and labels of the proposition that the car is not out of gas (shaded boxes).

environments, each of which is consistent. These are shaded in the figure. As before, we ignore nogoods, so this rules out the environment in which the plugs are wet and the car is out of gas, and the environment in which the carburetor is flooded and the car is out of gas.

Obviously, the proposition also holds in the environment characterized by the join of these two environments, or in any environment that extends either of the two. However, it is hardly worth recording this fact. We would rather that the label only contained those environments characterized by the minimal sets of assumptions needed for the proposition to hold.

In summary, the basic purpose of an ATMS is to construct a list of the interesting environments in which a proposition holds. Such a list is defined as a *sound, complete, consistent* and *minimal label*. This terminology can be explained as follows.

A label for a propositional node is

- *sound* if the proposition is indeed derivable from each environment in its label, that is, if it is *in* the context characterized by each such environment;
- *complete* if every consistent environment in which the proposition holds is either in the label or a superset of an environment in the label;
- *consistent* if every environment in the label is consistent; and
- *minimal* if no environment in the label is a superset of any other.

If a propositional node has an empty label, this means that the proposition is not derivable from any consistent set of assumptions. In other words, it is not to be found in the context of any environment that is consistent with the justifications. Thus the node standing for the proposition that the car is out of gas *and* its plugs are wet would have an empty label.

19.4.2 Model-based diagnosis using ATMS

We have seen that most rule-based expert systems perform diagnosis by the method of heuristic classification (see Chapters 11 and 12). In this method, diagnostic knowledge is represented mainly in terms of heuristic rules, which perform a mapping between data abstractions (typical symptoms) and solution abstractions (typical disorders). Such a representation of knowledge is sometimes called 'shallow' because it does not contain much information about the causal mechanisms underlying the relationship between symptoms and disorders. The rules typically reflect empirical associations derived from experience, rather than a theory of how the device (or organism) under diagnosis actually works. The latter is sometimes called 'deep' knowledge, because it involves understanding the structure of the device and the way its components function.

Model-based diagnosis tends to approach the problem from another angle. Rather than assume the existence of an expert experienced in diagnosing the device, we assume the existence of a system description: a complete and consistent theory of the correct behavior of the device. Given a data set supplying evidence of that system's malfunction, the idea is that it should be possible to conjecture one or more minimum perturbations to the system description that would account for the data.

The apparent advantages of this 'first principles' approach over heuristic classification are as follows:

- Given a device description, the program designer is able to short-cut the laborious process of eliciting empirical associations from a human expert.
- The reasoning method employed is device independent, so it is not necessary to tailor the inference machinery for different applications.
- Since only knowledge of correct device behavior is required, the method ought to be able to diagnose faults that have never occurred before.

The DART program (Genesereth, 1984) was a prototype for such a diagnostic system in the domain of digital circuits. A distinguishing feature of this system was that both the representation language and the inference mechanism were more or less device independent. Genesereth used the predicate calculus to encode design descriptions of devices under diagnosis, and a form of theorem proving (called resolution residue) to generate both sets of suspect components and tests to confirm or refute fault hypotheses. DART's problem solving method relied on three simplifying assumptions:

(1) The connections in the device are assumed to be working properly, so we seek faulty components to account for symptom data.
(2) Faults are non-intermittent, that is, components behave consistently for the duration of the diagnosis.
(3) There is only a single fault in the device.

Each of these assumptions is quite limiting in real applications, but De Kleer and Williams (1987) found that ATMS could be used to address (3) in a program called GDE (General Diagnostic Engine).

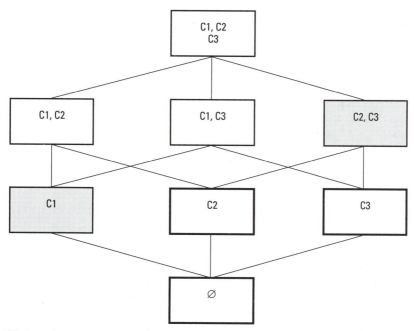

Figure 19.6 An environment lattice representing a candidate space, showing nogoods (dark border) and minimal candidates (shaded boxes).

The trouble with allowing multiple faults is that the hypothesis space now grows exponentially, because we now have to consider sets of hypothetical faults, rather as in the INTERNIST program of Chapter 13. It is therefore important to generate hypotheses in rough order of 'goodness' and then apply tests that will differentiate between competing hypothesis sets in a minimum number of measurements. The inherent complexity of the problem is addressed by a combination of assumption-based truth maintenance and probabilistic inference.

As we saw earlier in this section, ATMS is a method of maintaining a lattice of environments: alternative states of the world which are consistent with some theory but in which different assumptions hold. In diagnostic applications, this (implicit) theory is the device description, and the alternative states of the world are characterized by the 2^n different ways in which n components can fail. The environments are arranged in a lattice by set inclusion: the least element is the empty set of faulty components, while the greatest element is the set of all components. Each such environment is called a *candidate*: a hypothesis about the way in which a faulty device actually deviates from its description. The environment lattice is called the *candidate space*.

If the device is working perfectly, the least element (representing no faulty components) 'explains' the observation of the correct outputs. Otherwise, faulty outputs are seen as evidence for some component failure in the candidate space. Because the size of this space is exponential in the number of components, we need some way of focusing the search for candidates.

The key notion is that of a *conflict set*: a set of components that cannot all be functioning correctly, given the symptom data. The conflict sets are just those assumption sets in the ATMS which generate environments inconsistent with the data. They can be determined by forming the deductive closure of an environment with the data, and then looking for a contradiction. This is obviously a form of constraint propagation, as outlined in Section 19.1 above. The main goal of the truth maintenance system is to identify the complete set of minimal conflicts, that is, to detect those conflict sets which subsume all others by set inclusion. From these, one can compute the minimal sets of faulty components that account for all the symptoms.

As a simple example, let C1, C2 and C3 be system components, and let S be an observation that is a symptom of system failure (see Figure 19.6). Suppose we know that if S occurs then Cl and C2 cannot both be working, and neither can Cl and C3. Thus we can rule out the environments labeled Ø, C2 and C3 (marked as nogoods in the figure), because each has some forbidden conjunction of components working. All other environments are candidate diagnoses, but the minimal candidates are obviously {C1} and {C2, C3}.

The ATMS uses a number of strategies to control the complexity of the candidate space, for example:

- exploiting a preference for minimal explanations by beginning the search for solutions from the smallest conflict sets;
- recording inferences (such as predictions of device behavior based on assumption sets) in the ATMS, so that they are never drawn twice.

GDE also uses an information-theoretic measure of uncertainty to determine the best next measurement to make. The best measurement is that which minimizes entropy (see Chapter 20), that is, that which causes the greatest diversity among the probabilities of the candidates. They assume that the prior probability of failure is known for each component and that components fail independently of each other. These probabilities are also used to guide the generation of candidates. The search of the environment lattice is conducted best-first (see Chapter 2) on the joint probabilities of multiple faults.

19.5 Summary and comparison of TMSs

The function of a truth maintenance component in the context of a larger problem solving program is

- to cache inferences made by the problem solver, so that conclusions that have once been derived need never be derived again;
- to allow the problem solver to make useful assumptions and see if useful conclusions can be derived from them; and
- to handle the problem of inconsistency, either by maintaining a single consistent world model, or managing multiple contexts which are internally consistent but which may be mutually inconsistent.

TMSs such as those of Doyle and McAllester are useful for finding a single solution to a constraint satisfaction problem. For example, the use of a dependency net in the VT expert system described in Chapter 15 is an excellent example of how a simple TMS can be used to good effect. Only one solution to the problem is required; we are not really interested in generating the whole range of alternative designs.

Extra control machinery is required if you want more than one solution, or all solutions. The fact that you are all the time dealing with a single state of the network makes it difficult to compare alternative solutions to a problem, if you really need to do this. For example, in differential diagnosis, it is usually important to compare hypotheses with their competitors to arrive at a composite hypothesis which covers the data and gives the best account of it (as in Chapter 13).

De Kleer's ATMS is more oriented towards finding all solutions to constraint satisfaction problems, that is, finding all the interesting environments which satisfy the constraints. Extra control machinery is required if you want to find fewer solutions, or a single 'best' solution according to some criteria, as we saw in the diagnostic example given in the last section. However, since you can maintain more than one context, this obviates the need for dependency-directed backtracking in the basic version outlined here.

BIBLIOGRAPHICAL NOTES

Dependency networks are well described in Charniak *et al.* (1987). The original papers by Doyle (1979) and de Kleer (1986) are not very readable, and do not make good introductions to this area. But TMSs are well covered in Chapters 6–14 of Forbus and de Kleer (1993). Program listings are available for most of the examples in a companion volume. Readers interested in the theoretical background to truth maintenance may wish to consult papers in Ginsberg (1987), while Martins and Reinfrank (1991) is a later collection of research papers from a specialist conference on TMSs.

STUDY SUGGESTIONS

1. What do you understand by the term 'relaxation' in a dependency network?

2. Explain the difference between monotonic and nonmonotonic revisions.

3. What is the difference between a justification and an assumption in belief revision?

4. If $(\{\}, \{\neg p\})$ is a reason for p, and $(\{\}, \{\neg p\})$ is a reason for q, what happens to p and q if we add $\neg p$ to the database of a nonmonotonic TMS?

5. If $(\{q\}, \{\})$ is a reason for p, and $(\{\}, \{\neg q\})$ is a reason for q, what happens to p and q if we add $\neg q$ to the database of a nonmonotonic TMS?

6. Fill in the truth value of r in the McAllester-style TMS of Figure 19.7.

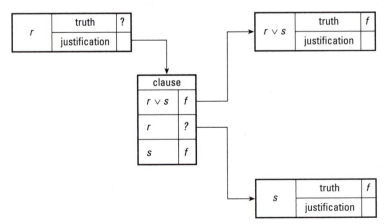

Figure 19.7 A support structure for Exercise 6.

continued

7. Consider the ATMS justifications:

$p \wedge q \supset r$

$\neg p \wedge q \supset s$

$p \wedge \neg q \supset t$

$\neg p \wedge \neg q \supset u.$

Assume that there are four possible assumptions that can be made, singly or in combination: p, $\neg p$, q, and $\neg q$. What are the consistent environments of this justification set, based on these assumptions?

8. Extend the templates and rules given in Box 19.1, so that we can draw inferences of the form

'P implies Q' and 'not Q' imply 'not P'

and record the corresponding support for 'not P.'

20 Machine Learning

In Chapter 1, the problem of knowledge acquisition was mentioned, and its relation to machine learning. We noted that knowledge acquisition was considered a 'bottleneck' in expert systems development, owing to the time and effort required to construct the appropriate production rules and structured objects. In Chapter 10 *et seq.*, a variety of tools and methods for knowledge elicitation were examined, but none of these eliminate the need for significant human labor.

There appear to be only three alternatives to the 'hand-building' of a knowledge base by a combination of domain expert and knowledge engineer:

(1) Interactive programs which elicit knowledge from the expert during the course of a 'conversation' at the terminal. Various attempts to deploy this method were discussed in previous chapters. We saw that the approach showed great promise, if it were guided by domain knowledge.
(2) Programs which learn by scanning texts, rather as humans read technical books. This method is hampered by the general problem of natural language understanding by machine. Since this is at least as hard as knowledge acquisition, it does not appear to be a promising avenue of research at the moment.
(3) Programs which learn the concepts of a domain under varying degrees of supervision from a human teacher. In one approach, the teacher presents the program with a set of examples of a concept, and the program's task is to identify what collection of attributes and values defines the concept. This approach has been applied to knowledge acquisition with some success, and the basic techniques form the main subject matter of this chapter.

The field of machine learning has enjoyed a period of continuous growth and progress over the past 10 years. Rather than attempt a broad but shallow review of the whole, this chapter will concentrate on methods that have had direct application to expert systems technology, namely those which concentrate upon

- deriving sets of decision rules from examples;
- evaluating the importance of individual rules; and
- optimizing the performance of sets of rules.

There are other fields of learning research that we shall not touch upon at all, because they have yet to make a significant impact upon expert systems. (This is not to say that they will not have a significant impact in the future.) The interested reader is referred to citations in the bibliography at the end of the chapter for a broader coverage than can be attempted here.

20.1 Overview of inductive learning

Precise definitions of learning are hard to find, but most authorities would agree that it is a characteristic of *adaptive systems* which are capable of improving their performance on a problem as a function of previous experience, for example, in solving similar problems (Simon, 1983). Thus learning is both a capability and an activity. Any learning program must have the ability to represent and reason about problem solving experiences, as well as the ability to apply such representations and inferences to the solution of the current problem.

Carbonell *et al.* (1983) present a classification of learning programs in terms of the underlying strategy employed. Roughly speaking, the strategy used depends upon the amount of inference that the program has to perform on the information available to it.

At one extreme, programs which learn by the direct implanting of new knowledge (for example by being reprogrammed, or being supplied with new data), are performing no inference at all. This is usually referred to as *rote learning*: a reasonable human analog would be the learning of multiplication tables. At the other extreme, there is *unsupervised learning*: a generic term which covers tasks such as theory formation, which more closely resemble human efforts at scientific discovery.

In this chapter, the emphasis is upon *supervised learning*, which can be regarded as having a strategy which is halfway between the two extremes mentioned above. In supervised learning, a program is typically presented with examples which help it to identify the relevant concept. These examples have known properties, which are normally represented as attribute–value pairs. The learning involved is supervised, because the examples provide the program with clues as to what it is looking for, as well as providing a space of attributes for its consideration.

The most common form of supervised learning task is called *induction*. An inductive learning program is one which is capable of learning from examples by a process of generalization. The learning process is then

> 'a heuristic search through a space of symbolic descriptions, generated by the application of various inference rules to the initial observational statements.'
> (Michalski, 1983, p. 83)

The symbolic descriptions usually represent generalizations that could be made about the observations, and these generalizations are a form of inference, that is, they involve law-like transformations of symbolic descriptions representing observations.

Instance	Nationality	Size	Vintage	Pos or Neg
Oldsmobile Cutlass	American	Large	No	Neg
BMW 316	German	Small	No	Pos
Thunderbird Roadster	American	Small	Yes	Neg
VW Cabriolet	German	Small	No	Pos
Rolls-Royce Corniche	British	Large	Yes	Neg
Chevrolet Bel Air	American	Small	Yes	Neg

Figure 20.1 A training set.

One form of inductive learning is when a learner is provided with a set of data, some of which are examples of a concept and some of which are not (the counterexamples). The learning task is to identify or construct the relevant concept, that is, the concept which includes all of the examples and none of the counterexamples. Examples are called *positive instances*, while counterexamples are sometimes called *negative instances*. This kind of learning is often called *concept learning*.

Consider the data set

```
{Oldsmobile Cutlass, BMW 316, Thunderbird Roadster,
  Chevrolet Bel Air, Rolls Royce Corniche, VW Cabriolet}.
```

Suppose that the concept we wanted the program to learn was **German car**. Then the only positive instances of a concept are BMW 316 and VW Cabriolet; the rest are negative instances. But if the target concept were **Vintage American Car**, then Thunderbird Roadster and Chevrolet Bel Air would be the positive instances and the rest would be negative instances.

Giving a program both positive and negative examples is important to learning. In the first learning task considered above, both the BMW and the VW are small vehicles. So without the negative example of the Chevy, the program might have drawn the wrong inference and chosen the concept **Small Car**. Similarly, without the negative example of the Oldsmobile Cutlass, a program could be forgiven for arriving at the too general concept **American Car** in the second task.

More formally, we can consider any data set that contains an assignment of 'positive' or 'negative' to each element as a *training set* that can be given to an inductive learning program. The training set will also specify some attributes relevant to the task, and the values that each instance has for each of those attributes. Figure 20.1 shows a training set for the concept **German Car**.

Another supervised learning task has been called *descriptive generalization*. Here one is given a class of objects, representing a concept, and the learning task is to derive a description that specifies the properties of objects belonging to that class. Thus, for a training set with members

```
{Cadillac Seville, Oldsmobile Cutlass, Lincoln Continental}
```

characterized with respect to the attributes size, comfort, and gas consumption, an appropriate descriptive generalization might be:

```
large, comfortable, gas-guzzling.
```

We can distinguish between concept learning and descriptive generalization as follows.

- In concept learning, one is given a set of positive and negative instances of some concept which belongs to a pre-enumerated set of concepts, and the task is to generate a rule that will 'recognize' unseen instances of the concept.
- In descriptive generalization, one is given a set of instances which belong to a particular class, and the task is to derive the most parsimonious description which applies to each member of that class.

Both are examples of supervised learning, because the program is given both a set of examples and an attribute space to work with.

The next section looks at two learning programs that have been associated with an early expert system called DENDRAL. The initial implementation does not fit precisely into either of the categories of supervised learning outlined above, but the second implementation uses an inductive learning technique called *version spaces*, which closely resembles the typical concept learning task involving the presentation of positive and negative instances. It is interesting to compare the two approaches, and see how domain-specific knowledge about chemistry can be employed by a domain-free learning algorithm.

Section 20.3 describes a state of the art program for inductive learning, which has seen successful application to the generation of rules for expert systems, while Section 20.4 describes work on evaluating individual rules and tuning rule sets.

20.2 Early work: Meta-DENDRAL

The DENDRAL project began at Stanford University in 1965, and was perhaps the first system to demonstrate that it was possible for a computer program to rival the performance of domain experts in a specialized field. The task was to determine the molecular structure of an unknown organic compound, and the method that the system used was a modified form of generate and test. DENDRAL is concerned with the interpretation of data obtained from a laboratory device called a mass spectrometer, which works by bombarding a chemical sample with a beam of electrons, causing the compound to fragment and its components to become rearranged. Atom migrations correspond to the detachment of nodes from one subgraph and their attachment to another subgraph; these charged fragments are collected by mass to form a spectrum.

The problem is that any complex molecule can fragment in more than one way; that is, different bonds can be dissolved as a result of the bombardment, accompanied by different patterns of migration. The theory of mass spectrometry is therefore incomplete, in the following sense. We can make some predictions concerning which bonds in a given molecule are *likely* to break (and therefore contribute to peaks in the mass spectrum), but we are not always sure *exactly* how the molecule will fragment.

CONGEN is a DENDRAL program which constructs complete chemical structures by manipulating symbols that stand for atoms and molecules. It receives as its input a molecular formula, together with a set of constraints which serve to restrict the possible interconnections among atoms. Its output is a list of all possible ways of assembling the atoms into molecular structures, given the constraints imposed.

DENDRAL also has programs to help the user rule out some hypotheses and order the others by using knowledge of mass spectrometry to make testable predictions about candidate molecules. Thus the program MSPRUNE eliminates candidates which are not worth considering because the fragmentations one would expect them to undergo are not found in the spectral data. MSRANK orders the remaining candidates according to the number of predicted peaks which appear in the data and the number of peaks not found. The scores for the presence and absence of these features are weighted according to the importance of the underlying spectral processes. This is basically a strategy of 'hypothesize and test.' Initial data suggest some space of hypotheses, each of which predicts the presence or absence of certain other data, and can be verified or eliminated as a consequence.

20.2.1 Rule generation and refinement

Meta-DENDRAL can be distinguished from DENDRAL in the following way. DENDRAL is a program which uses a set of rules to reason about the domain of mass spectrometry. Meta-DENDRAL is a program which reasoned about the rules that DENDRAL uses to perform this task. The initial implementation of Meta-DENDRAL generated rule hypotheses by a process of heuristic search similar to that used by DENDRAL itself (in the generation of structural hypotheses for chemical compounds). In other words, it applied DENDRAL's own search strategy to the problem of deriving DENDRAL rules.

The role of Meta-DENDRAL was to help a chemist determine the relationship between molecular fragmentations (spectral processes) and the structural features of compounds. Working together, program and chemist decided which data points were interesting, and then looked for processes which might explain them. Finally, the program tested and modified the derived rules, rather as a chemist would.

The rules of mass spectrometry that chemists use to describe a fragmentation can be expressed symbolically as production rules. Thus the following cleavage rule would be a way of encoding the fact that a particular molecule fragments in a particular way in a mass spectrometer, assuming that '$-$' stands for a bond and '$*$' stands for a break:

$$N - C - C - C \rightarrow N - C * C - C$$

The left-hand side of such a rule describes a structural feature, while the right-hand side describes a spectral process.

Meta-DENDRAL's training data was a set of molecules whose three-dimensional structure and mass spectra were known. Thus the input–output pairs which constituted its training instances were respectively: (i) a molecular structure, and (ii) a point from the histogram of the relative abundances of fragment masses, that is, a spectral peak.

It is important to realize that although the 'vocabulary' for describing atoms in subgraphs is small, and the actual 'grammar' for constructing subgraphs is simple, the number of subgraphs that can be generated is very large. In coping with this potential for combinatorial explosion, Meta-DENDRAL (like DENDRAL) used a problem solving strategy of 'plan, generate and test.' Thus Meta-DENDRAL had a planning phase, involving a program called INTSUM, which stands for the interpretation and summary of data. Its job was to propose simple spectral processes which might have occurred in the training instances. These processes were represented as simple cleavage rules similar to the one shown above, where a whole molecular structure is mapped onto a single broken bond.

The output of INTSUM went to a heuristic search program called RULEGEN. RULEGEN was like DENDRAL's CONGEN, except that its task was to generate more general cleavage rules, for example allowing multiple broken bonds, which would cover the cases covered by INTSUM's output. Once candidate rules had been generated, the last phase of Meta-DENDRAL, called RULEMOD, tested and modified them.

The division of labor between RULEGEN and RULEMOD was as follows. RULEGEN did a comparatively coarse search of the space of rules that could be constructed from INTSUM's output, generating approximate and possibly redundant rules. RULEMOD performed a finer search to tune the set of rule hypotheses.

The workings of RULEMOD are still interesting today, because the tasks that it performed are typical of rule refinement programs:

(1) *Removing redundancy.* The data may be overdetermined, that is, many rule hypotheses generated by RULEGEN may explain the same data points. Usually only a subset of the rules is necessary, and there may also be rules which make incorrect predictions.

(2) *Merging rules.* Sometimes a set of rules, taken together, explain a pool of data points that could be accounted for by a single, slightly more general, rule which includes all the positive evidence, but does not introduce any negative evidence. If such a rule can be found, the overlapping rules are deleted and the compact rule retained.

(3) *Making rules more specific.* Often rules are too general, and therefore make incorrect predictions. RULEMOD tries adding feature descriptions to atoms in each rule to try to delete the negative evidence, while retaining the positive evidence of correct predictions.

(4) *Making rules more general.* Given that RULEGEN is reasoning from particular cases, it frequently makes rules that are more specific than they should be. RULEMOD will try to make rules more general, so that they cover the same data points, perhaps including new data, without making any incorrect predictions.

(5) *Selecting the final rules.* It is possible that redundancies may have been introduced by the generalization and specialization operations of RULEMOD. Consequently, the selection procedure of step (1) is applied again to remove them.

The stages of selection, merging, deletion and so on could be applied iteratively by RULEMOD until the user was reasonably satisfied with the rule set. These tasks pretty well exhaust what can be done to a rule set, with the exception of adding weights to rules and then tuning those weights. We shall see examples of this practice later in the chapter.

The quality of rules generated by Meta-DENDRAL was assessed by testing them on structures not in the training set, by consulting mass spectroscopists, and by comparing them with published rules. The program succeeded in rediscovering known rules of spectrometry that had already been published, as well as discovering new rules, for example, for certain subfamilies of compounds called androstanes. Its ability to predict spectra for compounds outside the original set of instances was impressive. However, neither DENDRAL nor Meta-DENDRAL proved marketable, even though many ideas from these projects found their way into computational chemistry. These programs have since been disassembled and various modules have found their way into other tools, such as chemical database management systems (Feigenbaum and Buchanan, 1993).

20.2.2 Version spaces

In this section, we review an application of a learning technique known as *version spaces* (Mitchell, 1978, 1982, 1997) to the reimplementation of Meta-DENDRAL. In attempting to derive a general rule of mass spectrometry from a set of examples of how particular molecules fragment, Meta-DENDRAL is tackling a concept learning problem. Mitchell (1978) defines such problems as follows.

> A concept can be conceived of as a pattern which states those properties which are common to instances of the concept. Given (i) a language of patterns for describing concepts, (ii) sets of positive and negative instances of the target concept, and (iii) a way of matching data in the form of training instances against hypothetical descriptions of the concept, the task is to determine concept descriptions in the language that are consistent with the training instances.

In this context, 'consistency' means that the description must match all the positive instances but none of the negative ones.

In order to reason about the rules for mass spectrometry, Meta-DENDRAL needs a language for representing concepts and relationships in that domain. The pattern language used by Meta-DENDRAL is a structured object language (see Chapter 6) in which nodes and links are connected together in a network. The nodes stand for atoms, or configurations of atoms, while the links stand for chemical bonds. A pattern in this language matches some training instance just in case there is a mapping from the nodes and links of the instance to the nodes and links of the pattern that satisfies all the constraints placed upon the nodes and links of the pattern. Thus, in order to match a pattern of nodes and links representing atoms connected by chemical bonds, the components of an instance must not have properties or relationships which violate the stated constraints.

In the context of a concept learning problem, a *version space* is simply a way of representing the space of all concept descriptions consistent with the training instances seen so far. The principal advantage of Mitchell's technique for representing and updating version spaces is that they can be determined instance by instance, without looking back to examine either past training instances or previously rejected concept descriptions.

Mitchell found the key to the problems of efficient representation and update of version spaces by noting that the search space of possible concept descriptions is not without structure, that is, it contains redundancy. In particular, he observed that a partial order can be defined over the patterns generated by any concept description language of the kind described above. Most important is the relation 'more specific than or equal to,' which can be defined as follows:

> Pattern P1 is more specific than or equal to pattern P2 (written as P1 $\leq$ P2) if and only if P1 matches a subset of all the instances that P2 matches.

Consider the following simple example from Winston's (1975a) 'blocks world' learning program. In Figure 20.2, the pattern P1 is more specific than pattern P2 because the constraints imposed by P1 are only satisfied if the weaker constraints

Figure 20.2 Relations between patterns.

imposed by P2 are satisfied. Another way of looking at this is to say that if P1's constraints are satisfied, then so are P2's, but not conversely.

Note that for a program to appreciate an example of partial ordering such as that shown above, it would need to understand a number of concepts and relationships, constituting domain-specific knowledge:

- It would need to know that if B is a brick then B is a shape, that is, to have some criteria for categorizing the kinds of entities in the domain that are represented by nodes in the structural language.
- It would need to know that if A supports B then A touches B in the blocks world, that is, to realize that there is redundancy in the domain relations.
- It would need to understand the logical meaning of terms such as NOT, ANY and OR, in terms of the restrictions or permissions that they imply for the matching process.

The program needs to know these things in order to satisfy itself that there is a mapping between P1's nodes and links and those of P2 such that each constraint in P1 is in fact more specific than the corresponding constraint in P2. Once it can grasp this relationship of specificity, the way is open for a representation of version spaces in terms of their maximally specific and maximally general patterns. This is because the program can then consider the version space as containing:

- the set of maximally specific patterns;
- the set of maximally general patterns;
- all concept descriptions which occur between these two sets in the partial ordering.

This is called the *boundary sets* representation for version spaces, and it is both compact and easy to update. It is compact because one is not explicitly storing every concept description in the space. It is easy to update, because defining a new space corresponds to moving one or both of the boundaries.

20.2.3 The candidate elimination algorithm

A version space, as described so far, is no more than a data structure for representing a set of concept descriptions. However, the term 'version spaces' is often applied to a learning technique which applies a particular algorithm, known as the *candidate elimination* algorithm, to such data structures. This algorithm works by manipulating the boundary sets that represent a given version space.

The algorithm begins by initializing the version space to the set of all concept descriptions consistent with the first positive training instance. In other words, the set of maximally specific patterns (S) is initialized to the most specific concept descriptions that the pattern language is capable of generating, while the set of maximally general patterns (G) is initialized to the most general concept descriptions available in the language. As each subsequent instance is processed, the sets S and G are modified in order to eliminate from the version space just those concept descriptions which are inconsistent with the current instance.

In the course of learning, the boundaries should move towards each other monotonically, that is, without back and forth movement in which they sometimes move further apart. Moving the S boundary in the direction of greater generality can be considered as a breadth-first search from specific patterns to more general ones. The object of the search is to compute a new boundary set which is just sufficiently general that it does not rule out a newly encountered positive instance. In other words, S moves when the program encounters a new positive instance which does not match all of the patterns in S. Correspondingly, moving the G boundary in the direction of greater specificity can be considered as a breadth-first search from general patterns to more specific ones. The object of this search is to compute a new boundary set which is just specific enough to rule out a newly encountered negative instance. Thus G moves when the program encounters a negative training instance which matches some pattern in G.

This algorithm does not employ heuristic search, because the constraints are exact and they are guaranteed to cause the algorithm to converge on a solution. The monotonicity of the search is the key to controlling the combinatorics of the update problem. As hinted earlier, the version spaces technique has a number of pleasing properties, which are worth listing:

- All concept descriptions that are consistent with all of the training instances will be found.
- The version space summarizes the alternative interpretations of the observed data.
- The results are independent of the order in which training instances are presented.
- Each training instance is examined only once.
- One never needs to reconsider discarded hypotheses.

The fact that the version space summarizes the data so far means that it can be used as a basis for generating new training instances, that is, instances that might bring the boundaries closer together. The fact that you consider each instance only once means that the program doesn't need to store past instances. Thus the time required by the algorithm will be proportional to the number of observed instances, rather than some explosive function of this number. The avoidance of backtracking also contributes to the efficiency and simplicity of the algorithm. However, it is well known that the introduction of disjunctive concepts causes severe combinatorial problems, by increasing the branching factor in the partial order of patterns.

20.2.4 Matching instances to patterns in Meta-DENDRAL

Meta-DENDRAL uses the same language to describe training instances as it uses to describe patterns, although only a subset of the pattern language is required to do this. Each training instance is a complete molecule with a particular site in the compound, rather than a constrained description of a molecule.

Matching instances to patterns involves defining a connected mapping from pattern nodes to instance nodes. A mapping, X, is *connected* if the mapping is one-to-one and injective, and if every pair of instance nodes, X(p1) and X(p2), corresponding to pattern nodes p1 and p2 share a common link if and only if p1 and p2 also share a common link. We also require that the feature values of each instance node of the form X(p) satisfy the feature constraints of the corresponding pattern node, p.

It is now possible to give Mitchell's domain-specific definition of partial order for Meta-DENDRAL, using the definitions given above. Lower case letters stand for pattern nodes, while upper case letters stand for whole patterns. Pattern P1 is more specific than or equal to pattern P2 if and only if there is a connected mapping, X, of nodes in P2 into nodes of P1 such that for each pair of nodes, p2, X(p2), the feature constraints associated with X(p2) are more specific than or equal to the feature constraints associated with p2. In trying to understand this definition, and how it applies to the mass spectrometry domain, it is worth looking back to the blocks world example given earlier. In the world of chemical structure elucidation, the analog of blocks are the atoms and superatoms, while the analog of spatial relationships such as 'supports' and 'touches' are chemical bonds.

Knowledge of chemistry can be employed by the candidate elimination algorithm in two ways.

(1) The representation language for chemical substructures allows forms which are syntactically distinct but semantically equivalent patterns; that is, it can generate expressions which are different in form but have the same meaning. Knowledge of the meaning of these patterns can therefore be used to delete redundant patterns from the version space boundaries. This has no effect upon the completeness of the version space approach.
(2) Version space boundaries grow quite large for some problems. It is therefore useful to apply various rules of thumb to prune these boundaries. However, if heuristic methods are used, one can no longer be sure that the program will determine all of the concept descriptions that are consistent with the training instances.

Mitchell claimed that the version space approach added the following new capabilities to the original Meta-DENDRAL program.

- Additional training data can modify existing rules without the original data having to be reconsidered.
- The learning process is properly incremental, in that one can determine to what degree each rule has been learned and reliably employ partially learned rules.
- The new rule formation strategy avoids the expensive 'coarse search' of RULEGEN and focuses upon the most 'interesting' training data first.
- The method for considering alternative versions of each rule is more complete than the generalization and specialization operations of RULEMOD.

In summary, the version spaces approach appears to provide an incremental learning methodology that is both principled and efficient. Candidate elimination can be contrasted with depth- and breadth-first search strategies in that it determines every concept description consistent with the training instances, rather than finding a single acceptable concept description (depth-first search), or all maximally specific such concept descriptions (breadth-first search). As Mitchell points out, the chief manpower cost involved in applying this kind of technology to real problems is the construction of the set of training instances.

20.3 Building decision trees and production rules

Rules are not the only way of representing attribute–value information about concepts for the purposes of classification. *Decision trees* are an alternative way of structuring such information, and there are efficient algorithms for constructing such trees from data. We discuss these representations in Section 20.3.1.

The past 30 years have seen the emergence of a family of learning systems that work in this way, for example, CLS (Hunt *et al.*, 1966), ID3 (Quinlan, 1979), ACLS (Paterson and Niblett, 1982), ASSISTANT (Kononenko *et al.*, 1984) and IND (Buntine, 1990). ACLS (a generalization of ID3) has given rise to a number of commercial derivatives, such as Expert-Ease and RuleMaster, which have seen successful application in industry. Section 20.3.2 covers the ID3 algorithm in some detail.

C4.5 (Quinlan, 1993) is a suite of programs based on the ID3 algorithm which includes C4.5Rules, a module that generates production rules from a decision tree. It is both well-documented and publicly available, so we shall focus upon it here. The latest version of this system is called C5.0, which offers a tighter integration between the decision tree and decision rule formats.

20.3.1 The structure of decision trees

A decision tree represents a particular way of breaking up a data set into classes or categories. The root of the tree implicitly contains all the data to be classified, while the leaf nodes represent the final classes after categorization. Intermediate nodes represent choice points, or tests upon attributes of the data, which serve to further subdivide the data at that node.

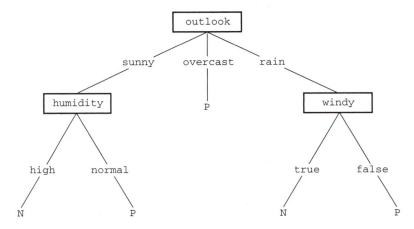

Figure 20.3 A decision tree (after Quinlan, 1986a).

```
if       outlook = overcast

         ∨
         outlook = sunny &
         humidity = normal

         ∨
         outlook = rain &
         windy = false
then     P
```

Figure 20.4 A classification rule based on the tree in Figure 20.3.

Thus, Quinlan (1993) defines decision trees as structures that consist of

- leaf nodes, representing a class, or
- decision nodes, specifying some test to be carried out on a single attribute value, with one branch for each possible outcome of the test.

Another way of looking at decision trees is that nodes correspond to attributes of the objects to be classified, while the arcs correspond to alternative values for these attributes. A sample tree is shown in Figure 20.3.

The tree of Figure 20.3 has as its non-terminal nodes the weather attributes out-look, humidity and windy. The leaves are labeled by one of two classes, P or N. One can think of P as the class of positive instances of the concept we are using, and N as the class of negative instances. For example, P might stand for 'play outside' while N might stand for 'don't play' or 'stay indoors.'

Although decision trees are obviously a different form of representation than production rules, one can think of a decision tree as a kind of rule: a classification rule that decides, for any object to which the attributes apply, whether it belongs in P or N. Indeed, it is possible to translate the tree of Figure 20.3 into such a rule directly (see Figure 20.4).

The single rule of Figure 20.4 could also be split into three separate rules that do not need disjunction, and then represented in a production rule language such as CLIPS.

```
if outlook = overcast
then P

if outlook = sunny &
   humidity = normal
then P

if outlook = rain &
   windy = false
then P
```

The reason for using decision trees rather than rules is that there exist comparatively simple algorithms for taking a training set and deriving a decision tree that will correctly classify unseen objects. The ID3 algorithm which performed this task is conceptually quite simple, as we shall see in the next section. It is also computationally efficient, in that the time taken to build such trees only increases linearly with the size of the problem.

No.	Outlook	Temperature	Humidity	Windy	Class
1	sunny	hot	high	false	N
2	sunny	hot	high	true	N
3	overcast	hot	high	false	P
4	rain	mild	high	false	P
5	rain	cool	normal	false	P
6	rain	cool	normal	true	N
7	overcast	cool	normal	true	P
8	sunny	mild	high	false	N
9	sunny	cool	normal	false	P
10	rain	mild	normal	false	P
11	sunny	mild	normal	true	P
12	overcast	mild	high	true	P
13	overcast	hot	normal	false	P
14	rain	mild	high	true	N

Figure 20.5 A small training set (from Quinlan, 1986a).

The training set used to derive the tree in Figure 20.3 is shown in Figure 20.5; the reader can check that the tree correctly classifies each of the 14 instances in the set. Note that the temperature attribute does not appear in the tree: it is not needed for classifying the instances.

20.3.2 The ID3 algorithm

The problem that ID3 sets out to solve is easy to state. Given

- a set of disjoint target classes $\{C_1, C_2, ..., C_k\}$, and
- a set of training data, S, containing objects of more than one class,

ID3 uses a series of tests to refine S into subsets that contain objects of only one class. The heart of the algorithm is a procedure for building a decision tree, where non-terminal nodes in the tree correspond to tests on a single attribute of the data, and terminal nodes correspond to classified subsets of the data set. As we shall see, the trick to doing this effectively is selecting the tests.

Let T be any test on a single attribute of the data, with $O_1, O_2, ..., O_n$ representing the possible outcomes of applying T to any object x, which we shall write as $T(x)$. T will therefore produce a partition $\{S_1, S_2, ..., S_n\}$ of S such that

$$S_i = \{x \mid T(x) = O_i\}.$$

This partition is shown graphically in Figure 20.6.

If we proceed recursively to replace each S_i in Figure 20.6 with a decision tree, we would have a decision tree for S. As noted earlier, the crucial factor in this problem reduction strategy is the choice of test. For each subtree, we need to find a 'good' attribute for partitioning the objects.

In making this decision, Quinlan employs the notion of *uncertainty* from information theory. Uncertainty is a number describing a set of messages,

$$M = \{m_1, m_2, ..., m_n\}.$$

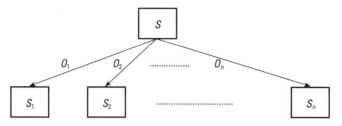

Figure 20.6 **A tree structuring of partitioned objects.**

Each message m_i in the set has probability $p(m_i)$ of being received and contains an amount of information, $I(m_i)$, defined as

$$I(m_i) = -\log p(m_i). \tag{20.1}$$

Thus information is an inverse monotonic function of probability. Information and uncertainty are measured in bits, so logarithms are taken to base 2.

The uncertainty[1] of a message set, $U(M)$, is just the sum of the information in the several possible messages weighted by their probabilities:

$$U(M) = -\Sigma_i\, p(m_i)\log p(m_i) \qquad\qquad \text{for } i = 1 \text{ to } n. \tag{20.2}$$

Speaking intuitively, we are uncertain about which message from the set will be sent to the degree to which we expect the messages to be informative. Consequently, we compute the average information of the possible messages that could be sent. If all messages in a set are equiprobable, then uncertainty is at a maximum.

Quinlan's use of this measure is based on the following assumptions.

- A correct decision tree for S will classify objects in the same proportion as their representation in S.
- Given a case to classify, a test can be regarded as the source of a message about that case.

Let N_i stand for the number of cases in S that belong to class C_i. Then the probability that a random case, c, drawn from S belongs to class C_i is estimated by

$$p(c \in C_i) = N_i\,/\,|S|$$

so the information such a message would convey amounts to

$$I(c \in C_i) = -\log_2 p(c \in C_i) \text{ bits.}$$

We next consider the uncertainty associated with the set of target classes viewed as a message set $\{C_1, C_2, \ldots, C_k\}$. This quantity is derived by computing a weighted sum over these classes, using weights in proportion to their representation in S.

$$U(S) = -\Sigma_{i\,=\,1\text{ to }k}\, p(c \in C_i) \times I(c \in C_i) \text{ bits.}$$

Note that the parameter S is embedded in both the probability and information terms inside the summation. The uncertainty, $U(S)$, measures the average amount of information needed to determine the class of a random case, $c \in S$, prior to partitioning by any test.

---

[1] Uncertainty is sometimes called *expected information*, or *entropy*.

We now consider a similar uncertainty measure *after* S has been partitioned into $\{S_1, S_2, ..., S_n\}$ by a particular test, T. This is given by

$$U_T(S) = \Sigma_{i = 1 \text{ to } n} \frac{|S_i|}{|S|} \times U(S_i).$$

This number measures how much information is needed after the partition has been performed; it is simply the sum of the uncertainties of the subsets so created, weighted in proportion to the size of the subset.

Thus the heuristic that ID3 uses in deciding what attribute to branch on next is to *select the test that gains the most information*. The *information gain* derived from carrying out a test T on a set S is given by

$$G_S(T) = U(S) - U_T(S).$$

Such heuristics are sometimes described as 'minimum entropy,' because maximizing information gain corresponds to minimizing uncertainty or disorder.

Let us return to our 'play, don't play' example and look at this formula in the simple, two-message case. Suppose that p denotes the number of objects of class P in the set of all cases S and n denotes the number of objects of class N in S. Thus an unseen object will belong to class P with probability $p/(p + n)$ and to class N with probability $n/(p + n)$. The expected information associated with the message set $M = \{P, N\}$ is therefore

$$U(M) = - p/(p + n) \log_2 p/(p + n) - n/(p + n) \log_2 n/(p + n).$$

Given a test T producing a partition $\{S_1, S_2, ..., S_n\}$ of S as before, suppose that each S_i contains p_i objects of class P and n_i objects of class N. The uncertainty inherent in any subclass S_i is given by

$$U(S_i) = - p_i /(p_i + n_i) \log_2 p_i /(p_i + n_i) - n/(p_i + n_i) \log_2 n_i /(p_i + n_i).$$

The expected information of the larger tree with S at its root is then given by the weighted average:

$$U_T(S) = \Sigma_{i = 1 \text{ to } n} \frac{(p_i + n_i)}{(p + n)} \times U(S_i)$$

The ratio $(p_i + n_i)/(p + n)$ corresponds to the weight for the *i*th branch in a tree such as that shown in Figure 20.6. It represents the proportion of the objects in S that belong to S_i.

We shall see in the next section that Quinlan has chosen a slightly different heuristic for use in C4.5, the latest incarnation of the ID3 algorithm. The problem with information gain as defined above is that it favors tests with many outcomes.

Nevertheless, the ID3 algorithm has been successfully applied to fairly large training sets (see for example, Quinlan, 1983). Its computational complexity hinges on the cost of choosing the next test to branch on, which is itself a linear function of the product of the number of objects in the training set and the number of attributes used to describe them. The system has also been adapted to cope with noisy and incomplete data, although we shall not discuss these extensions here (see Quinlan, 1986b).

The simplicity and efficiency of Quinlan's algorithm make it a feasible alternative to knowledge elicitation if sufficient data of the right kind are available. However, unlike the version spaces approach to concept learning, this method is not incremental. In other words, you cannot consider additional training data without reconsidering the classification of previous instances.

ID3 is not guaranteed to find the simplest decision tree that characterizes the training instances, because the information-theoretic evaluation function for choosing attributes is only a heuristic. Nevertheless, experience with the algorithm has shown that its decision trees are relatively simple and perform well in classifying unseen objects. Continuing the search for the 'best' solution would increase the complexity of the algorithm; as we noted in Chapters 14 and 15, it is sometimes better to settle for a satisficing solution to a hard problem.

20.3.3 Changes and additions to ID3 in C4.5

C4.5 is a suite of programs that embody the ID3 algorithm, and include a module, called C4.5RULES, that can generate a set of production rules from any resultant decision tree. The program uses *pruning heuristics* to simplify decision trees in an attempt to produce a result that is both easier to understand and less dependent upon the particular training set used. As mentioned in the last section, the test selection criterion has also been changed.

The original test selection heuristic based on information gain proved unsatisfactory because it tends to favor tests with a large number of outcomes over tests with a smaller number. To take an extreme example, vacuous tests that split the data into a large number of singleton classes, for example, classifying patients in a medical database by their name, will score well, because $U_T(S)$ will equal zero, thereby maximizing $G_S(T) = U(S) - U_T(S)$.

Given a test T on a data set S, with information gain $G_S(T)$, the gain criterion is now defined as a *gain ratio*, $H_S(T)$:

$$H_S(T) = G_S(T) / V(S)$$

where

$$V(S) = - \Sigma_{i = 1 \text{ to } n} \frac{|S_i|}{|S|} \times \log_2 \left(\frac{|S_i|}{|S|} \right)$$

It is important to understand the difference between $V(S)$ and $U(S)$. The message set upon which V is based is the set of outcomes, or equivalently, the set of subsets $\{S_1, S_2, ..., S_n\}$ associated with those outcomes, not the set of classes $\{C_1, C_2, ..., C_k\}$. So, in $V(S)$, the message indicates the *outcome* of the test, rather than the class to which a case belongs. Thus the focus is much narrower than in $U(S)$, even though we are looking at the same division of S into subsets. Now we merely consider the uncertainty associated with the outcomes themselves, not the uncertainty associated with the ultimate classification of a case.

The new heuristic is to select a test that maximizes the gain ratio defined above. Vacuous tests such as that described above will now score poorly, because the denominator will be $\log_2(N)$ for N training cases.

Another problem with ID3 is that it often builds a complex tree that *overfits* the data, that is, it finds distinctions in the training examples which are not in fact relevant to the classification problem as a whole. One way of dealing with the overfitting problem would be to have a 'stopping rule' which told ID3 when to stop splitting the tree and thereby making distinctions between data. However, it is hard to choose such a rule, so instead Quinlan chose to prune the decision tree after ID3 has run its course. It can be shown that, although pruning will make the tree more errorful on the training data set, it will typically perform better than the original tree on test data. Pruning is a complex issue that we shall not discuss here (see, for example, Mingers, 1989b; Mitchell, 1997), while the details of C4.5's pruning heuristics can be found in Quinlan (1993, Chapter 4).

In the interests of making ID3's output more understandable, C4.5 also provides a mechanism for translating the decision tree into a set of production rules. We saw in the last section that there is an equivalence between a single path through a decision tree from the root to a leaf and a rule. The conditions of the rule are simply the tests that we performed along the way, and the conclusion is the class assigned.

However, it is not very satisfactory to form a rule set by exhaustively enumerating all these paths. Some of the tests may largely serve to the split the tree and thereby narrow the space of cases into subsets that are subsequently refined by more meaningful attribute tests. This is because not all attributes are relevant to all classes.

Quinlan employs the following strategies for forming a final rule set from a decision tree:

(1) Derive an initial rule set by enumerating paths from the root to the leaves.
(2) Generalize the rules by possibly deleting conditions deemed to be unnecessary.
(3) Group the rules into subsets according to the target classes they cover and then delete any rules that do not appear to contribute to overall performance on that class.
(4) Order the sets of rules for the target classes, and choose a default class to which cases will be assigned.

This ordering of rule sets in step (4) can be seen as a primitive form of conflict resolution (see Chapter 5). The order of rules within a particular class is now irrelevant. Having a default class is like having a default rule which applies when no other rule is relevant.

The resultant set of rules will probably not have the same coverage as the decision tree, but its accuracy will be comparable. The advantage is that the rules are much easier to understand than the tree, and so they can be tuned by hand, if additional knowledge engineering is required.

Quinlan is careful to outline the circumstances under which C4.5 is an appropriate learning tool and can be expected to perform well. Not all classification tasks lend themselves to a decision tree approach, or to the particular algorithms embodied in C4.5. The following requirements are crucial.

- The classes into which data will be divided must be determined ahead of time. In other words, C4.5 and similar methods will not discover groupings of data. Also, the classes are 'crisp,' not fuzzy; either a datum belongs to a particular class or it doesn't. In addition, the classes must be disjoint.
- These methods require large data sets, the larger the better. Training sets that are too small will lead to overfitting, that is, the classification will be too heavily influenced by individual data items, and the classifier will then perform badly on

unseen data. C4.5's pruning methods will not correct for the problems cause by a small sample containing atypical data.

- The data must be in a regular attribute–value format; that is, each datum must be capable of being characterized in terms of a fixed set of attributes and their values, whether symbolic, ordinal or continuous. There are methods for handling missing attributes: C4.5 assumes that unknown test outcomes are distributed probabilistically according to the relative frequency of outcomes that are known. Continuous values are tested by thresholding, and there are methods for finding appropriate thresholds.

There are a number of advantages in electing to use decision tree methods over more conventional statistical methods where appropriate. Methods like C4.5 make no assumptions about the distribution of the attribute values (for example, that they are normally distributed), or about the conditional independence of attributes (as would be required by Bayesian classifiers). Studies have concluded that tree-based classifiers compare favorably with other methods, in terms of accuracy, robustness across different tasks, and speed of computation.

20.4 Tuning rule sets

Researchers are also working on the problems of debugging and justifying weighted rules which perform inexact reasoning. Here we shall do no more than consider two recent examples, which will serve to give the reader the flavor of current work and provide pointers to the relevant literature. Despite the theoretical orientation of such work, its practical significance is obvious, in that any reliable tool which helped improve the performance of sets of weighted rules would be welcomed by knowledge engineers.

Given a set of rules, derived by induction or from an expert, we are most interested in

(1) evaluating the contribution of individual rules, and
(2) evaluating the performance of the rule set as a whole.

Under (1), our chief concern is the applicability of the rule: how often will it be correctly applied, and how often will it contribute towards error, that is a wrong decision on the part of the system? Under (2), our main concern is with properties of the rule set, rather than the quality of individual rules. Is the rule set complete, that is will it handle all the cases that it is likely to encounter? Is it redundant, that is are there rules that we could delete from the rule set without adversely affecting performance? Bear in mind that such rules may not be 'bad' or 'wrong' in themselves, but their deletion might improve performance because they interact adversely with other rules in the set.

Langlotz *et al.* (1986) present a decision-theoretic method for evaluating individual production rules. Where trade-offs are involved in the specification of a rule, for example between probability and utility, it is useful to know how robust the recommendations of a system are. In other words, how finely balanced is the judgment to which the rule contributes, and how far would an alteration to the weight of the rule affect the final outcome?

> IF   1) The therapy under consideration is tetracycline
>   2) The age (in years) of the patient is less than 8
> THEN There is strongly suggestive evidence (.8) that tetracycline is not an appropriate therapy for use
>   against the organism.

Figure 20.7 **The MYCIN tetracycline heuristic.**

As an illustration, they consider a simplified MYCIN rule (see Figure 20.7) which militates against the prescription of tetracycline to children because, although it is effective against some infections, it causes dental staining. This rule involves a trade-off between curing an infection and risking a negative side-effect. The expected utility of applying this rule is a function of both the utility of the various outcomes and the probability of their occurrence.

In decision-theory, the *expected utility* of an action A, with possible outcomes O_1, O_2, ..., O_n having probabilities p_1, p_2, ..., p_n is given by

$$EU(A) = \Sigma_i\, p_i\, u(O_i) \qquad \text{for } i = 1 \text{ to } n$$

where $u(O_i)$ denotes the utility of the outcome O_i. Thus we are interested in how the utility of the action that a rule supports will vary as a function of variations in the parameters p_i and $u(O_i)$. For example, if the infection is resistant to all drugs except tetracycline, and the probability of dental staining is actually quite low, then $EU(A)$ will be high compared to a situation where other drugs are available and the probability of dental staining is high.

The authors describe an application of sensitivity analysis which plots the utility of an outcome against its probability. The point at which alternative therapy recommendations have equal utility represents a probability threshold, thus determining how far the probability assessment in the model must vary before the optimal decision changes. Arguably, the extra effort required to perform the analysis is repaid by the knowledge engineer and domain expert having to be more precise about the rationale behind a rule. In particular, decision analysis makes explicit those variables upon which the applicability of a given rule depends. This may help knowledge engineers to identify unwanted interactions between rules in a rule set, including those which result from probabilistic dependencies of the kind discussed in Chapter 9.

Wilkins and Buchanan (1986), on the other hand, concentrate upon debugging whole sets of heuristic rules. They argue that the incremental modification of individual rules, using tools such as TEIRESIAS (see Chapter 10), does not guarantee that the knowledge engineer will converge on an optimal rule set. They caution against a strategy of making rules more general or specific, and strengthening or weakening their weights in response to false positive and false negative results. Heuristic rules are inexact and should not be modified simply because they fail; their weights are intended to code for their reliability. In fact, all heuristic rules represent a trade-off between generality and specificity in terms of some overall policy, and it is better to maintain that policy than make arbitrary changes.

The authors define the optimum rule set as that element of the power set of rules in the original set that minimizes error. They assume that individual rules in the rule set all meet some standard of goodness, and then concentrate on deriving the best subset of this original set. The process of deriving such an optimal set is formulated as a *bipartite graph minimization problem*, based on the mapping between a set of nodes representing the training instances and a set of nodes representing the initial rule set. This problem is shown to be intractable in general, but a heuristic method for solving it is presented. The solution proposed is mainly intended to minimize deleterious interactions between good heuristic rules in rule sets that have been derived by induction methods.

Other work on knowledge refinement includes the Learning Apprentice System (LAS) of Smith *et al.* (1985). LAS is an interactive aid for building and improving knowledge bases. It partially automates both the generation of heuristic rules from a domain theory and the debugging of such rules as problems occur during routine use. It uses a kind of dependency network (see Chapter 19) to specify the justification of a rule in terms of the underlying theory, and uses this structure to construct possible explanations for system failures.

The systems mentioned in this chapter all demonstrate the feasibility of construct-ing aids that could partially automate the task of constructing or improving a knowl-edge base. Although some of this work is still at the research stage, it is clear that such progress as has been made derives from more rigorous analyses of the different kinds of knowledge and problem solving strategy that expert systems use. Theoretical advances such as these are beginning to have practical pay-offs which will result in sys-tems which are easier to design, construct and debug.

In summary, we can see that machine learning research has the potential to make a profound contribution to the theory and practice of expert systems, as well as to other areas of artificial intelligence. Its application to the problem of deriving rule sets from examples is already helping to circumvent the knowledge acquisition bottleneck dis-cussed in Chapter 10. However, such techniques are also finding application to the problem of evaluating and tuning sets of decision rules, regardless of the manner in which they have been derived.

BIBLIOGRAPHICAL NOTES

As noted in the introductory paragraphs of this chapter, there are many areas of machine learning that we have not attempted to cover here. For the reader interested in a more rounded view, the papers in Michalski *et al.* (1983, 1986) make a reasonable starting point, prefaced perhaps by Winston (1984, Chapter 11). These papers cover many different kinds of learning, not all of which are immediately relevant to expert system applications.

Some issues of *Artificial Intelligence* journal also contain papers, such as Winston (1982) and Lenat (1982), which describe significant pieces of AI research into machine learning. Again, these are somewhat broader in scope than the material covered here. For example, Winston's program creates rules by analogical reasoning, while Lenat's program uses heuristics to discover mathematical concepts in a form of discovery learning.

For a classification of learning programs based on an analysis of basic algorithms, rather than kinds of learning behavior, see Bundy *et al.* (1985). However, this paper assumes some prior knowledge of the programs being compared, and should therefore be consulted after some of the references cited above. O'Rourke (1982) compares ID3 with other learning programs, while Dietterich and

   Michalski (1983) analyze a number of concept learning programs, including the original Meta-DENDRAL.

Buchanan and Wilkins (1993) collects together an excellent set of readings on knowledge acquisition and machine learning. The definitive reference on C4.5 is Quinlan (1993), which also contains a source listing of the program. Version spaces are well described in Mitchell, 1997, Chapter 2).

1. What is the difference between supervised and unsupervised learning?

2. Distinguish between concept learning and descriptive generalization.

3. Construct training sets for the following concepts, along the lines of Figure 20.1.
   (i) **Foreign Car.**
   (ii) **Small Foreign Car.**
   (iii) **Small American Car.**
   Do you see any problems with forming training sets for (ii) and (iii), if you stick to the six instances used in the figure? What does this tell you about the construction of training sets?

4. Figure 20.8 shows three pairs of patterns. For each pair, say which, if any, is the most specific of the two.

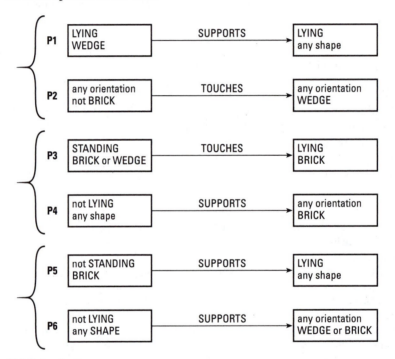

Figure 20.8 Pairs of patterns.

5. Look at the training data in Figure 20.5. Of the 14 objects, 9 are of class P and 5 are of class N. The uncertainty of the message set $M = \{P, N\}$ is therefore given by

$$-\frac{9}{14} \log_2 \frac{9}{14} - \frac{5}{14} \log_2 \frac{5}{14} = 0.940 \text{ bits.}$$

   (i) What is the expected information for the attribute outlook?
   (ii) What is the information gain of branching on outlook?

continued

(iii) Repeat this analysis for the attributes `humidity` and `windy`.
(iv) Which attribute has the highest information gain?

6. List some of the different kinds of learning that humans engage in, and attempt to distinguish clearly between them. For example, learning multiplication tables is rather different from learning to play a musical instrument, because the latter involves motor skills as well as rote memory. Which of these different kinds of learning do you think will be easiest to program, and what are your reasons?

21 Belief Networks[†]

In this chapter, we consider two quantitative methods for reasoning under uncertainty in a structured space of hypotheses. It is arguable that both of them handle belief updating in a more convincing manner than certainty factors do. These methods also represent alternatives to more heuristic methods, such as those employed by the INTERNIST and CENTAUR systems described in Chapter 13, which have no mathematical basis.

Gordon and Shortliffe (1985) and Pearl (1986) have each suggested ways in which evidential reasoning in a hierarchical hypothesis space can be managed in the context of the Dempster–Shafer theory of evidence and a Bayesian formalism respectively. Each approach involves defining a belief function over a hypothesis set, and then providing mechanisms for updating the current set of beliefs as new evidence is gathered.

The approaches are described in detail, and an attempt is made to compare and contrast them. Finally, we consider a general framework for effecting such comparisons.

21.1 Dempster–Shafer theory

The hypothesis space in Dempster–Shafer (D–S) theory is called the *frame of discernment*, denoted by Θ. It is assumed that the hypotheses in this space are both exhaustive and mutually exclusive. It is also assumed that we may have means of obtaining evidence not merely for single hypotheses $h_1, ..., h_n$ in Θ, but also about one or more subsets $A_1, ..., A_k$ of Θ, which are allowed to overlap.

We can think of these pieces of evidence as being members of a set, Ψ, and construct a mapping,

$$\Gamma: \Psi \rightarrow 2^\Theta$$

which associates each element of Ψ with a subset of Θ. Such a subset is called a *focal element*. Note that the assumption of exhaustiveness means that we do not map any $\psi \in \Psi$ onto the empty set. In other words, each piece of evidence points to at least one known hypothesis.

Dempster–Shafer theory provides a means for computing a belief function over these hypothesis sets, together with a rule for combining belief functions derived from different pieces of evidence.

21.1.1 Belief functions

The *basic probability assignment* (bpa) of D–S theory, m, is a function from 2^Θ to $[0,1]$ such that

$m(\varnothing) = 0$; and

$\Sigma_{A_i \in 2^\Theta} (m(A_i)) = 1.$

The total belief, Bel, in any focal element A can be found by summing the bpas of all subsets of A. Thus Bel is a function from 2^Θ to $[0,1]$ such that

$\mathrm{Bel}(A) = \Sigma_{B \subset A}\, m(B).$

Bel(Θ) is always 1, regardless of the value of $m(\Theta)$. This follows from the definition of a bpa. Bel(Θ) = 1 represents the fact that the correct hypothesis is always believed to be in Θ (exhaustiveness again). $m(\Theta)$ reflects the weight of evidence as yet uncommitted to subsets of Θ. Bel and m will be equal for singleton sets.

The probability of a focal element A is bounded below by the belief in A, and above by the plausibility of A, given by $1 - \mathrm{Bel}(A^c)$, where A^c is the complement of A.

The plausibility of A, $\mathrm{Pls}(A)$, represents the degree to which the evident is consistent with A, and can be calculated as follows:

$\mathrm{Pls}(A) = \Sigma_{A \cap B \neq \varnothing}\, m(B).$

Since the plausibility of A is simply the degree to which we do not believe in $\neg A$, we can also write:

$\mathrm{Pls}(A) = 1 - \mathrm{Bel}(\neg A).$

The plausibility of A can be thought of as the extent to which A is capable of improving, given the evidence for competitors of A. It is therefore convenient to think of the information contained in Bel for a given subset as a *belief interval* of the form $[\mathrm{Bel}(A), \mathrm{Pls}(A)]$. The width of the belief interval can be regarded as the amount of uncertainty with respect to a hypothesis, given the available evidence.

Dempster's rule computes a new belief function, given two belief functions based on two different observations. Let Bel_1 and Bel_2 denote two belief functions with their respective bpas, m_1 and m_2. The rule computes a new bpa, $m_1 \oplus m_2$, and then a new belief function $\mathrm{Bel}_1 \oplus \mathrm{Bel}_2$ based on the definition of Bel given above.

$m_1 \oplus m_2(A)$, for a given hypothesis A, is given by the sum of all the products of the form $m_1(X)m_2(Y)$, where X and Y range over all subsets of Θ whose intersection is A. When there are empty entries in the intersection table, a normalization is applied which defines κ as the sum of all the non-zero values assigned to $\varnothing$, assigns $m_1 \oplus m_2(\varnothing)$ as zero, and then divides $m_1 \oplus m_2$ for all other hypothesis sets by $1 - \kappa$.

In summary,

$$m_1 \oplus m_2(A) = \frac{\Sigma_{X \cap Y = A} \, m_1(X)m_2(Y)}{1 - \Sigma_{X \cap Y = \emptyset} \, m_1(X)m_2(Y)}$$

but we insist that m_1 and m_2 are induced by independent evidential sources within the same frame of discernment. Note that the commutativity of multiplication ensures that Dempster's rule gives the same result regardless of the order in which evidence is combined.

21.1.2 Applying Dempster–Shafer theory to MYCIN

Gordon and Shortliffe advocate the use of Dempster–Shafer theory as an alternative to MYCIN's certainty factors. They note that, when searching for the identity of an organism, MYCIN often narrows the hypothesis set of all possible organisms down to a proper subset, for example, the gram-negative organisms. (This is an example of what Clancey would call the application of structural knowledge.) Moreover, the rules which produce this narrowing typically have nothing to say about the relative likelihoods of organisms in that subset.

A Bayesian approach might assume that each organism in the subset has an equal prior probability, and so distribute the weight of evidence for the subset equally among its elements. But this tends to confound the case of equal evidence for each of the organisms with the case where there is no evidence at all. The Dempster–Shafer bpa does not distinguish prior and posterior probabilities in this way, and so does not sanction such a distribution of probabilities.

Dempster–Shafer belief functions also avoid another counter-intuitive aspect of the Bayesian view. In the latter, a subjective interpretation of probabilities means that a degree of belief in a hypothesis, H, implies that one's remaining belief is committed to its negation, that is, that

$$P(H) = 1 - P(\neg H).$$

However, one of the desiderata of the confirmation model that gave rise to the use of certainty factors in MYCIN was that evidence partially in favor of a hypothesis should not be construed as evidence partially against the same hypothesis. In D–S, the commitment of belief to a subset A does not force the commitment of the remaining belief to its complement, thus $\text{Bel}(A) + \text{Bel}(A^c) \leq 1$. The amount of belief committed to neither A nor A^c is the degree of ignorance concerning A.

Gordon and Shortliffe go on to show how D–S theory could be applied to evidential reasoning in MYCIN. (object attribute value) triples found in the conclusions of rules represent singleton hypotheses concerning the value of a particular attribute for a particular object. So any set of such triples having the same object and attribute, for example (ORGANISM-1 IDENTITY value), constitutes a frame of discernment in its own right. So long as the parameters are single-valued, the condition concerning mutual exclusivity of hypotheses will be met. The set of values should also exhaust the range.

Rules can therefore be construed as belief functions of a certain sort. If the premises confirm the conclusion of a hypothesis H with degree d, and d is above the threshold set for rule activation, then the CF associated with the H can be regarded as a bpa which assigns d to the singleton set, {H}, and $1 - d$ to Θ. If the premises disconfirm a conclusion with degree d, then we assign d to $\{H\}^c$, and $1 - d$ to Θ, and the CF associated with H is $-d$.

The authors identify three different ways in which evidence could be combined as a consequence of rule triggering in MYCIN, according to the D–S model.

(1) Two rules either both confirm or both disconfirm the same conclusion, $\{H\}$, with bpas m_1 and m_2. In this case, some weight of evidence will be transferred between $\{H\}$ and Θ. The updated belief in these two sets will be

$$m_1 \oplus m_2(\{H\})$$

and

$$m_1 \oplus m_2(\Theta).$$

There is no need to apply the k normalization, since $\{H\} \cap \Theta \neq \emptyset$. It turns out that the original certainty factor model gives the same results as Dempster's rule here.

(2) One rule confirms $\{H\}$ to degree m_1 and one rule disconfirms $\{H\}$ to degree m_2, that is, confirms $\{H\}^c$ to degree m_2. In this case, normalization will be necessary, since

$$\{H\} \cap \{H\}^c = \emptyset.$$

Otherwise bpa values are combined as before to derive

$$m_1 \oplus m_2(\{H\})$$
$$m_1 \oplus m_2(\{H\}^c)$$

and

$$m_1 \oplus m_2(\Theta).$$

Here the results will not agree with the CF model. The application of Dempster's rule will result in reduced support for both $\{H\}$ and $\{H\}^c$, with a corresponding gain for Θ. Thus conflicting evidence increases our uncertainty concerning both $\{H\}$ and $\{H\}^c$ by widening their belief intervals. (Each also becomes more plausible as a result of conflicting evidence, since support for its complement is weakened. This may seem less intuitive, if one gives 'plausible' its everyday meaning. However, given the definition of Pls, it is clear why this must be so.) By contrast, MYCIN's combination function (see Chapter 3) tends to come down on the side of the hypothesis with the largest CF.

(3) The rules conclude about competing singleton hypotheses, $\{H_1\}$ and $\{H_2\}$. In this case, normalization will be required if $\{H_1\} \cap \{H_2\} = \emptyset$, and we calculate

$$m_1 \oplus m_2(\{H_1\})$$
$$m_1 \oplus m_2(\{H_2\})$$

and

$$m_1 \oplus m_2(\Theta).$$

Dempster's rule can be seen to be more general than MYCIN's combination function in that, if a subset relation exists between $\{H_1\}$ and $\{H_2\}$, belief in the subset will be counted as belief in the superset, but not conversely. Thus the pooling of evidence has a wider impact here than in the CF model.

Gordon and Shortliffe propose an approximation technique to the Dempster–Shafer method which attempts to minimize computational cost. They also point out that partitioning of the search space, such as that performed by INTERNIST, can help to keep the set of competitors constituting the current frame of discernment sufficiently small. However, the problem remains that systems such as INTERNIST cannot allow a strict mapping such as

$$\Gamma: \Psi \to 2^\Theta$$

between evidential elements and hypothesis sets in the construction of a set of competing hypotheses, given that symptoms may have implications for disjoint hypothesis sets in different parts of the hierarchy.

Dempster–Shafer theory has slowly gained in popularity over the past 10 years. It has been applied in diverse areas such as diagnosis (Biswas and Anand, 1987) and computer vision (Provan, 1990). It does not solve the problem of conditional dependencies noted in Chapter 9, but it does provide knowledge engineers with a certain amount of flexibility, in that they can assign belief mass to non-singleton subsets of the hypothesis space. Such assignments can code for dependencies among evidential groupings. The hierarchical arrangement of the frame of discernment is a useful tool that facilitates this kind of thinking.

21.2 Pearl's theory of evidential reasoning in a hierarchy

Pearl's (1986) alternative to Dempster–Shafer theory for evidential reasoning in a hierarchy is based on a Bayesian view of evidence aggregation and updating by propagation. As with Gordon and Shortliffe, it assumes that some subsets of the total hypothesis space are of semantic interest and can be arranged in a hierarchy.

Initially, it is assumed that each singleton hypothesis has a prior degree of belief associated with it. Pearl does not say where the priors come from, but presumably a domain expert provides them.

The expert is also required to determine the set of hypotheses, S, upon which a given piece of evidence, E, bears directly. If E bears directly on S, then this can be taken to mean that there is some causal mechanism giving rise to E, and this mechanism is a unique property of the members of S. However, E conveys no information which allows us to prefer one member of S over another, as an explanation of E.

This mapping therefore introduces the notion of conditional independence between evidence and singleton hypotheses, such that

$$P(E|S, h_i) = P(E|S), \text{ for all } h_i \in S.$$

The degree to which E confirms or disconfirms S can be estimated using the likelihood ratio

$$\lambda S = \frac{P(E|S)}{P(E|\neg S)}.$$

The impact of evidence E on the set S is calculated as follows. Each singleton hypothesis, h_i, in S obtains the weight $W_i = \lambda_S$, while every hypothesis in S^c receives a unity weight, $W_i = 1$. This is the weight distribution phase.

Then updating begins, by computing a new value for the belief function, $\mathrm{BEL}'(h_i)$, from $\mathrm{BEL}(h_i)$:

$$\mathrm{BEL}'(h_i) = P(h_i|E) = \alpha_S W_i \mathrm{BEL}(h_i)$$

where α_S is the normalization given by

$$\alpha_S = \frac{1}{\Sigma_i W_i \mathrm{BEL}'(h_i)}$$

and $\mathrm{BEL}(h_i)$ is just the prior degree of belief.

Thus the belief assigned to a set of hypotheses is distributed among its singleton elements as a function of their prior probabilities, while belief assigned to a non-singleton hypothesis is the sum of the belief in its singleton elements. Updating can proceed recursively, so that posterior beliefs serve as prior beliefs for the next evidence.

The justification for this scheme is that the assumption of conditional independence, together with the symmetrical assumption for the complement of S,

$$P(E|S^c, h_i) = P(E|S^c) \text{ for all } h_i \in S^c,$$

gives

$$P(E|h_i) = P(E|S) \text{ if } h_i \in S, \text{ else } P(E|S^c).$$

Put this together with the odds-likelihood form of Bayes' Rule, and it follows that

$$P(h_i|E) = \alpha_S \lambda_S P(h_i) \text{ if } h_i \in S, \text{ else } \alpha_S P(h_i).$$

But although Pearl's formalism is Bayesian, partial evidence in favor of a hypothesis can no longer be construed as partially supporting its negation. Evidence for a subset S is never construed as evidence for S^c, while mass assigned to singleton, h, is quite distinct from the mass assigned to its competitors. In this, it resembles D–S theory's tolerance for ignorance of how mass should be assigned.

Distributing evidence from subsets to singletons recovers a point probability distribution for the hypothesis space, but at the expense of being more precise about individual hypotheses than the evidence actually warrants. However, Pearl claims that one need not distribute the mass at a subset S to its constituents until further (or all of the) evidence has been received. Normalization can also be postponed, until several pieces of evidence have impacted upon (possibly different) hypotheses. Thus given evidence $E_1, ..., E_n$ for hypotheses $S_1, ..., S_n$ respectively, the weights are combined multiplicatively by

$$W_i(E_1, ..., E_n) = W_{1,i} W_{2,i} ... W_{n,i}$$

where $W_{k,i} = \lambda_{S_k}$ if $h_i \in S_k$ and 1 otherwise.

Pearl puts forward an alternative mechanism for updating which avoids the normalization step altogether and involves propagating revisions up and down the hierarchy using message passing. This appears to be more attractive than Dempster's rule from an implementational point of view. Pearl claims a peculiar transparency for this method of updating by message passing, since influence flows along pathways that have some semantic justification. Doing away with global normalizations, such as κ and α, makes the intermediate steps easier to understand. This leaves only one numerical parameter, the likelihood ratio, whose significance is easily comprehended.

BOX 21.1

Pearl (1988) presents a formalism called *Bayesian networks* which can be seen as a generalization of the hierarchical belief networks described here. In Bayesian nets, arcs between nodes also represent causal dependencies, but we allow nodes to have multiple parents, and networks may even contain loops. Belief update proceeds by message passing, as in the hierarchical case, although this is only straightforward for *polytrees*, that is, networks in which there exists no more than a single path between any two nodes.

It is interesting to contrast further Pearl's formalism with that of Dempster–Shafer theory.

- In Pearl's system, one is still assigning prior degrees of belief to singleton events, while in D–S, one is distributing mass over the whole frame of discernment.
- Pearl's identification of BEL(h_i) with $P(h_i)$ and BEL'(h_i) with $P(h_i|E)$ gives these functions a firmer foundation in probability theory than Dempster's rule of combination, which has no strong argument associated with it, as Shafer (1976) admits.
- As Yen (1986) points out, in Pearl's formalism one loses the D–S notion of a belief interval within which probability estimates may vary. Belief intervals could be useful for scheduling purposes in the context of expert systems, since they give some indication of the goodness of a hypothesis, its room for improvement, and the degree of uncertainty associated with it.

Pearl (1988) correctly points out that D–S theory accepts an incomplete probabilistic model and resigns itself to providing partial answers. Rather than directly estimating how close a hypothesis is to being true, it estimates how far the evidence forces us to accept the truth of a hypothesis. In this, it resembles objectivist methods of significance testing using confidence intervals more closely than subjectivist Bayesian approaches (Neapolitan, 1990).

However, despite these differences, there are also basic similarities between the two formalisms, which justify their joint treatment here. The association between evidential elements and hypothesis sets in Pearl's method is not unlike the mapping in Dempster–Shafer theory. Both can be viewed as using a 'mass distribution' metaphor, in that they are concerned with the sharing out of evidence in the context of a structured space of alternatives, and both allow for the computation of belief functions based upon simple probability estimates.

It is not easy to make systematic comparisons between alternative quantitative methods of plausible inference. Apart from problems of terminology and notation, comparing two methods is difficult unless they can both be viewed in terms of some common framework. In the next section, we look at just such a framework of comparing different methods which has the advantage of being rooted in probability theory.

21.3 Comparing methods of inexact reasoning[†]

Horvitz *et al.* (1986) propose a general model of belief entailment as a framework for comparing alternative formalisms that sheds further light on the problems of MYCIN. Drawing on the work of Cox (1946), they identify a number of essential properties that a measure of belief should possess. The idea is to provide an intuitive basis for probability theory from which the usual axioms follow.

The properties Horvitz presents can be summarized as follows:

(P1) *Clarity.* Propositions should be precisely defined, so that their truth conditions can be determined.

(P2) *Scalar continuity.* The degree of belief in a proposition should be a single real number which varies continuously between certain truth and certain falsehood.

(P3) *Completeness.* It is possible to ascribe a degree of belief to any well-defined proposition.

(P4) *Context dependency.* Degree of belief in a proposition may depend upon degree of belief in other propositions.

(P5) *Hypothetical conditioning.* There should be a function such that belief in a conjunction of propositions can be calculated from belief in one proposition and belief in the other given that the first is true.

(P6) *Complementarity.* Belief in the negation of a proposition is a monotonically decreasing function of belief in the proposition itself.

(P7) *Consistency.* Propositions with the same truth value will have equal degree of belief.

It can be shown that the axioms of probability theory follow as a logical consequence of these axioms, that is, there exists a continuous monotonic function, Φ, such that

(A1) $0 \leq \Phi(Q|e) \leq 1$
(A2) $\Phi(\text{TRUE}|e) = 1$
(A3) $\Phi(Q|e) + \Phi(\sim Q|e) = 1$
(A4) $\Phi(QR|e) = \Phi(Q|e)\Phi(R|Qe)$.

The semantic properties of belief, (P1)–(P7), can serve as a basis for comparison between formalisms whose axiomatizations are hard to compare. They can also help researchers identify areas of dissatisfaction with probability theory as a basis for reasoning about degree of belief. Finally, they may help identify points where various formalisms actually diverge from the axioms of probability theory.

Horvitz uses four categories to classify non-probabilistic approaches to belief entailment:

(C1) *generalization*, where particular properties are weakened or eliminated;
(C2) *specialization*, where existing properties are strengthened or new ones are added;
(C3) *self-inconsistency*, where (C2) results in the set of properties becoming inconsistent;
(C4) *substitution*, where properties are changed in a manner other than generalization or specialization.

Horvitz then demonstrates the utility of the framework by using it to compare fuzzy logic (see for example Zadeh, 1981), Dempster–Shafer theory (Shafer, 1976), and MYCIN certainty factors with probability theory.

- *Fuzzy logics* concerned with vagueness weaken the clarity property (P1), in that ill-defined propositions may still be assigned a degree of belief. They therefore fall into the generalization category (C1) listed above. On the other hand, fuzzy logics concerned with the fuzzification of truth values are inconsistent with the hypothetical conditioning property (P5). This is because degree of belief in a conjunction is given as the min of the degree of belief in the conjuncts, in contrast with axiom (A4). So such logics fall into the substitution category (C4).

- The central difference between *Dempster–Shafer theory* and probability theory appears to be a weakening of the completeness property (P3). Dempster–Shafer theory allows one to state that certain prior and conditional probabilities cannot be assessed, and provides the notion of a compatibility relation between beliefs. This difference leads to a violation of both the scalar continuity property (P2) and the complementarity property (P6). Thus Dempster–Shafer theory can be considered as a generalization of probability theory, instead of being in the substitution category.
- The *certainty factor* model used by MYCIN makes stronger assumptions than probabilistic models of belief, and so it could be considered as falling into the specialization category (C2). Yet we have seen that it is also self-inconsistent, and so it really falls into category (C3). Heckerman's (1986) reformulation of certainty factors in terms of the likelihood ratio is a genuine specialization, however.

21.4 Summarizing the state of uncertainty

Horvitz and Heckerman's work is typical of a theoretical approach to uncertainty which is concerned with comparing the semantics of different formal languages for calculating degrees of belief. However, it is worth bearing in mind that standard probability theory may itself admit of more than one semantic interpretation. For example, Shafer and Tversky (1985) note three such ways of vivifying the Bayesian formalism:

- the *frequency* semantics, where we ask how often, in evidential situations, a hypothesis would turn out to be true;
- the *betting* semantics, where we determine at what odds we would be willing to bet on a hypothesis in the light of evidence.
- the *propensity* semantics, where we study a causal model of the situation and ask how well a hypothesis explains the evidence.

Very few expert systems appear to employ a frequency interpretation of measures of belief. Thus Buchanan and Shortliffe (1984, Chapter 11) move away from the notion of relative frequency towards Carnap's notion of degree of confirmation, which is at least consistent with the betting semantics. The betting semantics is also consonant with the view of MYCIN's rules as heuristics which bear a degree of risk. Clearly some of the rules encode causal information, for example the rules concerning compromised hosts. However, we have already established that such information is compiled into the rules and therefore mixed in with non-causal considerations. Hence it can hardly be said that certainty factors encode the degree to which a hypothesis explains the evidence on the basis of a propensity semantics. The INTERNIST model, where considerations concerning explanatory power and causal factors have the potential to be more explicit, would be a better candidate for a propensity semantics, except that INTERNIST employed rather *ad hoc* scoring methods. To the extent that they are analyzable, such methods appear to suffer from the confusion of absolute belief and belief update found in MYCIN (Horvitz and Heckerman, 1986, Section 12) that we mentioned in Chapter 9.

Thus we see a trend towards increasing sophistication in both the theoretical underpinnings of methods for coping with uncertainty and the practical aspects of providing tools for its management. It is possible that such work needs to be integrated with the more differentiated view of knowledge outlined in Chapters 11–15 for real advances to be made. As expert system applications become more complex, and are involved in the execution of critical tasks, mechanisms for handling uncertainty will require both a more rigorous formal justification and a greater degree of transparency.

BIBLIOGRAPHICAL NOTES

Pearl (1988) argues strongly in favor of Bayesian methods, and covers much of the relevant AI background. This book is not a bad place to start, since it is relatively self-contained. It is also structured in such a way that readers can skip highly technical sections and still get the flavor of the debate. However, the author is clearly arguing from a particular point of view. Pearl (1997) is a more up-to-date book dealing with the theory and application of belief networks, while Jensen (1996) is recent introductory text that could be used as an alternative starting point. Shafer and Pearl (1990) is an excellent book of readings.

STUDY SUGGESTIONS

1. A simple frame of discernment for automotive troubleshooting is given in Figure 21.1. The root node, *car fault*, can be thought of as standing for the set of faults {*fuel fault, electrical fault*}, while *fuel fault* stands for the fault set {*carburetor fault, fuel lead fault*} and *electrical fault* stands for the fault set {*battery fault, distributor fault*}. Thus *car fault* can be seen to stand for the whole frame of discernment

$$\Theta = \{fuel\ fault,\ electrical\ fault,\ carburetor\ fault,\ fuel\ lead\ fault\}.$$

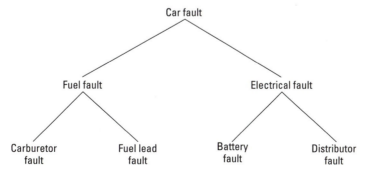

Figure 21.1 A frame of discernment for automotive troubleshooting.

continued

(i) Suppose that the evidence confirms the diagnosis of *carburetor fault* to degree 0.8. Compute m(*fuel lead fault*), m(*electrical fault*), and m(Θ).

(ii) Suppose that the evidence disconfirms *fuel fault* to degree 0.6. Compute m(*electrical fault*).

(iii) Suppose that the evidence confirms *carburetor fault* to degree 0.2 and *fuel lead fault* to degree 0.5. Compute m(*fuel fault*).

2. With reference to Figure 21.1, suppose that evidence confirms *fuel fault* to degree 0.3 and *battery fault* to degree 0.6. Compute *m* values for all nodes in the tree, using Dempster's rule.

3. Again with reference to Figure 21.1, suppose that the prior probabilities of the singleton hypotheses are as follows:

P(*carburetor fault*) = 0.4
P(*fuel lead fault*) = 0.1
P(*battery fault*) = 0.3

Suppose further that we have some evidence, *e*, such that

P(*e* | *carburetor fault*) = 0.3
P(*e* | *carburetor fault*) = 0.5
P(*e* | *fuel lead fault*) = 0.2
P(*e* | ¬*fuel lead fault*) = 0.4
P(*e* | *battery fault*) = 0.6
P(*e* | ¬*battery fault*) = 0.3
P(*e* | *distributor fault*) = 0.7
P(*e* | ¬*distributor fault*) = 0.1

Compute the new belief in each of the singleton hypotheses using Pearl's method of evidential reasoning in a hierarchy.

22 Case-Based Reasoning

We saw in Chapter 2 that early AI programs tended to apply rather uniform problem solving methods, reasoning from a small set of assumptions or axioms, using a relatively small set of rules to generate new problem states which were then evaluated by rules of thumb. The classic domains of game playing and theorem proving are formal systems which lend themselves to this combination of logical analysis and heuristic search. Most expert systems apply a larger number of domain-specific rules, and use less uniform problem solving methods, but the way they perform search and inference under the hood is not so very different from these earlier programs.

For example, a production system works by progressively rewriting the problem state in its working memory so that it more closely resembles a solution state. This step-by-step approach is quite similar to making moves according to the rules of a game, the main difference being that an expert system's rules encode much more than the legal ways to move a knight. A knowledge-based chess program would also encode strategies, simple board patterns, ways of recognizing the shift from middle game to end game, and so on.

However, there are many tasks that humans routinely perform which do not fit this paradigm very well. It is hard to believe that people do logical analysis or heuristic search when selecting a restaurant or a movie for a night on the town. To take less trivial examples, it is also hard to believe that a judge or an architect or a chef functions by reasoning in this way. Even human mathematicians and chess players rarely discover proofs or win games solely by these means. Consequently, one suspects that other styles of reasoning and decision making are at work in many everyday situations.

To state the obvious, human problem solving is hard work and, unlike machines, we get bored and tired, and we like to economize on time and energy. Nevertheless we effortlessly acquire memories and experiences, and we are much better at recognizing solutions than generating them. It would be surprising, therefore, if we did not attempt to solve new problems by reusing solutions to old problems.

But how would this work as a computational model? We know that memories and experiences are not easily reduced to rules, but we can imagine a 'library' of past cases relevant to a given problem, for example, a chef's repertoire of recipes, or a judge's knowledge of past decisions, or an architect's blueprints for different styles of building. However, a library must be indexed in some way, so that we can recognize problems similar to the one at hand, and there must be some machinery for adapting the old solution to the new problem.

This approach is the essence of case-based reasoning (CBR). We explore this new technology with the aid of three examples, drawn from the different domains of cooking, legal reasoning, and report writing. Then we resume our comparison of CBR with more conventional expert systems and suggest that these methods are complementary rather than antagonistic: a thesis that will be exemplified and further propounded in Chapter 23.

22.1 The case base

The 'library' analogy employed above is useful but not perfect. Cases are not books; they have some abstract features in common, but there are important differences.

- A case resembles a (non-fiction) book in that it contains specific content embedded in some context. The content is knowledge, and the context describes some state of the world in which that knowledge could be applied. However, a case embodies that knowledge in a manner that makes it usable by a program. In other words, the knowledge is ready to be 'operationalized,' in the same sense as a production rule is ready to be applied.
- A case should present a solution to a problem in a particular context. It should also describe the resulting state of the world if the solution is adopted. Books sometimes do both of these things, but again not in a manner that enables this information to be manipulated by a program.
- Cases, like books, come in all shapes and sizes, but the granularity of a case is typically much smaller than that of a book. In other words, it is more focused and more specialized. A case is also more terse, being written in a formal language.

Given that a case is a computer-readable module of knowledge, how is it different from some of the other knowledge representations we have hitherto examined? The short answer is that a case is typically implemented as a frame (see Chapter 6) that structures information about the problem, the solution, and the context. Like a frame, or a production rule, it can be pattern-directed, that is, it can be evoked by matching some of its components against goals or data. However, unlike a production rule or a simple frame, selecting a case from a case base involves a different kind of retrieval process and subsequent application of the case involves first adapting it to the current situation. Thus finding a case involves more complex indexing considerations, and using a case involves something more than mere instantiation.

22.1.1 The CHEF program

To illustrate how case-based reasoning works, we shall examine a planning program called CHEF (Hammond, 1986), which creates recipes in the domain of Szechwan cooking. CHEF's input is a list of goals that specify different types, tastes and textures of dishes, and its output is a single recipe that satisfies these constraints. For example, the program might be given the following goals:

> *create a beef dish;*
> *include broccoli;*
> *use stir-fry method;*
> *achieve a crisp texture*

in some formal language, for example:

```
dish(beef), include(broccoli), method(stir-fry), texture(crisp)
```

and its output is a plan (recipe) to make such a meal.

How CHEF achieves this is to look in its case base for a recipe that makes a similar meal and then adapt this recipe to solve the new problem and achieve its goals. So, if it already has a recipe for beef with green beans, it might make a copy of this recipe, and substitute broccoli for green beans. Of course, the problem is not yet solved, because the green beans were boiled, not stir-fried. Stir-frying suggests that the broccoli be chopped up small, instead of being left whole for boiling, so there needs to be a plan modification rule to cover this. Also, stir-frying the beef and the broccoli together will probably make the broccoli soggy, so there needs to be a rule that detects this, and repairs this naive plan, suggesting that the broccoli be fried first and then removed from heat.

Figure 22.1 presents a simplified view of the CBR part of CHEF's architecture, illustrating how the case base interacts with key modules of the program.

The RETRIEVER finds recipes in the case base that best match the current problem specification, which would be input as a goal list, such as the 'beef-and-broccoli' example displayed above. The RETRIEVER module searches for a recipe that satisfies some or all of these goals, and returns a partial match, for example a recipe for stir-fried beef and green beans. Clearly, this module needs to be able to treat the case base as a content-addressable memory, and must have some similarity measure for ranking stored cases with respect to problem specifications.

The MODIFIER then copies and renames the found recipe, and attempts to adapt it to the goals, so that it matches more closely. Substituting broccoli for green beans

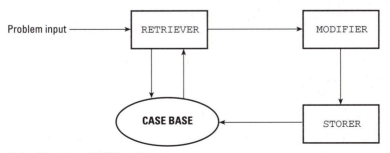

Figure 22.1 A simplified view of CHEF's architecture.

would achieve this in our example, but a seemingly simple fix of this kind can cause problems, for example, broccoli will not remain crisp if cooked like beans. Consequently, the MODIFIER needs access to 'critics' that will spot such problems and suggest fixes.

Finally, the STORER adds the new recipe to the case base for subsequent use.

In CHEF, the repair of a failed plan (proposed recipe) is actually handled by another module which has access to a domain-specific vocabulary of failure description terms and an indexed set of repair strategies to try. There is also a simulator which 'executes' the recipe, looking for problems, such as soggy broccoli. But the basic CBR modules are as outlined above.

22.1.2 Retrieval and adaptation methods

Different case-based reasoners use a variety of different schemes for retrieving cases and adapting them to new problems.

For many programs, such as CHEF, retrieval and adaptation both involve matching goal lists to the problem descriptions associated with a case with the aid of a semantic network (see Chapter 6). In our running example, the RETRIEVER and the MODIFIER know that broccoli and green beans are both green vegetables. The RETRIEVER can therefore use this information in computing the degree of match between problem and case, and the MODIFIER can use it to propose substitutions. Such background knowledge is essential to both tasks.

Index terms tend to be features that strongly determine solutions or distinguish cases from each other. Clearly cases in a case base are competing for the attention of the RETRIEVER, rather as production rules compete for the attention of an interpreter under some conflict resolution strategy. To this end, a case must contain at least some features that both attach to classes of problems and render it distinct from its fellows. Thus CHEF indexes cases with respect to taste, texture, ingredients and method of preparation, since these relate directly to diner preferences and also serve to distinguish one recipe from another. However, the emphasis in CHEF is mostly on similarity with respect to relatively superficial features of a dish.

Matching needs to be done efficiently, as an exhaustive serial search through the cases is only feasible for very small bases. One popular method is to use a *shared feature network*. Cases that share features are clustered together, resulting in a taxonomy of different case types. Matching in a shared-feature network involves a breadth-first, non-backtracking search of this hierarchy which can be conducted in logarithmic time. Individual matches are typically conducted as follows.

Each feature, or *dimension*, is given a weight which codes for how important that feature is. Thus, if cases represent customer accounts, a customer's name is probably not at all important when we are looking to group or retrieve accounts by similarity. Consequently, the name feature might have a weight of 0. The dollar value of the account, on the other hand, might be very significant, and would therefore receive a weight closer to 1.0. Weights are often assigned as real numbers in the range [0, 1].

This leads to the simple algorithm for matching one case against another shown in Figure 22.2. The basic procedure is called *Nearest-Neighbor* matching, because cases that have similar feature values are conceptually 'closer' than those that do not. This

```
Set MATCH = 0.0;
For each feature in the input case
{

    (1) Find the corresponding feature in the stored case.
    (2) Compare the two values and compute the degree of match, m.
    (3) Factor in a coefficient, c, coding for the feature's importance.
    (4) Set MATCH = MATCH + cm.

}
Return MATCH.
```

Figure 22.2 **Nearest-Neighbor matching algorithm.**

may also be reflected in the fact that the cases are closer together in the network, depending upon how the net is implemented.

The value MATCH is usually called the *aggregate match score*. The case selected from the case base will obviously be that with the highest score, and if subsequent cases are needed these will be processed in rank order. Most CBR products on the market use this simple algorithm. The actual method used at step (2) for computing the degree of match between two feature values will depend upon the data type. Qualitative comparisons may result in binary values, or involve computing distance in an abstraction hierarchy. Thus 'broccoli' is closer to 'peas' than it is to 'chicken' in a food hierarchy, and the corresponding values of m should reflect this. Quantitative comparisons will involve scaling.

Having found a case, CBR programs also use different adaptation methods to apply old solutions to new problems. In most instances, adaptations are really performing substitutions on old solution elements, for example exchanging green beans for broccoli, or performing transformations on old solutions, for example changing the order of actions in a plan. Some alternative approaches are outlined below.

- *Reinstantiation.* This involves reinstantiating variables in an existing case with new values, for example, matching the vegetable variable with broccoli instead of green beans.
- *Parameter adjustment.* Some cases may contain numerical values, such as cooking time, which can be adjusted to correct problems, for example, overcooking a vegetable.
- *Memory search.* Search the case base, or other knowledge structures, for anticipated problems, for example, what causes vegetables to turn soggy.

Most of these methods depend on using some form of abstraction hierarchy, whether a frame system or a semantic net, to organize the concepts that can be substituted for each other. This is typically the same net that is used for matching and indexing.

In the next section, we examine a system that requires a rather specialized knowledge representation to model its domain. The fundamental organization of cases is not according to shared features but with respect to higher-level factors derived from the domain by abstraction. This representation demands more sophisticated indexing and search machinery than CHEF's RETRIEVER.

22.2 Computer-aided instruction: the CATO system

We saw in Chapters 11 and 12 that second-generation expert system researchers had been quick to surmise that the knowledge represented inside an expert system might be harnessed for computer-aided instruction (CAI). Given that a successful program could solve problems in some domain, surely such a program could be used to teach students to solve similar problems. Indeed, one of the main criticisms that was leveled at CAI programs in the 1970s was that they did not incorporate modules that were capable of solving the problems that they set students, much less 'debug' a student's faulty work.

However, it turned out that adapting an expert system for instructional purposes was a far more difficult enterprise than one might imagine. The program had to be aware of how it had solved the problem, and why it had chosen to apply various pieces of knowledge at various points in its reasoning in preference to others. Researchers came to realize the importance of teaching a set of *problem solving strategies*, and that these strategies would have to be represented explicitly in the program, and not merely be implicit in the way that the program was written.

This section describes a program called CATO which attempts to teach legal research skills to law students based on an abstract model of the process of argument. It derives in part from a CBR system called HYPO, which evaluates the legal issues associated with a case by comparing and contrasting them with case reports stored in a case knowledge base. We shall see that 'compare and contrast' is a powerful problem solving method of the kind that we have met in earlier chapters, such as 'hypothesize and test' or 'propose and apply.'

22.2.1 The domain of caselaw

The system of US appellate courts hands down approximately 500 new rulings every day. These appear in case reports, which are collected together by jurisdiction in 'reporters' available in bound form, on CD-ROM, and increasingly on the World Wide Web. Appellate-level decisions collectively comprise 'caselaw': a body of law which both interprets legal codes (such as statutes and regulations) and sets precedents to guide subsequent decisions. One part of 'knowing the law' in a particular area, such as products liability or bankruptcy, consists in knowing (or knowing how to find) past cases that are relevant to particular topics in that area.

Another part of knowing the law is knowing how to argue for or against a particular outcome in a specific case. Since a lawyer may be called upon to act on behalf of either side of a dispute, this knowledge must be perfectly general; it must consist of strategies that depend upon whom one is representing and under what circumstances. These circumstances consist largely of the constellation of facts surrounding the case, that is, who did or said exactly what to whom and in what context.

Although it seems unlikely that a computer program could play the role of legal counsel in a court of law, lawyers and paralegals do routinely make use of computer-based search tools to research cases that might be relevant to their current caseload. Finding and interpreting such cases is a non-trivial task that could use more support in the way of an intelligent system than current online services provide. However, our focus here is upon the design of a program to teach the requisite skills, rather than an expert system to perform the actual research task.

22.2.2 Legal research and legal reasoning

Legal research and reasoning are both driven by argumentation, more specifically by *adversarial* argument, in which opposing counsel attempt to convince a judge or jury that their interpretation of both the relevant law and the facts of a case is correct. The lawyer's job is not primarily to determine the truth of the matter (that is the job of the judge or jury), but rather to represent a client's interests in a proceeding. Consequently, there is game-like aspect to conflict in the courtroom, in which opposing sides can be seen to make various moves and counter-moves as they struggle for advantage.

The basic premise behind CATO is that these moves can be systematically described and then taught in a computer-based framework. The moves involve the selection of prior legal cases from a case knowledge base in a manner that is driven by both the facts of the current case and the moves available to opposing counsel. Thus both parties can be viewed as planning in a three-ply game, in which

- one counsel advances a position with one set of cases,
- opposing counsel advances another set of cases to present the other side of the argument, and then
- the original party counters, having anticipated the opposing argument to some degree.

These three moves are usually called a *point*, a *response*, and a *rebuttal*. The moves and counter-moves have a finer structure, however, which can be analyzed in terms of case-based reasoning. Ashley (1990) identifies the following processes underlying such a model of argumentation.

(1) Comparing the current case to a past case with a view to justifying a similar outcome.
(2) Distinguishing the current case from a past case to argue against the same outcome.
(3) Finding counterexamples to (1) in which similar cases led to different outcome.
(4) Posing hypothetical cases to argue for or against a particular position.
(5) Combining a number of comparisons and contrasts into an argument that includes an assessment of the competing arguments.

This model of argument is implemented in the HYPO system, using such CBR processes. HYPO creates an argument in six steps:

(1) *Analyze* the current case for relevant factors.
(2) *Retrieve* cases using these factors.
(3) *Arrange* the retrieved cases with respect to the current case.
(4) *Select* the most relevant cases, both for and against your position.
(5) *Generate* three-ply arguments for each of the issues in a case.
(6) *Test* the resultant analysis on hypothetical cases.

Step (5) is complicated by the fact that a legal case can contain more than one issue, or point of law. Thus a divorce case could contain a variety of financial issues, issues relating to child custody, and so on, each of which has to be argued and decided. In addition to matters of fact and law, there may also be the question of what amount of damages a client is seeking.

22.2.3 CATO as an intelligent teaching system

The stated goal of CATO is to provide beginning law students with an environment in which they can learn how to reason with cases, and also how to test hypotheses about the law (Ashley and Aleven, 1997; Aleven and Ashley, 1997). As we have seen, reasoning with cases involves constructing arguments and anticipating the arguments of an opponent. Similarly, forming and testing hypotheses about the law is an important activity that takes students deeper into caselaw.

The student's task in this environment is to take a legal problem, in the form of a factual history behind a dispute or claim, analyze it, and build arguments on behalf of both the plaintiff (the person who brought the suit) and the defendant (the person answering the suit). These arguments should include a list of the relevant cases from the CATO database that each party can cite to support their cause. CATO's current domain is trade secret law, that is, the law governing the control of confidential and competitive commercial information.

In a typical trade secrets case, the plaintiff's complaint is that the defendant somehow gained access to confidential information and then used it to gain an unfair competitive advantage. The parties to such a case are typically, but not always, companies, and the information is normally technical in nature. In any such case, certain issues commonly occur, such as whether the plaintiff took steps to protect the information from public knowledge, and whether the defendant had agreed not to use the information or disclose it to others.

There is a vocabulary associated with such themes which can be used to analyze a given case. The CATO database contains about 150 cases which are analyzed with respect to a set of factors. Figure 22.3 shows some typical factors, with their associated definitions.

Such factors are used to index cases. The factors are classified according to whether they tend to support the argument of the plaintiff or the defendant. This information, together with knowledge of which side actually won the case, allows for interesting searches over the case base:

- A student can retrieve cases that feature some Boolean combination of factors and then see how many cases containing that factor pattern were won by which side.
- A student can retrieve cases that 'match' (share factors with) the current case and see how they turned out.

CATO's database does not contain the full text of the cases, but rather a 'squib', that is, a short abstract that outlines the salient facts and issues in a case. However, case retrieval is performed via the factors, not via the squibs. Searching by factors, rather than performing a textual search for fact and issue language over the squibs, makes the student's job easier in a number of ways.

Competitive-Advantage. The defendant's access to the plaintiff's secret information gave the defendant a competitive advantage.

Disclose-Secrets. The plaintiff did not voluntarily disclose his secrets to outsiders.

Bribe-Employee. The defendant bribed the plaintiff's employees to switch employment.

Figure 22.3 Sample factors from the trade secrets domain (after Ashley and Rissland, 1988).

- The student does not have to use the 'right' query terms to match the language of the squib.
- The student does not have to read the squib right away in order to understand what role a fact or issue plays in the stored case.

When a case is retrieved, it is presented along with additional information made possible by the factors. Each case sports a list of factors that it contains, together with an indication of whether or not that factor is shared by the current case, or was in the query. Each factor is also marked to show whether it tends to favor the plaintiff or the defendant.

This more complex indexing and retrieval apparatus allows for the modeling of some rather sophisticated reasoning strategies.

If you are a lawyer, then your top-level goal is to justify a favorable decision on this issue. To do so, you will typically make one or more points that play to the strengths of your case, and exhibit cases in which these strengths led to the desired outcome. However, such an approach, unaugmented, does not constitute much of a strategy. The opposing counsel will have their own points to make, with cases to back them up. They will also find weaknesses in your case, for example past cases that had some of the features of your case and in which the decision went the other way. Consequently it may be necessary for you to discuss the weaknesses in your case, perhaps anticipating the arguments of opposing counsel, and thereby taking some of the wind from their sails. One way that you can do this is to find cases that had an outcome favorable to your side in spite of these weaknesses.

Thus, depending upon the situation, you may wish to argue that two cases are similar, or you may wish to distinguish two cases. Of course, most cases are similar to some extent, if viewed at a sufficiently high level of generality, in that they are all based on a grievance, involve opposing parties, and seek some form of redress. On the other hand, all cases are unique, in that the pattern of facts and circumstances in a given case is rarely repeated elsewhere. Also, as noted above, a case may involve more than one issue. Two cases may resemble each other on one issue, for example, the type of crime, but differ on another issue, for example the mode of arrest.

So a large part of arguing about similarities and differences involves choosing a particular level of abstraction. In so doing, you are selecting a particular interpretation of the issues in current case with respect to the earlier case. To argue for similarity, you must select factors that the two cases have in common and characterize them as significant at the chosen level of abstraction, while downplaying contrasting factors which the cases don't share. To distinguish the current case from the earlier case, you must find factors that differentiate the two cases.

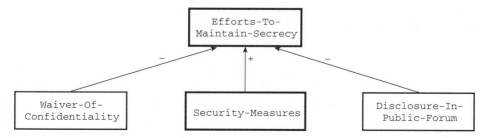

Figure 22.4 **Fragment of CATO's factor hierarchy (adapted from Ashley and Aleven, 1997).**

This kind of reasoning requires more than a conventional semantic net. In addition to labeling each factor in the hierarchy as to whether it supports the plaintiff or the defendant, relations between factors must be explicitly represented. This is best illustrated by an example.

Figure 22.4 shows a small fragment of the factor hierarchy for CATO's trade secrets domain. The top node of the fragment, Efforts-To-Maintain-Secrecy, stands for the factor whereby the plaintiff who is alleging a violation maintains that efforts were made to guard the trade secret to preserve competitive advantage. (A dark border indicates a factor that supports the plaintiff.)

There are subfactors that support such a claim, for example the fact that certain security measures were taken to prevent the secret from becoming public knowledge, and these clearly support the plaintiff's position. (As a result, they are marked with plus signs, because they support their parent node.) However, there are also subfactors that can mitigate such a claim, for example if the plaintiff at some point signed a waiver of confidentiality, or if the plaintiff allowed an employee to disclose the secret in a public forum, such as a technical conference. These factors detract from the position established by their parent node, and are therefore marked with minus signs.

Such subfactors may themselves have subfactors with positive or negative links, and these connections are also divided into strong and weak links. CATO can then use a number of algorithms to decide at what level of abstraction in the hierarchy an argument should be focused, depending upon whether we want to emphasize or downplay a distinction. The details of these algorithms are beyond the scope of this text, but the point is that they require a highly domain-specific, knowledge-based indexing scheme.

HYPO and CATO use another data structure called a *claim lattice* to organize retrieved cases with respect to their similarities and differences. This lattice is a hierarchical structure with the current issue at its root and with retrieved cases arranged by relevance below the root, so that the most relevant cases are closest to the root. Nodes in the lattice are labeled by factors, such as Competitive-Advantage and Agreed-Not-To-Disclose. The structure is called a claim lattice because each such lattice addresses a particular claim associated with the current case. Most cases involve more than one claim, and so a case would typically need more than one lattice in order to represent them all. Once again, we see a highly specialized knowledge representation being used to support a particular kind of inference.

In the next section, we examine another program, which shows how a CBR module can be integrated into a larger AI system that also performs a complex reasoning task.

22.3 Case-based report generation in FRANK

A writer can have any number of different goals in writing a report, for example, attempting an even-handed survey, arguing for a particular outcome, or presenting a justification for a decision that has already been taken. These goals will have a marked effect upon the information-gathering and presentation strategies of the writer. For example, a scientist writing a survey for a scientific journal is obliged to sample widely among opposing views, while a defense lawyer is obliged to present only those cases which further his or her client's interest.

The FRANK system (Rissland *et al.*, 1993) is a blackboard system that integrates case-based and rule-based reasoning paradigms to generate medical diagnostic reports. (FRANK is a failed acronym for Flexible Report and Analysis System.) The main emphasis is upon the interaction between writers' high-level goals and their information subgoals, such as retrieving relevant cases.

22.3.1 Components of FRANK

FRANK's architecture (Figure 22.5) consists of three components:

- a Planner that provides control by selecting a skeletal plan from a plan library and then doing the hierarchical planning needed to instantiate it;
- a CBR module and a production system module (actually OPS5) which perform domain reasoning, in conjunction with other knowledge sources; and
- a Report Generator which has various strategies for generating reports for the user, based on rhetorical knowledge.

Much of the knowledge in FRANK is contained in three hierarchies:

- a Report Hierarchy that classifies reports according to their overall goals, for example whether they are argumentative or summarizing, whether they adopt a particular position or attempt a neutral stance;
- a Problem Solving Strategies Hierarchy that represents knowledge about how to gather information for a particular kind of report, for example how to find relevant data and deal with data that supports contrary conclusions;
- a Presentation Strategies Hierarchy that guides the system in how to lay out the conclusions of a report, for example putting forward a strong argument first, or examining the strengths and weaknesses of alternatives.

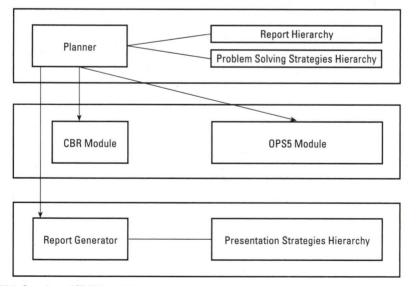

Figure 22.5 **Overview of FRANK architecture.**

The coordination of these various modules and knowledge sources requires a fairly sophisticated control regime, hence the choice of a blackboard architecture as outlined in the next section.

22.3.2 FRANK's blackboard system

The flow of control in FRANK can be summarized in terms of a series of processing steps in which knowledge sources (KSs) manipulate data on a blackboard (see Chapter 18). Rather than describe each of the knowledge sources in turn, we provide an overview of the main steps by which a problem posed to the system results in plan selection and execution. An input problem for FRANK takes the form of an issue, such as whether or not a certain medical procedure is justified in a particular case, while the output solution is a report that addresses this issue according to whatever preferences the user may have specified in advance, for example, a preference for an argumentative report that justifies the procedure.

- An initial KS draws any quick, credible inferences that it can from the input and creates a skeletal report that contains pointers to the various pieces of context that the problem solver will need as its processing proceeds.
- Various KSs then look up the strategies associated with the specified report type and use them to choose a plan from the plan library. (The plan having the greatest number of strategies in common with the report type is the one selected.)
- A KS then instantiates the plan and executes it by activating its top-level goal. After goal–subgoal generation, lower-level goals are satisfied by one of the reasoning components. These goals typically fill slots in the report template.
- Another KS then evaluates the resultant report to see if it is coherent. If so, it is output using the appropriate presentation strategies, otherwise a change of plan or report type may be indicated.

Thus, the system will first select a medical report type based on user input, either using the default problem solving strategies associated with that type, or else using strategies specified in the input. The input might state that the user wants a 'pro position' report to justify a particular diagnosis. FRANK might then select the report type *Diagnosis-with-Alternatives*, and use its default strategy of 'equitable comparison.'

22.3.3 The CBR module of FRANK

Thus the combination of report type and strategy outlined above lead to the selection of a particular plan, which sets out to find cases relevant to the current diagnosis. A case might be deemed most relevant if it shares a greater number of overlapping symptoms with the current problem than other cases in the database. Or, if the strategy is less equitable, a case might be deemed relevant only if it supports the current diagnosis and no other diagnosis.

For example, a more argumentative strategy might require that a case be deemed relevant only if:

(1) it overlaps with the current problem;
(2) it advocates the same diagnosis; and

(3) it does not share any properties with other relevant cases that indicate another diagnosis.

But what happens if no such cases can be found? Then the above criteria must be relaxed, say by deleting (3), and the search must be run anew. In any event, the system must use knowledge to recover from this failure.

Queries to the case base are controlled by a knowledge source that serves as a task scheduling mechanism. Such queries may be partial, and may therefore need to be completed using default values. This module also has a number of behaviors for dealing with search failure.

Faced with an unsuccessful query, the knowledge source may vary these values within permitted bounds and resubmit. It may manipulate parameters which allow near-misses to be returned, or cases that only partly overlap with the current problem. Or it may weaken the definition of what constitutes a relevant case, as outlined above.

FRANK also supports two CBR methodologies:

- a nearest-neighbor style based on *lower-level features*, as in CHEF; and
- a lattice of cases grouped by similarity according to a set of *higher-level factors*, as in CATO.

Thus it may also select what appears to be the best CBR methodology or matching criteria for retrieving cases depending upon the context. For example, lower-level features of the input case, such as age and sex of patient, may be less important than higher-level factors used to classify medical procedures. Alternatively, no such factors may usefully apply to a particular problem, in which case low-level features are the only option.

This kind of flexibility in the choice of methodology allows a symmetry in the way that high-level goals and lower-level results are allowed to influence each other, in that

- the current context can govern lower-level strategies for retrieving and assembling information, and
- the (negative) results of these strategies can affect the current plan or task orientation.

It is hard to see how this level of sophistication could be achieved in a non-hybrid system, such as a monolithic production system. The use of meta-rules, as in MYCIN, allows a limited selection of reasoning strategies, but has no way to respond to feedback in the form of unsatisfactory results. Without some mechanism for recognizing success, partial success, or failure, the system has no way of knowing how well it is doing or whether a change in strategy is called for. Having a blackboard architecture drive a CBR or a production rule system introduces another stratum of control which allows for this kind of meta-level reasoning. The complexity of this kind of architecture is rendered tractable only by the extreme modularity of the design and the relatively declarative nature of the knowledge encoded in knowledge sources.

22.4 Comparing case-based and rule-based systems

There are certain superficial similarities between the case-based and rule-based approaches to reasoning. Both cases and rules have to be indexed for subsequent retrieval. Both are selected on the basis of matching, and this selection and ranking process may be assisted by background knowledge stored in auxiliary structures, such as frames (for example, MYCIN's knowledge tables).

However, the differences are more interesting, as have been summarized by Kolodner (1993) along the following lines.

- Rules in a rule base are patterns, whereas cases in a case base are constants. Clearly, rules contain variables; they do not describe solutions directly.
- A rule is selected on the basis of an exact match between data in working memory and its antecedent. A case is retrieved on the basis of a partial match, facilitated by knowledge about its features.
- Rules are applied in an iterative cycle; a series of steps towards a solution. Cases can be viewed as approximations to an entire solution, although it is also possible to draw analogies to different cases iteratively to solve different parts of a problem.

So there is a sense in which CBR supports yet another problem solving strategy, call it 'retrieve and adapt,' which is distinguishable from heuristic classification, 'propose and revise,' and all the rest, as described in Chapters 11–15. There is something very intuitive about this approach, in that it seems more tailored to everyday human problem solving than strategies that start from scratch. The relative ease with which humans are reminded of past events and their outcomes is in sharp contrast with the effort involved in actual ratiocination upon almost any topic.

However, there are a number of cautionary remarks that should be made, lest we believe that we can dispense with the hard work of reasoning from first principles. In compiling a case base, it is tempting to think that one can sidestep all of the knowledge engineering difficulties associated with building a rule base, since one is merely accumulating experiences. Arguably, this is not the case, because of the following considerations.

Veracity. Human memory is notoriously influenced by emotional and motivational factors; people tend to remember their past endeavors as being successful, regardless of whether they actually were or not. This tendency can lead to a rather unreliable case base of cozy memories based on wishes rather than reality.

Consistency. Although a case base does not have to be consistent to the degree that a rule base should be, there must still be mechanisms in place to resolve conflicts among cases. These mechanisms are as yet less sophisticated than those associated with rule-based systems.

Scale. The problem of how to reason with very large numbers of cases has yet to be satisfactorily addressed. Most systems in the literature deal with tens of cases, rather than hundreds or thousands.

But we expect to see CBR featured in many future systems, both as the main paradigm, as in CHEF, and as a module of a hybrid system, as in FRANK. CBR is certainly one way for a program to accumulate experience as it encounters more and more problems, and it will be interesting to see how researchers and engineers take advantage of this technology. In the next chapter, we focus on three more hybrid systems, each of which has a learning component, and discuss the problems and promise of multiple paradigm systems generally.

BIBLIOGRAPHICAL NOTES

The single best text on case-based reasoning is Kolodner (1993). Shorter review articles include Slade (1991), Harmon (1992), Kolodner (1992), and Watson and Marir (1994). For a review of CBR tools, see Harmon and Hall (1993).

The single most popular application of CBR in the 1990s has been customer support. In this scenario, support agents use a case-based expert system to retrieve information about products and problems. See, for example, Acorn and Walden (1992), Allen (1994), Nguyen *et al.* (1993), Hislop and Pracht (1994) and Borron *et al.* (1996) for recent papers on this topic.

STUDY SUGGESTIONS

1. What is a case library, and how does a case differ from a book?

2. What are the main differences between case-based reasoning and rule-based reasoning?

3. What is the relationship between cases and frames? How could frame concepts be applied to a case library?

4. Suppose that you have bought a lobster, and wish to create a lobster dish for yourself and a friend. Your case library of lobster dishes consists of records of the following form.

Feature	Weight
Name	0.0
Primary sauce	0.9
Spices	0.7
Alcoholic content	0.5

The weights indicate the relative importance of listed features, such as sauce, spice and alcohol content, as a feature of the recipe.

For example, one might represent the dish 'Lobster in Cream' by the following record.

Feature	Value
Name	Lobster in Cream
Primary sauce	Cream
Primary spice	Paprika
Alcoholic content	Sherry

continued

(i) How might the nearest-neighbor algorithm compute a match between the 'Lobster in Cream' recipe and the following recipe for 'Lobster Au Gratin'?

Feature	Value
Name	Lobster au Gratin
Primary sauce	Cream
Primary spice	Paprika
Alcoholic content	Cognac

(ii) Is 'Lobster in Cream' more similar to 'Lobster au Gratin' than 'Lobster Franco-American' or vice versa?

Feature	Value
Name	Lobster Franco-American
Primary sauce	Meat glaze
Primary spice	Pimiento
Alcoholic content	Sherry

(iii) Consider how one might perform more sophisticated matching between recipes, given that

- dishes can have more than one sauce, for example 'Lobster au Gratin' actually has a Hollandaise sauce as well as cream;
- dishes can contain more than one alcohol additive, for example 'Lobster au Gratin' contains both white wine and cognac;
- some spices, sauces and alcohols are more similar than others, for example paprika is closer to curry than it is to oregano, while sherry can be substituted for Madeira, but not cognac.

What implications would these considerations have for nearest-neighbor matching?

5. Consider the following factors for deciding whether or not a person was justified under Penal Law Article 35 in using 'deadly force' to defend themselves against attack.
   Such conduct is deemed justifiable when

   - used as an emergency measure to avoid injury imminent due to no fault of the actor;
   - the actor cannot retreat or otherwise avoid the necessity of using force;
   - the actor perceives that the other person is committing or attempting to commit kidnapping, rape or robbery.

   Such conduct is not deemed justifiable when

continued

- the actor was the initial aggressor;
- the physical force was applied in a combat not authorized by law, for example a duel;
- the actor could have retreated or otherwise escaped the threat upon their person.

However, there are complicating factors, for example:

- a person is not obliged to retreat when in his or her home;
- deadly force is not permitted in response to threats or damage to property only;
- deadly force is not permitted if it is out of proportion to the danger or threat.

Organize these factors into a HYPO-style factor hierarchy (see Figure 22.4) in which the top node is **Justified-Use of-Deadly Force**. Assume that the user of deadly force is the defendant. How should these various factors be arranged in order to demonstrate how they impinge upon each other? Indicate whether a factor favors the defense or the prosecution.

23 Hybrid Systems

We are already familiar with the idea that an expert system may contain more than one representation of knowledge. Even early programs such as MYCIN (see Chapter 3) stored domain-specific information in more than one form, for example, diagnostic production rules and tables of medical parameters. Similarly, programs like CENTAUR (see Chapter 13) were hybrids in the sense that they integrated different knowledge representations and then put that knowledge to more than one use, for example, both for problem solving and for generating explanations.

Later research vehicles, such as XPLAIN (see Chapter 16), had more sophisticated architectures that attempted to incorporate a variety of software tools and modules to aid in the development and maintenance of an expert system. Such programs move somewhat further away from the notion of a simple shell which supports a particular programming paradigm. Meanwhile blackboard systems (see Chapter 18), like HEARSAY and BB*, combine multiple knowledge sources, which can have widely differing internal structures.

The systems that we shall examine in this chapter go even further down this road in that they combine a traditional problem solving program with a learning or critiquing component. The ODYSSEUS system (Wilkins, 1990) learns how to refine a knowledge base using two different methods: case-based learning and explanation-based learning. These are both relatively recent machine learning methods, and we provide an introduction to each of them here. Next we describe a program which uses case-based reasoning to handle exceptions to rules in a rule based system and has the potential to learn new rules (Golding and Rosenbloom, 1991). Finally, we examine an information retrieval system called SCALIR (Rose, 1994) which combines more conventional symbolic methods with a connectionist approach.

Although these systems are research vehicles rather than commercially available products, we review them here because we believe they are indicative of things to come, and they serve to illustrate the increasing sophistication of expert system architectures which combine specialized methods for learning and reasoning in a nontrivial way.

23.1 Learning methods in ODYSSEUS

Methods such as version spaces and ID3 are sometimes characterized as *similarity-based* learning methods. This is because they perform induction by searching through sets of features that the training instances all share, in order to decide which of them are relevant to the task of concept attainment. They are typically data-intensive, requiring a large number of positive (and sometimes negative) examples for the defining properties of the general concept to emerge.

Explanation-based learning (EBL) can be mostly clearly contrasted with such methods by saying that it is typically used to generalize from a *single* training instance. It is able to do this because it uses domain-specific knowledge to guide the generalization process. This is quite different from ID3's approach, where the algorithm requires nothing more than attribute–value information about the training examples, together with an indication of whether they are positive or negative instances. Another way of looking at this is to say that EBL is *analytic* and *deductive*, rather than *empirical* or *inductive* (Bergadano and Gunetti, 1996). In other words, it infers a new concept description by examining a fresh instance in the light of background knowledge. This is quite different from a situation in which you examine a large number of examples and then use clever domain-free heuristics to figure out which properties of these objects are relevant.

Case-based reasoning (CBR) formed the main subject matter of Chapter 22, where we saw that new problems could sometimes be solved by adapting old solutions to similar problems. Case-based reasoning forms the basis of a learning method, because once one has adapted an old solution to a new problem, one has a new case to add to the case base for future use. Thus, a program with a case base learned from experience should become more efficient at solving problems.

In the next two sections, we examine explanation-based generalization in some detail, and examine CBR more closely as a basis for machine learning.

23.1.1 EBG as abstraction

Explanation-based generalization (EBG) is an abstraction over individual EBL methods (Mitchell *et al.*, 1986). Succinctly put, it is a domain-independent method for using domain-specific knowledge to guide the process of generalization from a single example. As such, it rather resembles some of the 'abstract architectures' we have seen elsewhere, which embody an implicit methodology for applying knowledge from whatever domain is currently the subject of an expert systems application.

The EBG method requires the following inputs:

- a (positive) training example;
- a domain theory;
- a definition of the concept to be learned.

The language of logic programming is usually employed to formalize these ideas (see Chapter 8). Thus a concept is typically a *predicate* which characterizes some subset of the universe of objects we are interested in. For example, the predicate cup(X) could stand for the concept of 'cuphood,' defined as being a small, stable, open vessel in the PROLOG style. Recall that

$$\alpha :\!- \beta.$$

can be read as 'α is true if β is true.'

```
cup(X)  :- small(X), stable(X), open(X).
```

Domain knowledge might include under what conditions an object can be said to be stable, for example by having a flat bottom, and what it means to be open, for example by being concave in shape and having the concavity point upwards in the frame of reference.

Given a training instance which is a few inches in diameter, flat-bottomed, concave-topped object, we recognize it as an instance of cuphood by constructing an explanation, that is, by showing that it has sufficiently cup-like properties. An instance is usually described by some number of *ground literals*, for example:

```
color(red, obj).
diameter(4, obj).
flat(bottom, obj).
concave(top, obj).
```

would denote a particular red object, obj, four inches in diameter, with a flat bottom and a concave top. The domain knowledge given below enables us to recognize the example as an instance of the concept:

```
small(X)  :- diameter(Y, X), Y < 5.
stable(X)  :- flat(bottom, X).
open(X)  :- concave(top, X).
```

Note that the fact that obj is a cup also follows logically from this body of knowledge. Thus, our explanation of why obj is a cup is actually a *proof*. This concludes the *explanation* phase of EBG.

What follows is a *generalization* phase, in which we work out a set of sufficient conditions under which the explanation holds. Without going into technical details (which involve unification – see Chapter 8), what we want to do is determine the weakest conditions under which we can use the domain knowledge to infer that obj is a cup. The resulting concept generalization is that a flat-bottomed, concave-topped object with a diameter less than 5 is a cup:

```
cup(X)  :- flat(bottom, X), concave(top, X), diameter(Y, X), Y < 5.
```

Note that this generalization follows logically from the original definition of cuphood that we were given, plus the background knowledge about smallness, stability and openness. In a sense, the new generalization was implicit in our prior knowledge; seeing the single training example allowed us to make the generalization explicit. Note also that, since we already have a general-purpose definition of cuphood, we can safely ignore irrelevant features (such as color) which an inductive concept learner would have to consider.

23.1.2 Case-based learning

Case-based learning (CBL) is in sharp contrast to EBG's approach to learning, which can be explained and justified in terms of a proof. As we saw in Chapter 22, the case-based approach to retrieval is based upon an argument from similarity, rather than a logical argument. It is also true to say that the process by which an old case is adapted to generate a new solution is not one that involves generalization in the logic programming sense. An abstraction hierarchy, such as a semantic net, may be used as an adjunct to provide knowledge about relations between domain entities. However, the output is *not* a new rule containing variables, but rather a new case, derived from the old case by substituting constants.

CBR is much more like reasoning by analogy than logical reasoning. If one concludes that John, a Porsche owner, is a dangerous driver because a previous case, Jack, a Ferrari owner, is a dangerous driver, then you are arguing that John is like Jack because a Porsche is like a Ferrari. Now one can argue that each case implicitly generates a rule when it is analogized in this way. To pursue our example, the general rule might be that people who drive sports cars are dangerous drivers. But there is a sense in which case-based reasoning defers the process of deciding what the rule actually is. Are all sports car owners dangerous, or is it just male sports car owners, or young male sports car owners? A CBR program does not have to decide this in order to use the old case as a basis for a solution. It simply has to find the most similar case to the current problem.

CBL and EBG do share some features. They can both be contrasted with the inductive methods of Chapter 20, in that neither method involves looking for regularities in large amounts of data. As we have seen, EBG can learn from a single example, while a case base need only contain one relevant case to generate a good analogy.

However, learning is more than just accumulation. A case-based reasoner should be able to detect and recover from instances where it fails to find a genuine solution to some problem. Otherwise, it will happily accumulate new cases with erroneous solutions, in much the same manner as people who never learn their own limitations.

The CHEF program described in Chapter 22 is often able to detect when it has generated a bad recipe, and will try to repair it. To do this, it must be able to *explain* why the recipe is no good. This requires domain knowledge, of course, in the form of causal rules.

For example, the RETRIEVER and MODIFIER modules might produce a recipe that suggests marinading shrimp and then shelling them afterwards. But then the shrimp will be too slippery to handle, and the precondition 'shell the shrimp' will fail when the program attempts to simulate the recipe. Another module, the REPAIRER, uses knowledge of failure types and indexed repair strategies to reorder the steps of the recipe, so that the shrimp are shelled first.[1]

Even if a new case is solved, it may not be indexed properly unless the program understands why the solution was successful. If a user wants a light, low-fat dish, and a recipe program comes up with something suitable by chance manipulation of an old case, then the resultant case will not be readily available for future use unless the

---

[1] The problem of debugging faulty plans is well known in AI, and work in this area dates back at least to Sacerdoti (1974) and Sussman (1975).

properties 'light' and 'low-fat' are associated with it. As Kolodner (1994) points out: 'Cases that are accumulated are only as good as the indexes associated with them.'

23.2 The ODYSSEUS and MINERVA systems

ODYSSEUS is an 'apprenticeship' program, which learns how to improve the knowledge base of an expert system for heuristic classification problems (see Chapters 11 and 12). It observes an expert solving a problem and constructs an explanation for each of the expert's actions (such as asking for the value of some attribute) based on its knowledge of the domain and the underlying problem solving strategy. When the program fails to construct such an explanation, it initiates a process of knowledge base repair.

23.2.1 The MINERVA expert system shell

MINERVA is the expert system shell derived from EMYCIN and NEOMYCIN (see Chapters 10–12) which provides the knowledge base and problem solving method for ODYSSEUS, and it was specifically designed to support EBL. One of the differences between MINERVA and EMYCIN is that MINERVA represents more than just domain knowledge; it also represents strategic knowledge which is meant to mirror the problem solving strategies of a human physician. This can be looked upon as a further development of the use of meta-rules in MYCIN, EMYCIN and NEOMYCIN.

The main knowledge base used in this work is a medical one for the diagnosis of meningitis and other neurological diseases. MINERVA is implemented in PROLOG, so it is convenient to represent domain knowledge by Horn clauses (see Chapter 8), but otherwise the rules are similar in content to the productions we saw in the MYCIN expert system. For example, the following clause encodes the fact that photophobia is suggestive of a migraine headache.

```
conclude(migraine-headache, yes) :- finding(photophobia, yes).
```

Problem state knowledge is recorded in fact clauses during an expert system run, for example

```
rule-applied(rule163).
```

would state that Rule 163 has been applied during execution, and this information is available to the program as it continues to run. Alternatively, a simple clause such as

```
differential(migraine-headache, tension-headache).
```

would record the fact that migraine headache and tension headache are the program's current hypotheses regarding the patient's disorder.

Clearly such information could be represented and recorded in any number of ways behind the scenes, for example, by setting variables or flags, but representing it in the same way as domain knowledge brings substantial benefits. Because it is represented explicitly, it can now be reasoned about using the same sophisticated mechanisms as apply to domain knowledge.

An example of a simple meta-rule might be the following:

```
goal(findout(P)) :- not(concluded(P)), ask-user(P).
```

which simply states that if it is a current system goal to find the value of the parameter P, and the system cannot conclude P from what it already knows, then it can ask the user for the value. P is a variable, so that the head of the clause

```
goal(findout(P))
```

can match (that is, unify with) an explicit system goal, such as

```
goal(findout(temperature)).
```

and a subgoal like

```
not(concluded(P))
```

could match (or fail to find) a system datum describing the current state of the computation, such as

```
concluded(temperature).
```

Thus strategic knowledge can be used to reason about the current state of the problem and decide what domain knowledge is known or relevant at a particular point in the problem solving process. Additionally, it then becomes easier to build a learning program that can access the knowledge structures used by the meta-level reasoning facility of the expert system, as we shall see. MINERVA contains other refinements over a standard expert system shell; for example, it uses a blackboard scheduler instead of a fixed EMYCIN-like goal tree in deciding what is the next reasoning task to perform. It also supports both certainty factors (described in Chapter 9) and belief networks (described in Chapter 21). However, we are less interested in the details of MINERVA here than the way in which a more sophisticated shell can support a kind of machine learning in an expert system context.

23.2.2 Learning in ODYSSEUS

The kind of learning that ODYSSEUS exhibits is somewhat different from that described in Chapter 20. The system is designed to extend an existing knowledge base that is incomplete, rather than inducing some new concept from large amounts of training data. It learns by watching a human expert solve a problem, rather as a real apprentice would, and employs explanation-based generalization.

The principal problem solving activity involved in an diagnostic session is finding out values for various variables, that is, properties of the person or object under diagnosis, such as a patient's temperature or the demise of a device component. In ODYSSEUS terminology, these are called *findout* questions. The program extends its knowledge base as a by-product of understanding why such questions are asked.

Thus the concept of learning in ODYSSEUS is closely linked with that of constructing an explanation. In fact, explanation has a rather specialized meaning in the context of ODYSSEUS, one which differs from both the everyday meaning of the word and the expert system meaning, where we speak of a program justifying its solution.

An *explanation* in ODYSSEUS is a kind of proof, just as it is EBG. It is a proof that demonstrates why the human expert asked a particular question at a particular time during a diagnosis. The question is related to both the current state of the problem and the underlying strategy that the expert is using, so understanding why the question was asked involves inferring that strategy.

If the program's knowledge is complete, then it ought to be able to derive the question (or rather the proposition underlying it) as a logical consequence of the current problem state, the strategic knowledge embodied in meta-rules, the domain knowledge, and one of the current high-level goals.

For example, chaining backward from a question like

```
askuser(temperature).
```

would lead us to the immediate goal

```
goal(findout(temperature)).
```

However, this goal was itself generated by a higher-level goal, such as applying a particular rule or testing a hypothesis in the differential. The presence of this higher goal in the current state of the computation explains why the lower-level goal was generated and hence why the question was asked, given that the system did not already know the answer. This reasoning back from subgoals to goals is accomplished by backward chaining in the usual PROLOG, or even MYCIN, style – but note that this is reasoning at the *meta-level*, that is, reasoning about how the program solves problems, rather than reasoning about the problems themselves.

If we look at ODYSSEUS's apprenticeship learning strategy in more detail, we see that it breaks down into three phases:

- *Detect a deficiency in the knowledge base.* Such deficiencies are suggested by the failure to construct an explanation for one of the expert's actions using the backward chaining method described above. Failures of this kind represent an opportunity for learning.
- *Propose a knowledge base repair.* The failed proof suggests that a piece of domain or problem-state knowledge is missing from the knowledge base. If domain knowledge is missing, we can temporarily add an appropriate clause and see if the proof succeeds. If problem-state knowledge is missing, the program must look for a different proof.
- *Validate the knowledge base repair.* The method used to evaluate a repair is called the 'confirmation decision procedure' method. Briefly, this requires the designer of the system to construct a procedure that will evaluate new MINERVA rules, for example, by determining how many competing hypotheses could be eliminated by the knowledge gained from applying the rule.

The details of how these phases are implemented is beyond the scope of this discussion, but the basic principles are relatively straightforward. Apprenticeship learning using explanation-based generalization can be distinguished from other kinds of machine learning in that it occurs during an actual problem solving session. A training instance is now a single attribute–value pair, although many training instances may arise during a session, as the program tries to explain why each training instance it encounters is significant. When it fails to do so, it attempts to modify its knowledge base in such a way that it can then show why the attribute–value pair is important in the current context.

ODYSSEUS also employs a primitive form of *case-based learning* to modify rules or add rules to the knowledge base in the following way. It has a library of cases, together with their correct diagnoses, that it can use for test purposes. When a case is misdiagnosed, a kind of credit and blame assignment takes place with respect to the rules that were, or could have been, employed in producing the diagnosis.

The premises of those rules which drew the wrong conclusions are weakened by specialization, that is, their scope of applicability is made narrower, while the premises of rules which were key to the correct diagnosis are strengthened, rather as in the Meta-DENDRAL system described in Chapter 20. This form of rule modification is not guaranteed to solve the problem, however, and so it may be necessary to induce new rules from the case library in various ways. The rule modifications and any new rules derived are subject to the same test procedures as employed in the apprenticeship learning part of the program.

23.3 Using cases to handle exceptions

In this section, we explore an architecture for combining rules and cases in a more convincing manner than ODYSSEUS. Rather than using cases to modify rules, their role is to supplement the knowledge in the rule base, mostly by handling exceptions. This allows rules to do what they are good at, capturing domain generalizations, while letting cases do what they are good at, namely particularizing individual pockets of the domain.

Building a rule set is a non-trivial enterprise, as we have seen in earlier parts of this book, for example, Chapters 10–15. In addition to the difficulty of acquiring knowledge and representing it, there are problems of how to ensure rule quality and rule base coverage. Ideally, a rule base should be complete, consistent (at least with respect to the conflict resolution strategy), and correct. But this lofty goal becomes harder to attain as the rule set grows and many incremental additions and changes are made to it, perhaps by multiple people.

Individual rules can be greatly complicated by trying to handle every exception. It is a cliché that every rule admits of an exception,[2] and attempting to qualify rules to capture these irregularities can lead to large numbers of rule conditions that make the rules harder to understand and slower to execute. Similarly, adding extra rules to capture domain minutiae may not be the best way to handle the problem. Rules, by their very nature, are general. They are meant to capture regularities rather than peculiarities.

Golding and Rosenbloom (1996) present a new architecture which combines rule-based reasoning (RBR) with CBR to solve this problem. The idea is that CBR is used as a critic of RBR, by looking for analogies between the current case and a case in the case library that seems to be an exception to the rule. This approach requires that cases by indexed with respect to rules that they might impact, and that there be some similarity metric that says how good the analogies are (see Figure 23.1).

The basic idea is very simple and elegant. First apply rules to a problem to generate a solution, then check a case base to see if there is a known exception that applies in this case. Thus the algorithm can be sketched as in Figure 23.2. Note that rule- and case-based reasoning may be interleaved at each new cycle. (If no applicable rules or cases are found, the program will halt.)

---

[2] Including this very rule; it is its own exception.

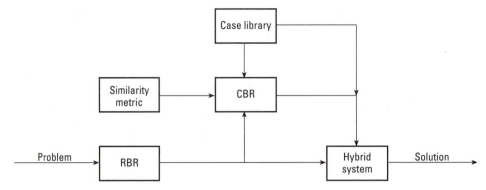

Figure 23.1 Architecture for combining CBR and rule-based reasoning (RBR).

For this to work, cases must be indexed with respect to the rules that they contradict. Thus an insurance rule to the effect that

'Males under 25 pay high motor vehicle insurance premiums'

might have an associated case in the database where an 18-year-old male who had completed an advanced driving test was offered a reduced rate.

How do we decide whether or not a case is compelling? Golding's solution is as follows. When we draw an analogy between an old case and the current case, there is an implicit rule lurking in the background. Suppose, in our simple example above, the current case is a 20-year-old male driver with an advanced driving qualification, and we discover the analogous case of the 18-year-old. The implicit rule generated by this analogy would be:

'Males under 25 with an advanced driving course pay a reduced rate.'

We assume that the similarity metric for retrieving cases splits ages into ranges, such as 'under 25,' 'over 25 and under 65,' and 'over 65.' This metric will have rated the two cases as being highly similar, given the agreement with respect to sex and age.

We can test this rule on the rest of the case base, and score it with respect to the percentage of cases that it covers. Any male under 25 with an advanced course who paid a high premium would count as an exception to this case, thereby lowering its score. If the cases are similar enough, and the rule is accurate enough, then the analogy is deemed to be compelling, and the CBR component 'wins.' Otherwise, RBR 'wins' and the proposed rule application goes ahead.

```
UNTIL problem is solved
{
    (1) Use the rules to select the next operation to perform.
    (2) Search the case base for compelling cases that would contradict that choice of operation.
    (3) If such a case is found, apply the operation associated with the case, else apply the operation
        associated with the rule.
}
```

Figure 23.2 Basic algorithm for combining rules and cases.

'Compellingness' is therefore a function of the following three things:

- the *similarity* between the two cases, which must exceed a certain threshold;
- the *accuracy* of the implicit rule proposed by the analogy, in terms of what proportion of those extant cases to which it could apply are in fact correctly determined by it; and
- the *significance* of this accuracy score, given the sample size, given by one minus the probability of obtaining such a score by chance.

The authors demonstrate this architecture in the context of a name pronunciation task. The system contains about 650 linguistic rules and about 5000 cases. They show that by combining rules and cases, they get better performance than with either rules or cases alone. They also show that their name pronunciation program, called Ana-pron, performs at least as well as commercial systems designed for this task. However, our interest here is in the result which shows that CBR and RBR can be profitably combined to form a high performance hybrid system.

23.4 Hybrid symbolic and connectionist approaches

In this section, we examine an alternative to symbolic knowledge representation, called *connectionism*, which constitutes a radically different model of computation from that which we normally associate with expert systems. After comparing and contrasting the two approaches, we shall see how they can be combined to form an interesting hybrid that attempts to capitalize on their respective strengths and compensate for their weaknesses. In so doing, we shall concentrate on a particular system, called SCALIR (Rose, 1994), which stands for Symbolic and Connectionist Approach to Legal Information Retrieval.

SCALIR is a system that acts as an aide to an online researcher attempting to find legal documents, such as cases or statutes, relevant to his or her current concerns. Since legal issues cover almost every sphere of human activity, a purely knowledge-based approach to legal information retrieval would require the representation of a great deal of knowledge, much of it non-trivial, involving sophisticated concepts to do with rights, permissions, obligations, agreements, and so forth. The natural language problems alone would render such an enterprise daunting; most 'natural language' query systems for information retrieval, such as those on the World Wide Web, employ statistical, rather than knowledge-based, methods.

SCALIR attempts to finesse this problem by combining a statistical approach to information retrieval based on term weighting with a more knowledge-based approach based on factual relations between documents within a connectionist paradigm. The result is an interesting hybrid system which takes an unusual approach to a well-known problem. The fact that it also incorporates a learning mechanism makes it particularly interesting in the present context.

23.4.1 Why connectionism?

Two criticisms have often been leveled at AI systems in general and expert systems in particular.

- They are 'brittle,' meaning that if they encounter any situation not anticipated by the designers or programmers, they either generate an error or produce an unsatisfactory result (just like any other program). In other words, they break easily.
- They do not learn continuously from experience as human problem solvers do.

Many researchers since the mid-1980s have embraced connectionism as a cure for these, and other, ills.

Connectionism will be defined more rigorously below, but it can most easily be understood as a way of modeling intelligence loosely based on the organization of the human brain. The cerebral cortex mainly consists of a richly connected set of about 10^{10} simple processing units, called *neurons*. Thus, one sees the terms neural computing, and particularly *neural network*, associated with connectionist programs.

A neuron receives input from a large number of other neurons in the form of electrical stimulation. Some inputs are excitatory, in that they tend to cause the recipient to 'fire' by sending its own signal, while others are inhibitory, in that they tend to prevent the recipient from firing. Each neuron has an internal state and a threshold, such that if the sum of excitatory and inhibitory inputs causes the internal state to exceed a certain value, then that neuron will fire. When a neuron fires, it propagates a signal to other neurons along its outgoing connections in the form of a train of impulses. A typical neuron can be connected to as many as 10^3 other neurons.

Given the somewhat slow switching time of a neuron (a few milliseconds), and the rather narrow frequency band of its output (up to about 100 Hz), it seems that the brain is made up of processing elements which are much slower than man-made computing devices and which exchange only a few bits of information. Thus researchers have concluded that the processing power of the brain is a function of the sheer number of such elements, their connectedness, and their capacity for parallel operation. Hence the popularity of the term 'massive parallelism' in the connectionist literature.

Connectionist approaches are often deemed to be nonsymbolic, or *subsymbolic*, because the basic unit of computation is not a symbol (as defined in Chapter 4), but something more primitive and generic. For example, a symbol in some LISP program, such as MY_LAPTOP, might be represented by a pattern of activity in some number of connected neurons in a connectionist system. However, neural networks are often simulated in software, so the neurons will typically have some internal structure, and may even be implemented using symbols. For example, the role of a neuron could be played by some data object, suitably endowed with properties and methods, connected by pointers to other objects in the net. This is only confusing if you forget what we said in Chapter 10 about different levels in the analysis of knowledge representations. There is, in fact, nothing paradoxical in a subsymbolic system (at the conceptual level) being realized as a computer program that contains symbols (at the implementation level).

Regardless of how it is implemented, a *connectionist network* can be considered as a weighted directed graph of the kind described in Chapter 6. Thus nodes in the graph stand for neurons, while links between them stand for connections. Real-valued weights on the links can be thought of as encoding the strength of the connection between two neurons, and hence the amount of excitation or inhibition that is conveyed to the recipient when the sender fires.

Given the dynamic nature of such systems, time is more of a factor in connectionist networks than in other forms of knowledge representation. Levels of activation change over time, and visible patterns of activation representing concepts will decay in the absence of stimulation. Time is usually handled discretely, in that the state of the net is considered in a series of snapshots, with each new state depending only upon the state corresponding to the last cycle of neuron firings.

Certain other conventions are required to perform computation with such a network. For a network to become activated, it must receive some input, so some nodes will typically serve as 'sensors,' deriving their activation from an external source. These input nodes will then propagate excitatory activity to other internal nodes in the network. This is normally done by *clamping* the sensory nodes, that is, setting their activation level to some high value for some number of firing cycles. Subsequently, such nodes are unclamped and allowed to decay.

It may also be useful to have some nodes designated as output or 'response' nodes whose pattern of activation will be read at the end of the computation. Alternatively, we may be interested in the state of the whole network after the computation is deemed to be over, or we may be interested in only those nodes with high levels of activation. In some circumstances we may be interested in watching the network settle into a stable state, while in others we may prefer to record activation levels in certain nodes before that activation decays.

Figure 23.3 shows a simple network fragment in which four sensory nodes, S_1–S_4 feed input to the other nodes, one of which, R, is a response node. Without knowing the weights on the links, one can tell that R will be activated when S_1 and S_4 alone are active. But when S_2 and S_3 become active, they will tend to suppress R, even if S_1 and S_4 are active. Whether or not R actually becomes active in this case will depend upon the weights on the competing links.

The design space of possible configurations for networks of this type is extremely large. Also, there are very many ways one could compute the output of a neuron, given the sum of its inputs. Such details and variations are beyond the scope of this text; here we shall follow Rose and concentrate upon a rather plain network model which allows any node to be connected to any other node, and which makes no distinction between the activation of a node and its output.

To get more precise about such networks, we will need a little notation.

- Let w_{ij} denote the weight on the link from node j to node i.
- Let $net_i = \Sigma_j\, w_{ij}$ denote the *net input* to node i from other nodes at a given time.

Any definition of a connectionist network must take *time* into account, since the state of a neuron at any time will depend upon its former state and the former state of its input nodes.

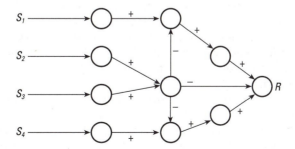

Figure 23.3 **A collection of neurons with excitatory and inhibitory connections.**

> **Definition**   A *connectionist network* can be considered as a weighted directed graph
> such that, for any node, *i*,
> (1) it will have a real-valued activation at time *t*, which we shall write as $a_i(t)$;
> (2) it may be connected to any other node *j* by a link with real-valued weight w_{ij};
> (3) its activation at time *t*+1 is a function of
>   (i)   its activation at time *t*, $a_i(t)$,
>   (ii) the weighted sum of the states of its input nodes, net_i, at time *t*, and
>   (iii) any external input, $x_i(t)$.

A simple function for rendering the new level of activation in a node i satisfying (3) in the above definition would be:

$$a_i(t+1) = \Sigma_j\, w_{ij} a_j(t) + x_i(t).$$

However, other activation functions are possible. Some involve the addition of bias or decay terms, while others use a differentiable nonlinear function (see, for example, Hinton, 1989). We shall not pursue such matters here.

In designing a network, weights on links can be assigned *a priori*, or tuned over time, as a by-product of activation. The weights are deemed to encode knowledge, while adjustment of weights is seen as a learning process. Since the weights determine how activation spreads along connections, there is a real sense in which they determine how the network behaves, and consequently changes in the weights will modify that behavior, hopefully in the direction of improvement.

As noted above, knowledge is represented implicitly in a connectionist network, in that no single processing element codes for a domain entity or a domain rule. Rather it is weighted connections between constellations of elements that embody the knowledge. The representation is therefore *distributed* over many elements, and consequently the knowledge so stored is not amenable to a simple listing of numeric and symbolic elements. Nor is it necessarily the case that a neuron involved in representing some entity is actually encoding some human-comprehensible part of it, such as its color or shape, that we might normally associate with a symbol. Hence connectionist networks are sometimes described as performing *subsymbolic processing*.

Far from separating knowledge and inference, in the manner of a rule-based system, a connectionist network more or less abolishes the distinction. Knowledge is not stored as declarative facts; neither is the knowledge in the system accessible to interpretation by a separate processor (Rumelhart and McClelland, 1986). Knowledge access and inferential behavior are both describable only in terms of patterns of activation.

Of course, there is nothing to prevent a network architect from making nodes stand for domain entities, and that is what Rose does in the SCALIR system, as we shall see in the next section. However, such a mapping between nodes and entities does not alter the fact that the relationships that hold between these entities are still implicit in the connections, and are not formally stated in rules. Thus, the mystery of what nodes stand for may be solved, but the significance of the weighted connections between them remains 'subsymbolic.'

Even if nodes represent domain entities, patterns of activation in constellations of such nodes may still code for higher-order concepts which combine aspects of the nodes involved. For example, if the nodes represent words, and the nodes 'race,' 'car' and 'driver' are active, then this may code for the concept of a racing car driver or, alternatively, the act of driving a racing car. In any event, such a representation could still be deemed subsymbolic, because the constituent nodes are not arranged in a syntactic structure which makes the meaning explicit, neither is the constellation of nodes amenable to semantic analysis by an external set of rules.

23.4.2 SCALIR: a hybrid system for legal information retrieval

Nodes in SCALIR stand for cases (court reports), statutes, and important words that occur in such documents. The network therefore has a basic tripartite structure, as shown in Figure 23.4, where a case node layer and a statute node layer are separated by a word node layer. These words (hereafter *terms*, in the parlance of information retrieval) are linked to the documents in which they occur.

Thus the basic structure connects term nodes to document nodes to form an *indexing scheme* based on weighted links. So there is a mapping between term nodes and case nodes, and between term nodes and nodes representing statute sections. (Statutes are complex documents which are usually broken down into sections for indexing purposes.)

Rather than link every word to every document in which it occurred, SCALIR computes a *term weight* for each term associated with a document, as a function of how frequently it occurs in that document and how frequently it occurs in the document collection as a whole. Intuitively, a good indexing term for a document is one that occurs frequently in the document but infrequently in the rest of the collection. This value was then thresholded, so that each document was indexed by approximately 10 terms, and terms below the threshold were discarded. (Note that links are bidirectional; in fact there are two directed links between each pair of connected nodes, and these can bear different weights. Thus terms suggest documents, but documents also suggest terms.)

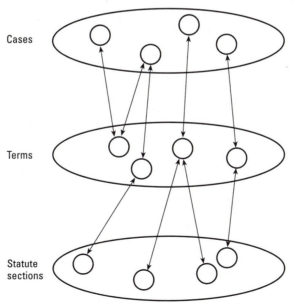

Figure 23.4 **SCALIR network showing links between terms and documents (after Rose, 1994).**

The SCALIR network was therefore constructed by first of all selecting terms from the documents, and then linking these terms to documents with a link weight proportional to the term weight for that term in the context of that document.

However, these connectionist-style links (called 'C-links') are not the only kind of link in the architecture. There are also *symbolic links* ('S-links'), which are more like the links of a semantic network, having labels and a constant weight. These describe factual relationships among documents; for example, one document may cite another, one court decision may criticize another, one statute section may contain another, and so on. These links are necessitated by the complexity of the relationships that may hold between legal documents, irrespective of indexing considerations. S-links represent such domain knowledge explicitly.[3]

The resultant network contained about 13 000 term nodes, 4000 case nodes and 100 statute nodes. There were about 75 000 links between cases and terms and 2000 links between statutes and terms. The remaining 10 000 links were mostly symbolic links between cases. Rose does not report how much effort was involved in building this initial network, but one assumes that key tasks like term extraction and citation extraction were done programmatically, and that nodes and links could be generated automatically on the basis of such information. He was also assisted by the fact that the documents had already been editorially enhanced with various kinds of cross-referencing information by a legal publisher.

This structure is then used as the basis for a knowledge-based document retrieval engine, in which the primary inferential mechanism is *spreading activation*. The use of spreading activation as a vehicle for reasoning is not new; it dates back to Quillian's work on semantic nets (see Chapter 6). In that formalism, we could tell if two nodes stood in a certain relationship by allowing activation in the form of markers to pass along labeled links and then seeing if the markers collide at some point in the network.

The basic idea underlying SCALIR is that the level of activity in a given node should be proportional to its relevance. More precisely, if we 'excite' some number of term nodes to form a query, then this should induce a proportional degree of activity in those document nodes that are relevant to that query. Query nodes are simply sensory nodes, as described above, in that they receive their excitation from outside of the network. These nodes then excite selected document nodes via C-links, and these documents excite other documents via S-links.

Symbolic links assure us that if a given document is retrieved, then related documents will also have a good chance of being retrieved. These weights are fixed because the strength of such associations has been decided in advance. Activity is propagated along S-links by a form of marker passing.

There are two properties that were deemed desirable in an activation function for an information retrieval application, and these impact the way query nodes are clamped, the way weights are assigned to links, and the nature of the activation function.

(1) The amount of activity pumped into the system should be independent of the size of the query.

---

[3] SCALIR uses another type of symbolic link, called an H-link, to code for occasions when a higher court criticizes a lower court decision. These are symbolic links with adjustable weights. However, we shall not get into that level of detail here, and confine our discussion to C-links and S-links.

(2) Propagation should not create more activity than it receives.

Clearly, if (1) is ignored, then one-word queries will result in less activation than multi-word queries, therefore leading to fewer retrievals than a more restrictive query containing additional terms. This would be counter-intuitive, to say the least. If (2) is violated, then too many documents might be retrieved, many of them only marginally relevant.

To enforce (1), a fixed amount of activation is divided equally between the query nodes at the clamping stage. To enforce (2), weights on outgoing links must always sum to 1.0 or less, and the activation function must always be less than or equal to its argument.

C-links use a linear activation function which contains a *retention constant*, ρ, as shown in the equation below. This value determines what proportion of a node's activity is retained for the next firing cycle, and what proportion is propagated to its neighbors. It clearly satisfies the constraint outlined above, since $a_i(t+1) \leq a_i(t)$ as long as $\Sigma_j w_{ij} \leq 1$.

$$a_i(t+1) = \rho a_i(t) + (1 - \rho)\Sigma_j w_{ij}a_j(t)).$$

A similar function was employed by Belew (1986). Rose also follows Belew in using two other parameters to control activation in the SCALIR network.

- The *significance threshold*, θ_s, determines which nodes have activity high enough to merit retrieval. This value is progressively lowered from its initial value to compensate for the decay of activity in the network.
- The *quiescence threshold*, θ_s, determines which nodes have activity low enough to be considered inactive and therefore ignored. This prevents the system from spending time on nodes that are unlikely to be retrieved, and guards against errors in arithmetic precision.

These quantities feature in SCALIR's retrieval algorithm, a simplified version of which is given in Figure 23.5. It describes a breadth-first search through the network from the set of clamped query nodes (QUERY-NODES) along the weighted links.

Set θ_s to initial value.
Let the set of ACTIVE-NODES be QUERY-NODES
Repeat
{
    If still clamping, set activity levels of nodes in QUERY-NODES.
    Set RESPONSE-SET to be all nodes in ACTIVE-NODES with activity above θ_s.
    Remove from ACTIVE-NODES all nodes with activity below θ_q.
    Add neighbors of nodes in ACTIVE-NODES to ACTIVE-NODES.
    Update activities of all nodes in ACTIVE-NODES using activation function.
    Sort ACTIVE-NODES by activity level.
    Decay θ_s.
}
Until $(\theta_s \leq \theta_q)$ or (ACTIVE-NODES = $\varnothing$).

Figure 23.5 **SCALIR's retrieval algorithm, slightly simplified.**

The simplification involves omitting from consideration a shrinking parameter which controls the breadth of this search, narrowing it at each level. We also omit a parameter which determines the maximum size that the response set is allowed to achieve before halting search. There is also an implicit parameter which tells the algorithm when to stop clamping the query nodes.

If we look at the termination condition of the loop in Figure 23.5, we see that propagation continues until significance decays to quiescense, in which case no more nodes will ever be retrieved, or we run out of active nodes. As hinted above, there are actually two other termination conditions. Propagation can be halted when the response set reaches some arbitrary maximum size, or when the parameter controlling the breadth-first search shrinks to zero.

It is obvious that the values of most of these parameters have to be determined empirically, and these values will depend to some extent on the context in which the system is tested or actually used. The same is true of various parameters that govern machine learning by the tuning of weights. This forms the subject matter of the next section.

23.5 Learning in SCALIR

Since C-links have adjustable weights, relevance judgments from a user concerning the documents retrieved enable the system to tune itself. One method of doing this within the connectionist paradigm is called *reinforcement*, in which the system gets a 'reward' whose size depends upon the correctness of its outputs. We describe a variant of this method here, providing a somewhat simplified account of the issues as they pertain to SCALIR.

Suppose that a node i receives input from a node j along a connection with weight w_{ij}. If node i represents a relevant document, then we would like to strengthen the link by increasing w_{ij}, whereas if the document is deemed irrelevant we would rather weaken it. The question then arises as to how much the weight should be changed. One simple rule for computing the weight change, Δw_{ij}, is given by

$$\Delta w_{ij} = \eta f_i a_j$$

where η is a constant *learning rate*, and f_i is a feedback term, which could be +1 or − 1, for example.

However, the application of such a rule is not straightforward, for a number of reasons.

- Determining the value of the activity level a_j is difficult, because a clamped query node, for example, may decay once it is unclamped.
- Neighbors of nodes that receive feedback should probably receive some feedback too, in that they also represent relevant documents.
- Node i may be at the end of a chain of propagations, and so feedback needs to be propagated back along the chain.

For these reasons, feedback is allowed to propagate through the network, just like activity. The maximum feedback at each node is recorded and updated during propagation, and these values subsequently become the f_i and a_j of the equation shown above. Weights are then normalized, so that weights out of any given node sum to 1.0.

The details of how SCALIR actually works are a bit more complex than outlined here, thanks to the presence of different link types; the interested reader is referred to Rose (1994). But the idea of combining symbolic and connectionist methods is an intriguing one that merits further study. SCALIR effects a very pragmatic compromise between a purely statistical approach to information retrieval, using readily available numbers, and a conventional AI approach that requires large amounts of domain knowledge.

23.6 The future of hybrid systems

In summary, we see that hybrid systems are a potentially powerful tool that may enable us to address and solve problems that are just too complex for more conventional approaches. If we contrast ODYSSEUS with EMYCIN, we see a methodology for building and refining knowledge bases that is far more sophisticated than the syntactic checks performed by the latter. Expert systems have yet to emulate the continuous improvement that we associate with human experts, but research is beginning to address this vital issue.

Similarly, the augmentation of rule-based systems with CBR allows us to handle exceptions gracefully, without making a rule set overly complicated. A rule, by definition, is meant to capture a generalization; it loses its power if it is too heavily qualified. Attempts to handle exceptions within the framework of mathematical logic have not yielded much in the way of theoretical consensus or practical results. As we saw in Chapter 6, exception handling inframe systems can involve a clash of intuitions, and so it is unlikely that any one formalism will satisfy all parties, or be appropriate for all domains. CBR provides a mechanism for domain-dependent inference that fills a gap in our current toolkit.

SCALIR's attempt to blend two paradigms, the symbolic and the subsymbolic, which are often viewed as being mutually exclusive competitors, dramatically illustrates that even apparently heterogeneous approaches can be combined advantageously within a hybrid system.

In the future, one expects to see more efforts along these lines. However, there are a number of continuing trends in AI which militate against the construction of hybrid systems. It is worth mentioning them briefly here; I doubt if these points are controversial.

- AI software is mostly platform-dependent and implemented in languages that no one outside of the AI community uses.
- AI software methodology has fallen behind the state of the art with respect to the good practices associated with object-oriented analysis and design, as well as emerging component technologies.
- AI software still tends to be brittle, poorly documented, and usable only inside its laboratory of origin. This means that software modules are often not available as building blocks in novel systems under construction elsewhere. Commercial systems are typically of higher quality, but their proprietary nature does not encourage reuse.

There are also psychological barriers to collaboration across theoretical divides, but these will hopefully be overcome by future generations of researchers and developers.

BIBLIOGRAPHICAL NOTES

Various software products combine rule-based and case-based reasoning, for example, CBR Express from Inference Corp, which runs on top of ART-IM. ART-IM itself supplies a basic CBR facility, namely nearest-neighbor indexing coupled with associative retrieval. CBR Express adds more functionality and a graphical user interface – see Davies and May (1995) for an assessment. CBR Express was initially targeted at help-desk applications; the latest version is called CBR Content Navigator and features tools for the indexing and retrieval of unstructured information.

Expert system shells that combine rule-based reasoning with learning or with neural nets are less well developed. However, researchers have coupled expert systems with neural nets in various ways, often using rules to screen a problem and then using neural networks to classify it (see for example, Kam *et al.*, 1991). Similarly, a product like NeuroShell 2 from Neuron Data will allow a user to preprocess data with production rules before feeding it to the network; one can also use the rules to post-process the network's outputs.

STUDY SUGGESTIONS

1. To what extent are MYCIN and CENTAUR hybrid systems?

2. To what extent is a blackboard system a hybrid system?

3. Why is learning such an important component for an expert system, and why do so few expert systems feature such a component?

4. What do you understand by the term 'explanation-based generalization'? What is the main feature that distinguishes it from the learning methods examined in Chapter 20?

5. Consider the following definition of an arch consisting of two pillars and a lintel.

```
arch(X, Y, Z) :-
  left_pillar(X),
  right_pillar(Y),
  lintel(Z),
  supports(X, Z),
  supports(Y, Z),
  apart(X, Y).

supports(X, Y) :-
  on(X, ground),
  on(Y, X),
  not(on(Y, ground)).

apart(X, Y) :- not(touch(X, Y)).
```

together with the following set of facts

```
left_pillar(obj1).
right_pillar(obj2).
on(obj1, ground).
on(obj2, ground).
```

continued

```
lintel(obj3).
on(obj3, p1).
on(obj3, p2).
```

What kind of explanation-based generalization is possible from these facts and rules about 'archhood'?

6. What are the strengths and weakness of rule-based reasoning and case-based reasoning, and how might they be used in parallel?

7. How worthwhile is it to try to derive rules from cases, or cases from rules?

8. What is 'connectionism'? What advantages might connectionist models of intelligence offer over symbolic models?

9. Examine the connectionist network in Figure 23.6.
   (i) What will tend to happen to node R when nodes S_1 and S_3 are activated?
   (ii) How will R respond differently when S_2 is also activated?

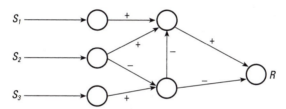

Figure 23.6 A connectionist network featuring excitation and inhibition.

10. Can you think of ways of blending symbolic and subsymbolic paradigms that differ from the SCALIR approach? Think first about the information retrieval application, but then also consider other data-intensive applications, such as speech recognition.

24 Summary and Conclusion

This chapter attempts a retrospective roundup of the topics that we have covered and provides some suggestions for further study. This overview is organized around a number of themes that recur throughout the book, and serves to summarize the contents from a different perspective that pulls various strands of thought closer together. The discussion will include some back pointers to the chapters themselves, but not so many as to detract from the readability of the text. The chapter contains some opinions and predictions about the future of expert systems and AI generally, which may provide grounds for class discussion and lively debate. Unless otherwise attributed, these are my personal views, and the reader should approach them in a spirit of critical evaluation and healthy skepticism.

24.1 The riddle of artificial intelligence

Artificial intelligence[1] has always been the 'badlands' of computer science, populated by unruly problems that have never been brought under the control of more conven-

---

[1] Some people are put off by the phrase 'artificial intelligence,' just as there are people who cannot tolerate the phrase 'fuzzy logic.' Alternative suggestions, such as 'complex information processing' for the former, and 'continuous set theory' for the latter, do not capture the thrill of discovery that engendered these fields, nor the romance of such domains for those who came after. There will no doubt come a time when all poetry will be purged from human language, but in the meantime we will continue to use phrases that connote affection and adventure.

tional methods. The discipline initially attracted multidisciplinary people who were not afraid of these wide open, rather lawless, spaces – people who welcomed the challenge of reinventing the way we think about thinking. Frontiersmen such as Marvin Minsky, John McCarthy, Herbert Simon, Pat Hayes, Donald Michie and Bernard Meltzer blazed a tantalizing trail through computer science, human psychology, and mathematical logic for the rest to follow.

The question I want to address is: In building expert systems, why do we need artificial intelligence techniques at all? What is wrong with other kinds of technique, such as mathematical modeling, from other disciplines, such as mainstream computer science? Put another way, is the engendering of expert systems within AI an historical accident, or something more like a necessity?

The short answer is that there is nothing wrong with using 'non-AI' techniques, as and when they are appropriate. Thus, DENDRAL's hypothesis generation (see Chapter 20) was founded upon an algorithm for enumerating planar graphs, while MYCIN (see Chapter 3) relied upon a straightforward statistical approach to therapy based on drug sensitivities. The use of AI architectures, search methods or programming languages does not prevent knowledge engineers from availing themselves of suitable methods from applied mathematics, computer science, operations research or any other relevant discipline. Knowledge engineers building an application should *always* examine existing methods for solving the problem and take the trouble to analyze their strengths and weaknesses. Some parts of the problem may yield to purely algorithmic or mathematical solutions, in which case it is foolish not to use such methods as long as they are computationally efficient.

The long answer (which I shall make short) is that expert systems would *not* exhibit the variety, generality, and utility that they do today without significant input from AI. What Artificial Intelligence offers is a collection of *insights*, *techniques* and *architectures* for complex problem solving in cases where purely algorithmic or mathematical solutions are either unknown or demonstrably inefficient. Some of the work that has gone on over the past 30 years has involved adapting theoretical and practical results from related areas in mathematics, computer science and the social sciences. However, it usually turns out that translating results from diverse disciplines in such a way that they can be harnessed for computational purposes is a non-trivial exercise that requires novel approaches to representation and control. AI has both nurtured such approaches (for example, connectionism) and synthesized 'best of breed' approaches found elsewhere (for example, object-orientation).

The insights documented in the early chapters of this book include

- the realization that all problems, from solving simple puzzles to learning new concepts, can be reduced to *search problems* if we are able to specify them precisely enough;
- the realization that search must be *knowledge-based*, in the sense of being guided by knowledge about the problem domain, if it is to address problems which are inherently intractable, that is, problems which are isomorphic with abstract problems (such as maze traversal, optimal tours, and so on) which are known to require exponential resources; and
- the realization that *knowledge representation* is just as crucial to solving hard problems as inference techniques, since it is the representation of knowledge that determines the underlying search space which inference unfolds.

The corresponding techniques documented in the middle chapters consist of

- a range of *high-level languages* for representing knowledge of different kinds, such as empirical associations and conceptual hierarchies;
- a range of *interactive strategies* for eliciting knowledge, compiling it into such representations, and controlling its application to problems of realistic complexity; and
- *design methodologies* for making systems that use such representations transparent to both the end user and the knowledge engineer.

These techniques were then assembled into architectural building blocks of the kind described in the later chapters which provide

- ways of *combining* different knowledge representation paradigms to trade on their strengths and compensate for their weaknesses;
- ways of *layering* computational structures so that domain, task and problem solving knowledge are cleanly separated yet well integrated; and
- useful tools for *extending* problem solvers with components that perform tasks such as learning and recording inferences.

We shall return to the subject of expert systems architecture later in this summary. What is important is that we would have had none of these practical benefits without the theoretical insights documented in the early chapters. Even pioneering systems like MYCIN and DENDRAL, which were surprisingly successful for their time, did not emerge *sui generis* but are recognizable products of artificial intelligence research.

While other disciplines contributed to these advances (for example, operations research and search strategies), it was within AI that their full significance and potential was realized and exploited. It is now a cliché that the domain of AI is, by definition, that set of computer science problems which we do not know how to solve by conventional means. My sense is that this will continue to be the case, and that it will continue to be AI's mingled curse and blessing. It is a curse, because in the short term one always appears to fail, but also a blessing, because one gets to work on the more interesting problems.

24.2 Knowledge representation revisited

In a sense, all computer programs contain knowledge. A 'bubble sort' program written in BASIC contains the programmer's knowledge about how to order the elements in an array or list. So what is it that makes knowledge representation different from ordinary programming?

Computer programs for tasks harder than sorting lists are notoriously hard to understand. Certainly they contain the programmer's knowledge about how to perform the task. But they also contain his or her knowledge about

- how to wrestle with constructs in the programming language,
- how to trade clarity for efficiency, and
- how to make important but low-level decisions about data manipulation and flow of control.

Knowledge representation languages are high-level languages developed expressly for the purpose of encoding 'chunks' of human knowledge, such as rules of thumb and prototypical objects, in a manner that hides the minutiae of data and control structure from the user as far as possible. Users can delve into the internals, of course; but the idea is that they should not have to do this in order to write programs. Such languages tend to be extremely economical of code, compared with more conventional programming languages, just because so many of the programming details are taken care of by the interpreter of the language. Yet most of them can be shown to have the power of a Turing machine. In other words, they can in theory compute any function that can be computed using more conventional programming languages.

To the extent that a knowledge engineering tool reintroduces the complexities of procedural programming, it has failed to provide the user with the right level of abstraction for specifying and solving the problem, as we suggested in Chapter 17.

However, although there are substantial benefits associated with this ascent to a higher-level language, certain computational problems remain and should not be forgotten.

- The step from having a domain description in human language to having a representation in some computer-readable formalism is essentially magical, in that we have *no* firm idea as to how this translation could be achieved mechanically. Since the nature and scope of a program's inferences depend crucially upon the choice of representation, I believe that *this* is the major pitfall facing expert systems builders, not knowledge acquisition *per se* (Chapter 3).
- There is an adverse trade-off between the *expressivity* of a knowledge representation language and the *tractability* of its inference procedures, if we wish to retain soundness and completeness. In other words, the more you can say, the less you can prove about what you say in a finite time. Sometimes, thanks to undecidability, you may not be able to prove what you say at all (Chapter 8).
- Much of the knowledge that we wish to represent is complicated by *vagueness* and *uncertainty*. Our knowledge is often radically incomplete, and therefore contains estimates and assumptions. Data can be partial, noisy or inherently variable. Furthermore, the concepts that humans use are not crisply defined, and may resist attempts to render them more precise (Chapter 9).

The challenge of knowledge representation is that we cannot let ourselves be paralyzed by the problems of translatability, tractability and uncertainty. It is this engineering approach that separates artificial intelligence from mathematical logic; a distinction that has sometimes been lost in the desire for rigor on the part of AI researchers. We ought to be in the business of solving problems, not proving theorems, or 'doing philosophy in front of a computer.'

- We adopt a somewhat empirical approach to translating domain knowledge into formalisms such as production rules or objects. This is really an art rather than a science, and the more rules or objects you create the more skilled you tend to become. Contrary to popular opinion, not just anyone can do a good job of this.
- We are often willing to give up logical completeness in the face of intractability, so long as we can still get all the solutions that we are likely to need. Sometimes we do not need to consider all the logically possible solutions to some problem, or find an optimal solution, if we can find one that satisfies all the important constraints.

- We are also willing to make some compromises with respect to mathematical correctness when faced with uncertainty. Although many of the inference schemes we use are not quite in accordance with the axioms of probability theory, we typically take some short cuts which simplify the computation of belief measures for practical purposes.

The last paragraphs are not intended to sound complacent, merely realistic. Further research on knowledge representation and inference will ultimately enable us to have a better understanding of these trade-offs, but in the meantime we have methods that suffice for many applications. However, one suspects that the representation of human knowledge will *always* remain a pragmatic enterprise, at least until psychology becomes an exact science.

Thus knowledge representation is an empirical and experimental research area, and not merely an arena for philosophical debate. The old issues – such as 'Can machines think?' and 'How is knowledge *really* represented in the human brain?' – seem increasingly irrelevant. The key question is rather 'What can we do with this technology?', and it can only be answered by a concerted programme of theoretical and practical work, as opposed to metaphysical speculation.

24.3 AI programming languages

Artificial intelligence did not invent rewrite rules, directed graphs or predicate logic; rather AI researchers have creatively adapted these formalisms to the practical ends of knowledge representation and found highly efficient implementations for them. The development of modern *production systems*, *object-oriented systems* and *procedural deduction systems* has been driven by AI applications involving classification and construction problems of the kind described in the middle chapters. Without that impetus, and the empirical enterprise of trying to solve such problems, it is doubtful that many of these innovations would have occurred.

Although AI has produced a variety of representation languages, they all have certain things in common.

Firstly, they are *declarative*, in the sense that they describe knowledge relevant to solving some task rather than prescribing how the task should be done. The separation between knowledge base and inference engine implicit in most expert systems architectures means that one can experiment with applying the same knowledge under different control regimes; at least, you can if you are crafting the inference engine yourself. Some architectures, such as blackboards, allow you to represent control knowledge declaratively, and reason about it just like any other kind of knowledge.

Secondly, they are highly *modular*. As well as concealing implementation details from the user of the language, modules of knowledge conceal implementation detail from each other, communicating through global data structures (as in production systems and blackboard systems) or via strict protocols (as in object-oriented systems). This feature encourages the piecemeal and incremental encoding of knowledge and supports fast prototyping.

Thirdly, the analog of procedure invocation in such languages tends to be *pattern-directed*. Thus the firing of rules in production systems, the triggering of knowledge sources in blackboard systems, and the resolution of clauses in deduction systems all rely on a form of pattern matching. This is a very powerful and general mechanism, which aids modularity, although it does not come without computational cost.

Knowledge representation languages of whatever kind are normally implemented as *pattern-directed inference systems*. The resultant programs consist of a number of relatively independent modules (for example, rules, structures or clauses) which are matched against incoming data and which manipulate data structures. There are three essential ingredients to any such system:

- A collection of *modules* which are capable of being activated by incoming data which match their 'trigger' patterns.
- One or more *dynamic data structures* that can be examined and modified by an active module.
- An *interpreter* that controls the selection and activation of modules on a cyclic basis.

Artificial Intelligence research has concentrated upon a number of topics related to pattern-directed inference:

- the *efficient implementation* of such interpreters;
- turning relatively 'pure' formalisms into usable *software tools*;
- experimenting with *mixed formalisms* which combine different paradigms.

Today, languages such as CLIPS offer the user a powerful collection of tools for knowledge representation and inference which, in the hands of skilled personnel, are able to solve a wide range of problems. By packaging an OPS-style production rule interpreter with a CLOS-style object system and a LISP-style procedural language, CLIPS offers a consistent multi-paradigm language that combines 'best of breed' components and is not hard to learn. Users can then pick and choose which modules to utilize for what purposes, hopefully based on an understanding of the strengths and weaknesses of these approaches, based on their own experience or derived from sources such as this book.

24.4 Practical problem solving

In Chapters 10–15, we explored the idea that there are generic tasks which are exemplified again and again in expert systems applications. In particular, we looked at the difference between classification and construction tasks, and saw that in their purest forms they required rather different search strategies for their solution.

- In *classification tasks*, the emphasis is upon finding a useful but approximate mapping between data and solutions at some level of abstraction. We have to consider all the evidence, combine it in some way, then refine and rank candidate solutions accordingly. The solution space is usually known in advance, and its categories are capable of being enumerated. Exhaustive search methods which use certainties to order and prune solution paths are adequate for many purposes, for example if the search space is small or factorable into more or less independent subproblems. Large search spaces which represent interacting subproblems require stronger methods that impose some form of organization on the hypothesis space (for example, hierarchical or causal) and allow for the explicit scheduling of subtasks (for example, subclassification or tracing a causal path).

- In *construction tasks*, we are typically building some complex entity that must satisfy certain constraints, and the solution space may be very large indeed. Consequently, the emphasis is upon keeping one's options open, being prepared to guess when a problem is under-constrained, and being able to recover from bad decisions. We will not normally explore all solution paths in search of an optimal solution; rather we are satisfied if we find one that fits the constraints. Constraints may interact, and domain-specific knowledge may be required for the resolution of conflicts. The most general strategy appears to be one of 'propose and revise,' in which partial solutions are extended until a constraint is violated, and then such violations are 'fixed' by heuristics.

Although it is tempting to think of tasks like diagnosis as being classification tasks and tasks like planning as being construction tasks, the mapping between individual applications and generic tasks is more complicated than that.

- We saw that programs such as INTERNIST can view diagnosis as a construction task: the solution elements are disorders which can be combined into composite hypotheses. It is therefore not practical to enumerate the solution space in advance, given that a patient may be suffering from 10 or more disorders. Furthermore, the general problem of finding the 'best' explanations of a set of symptoms is intractable and cannot even be approximated without powerful mechanisms for focusing the attention of the program. In this respect, tasks such as differential diagnosis share many of the features of constructive problem solving. To the extent that this is true for a given task, strategies such as 'least commitment' and 'propose and revise' become appropriate.
- We also saw that programs such as R1/XCON sometimes have enough knowledge to perform a construction task without recourse to guessing or backtracking. Given an overall strategy of 'top-down refinement,' which analyzes the computer configuration task into nearly independent subtasks, R1 can afford to reason wholly bottom up. In other words, it can 'propose and extend' without having to revise. In addition, we studied a planner (ONCOCIN) which essentially performs a constructive task by the method of heuristic classification. Thanks to the restricted form of cancer-treatment protocols, the system could merely select skeletal plans from a 'plan library,' and then adapt them to the current situation by a process of plan refinement.

Nevertheless, the theoretical distinction between classification and construction is extremely useful, not least because it aids the process of knowledge acquisition and its automation. We saw that the functionality of a knowledge elicitation tool could be greatly enhanced if it possessed both a declarative model of the domain and some knowledge of how the task would be performed, that is how domain knowledge would be used by the applications program. Although role-limiting acquisition systems such as MORE and RIME are still in their infancy, they point the way to powerful methodologies for building knowledge bases. The key insight, that automatic knowledge elicitation should itself be knowledge based, will ultimately lead to effective tools for dealing with the 'knowledge acquisition bottleneck.' Automatic consistency checking and compilation into an executable form is also facilitated by access to a domain model and a set of problem solving principles.

24.5 Expert system architectures

We presented a classification of tools for building expert systems that depended largely upon different approaches to the trade-off between making representation and control decisions for users and providing them with the tools for implementing their own decisions. In particular, we distinguished between

- *expert system shells* which provide a single representation language and control regime combination which has worked well in the past;
- *high-level programming languages*, such as production rule interpreters and object-oriented systems, which provide basic building blocks for representation and control;
- *mixed-paradigm programming environments* which provide a wide range of representational devices and control mechanisms;
- *problem solving architectures*, such as blackboard systems, where task-oriented frameworks can be instantiated for particular applications;
- *useful packages*, for subtasks such as simulation or truth maintenance, which can be interfaced to the main problem solving program.

We saw that the first generation of software tools for building expert systems were essentially abstractions over successful applications programs. Many of these attempts at generalization were themselves successful. Thus the EMYCIN shell was applied to problems far from the original domain of blood infections, including structural analysis and troubleshooting electronic circuits. Special-purpose programming languages, such as OPS5 and Flavors, also emerged during this period. These eventually made the transition from the research laboratory to more general use, providing the skilled programmer with a viable alternative to shells.

The second generation supported a 'mix and match' style of architecture, which encouraged knowledge engineers to select and combine programming paradigms that features of the problem appeared to demand. Arguably, this was something of a black art, and required a level of experience and sophistication beyond the average consumer. Nevertheless, these tools demonstrated the enormous range of possible architectures that could be built around different representations and control regimes.

As far as usability is concerned, it has sometimes been assumed in the past that giving the programmer 'powerful' tools makes programming easier. However, there is also a trade-off between making decisions for the programmer and allowing him or her more flexibility. To oversimplify, shells sometimes err on the side of constraining the programmer, while mixed programming paradigms give some programmers more options than they can cope with. 'Powerful' programming environments are often hard to master, and so the learning curve can be quite steep. Nevertheless, the provision of well-engineered modules, such as truth maintenance systems, which perform essential tasks and which are non-trivial to program efficiently, obviously speeds expert systems development.

Hopefully, the next generation of tools will provide a more structured approach to the problem of deciding which architecture to use for which problems. Much current research is focusing upon the construction of tools for particular generic tasks, and the various approaches in the literature appear to be converging on some fundamental principles for the promotion of knowledge reuse. Thus, the principle of separating domain from problem solving knowledge and the principle of constructing domain ontologies appear to be firmly entrenched in new tools such as CommonKADS and PROTEGE.

Such evidence as there is suggests that knowledge engineering environments need to be more specialized to particular kinds of task. One doubts that these environments will have a gentler learning curve than earlier tools, or that they will help non-programmers build expert systems painlessly. On the other hand, although knowledge engineering may not get easier, good knowledge engineers may be able to get more done.

24.6 Expert systems research

The latter chapters of this book contain a representative sample of current research problems that impinge upon practical aspects of expert systems, such as inexact reasoning, rule induction, case based reasoning, and hybrid systems These topics were chosen because they are intrinsically interesting, and because any progress in these areas will have great impact upon the expert systems of the future. In particular, each of these topics has implications for the central problem of knowledge acquisition.

Research on *inexact reasoning* is suggesting ways in which belief update can be more closely tied to the structure of the problem. Thus both Dempster–Shafer theory and Bayesian belief updating can be adapted for modeling probabilistic inference in hierarchical hypothesis spaces. The link between Bayesian methods and causal networks suggests another way of tying inexact methods to deeper knowledge of the domain, instead of attaching certainties to more superficial associations between causes and effects. Having a model of hierarchical or causal relationships among data and hypotheses may make the assignment of weights of evidence to hypotheses easier than the assignment of certainties to the conclusions of individual decision rules. For example, having the explicit model to hand may encourage the expert and the knowledge engineer to devise and enforce a coherent policy on the assignment of weights, and help the knowledge engineer to design a knowledge acquisition program to check that this policy is consistently applied. The management of uncertainty is now an extremely active and somewhat controversial research area which is far too large and diverse to review in an introductory text. Thus attention has been focused on proposals which can be seen to have seen some direct application to expert systems.

Research on *rule induction* is providing a methodology for deriving, evaluating and tuning sets of decision rules. It seems certain that such methods will be required if we are to build and maintain really large knowledge bases. Also, machine learning is fundamental to the whole area of 'self-improving' systems, which gain in knowledge from their problem solving experiences.

We saw that the following techniques were of direct relevance to expert systems applications.

- Programs have been built which are capable of learning concepts from examples, by constructing rules which correctly classify a set of positive and negative training instances, and then using these rules to classify unseen data with a high degree of accuracy.
- Work is being done on the application of decision theory to the evaluation of individual heuristic rules and the optimization of sets of such rules, with a view to improving the quality of rule sets in terms of both analyzability and performance.

Research on inductive learning has made great progress in the past 15 years, and is certain to contribute to future knowledge engineering methodologies. Meanwhile, research on the evaluation of heuristic rules seeks to demystify the art of encoding expertise in rules by showing to what extent rule weights can be varied before the output of a program is affected. Greater understanding in this area will facilitate knowledge elicitation and lead to more robust systems.

Case-based reasoning, on the other hand, takes a different path towards the interaction between learning and problem solving. It is based on the simple observation that humans solve problems by using, and adapting, techniques that have worked in the past. We are much better at remembering solutions to problems than we are at devising wholly new approaches.

CBR is in some ways simpler and more intuitive than many other problem solving methods proposed by AI:

- CBR works with concrete examples of previous solutions, rather than abstract operations which form novel solutions.
- CBR works by manipulating whole cases, rather than analyzing or synthesizing solution fragments.

Reasoning therefore tends to take place within the context of a particular case, rather than within some more abstract space of hypotheses. This makes solutions easier to understand and explain. It also makes knowledge acquisition incremental, as the reasoner accumulates more cases.

Hybrid systems are systems which combine more than one problem solving method, often including a learning or critiquing component which is distinguishable from the main inference engine. There are both theoretical and practical issues of interest emerging here.

- On the theoretical side, we are interested in how such hybrids can extend and refine expert system architectures for classification and construction problems.
- On the practical side, we are interested in how such architectures can be implemented in a manner that leverages the learning or critiquing component to give significantly better performance.

Such facilities are bound to find their way into the expert system tools of the future, making programs easier to construct and maintain.

24.7 Conclusion

Although artificial intelligence has gone in and out of fashion several times over the past 40 years, no one can seriously doubt that computers present us with a unique tool for emulating and extending human cognitive abilities. Neither can anyone doubt that, in the twenty-first century, human knowledge will be one of the world's most important commodities. At present, it is a scarce resource, and there are signs that education may not be able to keep pace with the future global demand for expertise.

Expert systems research is developing a methodology for not merely codifying knowledge, but representing it in a form whereby its application to real problems can be wholly or partly automated. Expert systems are capable of amplifying human expertise in a manner that increases productivity on hard problems and enhances our potential to deal with the even harder problems we shall face in the twenty-first century. Although advances in computer architecture and the falling price of memory will facilitate AI applications, none of the techniques described in this book require very special hardware; most run on workstations which are getting cheaper, more powerful and more widespread every year.

Every day, the technology that supports all aspects of modern life, from the medical to the military, becomes more complex and sophisticated, yet our ability to harness this technology to sensible ends sometimes seems to lag behind. It is this 'knowledge explosion,' rather than the 'information explosion' beloved of technical journalists, which will present the computer and cognitive sciences with their greatest challenge. Artificial intelligence is one of the tools that can help us meet that challenge, so long as it is applied with humanity and common sense.

BIBLIOGRAPHICAL NOTES

AI Magazine is a good way for the general reader to keep abreast of what is new and interesting in AI research, particularly with regard to novel applications. *Knowledge Engineering Review* is an excellent source of survey and tutorial articles on subjects likely to interest both students and knowledge engineers.

To keep up with a particular area of AI research, one can look through the proceedings of conferences such as

- IJCAI (*International Joint Conference on Artficial Intelligence*);
- AAAI (The *National Conference on Artificial Intelligence* sponsored by the American Association for Artificial Intelligence);
- ECAI (*European Conference on Artificial Intelligence*);

as well as various other national conferences.

To keep up with new applications of AI, there are now numerous specialist conferences in areas such as aerospace, defense, design, manufacturing, and so forth. These are normally listed in the calendars of publications such as *AI Magazine* and *Communications of the Association for Computing Machinery*. The Association for Computing Machinery has a *Special Interest Group on Artificial Intelligence* (SIGART) which publishes a quarterly newsletter.

The *Artificial Intelligence* journal is an excellent source of archival papers. The *Journal of Artificial Intelligence Research* is an electronic journal of refereed papers distributed on the Internet since 1993 and also published in bound volumes. The URL is:

```
http://www.cs.washington.edu/research/jair/home.html
```

Other URLs on the World Wide Web are good sources of information about AI and expert systems. Here are just a few suggestions.

- `http://www.aaai.org` – the home page of the American Association for Artificial Intelligence.
- `http://www.cs.cmu.edu/Groups/AI/html/repository.html` – the Artificial Intelligence Repository at Carnegie-Mellon University.
- `http://www.comlab.ox.ac.uk/archive/comp/ai.html` – includes a directory of AI laboratories
- `http://www.jsc.nasa.gov/~clips/CLIPS.html` – CLIPS home page, includes history of CLIPS, how to obtain CLIPS, CLIPS links, and so on.

> continued
>
> - `http://www.ai-cbr.org/theindex.html` – a case-based reasoning resource.
>
> AI-related newsgroups have languished in recent years. (`comp.ai` receives fewer postings each day than `alt.guitar.rickenbacker`.) The Web is a far better resource.

Check out some of the links listed above and find new ones. Then take the rest of the day off.

CLIPS Programming

A1 A short history of CLIPS

CLIPS stands for C Language Integrated Production System: a programming language developed at NASA's Johnson Space Center[1] in the mid-1980s. It is patterned on LISP-based tools such as OPS5 and ART, and supports many of the features of these tools, including a procedural language that looks a lot like LISP. The shift to C as the implementation language was prompted by the restricted availability of LISP compilers for many hardware platforms, the costly nature of industrial-strength LISP environments, and the difficulty of integrating LISP code with non-LISP applications. C-based AI tools were just becoming available at that time, at a price, but the NASA folks decided to go ahead and develop their own. The resulting system is now cheaply and easily available to the world at large, and one has to say that it is as good as many of the more expensive commercial offerings for the majority of applications.

The initial version was really a production rule interpreter; the procedural language and the CLIPS Object-Oriented Language (COOL) were not added until the 1990s. The current version runs on UNIX, DOS, Windows, and Macintosh platforms. It is maintained as public domain software[2] and is well documented, as well as being downloadable by anonymous FTP from a number of university sites[3]. CLIPS source code is freely available, so that the basic tool can be installed on any platform with a standard C compiler. However, it is worth getting the official release for your platform in order to obtain the user interface with its command menus and integrated editor.

---

[1] See http://www.jsc.nasa.gov/~clips/CLIPS.html

[2] See http://www.cosmic.uga.edu/

[3] See http://www-cgi.cs.cmu.edu/afs/cs/project/ai-repository/ai/areas/expert/systems/clips

The plan of this appendix is as follows. Section A2 explores the basic features of both the rule language and the procedural language. Section A3 takes a look at objects in CLIPS and shows how they can be made to work together with rules and procedures. Section A4 contains a worked example that demonstrates some advanced techniques in rule-based programming. Section A5 summarizes CLIPS and suggests further study topics.

A2   Rules and functions in CLIPS

As outlined above, the original CLIPS consisted of

- a production rule language, and
- a procedural language.

In this section, we shall look at these two modules, illustrating their main features with examples.

The main components of the rule-based language are the *fact base* and the *rule base*. These serve the following functions.

- The fact base represents the initial state of the problem (see Chapter 2).
- The rule base contains operators which can transform the problem state into a solution (see Chapters 2 and 3).

The CLIPS inference engine matches these facts against the rules to see which rules are applicable. It works in a cyclic fashion as follows:

(1) *Match* the facts against the rules.
(2) *Choose* which rule instantiation to fire.
(3) *Execute* the actions associated with this rule.

This three-step process is sometimes called the recognize–act cycle (see Chapter 5).

A2.1   Facts

Once you have launched the CLIPS application, you should see the CLIPS prompt in a buffer, which tells you that you are interacting with an interpreter.

```
CLIPS>
```

Various commands are then available to you. Thus facts can be asserted into the fact base explicitly at the top level of the interpreter, using the assert command, for example:

```
CLIPS> (assert (today is sunday))
<Fact-0>

CLIPS> (assert (weather is warm))
<Fact-1>
```

For convenient identification, user inputs will be rendered in italics here, while system prompts and responses will be in plain type.

Facts in the fact base can then be listed with the facts command:

```
CLIPS> (facts)
```

```
f-0 (today is sunday)
f-1 (weather is warm)
```

In more recent versions of CLIPS, for example for Windows, commands such as 'facts' are available in pull-down menus.

Facts can also be removed from the fact base with the retract command.

```
CLIPS> (retract 1)
CLIPS> (facts)
f-0 (today is sunday)
```

However, assert and retract are more commonly used in the action part of rules in order to manipulate the fact base. A useful command that one would use at the top level of the interpreter (usually via a pull-down menu) is clear, which destroys all the current facts.

```
CLIPS> (clear)
CLIPS> (facts)
```

Play with these commands briefly to get the feel of the system.

Rather than have you fool around with individual assert statements, CLIPS provides a mechanism for defining a whole bunch of facts at one time, using the deffacts command.

```
(deffacts today
  (today is sunday)
  (weather is warm)
)
```

The deffacts statement is therefore a LISP-like expression that starts with the deffacts command, then cites a name for the list of facts you are about to define, such as 'today,' and then defines as many facts as you like for addition to the list. This set of facts can later be undefined or cleared by

```
CLIPS> (undeffacts today)
```

One could type the deffacts statement into the CLIPS buffer, but the smart thing to do is to load it from a file you have created using the CLIPS editor, or some other editor of your choice. Loading of files is typically accomplished via the File menu, although

```
CLIPS> (load "myfile")
```

would also work if the statement deffacts was in a file called 'myfile.'

However, once the file is loaded, the defined facts are still not actually in the CLIPS fact base. deffacts simply defines 'today' to be a potential set of facts. The key command to install the facts is called reset.

```
CLIPS> (reset)
```

reset removes any facts already in the fact base and inserts the facts associated with *all* currently defined sets of facts. It also adds a single system-defined fact:

```
f-0 (initial-fact)
```

This is provided as a convenience, because it often makes sense to write a 'start rule' which matches against this fact and gets the recognize–act cycle going. However, you don't have to use it.

You can watch `reset` at work if you follow the example given above after the Watch command in the Execution menu is turned on for Facts.

A2.2   Rules

CLIPS rules have the following syntax.

```
(defrule <rule-name>
 <optional comment>
 <optional declaration>
 <premise₁>
 ...
 <premiseₘ>
 =>
 <action₁>
 ...
 <actionₙ>
)
```

For example,

```
(defrule chores
 "Things to do on Sunday"
 (salience 10)
 (today is sunday)
 (weather is warm)
 =>
 (assert (wash car))
 (assert (chop wood))
)
```

'Chores' is just an arbitrary name for the rule. The premise part of the rule

```
(today is Sunday)
(weather is warm)
```

matches against the fact base, while action part after the '=>' will insert the two facts

```
(wash car)
(chop wood)
```

into the fact base, whenever the rule fires. The comment

```
"Things to do on Sunday"
```

is simply a piece of documentation that you will be glad you wrote when the rule base has scores of rules in it, while the statement

```
(salience 10)
```

says how important the rule is, roughly speaking. For example, if there was a competing rule

```
(defrule fun
 "Better things to do on Sunday"
 (salience 100)
 (today is sunday)
```

```
(weather is warm)
=>
(assert (drink beer))
(assert (play guitar))
)
```

then, all other things being equal, the 'fun' rule would be selected by the inference engine in preference to the 'chores' rule, because its salience is higher. Saliences can be set to any integer in the range [–10 000, 10 000]. If you do not set a salience, it defaults to 0.

Of course, rules will typically contain variables, to make them more applicable. Thus

```
(defrule pick-a-chore
  "Allocating chores to days"
  (today is ?day)
  (chore is ?job)
  =>
  (assert (do ?job on ?day))
)
```

would match against a fact base containing

```
(today is sunday)
(chore is carwash)
```

and would insert

```
(do carwash on sunday)
```

into the fact base, if that rule were selected to fire. Similarly, the rule

```
(defrule drop-a-chore
  "Allocating chores to days"
  (today is ?day)
  ?chore <- (do ?job on ?day)
  =>
  (retract ?chore)
)
```

would cancel a chore. Note that both instances of ?day must be bound to the same value. Note also that we have to assign a variable, ?chore, to the fact that we want to retract, and that this assignment occurs through the premise that was matched.

So this rule would match against a fact base containing

```
(today is sunday)
(do carwash on sunday)
```

and delete

```
(do carwash on sunday)
```

from the fact base, if that rule were selected to fire.

The details of the pattern matching supported in CLIPS can be found in the manual, but the fact

```
(do carwash on sunday)
```

would match any of the following patterns

```
(do ? ? sunday)
(do ? on ?)
(do ? on ?when)
(do $?)
(do $? sunday)
(do ?chore $?when)
```

Note that the $? prefix denotes a segment variable that will bind to a list segment. Thus the variable $?when would bind to

```
(on sunday)
```

in the last example. Plain ? and $?, occurring without a variable name suffix, are simply wildcards that match single list items or segments respectively, but do not bind to anything.

A2.3   Watching and dribbling

Let's begin with a simpler example to illustrate some debugging features provided by the CLIPS environment.

```
(defrule start
  (initial-fact)
  =>
  (printout t "hello, world" crlf)
)
```

Type this into a file and then load it into CLIPS. Execute a reset, either by typing

```
CLIPS> (reset)
```

or by selecting Execution/Reset from the command menu (in the Windows version), or by typing CTRL-U (in the Windows version).

Then run the program, either by typing

```
CLIPS> (run)
```

or by selecting Execution/Run from the command menu (in the Windows version), or by typing CTRL-R (in the Windows version).

The program should then print the immortal words 'hello, world.' To invoke the program again, simply reset and run as before.

If you had the Rules box checked in the Execution/Watch menu selection, or typed

```
CLIPS> (watch rules)
```

before running the program, then you would see the trace

```
CLIPS> (run)
FIRE 1 start: f-0
hello, world
```

where FIRE denotes a rule firing, start is the name of the rule that fired, and f-0 is the name of the fact that satisfied it. The 'watch' facility affords various levels of trace, as described in the manual.

If you had typed

```
CLIPS> (dribble-on "dribble.clp")
TRUE
```

before running, then

```
CLIPS> (run)
FIRE 1 start: f-0
hello, world
```

would be saved in the file 'dribble.clp' after

```
CLIPS> (dribble-off)
TRUE
```

was executed. This is a useful facility, especially when you are starting out.

A2.4 Using templates

Rather than use list-like structures for facts, it is usually more convenient to use templates, which resemble simple records. (They bear no resemblance to C++ templates.) Templates look like this:

```
(deftemplate student "a student record"
  (slot name (type STRING))
  (slot age (type NUMBER) (default 18))
  )
```

Each template declaration consists of an arbitrary name for the template, an optional comment, and some number of slot declarations. A slot consists of a data field, such as 'name' and a data type, such as 'STRING.' Default values can also be declared, as in the above example.

Following such a declaration, the statement

```
(deffacts students
  (student (name fred))
  (student (name freda) (age 19))
  )
```

would result in

```
(student (name fred) (age 18))
(student (name freda) (age 19))
```

being added to the fact base at reset time.

A2.5 Defining functions

A CLIPS function has a LISP-like appearance (see Chapter 4), with the important difference that variables must begin with a ? prefix, as in the following definition.

```
(deffunction hypotenuse (?a ?b)
  (sqrt (+ (* ?a ?a) (* ?b ?b)))
  )
```

In general, CLIPS functions have the following form:

```
(deffunction <function-name> (<arg> ... <arg>)
```

```
  <expression>
  <expression>
  )
```

The value of the last expression is the value returned by the function.

But often functions are really executed for their side effects, for example:

```
(deffunction init (?day)
  (reset)
  (assert (today is ?day))
  )
```

Thus

```
CLIPS> (init sunday)
```

would execute a reset, thereby clearing the fact base, and then insert

```
(today is sunday)
```

into the fact base.

A3 Object-orientation in CLIPS

Objects are useful for managing complexity in CLIPS because they allow the programmer to keep the rules clean and simple by implementing mechanisms for data update as message handlers associated with a class. We will illustrate this principle in this section by writing code which simulates the safe handling and firing of a semi-automatic pistol. Rules will still drive the computation, but they will hand off the details of the simulation by message passing.

First, let us define the class 'pistol' in the CLIPS object-oriented language, COOL, along with some properties needed for the simulation.

```
(defclass pistol
  (is-a USER)
  (role concrete)
  (pattern-match reactive)
  (slot safety (type SYMBOL) (create-accessor read-write))
  (slot slide (type SYMBOL) (create-accessor read-write))
  (slot hammer (type SYMBOL) (create-accessor read-write))
  (slot chamber (type INTEGER) (create-accessor read-write))
  (slot magazine (type SYMBOL) (create-accessor read-write))
  (slot rounds (type INTEGER) (create-accessor read-write))
  )
```

The first three slots are 'system slots' needed by COOL. They tell COOL that

- 'pistol' is a user-defined class;
- 'pistol' is a concrete class that will have instances, as opposed to an abstract class, which would not be instantiated, but exist solely to structure the class hierarchy;
- instances of 'pistol' should be available as data objects to match against rule conditions and be affected by rule actions.

The next five slots declare the following properties or data members of the class:

- the safety slot will contain the symbol 'on' or 'off';
- the slide slot will contain 'forward' or back' to denote the position of the slide;
- the hammer slot says whether the hammer is 'back' or 'down';
- the chamber slot will hold '1' or '0,' depending upon whether or not there is a round in the chamber;
- the magazine slot will hold 'in' or 'out,' depending upon whether or not there is a magazine seated in the pistol's butt;
- the rounds slot will keep track of how many rounds are in the magazine.

If we want to be able to 'put' and 'get' values to and from these slots, we need to enable this by creating an automatic accessor function via the create-accessor facet.

We can now define an instance of pistol, as follows.

```
(definstances pistols
  (PPK of pistol
    (safety on)
    (slide forward)
    (hammer down)
    (chamber 0)
    (magazine out)
    (rounds 6))
  )
```

Thus the PPK is correctly stowed with the magazine out, the safety on, the slide forward, and the hammer down on an empty chamber. The magazine is already loaded with six rounds.

Now that we have a class and an instance, we want to write rules and message handlers that take us through the steps of safely loading the gun, firing it once, and then unloading it. One way to do this is to build a task template that will guide the application of the rules. We want to keep track of two things:

- whether or not there is a round in the chamber;
- whether or not we have fired the gun.

The following template will serve this purpose.

```
(deftemplate range-test
  (field check (type SYMBOL) (default no))
  (field fired (type SYMBOL) (default no))
  )
```

Our first rule will set up range-test as a task in working memory.

```
(defrule start
  (initial-fact)
  =>
  (assert (range-test))
  )
```

This rule will add

```
(range-test (check no) (fired no))
```

to working memory when it fires. Our next three rules will check that the weapon was indeed stowed correctly.

```
(defrule check
  (object (name [PPK]) (safety on) (magazine out))
  ?T <- (range-test (check no))
  =>
  (send [PPK] clear)
  (modify ?T (check yes))
)
```

The rule check says that if the safety is on, the magazine is out, and we haven't checked the pistol, we should clear the chamber, or check that it is clear. We can write a message handler clear for the class pistol as follows.

```
(defmessage-handler pistol clear ()
  (dynamic-put chamber 0)
  (ppinstance)
)
```

The first line simply declares that clear is a message handler for the class pistol, and that it takes no arguments. The second line empties the chamber. Of course, the chamber may already be empty, but we do the assignment anyway. The third line tells the instance to 'pretty print' itself, so that we see the state of its slots.

The next two rules deal with the case where the pistol has been stowed incorrectly, with the safety off, or the magazine in. The rule correct1 puts the safety on, while the rule correct2 drops the magazine.

```
(defrule correct1
  (object (name [PPK]) (safety off))
  (range-test (check no))
  =>
  (send [PPK] safety on)
)

(defrule correct2
  (object (name [PPK]) (safety on) (magazine in))
  (range-test (check no))
  =>
  (send [PPK] drop)
)
```

As before, we must associate message handlers with the messages safety and drop.

```
(defmessage-handler pistol safety (?on-off)
  (dynamic-put safety ?on-off)
  (if (eq ?on-off on)
  then (dynamic-put hammer down)
  )
)
```

The safety message handler takes a single argument, which is either the symbol on or the symbol off. Instead, we could have written two message handlers, one for safety-on and one for safety-off. Note that, on a Walther PPK, the safety also functions as a decocker, so that putting the safety on will safely drop the hammer if it is drawn back.

The drop message handler simply drops the magazine from the mag well.

```
(defmessage-handler pistol drop ()
 (dynamic-put magazine out)
)
```

Now that the gun has been rendered safe, we can prepare it to fire. The next rule leads to the insertion of the magazine.

```
(defrule mag-in
 (object (name [PPK]) (safety on) (magazine out))
 (range-test (fired no) (check yes))
 =>
 (send [PPK] seat)
)
```

The message handler seat is just the inverse of the drop operation.

```
(defmessage-handler pistol seat ()
 (dynamic-put magazine in)
)
```

Of course, we could have written mag-in as

```
(defrule mag-in
 ?gun <- (object (name [PPK]) (safety on) (magazine out))
 (range-test (fired no) (check yes))
 =>
 (modify ?gun (magazine in))
)
```

but we adhere to the principle of having objects manage their own data. The next rule loads a round into the chamber.

```
(defrule load
 (object (name [PPK]) (magazine in) (chamber 0))
 =>
 (send [PPK] rack)
)
```

The body of the rack message handler shows the advantage of allowing objects to manage their own data, since it must contain a little logic of its own.

```
(defmessage-handler pistol rack ()
 (if (> (dynamic-get rounds) 0)
 then (dynamic-put chamber 1)
 (dynamic-put rounds (- (dynamic-get rounds) 1))
 (dynamic-put slide forward)
 else (dynamic-put chamber 0)
 (dynamic-put slide back)
 )
)
```

Racking the slide will completely cycle the action and load a round into the chamber only if the magazine is non-empty. If the magazine is empty, then the chamber stays empty and the slide will stay back and not return to battery. The next rule makes the gun ready to fire. Note that we get to reuse the safety message handler.

```
(defrule ready
  (object (name [PPK]) (chamber 1))
  =>
  (send [PPK] safety off)
)
```

We are finally ready to fire the gun.

```
(defrule fire
  (object (name [PPK]) (safety off))
  ?T <- (range-test (fired no))
  =>
  (if (eq (send [PPK] fire) TRUE)
    then (modify ?T (fired yes)))
)
```

Note that the message handler returns a value when it is invoked and we can test this value to see if the gun actually fired. If the chamber is loaded and the safety is off, then the gun will fire, and the function returns TRUE (after printing out BANG!). Otherwise it returns FALSE (after printing out click). The rule only marks the range test as having led to the successful firing of the gun if the right value is returned.

```
(defmessage-handler pistol fire ()
  (if (and
          (eq (dynamic-get chamber) 1)
          (eq (dynamic-get safety) off)
      )
    then (printout t crlf "BANG!" t crlf)
         (RUE
    else (printout t crlf "click" t crlf)
       FALSE
  )
)
```

It is OK for the message handler to check a condition (the safety's being off) that we already checked in the rule, because we may want to call this message handler from another rule that doesn't perform this test. The point is to make the code in the handler as self-contained as possible.

Having fired the gun, we must now make it safe, which begins with putting the safety back on, using the safety message-handler we already wrote.

```
(defrule unready
  (object (name [PPK]) (safety off))
  (range-test (fired yes))
  =>
  (send [PPK] safety on)
)
```

Next we drop the magazine. Note that we can reuse the drop message handler.

```
(defrule drop
  (object (name [PPK]) (safety on))
  (range-test (fired yes))
  =>
  (send [PPK] drop)
```

```
    )
```

Finally we clear the chamber, reusing the `clear` messagehandler.

```
(defrule unload
  (object (name [PPK]) (safety on) (magazine out))
  (range-test (fired yes))
  =>
  (send [PPK] clear)
)
```

This program illustrates the ways in which rules and objects coexist in CLIPS. Rules retain control of the computation, but delegate certain data management tasks to objects. Object do not reside in working memory, but the left-hand side of rules can match against their slots. Rules can also side-effect their slots, although I would argue that it is better programming practice to let objects perform their own data manipulation. Objects do not 'call' rules, but they can return values to rules to feed logic in their right-hand sides.

A4   The 'Knights and Knaves' example

I have chosen a puzzle as the main vehicle for illustrating advanced CLIPS features, rather than an actual expert systems application. The puzzle concerns an island inhabited by two kinds of persons: those who always tell the truth (knights) and those who always lie (knaves). Many variants of this puzzle are discussed in Raymond Smullyan's wonderful work entitled *What is the Name of this Book?*.

Here are some examples of these puzzles:

P1. There are two people, A and B, each of whom is either a knight or a knave. Suppose A says: 'Either I am a knave or B is a knight.' What are A and B?

P2. There are three people, A, B, and C. Suppose A says: 'All of us are knaves' and B says: 'Exactly one of us is a knight.' What are A, B, and C?

P3. There are three people, A, B, and C. A stranger asks A: 'How many knights are among you?' A answers indistinctly, but B says: 'A said that there is one knight among us.' Then C says: 'B is lying!' What are B and C?

A general solution to a class of such problems will fully exercise the rule-based features of CLIPS and provide the opportunity to demonstrate some advanced programming techniques, such as the use of contexts and dependency-directed backtracking. We shall also show how to construct and test prototypes which provide successive approximations to the behavior that we want. This kind of incremental system building is the key to rapid, but structured, expert systems development.

A4.1   Understanding the problem

As in any software project, no matter how large or small, someone needs to understand both the nature and scope of the problem. Your in-house expert needs to be able to actually solve the problem, while your knowledge engineers need to understand what a solution involves. In the 'Knights and Knaves' example, we can serve as our own experts.

One way to solve such puzzles is to systematically explore what happens when you assume that a speaker is telling the truth or when you assume that a speaker is lying. Let

$T(A)$

denote that A is telling the truth and is therefore a knight, and let

$F(A)$

denote that A is lying and is therefore a knave. Looking at P1, we can write

$T(A) \Rightarrow F(A) \lor T(B)$

to represent the fact that, if we assume that A is a knight, then it follows that either A is a knave or B is a knight, based on A's statement 'Either I am a knave or B is a knight.' Since A cannot be both a knight and a knave, it follows that

$T(A) \Rightarrow T(B)$.

Similarly, we can write

$F(A) \Rightarrow \lnot(F(A) \lor T(B))$

to represent that fact that, if we assume that A is a knave, then it follows that his statement is false, so we place it in the scope of negation. Simplifying, we can rewrite this as

$F(A) \Rightarrow \lnot F(A) \land \lnot T(B)$

or, better still,

$F(A) \Rightarrow T(A) \land F(B)$.

Visual inspection of these two alternative worlds, the one in which A is a knight versus the one in which he is a knave, makes it clear that only the former is viable, since the latter generates an inconsistency. A must be a knight, which makes B a knight too.

The problem is clearly one in which solutions are found by making assumptions and then looking for contradictions, or the lack of them. We assume that a given speaker is telling the truth and see if we can then construct a unique consistent assignment of truth and falsity to statements and hence knighthood and knavehood to the target characters. In the jargon of mathematical logic, an assignment of truth and falsity to a set of statements is called an *interpretation*, while a consistent assignment that renders a set of statements true is called a *model*.

However, our puzzle is a little more involved than the typical logic problem, because there can be more than one speaker (as in P2) as well as reported speech (as in P3). The initial version of the program does not have to address such complications, but the final version should extend the restricted scope of earlier prototypes. We will see that the rule-based approach is particularly well suited to the incremental addition of complexity.

In fact, it is sometimes useful to address a 'degenerate case' of a problem in the first version of the program, that is, to set out to solve a trivial problem which nonetheless has many of the features of the real problem. Here is an instance of such a problem for 'Knights and Knaves.'

P0. A says: 'I am a knave.' Is A a knight or a knave?

P0 is simply a way of stating the well-known Liar Paradox. If A is a knave, then he is lying, so he is really a knight, but that leads to a contradiction. If A is a knight, then he is telling the truth, so he really is a knave, but that also leads to a contradiction. There is no consistent way to assign truth or falsity to A's self-referential statement, that is, it has no model.

There are a number of advantages to starting with P0.

- There is a single speaker and only one character.
- The statement does not contain logical connectives, such as 'or' and 'and,' or quantifiers, such as 'all,' 'some' and 'exactly one.'
- There is no reported speech.

At the same time, the essential features of the problem are still present. We still have to try to construct a consistent interpretation of A's statement, which means we have to accomplish two tasks common to more complex versions of the puzzle:

- assign alternative interpretations to statements, and
- detect contradictions, if they occur.

We shall see that the mechanisms required to perform these two tasks strongly resemble some of the truth maintenance machinery described in Chapters 17 and 19.

A4.2   Ontological analysis and knowledge representation

The next step is to determine what kinds of data one needs to deal with. What are the objects of interest in our 'Knights and Knaves' universe? And which of their attributes do we need to represent in order to solve a puzzle?

Clearly, the following objects and attributes are essential.

- There are *speakers*. Speakers make claims about themselves or other persons. A speaker is either always lying or always telling the truth.
- There are *claims* made by speakers. These can either be true or false. In the most general case, a claim can contain reported speech.

But a little thought will show that there are other objects and attributes that are important in solving one of these puzzles.

- There are what we have called *worlds*, which are created by sets of assumptions. For example, there is the world in which we assume that A is a knight, and is therefore telling the truth. Various consequences follow from this assumption, but they will be confined to the context of this hypothetical world.
- There are what we might call *reasons*, which represent consequential links between statements in a world. If A says 'B is a knave,' and we assume that A is a knight, then this statement is a reason for believing that B is a knave, and for further assuming that anything that B says is false. Keeping track of these relationships between statements is essential if we want to recover from contradictions derived from assumptions that turn out to be false.

There are obviously many ways in which one could choose to represent these objects, together with their attributes and relationships. Ontological analysis almost never determines a unique representation. Cutting to the chase, I chose to encode these entities in the following way for the first version of my CLIPS program.

```
;; A statement has a speaker.
;; A statement makes a claim.
;; A statement has a ground (a reason for believing it)
;; and a tag (which is just an arbitrary identifier).
(deftemplate statement
  (field speaker (type SYMBOL))
  (multifield claim (type SYMBOL))
  (multifield reason (type INTEGER) (default 0))
  (field tag (type INTEGER) (default 1))
)
```

Rather than focus on the speaker, I focus on the statement, and make the speaker an attribute of it. I want to be able to set up a puzzle with a template instantiation such as:

```
(statement (speaker A) (claim F A))
```

This can be read as follows: There is a statement made by A which claims that A is a knave, and it will get a default tag of 1. Note that its reason will also be set to 0 by default; that is, we can assume there is no previous statement that justifies it, since none was explicitly stated.

Note that claim and reason are 'multifields,' because they may need to contain more than one datum (see manual).

However, merely representing statements is not enough, because we will want to unwrap statements in order to reason about the claims themselves. In so doing, we need to know whether we are in the scope of truth or falsity, that is, whether the claim follows from an assumption that the speaker was telling the truth, or an assumption that the speaker was lying. We also want each claim to have a unique numeric identifier, for reasons that will become apparent.

```
;; A claim has content, for example,
;; T A ...' meaning A is a truth-teller (knight)
;; F A ... meaning A is a liar (knave).
;; A claim has a reason which supports it,
;; typically the tag of a statement
;; or the tag of another claim.
;; A claim has a scope, which is truth or falsity.
(deftemplate claim
  (multifield content (type SYMBOL))
  (multifield reason (type INTEGER) (default 0))
  (field scope (type SYMBOL))
)
```

Thus, when we unwrap our sample statement with an assumption that A is telling the truth, we want the following claim to emerge:

```
(claim (content F A) (reason 1) (scope truth)).
```

Thus a claim inherits its content from the statement it derives from. This statement is the reason we entertain the claim. We are in the scope of an assumption of the truth with respect to this statement.

Finally, we need to represent the world we are currently in. Such worlds come into being when we make assumptions. We need to be able to identify and distinguish them, particularly when detecting contradictions. For example, there is no contradiction between T(A) and F(A) if these expressions are deemed to be true in different worlds, that is, under different sets of assumptions. Refer back to the example in A4 if this seems unclear.

We can represent such worlds as follows:

```
;; A world is a context created by an assumption.
;; It has a unique identifier or tag, and its scope
;; is truth or falsity, depending upon assumption type.
(deftemplate world
  (field tag (type INTEGER) (default 1))
  (field scope (type SYMBOL) (default truth))
)
```

Note that, thanks to default values, we can start each computation with a world labeled 1 which we plan to populate with statements based on an assumption of truth. So we can initialize our fact base, called the-facts, for puzzle P0 as follows:

```
;; A claims that A is a liar.
(deffacts the-facts
  (world)
  (statement (speaker A) (claim F A))
)
```

If we keep this deffacts statement in the same file as our template declarations (and the rules that we are about to write) then, after loading the file into the CLIPS environment, all we need do is execute a reset, and we are ready to run the rule set on this problem.

A4.3 Writing the rules

Without further ado, let's look at a set of rules that solve the degenerate case of P0. The first two rules, unwrap-true and unwrap-false, assume that the speaker is telling the truth or lying respectively, and generate the appropriate claims.

```
;; Unwrap statements
(defrule unwrap-true
  (world (tag ?N) (scope truth))
  (statement (speaker ?X) (claim $?Y) (tag ?N))
  =>
  (assert (claim (content T ?X) (reason ?N) (scope truth)))
  (assert (claim (content $?Y) (reason ?N) (scope truth)))
)

(defrule unwrap-false
  (world (tag ?N) (scope falsity))
  (statement (speaker ?X) (claim $?Y) (tag ?N))
  =>
  (assert (claim (content F ?X) (reason ?N) (scope falsity)))
  (assert
    (claim (content NOT $?Y) (reason ?N) (scope falsity)))
)
```

The first action item of each rule makes the assumption that the speaker is a knight or a knave respectively, which the second action item propagates this assumption to the claim being made.

Next we need some rules to drive negation into expressions. Since ¬T(A) is equivalent to F(A), and ¬F(A) is equivalent to T(A), we can have rewrite rules that perform this simple transformation. The output of such rules will make it easier to detect contradictions following from assumptions.

```
;; Negation rules
(defrule not1
  ?F <- (claim (content NOT T ?P))
  =>
  (modify ?F (content F ?P))
)

(defrule not2
  ?F <- (claim (content NOT F ?P))
  =>
  (modify ?F (content T ?P))
)

;; Find contradiction between assumption of truth
;; and derived fact.
(defrule contra-truth
  (declare (salience 10))
  ?W <- (world (tag ?N) (scope truth))
  ?S <- (statement (speaker ?Y) (tag ?N))
  ?P <- (claim (content T ?X) (reason ?N) (scope truth))
  ?Q <- (claim (content F ?X) (reason ?N) (scope truth))
  =>
  (printout
    t crlf
    "Statement is inconsistent if " ?Y " is a knight."
    t crlf)
  (retract ?Q)
  (retract ?P)
  (modify ?W (scope falsity))
)
```

If we detect a contradiction in the scope of truth, we delete the contradictory pair of claims   and move to an assumption of falsity. If we detect a contradiction in the scope of falsity, then we are out of options, and we are left with a global contradiction, that is, a paradox.

```
;; Find contradiction between assumption of falsity
;; and derived fact.
(defrule contra-falsity
  (declare (salience 10))
  ?W <- (world (tag ?N) (scope falsity))
  ?S <- (statement (speaker ?Y) (tag ?N))
  ?P <- (claim (content F ?X) (reason ?N) (scope falsity))
  ?Q <- (claim (content T ?X) (reason ?N) (scope falsity))
  =>
  (printout
    t crlf
    "Statement is inconsistent if " ?Y " is a knave."
    t crlf)
```

```
(modify ?W (scope contra))
)
```

The sweep rule is needed to make sure that we retract all the consequences of our assumptions.

```
;; Clear out all claims based on assumption of truth
;; of a claim once falsity is assumed.
(defrule sweep
  (declare (salience 20))
  (world (tag ?N) (scope falsity))
  ?F <- (claim (reason ?N) (scope truth))
  =>
  (retract ?F)
)
```

Note that contra-truth, contra-falsity and sweep have a higher salience than the other rules, to make sure that contradictions are detected as soon as possible and that consequences of failed assumptions are retracted as soon as an assumption fails.

If we now run the complete program on the 'I am a knave' example, the program quickly detects that both contexts are contradictory. In other words, whether we assume that A is telling the truth or lying, we get an inconsistent world. Refer to Figure A.1 for a trace of the program. Lines in italics are output by print statements in the program. I have emboldened the rule firings for ease of reading.

```
CLIPS> (reset)
==> f-0   (initial-fact)
==> f-1   (world (tag 1) (scope truth))
==> f-2   (statement (speaker A) (claim F A) (reason 0) (tag 1))
CLIPS> (run)
FIRE 1 unwrap-true: f-1,f-2
Assumption:
  A is a knight, so (T A) is true.
==> f-3   (claim (content F A) (reason 1) (scope truth))
==> f-4   (claim (content T A) (reason 1) (scope truth))
FIRE 2 contra-truth: f-1,f-2,f-4,f-3
Statement is inconsistent if A is a knight.
<== f-3   (claim (content F A) (reason 1) (scope truth))
<== f-4   (claim (content T A) (reason 1) (scope truth))
<== f-1   (world (tag 1) (scope truth))
==> f-5   (world (tag 1) (scope falsity))
FIRE 3 unwrap-false: f-5,f-2
Assumption
  A is a knave, so (T A) is false.
==> f-6   (claim (content NOT F A) (reason 1) (scope falsity))
==> f-7   (claim (content F A) (reason 1) (scope falsity))
FIRE 4 not2: f-6
<== f-6   (claim (content NOT F A) (reason 1) (scope falsity))
==> f-8   (claim (content T A) (reason 1) (scope falsity))
FIRE 5 contra-falsity: f-5,f-2,f-7,f-8
Statement is inconsistent if A is a knave.
<== f-5   (world (tag 1) (scope falsity))
==> f-9   (world (tag 1) (scope contra))
```

Figure A.1 A trace of the first Knights and Knaves program.

Now refer to Exercise 1 for a desirable extension to the program.

Exercise 1

Consider the following 'Knights and Knaves' puzzle, which is also a degenerate case.

A: 'I am a knight.'

What if anything can we conclude about the speaker, A? Obviously he could be either a knight or a knave, so the solution to the puzzle is indeterminate. You can verify that the program will find no solution.

Your task is to modify the program so that it indicates when A's knighthood or knavehood is consistent with the known facts. In this case, it would be consistent either way. One way to do it would be to write rules **consist-truth** and **consist-falsity** modeled on **contra-truth** and **contra-falsity** which fire when no other rules want to fire and which let the user know that no contradictions have been found in the current scope.

Note that, even if the assumption of truth provokes no inconsistency, you might still want to go ahead and see what the assumption of falsity brings. If that assumption is also consistent, then the solution is indeterminate, as noted above. Otherwise, the single consistent interpretation provides the solution.

A4.4   Extending the rules: logical compounds

The next step is to extend the program so that it handles compound statements. This will allow us to state more interesting puzzles than the degenerate cases handled above. Let's work with the following example:

P4. There are two people, A and B, each of whom is either a knight or a knave. Suppose A says: 'Both of us are knaves.' What are A and B?

Now we have to be able to handle conjunction, since we will model A's claim as

$F(A) \wedge F(B)$.

This conjunction needs to be broken down into its component statements, so that we can check for inconsistency. Clearly, A cannot be a knight, because it follows from this assumption that he is a knave. But the program must be able to 'unpack' the conjunction to find this out.

However, we also need to be able to handle disjunction, because when we assume that A is lying we have to drive negation into the compound statement, turning

$F(A) \wedge F(B)$

into

$T(A) \vee T(B)$.

This involves both writing rules to drive negation through connectives like conjunction and disjunction, and writing rules which understand that a disjunct like $T(A)$ is really an assumption. We will evaluate $T(A) \vee T(B)$ by first assuming $T(A)$ and looking for a contradiction. If we fail to find one, then we can assume that $T(A) \vee T(B)$ is consistent with the assumption that A is lying, F(A). But if T(A) generates an inconsistency, then we have to undo the assumption of T(A), and assume T(B). If T(B) generates an inconsistency, then T(A) ∨ T(B) is inconsistent with the assumption of F(A). Otherwise, T(B) forms part of a consistent interpretation of the initial statement.

The easiest way to represent compound statements in CLIPS is to write the contents of a claim as a 'Polish' expression. Polish is a notation in which operators are given before arguments. The operators have a fixed arity (that is, they always take a certain number of arguments), so we can always reconstruct the scope of an operator, even when operators are nested. Thus, the parenthesized expression

¬(F(A) ∧ T(B))

can be represented by the flat expression

NOT AND F A T B.

You can most easily recover the structure of such an expression by working from right to left, placing arguments on one side until you encounter an operator that will consume them. The operator–argument compound can then be construed as an argument for the next operator. Thus B is immediately consumed by T, but we must discover both T(B) and F(A) before we have two arguments to feed AND.

Given this representation, the logical rules for driving negation through the connectives are fairly straightforward, so long as we define a CLIPS function, called flip, which turns 'T' into 'F' and vice versa.

```
(defrule not-or
 ?F <- (claim (content NOT OR ?P ?X ?Q ?Y))
 =>
 (modify ?F (content AND (flip ?P) ?X (flip ?Q) ?Y))
)
(defrule not-and
 ?F <- (claim (content NOT AND ?P ?X ?Q ?Y))
 =>
 (modify ?F (content OR (flip ?P) ?X (flip ?Q) ?Y))
)
```

The flip function is needed because it is more convenient to go direct from, for example:

NOT AND F A T B

to

OR T A F B

rather than

OR NOT F A NOT T B.

flip is easily defined.

```
(deffunction flip (?P)
 (if (eq ?P T) then F else T))
```

For ease of exposition, we will confine ourselves to claims that consist of simple conjunctions and disjunctions, for example:

$$T(A) \vee T(B)$$

or

$$F(A) \wedge T(B)$$

but not

$$F(B) \wedge (T(A) \vee T(B))$$

or

$$\neg(F(A) \vee F(B)) \wedge (T(A) \vee T(B)),$$

but the simpler expressions suffice for most interesting puzzles.

The hard part of this extension to our program lies in processing disjunctions, because we need to ensure that we don't cry 'contradiction!' until we have run out of disjuncts. For example, F(A) is not inconsistent with T(A) (F(B). When we process T(A) by assuming it, the resulting contradiction is merely local to the context of that assumption. If we then back out of that context and try F(B), we derive no contradiction, and so we have found an interpretation.

One way to implement this distinction between a local and a global contradiction is to add a 'context' attribute to our 'claim' template, thus:

```
(deftemplate claim
  (multifield content (type SYMBOL))
  (multifield reason (type INTEGER) (default 0))
  (field scope (type SYMBOL))
  (field context (type INTEGER) (default 0))
)
```

A context of '0' is global, so claims inhabit a global context by default. We shall use '1' to denote the context of the left disjunct, and '2' the context of the right disjunct. Thus, given

$$T(A) \vee F(B),$$

T(A) would be true in context 1 and F(B) would be true in context 2. The whole disjunction is true globally in context 0.

The 'world' data structure also needs a context field, to keep track of the current focus of the computation. Thus a world vector like

```
(world (tag 1) (scope truth) (context 2))
```

stands for the world created by assuming that the statement tagged '1' is true, and then assuming the right disjunct of the claim associated with this statement. The new declaration for the world template is given below.

```
;; A world is a context created by an assumption.
;; It has a unique identifier or tag, and its scope
;; is truth or falsity, depending upon the assumption.
;; The context field keeps track of where we are in a
;; disjunction:
;; 0 means no disjunction,
;; 1 means left disjunct,
;; 2 means right disjunct.
```

```
(deftemplate world
  (field tag (type INTEGER) (default 1))
  (field scope (type SYMBOL) (default truth))
  (field context (type INTEGER) (default 0))
)
```

We are now ready to write some rules that manipulate these context values. The following rule simply creates a new context for the left disjunct of a disjunction.

```
(defrule left-or
  ?W <- (world (tag ?N) (context 0))
  (claim (content OR ?P ?X ?Q ?Y) (reason ?N) (scope ?V))
  =>
  (modify ?W (context 1))
  (assert
    (claim
      (content ?P ?X) (reason ?N) (scope ?V) (context 1)))
)
```

It does this by creating a new world context, labeled '1', and then asserting the left disjunct qualified by that new context.

Similarly, the next rule creates a context for the right disjunct.

```
(defrule right-or
  ?W <- (world (tag ?N) (context 1))
  (claim (content OR ?P ?X ?Q ?Y) (reason ?N) (scope ?V))
  =>
  (modify ?W (context 2))
  (assert
    (claim
      (content ?Q ?Y) (reason ?N) (scope ?V) (context 2)))
)
```

Exercise 2

Write a single rule to take a claim that is a conjunction, such as

```
(claim (content AND T A F B) (reason 1) (scope truth))
```

and split it by asserting two new claims, one to the effect that A is a knight, and the other to the effect that B is a knave. The new claims should live in the current context identified by the 'world' vector.

Once we have the rules given above, and the rule for handling conjunctions described in Exercise 2, all we need are context-sensitive rules for detecting contradictions.

```
;; Find contradiction between assumption of truth and
;; a derived fact in same world, but different contexts.
(defrule contra-truth-scope
  (declare (salience 10))
  (world (tag ?N) (scope truth) (context ?T))
  (claim
    (content T ?X) (reason ?N) (scope truth)
```

```
      (context ?S&:(< ?S ?T)))
  ?Q <- (claim (content F ?X) (reason ?N) (scope truth)
                (context ?T))
  =>
  (printout t "Disjunct " ?T
    " is inconsistent with earlier truth context." crlf)
  (retract ?Q)
)

;; Find contradiction between assumption of falsity and
;; derived fact in same world, but different contexts.
(defrule contra-falsity-scope
  (declare (salience 10))
  ?W <- (world (tag ?N) (scope falsity) (context ?T))
  (claim
    (content F ?X) (reason ?N) (scope falsity)
    (context ?S&:(< ?S ?T)))
  ?Q <- (claim (content T ?X) (reason ?N) (scope falsity)
                (context ?T))
  =>
  (printout t "Disjunct " ?T
    " is inconsistent with earlier falsity context." crlf)
  (retract ?Q)
)
```

We also need to modify our original rules to accommodate contexts. A flat contradiction now exists if the contradictory statements exist in the same context.

```
;; Find contradiction between assumption of truth and
;; derived fact in the same world and the same context.
(defrule contra-truth
  (declare (salience 10))
  ?W <- (world (tag ?N) (scope truth))
  ?P <- (claim (content T ?X) (reason ?N) (context ?S)
                (scope truth))
  ?Q <- (claim (content F ?X) (reason ?N) (context ?S)
                (scope truth))
  =>
  (printout t
    "Statement is inconsistent if " ?X " is a knight" crlf)
  (retract ?Q)
  (retract ?P)
  (modify ?W (scope falsity) (context 0))
)

;; Find contradiction between assumption of falsity and
;; derived fact in the same world and the same context.
(defrule contra-falsity
  (declare (salience 10))
  ?W <- (world (tag ?N) (scope falsity))
  ?P <- (claim (content F ?X) (reason ?N) (context ?S)
                (scope falsity))
  ?Q <- (claim (content T ?X) (reason ?N) (context ?S)
                (scope falsity))
```

```
  =>
  (printout t
   "Statement is inconsistent whether " ?X
    " is knight or knave."
   crlf)
  (modify ?W (scope contra))
)
```

Now that we are no longer dealing with degenerate cases, it is also worth printing out the solution, that is, printing the assignment of knighthood and knavehood to the characters mentioned in the statements.

```
(defrule consist-truth
  (declare (salience -10))
  ?W <- (world (tag ?N) (scope truth))
  (statement (speaker ?Y) (tag ?N))
  =>
  (printout t "Statement is consistent:" crlf)
  (modify ?W (scope consist))
)

(defrule consist-falsity
  (declare (salience -10))
  ?W <- (world (tag ?N) (scope falsity))
  (statement (speaker ?Y) (tag ?N))
  =>
  (printout t "Statement is consistent:" crlf)
  (modify ?W (scope consist))
)

(defrule true-knight
  (world (tag ?N) (scope consist))
  ?C <- (claim (content T ?X) (reason ?N))
  =>
  (printout t ?X " is a knight" crlf)
  (retract ?C)
)

(defrule false-knave
  (world (tag ?N) (scope consist))
  ?C <- (claim (content F ?X) (reason ?N))
  =>
  (printout t ?X " is a knave" crlf)
  (retract ?C)
)
```

Note that the consistency rules provide an answer to Exercise 1. An answer to Exercise 2 is given by the following rule for splitting conjunctions. Notice that it has to track contexts, even though it doesn't depend on them, in the way that disjunction elimination does.

```
(defrule conj
  (world (tag ?N) (context ?S))
```

```
CLIPS> (reset)
==> f-0  (initial-fact)
==> f-1  (world (tag 1) (scope truth) (context 0))
==> f-2  (statement (speaker A) (claim OR F A T B) (reason 0) (tag 1))
CLIPS> (run)
FIRE 1 unwrap-true: f-1,f-2
Assumption
  A is a knight, so (OR F A T B) is true.
==> f-3  (claim (content OR F A T B) (reason 1) (scope truth) (context 0))
==> f-4  (claim (content T A) (reason 1) (scope truth) (context 0))
FIRE 2 left-or: f-1,f-3
==> f-5  (claim (content F A) (reason 1) (scope truth) (context 1))
<== f-1  (world (tag 1) (scope truth) (context 0))
==> f-6  (world (tag 1) (scope truth) (context 1))
FIRE 3 contra-truth-scope: f-6,f-4,f-5
Disjunct 1 is inconsistent with earlier truth context.
<== f-5  (claim (content F A) (reason 1) (scope truth) (context 1))
FIRE 4 right-or: f-6,f-3
==> f-7  (claim (content T B) (reason 1) (scope truth) (context 2))
<== f-6  (world (tag 1) (scope truth) (context 1))
==> f-8  (world (tag 1) (scope truth) (context 2))
FIRE 5 consist-truth: f-8,f-2
Statement is consistent:
<== f-8  (world (tag 1) (scope truth) (context 2))
==> f-9  (world (tag 1) (scope consist) (context 2))
FIRE 6 true-knight: f-9,f-7
B is a knight
<== f-7  (claim (content T B) (reason 1) (scope truth) (context 2))
FIRE 7 true-knight: f-9,f-4
A is a knight
<== f-4  (claim (content T A) (reason 1) (scope truth) (context 0))
CLIPS>
```

Figure A2. Trace of the second knights and knaves program.

```
(claim (content AND ?P ?X ?Q ?Y) (reason ?N) (scope ?V))
=>
(assert
  (claim
    (content ?P ?X) (reason ?N) (scope ?V) (context ?S)))
(assert
  (claim
    (content ?Q ?Y) (reason ?N) (scope ?V) (context ?S)))
)
```

To run this program on the example P4, the facts must be defined by

```
(deffacts the-facts
  (world)
  (statement (speaker A) (claim AND F A F B) (tag 1))
)
```

If we run our program on these facts, we get the output shown in Figure A2.

A4.5 Backtracking and multiple contexts[†]

The next step in making this program solve harder problems is to deal with the fact that a puzzle may present itself with more than one speaker. For example, consider the multi-speaker puzzle in Exercise 3.

Exercise 3.

P5. There are two people, A and B, who make the following statements.

A: 'I am a knight or B is a knave.'
B: 'A is a knight or I am a knave.'

What are A and B? Solve this by hand, using the logical notation we developed earlier in this appendix.

The task of accommodating multiple speakers requires a version of a slightly complicated technique called dependency-directed backtracking.

The program needs to be able to backtrack under the following circumstances:

- when there is a clash between the current world and an earlier world, where the old world assumes the truth of a statement, but has not checked out its falsity;
- when there is a clash between the current world and an earlier world, where the old world has checked out one disjunct in a disjunction but not the other.

A single example will make this clear.

P6. There are two people, A and B, who make the following statements.
A: 'At least one of us is a knight.'
B: 'At least one of us is a knave.'
What are A and B?

We can encode this problem as follows:

A: $F(A) \vee F(B)$
B: $T(A) \vee T(B)$

Beginning with B's statement:

$T(B) \Rightarrow F(A) \vee F(B)$

and checking out the left disjunct, we generate a consistent interpretation in which B is a knight and A is a knave.

Since we have a consistent interpretation of B's statement, we move on to A's statement:

$T(A) \Rightarrow FALSE,$

since the assumption of A's truthfulness contradicts the interpretation we have chosen for B's statement. Thus we assume that A is a liar.

$F(A) \Rightarrow \neg(T(A) \vee T(B)) \Rightarrow F(A) \wedge F(B) \Rightarrow FALSE.$

This assumption does not work out either, since it contradicts the assumption of B's truthfulness in the interpretation we chose for B's statement.

But our work is not done, because we have not checked out all the interpretations. We did not check the right disjunct while looking for an interpretation of

$$T(B) => F(A) \vee F(B),$$

nor did we check the interpretation that follows from assuming that B is a knave. Until we explore these possibilities, we cannot be sure that these two statements are inconsistent.

So we need to backtrack to the point at which we chose to assume the left disjunct, undo this choice, and try the right one, F(B), instead. In fact, this generates an immediate contradiction with the assumption of B's truthfulness, but without backtracking we could not possibly know this. Even now we are not done, because we need to check out the interpretation that follows from the assumption that B is a liar.

$$F(B) => \neg(F(A) \vee F(B)) => T(A) \wedge T(B) => FALSE.$$

Now we know that there is no consistent interpretation of these two statements. The assumption of B's truthfulness leads to a clash with A's statement, while the assumption of B's untruthfulness is self-inconsistent.

Backtracking in a rule-based system is a little tricky, because you have to be able to restore the previous context that held before you made the assumption you now want to undo. As we saw in Chapter 5, one of the strengths of production systems like CLIPS is that they do not save old states of the current computation, unlike fundamentally recursive programming languages, such as LISP and PROLOG. However, when the need to backtrack arises, it can be accomplished by undoing everything that has been added to working memory between the current state and the backtrack point. But this assumes that nothing essential from the earlier state has been deleted, that is, important changes to working memory since the backtrack point have been purely additive.

Examples such as P6 complicate life considerably because the program now has to be able to perform some additional tasks that were not required in the single statement case:

(1) Save backtrack points to return to.
(2) Decide whether or not to backtrack when met with a contradiction, and where to backtrack to.
(3) Undo everything that has been done between the contradiction and the backtrack point.
(4) Restart the computation from the backtrack point.

Let's address each of these tasks in turn.

- A world already has a unique identifier associated with it, its TAG. This facility was probably not needed to solve the single statement case, since we are always working within a single world, then world generated by that statement. But now this identifier will come into its own, since we must be able to distinguish between claims that are generated by different statements in different worlds. As we work our way systematically through multiple statements, we will generate multiple worlds. We need to leave these worlds in such a state that we can return to them if we need to. This means that the world vector of an 'old' world we have left behind should contain all the information needed for the program to pick up where it left off if we ever backtrack to this point. This boils down to knowing which assumptions were made concerning the truthfulness of the speaker and which disjuncts were checked out, should the speaker's claim contain a disjunction.

- Given that worlds have unique identifiers, and every claim is indexed with the identifier of the world in which it was derived, it is easy to detect 'transworld' contradictions, that is, contradictions that occur between claims in different worlds. The only issue then is whether or not to backtrack to an earlier world if the current world generates a transworld contradiction. Our (depth-first) strategy will be to do this only when we have run out of options in the current world.

- If we number worlds sequentially as we generate them, we should be able to write rules that will take us back to a previous world, destroying both the current world and all intervening worlds (which may have to be regenerated subsequently).

- If the old world vector faithfully reflects the state in which the world was left, and the claims in that world are consistent with that state, then we should be able to restart the computation successfully.

Let's start by creating a slot in the world template to record the prior world with which the current world disagrees. We do this for two reasons:

(1) We need to distinguish the case where a contradiction arises within a world with the case where there is a contradiction between worlds. We do not need to back-track to previous world if the current statement is paradoxical and therefore can-not generate a consistent world.

(2) We might want to write rules which backtrack directly to the prior world.

We shall see that implementing (2) is not actually necessary to solve the problem, nor is it as easy as it sounds, but (1) is both necessary and straightforward.

```
;; A WORLD is a set of claims generated by making an
;; assumption about the truth or falsity of a statement.
;; It has a unique identifier or TAG and its SCOPE
;; is truth or falsity, depending upon the assumption.
;; The PRIOR field can hold the tag of the previously processed
;; world to which it relates usually by generating an
;; inconsistency with it.
;; The CONTEXT keeps track of where we are in disjunctions.
(deftemplate world
  (field tag (type INTEGER) (default 1))
  (field scope (type SYMBOL) (default truth))
  (field prior (type INTEGER) (default 0))
  (field context (type INTEGER) (default 0))
)
```

We now have a place to store the information that we need to implement back-tracking. In addition, there are various tasks that we need new rules to perform, and these tasks need to be keyed to the state of the current world. The main tasks are as follows, and we shall associate keywords with them.

CHECK. This task describes the normal forward movement of the program as it checks out assumptions of truth or falsity.

CONTRA. Analyze a contradiction that has just occurred. Is it between two statements in the same world? Is it between two statements in the same world but in different contexts, for example different forks in a disjunction? Is it between two worlds derived from different statements?

CLEAN. Having diagnosed the contradiction, remove the claims in the most recently generated world, prior to backtracking.

BACK. If we have a contradiction between the current world and an earlier world, then simply backtrack to the last world that has not been checked for falsity or has dangling disjuncts that need to be checked out.

QUIT. We have to know when we have checked out all possible interpretations of a set of statements, that is, when we have checked all disjunctive branches and tried assigning in turn both truth and falsity to all statements and claims. At that point, if we have failed to find a consistent interpretation, we know that the set of statements is inconsistent, and there is no solution in terms of assigning knighthood or knavehood to the speakers.

Here is an extended declaration of the 'world' template which has a TASK field to encode these tasks for the benefit of as yet unwritten rules. This mechanism will work rather like the control tokens we encountered in Chapters 5 and 14, which encourage certain rules to fire. However, we will not count on the MEA strategy to make this work, nor will we use a specially defined vector to achieve this. The controlling tokens will simply be kept in a particular field of the world template. But the net outcome will be the same, in that particular rules will be driven by these task tokens, and will also manipulate them in order to sequence tasks that must be performed in a particular order.

```
;; A WORLD is a set of claims generated by making an
;; assumption about the truth or falsity of a statement.
;; Its TAG corresponds to the tag of that statement.
;; Its SCOPE says whether we are assuming truth or falsity.
;; Its TASK will be one of:
;; CHECK - check out the truth or falsity of a statement
;; CONTRA - check out a contradiction
;; CLEAN - remove claims from an inconsistent world
;; BACK - backtrack to a particular world
;; QUIT - give up.
;; The PRIOR field can hold the tag of a previously processed
;; world to which it relates usually by generating an
;; inconsistency with it.
;; The CONTEXT keeps track of where we are in disjunctions.
(deftemplate world
  (field tag (type INTEGER) (default 1))
  (field scope (type SYMBOL) (default truth))
  (field task (type SYMBOL) (default check))
  (field prior (type INTEGER) (default 0))
  (field context (type INTEGER) (default 0))
)
```

We now need to write rules which perform the operations of contradiction detection, retraction, backtracking, and context reinstatement outlined above. Some modification to the old rules will also be necessary to capture some of the new distinctions we are making about worlds. It is an unfortunate fact of life that making a rule-based program (or any program) more sophisticated almost always involves more than merely adding code.

Contradiction detection

There are two basic cases in which a contradiction can occur:

- between statements in the same world, but possibly different disjunctive contexts;
- between statements in different worlds.

It is convenient to analyze these modes using four different rules. We split the first case into two cases:

- one where the contradictory statements are in the same context, for example where the assumption of T(A) leads straight to the conclusion that F(A), as in the statement A: F(A), and
- one where a disjunctive split intervenes, as in the statement A: T(B) ∨ F(A).

When the conflicting statements are in different worlds, then it pays to separate the case where the current world is in the scope of truth from the case where the scope is falsity. This is because if an assumption of truth fails, the program can try assuming falsity, but if the assumption of falsity fails we will need to backtrack.

These four rules are given below. Note that they are all given high salience values, to make sure that they will be selected by conflict resolution, since there is no point in proceeding down a path that is doomed to fail. We make the intra-world rules more salient than the transworld rules just because it is easier to fix a contradiction involving a single world, and we want to avoid backtracking between worlds if possible.

```
;; IF we find a contradiction between assumption and derived fact
;; in the same world and the same context
;; THEN record the contradiction and retract the offending claims.
(defrule contradiction
  (declare (salience 100))
  ?W <- (world (tag ?N) (task check) (context ?S) (prior 0))
  ?P <- (claim (content ?F ?X) (reason ?N) (context ?S))
  ?Q <- (claim (content ?G&:(not (eq ?G ?F)) ?X) (reason ?N)
  (context ?S))
  =>
  (printout
   t crlf
   "CONTRADICTION: " ?F ?X " versus " ?G ?X " in world " ?N
   t crlf)
  (retract ?P)
  (retract ?Q)
  (modify ?W (task contra))
)

;; IF we find a contradiction between assumption and derived fact
;; in same world, but at different contexts
;; THEN record the contradiction.
```

```
(defrule transcontext
 (declare (salience 90))
 ?W <- (world (tag ?N) (task check) (context ?T) (prior 0))
 (claim (content ?F ?X) (reason ?N) (context ?S&:(< ?S ?T)))
 (claim (content ?G&:(not (eq ?G ?F)) ?X) (reason ?N)
 (context ?T))
 =>
 (printout
 t crlf
 "TRANSCONTEXT CONTRADICTION: " ?F ?X " versus " ?G ?X " in
 world " ?N
 t crlf)
 (modify ?W (task contra))
)

;; IF we find a contradiction between world in the scope of truth
;; and an earlier world
;; THEN record the contradiction.
(defrule transworld-truth
 (declare (salience 80))
 ?W <- (world (tag ?N) (scope truth) (task check) (prior 0))
 (claim (content ?F ?X) (reason ?N))
 (claim (content ?G&:(not (eq ?G ?F)) ?X)
 (reason ?M&:(< ?M ?N)))
 =>
 (printout
 t crlf
 "TRANSWORLD CONTRADICTION: "
 ?F ?X " versus " ?G ?X " in worlds " ?N "|" ?M
 t crlf)
 (modify ?W (task contra))
)

;; IF we find a contradiction between world in the scope of falsity
;; and an earlier world
;; THEN prepare to backtrack to that prior world.
(defrule transworld-falsity
 (declare (salience 80))
 ?W <- (world (tag ?N) (scope falsity) (task check))
 (claim (content ?F ?X) (reason ?N))
 (claim (content ?G&:(not (eq ?G ?F)) ?X) (reason ?M&:(< ?M ?N)))
 =>
 (printout
 t crlf
 "TRANSWORLD CONTRADICTION:
 " ?F ?X " versus " ?G ?X " in worlds " ?N "|" ?M
 t crlf)
 (modify ?W (task contra) (prior ?M))
)
```

Note that the last rule records the prior world that the current world is in conflict with at the same time that it records the contradiction. This information will then be available to the backtracking rules listed in a following subsection.

Retraction

There are only two cases here.

- A choice of disjunct has led to a contradiction, so we wish to destroy the context created by that choice.
- The assumption of truth has led to a contradiction, so we want to undo that context and try the assumption of falsity.

In each case, claims need to be removed from working memory. Since we will never want to backtrack into a contradictory context, this destruction of data will not affect completeness. If we need to recompute these contexts under another set of assumptions, we will do this from scratch.

```
;; IF a world has a contradiction in one of its disjunctive
;; contexts THEN delete all claims from that context.
;; NOTE rule will fire repeatedly until there are no more claims.
(defrule clean-context
  (declare (salience 50))
  (world (tag ?N) (task contra) (prior 0) (context ?S&~0))
  ?F <- (claim (reason ?N) (context ?S))
  =>
  (retract ?F)
)

;; IF current contradictory world has only been explored under
;; truth THEN check it out under falsity.
(defrule switch-context
  (declare (salience 40))
;; As long as there is no dangling right disjunct
  ?W <- (world
        (tag ?N) (scope truth) (task contra)
        (prior 0) (context ?S&~1))
  =>
;; change the scope and reset the context.
  (modify ?W (scope falsity) (task check) (context 0))
)

;; Clear out all claims based on assumption of truth of statement
;; once falsity is assumed.
;; NOTE rule will fire repeatedly.
(defrule sweep-truth
  (declare (salience 100))
  (world (tag ?N) (scope falsity))
  ?F <- (claim (reason ?N) (scope truth))
  =>
  (retract ?F)
)
```

The last rule shows how the reason and scope fields keep track of claims. As in a truth maintenance system (see Chapter 19), we keep track of which claims are based in which worlds and under what assumptions

We are now in a position to write the backtracking rules.

Backtracking

Each individual statement in a puzzle generates a world. Since we have to process the statements in sequence, it is possible that a later world will turn out to be in conflict with a world earlier in the sequence. What we do then depends upon the assumptions upon which the two worlds are based.

If the current world has only been explored under the assumption of truth, then we should go ahead and check it out under falsity before thinking about backtracking. If a world is inconsistent with an earlier world under the assumption of falsity, then we have used up all our local options, and we have to consider backtracking to an earlier world and redoing part of the computation under a different set of assumptions.

But we only want to backtrack if there are alternative arms of the computation to explore. One condition under which this occurs is if an earlier world was only explored under the assumption of truth and not the assumption of falsity. It is then conceivable that we could recover from the present contradiction by going back to that world and undoing the assumption of truth and assuming that the speaker in the world was in fact lying.

The rule `undirected-falsity` prepares to do this. It is called 'undirected' because it implements chronological backtracking; that is, we return to the last choice point and try a different assumption. CLIPS conflict resolution contains a recency preference which will insure that we backtrack to the most recent world that satisfies the conditions. But we make no attempt to locate the choice point that caused the problem, for example by backtracking to the world that contradicts the current world.

```
;; Chronological backtracking to an assumption of truth
(defrule undirected-falsity
  (world (tag ?N) (scope falsity) (task contra))
  ?W <- (world (tag ?M&:(< ?M ?N)) (scope truth) (task check))
  =>
  (modify ?W (task back))
)
```

An alternative scenario is where we checked out one of the disjuncts in a previous world but not the other. At the time, the disjunct did not generate a contradiction. But now, we want to go back and redo part of the computation with the other disjunct.

The rule `undirected-disjunct` prepares to do this chronologically.

```
;; Backtrack chronologically to an unexplored disjunct.
(defrule undirected-disjunct
  (world (tag ?N) (scope falsity) (task contra))
  ?V <- (world (tag ?M&:(< ?M ?N)) (task check) (context 1))
  (claim (content OR ?P ?X ?Q ?Y) (reason ?M) (scope ?S))
  =>
  ;; Assume the unexplored disjunct in the earlier world.
  (assert (claim (content ?Q ?Y) (reason ?M) (scope ?S) (context 2)))
  ;; Start backtracking to that world.
  (modify ?V (task back))
)
```

Chronological backtracking isn't our only option. We could also write 'directed' versions of these two rules which take note of which previous world contains the claim that generates a contradiction in the current world. The following two rules implement this, using the 'prior' slot associated with the current world, which records the number of the previous world.

```
;; IF we have a contradiction between worlds M and N
;; AND M is an earlier world than N which was not checked out
;; wrt the falsity of its founding statement
;; THEN backtrack to world M and check out the falsity option.
(defrule directed-falsity
  (world (tag ?N) (scope falsity) (task contra) (prior ?M&~0))
  ?W <- (world (tag ?M) (scope truth) (task check))
  =>
  (modify ?W (task back))
)

;; IF we have a contradiction between worlds N and M
;; AND M is an earlier world than N which was not checked out
;; wrt both arms of a disjunction
;; THEN get ready to backtrack to that earlier world.
(defrule directed-disjunct
  (world (tag ?N) (scope falsity) (task contra) (prior ?M&~0))
  ?V <- (world (tag ?M) (task check) (context 1))
  (claim (content OR ?P ?X ?Q ?Y) (reason ?M) (scope ?S))
  =>
  ;; Assume the unexplored disjunct in the earlier world.
  (assert (claim (content ?Q ?Y) (reason ?M) (scope ?S) (context 2)))
  ;; Start backtracking to that world.
  (modify ?V (task back))
)
```

We might suppose that these two rules cover all the cases in which we need to back-track, obviating the need for the chronological rules, but we would be wrong. There are situations where there is a contradiction between worlds W and V, but both have been checked out wrt assumptions of truth and falsity and all their disjuncts. The problem lies in some other world which has unchecked assumptions or disjuncts (see Exercise 4), and which must be checked in the interests of completeness.

Exercise 4.

What backtracking problem is posed by the puzzle given below?

> A: 'B is a knave.'
> B: 'C is a knave.'
> C: 'B is a knight.'

Identify the world that needs to be backtracked to, and explain why the directed backtracking rules will not do the Right Thing.

In fact, the second and third statements can be seen at a glance to be inconsistent, so there is no assignment of knighthood and knavehood to the characters that works.

We might suppose that we could combine the directed and undirected rules, but this is not straightforward. The conditions under which undirected-falsity will fire are essentially the same as the conditions under which `directed-falsity` will fire. This means we can only control which rule fires by manipulating salience values, so that one or the other rule of the pair will always dominate. The directed rules are usually more efficient, because they often go straight back to the problem world, but they sometimes sacrifice completeness, while the complete chronological rules are complete but somewhat pedestrian. I leave it up to the reader to convince himself or herself that this is the case, for example by experimenting with different versions of the program. Going forward, we will use the undirected rules only.

Context reinstatement

Returning to an earlier context involves destroying intervening contexts, including the claims that were generated in them. We do not want to destroy the statements upon which they were founded, however, since we may need to regenerate these worlds later on. But we do want to mark these statements as not being 'done,' else they will not be unwrapped again.

```
;; Undo past worlds.
;; IF we are backtracking to world M
;; THEN destroy all worlds later than M.
;; NOTE rule will fire repeatedly.
(defrule undo-world
  (declare (salience 40))
  (world (tag ?M) (task back))
  ?W <- (world (tag ?N&:(> ?N ?M)))
  ?S <- (statement (tag ?N) (done ?X&~0))
  =>
  (retract ?W)
  (modify ?S (done 0))
)

;; Undo past claims.
;; IF we are backtracking to world M
;; THEN destroy all claims in all worlds later than M.
(defrule unclaim
  (declare (salience 30))
  (world (tag ?M) (task back))
  ?F <- (claim (reason ?N&:(> ?N ?M)))
  =>
  (retract ?F)
)

;; Restart computation at backtrack point.
;; IF we have done destroying worlds later than M
;; THEN begin recomputing the world M under the assumption
;; of falsity.
(defrule restart
  (declare (salience 20))
  ?W <- (world (tag ?M) (scope truth) (task back) (context ?C&~1))
  =>
  (retract ?W)
  (modify ?W (scope falsity) (task check) (context 0))
)
```

The last rule given above merely restarts the computation once we have arrived back at the chosen world. Note that its salience is lower than the other two rules, ensuring that they fire first.

These mechanisms should be sufficient to ensure completeness, in the sense that the program will not halt while there is a path through the worlds worth exploring. If we deleted the directed backtracking rules, the program should still be complete, since we would always backtrack to the last world that offers an alternative assumption (of truth or falsity) or an unchecked disjunct. But these rules make the program more efficient without sacrificing completeness, in that any program that contains them will tend to do less backtracking.

Exercise 5.[†]

Consider the following puzzle.
P7. There are two people, A and B, who make the following statements.

> A: 'B says that he is a knight.'
> B: 'A says that he is a knave.'

What are A and B? And how would you extend the current program to solve puzzles of this kind? Here are some ontological hints to help you extend your domain model.

In the beginning, we were concerned with the consistency of a single world; the world in which a single statement was true. With the advent of multiple statements, we extended this to assume that there is just one 'layer' of worlds, that is, that each statement generates a single world, namely the world in which the claim expressed by that statement is true. Our sole concern was then

- are these worlds internally consistent, that is, are they possible worlds?
- are these worlds consistent with each other, that is, could they decribe the same reality?

Reported speech complicates this picture, because statements can beget worlds in which statements (and not claims) are held to be true. But these statements must themselves be unwrapped to generate further worlds.
Given a statement like

> A: 'B says that he is a knight.'

and the assumption that A is telling the truth, we generate the world in which B really says that he is a knight, but there is also the inner world in which B really is a knight. Keeping track of these embedded worlds is another task for truth maintenance.

But what can we say about the world in which A is lying? We must show that B could not have said that he is a knave without generating a contradiction.

A4.6   Handling reported speech

Once the basic backtracking mechanism is in place, we can go on and adapt it deal with statements about statements. This will enable us to solve puzzles such as P6 (see Exercise 5 above).

Given a statement like

A: 'B says that he is a knight.'

we must generate the world in which B says that he is a knight, but there is also the inner world in which B really is a knight. These embedded worlds form another set of dependencies that must be tracked by truth maintenance. We begin by making each world know what its outer world is, for bookkeeping purposes, by modifying the world template accordingly.

It turns out that, in this more complex scenario, it is also useful to track when we have already unwrapped a statement, so that we don't go back and unwrap it again. We therefore add a 'done' field to both the world template and the statement template.

```
;; A WORLD is a set of claims generated by making an assumption
;; about the truth or falsity of a statement.
;; Its TAG corresponds to the tag of that statement.
;; Its SCOPE will be truth or falsity, depending upon the
;; assumption that is being made.
;; Its TASK will be one of
;; CHECK - check out the truth or falsity of a statement
;; CONTRA - check out a contradiction
;; CLEAN - remove claims from an inconsistent world
;; BACK - backtrack to a particular world
;; QUIT - give up.
;; The PRIOR field can hold the tag of a previously processed world
;; to which it relates usually by generating an inconsistency with it.
;; The UPPER field holds the name of another world within which
;; the current world is embedded, due to an embedded statement,
;; for example, A says that B says that A is a liar.
;; The CONTEXT field keeps track of where we are in disjunctions.
;; The DONE field says we unwrapped a statement for this world
;; already.
(deftemplate world
  (field tag (type INTEGER) (default 1))
  (field scope (type SYMBOL) (default truth))
  (field task (type SYMBOL) (default check))
  (field prior (type INTEGER) (default 0))
  (field upper (type INTEGER) (default 0))
  (field context (type INTEGER) (default 0))
  (field done (type INTEGER) (default 0))
)

;; A STATEMENT is a SPEAKER uttering a CLAIM.
;; Its REASON will be 0, unless it derives from another statement.
;; Its TAG is just a unique number > 0.
;; DONE ::= 0 | 1 | 2
;; 0 means not yet 'unwrapped' for processing.
;; 1 means unwrapped for truth.
;; 2 means unwrapped for falsity.
(deftemplate statement
  (field speaker (type SYMBOL))
  (multifield claim (type SYMBOL))
  (field scope (type SYMBOL) (default truth))
  (multifield reason (type INTEGER) (default 0))
```

```
    (field tag (type INTEGER) (default 0))
    (field done (type INTEGER) (default 0))
)
```

The next task is to write rules that will unwrap statements about statements.

```
;; IF our world is to be based on the truth of a meta-statement
;; THEN assume that the speaker speaks the truth
;; AND assume that the statement is true.
(defrule unwrap-true-state
  ?W <- (world (tag ?N) (scope truth) (task check) (done 0))
  ?S <- (statement (speaker ?X) (claim SAY ?Z $?Y) (done 0))
  =>
  (printout
    t crlf
    "Assuming " T ?X " and " ?Z " says " $?Y " in world " ?N
    t crlf
  )

;; Record that we have unwrapped the statement for truth.
  (modify ?S (tag ?N) (done 1))
;; Assume that the speaker is truthful in the current world.
  (assert (claim (content T ?X) (reason ?N) (scope truth)))
;; Record that world has had a statement unwrapped in it.
  (modify ?W (done 1))
;; Create a new world for the embedded statement and record that
;; it has the original world, ?N, as its upper world, or world of
;; origin.
  (assert (world (tag (+ ?N 1)) (scope truth) (upper ?N)))
;; Record the embedded statement in the new world.
  (assert (statement (speaker ?Z) (claim $?Y) (reason ?N)))
)

;; IF our world is to be based on the falsity of a meta-statement
;; THEN simply assume that the speaker lies.
;; Don't assume anything about the claim.
(defrule unwrap-false-state
  ?W <- (world (tag ?N) (scope falsity) (task check))
  ?S <- (statement (speaker ?X) (claim SAY ?Z $?Y) (tag ?N) (done 1))
  =>
  (printout
    t crlf
    "Assuming " F " " ?X " and NOT " ?Z " says " $?Y " in world " ?N
    t crlf
  )
;; Change scope of current world.
  (modify ?W (scope falsity) (done 2))
;; Note that statement has been unwrapped for falsity.
  (modify ?S (scope falsity) (done 2))
;; Assume that outer speaker is lying in current world.
  (assert (claim (content F ?X) (reason ?N) (scope falsity)))
)
```

To make our lives easier, we will assume that reported speech is never governed by negation, that is, that there are no initial statements such as:

A: 'B does not say that he is a knight.'

Furthermore, if A says that B made a claim, then (according to the conventions of the puzzle) all we need to do in order to prove A a liar is to show that there is no possible world in which B could have truthfully made that claim. Thus we don't need to drive negation into the embedded statement and check out its consistency. This convention is reflected in the rule `unwrap-false-state`, which simply assumes that A is lying if the assumption of truth did not work out, without any further checking.

Of course, this tactic follows Smullyan in assuming that B would not make irrational statements (see Box A1).

BOX A.1

Epistemological Problems

Ontologically, we assume that every character is either a knight or a knave and not both. However, if we carry this assumption into the context of reported speech, it gives rise to some odd outcomes. For example, the statement

A: 'B says that he is a knave.'

leads us to conclude that A is a knave in the outer world, because there is no consistent inner world in which B can truthfully say that he is a knave, because if he's a knave, then he's a knight, and vice versa. Thus, anyone who actually reports a paradoxical statement in one of these puzzles would be judged a knave.

This seems unfair to A. One could argue that there should be a possible world in which A is a knight and B is being deliberately nonsensical. Do you agree?

A4.7 Complete program listing

Below is a complete listing of the CLIPS program which handles multiple compound statements which may contain reported speech.

```
;; Truth games for multiple compound statements
;; Detects inconsistency and reports first consistent
;; interpretation
;; Deals with conjunction and disjunction
;; Deals with multiple statements
;; Deals with embedded statements (reported speech)

;; TEMPLATES

;; A CLAIM has the following fields:
;; CONTENT, for example,
;; T A ... meaning A is a truth-teller (knight)
;; F A ... meaning A is a liar (knave)
;; OR T A F B ... meaning A is a knight or B is a knave, etc.
;; REASON signifying what original statement gave rise to it.
;; The reason of a claim will equal the tag of this statement.
;; Original statements have a reason of 0, since they are
;; unsupported.
;; CONTEXT ::= 0 | 1 | 2
;; 0 means claim follows from the content of the statement, or
```

```
;; is an assumption about the speaker of the statement.
;; 1 means the context of a left disjunctive split.
;; 2 means the context of a right disjunctive split.
(deftemplate claim
  (multifield content (type SYMBOL))
  (field reason (type INTEGER))
  (field scope (type SYMBOL))
  (field context (type INTEGER) (default 0))
)

;; A STATEMENT is a SPEAKER uttering a CLAIM.
;; Its REASON will be 0, unless it derives from another statement.
;; Its TAG is just a unique number > 0.
;; DONE ::= 0 | 1 | 2
;; 0 means not yet 'unwrapped' for processing.
;; 1 means unwrapped for truth.
;; 2 means unwrapped for falsity.
(deftemplate statement
  (field speaker (type SYMBOL))
  (multifield claim (type SYMBOL))
  (field scope (type SYMBOL) (default truth))
  (multifield reason (type INTEGER) (default 0))
  (field tag (type INTEGER) (default 0))
  (field done (type INTEGER) (default 0))
)

;; A WORLD is a set of claims generated by making an assumption
;; about the truth or falsity of a statement.
;; Its TAG corresponds to the tag of that statement.
;; Its SCOPE will be truth or falsity, depending upon the
;; assumption that is being made.
;; Its TASK will be one of
;; CHECK - check out the truth or falsity of a statement
;; CONTRA - check out a contradiction
;; CLEAN - remove claims from an inconsistent world
;; BACK - backtrack to a particular world
;; QUIT - give up.
;; The PRIOR field can hold the tag of a previously processed world
;; to which it relates usually by generating an inconsistency with
;; it. The UPPER field holds the name of another world within which
;; the current world is embedded, due to an embedded statement,
;; for example, A says that B says that A is a liar.
;; The CONTEXT field keeps track of where we are in disjunctions.
(deftemplate world
  (field tag (type INTEGER) (default 1))
  (field scope (type SYMBOL) (default truth))
  (field task (type SYMBOL) (default check))
  (field prior (type INTEGER) (default 0))
  (field upper (type INTEGER) (default 0))
  (field context (type INTEGER) (default 0))
  (field done (type INTEGER) (default 0))
)
```

```
;; FUNCTIONS

;; Changes the scope of the truth predicate from T to F
;; and vice versa.
(deffunction flip (?P)
 (if (eq ?P T) then F else T))

;; RULES

;; Unwrap statements

;; IF our world is to be based on the truth of a statement
;; THEN assume that the speaker speaks the truth
;; AND assume that the statement is true.
;; The TAG of the statement becomes the reason of these claims.
;; NOTE that this rule does not apply to embedded statements.
(defrule unwrap-true
 ?W <- (world (tag ?N) (scope truth) (task check) (done 0))
 ?S <- (statement (speaker ?X) (claim ?P&:(not (eq ?P SAY)) $?Y)
(done 0))
 =>
 (printout
   t crlf
   "Assuming " T ?X " and " ?P $?Y " in world " ?N
   t crlf
 )

;; Record that we have unwrapped the statement for truth.
  (modify ?S (tag ?N) (done 1))
;; Record that world was started for truth.
  (modify ?W (done 1))
;; Assume that the speaker is telling the truth.
  (assert (claim (content T ?X) (reason ?N) (scope truth)))
;; Assume that what the speaker says is true.
  (assert (claim (content ?P $?Y) (reason ?N) (scope truth)))
)

;; IF our world is to be based on the truth of a statement
;; THEN assume that the speaker speaks the truth
;; AND assume that the statement is true.
;; NOTE For embedded statements, not simple claims.
(defrule unwrap-true-state
 ?W <- (world (tag ?N) (scope truth) (task check) (done 0))
 ?S <- (statement (speaker ?X) (claim SAY ?Z $?Y) (done 0))
 =>
 (printout
   t crlf
   "Assuming " T ?X " and " ?Z " says " $?Y " in world " ?N
   t crlf
 )

;; Record that we have unwrapped the statement for truth.
  (modify ?S (tag ?N) (done 1))
;; Assume that the speaker is truthful in the current world.
  (assert (claim (content T ?X) (reason ?N) (scope truth)))
```

```
;; Record that world has had a statement unwrapped in it.
  (modify ?W (done 1))
;; Create a new world for the embedded statement and record that
;; it has the original world, ?N, as its upper world, or world
;; of origin.
  (assert (world (tag (+ ?N 1)) (scope truth) (upper ?N)))
;; Record the embedded statement in the new world.
  (assert (statement (speaker ?Z) (claim $?Y) (reason ?N)))
)

;; IF our world is to be based on the falsity of a statement
;; THEN assume that the speaker lies
;; AND assume that the statement is false.
;; NOTE that this does not handle embedded statements or
;; claims in the scope of negation.
(defrule unwrap-false
  ?W <- (world (tag ?N) (scope falsity) (task check))
  ?S <- (statement
    (speaker ?X)
    (claim ?P&:(not (or (eq ?P NOT) (eq ?P SAY))) $?Y)
    (tag ?N) (done 1))
  =>
  (printout
    t crlf
    "Assuming " F ?X " and NOT " ?P $?Y " in world " ?N
    t crlf
  )

;; Record that we are checking the falsity of the statement.
  (modify ?S (scope falsity) (done 2))
;; Record that the world has been done for falsity.
  (modify ?W (done 2))
;; Assume that the speaker is a liar.
  (assert (claim (content F ?X) (reason ?N) (scope falsity)))
;; Negate the claim that has been made.
  (assert (claim (content NOT ?P $?Y) (reason ?N) (scope falsity)))
)

;; IF our world is to be based on the falsity of a meta-statement
;; THEN simply assume that the speaker lies.
;; Don't assume anything about the claim.
;; NOTE for embedded statements which must be positive
;; that is, there is no coverage of A: "B did not say he was a
;; knave" or A: "B says that he is not a knave".
(defrule unwrap-false-state
  ?W <- (world (tag ?N) (scope falsity) (task check))
  ?S <- (statement (speaker ?X) (claim SAY ?Z $?Y) (tag ?N) (done 1))
  =>
  (printout
    t crlf
    "Assuming " F " " ?X " and NOT " ?Z " says " $?Y " in world " ?N
    t crlf
  )
```

```
;; Change scope of current world.
 (modify ?W (scope falsity) (done 2))
;; Note that statement has been unwrapped for falsity.
 (modify ?S (scope falsity) (done 2))
;; Assume that outer speaker is lying in current world.
 (assert (claim (content F ?X) (reason ?N) (scope falsity)))
)

;; HANDLING LOGICAL OPERATORS

;; Negation rules
;; IF someone is not a truth-teller
;; THEN they are a liar.
(defrule not1
 (declare (salience 5))
 ?F <- (claim (content NOT T ?P))
 =>
 (modify ?F (content F ?P))
)

;; IF someone is not a liar
;; THEN they are a truth-teller.
(defrule not2
 (declare (salience 5))
 ?F <- (claim (content NOT F ?P))
 =>
 (modify ?F (content T ?P))
)

;; Distribute NOT over OR.
(defrule not-or
 (declare (salience 5))
 ?F <- (claim (content NOT OR ?P ?X ?Q ?Y))
 =>
 (modify ?F (content AND (flip ?P) ?X (flip ?Q) ?Y))
)

;; Distribute NOT over AND.
(defrule not-and
 (declare (salience 5))
 ?F <- (claim (content NOT AND ?P ?X ?Q ?Y))
 =>
 (modify ?F (content OR (flip ?P) ?X (flip ?Q) ?Y))
)

;; Conjunction elimination.
(defrule conj
 (world (tag ?N) (scope ?V) (task check) (context ?L))
 (claim (content AND ?P ?X ?Q ?Y) (reason ?N) (scope ?V) (context ?L))
 =>
 (assert (claim (content ?P ?X) (reason ?N) (scope ?V) (context ?L)))
 (assert (claim (content ?Q ?Y) (reason ?N) (scope ?V) (context ?L)))
)

;; DEALING WITH DISJUNCTIONS
```

```
;; IF we have a disjunction at context 0
;; THEN first try asserting its left disjunct.
;; NOTE we increase the context parameter of the world
;; as well as setting the context of the new claim to 1.
(defrule left-disjunct
  ?W <- (world (tag ?N) (task check) (scope ?V) (context 0))
  (claim (content OR ?P ?X ?Q ?Y) (reason ?N) (scope ?V) (context 0))
  =>
  (assert (claim (content ?P ?X) (reason ?N) (scope ?V) (context 1)))
  (modify ?W (context 1))
)

;; IF the left disjunct fails
;; THEN assert the right disjunct.
(defrule right-disjunct
  (declare (salience 10))
  ?W <- (world (tag ?N) (task contra) (context 1))
  (claim (content OR ?P ?X ?Q ?Y) (reason ?N) (scope ?V))
  =>
  (assert (claim (content ?Q ?Y) (reason ?N) (scope ?V) (context 2)))
  (modify ?W (task check) (context 2))
)

;; IF we ever backtrack to the right disjunct
;; THEN assert it.
(defrule resume-disjunct
  ?W <- (world (tag ?N) (task back) (context 1))
  (claim (content OR ?P ?X ?Q ?Y) (reason ?N) (scope ?V))
  =>
  (assert (claim (content ?Q ?Y) (reason ?N) (scope ?V) (context 2)))
  (modify ?W (task check) (context 2))
)

;; IF both disjuncts fail in the scope of truth
;; THEN try the scope of falsity.
(defrule false-disjuncts
  ?W <- (world (tag ?M) (scope truth) (task contra) (prior 0)
  (context 2))
  (not (claim (reason ?M) (context 2)))
  =>
  (modify ?W (scope falsity) (task check) (context 0))
)

;; IF an assumption of truth clashes with another world
;; THEN try falsity.
(defrule other-world
  ?W <- (world (tag ?N) (scope truth) (task contra) (prior ?M&~0)
  (context 0))
  =>
  (modify ?W (scope falsity) (task check))
)

;; HANDLING CONTRADICTIONS

;; Find contradiction between assumption of truth and derived fact
```

```
;; in the same world and the same context.
(defrule contradiction
  (declare (salience 100))
  ?W <- (world (tag ?N) (task check) (scope ?V) (context ?S))
  ?P <- (claim (content ?F ?X) (scope ?V) (reason ?N) (context ?S))
  ?Q <- (claim (content ?G&:(not (eq ?G ?F)) ?X) (scope ?V) (reason
  ?N) (context ?S))
  =>
  (printout
    t crlf
    "CONTRADICTION: " ?F ?X " versus " ?G ?X " in world " ?N
    t crlf)
  (retract ?P)
  (retract ?Q)
  (modify ?W (task contra))
)

;; Find contradiction between assumption and derived fact
;; in same world, but at different contexts.
(defrule transcontext
  (declare (salience 90))
  ?W <- (world (tag ?N) (task check) (scope ?V) (context ?T))
  (claim (content ?F ?X) (scope ?V) (reason ?N) (context ?S&:(< ?S
  ?T)))
  (claim (content ?G&:(not (eq ?G ?F)) ?X) (scope ?V) (reason ?N)
  (context ?T))
  =>
  (printout
    t crlf
    "TRANSCONTEXT CONTRADICTION: " ?F ?X " versus " ?G ?X " in world " ?N
    t crlf)
  (modify ?W (task contra))
)

;; Find contradiction between current world in the scope of truth
;; and an earlier world.
(defrule transworld-truth
  (declare (salience 80))
  ?W <- (world (tag ?N) (scope truth) (task check) (upper 0))
;; Current world has a claim in conflict with another world.
  (claim (content ?F ?X) (reason ?N))
;; Conflicting world is earlier than current world.
  (claim
    (content ?G&:(not (eq ?G ?F)) ?X)
    (reason ?M&:(< ?M ?N)))
  =>
  (printout
    t crlf
    "TRANSWORLD CONTRADICTION:"
      ?F ?X " versus " ?G ?X " in worlds " ?N "|" ?M
    t crlf)
  (modify ?W (task contra))
)
```

```
;; Find contradiction between current world in the scope of fal-
sity
;; and an earlier world.
(defrule transworld-falsity
 (declare (salience 80))
 ?W <- (world (tag ?N) (scope falsity) (task check) (upper 0))
 (claim (content ?F ?X) (reason ?N))
 (claim
   (content ?G&:(not (eq ?G ?F)) ?X)
   (reason ?M&:(< ?M ?N)))
 =>
 (printout
   t crlf
   "TRANSWORLD CONTRADICTION: "
     ?F ?X " versus " ?G ?X " in worlds " ?N "|" ?M
   t crlf)
 (modify ?W (task contra) (prior ?M))
)

;; IF we find a contradiction between embedded world and
;; an earlier world
;; THEN record it and retract the statement associate with the
;; former.
(defrule upper-world
 (declare (salience 80))
 ?W <- (world (tag ?N) (task check) (upper ?U&~0))
 (claim (content ?F ?X) (reason ?N))
 (claim
   (content ?G&:(not (eq ?G ?F)) ?X)
   (reason ?M&:(< ?M ?N)))
 ?S <- (statement (tag ?N) (reason ?U))
 =>
 (printout
   t crlf
   "TRANSWORLD CONTRADICTION: "
     ?F ?X " versus " ?G ?X " in worlds " ?N "|" ?M
     t crlf)
 (retract ?S)
 (modify ?W (task contra) (prior ?U))
)

;; SIMPLE RETRACTION MECHANISMS

;; Prune a failed branch in a disjunction.
(defrule clean-context
 (declare (salience 50))
 (world
   (tag ?N)
   (task ?T&:(or (eq ?T contra) (eq ?T back)))
   (context ?S&~0))
 ?F <- (claim (reason ?N) (context ?S))
 =>
 (retract ?F)
)
```

```
;; IF current world has only been explored under truth
;; THEN check it out under falsity.
(defrule switch-scope
  (declare (salience 40))
  ?W <- (world (tag ?N) (scope truth) (task contra) (context ?C&~1))
  =>
;; Change the scope.
  (modify ?W (scope falsity) (task check))
)

;; Clear out all claims based on assumption of truth of claim
;; before falsity is assumed.
(defrule sweep-claims
  (declare (salience 100))
  (world
    (tag ?N) (scope truth) (context ?C&~1)
    (task ?T&:(or (eq ?T contra) (eq ?T back))))
  ?F <- (claim (reason ?N) (scope truth) (context ?D&~1))
  =>
  (retract ?F)
)

;; Clear out any statement based on assumption of truth of
;; statement before falsity is assumed.
(defrule sweep-statements
  (declare (salience 100))
  (world
    (tag ?N) (task ?T&:(or (eq ?T contra) (eq ?T back)))
    (scope truth) (context 0))
  ?F <- (statement (reason ?N) (scope truth))
  =>
  (retract ?F)
)

;; Remove claims from an inconsistent world.
(defrule kill-claims
  (declare (salience 100))
  (world (tag ?N) (task clean))
  ?F <- (claim (reason ?N))
  =>
  (retract ?F)
)

;; Stop when there are no more such claims or statements
;; and remove the cleaning task.
(defrule stop-killing
  (declare (salience 100))
  ?W <- (world (tag ?N) (task clean))
  (not (claim (reason ?N)))
  =>
  (retract ?W)
)

;; BACKTRACKING MECHANISMS
```

```
;; Backtrack chronologically through assumptions.
(defrule undirected-falsity
  (declare (salience 20))
  (world (tag ?N) (scope falsity) (task contra))
  ?W <- (world (tag ?M&:(< ?M ?N)) (scope truth) (task check))
  =>
  (modify ?W (task back))
)

;; Backtrack chronologically through disjunctions.
(defrule undirected-disjunct
  (declare (salience 20))
  (world (tag ?N) (scope falsity) (task contra))
  ?V <- (world (tag ?M&:(< ?M ?N)) (task check) (context 1))
  (claim (content OR ?P ?X ?Q ?Y) (reason ?M) (scope ?S))
  =>
  ;; Assume the unexplored disjunct in the earlier world.
  (assert (claim (content ?Q ?Y) (reason ?M) (scope ?S) (context 2)))
  ;; Start backtracking to that world.
  (modify ?V (task back))
)

;; Undo past worlds.
;; IF we are backtracking to world M
;; THEN destroy all worlds later than M.
(defrule undo-world
  (declare (salience 50))
  (world (tag ?M) (task back))
  ?W <- (world (tag ?N&:(> ?N ?M)))
  =>
  (retract ?W)
)

;; Undo past statements.
(defrule restate
  (declare (salience 50))
  (world (tag ?M) (task back))
  ?S <- (statement (tag ?N&:(> ?N ?M)) (reason 0) (done ?X&~0))
  =>
  (modify ?S (done 0))
)

;; Undo past claims.
;; IF we are backtracking to world M
;; THEN destroy all claims in all worlds later than M.
(defrule unclaim
  (declare (salience 30))
  (world (tag ?M) (task back))
  ?F <- (claim (reason ?N&:(> ?N ?M)))
  =>
  (retract ?F)
)

;; Undo past statements.
```

```
;; IF we are backtracking to world M
;; THEN destroy all statements in all worlds later than M.
(defrule unstate
 (declare (salience 30))
 (world (tag ?M) (task back))
 ?F <- (statement (reason ?N&:(> ?N ?M)))
 =>
 (retract ?F)
)

;; Restart computation at backtrack point.
;; IF we have done destroying worlds later than M
;; THEN begin recomputing the world M under the assumption of
;; falsity.
(defrule restart
 (declare (salience 20))
 ?W <- (world (tag ?M) (scope truth) (task back) (context ?C&~1))
 =>
 (modify ?W (scope falsity) (task check) (context 0))
)

;; MOVE TO NEXT WORLD & REPORTING

;; Move to next world.
;; IF no other rule will fire
;; THEN we are done with this world, so move on
;; as long as there are ungrounded statements to check.
;; NOTE this rule has a salience lower than any other rule
;; except the rules that report results.
(defrule move
 (declare (salience -50))
;; There is a world generated by an original statement.
 ?W <- (world (tag ?N&:(> ?N 0)) (task check))
;; There is no extant world later than this,
;; that is, it is the current world.
 (not (world (tag ?T&:(> ?T ?N))))
;; There exists a statement ready to generate a new world.
 (statement (reason 0) (done 0))
 =>
;; Start new world for statement
 (assert (world (tag (+ ?N 1))))
)

;; IF there are no contradictory worlds
;; THEN print out results.
;; NOTE rule will fire repeatedly to output
;; a consistent interpretation.
(defrule report-results
 (declare (salience -40))
 (not (world (task contra)))
 (not (statement (reason 0) (done 0)))
 (statement (tag ?N) (done ?M&~0))
 (claim (content ?P ?X) (reason ?N))
 =>
```

```
      (printout
        t crlf
        "RESULT: " ?P ?X " from statement " ?N
        t crlf)
    )

    ;; IF we have a contradictory world and no backtrack point
    ;; AND no other rule will fire
    ;; THEN get ready to halt.
    (defrule sanity-check
      (declare (salience -100))
      (world (tag ?N) (task ?T&:(or (eq ?T contra) (eq ?T back))))
      (not (world (tag ?M&:(< ?M ?N)) (scope truth) (task check)))
      =>
      (printout
        t crlf
        "FAIL: Statements inconsistent, detected in world " ?N
        t crlf)
      (halt)
    )
```

I am sure that this program could be improved upon, for example by finding a way to combine directed backtracking with chronological backtracking. But the current program covers the examples while retaining completeness. It shows that CLIPS can be used to implement a number of different computational mechanisms we have discussed in the text, for example:

- forward reasoning with conflict resolution (Chapter 5)
- goal-directed reasoning using task tokens (Chapters 5 and 14)
- multiple contexts based on different assumptions (Chapters 17 and 19),

I think that this program also demonstrates that simple problems, such as the 'truth' puzzle, can get complicated rather quickly as new features are added to cover more complex cases, such as multiple statements and reported speech. It is not altogether easy to preserve the integrity of the original design as new code is added. The modularity of the rules buys you something in this regard, but old rules may need to be updated as the data templates are elaborated and extended to cover more properties of the situation.

A5   CLIPS programming style

Chapter 17 contains a survey of expert system building tools, as well as various maxims on the subject of successful expert systems development. Many of the tools described in that chapter have features similar to those found in CLIPS. Also, many of the maxims about rule-based programming apply to CLIPS, such as the one about trying to keep rules simple. You may want to revisit this chapter after working through the Appendix.

Our puzzle solver only consisted of 35 rules, but real-world expert systems may contain many more. The original 1980 prototype of R1/XCON (see Chapter 14) had about 750 rules, which grew to about 3300 rules by 1984. At that time, the average number of patterns in an R1 rule was six, while the average number of actions was three.

As in all forms of programming, the key to good code is to find the right abstractions for the states that the program must recognize and the operations that it must perform. Understanding the states leads to good templates and good patterns on the left-hand side of rules, while understanding the operations leads to good actions on the right-hand side. As we saw in Section A3, the use of objects and message handlers can contribute to the clarity of this analysis and the cleanliness of the implementation.

1. Write a simulation program that uses both rules and objects along the lines of the example in Section A3, using a different device as your exemplar.

2. Write a program to solve crime puzzles of the following kind (taken again from Smullyan, 1978). Three criminals, A, B and C, are brought in for questioning with respect to a robbery. At least one of them is guilty and there are no guilty parties other than A or B or C.

   Case (i): A never works without at least one accomplice. C has a solid alibi. Is B innocent or guilty?

   Case (ii): A never works with C. C never works alone. If A is guilty and B is innocent, then C is guilty. Which one must be guilty?

   Case (iii): If A is guilty, then he had exactly one accomplice. If exactly two are guilty, then A is one of them. B and C have given each other alibis. Who is guilty?

   Do not write a separate program for each puzzle.

3. Critique and extend any of the CLIPS examples from the chapter material.

Abelson H., Sussman G. J. and Sussman J. (1996). *Structure and Interpretation of Computer Programs*. Cambridge MA: MIT Press

Abu-Hakima S., Halasz M. and Phan S. (1993). An approach to hypermedia in diagnostic systems. In *Intelligent Multi-Media Interfaces* (Maybury M., ed.). AAAI Press/MIT Press

Acorn T. L. and Walden S. (1992). SMART: Support Management Automated Reasoning Technology for Compaq customer service. In *Proc. Innovative Applications of Artificial Intelligence* (IAAI-92), pp. 3–18

Adams J. B. (1976). A probability model of medical reasoning and the MYCIN model. *Mathematical Biosciences*, **32**, 177–86. See also Buchanan and Shortliffe (1984), Chapter 12

Aiello N. (1983). A comparative study of control strategies for expert systems: AGE implementation of three variations of PUFF. *In Proc. National Conference on Artificial Intelligence*, pp. 1–4

Aiello N. (1986). User-Directed Control of Parallelism: The CAGE System. *Technical Report No. KSL-86-31*, Knowledge Systems Laboratory, Stanford University

Aikins J. S. (1983). Prototypical knowledge for expert systems. *Artificial Intelligence*, **20**, 163–210

Aikins J. S., Kunz J. C., Shortliffe E. H. and Fallat R. J. (1984). PUFF: an expert system for interpretation of pulmonary function data. In *Readings in Medical Artificial Intelligence* (Clancey W. J. and Shortliffe E. H., eds), Chapter 19. Reading, MA: Addison-Wesley.

Aleven V. and Ashley K. D. (1997). Evaluating A Learning Environment For Case-Based Argumentation Skills. In *Proc. Sixth International Conference on Artificial Intelligence and Law*, ACM Press, p. 170

Alexander J. H., Freiling M. J., Shulman S. J., Staley J. L., Rehfuss S. and Messick S. L. (1986). Knowledge level engineering: ontological analysis. In *Proc. National Conference on Artificial Intelligence*, pp. 963–8

Allen B. (1994). Case-based reasoning: business applications. *Communications of the ACM*, **37**(3), pp. 40–2

Allen J. F. (1983). Maintaining knowledge about temporal intervals. *Communications of the ACM*, **26**(11), 832–43

Allen J. F. (1995). *Natural Language Understanding*, 2nd edn. Menlo Park, CA: Benjamin/Cummings

Amarel S. (1968). On representations of problems of reasoning about actions. In *Machine Intelligence 3* (Michie D., ed.), pp. 131–71. Edinburgh: Edinburgh University Press

Anderson J. R. (1976). *Language, Memory and Thought*. Hillsdale NJ: Lawrence Erlbaum

Andrews P. B. (1986). *An Introduction to Mathematical Logic and Type Theory: To Truth through Proof*. Orlando FL, Academic Press

Ashley K. D. (1990). *Modeling Legal Argument: Reasoning With Cases and Hypotheticals*. Cambridge MA: MIT Press

Ashley K. and Aleven V. (1997). Reasoning symbolically about partially matched cases. *International Joint Conference on Artificial Intelligence*, IJCAI-1997. San Francisco: Morgan Kaufmann, 335–41

Ashley K. D. and Rissland E. L. (1988). A case-based approach to modelling legal expertise. *IEEE Expert*, **3**(3), 70–7

Bachant J. (1988). RIME: preliminary work towards a knowledge acquisition tool. In *Automating Knowledge Acquisition for Expert Systems* (Marcus S., ed.), Chapter 7. Boston: Kluiver Academic

Baldwin J. F., ed. (1996). *Fuzzy Logic*. New York: Wiley

Barr A. and Feigenbaum E. A., eds (1981). *The Handbook of Artificial Intelligence* Vol 1. Los Altos CA: Morgan Kaufmann

Barr A. and Feigenbaum E. A., eds (1982). *The Handbook of Artificial Intelligence* Vol 2. Los Altos CA: Morgan Kaufmann

Baum L. S., Dodhiawala R. T. and Jagannathan V. (1989). The Erasmus System. In *Blackboard Architectures and Applications* (Jagannathan V., Dodhiawala R. and Baum L., eds.), pp. 347–70. New York: Academic Press

Belew R. K. (1986). Adaptive information retrieval: machine learning in associative networks. *PhD thesis*, University of Michigan, Computer Science Department, Ann Arbor, MI

Bennett J. S., Creary L., Englemore R. and Melosh R. (1978). SACON: A Knowledge Based Consultant for Structural Analysis. *Report No. HPP-78–23*, Computer Science Department, Stanford University

Bergadano F. and Gunetti D. (1996). *Inductive Logic Programming: From Machine Learning to Software Engineering*. Cambridge MA: MIT Press

Biswas G. and Anand T. S. (1987). MIDST: an expert system shell for mixed initiative reasoning. In *Proc. International Symposium on Methodologies for Intelligent Systems*, pp. 1–8

Bobrow D. G. and Collins A., eds (1975). *Representation and Understanding*. New York: Academic Press

Bobrow D. G. and Stefik M. (1983). *The LOOPS manual*. Xerox Corporation

Bobrow D. G. and Winograd T. (1977). An overview of KRL, a knowledge representation language. *Cognitive Science*, **1**(1)

Bobrow D. G. and Winograd T. (1979). KRL: another perspective. *Cognitive Science*, **3**(1)

Booch G. (1994). *Object-Oriented Analysis and Design with Applications*, 2nd edn. Redwood City CA: Benjamin/Cummings

Boose J. H. (1986). *Expertise Transfer for Expert System Design*. New York: Elsevier

Boose J. H. (1989). A survey of knowledge acquisition techniques and tools. *Knowledge Acquisition*, **1**(1): 3–37

Boose J. H. and Bradshaw J. M. (1987). Expertise transfer and complex problems: using AQUINAS as a workbench for knowledge based systems. *International Journal of Man-Machine Studies*, **26**, 1–28

Boose J. H. and Gaines B. (1988). *Knowledge Acquisition Tools for Expert Systems*. New York: Academic Press

Borron J., Morales D. and Klahr P. (1996). Developing and deploying knowledge on a global scale. In *Innovative Applications of Artificial Intelligence 8*, *Proceedings of AAAI-96*. Menlo Park CA: AAAI Press

Brachman R. J. and Levesque H. J. (1985). *Readings in Knowledge Representation*. Los Altos CA: Morgan Kaufmann

Brachman R. J. and Schmolze J. G. (1985). An overview of the KL-ONE knowledge representation system. *Cognitive Science*, **9**, 171–216

Bratko I. (1990). *PROLOG Programming for Artificial Intelligence*, 2nd edn. Wokingham, UK: Addison-Wesley

Breuker J. A. and van de Velde W., eds (1994). *The CommonKADS Library for Expertise Modelling*. Amsterdam: IOS Press

Brown D. C. and Chandrasekaran B. (1989). *Design Problem Solving: Knowledge Structures and Control Strategies*. Los Altos CA: Morgan Kaufmann

Brown J. S., Burton R. R. and De Kleer J. (1982). Pedagogical, natural language and knowledge engineering techniques in SOPHIE I, II and III. In *Intelligent Tutoring Systems* (Sleeman D. and Brown J. S., eds), Chapter 11. London: Academic Press

Brownston L., Farrell R., Kant F. and Martin N. (1985). *Programming Expert Systems in OPS5*. Reading MA: Addison-Wesley

Buchanan B. G. and Feigenbaum E. A. (1978). DENDRAL and META-DENDRAL: their applications dimension. *Artificial Intelligence*, **11**, 5–24

Buchanan B. G. and Shortliffe E. H., eds (1984). *Rule-Based Expert Systems*. Reading MA: Addison-Wesley

Buchanan B. G. and Wilkins D. C., eds (1993). *Readings in Knowledge Acquisition and Learning*. Los Altos, CA: Morgan Kaufmann

Buchanan B. G., Barstow D., Bechtel R., Bennet J., Clancey W., Kulikowski C., Mitchell T. M. and Waterman D. A. (1983). Constructing an expert system. In *Building Expert Systems* (Hayes-Roth F., Waterman D.A. and Levat D., eds), Chapter 5. Reading, MA: Addison-Wesley

Bundy A. (1978). Will it reach the top? Prediction in the mechanics world. *Artificial Intelligence*, **10** 129–46

Bundy A., Byrd L., Luger G., Mellish C. and Palmer M. (1979). Solving mechanics problems using metalevel inference. In *Expert Systems in the Micro-Electronic Age* (Michie D., ed.), pp. 50–64. Edinburgh: Edinburgh University Press

Bundy A., Silver B. and Plummer D. (1985). An analytical comparison of some rule-learning programs. *Artificial Intelligence*, **27**, 137–81

Buntine W. L. (1990). Myths and legends in learning classification rules. In *Proc. National Conference on Artificial Intelligence*, pp. 736–42

Bylander T. (1994). The computational complexity of propositional STRIPS planning. *Artificial Intelligence*, **69**, 165–204

Cannon H. I. (1982). FLAVORS: a non-hierarchical approach to object-oriented programming. Unpublished paper

Carbonell J. G., Michalski R. and Mitchell T. (1983). An overview of machine learning. In *Machine Learning* (Michalski R.S., Carbonell J.S. and Mitchell T.M., eds), Chapter 1. Palo Alto, CA: Tioga

Carver N. and Lesser V. (1994). The evolution of blackboard control architectures. In *Expert Systems with Applications: Special Issue on the Blackboard Paradigm and its Applications*, 7(1), 1–30.

Cendrowska J. and Bramer M. (1984). Insdie an expert system: A rational reconstruction of the MYCIN consultation system. In *Artificial Intelligence: Tools, Techniques and Applications* (O'Shea T. and Eisenstadt M., eds), Chapter 15. New York: Harper and Row

Chandrasekaran B. (l983). Towards a taxonomy of Problem solving types. *AI Magazine*, **4**(1), Spring, 9–17

Chandrasekaran B. (1984). Expert systems: matching techniques to tasks. In *Artificial Intelligence Applications for Business* (Reitman W., ed.). Norwood, NJ: Ablex

Chandrasekaran B. (1986). Generic tasks in knowledge-based reasoning: high-level building blocks for expert systems design. *IEEE Expert*, **1**(3), 23–30

Chandrasekaran B. (1988). Generic tasks as building blocks for knowledge-based systems: the diagnosis and routine design examples. *Knowledge Engineering Review*, **3**(3), 183–210

Chandrasekaran B. and Mittal S. (1984). Deep versus compiled knowledge approaches to diagnostic problem solving. In *Developments in Expert Systems* (Coombs M.J., ed.), Chapter 2. London: Academic Press

Chappell, D. (1996). *Understanding ActiveX and Ole*. Microsoft Press.

Charniak, E. and McDermott, D. (1985). *Introduction to Artificial Intelligence*. Reading, MA: Addison-Wesley

Charniak E., Reisbeck C. and McDermott D. (1987). *Artificial Intelligence Programming*, 2nd edn. Hillsdale, NJ: Lawrence Erlbaum

Cheeseman P. (1985). In defense of Probability. In *Proc. 8th International Joint Conference on Artificial Intelligence*, pp. 1002–9

Church A. (1941). *The Calculi of Lambda Conversion*. Annals of Mathematics Studies, Princeton University Press

Clancey W. J. (1983). The epistemology of a rule-based expert system: a framework for explanation. *Artificial Intelligence*, **20**, 215–51

Clancey W. J. (1985). Heuristic classification. *Artificial Intelligence*, **27**, 289–350

Clancey W. J. (1987a). *Knowledge-Based Tutoring. The GUIDON Program*. Cambridge, MA: MIT Press

Clancey W. J. (1987b). Intelligent tutoring systems: a tutorial survey. In van Lamsweerde and Dufour (1987), Chapter 3

Clancey W. J. (1987c). From GUIDON to NEOMYCIN and HERACLES in twenty short lessons. In *Current Issues in Expert Systems* (van Lamsweerde A. and Dufour P., eds, Chapter 4. London: Academic Press

Clancey W. J. (1993a). Notes on "Heuristic Classification." *Artificial Intelligence*, **59**, 191–6

Clancey W. J. (1993b). Notes on "Epistemology of a rule-based expert system." *Artificial Intelligence*, **59**, 197–204

Clancey W. J. and Letsinger R. (1984). NEOMYCIN: reconfiguring a rule-based expert system for application to teaching. In *Readings in Medical Artificial Intelligence* (Clancey W.J. and Shortliffe E.H., eds), Chapter 15. Reading, MA: Addison-Wesley

Clancey W. J. and Shortliffe E. H., eds (1984). *Readings in Medical Artificial Intelligence*. Reading, MA: Addison-Wesley

Clark K. L. and McCabe F. (1982). PROLOG: a language for implementing expert systems. In *Machine Intelligence 10* (Hayes J.E., Michie D. and Pao Y.H. eds). Chichester, UK: Ellis Horwood

Clark K. L. and Tarnlund S.-A., eds (1982). *Logic Programming*, London: Academic Press

Cohen P. and Feigenbaum E. A., eds (1982). *The Handbook of Artificial Intelligence*, Vol 3. Los Altos, CA: Morgan Kaufmann

Collins A. M. and Quillian M. R. (1969). Retrieval time from semantic memory. *Journal of Verbal Learning and Verbal Behavior*, **8**, 240–7

Coombs M. J., ed. (1984). *Developments in Expert Systems*. London: Academic Press

Cooper G. F. (1990). The computational complexity of probabilistic inference using Bayesian belief networks. *Artificial Intelligence*, **42**, 393–405

Corkill D. D. (1991). Blackboard systems. *AI Expert*, **6**(9), 40–7

Coyne R. (1988). *Logic Models of Design*. London: Pitman

Cox R. (1946). Probability frequency and reasonable expectation. *American Journal of Physics*, **14**(1), 1–13

Craig I. (1995). *Blackboard Systems*. Norwood, NJ: Ablex

Davies J. and May R. (1995). The development of a prototype "correctly dressed" case-based reasoner: Efficacy of CBR-Express. In *Progress in Case-Based Reasoning* (Watson I., ed.). Lecture Notes in Artificial Intelligence, 1020. Berlin: Springer-Verlag

Davis R. (1980a). Meta-rules: reasoning about control. *Artificial Intelligence*, **15**, 179–222

Davis R. (1980b). Applications of meta-level knowledge to the construction, maintenance and use of large knowledge bases. In Knowledge-Based Systems in Artificial Intelligence (Davis R. and Lenat D., eds) pp. 229–490. New York: McGraw-Hill

Davis R. (1982). Expert systems: Where are we? And where do we go from here? *AI Magazine*, **3**(2)

Davis R. (1984). Diagnostic reasoning based on structure and behavior. *Artificial Intelligence*, **24**, 347–410

Davis R. (1989). Expert systems: how far can they go? Part Two. *AI Magazine*, **10**(2), Summer 1989, 65–77

Davis R. and King J. (1977). An overview of production systems. In *Machine Intelligence 8* (Elcock E.W. and Michie D., eds), pp. 300–32. New York: Wiley

Davis R. and Lenat D. (1980). *Knowledge-Based Systems in Artificial Intelligence*. New York: McGraw-Hill

De Kleer J. (1986). An assumption based TMS. *Artificial Intelligence*, **28**, 127–62

De Kleer J. and Williams B. C. (1987). Diagnosing multiple faults. *Artificial Intelligence*, **32**, 97–130

Dean T. L. and Wellman M. (1991). *Planning and Control*. Los Altos, CA: Morgan Kaufmann

Dietterich T. G. and Mickalski R. (1983). A comparative review of selected methods for learning from examples. In *Machine Learning* (Michalski R. S., Carbonello J. G. and Mitchell T. M., eds), Chapter 3. Palo Alto, CA: Tioga

Doyle J. (1979). A truth maintenance system. *Artificial Intelligence*, **12**, 231–72

Dubois D., Prade H. and Yager R. R., eds (1996). *Fuzzy Information Engineering: A Guided Tour of Applications*. New York: Wiley

Elcock E. W. and Michie D., eds (1977). *Machine Intelligence 8*. New York: Wiley

Englemore R. and Morgan T., eds (1988). *Blackboard Systems*. Reading, MA: Addison-Wesley

Eriksson H., Shahar T., Tu S.W., Puerta A.R. and Musen M.A. (1995). Task Modeling with reusable problem-solving methods. *Artificial Intelligence*, **79** (2): 293–326

Erman L., Hayes-Roth F., Lesser V. and Reddy D. (1980). The HEARSAY-II speech understanding system: integrating knowledge to resolve uncertainty. *Computing Surveys*, **12**(2), 213–53

Erman L. D., London P. E. and Fickas S. F. (1983). The design and an example use of HEARSAY-III, In *Proc. National Conference on Artificial Intelligence*, pp. 409–15

Eshelman L. (1988). A knowledge acquisition tool for cover-and-differentiate systems. In *Automating Knowledge Acquisition for Expert Systems* (Marcus S., ed.), Chapter 3. Boston: Kluiver Academic

Eshelman L. and McDermott J. (1986). MOLE: a knowledge acquisition tool that uses its head. In *Proc. National Conference on Artificial Intelligence*, pp. 950–5

Eshelman L., Ehret D., McDermott J. and Tan M. (1987). MOLE: a tenacious knowledge acquisition tool. *International Journal of Man-Machine Studies*, **26**, 41–54

Feigenbaum E. A. (1977). The art of artificial intelligence: themes and case studies of knowledge engineering. In *Proc. 5th International Joint Conference on Artificial Intelligence*, pp. 1014–29

Feigenbaum E.A. and Buchanan B.G. (1993). DENDRAL and Meta-DENDRAL: roots of knowledge systems and expert systems applications. *Artificial Intelligence*, **59**, 233–40

Feigenbaum E. A. and Feldman J., eds (1963). *Computers and Thought*. New York: McGraw-Hill

Feigenbaum E. A., McCorduck P. and Nii H. P. (1988). *The Rise of the Expert Company*. Times Books

Feiner S. K. and McKeown K. R. (1991). Automating the generation of coordinated multimedia explanations. In *Intelligent Multi-Media Interfaces* (Maybury M., ed.), Chapter 5. AAAI Press/MIT Press

Fikes R. E. and Nilsson N. J. (1971). STRIPS: a new approach to the application of theorem proving to problem solving. *Artificial Intelligence*, **2**,189–208

Findler N. V., ed. (1979). *Associative Networks*. New York: Academic Press

Forbus K. and de Kleer J. (1993). *Building Problem Solvers*. Cambridge, MA: MIT Press

Forgy C. L. (1982). Rete: a fast algorithm for the many pattern/many object pattern match problem. *Artificial Intelligence*, **19**, 17–37

Gale W. A. (1986). *Artificial Intelligence and Statistics*. Reading, MA: Addison-Wesley

Gale W. A. (1987). Knowledge-based knowledge acquisition for a statistical consulting system. *International Journal of Man-Machine Studies*, **26**, 54–64

Genesereth M. R. (1984). The use of design descriptions in automated diagnosis. *Artificial Intelligence*, **24**, 411–36

Genesereth M. R. and Nilsson N. J. (1987). *Logical Foundations of Artificial Intelligence*. Los Altos, CA: Morgan Kaufmann

Giarratano J. and Riley G. (1994). *Expert Systems: Principles and Programming*, 2nd edn. Boston, MA: PWS Publishing

Gil Y. and Paris C. L. (1994). Towards method-independent knowledge acquisition. *Knowledge Acquisition*, **6**(2), 163–78

Ginsberg M., ed. (1987). *Readings in Nonmonotonic Reasoning*. Los Altos, CA: Morgan Kaufmann

Ginsberg M. (1993). *Essentials of Artificial Intelligence*. Los Altos, CA: Morgan Kaufmann

Givan R. and Dean T. (1997). Model minimization, regression, and propositional STRIPS planning. In *Proc. 15th International Joint Conference on Artificial Intelligence*, pp. 1163–8

Glaser H., Hankin C. and Till D. (1984). *Functional Programming*. Englewood Cliffs, NJ: Prentice-Hall

Goldberg A. and Robson D. (1983). *Smalltalk-80: The Language and its Implementation*. Reading, MA: Addison-Wesley

Golding A. R. and Rosenbloom P. S. (1991). Improving rule-based systems through case-based reasoning. In *Proc. National Conference on Artificial Intelligence*, pp. 22–7

Golding A. R. and Rosenbloom P. S. (1996). Improving accuracy by combining rule-based and case-based reasoning. *Artificial Intelligence*, **87**, 215–54

Goldman N. (1978). *AP3 User's Guide*. Information Sciences Institute, University of Southern California

Gordon J. and Shortliffe E. H. (1985). A method of managing evidential reasoning in a hierarchical hypothesis space. *Artificial Intelligence*, 26, 323–57

Graham P. (1994). *On Lisp: Advanced Techniques for Common Lisp*. Englewood Cliffs, NJ: Prentice-Hall

Haberl J.S., Norford L.K., and Spadaro G.V. (1989). Diagnosing building operational problems. *ASHRAE Journal*, June, 20–30

Hammond K. J. (1986). CHEF: a model of case-based planning. In *Proc. AAAI-86*

Harmon P. (1992). Case-based reasoning III. Intelligent Software Strategies, **8** (1)

Harmon P. and Hall C. (1993). *Intelligent Software Systems Development: An IS Manager's Guide*. New York: Wiley

Harmon P. and Sawyer B. (1990). *Creating Expert Systems for Business and Industry*. New York: Wiley

Hasling D. W., Clancey W. J. and Rennels G. (1984). Strategic explanations for a diagnostic consulting system. *International Journal of Man–Machine Studies*, **20**(1), 3–19

Hayes J.E. and Michie D., eds (1984). *Intelligent Systems – The Unprecedented Opportunity*. Chichester, UK: Ellis Horwood

Hayes J. E., Michie D., and Pao Y. H. eds (1982). *Machine Intelligence 10*. Chichester, UK: Ellis Horwood

Hayes-Roth B. (1985). Blackboard architecture for control. *Artificial Intelligence*, **26**, 251–321

Hayes-Roth F., Waterman D. A. and Lenat D., eds (1983). *Building Expert Systems*. Reading, MA: Addison-Wesley

Hayes-Roth B., Buchanan B., Lichtarge O., Hewett M., Altman R., Brinkley J., Cornelius C., Duncan B. and Jardetzky O. (1986). PROTEAN: deriving protein structure from constraints. In *Proc. National Conference on Artificial Intelligence*, pp. 904–9

Hayes-Roth B., Garvey A., Johnson M. V. and Hewett H. (1987). A Modular and Layered Environment for Reasoning About Action. *Technical Report No. KSL 86-38*, Knowledge Systems Laboratory, Stanford University

Hayes-Roth B., Johnson M. V., Garvey A. and Hewett H. (1988). Building systems in the BB* environment. In *Blackboard Systems* (Englemore R. and Morgan T., eds), Chapter 29. Reading, MA: Addison-Wesley

Heckerman D. (1986). Probabilistic interpretation for MYCIN's certainty factors. In *Uncertainty in Artificial Intelligence* (Kanal L.N. and Lemmer J.F., eds) 169–96. Amsterdam: North-Holland

Henderson P. (1980). *Functional Programming: Application and Implementation*. Englewood Cliffs, NJ: Prentice-Hall

Hendrix G. G. (1979). Encoding knowledge in partitioned networks. In *Associative Networks* (Findler N.V., ed.), pp. 51–92. New York: Academic Press

Henrion M., Shachter R. D., Kanal L. N. and Lemmer J. F., eds (1990). *Uncertainty in Artificial Intelligence 5*. Amsterdam: North-Holland

Hewitt C. (1972). Decription and Theoretical Analysis (Using Schemata) of PLANNER, a Language for Proving Theorems and Manipulating Models in a Robot. *Report No. TR-258*, AI Laboratory, MIT

Hinton G. E. (1989). Connectionist learning procedures. *Artificial Intelligence*, **40**, 185–234

Hislop C. and Pracht D. (1994). Integrated problem resolution for business communications. In *Innovative Applications of Artificial Intelligence 6, Proceedings of AAAI-94*, pp. 63–74, Menlo Park, CA: AAAI Press

Hopcroft J. E. and Ullman J. D. (1979). *Introduction to Automata Theory, Languages and Computation*. Reading, MA: Addison-Wesley

Horty J. F., Thomason R. H. and Touretzky D. S. (1987). A skeptical theory of inheritance in nonmonotonic semantic nets. In *Proc. National Conference on Artificial Intelligence*, pp. 358–63

Horvitz E. and Heckerman D. (1986). The inconsistent use of measures of certainty in artificial intelligence research. In *Uncertainty in Artificial Intelligence* (Kanal L. N. and Lemmer J. F., eds), pp. 137–51. Amsterdam: North Holland

Horvitz E., Heckerman D. and Langlotz C. P. (1986). A framework for comparing formalisms for plausible reasoning. In *Proc. National Conference on Artificial Intelligence*, pp. 210–14

Hunt E. B., Mann I. and Stone P. T. (1966). *Experiments in Induction*. New York: Academic Press

Jagannathan V., Dodhiawala R. and Baum L. S., eds (1989). *Blackboard Architectures and Applications*. New York: Academic Press

Jamshidi M., Tilti A., Zadeh L. and Boverie S., eds (1997). *Applications of Fuzzy Logic: Towards High Machine Intelligence Quotient Systems*. Englewood Cliffs, NJ: Prentice Hall

Jensen F. V. (1996). *Introduction to Bayesian Networks*. Berlin: Springer Verlag

Johnson M. V. and Hayes-Roth B. (1986). Integrating Diverse Reasoning Methods in the BB1 Blackboard Control Architecture. *Technical Report No. KSL 86–76*, Knowledge Systems Laboratory, Stanford University

Kahn G. (1988). MORE: from observing knowledge engineers to automating knowledge acquisition. In *Automating Knowledge Acquisition for Expert Systems* (Marcus S., ed.), Chapter 2. Boston: Kluiver Academic

Kahn G. and McDermott J. (1984). The MUD system. In *Proc. 1st IEEE Conference on Artificial Intelligence Applications*

Kahn G., Nowlan S. and McDermott J. (1985). MORE: an intelligent knowledge acquisition tool. In *Proc. 9th International Joint Conference on Artificial Intelligence*, pp. 581–4

Kahn G., Kepner A. and Pepper J. (1987). TEST: a model-driven application shell. In *Proc. National Conference on Artificial Intelligence*, pp. 814–18

Kahneman D. and Tversky A. (1972). Subjective probability: a judgement of representativeness. *Cognitive Psychology*, **3**, 430–54

Kahneman D., Slovic P. and Tversky A., eds (1982). *Judgement under Uncertainty: Heuristics and Biases*. Cambridge: Cambridge University Press.

Kam M., Chow J.-C. and Fischl R. (1991). Hybrid expert system/neural network architecture for classifying power system contingencies. In *Proc. First International Forum on Applications of Neural Networks to Power Systems*, pp. 76–82

Kanal L. N. and Lemmer J. F., eds. (1986). *Uncertainty in Artificial Intelligence*. Amsterdam: North-Holland

Keene S. E. (1989). *Object-Oriented Programming in COMMON LISP*. Reading, MA: Addison-Wesley

Kingston J. K. C. (1997). Designing knowledge based systems: The CommonKADS design model. In *Research and Development in Expert Systems XIV, Proceedings of BCS SGES, Expert Systems '97*, Cambridge University Press

Kingston J. K. C., Doheny J. G. and Filby I. M. (1995). Evaluation of workbenches which support the CommonKADS methodology. *Knowledge Engineering Review*, **10**, 3.

Klahr P. and Waterman D., eds (1986). *Expert Systems: Techniques, Tools, and Applications*. Reading, MA: Addison-Wesley

Kodratoff Y. and Michalski R. S., eds (1990). *Machine Learning: An Artificial Intelligence Approach*, Vol. III. Los Altos, CA: Morgan Kaufmann

Kolodner J.L. (1991). Improving human decision making through case-based decision aiding. *AI Magazine*, **12** (2) 52–68

Kolodner J. (1993). *Case-Based Reasoning*. Los Altos, CA: Morgan Kaufmann

Kononenko I., Bratko I. and Riskar E. (1984). *Experiments in Automatic Learning of Medical Diagnostic Rules*. Jozef Stefan Institute, Ljubljana, Yugoslavia

Korf R.E. and Reid M. (1998). Complexity analysis of admissible heuristic search. In *Proc. 15th National Conference on Artificial Intelligence (AAAI-98)*. pp. 305–10 AAAI Press

Kowalski R. A. (1979). *Logic for Problem Solving*. Amsterdam: North-Holland

Kowalski R. A. (1982). Logic as a computer language. In *Logic Programming* (Clark K. L. and Tarnlund S. -A., eds) Chapter 1. London: Academic Press

Kunz J. C., Fallat R. J., McClung D. H., Osborn J. J., Votteri R. A., Nii H. P., Aikins J. S., Fagan L. M. and Feigenbaum E. A. (1978). A Physiological Rule-Based System for Interpreting Pulmonary Function Test Results. *Report No. HPP 78-19*, Heuristic Programming Project, Computer Science Department, Stanford University

Kunz J. C., Kehler T. P. and Williams M. D. (1984). Applications development using a hybrid AI development system. *AI Magazine*, **5**(3), Fall, 41–54

Lan M. S., Panos R. M. and Balban M. S. (1987). Experience using S.1: an expert system for newspaper printing press configuration. *Knowledge Engineering Review*, **2**(4), 277–85

Langlotz C. P., Shortliffe E. H. and Fagan L. M. (1986). Using decision theory to justify heuristics. In *Proc. National Conference on Artificial Intelligence*, pp. 215–19

Laurent J. P., Ayel J., Thome F. and Ziebelin D. (1986). Comparative evaluation of three expert system development tools: KEE, Knowledge Craft, ART. *Knowledge Engineering Review*, **1**(4), 19–29

Lehnert W. and Wilks Y. (1979). A critical perspective on KRL. *Cognitive Science*, **3**, 1–28

Lenat D. B. (1982). The nature of heuristics. *Artificial Intelligence*, **19**, 189–249

Levesque H. and Mylopoulos J. (1979). A procedural semantics for semantic networks. In *Associative Networks* (Findler N. V., ed.), pp. 93–120. New York: Academic Press

Linster M. and Musen M. A. (1992). Use of KADS to create a conceptual model of the ONCOCIN task. *Knowledge Acquisition*, **4**, 55–87

MacGregor R. (1991). Inside the LOOM classifier. *SIGART Bulletin*, **2**(3), 70–6

Mamdani E. H. and Gaines B. R. (1981). *Fuzzy Reasoning and its Applications*. London: Academic Press

Marcus S., ed. (1988a). *Automating Knowledge Acquisition for Expert Systems*. Boston: Kluwer Academic

Marcus S. (1988b). A knowledge acquisition tool for propose-and-revise systems. In *Automating Knowledge Acquisition for Expert Systems* (Marcus S., ed.), Chapter 4. Boston: Kluiver Academic

Marcus S., Stout J. and McDermott J. (1988). VT: an expert elevator configurer that uses knowledge-based backtracking. *AI Magazine*, **9**(1), 95–112

Marir F. and Watson I. (1994). Case-based reasoning: a categorized bibliography. *Knowledge Engineering Review*, **9**(4), 355–381

Martins J. P. and Reinfrank M. (1991). *Truth Maintenance Systems*. Lecture Notes in Artificial Intelligence, No. 515. Berlin: Springer Verlag

Maybury M., ed. (1993). *Intelligent Multi-Media Interfaces*. Cambridge, MA: AAAI Press/ MIT Press

McAllester D. (1980). An Outlook on Truth Maintenance. *Report No. AIM-551*, Artificial Intelligence Laboratory, Massachusetts Institute of Technology

McArthur D., Klahr P. and Narain S. (1986). ROSS: an object-oriented language for constructing simulations. In *Expert Systems: Techniques, Tools and Applications* (Klahr P. and Waterman D., eds), Chapter 3. Reading, MA: Addison-Wesley

McCarthy J. (1960). Recursive functions of symbolic expressions and their computation by machine. *Communications of the Association for Computing Machinery*, April, 184–95

McCarthy J. and Hayes P. (1969). Some philosophical problems from the standpoint of artificial intelligence. In *Machine Intelligence 4* (Meltzer B. and Michie D., eds), pp. 463–502. Edinburgh: Edinburgh University Press

McCarthy J., Abrahams P. W., Edwards D. I., Hart T. P. and Levin M. I. (1965). *LISP 1.5 Programmer's Manual*, 2nd edn. Cambridge, MA: MIT Press

McDermott J. (1980). R1: an expert in the computer system domain. In *Proc. National Conference on Artificial Intelligence*, pp. 269–71

McDermott J. (1981). R1's formative years. *AI Magazine*, **2**(2)

McDermott, J. (1982a). R1: a rule-based configurer of computer systems. *Artificial Intelligence*, **19**, 39–88

McDermott J. (1982b). XSEL: a computer sales person's assistant. In *Machine Intelligence 10* (Hayes J. E., Michie D. and Pao Y. H., eds) pp. 325–37. Chichester, UK: Ellis Horwood

McDermott J. (1984). Building expert systems. In *Artificial Intelligence Applications for Business* (Reitman W., ed.). Norwood, NJ: Ablex

McDermott J. (1988). Preliminary steps towards a taxonomy of problem solving methods. In *Automating Knowledge Acquisition for Expert Systems* (Marcus S., ed.), Chapter 8. Boston: Kluiver Academic

McDermott J. (1993). R1 ("XCON") at age 12: lessons from an elementary school achiever. *Artificial Intelligence*, **59**, 241–7

McDermott J. and Bachant J. (1984). RI revisited: four years in the trenches. *AI Magazine*, **5**(3), Fall, 21–32

McDermott J. and Forgy C. L. (1978). Production system conflict resolution strategies. In *Pattern Directed Inference Systems* (Waterman D. A. and Hayes-Roth F., eds), pp. 177–99. New York: Academic Press

McNeill D. and Freiberger P. (1993). *Fuzzy Logic*. New York: Simon and Schuster

Meltzer B. and Michie D., eds (1969). *Machine Intelligence 4*. Edinburgh: Edinburgh University Press.

Meyers S. (1995). *More Effective C++ : 35 New Ways to Improve Your Programs and Designs*. Reading, MA: Addison-Wesley

Meyers S. (1997). *Effective C++ : 50 Specific Ways to Improve Your Programs and Designs*, 2nd edn. Reading, MA: Addison-Wesley

Michalski R. S. (1983). A theory and methodology of inductive learning. In *Machine Learning* (Michalski R.S., Carbonell J.G. and Mitchell T.M., eds), Chapter 4. Palo Alto, CA: Tioga

Michalski R. S., Carbonell J. G. and Mitchell T. M., eds (1983). *Machine Learning*. Palo Alto, CA: Tioga

Michalski R.S., Carbonell J.G. and Mitchell T.M., eds (1986). *Machine Learning Vol. II*. Palo Alto, CA: Tioga

Michie D., ed. (1968). *Machine Intelligence 3*. Edinburgh: Edinburgh University Press.

Michie D., ed. (1979). *Expert Systems in the Micro-Electronic Age*. Edinburgh: Edinburgh University Press

Mingers J. (1989a). An empirical comparison of selection measures for decision tree induction. *Machine Learning*, **3**, 319–42

Mingers J. (1989b). An empirical comparison of pruning methods for decision tree induction. *Machine Learning*, **4**, 227–43

Minsky M., ed. (1968). *Semantic Information Processing*. Cambridge, MA: MIT Press

Minsky M. (1972). *Computation: Finite and Infinite Machines*. London: Prentice-Hall

Minsky M. (1975). A framework for representing knowledge. In *The Psychology of Computer Vision* (Winston P. H., ed.) pp. 211–77. New York: McGraw-Hill

Mitchell T. M. (1978). Version Spaces: An Approach to Concept Learning. *Report No. STAN-CS-78-711*, Computer Science Department, Stanford University

Mitchell T. M. (1982). Generalization as search. *Artificial Intelligence*, **18**, 203–26

Mitchell T. M. (1997). *Machine Learning*. New York, NY: McGraw-Hill

Mitchell T. M., Keller R. M., and Kedar-Cabelli S. T. (1986). Explanation-based generalization: A unifying view. *Machine Learning*, 1(1), 47–80

Moore J. D. (1995). *Participating in Explanatory Dialogues*. Cambridge MA: MIT Press

Moser M. G. (1983). An Overview of NIKL, the New Implementation of KL-ONE. *Technical Report No. 5421*, Cambridge MA: Bolt, Beranek and Newman

Moore J. D. and Paris C. L. (1993). Planning text for advisory dialogues: capturing intentional and rhetorical information. *Computational Linguistics*, 19(4), 651–95

Moore J. D., Lemaire B. and Rosenblum J. A. (1996). Discourse generation for instructional applications: identifying and exploiting relevant prior explanations. *Journal of the Learning Sciences*, 5(1), 49–94

Musen M. A. (1992). Overcoming the limitations of role-limiting methods. *Knowledge Acquisition*, 4(2), 165–70

Musen M. A. (1989). Automated support for building and extending expert models. *Machine Learning*, 4(3–4), 347–76

Musen M. A., Gennari J. H. and Wong W. W. (1995). A rational reconstruction of INTERNIST-I using PROTEGE-II. Knowledge Systems Laboratory, Medical Computer Science, *KSL-95–46*

Neale I. M. (1988). First generation expert systems: a review of knowledge acquisition methodologies. *Knowledge Engineering Review*, **3**(2), 105–45

Neapolitan R. E. (1990). *Probabilistic Reasoning in Expert Systems: Theory and Algorithms*. New York: Wiley

Neches R., Swartout W. R. and Moore J. (1985). Explainable (and maintainable) expert systems. In *Proc. 9th International Joint Conference on Artificial Intelligence*, pp. 382–9

Newell A. (1981). Physical symbol systems. In *Perspectives on Cognitive Science* (Norman D. A., ed.), Chapter 4. Norwood, NJ: Ablex

Newell A. (1982). The knowledge level. *Artificial Intelligence*, **18**, 87–127

Newell A. and Simon H. A. (1972). *Human Problem Solving*. Englewood-Cliffs, NJ: Prentice-Hall

Newell A. and Simon H. A. (1976). Computer science as empirical enquiry. *Communications of the Association for Computing Machinery*, **19**(3), 113–26

Nguyen T., Czerwinski M. and Lee D. (1993). Compaq QuickSource: Providing the consumer with the power of artificial intelligence. In *Innovative Applications of Artificial Intelligence 5, Proceedings of AAAI-93*, pp. 142–51. Menlo Park, CA: AAAI Press

Nii H. P. (l986a). Blackboard systems (Part 1). *AI Magazine*, **7**(2), 38–53

Nii H. P (1986b). Blackboard systems (Part 2). *AI Magazine*, **7**(3), 82–106

Nii H. P. and Aiello N. (1979). AGE (Attempt to GEneralize): a knowledge-based program for building knowledge-based programs. In *Proc. 6th International Joint Conference on Artificial Intelligence*, pp. 645–55

Nii H. P., Aiello N. and Rice J. (1988). Frameworks for concurrent problem solving: a report on CAGE and POLIGON. In *Blackboard Systems* (Englemore R. and Morgan T., eds), Chapter 25. Reading, MA: Addison-Wesley

Nilsson N. J. (1971). *Problem Solving Methods in Artificial Intelligence*. New York: McGraw-Hill

Nilsson N. J. (1980). *Principles of Artificial Intelligence*. Palo Alto, CA: Tioga

Norman, D. A., ed. (1981). *Perspectives on Cognitive Science*. Norwood NJ: Ablex

Norvig P. (1992). *Paradigms of Artificial Intelligence Programming: Case Studies in Common Lisp*. Los Altos, CA: Morgan Kaufmann

O'Rourke P. (1982). A Comparative Study of Two Inductive Learning Systems AQ11 and ID3 Using a Chess Endgame Test Problem. *Report No. 82–2*, Department of Computer Science, University of Illinois

O'Shea T. and Eisenstadt M., eds (1984). *Artificial Intelligence: Tools, Techniques, and Applications*. New York: Harper and Row

Paterson A. and Niblett T. (1982). *ACLS Manual*, Version 1. Glasgow, UK: Intelligent Terminals

Pearl J. (1982). Reverend Bayes on inference engines: a distributed hierarchical approach. In *Proc. National Conference on Artificial Intelligence*, pp. 133–6

Pearl J. (1984). *Heuristics. Intelligent Search Strategies for Computer Problem-Solving*. Reading, MA: Addison-Wesley

Pearl J. (1986). On evidential reasoning in a hierarchy of hypotheses. *Artificial Intelligence*, **28**, 9–15

Pearl J. (1988). *Probabilistic Reasoning for Intelligent Systems*. Los Altos, CA: Morgan Kaufmann

Pearl J. (1997) *Probabilistic Reasoning in Intelligent Systems: Networks of Plausible Inference*. Los Altos, CA: Morgan Kaufmann

Pepper J. and Kahn G. (1987). Repair strategies in a diagnostic expert system. In *Proc. 10th International Joint Conference on Artificial Intelligence*, pp. 531–4

Peterson G. E., ed. (1987). *Object-oriented computing*, Vols I and 2. Washington DC: The Computer Society Press of the IEEE

Poeson M. C. and Richardson J. (1988). *Foundations of Intelligent Tutoring Systems*. Hillsdale, NJ: Lawrence Erlbaum

Pople H. E. Jr. (1977). The formation of composite hypotheses in diagnostic problem solving: an exercise in synthetic reasoning. In *Proc. 5th International Joint Conference on Artificial Intelligence*, pp. 1030–7

Pople H. E. Jr. (1982). Heuristic methods for imposing structure on ill-structured problems: the structuring of medical diagnosis. In *Artificial Intelligence in Medicine* (Szolovits P., ed.), pp.119–90. Boulder, Co: Westview Cress

Post E. L. (1943). Formal reductions of the general combinatorial decision problem. *American Journal of Mathematics*, **65**, 197–268

Poundstone W. (1988). *Labyrinths of Reason*. New York: Doubleday

Prerau D. S. (1990). *Developing and Managing Expert Systems*. Reading, MA: Addison-Wesley

Provan G. M. (1990). The application of Dempster Shafer theory to a logic-based visual recognition system. In *Uncertainty in Artificial Intelligence* (Henrion M., Shachter R. D., Kanal L. N. and Lemmer J. F., eds.), pp. 389–405. Amsterdam: North Holland

Puerta A. R., Neches R., Eriksson H., Szeleky P., Luo P. and Musen M. A. (1994). Toward ontology-based frameworks for knowledge acquisition tools. In *Proc. 8th Banff Knowledge-Based Systems Workshop*, **26**, 1–14

Quillian M. R. (1968). Semantic memory. In *Semantic Information Processing* (Minsky M., ed.), pp. 227–70. Cambridge, MA: MIT Press

Quine W. V. O. (1979). *Methods of Logic*. London: Routledge Kegan Paul

Quinlan J. R. (1979). Discovering rules from large collections of examples: a case study. In *Expert Systems in the Micro-Electronic Age* (Michie D., ed.), pp. 168–201. Edinburgh: Edinburgh University Press

Quinlan J. R. (1983). Learning efficient classification procedures and their application to chess endgames. In *Machine Learning* (Michalski A. S., Carbonell J. G. and Mitchell T. M., eds), Chapter 15. Palo Alto, CA:Tioga

Quinlan J. R., (l986a). Induction of decision trees. *Machine Learning*, **1**, 81–106

Quinlan J.R. (1986b). The effect of noise on concept learning. *In Machine Learning Vol. II* (Michalski R.S., Carbonell J.G. and Mitchell T.M., eds), Chapter 6. Palo Alto, CA: Tioga

Quinlan J. R., ed. (1987). *Applications of Expert Systems*. Sydney: Addison-Wesley

Quinlan J. R. (1993). *C4.5: Programs for Machine Learning*. San Mateo, CA: Morgan Kaufmann

Raphael B. (1976). *The Thinking Computer: Mind inside Matter*. San Francisco: W. H. Freeman

Rayward-Smith V. J. (1994) *Applications of Modern Heuristic Methods*. Alfred Waller

Rayward-Smith V. J., Osman I. H. and Reeves C. R., eds. (1996). *Modern Heuristic Search Methods*. New York: Wiley

Reichgelt H. and van Harmelen F. (1986). Criteria for choosing representation languages and control regimes for expert systems. *Knowledge Engineering Review*, 1(4), 2–17

Reitman W., ed. (1984). *Artificial Intelligence Applications for Business*. Norwood, NJ: Ablex

Reynolds D. (1988). MUSE: a toolkit for embedded, real-time, AI. In *Blackboard Systems* (Englemore R. and Morgan T., eds), Chapter 27. Reading, MA: Addison-Wesley

Rice J. (1986). POLIGON: A System for Parallel Problem Solving. *Technical Report No. KSL-86-19*, Knowledge Systems Laboratory, Stanford University

Rice J. (1989). The advanced architectures project. *AI Magazine*, **10**(4), 26–39

Rich E. and Knight K. (1991). *Artificial Intelligence*. New York: McGraw-Hill

Richer M. H. and Clancey W. J. (1985). A graphic interface for viewing a knowledge based system. *IEEE Computer Graphics and Applications*, 5(11), 51–64

Rine D. C., ed. (1975). *Computer Science and Multiple-Valued Logic Theory and Applications*. Amsterdam: North-Holland

Rissland E. L., Daniels J. J., Rubinstein Z. B. and Skalak D. B. (1993). Case-based diagnostic analysis in a blackboard architecture. In *Proc. 11th National Conference on Artificial Intelligence*, pp. 66–72

Robinson J. A. (1965). A machine-oriented logic based on the resolution principle. *Journal of the Association for Computing Machinery*, **12**, 23–41

Robinson J. A. (1979). *Logic: Form and Function*. Edinburgh: Edinburgh University Press

Robinson V., Hardy N. W., Barnes D. P., Pace C. J. and Lee M. H. (1987). Experiences with a knowledge engineering toolkit: an assessment in industrial robotics. *Knowledge Engineering Review*, 2(1), 43–54

Rose D. E. (1994). *A Symbolic and Connectionist Approach to Legal Information Retrieval*. Hillsdale, NJ: Lawrence Erlbaum

Rosenman M. A., Coyne R. D. and Gero I S. (1987). Expert systems for design applications. In *Applications of Expert Systems* (Quinlan J. R., ed.), Chapter 4. Sydney: Addison-Wesley

Rothenfluh T. E., Gennari J. H., Eriksson H., Puerta A. R., Tu S. W., and Musen M. A. (1994). Reusable ontologies, knowledge acquisition tools, and performance systems: PROTOGE-II solutions to Sisyphus-2. In *Proc. 8th Banff Knowledge-Based Systems Workshop*, **43**, 1–30

Rumelhart D. E. (1988). *Parallel Distributed Processing: Explorations in the Microstructure of Cognition*. Cambridge, MA: MIT Press

Rumelhart D.E. and McClelland J.L. (1986) *Parallel Distributed Processing: Explorations in the Microstructure of Cognition: Foundations*. Cambridge, MA: MIT Press

Russell S. J. and Norvig P. (1995). *Artificial Intelligence : A Modern Approach*. Englewood Cliffs, NJ: Prentice-Hall

Sacerdoti E. D. (1974). *A Structure for Plans and Behavior*. Amsterdam: Elsevier North-Holland

Sandewall E. (1986). Nonmonotonic inference rules for multiple inheritance with exceptions. In *Proc. IEEE*, **74**, 81–132

Sanford A. J. (1987). *The Mind of Man: Models of Human Understanding*. Brighton: Harvester Press

Schach, S. R. (1993). *Software Engineering*. Richard D. Irwin

Schank R. C. (1975). *Conceptual Information Processing*. Amsterdam: North-Holland

Schank R. C. and Abelson R. (1977). *Scripts, Plans, Goals and Understanding*. Hillsdale, NJ: Lawrence Erlbaum

Schank R. C. and Colby K., eds (1973). *Computer Models of Thought and Language*. New York: W. H. Freeman

Schmolze J. G. (1991). Guaranteeing serializable results in synchronous parallel production systems. *Journal of Parallel and Distributed Computing*, **13**(4), 348–65

Schreiber A. Th., Wielinga B. J. and Breuker J. A., eds (1993). *KADS: A Principled Approach to Knowledge-Based System Development*. London: Academic Press

Schubert L. K. (1976). Extending the expressive power of semantic networks. *Artificial Intelligence*, **7**, 163–98

Selman B. and Levesque H. J. (1989). The tractability of path-based inheritance. In *Proc. 11th International Joint Conference on Artificial Intelligence*, pp. 1140–5

Shafer G. (1976). *A Mathematical Theory of Evidence*. Princeton NJ: Princeton University Press

Shafer G. and Pearl J. (1990). *Readings in Uncertain Reasoning*. Los Altos, CA: Morgan Kauffman

Shafer G. and Tversky A. (1985). Languages and designs for probability judgment. *Cognitive Science*, **9**, 309–39

Shannon C. E. (1950). Automatic chess player. *Scientfic American*, **182**(48)

Shepherdson J. C. (1984). Negation as Failure. *Journal of Logic Programming*, **1**, 51–81

Shepherdson J. C. (1985). Negation as Failure II. *Journal of Logic Programming*, **3**, 185–202

Shortliffe E. H. (1976). *Computer-Based Medical Consultations: MYCIN*. New York: Elsevier

Shortliffe E. H., Scott A. C., Bischoff M. B., van Melle W. and Jacobs C. D. (1981). ONCOCIN: an expert system for oncology protocol management In *Proc. 7th International Joint Conference on Artificial Intelligence*, pp. 876–81

Sime M. E. and Coombs M. J., eds (1983). *Designing for Human Computer Communication*. London: Academic Press

Simon H. A. (1983). Why should machines learn? In *Machine Learning* (Michalski R. S., Carbonell J. G. and Mitchell T. M., eds), Chapter 2. Palo Alto, CA: Tioga

Slade S. (1991). Case-based reasoning: A research paradigm. *AI Magazine*, **12**(1), Spring, 42–55

Sleeman D. and Brown J. S., eds (1982). *Intelligent Tutoring Systems*. London: Academic Press

Smith B. C. (1982). Reflection and Semantics in a Procedural Language. *MIT-TR-272*, Massachusetts Institute of Technology. Also in *Readings in Knowledge Representation* (Brachman R. J. and Levesque H. J., eds), 1985. Los Altos, CA: Morgan Kaufmann

Smith R. G., Winston H. A., Mitchell T. and Buchanan B. G. (1985). Representation and use of explicit justifications for knowledge base refinement. In *Proc. 9th International Joint Conference on Artificial Intelligence*, pp. 673–80

Smullyan R. (1978). *What Is the Name of this Book?* New York: Simon and Schuster

Stefik M. (1979). An examination of a frame-structured representation system. In *Proc. 6th International Joint Conference on Artificial Intelligence*, pp. 845–52

Stefik M. (1981a). Planning with constraints. *Artificial Intelligence*, **16**, 111–40

Stefik M. (1981b). Planning and meta-planning. *Artificial Intelligence*, **16**, 141–69

Stefik M. (1995). *Introduction to Knowledge Systems*. San Francisco, CA: Morgan Kaufmann

Stefik M. and Bobrow, D. G. (1986). Object-oriented programming: themes and variations. *AI Magazine*, 6(4), 40–62

Stefik M., Aikins J., Balzer R., Benoit J, Bimbaum L., Hayes-Roth F. and Sacerdoti E. (1983). The architecture of expert Systems. In *Building Expert Systems* (Hayes-Roth F., Waterman D. A. and Lenat D., eds), Chapter 4. Reading, MA: Addison-Wesley

Sterling L. and Shapiro E. (1994). *The Art of Prolog*, 2nd edn. Cambridge, MA: MIT Press

Stroustrup B. (1997). *The C++ Programming Language*, 3rd edn. Reading, MA: Addison-Wesley

Studer R., Benjamins V. R. and Fensel D. (1998). Knowledge Engineering: Principles and Methods. *Data and Knowledge Engineering*, 25(1–2), 161–98

Sussman G.J. (1975). *A Computer Model of Skill Acquisition*. New York: American Elsevier

Suwa W., Scott A.C. and Shortliffe E.H. (1982). An approach to verifying completeness and consistency in a rule-based expert system. *AI Magazine*, **3** (4) 16–21

Swartout W. R. (1983). XPLAIN: a system for creating and explaining expert consulting programs. *Artificial Intelligence*, **21**, 285–325

Szolovits P., ed. (1982). *Artificial Intelligence in Medicine*. Boulder, CO: Westview Press

Tate A. (1977). Generating project networks. In *Proc. 5th International Joint Conference on Artificial Intelligence*, pp. 888–93

Teknowledge (1985). *S.1. Reference Manual*. Palo Alto, CA: Teknowledge

Thomason R. (1992). NETL and subsequent path-based inheritance theories. *Computers Math. Applic.*, **23** (2–5), 179–204

Tommelein I. D., Johnson M. V., Hayes-Roth B. and Levitt R. E. (1987). SIGHTPLAN – a blackboard expert system for the layout of temporary facilities on a construction site. In *Proc. IFIP WG5.2 Working Conference on Expert Systems in Computer-Aided Design*, Sydney, Australia

Touretzky D. S. (1986). *The Mathematics of Inheritance Systems*. London: Pitman

Touretzky D. S., Horty J. F. and Thomason R. H. (1987). A clash of intuitions: the current state of nonmonotonic multiple inheritance systems. In *Proc. 10th International Joint Conference on Artificial Intelligence*, pp. 476–82

Tu S.W. Eriksson H., Gennari J., Shahar Y. and Musen M.A. (1995). Ontology-based configuration of problem-solving methods and generation of knowledge-acquisition tools: application of PROTEGE-II to protocol-based decision support. *Artificial Intelligence in Medicine*, **7**, 257–89

Tversky A. and Kahneman D. (1974). Judgment under uncertainty: Heuristics and biases. *Science*, September. Also in *Readings in Uncertain Reasoning* (Shafer G. and Pearl J., eds), 1990. Los Altos, CA: Morgan Kaufmann

van Lamsweerde A. and Dufour P., eds (1987). *Current Issues in Expert Systems*. London: Academic Press.

van Melle W. J. (1981). *System Aids in Constructing Consultation Programs*. Ann Arbor MI: UMI Research Press

von Luck K. and Marburger H., eds (1994). *Management and Processing of Complex Data Structures, Third Workshop on Information Systems and Artificial Intelligence, Proceedings*. Lecture Notes in Computer Science Vol. 777. Berlin: Springer Verlag

Walker E. A. and Nguyen H. T. (1996). *A First Course in Fuzzy Logic*. Boca Raton, FL: CRC Press

Ward R. D. and Sleeman D. (1987). Learning to use the S.1 knowledge engineering tool. *Knowledge Engineering Review*, **2**(4), 265–76

Waterman D. A. (1986). *A Guide to Expert Systems*. Reading, MA: Addison-Wesley

Waterman D. A. and Hayes-Roth F. (1978). *Pattern Directed Inference Systems*. New York: Academic Press

Watson I. (1995). *Progress in Case-Based Reasoning*. Lecture Notes in Artificial Intelligence, 1020. Berlin: Springer-Verlag

Watson I. and Marir F. (1994). Case-Based Reasoning: A Review. *The Knowledge Engineering Review*, **9** (4), 355–81

Weiss S. M. and Kulikowski C. A. (1983). *A Practical Guide to Designing Expert Systems*. London: Chapman and Hall

Wielinga B. J. and Breuker A. J. (1986). Models of expertise. In *Proc. 7th European Conference on Artificial Intelligence*, pp. 306–18

Wielinga B. J. and Schreiber A. Th. (1994). Conceptual modelling of large reusable knowledge bases. In *Management and Processing of Complex Data Structures, Third Workshop on Information Systems and Artificial Intelligence, Proceedings* (von Luck K. and Marburger H., eds), pp. 181–200. Lecture Notes in Computer Science, Vol 777. Berlin: Springer Verlag

Wielinga B. J., Schreiber A. Th. and Breuker J. A. (1992). KADS: A modelling approach to knowledge engineering. *Knowledge Acquisition*, **4**(1)5–53. Special issue: The KADS approach to knowledge engineering. Reprinted in *Readings in Knowledge Acquisition and Learning* (Buchanan B.G. and Wilkins D.G., eds), 1992. Los Altos, CA: Morgan Kaufmann

Wilkins D. C. (1988). Knowledge base refinement using apprenticeship learning techniques. In *Proc. National Conference on Artificial Intelligence*, pp. 646–51

Wilkins D. C. (1990). Knowledge base refinement as improving an incomplete and incorrect domain theory. In *Machine Learning: An Artificial Intelligenmce Approach*, Vol. III (Kodratoff Y. and Michalski R. S., eds), pp. 493–514. Los Altos, CA: Morgan Kaufmann

Wilkins D. C. and Buchanan B. G. (1986). On debugging rule sets when reasoning under certainty. In *Proc. National Conference on Artificial Intelligence*, pp. 448–54

Winograd T. (1972). Understanding natural language. *Cognitive Psychology*, **1**, 1–191

Winograd T. (1975). Frame representations and the declarative/procedural controversy. In *Representation and Understanding* (Bobrow D. G. and Collins A., eds). New York: Academic Press

Winston P. H. (l975a). Learning structural descriptions from examples. In *The Psychology of Computer Vision* (Winston P.H., ed.), Chapter 5. New York: McGraw-Hill

Winston P. H., ed. (1975b). *The Psychology of Computer Vision*. New York: McGraw-Hill

Winston P. H. (1982). Learning new principles from precedents and examples. *Artificial Intelligence*, **19**, 321–50

Winston P. H. (1984). *Artificial Intelligence*. Reading, MA: Addison-Wesley

Winston P. H. (1992). *Artificial Intelligence*, 3rd edn. Reading, MA: Addison-Wesley

Winston P. H. and Brown R. H. (1979). *Artificial Intelligence: An MIT Perspective*, Vols 1 and 2. Cambridge, MA: MIT Press

Winston P. H. and Horn K. P. (1981). *LISP*. Reading, MA: Addison-Wesley

Winston P. H. and Horn K. P. (1984). *LISP*, 2nd edn. Reading, MA: Addison-Wesley

Winston P. H. and Horn K. P. (1988). *LISP*, 3rd edn. Reading, MA: Addison-Wesley

Winston P. H. and Shellard S. A. (1990). *Artificial Intelligence at MIT: Expanding Frontiers*, Vols 1 and 2. Cambridge, MA: MIT Press

Wise B. P. and Henrion M. (1986). A framework for comparing uncertain inference systems to probability. In *Uncertainty in Artifical Intelligence* (Kanal L.N. and Lemmer J.F., eds), pp. 69–83. Amsterdam: North-Holland

Woods W. (1975). What's in a link: Foundations for semantic networks. In *Representation and Understanding* (Bobrow D.G. and Collins A., eds). New York: Academic Press

Yager R. R. and Filev D. P. (1994). *Essentials of Fuzzy Modeling and Control*. New York: Wiley

Yen J. (1986). A reasoning model based on an extended Dempster–Shafer theory. In *Proc. National Conference on Artificial Intelligence*, pp. 125–31

Yen J., Juang H. and MacGregor R. (1991a). Using polymorphism to improve expert system maintainability. *IEEE Expert*, April

Yen J., Neches R. and MacGregor R. (1991b). CLASP: Integrating term subsumption systems and production systems. In *IEEE Transactions on Knowledge and Data Engineering*, **3**, 1, March

Zadeh L. A. (1965). Fuzzy sets. *Information and Control*, **8**, 338–53

Zadeh L. A. (1975). Fuzzy logic and approximate reasoning. *Synthèse*, **30**, 407–28

Zadeh L. A. (1978). Fuzzy sets as a basis for a theory of possibility. *Fuzzy Sets and Systems*, **1**, 3–28

Zadeh L. A. (1981). PUF – a meaning representation language for natural languages. In *Fuzzy Reasoning and its Applications* (Mamdani E. H. and Gaines B. D., eds), pp. 1–66. London: Academic Press